Believers Church
Bible Commentary

Elmer A. Martens and Willard M. Swartley, Editors

BELIEVERS CHURCH BIBLE COMMENTARY

Old Testament
Genesis, by Eugene F. Roop 1987
Exodus, by Waldemar Janzen 2000
Judges, by Terry L. Brensinger 1999
Ruth, Jonah, Esther, by Eugene F. Roop 1999
Proverbs, by John W. Miller 2004
Jeremiah, by Elmer A. Martens 1986
Ezekiel, by Millard C. Lind 1996
Daniel, by Paul M. Lederach 1994
Hosea, Amos, by Allen R. Guenther 1998

New Testament
Matthew, by Richard B. Gardner 1991
Mark, by Timothy J. Geddert 2001
Acts, by Chalmer E. Faw 1993
Romans, by John E. Toews 2004
2 Corinthians, by V. George Shillington 1998
Ephesians, by Thomas R. Yoder Neufeld 2002
Colossians, Philemon, by Ernest D. Martin 1993
1-2 Thessalonians, by Jacob W. Elias 1995
1-2 Peter, Jude, by Erland Waltner and J. Daryl Charles 1999
Revelation, by John R. Yeatts 2003

Old Testament Editors
Elmer A. Martens and Allen R. Guenther (for *Jeremiah*), Mennonite
    Brethren Biblical Seminary, Fresno, California

New Testament Editors
Willard M. Swartley and Howard H. Charles (for *Matthew*),
    Associated Mennonite Biblical Seminary, Elkhart, Indiana

Editorial Council
David Baker, Brethren Church
Lydia Harder, Mennonite Church Canada
Estella B. Horning, Church of the Brethren
Robert B. Ives, Brethren in Christ Church
Gordon H. Matties, Mennonite Brethren Church
Paul M. Zehr (chair), Mennonite Church USA

**Believers Church
Bible Commentary**

Romans

John E. Toews

HERALD PRESS
Scottdale, Pennsylvania
Waterloo, Ontario

Library of Congress Cataloging-in-Publication Data
Toews, John E., 1937-
  Romans / John E. Toews.
      p. cm. — (Believers church Bible commentary)
  Includes bibliographical references and index.
  ISBN 0-8361-9277-X (pbk. : alk. paper)
  1. Bible. N.T. Romans—Commentaries. I. Title. II. Series.
  BS2665.53.T64 2004
  227'.107—dc22
                                                    2003025237

BELIEVERS CHURCH BIBLE COMMENTARY: ROMANS
Copyright © 2004 by Herald Press, Scottdale, Pa. 15683
    Released simultaneously in Canada by Herald Press,
    Waterloo, Ont. N2L 6H7. All rights reserved
Library of Congress Control Number: 2003025237
International Standard Book Number: 0-8361-9277-X
Printed in the United States of America
Cover and charts by Merrill R. Miller

12 11 10 09 08 07 06 05 04   10 9 8 7 6 5 4 3 2 1

To order or request information, please call 1-800-759-4447 (individuals); 1-800-245-7894 (trade). Website: www.heraldpress.com

To the students in my Romans classes at
Mennonite Brethren Biblical Seminary,
Fresno, California, and Conrad Grebel
University College, Waterloo, Ontario,
from whom I learned so much.

Abbreviations/Symbols

*	The Text in Biblical Context (as starred in Contents)
+	The Text in the Life of the Church (as in Contents)
BCBC	*Believers Church Bible Commentary*
[bracketed term]	cross-reference to an entry in the essays
//	equal, parallel to
cf.	compare
ch/s.	chapter/s
e.g.	for example(s)
et al.	and other(s)
KJV	King James Version
Lit	literal
LXX	Septuagint
n	note
NIV	New International Version
note/s	Explanatory notes in sequence of chapters/verses
NRSV	New Revised Standard Version
NT	New Testament
OT	Old Testament
RSV	Revised Standard Version
TDNT	*Theological Dictionary of the New Testament*
TBC	The Text in Biblical Context
TLC	The Text in the Life of the Church
v./vv.	verse/verses

Contents

Series Foreword

The Believers Church Bible Commentary Series makes available a new tool for basic Bible study. It is published for all who seek more fully to understand the original message of Scripture and its meaning for today—Sunday school teachers, members of Bible study groups, students, pastors, and others. The series is based on the conviction that God is still speaking to all who will listen, and that the Holy Spirit makes the Word a living and authoritative guide for all who want to know and do God's will.

The desire to help as wide a range of readers as possible has determined the approach of the writers. Since no blocks of biblical text are provided, readers may continue to use the translation with which they are most familiar. The writers of the series use the *New Revised Standard Version*, the *Revised Standard Version*, the *New International Version*, and the *New American Standard Bible* on a comparative basis. They indicate which text they follow most closely, and where they make their own translations. The writers have not worked alone, but in consultation with select counselors, the series' editors, and the Editorial Council.

Every volume illuminates the Scriptures; provides necessary theological, sociological, and ethical meanings; and, in general, makes "the rough places plain." Critical issues are not avoided, but neither are they moved into the foreground as debates among scholars. Each section offers explanatory notes, followed by focused articles, "The Text in Biblical Context" and "The Text in the Life of the Church."

The writers have done the basic work for each commentary, but not operating alone, since "no . . . scripture is a matter of one's own interpretation" (2 Pet. 1:20; cf. 1 Cor. 14:29). They have consulted with select counselors during the writing process, worked with the editors for the series, and received feedback from another biblical scholar. In addition, the Editorial Council, representing six believers church denominations, reads the manuscripts carefully, gives churchly responses, and makes suggestions for changes. The writer considers all this counsel and processes it into the manuscript, which the Editorial Council finally approves for publication. Thus, these commentaries combine the individual writers' own good work and the church's voice. As such, they represent a hermeneutical community's efforts in interpreting the biblical text, as led by the Spirit.

The term *believers church* has often been used in the history of the church. Since the sixteenth century, it has frequently been applied to the Anabaptists and later the Mennonites, as well as to the Church of the Brethren and similar groups. As a descriptive term, it includes more than Mennonites and Brethren. *Believers church* now represents specific theological understandings, such as believers baptism, commitment to the Rule of Christ in Matthew 18:15-20 as crucial for church membership, belief in the power of love in all relationships, and willingness to follow Christ in the way of the cross. The writers chosen for the series stand in this tradition.

Believers church people have always been known for their emphasis on obedience to the simple meaning of Scripture. Because of this, they do not have a long history of deep historical-critical biblical scholarship. This series attempts to be faithful to the Scriptures while also taking archaeology and current biblical studies seriously. Doing this means that at many points the writers will not differ greatly from interpretations that can be found in many other good commentaries. Yet, these writers share basic convictions about Christ, the church and its mission, God and history, human nature, the Christian life, and other doctrines. These presuppositions do shape a writer's interpretation of Scripture. Thus this series, like all other commentaries, stands within a specific historical church tradition.

Many in this stream of the church have expressed a need for help in Bible study. This is justification enough to produce the Believers Church Bible Commentary. Nevertheless, the Holy Spirit is not bound to any tradition. May this series be an instrument in breaking down walls between Christians in North America and around the world, bringing new joy in obedience through a fuller understanding of the Word.

—The Editorial Council

Author's Preface

I have lived and slept with Paul's Letter to the Romans for over 30 years. It started with the simultaneous reading of Romans in Greek and Rudolf Bultmann's *Theology of the New Testament* during the summer of 1969 while in doctoral studies. I was persuaded that Bultmann misunderstood Paul. So began a life-long pilgrimage of reading and re-reading Romans and about Romans.

The work on this commentary began twenty years ago, and has gone through numerous drafts. Because I was involved in senior administration for most of this time—Academic Dean and Acting President at the Mennonite Brethren Biblical Seminary in Fresno, California (1980-93), and President of Conrad Grebel University College in Waterloo, Ontario (1996-2002)—I worked on Romans Saturday mornings and on sabbaticals (1988 and 1993 at Biblical Seminary, 2003 at Conrad Grebel). I would try to move the previous draft forward each sabbatical, but ended up re-writing much of the text.

My constant companions and dialogue partners over the years have been my students. They have pushed and challenged me, encouraged me, and forced me to clarify my thinking. To them I give my utmost thanks and to them I dedicate this commentary. Two of the most significant former students have been Gordon Zerbe and Wally Kroeker. The former helped me develop the initial bibliography of works on Romans in 1978, and later served as my peer reader for the Believers Bible Commentary Series. His helpful questions and thoughtful suggestions have helped me nuance my work and correct-ed numerous errors. Wally Kroeker edited the entire manuscript and made it much more readable. My deepest thanks to each of them for their tireless effort and friendship. Both have improved the quality of the commentary, but are not responsible for its interpretive stances or errors.

Willard Swartley, the New Testament editor of the Series, has been exceptionally helpful and patient. His counsel has been wise and his encouragement boundless. William Klassen read the entire manuscript in draft form and offered good counsel on numerous points. I am deeply grateful for the contribution of both of these friends.

Thanks are not sufficient for my wife, Arlene, and our three children—Delora, Dawn, and Mark. They have graciously endured my preoccupation with *Romans* and sacrificed more time and attention to this project than any of us care to recount. I will be forever grateful for their support and encouragement.

—*John E. Toews*
Fresno, California

Introduction to Romans

The New Testament letter to the Romans was written by Paul, apostle of Jesus Christ to the Gentiles. As an apostle, Paul spent his life traveling the Mediterranean area preaching the gospel and establishing churches. In the course of this missionary career he wrote numerous letters to the churches he had established as a way to pastor them in his absence [*Essay: Letter Form*].

Romans was written from Corinth between late A.D. 55 and early A.D. 57 at a turning point in Paul's career. He had established churches from Jerusalem in the East to Illyricum (Rom. 15:19—present day Serbia).

When writing Romans, Paul is about to leave Corinth for Jerusalem with an offering from the churches of Macedonia and Achaia (Rom. 15:23-29). Thereafter, he plans to visit the churches in Rome and then travel west to Spain.

Why Romans?

Romans is the longest and most complex of Paul's letters. Why would he write this letter to churches in the capital of the Empire—churches he had not founded? The introduction and conclusion of the letter, "the letter-frame," in 1:1-15 and 15:14-33, give four answers: 1) Paul wrote "to impart some spiritual gift" to the churches (1:11); 2) Paul wrote to "reap some harvest" among the Christians in Rome (1:13); 3) Paul wrote to remind the Romans of some things (15:15); 4) Paul wrote because he planned to visit Rome and hoped to gain support from the Roman churches for a mission in Spain (15:22-29).

The last reason helps explain parts of chs. 1 and 15, but it does not provide an adequate reason for the whole of Romans. The larger, real purpose must be to impart some gift, to reap some harvest, to remind the followers of Jesus of some things.

The importance of the first three reasons is underlined by the rhetorical form of Romans. The letter is concerned with more than communicating information. It is trying to persuade the churches of Rome about something. In the ancient world speech or writing that was designed to persuade took one of three forms—judicial (persuade to make a judgment about a past event), deliberative (persuade to take some action in the future), or epideictic or demonstrative (persuade to hold to or reaffirm a point of view in the present). There is general agreement that Romans is a demonstrative letter—it reaffirms values held in common and tries to persuade commitment to them. This affirmation of common values or beliefs is, of course, usually argued over against rival values or beliefs.

What is Paul trying to remind the Romans about? What common beliefs and values is he arguing for? There must be issues, problems, or disagreements that need attention among the Roman churches.

The Churches in Rome

We begin by describing what we know about the churches in Rome.

The Origin of the Church

We do not know how or when the churches in Rome were established. Paul did not establish them, since Romans 15:16 reports he is coming on his first visit to existing congregations. It is often suggested on the basis of Acts 2:10 that Roman Jews were present at Pentecost and brought the gospel back to Rome. However, the Roman Jews in Acts 2 are described as residents, rather than as visitors. It is possible that some of these people became followers of Jesus at Pentecost and later returned to Rome, but we do not know.

The first observation on the origin of the church in Rome comes from Ambrosiaster, a fourth-century Latin church leader. He reports that "it is established that there were Jews living in Rome in the times of the apostles, and that those Jews who had believed [in Christ] passed on to the Romans the tradition that they ought to profess Christ but keep the law . . . without seeing any signs or miracles and without seeing any of the apostles they nevertheless accepted faith in Christ, although according to a Jewish rite" (Works, III.73, cited from Donfried, 1991:47). Ambrosiaster's report makes it clear that Judaism and the Jewish communities provided the context of the Christian faith in Rome.

Precisely when these developments took place we do not know, but the evidence suggests the churches in Rome were founded relatively early in Christian history. Acts 18:2 reports that Aquila and Priscilla came from Rome in A.D. 49, because of the expulsion of the Jews from Rome by the emperor Claudius. The Christian mission in Rome had existed long enough to establish some churches. Paul's statement in the mid-50s that, "I have longed for many years to come to you" (Rom. 15:23), suggests that the churches had existed for some time. The Roman historian Tacitus reports that there was a large number of Christians in Rome in A.D. 64 at the time of the persecution by Nero. Sometime between Pentecost (A.D. 32-33) and A.D. 49, some Jews in Rome became followers of Jesus and witnessed to fellow Jews and Gentile "God-fearers" about their faith in Christ, and began to establish house churches.

From this limited historical evidence we can piece together the following picture: 1) the churches in Rome were founded by Jews who became followers of Jesus; 2) the Christian faith there was closely linked with the observance of the Jewish law and rituals; 3) the churches met in houses (see Rom. 16); 4) the churches were effected by Claudius's expulsion of the Jews from Rome in A.D. 49; 5) the churches grew; there are a good number by the time Paul writes Romans in the mid-50s, and many Christians by A.D. 64.

The Jewish Context in Rome

The Jewish context of these churches is important if we are to understand the pastoral setting for Paul's letter, which is dominated by concerns for Jew-Gentile relations and the Jewish people.

It is generally agreed that in the mid-first century there were between 20,000 to 50,000 Jews in Rome out of a population of one million. Many were slaves or former slaves.

History. The Jews were relative newcomers to Rome, the first reference to them being 139 B.C. Little is known about the Jewish community between 139 and 61 B.C. Its size increased significantly in 61 B.C., because of the captives Pompey brought from Jerusalem. Cicero reports in 59 B.C. that the Jews are a formidable element in Roman politics. In 49 B.C., the Jews support Caesar against Pompey, and Caesar rewards them with special privileges that allow them to practice their religion as long as they do not proselytize.

The Jews began to attract public attention during the Augustan era (30 B.C.—A.D. 14). By then a sizable Jewish population existed in Rome, and Roman writers began to criticize them for proselytizing activities, Sabbath observance, and dietary practices. Following the death of Augustus in A.D. 14 life in Rome became more difficult for the Jewish people, and in A.D. 19 they were expelled for proselytizing. The Roman Emperor, Gaius (37-41), nicknamed Caligula, faced a serious rebellion of the Jews in Alexandria, Egypt, in A.D. 38. A Jewish delegation from Alexandria to Rome was humiliated by Gaius with jeering support from his advisors. Gaius also insisted on placing his statue in the Temple in Jerusalem. Only the delaying tactics of a local governor and the death of Gaius prevented a rebellion in Judaea.

The emperor Claudius (A.D. 41-54) restricted the public assembly of the Jews in Rome in 41, because of their growing size and influence, and expelled them in 49 due to the agitations of a certain "Chrestus" ("since the Jews constantly made disturbances at the instigation of Chrestus, he [Claudius] expelled them from Rome." Suetonius, Claudius, XXV.4). The meaning of "expelled them" is uncertain—was it "all Jews," "some Jews," or "the Jews who made disturbances?" The traditional interpretation reads "Chrestus" as a misspelling of Christus. It then interprets it as a reference to Christian missionary activity within the Jewish community that stirred such controversy among the Jews that Claudius began to feel threatened and expelled "the Jews" from the city. However, "Chrestus" is probably a reference to a Jewish messianic pretender—actually present in Rome in A.D. 49—who nurtured Jewish zealot attitudes against the government. The political agitation within the Jewish community was so threatening that Claudius felt compelled to expel "the Jews" to maintain peace in the city [*Essay: Identity of Chrestus*]. "The Jews" were permitted to return to Rome following the death of Claudius in 54 (Walters, 1993:56ff.).

The Synagogue Structure. The central structure for the Jews in Rome was the house synagogue of 10 to 50 people. There were hundreds of such house synagogues in Rome, and their names and locations suggest great diversity, ranging from very conservative groups linked with Jerusalem to more liberal groups accommodating to Hellenistic culture. No central Jewish organization controlled the diverse groups of Jews in Rome, as in most cities of the Diaspora. The Jews had come to Rome comparatively late, and many were slaves. The lower class status of many of them as well as the rapid influx of new people from military conquests, immigration, and proselytizing required an organizational structure that could quickly assimilate new groups. Thus, independent house synagogues emerged in different parts of the city as need arose without strict accountability to a central governing body.

Proselytism. The Jewish population in the Diaspora was three times as large as in Palestine; Jews accounted for one-seventh of the total population of the empire. Natural growth alone cannot account for this increase. The growth in Rome was especially rapid; from 139 B.C. to A.D. 50, the Jewish population grew from a few people to many thousands. The spread of Judaism in the second and third centuries B.C. suggests some kind of missionary movement. Women were the most responsive to Jewish missionary activity. The big obstacle for men was circumcision.

Two identifiable groups of Gentiles attached themselves to the Jewish communities: proselytes and "God-fearers." Proselytes were full converts to Judaism. "God-fearers" were Gentiles who took part in synagogue worship services and observed some Jewish practices, but did not fully convert. During the Augustan period especially, it became fashionable for aristocratic members of Roman society to attach themselves to the synagogue; Sabbath observance and the practice of some dietary laws seem to be the common ground.

Summary on Judaism in Rome

The Roman Jewish community at mid-first century A.D. was a large, vital, diverse, and decentralized community. Its missionary activity, as well as its political influence and nationalist sympathies, concerned some Roman opinion makers and officials. These fears and hostilities meant the periodic disruption of life in the Jewish community, as in the expulsions of A.D. 19 and 49 (see Applebaum, 1974; Richardson, 1998; Wiefel, 1991 for more details).

Data on the Churches in Rome

What do we know about the churches of Rome that emerged in this context? Romans 16 tells us the church met in houses. This was the normal pattern throughout the empire until A.D. 200. The house church meeting places were known by the names of the owners, not by special Christian names; the Romans 16:5 reference to the church in the house of Aquila and Prisca was typical.

Archaeological reports on Rome indicate that diverse homes were used. Some of the houses belonged to craftsmen and artisans, others were apartments in large tenement complexes that belonged to lower class laborers. The house of Clement was close to a tenement house. The house of Pammachius was located in an industrial section with shops on the ground floor. The house of Cecilia included a granary. The house of Equitius looked like a barn or storeroom.

The Christians of Rome met in ordinary homes throughout the city. The words used to describe these churches, "the church in their home," designated both place and family. House meant a dwelling, but also signified a "family" or "household." The early Christian churches understood themselves as "families" or "households." Just as there was diversity of location and house style, so there was diversity in family composition and style of meeting and worship (see Branick, 1989).

The second thing we know about the churches of Rome is that there were groups with different theological identities. A surface reading of Romans reveals at least two different groups, Jewish Christians and Gentile Christians. The expression "Jew and also Greek," first encountered in 1:16, occurs in one form or another more often in Romans than in all the other letters of Paul combined: Jews/Greeks or Israel/Gentiles (1:16; 2:9-10; 3:9, 29; 9:24, 30-31; 10:12), circumcision/uncircumcision (2:25-29; 3:1, 30; 4:9-12; 15:8-12). Moreover, this pairing often marks the end of a section or the beginning of a new train of thought, thus suggesting it is important in the structure of Paul's argument. In addition, we find "you-they" language: "they are enemies of God for your sake" (11:28), "they are disobedient now . . . mercy shown to you" (11:31). Alternatively, chs. 14-15 talk about "strong Christians" and "weak Christians" who are putting each other down. Paul calls, in 15:7-13, for mutual acceptance of differences between the "strong" and the "weak."

The impression of group differences is reinforced by passages addressed directly to one or the other of the groups. Jewish Christians are addressed in: 2:12, 17; 3:1, 29; 4:1; 7:1, 4; Gentile Christians are addressed in: 1:5-6, 13; 2:12; 11:13, 17-18, 20; 15:14f.

Clearly there is a "Jewish problem" among the Roman house churches. Jewish Christians have a theology that exalts Jewish identity and excludes Gentile Christians. Chs. 3-11 contain 20 rhetorical questions: 3:1, 3b, 5c, 9, 27a, 31; 4:1, 9; 6:1, 15; 7:7, 13; 8:31; 9:14, 19, 30; 11:1, 7, 11, 19. All concern the problem of the Jew and the law. The issues raised in 3:1 and 3 are taken up again in the last four in 11:1, 7, 11, 19, thus forming an inclusio to the rhetorical questions.

But there is also a "Gentile problem" among the churches. The only exhortations in chs. 9-11 are directed against Gentile boasting and a Gentile theology which says the Gentile Christians do not need the Jewish people. This theology asserts that God has rejected the Jewish people. The warning to the "strong" in chs. 14-15 to nurture, rather than offend, the "weak" in the churches reinforces the same point.

The existence of such divisions in Rome is not surprising. The first believers were all Jews or Gentiles with Jewish sympathies and commitments. It is highly probable that these early Jewish Christians continued to worship in the house synagogues or in house churches in the same neighborhood as their former house synagogues. The interaction between Jewish Christians and Gentile Christians, and Jewish people was constant, intimate, and intense. Furthermore, there were clearly differing opinions on a variety of issues within the Jewish and Jewish Christian communities.

The first Jewish Christian missionaries converted people to their point of view. Thus, we encounter different types of Jewish-Gentile Christianity throughout the New Testament. At least four distinct types can be identified. Group 1 insisted on the full observance of the Mosaic Law, including circumcision. The group taught that Gentiles must become Jews to be Christian. This group is represented by the Jewish Christians of the circumcision in Acts 11:2 and the "false brothers" in Galatians 2:4. Group 2 insisted on keeping some Jewish observances, especially, the food laws, but not circumcision. James and Peter are spokespersons for this viewpoint (Acts 15 and Gal. 2). Group 3 rejected circumcision and food laws. Paul is the chief theologian for this position (Gal. 2, 1 Cor. 8). Group 4 rejected circumcision, the food laws, and the abiding significance of the Jewish cult. This point of view is represented by the Hellenists of Acts 6, the Gospel of John (2:19-21; 4:21; 10:33-36) and Hebrews (Jesus replaces the Temple and cult). All four groups are composed of Jews and Gentiles, and all are still closely linked with the Jewish community. The divisions among the Roman churches reflect the larger issues being debated between the Jewish and Christian communities and within the Jewish-Christian and Gentile-Christian communities (Brown and Meier, 1983).

The third thing we know about the Roman churches is that some people are leveling "slanderous charges" against Paul (3:8) and some people are creating dissension among the churches (16:17). The charges against Paul have something to do with the justice of God in relationship to Israel. The dissensions in the church concern teachings that are contrary to "the doctrine which you have been taught." The warning about these people, found in the final passage of the letter, is about the relationship between the community and specific individuals. Such "final warnings" are characteristic of Hellenistic letters, and reveal a purpose for the writing of the letter. Some problematic teaching is dividing the churches and needs correcting.

The Pastoral Context of the Churches in Rome

As noted earlier, we do not know how the churches of Rome emerged. We can only reconstruct the most likely scenario.

1) The first followers of Jesus in Rome were Jews, Jewish proselytes, and "God-fearers" from the Jewish house synagogues, who remained associated with these synagogues. The initial mission of these first converts was among their fellow Jews and "God-fearers."

2) The Christian faith in Rome was a thoroughly Jewish faith at the outset. The first believers were Jews and "God-fearers," who believed that Jesus was the Messiah and who continued to participate in Jewish life and to observe the law as Jews or the Sabbath and food laws as "God-fearers." In other words, the first Christians in Rome represented Groups 1 and 2 of the Jewish-Christians groups. The dominant form of Christianity at this stage was shaped by the Jerusalem Christianity of James and Peter. It was a Christian faith appreciative of Judaism and loyal to its customs, a picture confirmed by Ambrosiaster. Group 1 Jewish Christians continued to observe the whole Jewish law. Group 2 Christians observed Sabbath and food laws but not circumcision. The decentralized organizational structure of the Roman Jews meant that different house churches emerged in the city within or very close to house synagogues. It was easy for the early Christian missionaries to "evangelize" in house synagogues and win converts either within the synagogue or very close to it. Because the Christian movement was so Jewish in nature, it did not create major concerns among the Jewish leaders of the Roman community.

3) The expulsion edict of Claudius in A.D. 49 changed the face of the churches in Rome. From 49 to 54 it removed significant numbers of the Jewish people from the house synagogues and Jewish Christians from the house churches. During this time many house churches became Gentile-Christian churches of Group 3, but retained links to the house synagogues through the "God-fearers." When the expelled Jews and Jewish Christians returned to Rome, they encountered churches, maybe even some house synagogues, dominated by Gentile Christians who represented the viewpoints of Groups 3 and 4. Ch. 2 reflects tension, maybe even name calling, over circumcision. Chs. 14 and 15 indicate Roman believers who reject Sabbath and food laws. Chs. 9-11 presuppose Gentile Christians who reject the Jewish faith and heritage. The theology of Group 4 would be very consonant with anti-Jewish sentiments in Rome. It is possible that members of Groups 3 and 4 had been influenced by Paul's gospel of freedom from the Jewish law for Gentile Christians. At least ch. 16 suggests that friends of Paul were active and influential among the

churches. Whether influenced by Paul or not, the Gentile-Christian churches had shifted from the Jerusalem Christianity of Groups 1 and 2 toward the more Pauline Christianity of Group 3 or even the more radical Christianity of Group 4.

4) Over time tensions grew among the various house churches and between some of the house churches and the nearby house synagogues. The tensions center around the relationship of the Gentile Christians of Groups 3 and 4 with the Jewish Christians of Groups 1 and 2 and the relationship of Christian faith to the Jewish faith. Is Christianity an integral part of Judaism or not? Is it necessary for Gentile believers to observe the whole law or at least some Jewish ritual laws? Is the observance of Jewish laws a sign of weak faith? These tensions were fueled by the anti-Roman sentiment of the Jews and Jewish Christians following their return to Rome in A.D. 54. The zealot mentality that infected the Roman Jewish community in 49 was only intensified by the expulsion and by the growing hostility between the Jews of Palestine and the Roman government since that time.

The pastoral setting of the Roman churches at the time of Paul's Letter is the post-54 church-synagogue and church scene. There is diversity and tension among the churches and between the house churches and house synagogues. The churches of Rome represent the full-spectrum of Jew-Gentile groups.

The Purpose of Romans

Paul writes Romans to remind the churches of the purpose of God for both Jew and Gentile. His pastoral purpose is to resolve a crisis in Jewish-Christian, and in Jewish-Gentile, church relationships. He writes to aid in the reconciliation of disparate house churches and synagogues in Rome.

Written by Paul just prior to his fearful departure for Jerusalem, this letter addresses the same problem common in both Jerusalem and Rome: Jewish-Christian and Jewish-Gentile Christian antagonisms, which strike at the heart of Paul's gospel. It is important to emphasize that the issues in Rome and Jerusalem are both Christian and Jewish issues, but they are intra-Jewish and intra-Jewish-Christian church issues. The debate is a family one—at this time the Christian churches have not separated from Judaism. Paul is addressing the Jewish synagogues of Rome, as well as Jewish and Gentile Christian churches that have emerged out of Judaism and remain closely linked with Judaism. The central question is the nature of the people of God—its continuity or discontinuity with the Jewish people.

The pastoral theology Paul formulates for this problem centers in the equality of Jew and Gentile before God. Both are judged equally and both are made righteous equally by God through the faithfulness of Messiah Jesus. The emphasis is on the gospel for all, both Jew and Gentile. This equality blunts the assumption of Jewish privilege and the Gentile presumption of superiority. The gospel as the power of God affirms the election of Israel in continuity with the promises of God and includes the Gentiles in the people of God in a righteous way.

Paul argues for the entry of Gentiles into God's plan of salvation that originated in Israel. That is why he emphasizes both the equality of Jews and Gentiles and the priority of Israel. In the process he redefines Judaism. Paul outlines a gospel that opens the people of God to the Gentiles on the basis of a new way to be righteous before God. Gentile Christians are asked not to reject Israel, because God will yet keep the promises to this people.

Romans is about relationships between two people, Jews and Gentiles, in the gospel. It seeks the theological and social reorientation of both Jewish and Gentile Christians. Jewish-Christian and Gentile-Christian congregations can live together in peace with each other and with Jewish synagogues because both have been incorporated into the one people that God is creating in the world. Both people become real children of Abraham. The reconciliation of Christians and Jews and Jewish and Gentile Christians would make Paul welcome in Rome, and would provide a base of support for his mission to Spain.

Why Romans? Paul writes Romans to remind the Christians in the city that God is creating one people composed of Jews and Gentiles in the world. If that reminder is effective it will: 1) impart a spiritual gift to the churches; 2) bear fruit; 3) correct some false teachings about Paul and his gospel; and 4) prepare the churches to support his mission to the West.

This reading of Romans (the particular) fits with Paul's larger mission as the Apostle of Messiah Jesus to the Gentiles (the world). His vision is to build faithful and unified Christian communities in the Gentile world that demonstrate the faithfulness of God to the promises to Israel and Israel's scriptures (see esp. chs. 11 and 15).

The Perspective of This Commentary

The interpretive perspective of this commentary shares the "new perspective on Paul" with many contemporary scholars (J. D. G. Dunn introduced this phrase in 1982: see his note to this phrase used as a chapter title in 1990a:183). "The new perspective" refers to a new paradigm in the interpretation of Paul that focuses primarily on new understandings of Judaism and on Paul's view of the Law (the "faith of/in Jesus" issue is more long-standing, as a comparison of the KJV with the RSV/NIV/NRSV will attest). Everyone reads Paul's Letter to the Romans, as they do the entire Bible, through a perspective, a set of biases or glasses. Such perspectives are called "paradigms." A paradigm in biblical interpretation is the grid through which we see, read, and interpret the Bible, a perspective that shapes our reading and understanding of meaning. Periodically, paradigms shift. Such a paradigm shift has been and is taking place in Pauline studies right now, especially in the interpretation of Galatians and Romans. The groundbreaking work of E. P. Sanders, *Paul and Palestinian Judaism* (1977), contributed much to this shifting perspective.

The Dominant Paradigm since the Reformation

Traditionally, Romans has been interpreted through a paradigm that is characterized by three perspectives.

First, Paul is read as opposed to Judaism. Paul's theology, especially in Galatians and Romans, is shaped by a response to his Jewish critics and by his own reaction to his Jewish past. In other words, Paul's theology is seen as a polemic against Judaism. The center of the polemic is an attack on the idea that salvation can be earned by acts of obedience to the law, as supposedly held by the Jews and Paul's Jewish Christian opponents. Judaism is interpreted as a religion of works righteousness. The problem in Judaism is the law as a means of salvation. Human sin is fundamentally the drive for self-justification. Judaism and the law, in this perspective, are read negatively.

Second, Paul's answer to salvation by works is the gospel of salvation by the grace of God alone. The issue between Paul and his opponents is theological and theoretical. They are debating the merits of two rival answers to the question, how can individual men and women be accepted by God? Paul's answer is the doctrine of justification by faith. Human beings find acceptance before God by faith, by renouncing all forms of self-justification and accepting God's salvation in Christ by faith.

Third, Romans is read as a theological treatise in which Paul summarizes his gospel, his theology, of justification by faith through the grace of God.

The New Perspective Paradigm

The new paradigm reads Paul, and especially Romans, through a different set of perspectives.

First, Paul is a Jewish-Christian apostle to the Gentiles. His fundamental concern is the mission to the Gentiles, and the incorporation of Gentiles into the people of God. A major issue in Judaism from the return from the Babylonian Captivity in the late-sixth and fifth centuries B.C. on, and especially from about 200 B.C., was: what are the criteria for participation in the covenant people? Amid the vigorous debate about this question in Judaism, there is general agreement that covenant people were defined by circumcision and the proper observance of food and festival laws (often called purity laws). The central issue facing Paul in the Gentile mission is the implication of Jesus as God's Messiah for the incorporation of Gentiles into the people of God. Must Gentile converts become Jews to be part of the covenant people of God, to be Christians?

Second, the doctrine of justification is hammered out by Paul in two letters—Galatians and Romans—for the very specific purpose of enabling Gentile converts to be full and genuine heirs to the promises of God to Israel without becoming ethnic Jews.

Paul is a Jewish Christian concerned to see God's promises to Israel brought to complete fulfillment. Christianity is the fulfillment of Judaism, not the annulment of it. The fulfillment of Judaism means the incorporation of Gentiles into the people of God. Paul's argument in Romans is corporate. He is redefining the people of God to embrace Gentiles, as well as Jews. It is about God as the God of Jews as well as Gentiles; it is about the seed of Abraham; it is about incorporation into the new humanity of Christ over against the old humanity of Adam. Paul is redrawing the boundaries that mark out the covenant people of God.

Third, Judaism does not teach salvation by works. Salvation in Judaism is by God's election, by God's grace alone. Obedience to the Law is a means to maintain covenant salvation, not a means to earn it.

Fourth, Romans is read as a politically subversive letter. Over against the Roman imperial "good news" that Caesar is Lord, who brings justice and peace to the world, Paul proclaims a different "gospel"—Jesus is Lord, and he alone brings "righteousness" (justice) and peace. Jesus, not Caesar, is to be confessed and worshiped.

Finally, Romans is read as a pastoral letter addressing specific and concrete pastoral problems and issues among the house churches of Rome.

The Over-all Plan of Romans

Romans is a pastoral letter that aims to strengthen the life of the Roman house churches in the direction of unity. It is a genuine letter written to a specific audience facing a set of particular challenges and issues [*Essay: Letter Form*].

The goal of the letter is to persuade the Roman churches to adhere to shared beliefs and values, to see the gospel as the power of God for the salvation of all people, the Jew first and also the Gentile. The flip side is to persuade them to reject alternative beliefs and values which distinguish between people (e.g., that Gentiles must become Jews to be members of God's people, or that God has rejected the Jews as a people). Both the argumentative style and the repeated exhortations within the letter reflect this goal of persuasion.

A letter of persuasion (*epideictic* or *demonstrative letter*) follows a formal structural (*rhetorical*) pattern that is clearly evident in Romans. The formal outline of Romans is as follows:

Prescript	1:1-7
Thanksgiving	1:8-12
Disclosure Formula	1:13-15
Letter thesis	1:16-18
Argument	1:18-15:13
Conclusion	15:14-16:27

Within this formal structure, Paul uses many forms of communication which are familiar to his audience and are consistent with the goal of persuasion. For example, he uses chiasms—a parallel structure or word order that frames a central idea [*Essay: Chiasmus*]—or a diatribe, a dialogue between a teacher and an imaginary student [*Essay: Diatribe*]. The goal is always persuasion—to intensify commitment to and behavior consistent with the gospel as the power of God for the salvation of all people irrespective of ethnic origin.

The Larger Thought World of Romans

Romans must be understood within the larger structure of Paul's theology. The framework of this theology and of Romans is apocalyptic. Jewish apocalyptic theology is one type of OT covenant theology. Its foundation is the covenant between God and Israel. That covenant theology teaches that God acts in history to save Israel. Theologically that means God is in control of history, shaping events according to the divine will. On this basis the teachers of Israel taught that national disasters were God's response to Israel's infidelity to the covenant. In other words, OT covenant theology taught that God deals with evil within history. God raises up kings and nations to implement justice against sin. This theology bred the hope that in the future God would resolve the problem of evil by raising up a righteous nation and a righteous king out of Israel.

Apocalyptic theology represents a radicalization of this covenant theology that emerged during times of intense suffering and martyrdom in Israel. This radicalization accelerated especially after 167 B.C. and into the second century A.D.—the Maccabean period. Israel is a nation under siege. The oppression of these years gave birth to a profound awareness of the discrepancy between "what is" and "what should be." The conviction developed that "what is" is so evil that God can no longer effect the divine will from within history. The present world is ruled by Satan, death, and the forces of evil. Only a direct and radical intervention of God from outside of history will be able to change history.

History is the basic category in apocalyptic theology. The issue is God's plan and promises for Israel in history. The problem is God's apparent inability to overcome the power of evil. Once national disaster was a consequence of infidelity. Now fidelity seems to bring national disaster as an expression of cosmic evil. The experience of evil, and the nonfulfillment of divine promises, raises questions about God. The problem is resolved by developing a theology that says that God's future will not emerge out of the present or out of history, but will come from outside of and as a divine alternative to history.

The key theological category for this understanding of history was the concept of two ages, the present evil age and the future age to come. Two-age theology is fundamental to apocalyptic theology, whether or not the code phrases are used. The heart of apocalyptic theology is a view of history in which the present is discontinuous with the future. Such radical discontinuity is made necessary by the scope and intensity of evil in the present, and is made possible by the faith that the sovereignty of a righteous God will effect righteousness in the future. Apocalyptic theology is theodicy. It seeks to resolve the problem of suffering and evil among God's people with a fundamental dualism.

The knowledge of the reality of history and the future plan of God to transform reality totally with the introduction of a new age is secret. It can be known only by revelation (*apocalypsis*). Revelation imparts knowledge from the divine, privileged information, to selected prophets of God. The two-age theology combined with the revelatory communication of the present and the future creates a fundamental dualism that is characteristic of apocalyptic theology. The key components of the dualism are: 1) a temporal dualism: this age/the age to come; 2) an epistemological dualism: worldly knowledge/other-worldly knowledge; 3) a cosmic dualism: earth/heaven; and 4) a social dualism: the unrighteous/the righteous.

Jewish apocalyptic theology can be expressed diagrammatically as follows:

God's Intervention

The Present Evil Age | *The Age to Come*

The basic categories of Paul's theology, including Romans, are apocalyptic. He uses apocalyptic language and thought forms, e.g., "destined . . . for wrath," "the wrath to come," "the wrath of God," "the day of the Lord Jesus Christ," "the day of salvation," "redeemed," "redemption," "this age," "the rulers of this age," "the present evil age," "the ends of the ages," "new creation." But he also transforms Jewish apocalyptic thought in light of the death/resurrection of Jesus. Paul believes that in Jesus God has already begun the final act of transforming human history. The age to come has begun with Jesus. The present represents the juncture or the overlapping of the ages, as 1 Corinthians 10:11 states (literally, "upon whom the ends of the ages have met"). The diagram above of Jewish apocalyptic theology is thus modified by Paul as follows:

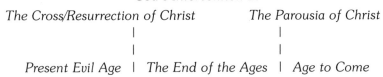

God's Intervention In

The Cross/Resurrection of Christ   *The Parousia of Christ*

Present Evil Age | *The End of the Ages* | *Age to Come*

In addition to this structural modification of Jewish apocalyptic theology, Paul introduces three other significant alterations, each of which is evident in Romans. First, he answers the theodicy question with God's act in the cross/resurrection of Jesus. Theodicy is an acute problem for people who see God as passive in the face of innocent suffering. Paul makes the case that God has acted, and acted righteously. The revelation of the righteousness of God, the theme of Romans in 1:16-18, answers the problem of theodicy. God is now acting righteously in behalf of sinners among all people. God is not absent from human suffering, but is suffering in and through Jesus to bring about cosmic righteousness. Paul can make that case, however, precisely because of his apocalyptic framework. He sees the death/resurrection of Jesus as eschatological events, which offer an alternative to the process of history that began with Adam. Paul's apocalyptic two-age theology enables him to grasp both the universality of the sin problem and the solution to it.

Second, Paul radicalizes the apocalyptic understanding of **Sin**. **Sin** for Paul is a power that enslaves (therefore, it is always in **bold**). It is bondage at one level to the power of the flesh. But it goes deeper; it is bondage to the power of the flesh which completely enslaves people and the world. **Sin**, in other words, is not simply a deed, but a power-force that conquers and enslaves all creation and all human beings.

Third, Paul's theology of salvation (*soteriology*) is christologically anchored and universal in scope. Much apocalyptic theology is ambivalent about a "messianic" figure and is nationalistic in proclaiming salvation/liberation for the Jews only. In some of the first-century B.C.-A.D. literature, a messianic figure plays a saving role, but in much of the literature there is no messianic figure. In contrast, Paul's doctrine of salvation is centered in Jesus as the Messiah of God. Messiah Jesus is decisive for salvation/liberation. He, and he alone, provides an alternative to Adam. Furthermore, Messiah Jesus' salvation in Paul does not vindicate Israel vis-à-vis the nations, but overcomes the division between Jews and Gentiles to create a new humanity.

Because God has acted decisively in Messiah Jesus to effect salvation for the world, Paul asserts that 1) **Sin** has been defeated (Gal. 1:4; 1 Cor. 15:3; Rom. 4:25); 2) death has been condemned (1 Cor. 15:54-57; Rom. 8:31-39); 3) creation itself has been reclaimed by God, although the battle goes on toward God's final victory (1 Cor. 15:2-28; Rom. 8:18-25); 4) God's sovereignty has been established (Rom. 8:31-39).

The theological grammar of Romans is apocalyptic. Paul's theology here shares the apocalyptic belief in the discontinuity of the present evil age with the age to come. But it also modifies this apocalyptic framework to announce the good news that God has now revealed end-time righteousness and salvation for all humanity and creation in Messiah Jesus. Jesus is God's apocalyptic answer to the problem of history introduced and defined by Adam (for a further discussion of Paul's apocalyptic theology, see Beker, 1980, Boomershine, 1989, deBoer, 1988 and 1989, Witherington, 1994).

The Problem of Language

Romans was written to mid-first century A.D. followers of Jesus, who shared an apocalyptic worldview. The letter is read today by Christians far removed from first-century language and realities. The house churches in the first century were part of Judaism. There was no Christian church distinct or separate from Judaism until sometime in the second century. The word "Christian" simply means the followers of the Jewish Messiah Jesus. Thus, to talk of the "Christian church" or of "Christianity" and Judaism is really to distort first-century realities. Romans is about an internal family debate concerning the nature, defining characteristics, and boundaries of the family faith. Or, to talk about sin as **Sin**, as a cosmic power that enslaves all people and creation, sounds strange to people in the twenty-first century.

Modern readers of Romans must constantly keep the family quality of the letter and the apocalyptic worldview of this family in mind. To accurately characterize first-century realities would require a wordiness that would be tiresome and irritating. When familiar language is used (e.g., Christian, church, sin), it is used with fear and trembling, and with the hope that modern readers can fill it with first century content and sensitivities.

This Commentary

This commentary is an attempt to provide a consistent re-reading of Romans on the basis of the new paradigm. This revised reading of Romans resonates more with Anabaptist-Mennonite perspectives on Christian faith and biblical interpretation than did the traditional Protestant understandings, which privileged the individual over the community. The person is valued indeed, but within the framework of the corporate. Salvation is for all, Jews and Gentiles. Romans hammers home the point that this salvation is for all humans, Jews and Gentiles, through God's faithfulness and the faith(fulness) of Jesus the Messiah/Christ.

The major literature on the new paradigm is found in the writings of people like J. C. Beker, D. A. Campbell, W. S. Campbell, K. P. Donfried, Neil Elliott, Mark Nanos, James Dunn, Richard Hays, Robert Jewett, Mark Reasoner, E. P. Sanders, Krister Stendahl, S. K. Stowers, James Walters, N. T. Wright (see bibliography for details). Not all these writers agree on the "faith of Jesus" translation and interpretation, but the proposal to translate the phrase as a subjective genitive appeared in articles and commentaries decades before the key points of the "new perspective" (E. P. Sanders, 1977, and J. D. G. Dunn, 1983:95-112; 1990a:183-214) emerged in scholarship, as described above.

Scripture cited in this commentary, as in other commentaries in the Believers Church Bible Commentary Series, appears in italic style and follows the NRSV, unless otherwise specified. However, in seeking to represent Paul's thought as precisely as possible, I have often rendered my own translation (indicated in the text with "JET trans."). Hence, in this Romans commentary scriptural citations in italic are either my own translation or from the NRSV. Translations from other versions are so designated.

Romans 1:1-15

Introduction

PREVIEW

Normally Greek letters begin with a prescript, a thanksgiving, and a disclosure formula. Paul follows this pattern in Romans. The Pauline introductions, however, are expanded due to the addition of significant theological content. The introduction to Romans is longer than any other Pauline letter. Paul has never been to Rome, and cannot take it for granted that he and his gospel will be accepted. Therefore, he must introduce himself in a way that will persuade the readers to accept and trust him. It is important that he create a positive relationship that will give him a hearing, and that will dispose the audience to accept and act on his message.

Paul frames his introduction very carefully. He introduces himself, his gospel, and his mission.

OUTLINE

Prescript, 1:1-7

Thanksgiving, 1:8-12

Disclosure Formula, 1:13-15

EXPLANATORY NOTES

Prescript 1:1-7

The prescript follows the structure common to ancient letters: author, addressee, greeting.

1:1-6 Author

Paul introduces himself boldly by setting forth his credentials on the model of the Old Testament prophets. He is *a servant* of Messiah Jesus, *called an apostle, set apart for the gospel of God.* A *servant* is literally a slave, a status most familiar to readers in Rome, but in this case a person chosen by God for special service. The verb *called* expresses divine calling in opposition to human self-appointment. *Apostle* denotes an authorized agent or representative. Paul is a slave, like many readers in his audience, who has been called to represent God. Specifically, as he will say in v. 5, he has been called as an apostle to the Gentiles. *Set apart or marked off* is OT language for election to a specific ministry. The phrase would remind Paul's readers of Jeremiah 1:5. The prophets discerned and proclaimed the intervention of God in human history. Paul is set apart to proclaim the good news of God's end-time (eschatological) intervention.

Having defined his own identity, Paul proceeds to define the gospel that he proclaims. The gospel concerns the fulfillment of past promises and the Messianic Son of God. Paul anchors it in God's prior history with Israel.

The gospel is about God's Son, Messiah Jesus our Lord. Verses 3-4 are a very carefully composed confession of faith that is poetically structured:

3a   concerning his Son
3b   who came about
3c   out of the seed of David
3d   according to the flesh
4a   who was appointed Son of God
4b   in power
4c   according to the Spirit of holiness
4d   out of the resurrection of the dead
4e   Messiah Jesus our Lord.

The confession also may be diagramed structurally as two parallel verses centered in the phrase *in power.*

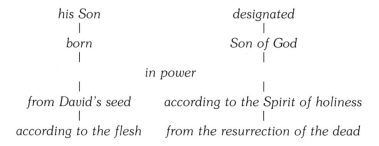

The center of the confession affirms Jesus as the Messiah in two titles, seed of David and Son of God. The confession says one thing about Jesus in two different ways. The first line confesses Jesus as the Davidic Messiah, as the fulfillment of Jewish messianic hopes. The second line declares Jesus as the Messiah in more exalted terms. The Son of God title here is not the full christological title used by the later church, but the messianic title of 2 Samuel 7 and Psalm 2:7. The language is OT enthronement language. Jesus has been enthroned as the Messiah in the resurrection. David as the Son of God, according to 2 Samuel 5:1ff., in intertestamental interpretation, is the anointed one who sums up Israel. The one represents the many, a theme that Paul will develop in ch. 5.

The confession begins with a reference to Messiah Jesus as the preexistent Son. The opening phrase *concerning his Son* (emphatic position) indicates that the one who was born of the seed of David was already the Son before and independent of *descending from David*. The confession concludes with a statement about Jesus' lordship. Jesus as the preexistent Son and the Messiah is the Lord of the world; he is the prime minister of God who sits at God's right hand and executes God's will in the world. The lordship theme is closely related to the revelation of the righteousness of God in 1:16-17 and the future acknowledgment of the nations in 15:10-12. It is at the same time a theme designed to subvert Roman imperial ideology—Jesus is Lord, not Caesar.

The parallel to *according to the flesh* in the first clause is not "according to the Spirit" but *according to the Spirit of holiness*. The phrase is rare (see Test. Levi 18:11) so that its precise meaning is difficult to determine. Jesus is enthroned as Son of God in power by the Spirit of holiness. The word *holiness* is used in only two other Pauline texts—1 Thessalonians 3:13 and 2 Corinthians 7:1. Both texts stress ethical obligation. *Spirit of holiness* suggests that the power involved in the resurrection entails moral obligation, or righteousness to use a thematic word from Romans. This theme will be developed in chapters 5–8 and 12–15.

Jesus is enthroned as Son of God *out of the resurrection **of** the dead* (JET). The phrase also is unique. Paul speaks of the resurrection of Jesus as *his resurrection* or *out of the resurrection **from** the dead*. Most translators assume the phrase refers to the resurrection of Jesus (NRSV, NEB, NIV). A minority read it as *by the resurrection of dead persons* (RV, Moffatt). The latter is preferable. The reference is to the general resurrection from the dead. The resurrection of Jesus is viewed in its cosmic function as

the beginning of the general resurrection. Early Christian apocalyptic thought linked the resurrection of Christ and the dawn of the
age of the general resurrection. Messiah Jesus is the first person to
rise from the dead; his resurrection makes possible the general resurrection. The language suggests the overlap of the ages [see the
earlier discussion of "The Larger Thought World of Romans" in the
Introduction to this commentary].

The one phrase that is without parallel in the confession, and
stands at the center of the confession, is *in power*. Jesus was
enthroned as Son of God *in power* by the end-time Spirit by means
of the resurrection. An act of end-time power is described. The evidence was the inauguration of the end-time resurrection of the dead.
The center of the confession is a statement about Spirit power that
enthrones Jesus as Son of God and Lord. The emphasis on power
attunes Paul's audience to what such power might mean and promise.
Paul answers that expectation at the outset by declaring that the
gospel is power, end-time power (1:16), and in his benediction by
asserting that hope abounds and the gospel is spread because of the
power of the Spirit (15:13, 19). Romans is about power; the letter is
bracketed by power language, particularly the confession of 1:4, the
theme of 1:16, and the benediction of 15:13, 19.

What is the function of the confession in Romans? An introduction is designed to introduce the author in an appealing way that will
lend credence to his concerns. It frequently also introduces topics to
be addressed in the letter. Of all Paul's letters only Romans includes
a confession in the introduction; it thus signals something important
for Paul and his audience. Paul introduces himself with a confessional statement designed to build common ground for the diverse
groups in the Roman churches. Its purpose is to be inclusive rather
than exclusive. It is not a litmus test of orthodoxy, but of the inclusiveness of the gospel. That is why the confession is grounded in
Israel's Scriptures and is centered christologically. It confesses Jesus
as Messiah in two different ways. It emphasizes the end-time role of
the Spirit in the enthronement of Jesus as Son of God, and
describes the activity of the Spirit as the powerful inauguration of
the end-time resurrection of the dead. The confession introduces
themes that Paul will expand in addressing the pastoral issues in
Rome.

Paul's mission concerns the gospel of God that consists in a message about Jesus as the Messiah. He is the Son of God, the Davidic
Messiah, whose messiahship and sonship are validated by the resurrection. This theological confession also is a political statement. The

good news is about Jesus, not Caesar. Paul opens the letter by addressing the seat of Roman power. He introduces Jesus as the true king and savior of the whole world. Jesus alone is the Lord of the world (see especially Elliott, 1994; Georgi, 1991; Horsley, 1997 and 2000).

Paul concludes Romans with a similar assertion (15:7-13). He makes the case through a carefully constructed sequence of Scripture passages that Messiah Jesus, from *the root of Jesse*, will *rule the Gentiles* (15:12). The hope of the world is Jesus, not Caesar. Paul frames Romans as a direct challenge to the imperial Roman proclamation that Caesar is the son of God and the ruler of the world.

Paul's third point in the prescript is to define his mission. Jesus' lordship is the basis of Paul's *apostleship* (v. 5), and the basis of his right to address the Roman churches (v. 6). Paul has been gifted with apostleship. *Grace (charis)*, a favorite word for Paul, is rarely used in Judaism. The Jews used "mercy" (*eleos*) to interpret God's saving activity. Paul replaces mercy with *grace*. He is the first early-Christian theologian to use it in a technical way to interpret the meaning of salvation. Grace interprets God's salvation as a gift that has nothing to do with human activity. Likewise, the office of apostle is a gift undeserved by Paul.

The purpose of the gift of apostleship is *to bring about the obedience of faith*. Paul uses the same phrase again in 16:26 to describe the purpose of his preaching. The phrase, unique to Romans, means "the obedience that consists in faith and the obedience that is the product of faith." Faith and obedience are closely linked and interchangeable for Paul [*Essays: Faith in Romans* and *Obedience*]. Obedience is exercised only from faith, and faith becomes a reality only in obedience. The phrase *obedience of faith* has an argumentative purpose in Romans. It marries the two watchwords of two major groups in tension in Rome. Faith was the watchword of the Gentile Christians, which they weakened by behavior without love. Obedience, in turn, was the slogan of the Jewish Christians, which they unhooked from faith. Furthermore, against the backdrop of faith's obedience in Jewish literature, it carries one other meaning. The covenant faithfulness of God's people Israel is now a possibility without assuming the identity of that people. To make the purpose of his apostleship "faith which is obedience" unifies the two people and the two theologies that are in tension among the house churches of Rome. There is one people of God that expresses obedience through faith and faith through obedience.

The purpose of Paul's mission *among all the Gentiles* (nations) is to make manifest the nature of God's name, literally "in behalf of his name." The phrase is borrowed from the OT (Ps. 106:8; Ezek. 20:14; Mal. 1:11). The name of God is connected with divine revelation. The gaining of new converts and their fidelity serves to commend the further revelation of God. The evangelism of the world does not just serve the good of those converted, but above all it discloses God's nature. In 1:8 Paul gives thanks for the faith of the Roman believers, which is known worldwide, in 15:18 he speaks of winning the obedience of the Gentiles, and in 16:19 of the obedience of the Roman Christians, which also is known throughout the world. All these things serve to manifest the name of God.

Unable to appeal to a history of personal acquaintance, as in his other letters, Paul relies on what he and the Romans share, the same faith and values. The prescript abounds with important faith symbols that build community: gospel, Messiah Jesus, God, Holy Spirit, prophets, holy writings, David, and divinely appointed apostleship. Paul's opening point is that we are one in the faith and belong to the same community of faith.

1:7a The Addressees

The readers are "all the ones being in Rome." The description of them is brief. The *all* is emphatic, and is reiterated in v. 8. All the followers of Jesus in Rome *are called.* Narrow definitions of who is in and/or out are rejected from the beginning of the letter. Furthermore, all are *loved of God* and *called saints.* God is pictured in the OT as the one who calls and loves a people. The Roman believers, all of them, are such a people.

1:7b Greetings

In the ancient world a letter's opening regularly concluded with a greeting, such as "be glad" or "good day." Paul changes the greeting formula. His greeting typically contains four elements: a wish (grace), the recipient (to you), a wish (peace), and a divine source (from God our Father and the Lord Jesus Christ). The use of grace (*charis*) in a greeting is without parallel. "Peace" (*shalom*) is the standard Hebrew greeting. The phrase "grace and peace" is a specifically Pauline creation (Lieu). Paul combines his distinctive theological term "grace" with the Hebrew peace greeting to form his own religious greeting. Another Pauline creation is the addition of the divine source of the greeting. Paul proclaims to the churches of Rome the gifts of salvation made available by God through Messiah Jesus.

Thanksgiving 1:8-12

Paul elaborates the traditional thanksgiving formula into a formal literary pattern in all his letters except Galatians. The thanksgiving formula in Romans is clearly defined. It begins with the principle clause of "thanksgiving to God" in v. 8 and concludes with v. 12. Verse 13 begins another text unit, as indicated by the use of the disclosure formula, *I want you to know*. The thanksgiving formula contains four parts: 1) the thanksgiving; 2) an oath; 3) a prayer sigh; and 4) the reasons. The thanksgiving continues to build the positive relationship begun in the prescript.

1:8 The Thanksgiving

The thanksgiving is *to God in behalf of all of you*. The *all of you* indicates a particular emphasis in Romans. All the followers of Jesus in Rome, whether Jew or Gentile, are included in the scope of Paul's prayer. The basis of Paul's thanksgiving is the faith of the Roman Christians, which *is proclaimed* worldwide. The presence of communities of disciples in the capital of the empire means a lot to Paul.

An important function of the thanksgiving in Paul's letters is to introduce themes he will elaborate later. The inclusiveness of the thanksgiving (*all of you*) and the importance of faith are both significant themes Paul will identify in the thesis and then discuss in the body.

1:9 An Oath

Paul introduces God as a witness that he regularly intercedes for the churches in Rome. Unable to prove it from a distance, Paul invokes God to underline his deep concern. He links God's witness role to a statement about the nature of his own ministry, which is a service offered to God. In both the LXX and the NT *service* (*latreuō*) is exclusively religious service offered either to the one true God or to pagan gods. For Paul it denotes all service that Christians offer to God. In v. 9 this service is defined specifically as the preaching of the gospel. The language here is parallel to 15:16, where Paul describes himself as a *servant of Messiah Jesus* who renders a *priestly service* by presenting to God *the offering* which the Gentile converts make.

1:10 A Prayer Sigh

The prayer formula within the thanksgiving is introduced by a verb for praying, and a phrase indicating the content of the prayer. The prayer in v. 10 is unusual in several respects. For one thing, it is the shortest petition found in the thanksgivings. Second, the request concerns the apostle himself rather than the recipients as in all other thanksgiving petitions. Third, the prayer is in the form of a question, similar to the sighs of the psalmists (e.g., 13:2; 35:17; 42:2). Paul's prayer is for a successful journey to Rome, a prayer he repeats in 15:30.

1:11-12 The Reasons

The reason for Paul's prayer is encouragement, *to impart some spiritual gift to strengthen you*. The particular gift is not specified. Verse 12 introduces a compliment or a correction. Paul wants to visit Rome to encourage and to be encouraged.

It is noteworthy that the focus of this thanksgiving, as in most thanksgivings in Paul's letters, is the *gospel, the proclamation* of the Romans' faith (v. 8), *the gospel of his son* (v. 9). The ground for thanksgiving is the gospel and its work among people. This emphasis on the gospel will continue into the next two text units in Romans, the disclosure formula, vv. 13-15 (*to proclaim the gospel* in v. 15), and the thesis statement, vv. 16-18 (*gospel* in v. 16).

Disclosure Formula 1:13-15

The thanksgiving is regularly followed by a disclosure formula in Greek letters. The purpose of this formula is to communicate important information to the readers. The formula contains four parts: 1) the verb *exhort* or *wish*; 2) a verb of knowing; 3) the person(s) addressed; and 4) the wish or information. Sometimes the direct form of address also is used (e.g., *brothers*, in v. 13).

Paul reinforces his previously stated desire to come to Rome. He wants the churches to know that he frequently made plans to visit, but was prevented. In 15:22 Paul refers again to having been prevented from coming to Rome. The purpose was to encourage the churches and to engage in missionary work.

Paul wants to visit and evangelize in the city because he is a *debtor*. A debtor owes another person money either because of a loan or because of a gift that obligates. But neither of these normal definitions fit Paul's relationship to the Roman churches. He does not know them, has not borrowed from them, and has not received anything from them. Instead, he has an apostolic obligation to them. The principle that Jesus made binding on his disciples had become binding on Paul: Christ's purpose in giving a gift to one disciple was that he/she might give it to another. This obligation is particularly important for Paul. God called him *to be a servant of Messiah Jesus to the Gentiles in order that the offering of the Gentiles might become acceptable* (15:16).

The object of the obligation embraces the entire Gentile world. Both pairs, *Greeks and barbarians* and *also wise and mindless* (JET), represent a Greek perspective on the categories of humanity. "Greek and barbarian" differentiates those Gentiles who possess Greco-Roman culture and the rest of the Gentiles, especially Orientals, which would include Jews. "Wise and also mindless" is an explanation of "Greek and barbarian"; it distinguishes those who are intelligent and educated from those who are not. In Rome this ethnocentric division of humanity was directed especially against immigrating "barbarians" from the Orient, which would include Jews and Jewish Christians returning to the city following the expiration of Claudius' edict of expulsion. Paul's apostolic obligation relativizes all cultural barriers between people. As an apostle of Messiah Jesus Paul crosses the conventions and prejudices that divide the world.

The Pattern

Running through "the thanksgiving" and "disclosure formula" and into the "thesis statement" is a pattern of argument designed to embrace the Roman Christians. Three times Paul asserts his desire to visit Rome and each time he gives the reasons for these intentions.

> Vv. 9-10 Intention—Paul's prayer to visit Rome
> > Vv. 11-12 Reason—to impart a spiritual gift, to be strengthened
> Vv. 13a Intention—Paul's long-standing desire to visit Rome
> > Vv. 13b-14 Reason—to reap some harvest among the Gentiles
> V. 15 Intention—Paul's long-standing eagerness
> > Vv. 16-18 Reason—the power of the gospel

The Framing 1:1-15 and 15:14-33

Romans is bracketed by an apostolic presence (*parousia* = coming). Paul encloses the letter in concerns about the Romans and about his coming, 1:1-15 and 15:14-33. The parallelism and overlap of information between the two sections is striking, as illustrated below (Figure 1).

The whole letter is framed by a formal structure (chiastic) that is designed to create a positive environment for hearing Paul:

> A 1:8 Paul gives thanks for the Romans' faith
> > B 1:9 Paul's prayer for the Romans
> > > C 1:10-11 Paul's desire to visit Rome
> > > > D 1:13 Paul prevented from visiting Rome
> > > > > E 1:14-15 Paul's mission to the Gentiles
> > > > > E 15:14-16 Paul's mission to the Gentiles

D 15:17-22 Paul hindered from visiting Rome
C 15:23-29 Paul will go to Rome after Jerusalem
B 15:30-32 Paul exhorts prayer for him
A 15:33 Paul invokes peace for the Romans

The parallelism between 1:1-15 and 15:14-33 reflects a deliberate composition. Paul wraps his pastoral concerns for the unity of Jews and Gentiles under the righteousness of God in the context of his apostolic presence.

TEXT IN BIBLICAL CONTEXT

Paul's central concern in the introduction is the gospel and its proclamation. The word gospel (both noun, *euangelion*, and verb, *euangelizein*) enjoys a prominence in Paul that is unparalleled in the rest of the NT (81 out of 130 uses; 23 in the LXX). But the idea is not unique to him. His use is grounded in a rich tradition of meaning.

Figure 1

1. I-you: dialogue	1:1, 6	15:14ff.
2. Praise of the Romans	1:8	15:14
3. Praying	1:8-10	15:30
4. The apostle's ministry	1:1, 5f., 8-17	15:15-33
4.1 Act of God's grace	1:5	15:15
4.2 Service character	1:1	15:16
	1:9	15:23, 31
4.3 For the nations	1:5, 13	15:16
	1:14-15	15:27
4.4 For obedience	1:5	15:18
4.5 Intention to visit	1:10, 11, 13, 15	15:22, 23, 24, 28, 29, 32
4.6 Bring a blessing	1:11	15:29
4.7 Dependence on God	1:10	15:32
4.8 Prevented so far	1:10, 13	15:22
4.9 Attitude	1:16	15:17
5. References to the gospel	1:1, 9, 15, 16	15:16, 19, 20
6. Power of the gospel	1:16	15:19 (2x)
7. Peace greeting	1:7	15:33
8. Wish for fruit	1:13	15:28
9. Sense of obligation	1:14	15:27

The basic meaning of the word is "good news" (to tell the good news in the verb form, or the content of the good news in the noun form). It is used in Greco-Roman literature to announce the good news of a military victory, or the accession of a new emperor, or the coming of the emperor to a community, or the birth of an heir to the emperor. For example, the accession of Augustus as Roman emperor is announced in 9 B.C., just a few years before the birth of Jesus, as follows:

> The providence which has ordered the whole of our life . . . has ordained the most perfect consummation for human life by giving to it Augustus, by filling him with virtue for doing the work of a benefactor among men, and by sending him, as it were, a saviour for us and those who come after us, to make war to cease, to create order everywhere . . . the birthday of the god [Augustus] was the beginning for the world of **the glad tidings** [gospel] that have come to men (sic) through him.

In the OT it was used to tell good news after a victory in battle (1 Sam. 31:9) or to announce the breaking-in of God's rule and the coming of salvation (Pss. 40:9; 96:2). But it is Isaiah 40-66 that shapes its meaning for the writers of the early church. Isaiah 40:9 and 52:7 are especially important in defining the meaning of "the gospel":

> Get you up to the high mountain,
> O Zion, herald of **good tidings** [gospel];
> lift up your voice with strength,
> O Jerusalem, herald of **good tidings** [gospel]
> lift it up, do not fear;
> say to the cities of Judah,
> 'Here is your God!'
> How beautiful upon the mountains
> are the feet of the messenger who **announces peace**
>   [lit., gospel's peace]
> who brings **good news** [gospel]
> who announces salvation,
> who says to Zion, 'Your God reigns.'

Gospel, in fact, becomes a technical term for the announcement of salvation proclaimed by the prophet. It announces God's universal victory, God's kingly rule, and God's enthronement as king. It is linked with the return of the Jewish people to Jerusalem and thus the end of exile, freedom from bondage, the coming eschatological salvation, the inclusion of the Gentiles in God's people, peace and righteousness, the anointing of the messenger with the Spirit.

This eschatological understanding of *gospel* continued into later Jewish literature. The most striking evidence comes from the Dead

Sea or Qumran Scrolls. The "Melchizedek Scroll" uses two texts from Isaiah, 52:7 and 61:1 (11Q13), to describe the good news as the eschatological liberation of the community from the domination of evil powers through the agency of a heavenly being.

Paul interprets the meaning of Jesus in continuity with this eschatological understanding of "good news" from Isaiah and Qumran. "Gospel" expresses in summary fashion the message that Paul announced to the world. It is his way of summing up the significance of the Jesus-event, and the meaning of the lordship of Jesus for human history. That Paul can use the term absolutely (at least 23 times) indicates that the term was already familiar to his readers.

The content and authorship of the gospel is stated succinctly by Paul. It is the *gospel of God* (Rom. 1:1; 15:16; 1 Thess. 2:2, 8; 2 Cor. 11:7), *the gospel of Christ* (1 Thess. 3:2; Gal. 1:7; Phil. 1:27; 1 Cor. 9:12; 2 Cor. 2:12; 9:13; 10:14; Rom. 15:19), *the gospel of our Lord Jesus* (2 Thess. 1:8), and *the gospel of his Son* (Rom. 1:9). The genitive *of* in each of these phrases indicates both content and authorship. The gospel is from God and about God, from Messiah Jesus and about Messiah Jesus. *My gospel* is unique to Romans (2:16; 16:25). It is a polemical framing of *the gospel* that stands over against other understandings of the good news.

Paul characterizes this gospel in various ways. It is promissory, having been promised by the prophets of Israel (Rom. 1:2). The gospel fulfills the promises of God. Second, it is revelatory, revealing the righteousness and wrath of God (1:17-18). It demonstrates for the world the reality of the new age. Third, the gospel is powerful, the power of God for salvation (1:16). It unleashes God's end-time power in history to effect salvation. Fourth, the gospel is universal. It is *for everyone who believes, for the Jew first and also for the Greek* (1:16). Finally, the gospel is normative. There is only one gospel (Gal. 1:7). People are expected to listen to it (Eph. 1:13), to welcome it (2 Cor. 11:4), to obey it (2 Thess. 1:8; Rom. 10:16). Those who diverge from it are to be corrected so that they may *walk straight according to the truth of the gospel* (Gal. 2:14).

The gospel is defined at the beginning of Romans as the announcement that Jesus is the Messianic King. He alone brings peace, righteousness, and salvation. This "good news" is at the same time a declaration that Caesar is not King, that Caesar does not bring real peace, that Caesar is not Savior.

TEXT IN THE LIFE OF THE CHURCH
Gospel

Romans centers the gospel in Messiah Jesus. Paul's own identity, the center of the gospel, the driving force of his mission, the hallmark of the church's confession is Messiah Jesus. In a world "where things fall apart, the center does not hold," Paul offers a bold claim. The people of God must be centered in the gospel of Messiah Jesus. Jesus, not Caesar, is Lord and King.

The gospel is first and foremost about a person, Messiah Jesus manifesting God's reign. It is the good news that "God is with us" in and through Messiah Jesus. What does it mean for the church in the post-modern West to proclaim and to live the good news? What does it mean for the church in the East and the South to be centered in the gospel? To what does the gospel say "no" in these cultures? What does the gospel stand over against? The gospel means that salvation and politics must be redefined in terms of Jesus as Messiah and Lord.

The gospel that Jesus is Messiah always involves fulfillment, new beginnings, new definitions of identity, and new obligations. The gospel is always two things at the same time, fulfillment and newness. It is about God keeping promises to bring redemption to humanity and to the world. It involves the beginning of a new era in history. That newness is identified most strikingly in this text as the beginning of the end-time resurrection of the dead.

This calls for a complete redefinition of group identity. The gospel is not for a few people, or a select group of "elect" people. The fulfillment of promises to the chosen people through Jesus involves redrawing the boundaries to include everyone. The gospel is inclusive, not exclusive. It is for "all the nations," for all people. The saints now include "Jews and Gentiles," "Greeks and barbarians," "wise and mindless," ethnic people of all tribes rather than just one. How does the gospel shape the church's identity today? Who is everyone in a post-modern world?

The Obedience of Faith

The gospel demands a response. It calls for obedience as an expression of faith. The gospel demands a new allegiance, loyalty to Jesus as Lord, rather than to Caesar as Lord. That allegiance must be expressed in trust that is demonstrated in life. The Radical Reformers of the sixteenth century understood the gospel to call for the transformation of loyalties and life. Jesus as Lord meant to follow Jesus in life and in death.

Romans 1:16-18

The Thesis Statement

PREVIEW

In the literary form of a Greek letter, the introduction is followed by a statement of its thesis. The precise dividing point between the opening of a letter, the statement of thesis, and the body of the letter itself can be somewhat fluid, as it is here in Romans.

In vv. 16-18, Paul clearly sets forth the three thematic statements of the letter: 1) the gospel is God's power for salvation, for Jews as well as Greeks (v. 16); 2) the gospel is *the revelation of the righteousness of God by means of faithfulness for the purpose of faithfulness* (v. 17); 3) the gospel is the revelation of the wrath of God against all ungodliness and unrighteousness (v. 18).

The thesis statement contains a chiasm, a symmetry of word order [*Essay: Chiasmus*]. Notice how the last two thematic statements, vv. 17-18, are parallel but contrasting:

A for the righteousness of God
   B is revealed
   B is revealed
A for the wrath of God

The same verb, "revealed," is used in both verses to relate contrasting ideas, the righteousness of God and the wrath of God. In the argument of the letter, Paul deals with these ideas in the reverse order of the thesis statement.

In addition to the chiasm, which frames the thesis statement, the thesis contains a repetition of a key word in Romans—faith: "to everyone who is **faithful**" (v. 16), "by means of **faithfulness** for the purpose of **faithfulness**" (v. 17), "the righteous one lives by means of **faithfulness**" (v. 17). The term "faith" represents a major translation issue. In English there is a difference between someone who is "faithful" and someone who "believes." The first means to keep faith with a promise or commitment, the latter to believe in someone or something. English lacks a verb "to faith." The word Paul uses here and throughout Romans really means "to be faithful," rather than to believe. Paul explains the meaning of this language as the letter proceeds [*Essay: Faith in Romans*].

Although vv. 16-18 state the thesis of the letter, they are also transitional; they are linked to what precedes and what follows. The statement of thesis tells us why Paul is eager to preach the gospel in Rome. He is eager (v. 15) *because*:

> –he is not ashamed of the gospel (v. 16a);
> –the gospel is the power of God for the salvation of all peoples (v. 16b);
> –the gospel reveals the righteousness of God (v. 17);
> –the gospel reveals the wrath of God against all sin (v. 18); and
> –people know about God (v. 19).

Not only are vv. 16-18 transitional, but they also formally introduce the first text unit of the argument. Verse 16 opens with "for not," and 2:11, the concluding verse of the first major text unit of the argument, begins with "for not." Paul is "not ashamed" of the gospel "for not" is there a distinction between peoples in the gospel.

OUTLINE

The Thesis, 1:16

The Explanation, 1:17-18

1:17   The gospel reveals the righteousness of God

1:18   The gospel reveals the wrath of God

EXPLANATORY NOTES
The Thesis 1:16

Paul introduces the thematic statement in a strange way, saying that he is *not ashamed of the gospel*. Why should he be ashamed? Most commentators explain these words psychologically saying Paul did not have a negative attitude toward the gospel. But that reading misses the radical point Paul is making.

Honor-Shame Language

The Roman world was an honor-shame culture, not a guilt-forgiveness culture [*Essay: Honor-Shame*]. Society was ordered according to a strict social status ladder that defined a hierarchy of honor. To violate the social order was to be shamed. *I am not ashamed of the gospel* is addressing questions of honor and shame in a caste society, a major theme in Romans (e.g., 1:21, 22, 24, 26, 31; 2:7, 19, 23; 6:21; 9:33; 10:11; 12:10; 13:7; 14:6). Christians among the Roman churches are ashamed of each other. They are calling each other names, like "circumcised penis" and "foreskin" (ch. 2), "weak" and "strong" (chs. 14-15), because they do not believe the gospel redefines social and religious status.

Paul's advice here, and in chs. 2, 14-15, is shocking to a society ordered by a hierarchy of honor. To say that circumcision is meaningless is revolutionary for both Jews and Romans, or to ask the strong to "bear" the weak, even to "welcome" them, is very problematic in a caste culture. For the strong to accept the weak is to make them equals and therefore to lose honor for themselves. To accept people from a different rung of the status ladder violates the standard social boundaries.

So to begin the thesis statement with *I am not ashamed of the gospel* is to assert at the outset that Paul expects the gospel to disrupt the established values of an honor-shame society. Paul's opening statement is polemical. He is arguing a point.

The Power of God

Paul is so confident about the transforming nature of the gospel, because it *is the power of God to salvation*. Power language is frequent in Paul (he uses *power* [*dunamis*] 48 times, eight times in Romans). *The power of God* (*dunamis theou*) describes the nature of God in OT covenant language. God exercises power in history on behalf of God's people because of the covenant relationship. The great models of God's power in the OT are the exodus event (Exod. 15:6, 13; Deut. 3:24; 9:26, 29) and the creation of the world (Jer. 34:5; 39:17). In Jewish apocalyptic literature the phrase "the power of God" is redefined eschatologically. That is, the end of history will be characterized by a worldwide demonstration of God's mighty power, known previously only by Israel. Paul has already referred to the exercise of this power in the present age in the resurrection of Jesus from the dead (1:4). Now he says the gospel is also the end-time, world-transforming power of God.

The gospel as *the power of God* is as polemical as *I am not ashamed*. According to 15:1 the different Christian groups are calling each other *strong* (*dunatoi*) and *weak* (*adunatoi*), all from the same root as *power* (*dunamis*). They are putting each other down instead of letting the power of God transform their cultural categories. Paul is eager to preach the gospel in Rome, because he knows the end-time, world-transforming power of God changes the honor-shame values.

The power language in the thesis statement also sets the stage for the discussion of **Sin** as power. The problem in the world, according to Romans, is the overwhelming reality of **Sin** as a cosmic power that enslaves all people and all creation. What is needed is an alternative power that can defeat the power of **Sin**. The gospel is the power of God that created the world, liberated Israel from Egypt, and raised Jesus from the dead. That power means something for the church.

Salvation

The power of God creates salvation (*sōteria*). In Hellenistic Greek and in the Septuagint (LXX), the Greek translation of the OT, "salvation" means deliverance from danger and death. It also is used in the LXX to describe God's great deliverances of Israel, e.g., the Exodus and the release from Babylonian captivity. This meaning was intensified in Jewish apocalyptic literature where it means God's end-time deliverance of Israel from the powers of Satan, death, and final judgment. That future power of deliverance is already present and operative in history through the death and resurrection of Messiah Jesus. That is why Paul is so confident in preaching his gospel. The gospel will effect end-time deliverance already now from whatever form of bondage exists in the church.

The gospel is the end-time power of salvation *to everyone [who is] being faithful*. The word *everyone* introduces another central theme of Romans, the universal scope of God's salvation. *Everyone* is more than a positive assertion; it is another polemical statement. The gospel includes **all** people. *All* or *everyone* (*pas*) occurs 71 times in Romans. It is used 25 times in such weighty expressions as *salvation to everyone who believes* (1:16), *all have sinned* (3:23), *that he might have mercy on all* (11:32), and five times with *Jews and Gentiles* (1:16; 2:9, 10; 3:9; 10:12). Paul is addressing partisans in Rome who are drawing the circle of inclusion too narrowly. The

Christian church includes everyone, irrespective of ethnic origin or social status.

But the gospel is also exclusive. It is for those *being faithful*, those who respond appropriately to the good news of God's salvation [*Essay: Faith in Romans*].

To the Jews first and also to the Greek explains *everyone. And also* indicates the fundamental equality of Jew and Gentile in the gospel. The word *first* denotes the historical reality that the Jews have precedence for the sake of God's plan. The letter *insists there is no distinction* (3:22; 10:12) yet supports the continuing validity of *the Jew first*. The thrust, on the one hand, is not to claim superiority for the Jew, but to argue for the equality of Jews and Gentiles. But, on the other hand, discrimination in Rome against Jews and Jewish Christians requires a reminder that God called the Jews first, and that God is and will be faithful to them. The tension between the priority of the Jew in salvation history and the equality of all people in the gospel is an issue to which Paul will return in the letter (see chs. 3, 9-11).

The Explanation 1:17-18

Righteousness

Verse 17, an explanation and confirmation of v. 16, introduces more key language in Romans, righteousness (*dikaiosunē*) and righteousness of God (*dikaiosunē theou*). Sixty percent of "righteousness" and 80% of "righteousness of God" language in Paul is used in Romans [*Essays: Righteousness and Righteousness of God*]. The translation of these words is a problem, because English does not have a verb form for "righteous." All of the Greek words for righteousness come from the same root word (*dik*), but this is lost in English because we use a different word, "justify," to translate the verb (*dikaioō*). Therefore, it is easy for English readers to miss the fact that Paul is talking about righteousness, about making right or justice, as essential to any notion of justification. To avoid this problem the words *make righteous* will be used consistently in this commentary for the verb. Paul is talking about *making right*, not some simple form of justifying.

The righteousness of God refers to the faithfulness of God to the promises of the covenant with Israel and to the promises to save all humanity, especially the Gentiles. It also refers to God's power "to make things right." The context for righteousness language in Romans is Jew/Gentile relations in the church, especially the legitimacy of Gentiles as equal partners with Jews in the new end-time community God is creating in Messiah Jesus. The question being answered by righteousness language is how God keeps faith with the promises to Israel by including the Gentiles in this people. Paul's concern is the end-time ordering of the world according to the covenant and the promises to Abraham.

The verb *revealed* describes the disclosure of end-time and cosmic secrets that are hidden from human beings. The tense of the verb is present, "is being revealed." A continuous revelation is taking place in the gospel. Paul's point in v. 17 is that an end-time, world-transforming revelation of God's righteousness is taking place now through the gospel.

Habakkuk 2:4

The phrase *by means of faithfulness for the purpose of faithfulness* (*ek pisteōs eis pistin*) must be understood on the basis of the quotation from Habakkuk 2:4 which follows it. Paul uses the specific phrase "from faithfulness to faithfulness" (*ek pisteōs eis pistin*) only in the two letters that quote the Habakkuk 2:4 text, but it is used 21 times in these letters so it is clearly an important concept. The phrase is best interpreted as translated above, by means of God's faithfulness for the purpose of humanity's faith. God takes the initiative. Human beings respond. Human faith is not a precondition for the revelation of God's righteousness, but a response to it.

Paul cites Habakkuk 2:4b, "as it is written, 'the righteous one shall live by faithfulness,'" in confirmation of v. 17a. Two critical issues affect the translation and interpretation of this citation. The first is the referent of "the righteous one" (*ho dikaios*). Traditional Protestant interpretation reads the phrase to mean the person who is declared righteous because he/she has responded in faith to God's revelation. But the phrase can also be understood as referring to the Messiah. "The righteous one" is the Messiah in the LXX of Habakkuk, and in a Jewish tradition of interpreting that text as a messianic prophecy. Other Jewish writings and the early church make the same identification (see *1 En.* 38:2; 53:6; Acts 3:14; 7:52; 22:14; 1 Pet. 3:18; 1 John 2:1, 29, 3:7). "The righteous one" in *1 Enoch* is the instrument of God's saving and judging power. He also is called the "Son of Man," and is glorified by God. In Peter's speech in Acts 3:14 "the righteous one" is the person God raised from the dead and glorified. His coming fulfills God's promises to Israel. In Stephen's speech in Acts 7, "the righteous one" is the Son of Man whose coming was "prophesied beforehand" (the same word as in Rom. 1:2) whom God now has exalted. *The righteous one* in Paul's speech in Acts 22:14 is linked with an apocalyptic vision and a commissioning to be a witness of Jesus as Messiah to the nations.

Each of these references to "the righteous one" appears in apocalyptic contexts. The *Enoch* and Acts 3:14 and 7:52 references are associated with another messianic title, Son of Man, suggesting a common messianic understanding of both titles. All of the Acts references associate "the righteous one" with the fulfillment of God's promises to Israel. The fact that all the Acts speeches that use this term occur before Jewish audiences suggests its common messianic connotation in some groups within first century Judaism. The 1 Peter 3:18 reference, which many believe is based on Isaiah 53:10-12, similarly links suffering unjustly to vindication and exaltation by God. The 1 John 2:1 reference is similar to the mention in 1 Peter—"the righteous one" makes atonement for the unrighteous. *The righteous one* in Romans 1:17 is likely a reference to the Messiah. The case for this reading is strengthened by the fact that both in Romans and in the other letters of Paul when "the righteous one" is used absolutely (not as a generic reference) it refers either to God, Christ, or the law, and never to human beings (in Romans see 2:13 and 5:7 for its reference to generic good people; 3:26 for reference God; 5:19 for reference to "the ones made righteous through the obedient one"; 7:12 for a description of the law). The Messiah, not human beings who trust in Jesus, is the confirmation of the end-time, world-transforming revelation of the righteousness of God (see D. Campbell, 1994b; Dodd, 1995; Hays, 1989b; Zorn, 1998).

The majority of modern translations give two readings of the Habakkuk quotation. The text usually reads, *he who through faith is righteous shall live*. The footnote gives an alternative reading, "The righteous (one) shall live by faith" (but see the NIV and the NRSV for this reading in the text). The translation in the footnote or the NIV and NRSV is the reading in all first century Jewish texts and interpretations. The emphasis is on the righteous one living out of faithfulness. It seems best to follow the common pattern of the first century. The point of the passage is its reference to faithfulness rather than righteousness.

But the question remains, whose faithfulness? The Hebrew text, the LXX, which Paul is quoting, and the Dead Sea Scrolls talk about the faithfulness of God, not the faith response of humans. The issue in Habakkuk is the faithfulness of God in the face of Chaldean oppression. In Habakkuk 2 the contrast is the self-assertion and boastfulness of the Chaldeans versus the faithfulness of God in whom the faithful Israelite trusts and stands firm. Paul omits the pronoun "my" from the Hebrew form of the Habakkuk quotation because of his messianic understanding of "the righteous one." The righteousness of God is revealed by the faithfulness of God. The confirmation of that thesis is that the Messiah lived out of the faithfulness of God.

This messianic reading of the Habakkuk 2:4 citation is proposed for several reasons: 1) Paul's concern throughout the introduction and thesis statement is the content of the gospel: i.e., *the gospel concerning his son* (1:2), *the gospel of his son* (1:9), and *the gospel is the power of God to salvation . . . for it reveals the righteousness of God* (1:16-17). The gospel is thus correlated with "the son" or with God; it is not here correlated with the human appropriation of the gospel. 2) The thesis statement is framed in theocentric and apocalyptic language—God is making an end-time, world-transforming revelation. To read the Habakkuk citation as a reference to the human appropriation of the gospel contradicts this profoundly theological frame. It is difficult to imagine how the human appropriation of the gospel could reveal the righteousness of God. It can receive the gospel, but it does not reveal God's end-time, world-transforming action. 3) This interpretation of v. 17 reads as an anticipation of Paul's more elaborate statement in 3:21-26. In fact, v. 17 is amazingly parallel to 3:22:

Romans 1:17	**Romans 3:22**
The righteousness of God is revealed	The righteousness of God continues to be manifested (revealed)
by means of faithfulness	through the faithfulness of Messiah Jesus
for the purpose of faithfulness.	to all who are faithful.

The good news of the gospel is that God is effecting end-time, world transformation through the Son, Messiah Jesus. Human beings may receive this good news and be transformed by it, but they do not reveal or effect it.

The Wrath of God

When we look at v. 18 it is helpful to remember that the structure of vv. 17 and 18 is parallel. The righteousness of God is revealed in v. 17; the wrath of God is revealed in v. 18. The gospel as the power of God reveals God's righteousness and God's wrath. Paul sees God's salvation and judgment as flip sides of the same coin.

The popular interpretation of this verse is that Paul is describing the revelation of God's wrath as taking place in the present frustration, futilities, and disasters that result from human ungodliness and unrighteousness. However, the parallel structure excludes this interpretation. The present tense of the verb in v. 18 has the same force as in v. 17. An end-time revelation is currently taking place.

The content of this revelation is *the wrath of God (orgē theou)*. The phrase describes the nature of God as revealed in God's activities. It is another OT term that describes God's reaction to sin within the covenant relationship [*Essay: Wrath*]. This wrath is revealed *from heaven*, a stereotyped Jewish phrase indicating the source of the wrath. The wrath is really God's wrath.

The point of v. 18 is that the end-time wrath of God is now being revealed in the world through the gospel just as the end-time righteousness of God is being revealed. It is being revealed *now*, in contrast to a Jewish emphasis on its *future* manifestation, though it will be revealed fully in the future. The wrath of God has both a present and a future dimension just as does the righteousness of God.

The linkage of God's righteousness and wrath in the thesis statement of the letter is important. The close relation of God's salvation and judgment, righteousness and wrath, is firmly rooted in the OT and Jewish literature. Salvation history moves toward God's consummate act of salvation, but there is always a corresponding movement toward God's ultimate judgment of disobedience and sin. This is expressed both in God's faithfulness to the covenant—God saves and judges the covenant people—and in the picture of God as a holy warrior: God does battle to save Israel and to defeat their enemies.

The placement of the Habakkuk quotation between the statements about the revelation of God's righteousness and God's wrath is significant. The Messiah in Jewish end-time expectation brings both salvation for the righteous and judgment for the wicked. The Habakkuk quotation as a messianic reference bonds vv. 17 and 18 together. God is revealing, and will reveal fully, divine righteousness and wrath in the gospel of Messiah ˌJesus. That revelation does not take place in the human response to the gospel, but in and through the faithfulness of Jesus.

The object of the wrath of God is *all ungodliness and unrighteousness of people the ones suppressing the truth in unrighteousness*. A single *all* embraces *ungodliness* and *unrighteousness*. The two words together offer a complete description of sin. *Ungodliness* focuses sin as an attack on the holiness and majesty of God. *Unrighteousness* defines sin as a violation of God's just order in the world. Both stand opposed to the righteousness of God, and both are characterized as assaults on the truth. They *hold down* or *bind* the truth. The word often is associated with demonic forces that bind and oppress. The phrase *who bind the truth by means of unrighteousness* is a profound description of the nature of sin, which will be subject to the wrath of God revealed in the gospel.

The structural parallelism of vv. 17-18 also contains a significant contrast. In v. 17 the human response is to the initiative of God. But in v. 18 human action is the cause of God's response. Humans can appropriate God's salvation in vv. 16-17. Human unrighteousness in v. 18 triggers divine judgment. God initiates salvation and judgment. Humans can accept only the first.

TEXT IN BIBLICAL CONTEXT

Righteousness

The language of Paul's thesis statement is rich in biblical history and meaning. It is covenant language that pictures God's relation to Israel, and Israel's relation to God and to fellow members of the community. "Righteousness" in relation to God in the OT usually refers to God's saving action, especially in Psalms and Isaiah 40-66. It describes God's saving action directed toward the well-being (shalom) of Israel. When "righteousness" (*tsedekah*) is used in relationship to Israel or individual people it most often is linked with "justice" (*mishpat*) to describe the appropriate conduct of the people in response to God's saving actions. The word-pair is concerned with the proper ordering of life in every sphere of human activity.

The basic Old Testament meanings are continued in the intertestamental literature, where righteousness describes the saving activity of God as well as denotes appropriate ethical conduct toward God and fellow Jews.

Righteousness language is quite limited in the gospels. The verb occurs only seven times, the noun 10 times. Many have, therefore, concluded that righteousness was not a major concern of Jesus or the writers of the gospels. But that conclusion is not warranted. In fact, Jesus' life and ministry provided the basis for the early Christian understanding of righteousness.

Jesus' proclamation of the reign of God could not be understood in first century Judaism without thinking of God's righteousness that characterizes this reign. The Psalms that proclaim God's kingship (e.g., 97, 98, 99) also declare God's righteousness. Intertestamental literature links the reign of God and the righteousness of God. The parable of the Pharisee and the Tax Collector (Luke 18:9-14) extends the OT picture of God forgiving the sinner (e.g., Ps. 51; Ezra 9:6-15; Neh. 9:9-37; Dan. 9:4-18) to Jesus' ministry. Jesus' practice of table fellowship with tax collectors and sinners dramatically illustrates this understanding. It also fulfills the prediction of *1 Enoch* 62:14 that the Son of Man will bring righteousness and salvation by the practice of table fellowship. God graciously extends righteousness to the needy and marginalized through Jesus' words and deeds. The ransom saying (Mark 10:45 par.) interprets Jesus' death as *for the many* to save them from God's righteous judgment. As Peter Stuhlmacher states, "through his willingness to make vicarious atonement Jesus gave a new direction to Old Testament language and experience precisely with respect to the righteousness of God and to the righteousness people have in the sight of God and live out in the world" (Stuhlmacher, 1986:3).

The early church prior to Paul began to develop the meaning of Jesus' death as a righteousness-demonstrating event and a righteousness-giving event. Seven "atonement formulas" are embedded in various NT writings (1 Cor. 1:30; 6:11; 2 Cor. 5:21; Rom. 3:24-26; 4:25; 1 Tim. 3:16; 1 Pet. 3:18). These atonement formulas clearly interpret the death of Jesus in terms of righteousness, and link this righteousness with forgiveness of sins, redemption, sanctification, and the Spirit.

Paul is the great interpreter of righteousness in the NT. Nearly half of all the righteousness language in the NT occurs in the Pauline letters (45.7%). Romans contains nearly a quarter (23.8%) of all NT righteousness language, and 52.2% of the "righteousness of God" language in Paul. The central concern of the language is the righteousness of God in making unrighteous people (Gentiles) righteous. That is, righteousness language is polemical. It argues that God makes Gentile people righteous through Messiah Jesus, and in so doing demonstrates God's righteousness in relation to the covenant.

In general, as we have seen, Paul's use follows OT-Jewish roots and picks up the lines of the seven early church atonement formulas. The main lines of interpretation in Paul relate to christology (Jesus as the righteous one who manifests the righteousness of God), salvation (Jesus as the one who makes people righteous), and ethics (Christians living righteously).

TEXT IN THE LIFE OF THE CHURCH

The exegesis reads v. 17 as a statement about God and about God's Messiah. Only inferentially, it speaks about God's gift to humanity; humanity's response to God is addressed later. Paul's thesis in Romans is that God, though faithful to Israel, is incorporating the Gentiles into this people in fulfillment of the promises to Abraham and Israel. Paul is confronting the problem of God's strange ways with Israel, explaining that God has not abandoned Israel, but is fulfilling the promises to Israel. The Habakkuk citation, interpreted messianically, confirms the faithfulness of God, a regular function of Habakkuk and Habakkuk 2:4 in Jewish apocalyptic literature. The Messiah, not human faith, confirms that God really is revealing righteous and end-time faithfulness in the gospel.

God Is Righteous

What difference does this interpretation make? It fundamentally alters the interpretation of the righteousness of God and of Romans, because at least three implications follow from it. First, it centers the righteousness of God in God's end-time and saving activity. The traditional Protestant interpretation centered the righteousness of God in what was given for human beings and brought about by human faith. The proposed interpretation centers the righteousness of God theologically. God is the righteous one who reveals this righteousness in and for the entire cosmos. This revelation is brought about by God's action in Messiah Jesus. Furthermore, the righteousness of God addresses primarily the question of personal and national purpose and the incorporation of new people into the people of God. Individual sin and guilt are addressed later, but always through the corporate lens set forth in this thesis statement.

Jesus Defines God's Righteousness

Second, it links the righteousness of God with the life and teachings of Jesus. In much of Protestantism, there is no necessary or logical connection between the interpretation of Jesus and righteousness. An act of having faith is simply substituted for the act of circumcision as the precondition for salvation. Christ, therefore, plays a passive role in justification. This all changes dramatically in the proposed interpretation where righteousness is shaped by christology and christology is shaped by righteousness. God's righteousness is revealed in the faithfulness of Messiah Jesus. Jesus is the definition of the righteousness of God. He is the only person who matters in justification because he is faithful to God in contrast to Adam's unfaithfulness. Without his faithfulness there would be no making righteous.

Righteousness and Ethics are Linked

Third, the new paradigm connects righteousness with ethics. In the traditional Protestant interpretation righteousness is a tranquilizer for the restless soul. God is all grace and love. The NT God of love is unhooked from the righteous God of the OT. In fact, since Luther, Protestant interpretation has suffered from a prejudice against law and judgment categories from the OT. Justification is the miracle in which God the righteous judge abdicates to become the Father of love and forgiveness. Justification is disconnected from sanctification. This highly individualistic doctrine then gets translated socio-politically into a two-kingdom theology where divine justice, God's grace and goodness, is separated from human justice. Therefore, the doctrine of justification has nothing to do with earthly justice; it cannot address social and communal issues and responsibilities.

The proposed interpretation, by contrast, states that righteousness is about God's end-time, world-transforming power to make the world right. It concerns faithfulness that rights wrong, especially that which includes the outcast and marginalized, e.g., the Gentiles. The righteousness of God is ethically and socially relevant. It creates a new community in the world that lives in right relationships. Thus righteousness addresses questions of social, communal, and cosmic order. God is making the world right, which means creating a people that is righteous in its social and ethical responsibilities.

Righteousness Concerns Peoplehood

The framework for the new paradigm is sociological and historical, rather than psychological and individualistic. Or, to put it in different terms, for Paul righteousness is an OT category that he refines in light of contemporary Jewish understandings and the meaning of Jesus as Messiah. That is why Paul's discussion of righteousness, primarily in Galatians and Romans, is so linked to the OT (53 OT references in Romans out of a total of 94 in all the Pauline letters). The people Paul is addressing were not troubled by inner feelings of sin and guilt, but by prejudice and fractured relationships with fellow Christians of different ethnic origin. That is why Paul uses righteousness language when he needs to straighten out problems in Jew-Christian and Gentile-Christian relations in the church in light of wrong understandings of OT teachings.

This way of reading Romans challenges not only traditional Protestant understandings, but also much modern evangelicalism. Evangelicals have tended to follow Luther in defining righteousness as the establishment of a personal relationship with God. This interpretation drives a wedge between righteousness (or justification) and the people of God. Much evangelicalism seeks to safeguard righteousness by insisting on a low view of the church, e.g., God wants inward religion (authentic, personal faith) instead of outward performance (institutional church, baptism, church going). When this happens we take righteousness (or justification) out of its covenantal context and reduce it to a subjective experience. The transformation of righteousness into inner personal religion is so attractive in the West, because it permits us to enjoy a bit of Christianity and a great deal of modern and post-modern subjectivism and individualism.

Righteousness is fundamentally concerned with being covenant people. It defines what it means to belong to the one family of Abraham, and to live within the covenant people God is creating. The righteousness of God does not involve an individualist charter, but a divine action that incorporates people into God's people. Righteousness declares that people are members of God's covenant community, which is called to live righteously. And that covenant people has a different king than Caesar.

God's Righteousness Again

The righteousness of God is a question again in our world, although in a different way than in Paul's time. Religious and racial wars abound—Auschwitz, Bosnia, Congo, Rwanda, Congo, Iraq—all of which raise questions about God and God's justice. September 11, 2001, raised profound questions about God. The mission of the church is to proclaim the gospel of God's righteousness through the faithfulness of Jesus for the purpose of creating one people out of many peoples, one human community that welcomes "the other" just as Jesus "welcomed us." The Creator God is the Righteous God who is "making right" people and creation in order to renew and restore the whole.

Socio-Political Implication

The announcement that the righteousness of God is revealed through the faithfulness of Jesus for the salvation of all people is more than a theological statement to address a pastoral problem among the Romans churches. It also is a bold political statement, what in fact Neil Elliott has called an "ideological intifada" (N. Elliott, 1994:190), aimed at the seat of Roman power and its imperial claims. Roman imperial propaganda makes the case in every way possible—decrees, coins, golden tablets, statues, images, festivals—that Augustus, the Roman emperor, has restored the "faith" of the Roman people by bringing "righteousness" (*ius*), "salvation" (*sōteria*), and "peace" (*eirēnē*) to all the people of the world. The Roman emperor alone is the savior of the world.

Paul's gospel makes a competing claim to the gospel of Caesar. The good news is that righteousness, the righteousness of God, is being revealed in the world for the salvation of all people through Messiah Jesus. Paul engages the kingship debate of the Roman empire by asserting that Jesus is King, the Messianic son of God who alone brings salvation by revealing the righteousness of God.

The gospel is simultaneously a religious and a political claim. Real salvation can only be effected by the true king, Messiah Jesus.

Romans 1:18–15:13

The Argument of
the Letter

From 1:18 through 15:13 Paul develops his theses by elaborating important themes and by answering theological and ethical objections to his arguments. He argues three main points: 1) the revelation of the wrath of God against all unrighteousness, 1:18-3:20; 2) the revelation of the righteousness of God for all humanity, 3:21-11:36; 3) the living sacrifice of the righteous community, 12:1–15:13.

The first argument develops the last thesis stated in v. 18, the revelation of the wrath of God. The second argument elaborates the meaning of the second thesis stated in vv. 16-17, the revelation of the righteousness of God. The third argument outlines the practical meaning of the gospel as the revelation of the righteousness of God for the people of God in Rome.

Romans 1:18–3:20

The Revelation of the Wrath of God

The first argument of the letter elaborates the statement of the thesis in v. 18, the revelation of the wrath of God against all unrighteousness. The central concern is God, not human sin. The text unit makes three major points to support the main argument:

1. the impartial judgment of God on all peoples, 1:18–2:11;
2. the equality of Gentiles and Jews before God's judgment, 2:12-29;
3. the objections of the Jews, 3:1-20.

These three points fit well into a Greco-Roman argumentative (rhetorical) pattern: proof of Paul's thesis (1:18-2:29), and refutation of objections (3:1-20). The argument is designed to persuade the audience of the justice of God in judging all people, Jews and Gentiles, of sin (see Bassler, 1982, 1984).

Two things about this larger text unit are remarkable. First, except for a reference to Messiah Jesus in connection with the future end-time judgment in 2:16, Jesus is not mentioned. Second, the word "sin" does not appear until 3:9, and is used only one other time, in 3:20. The beginning point for Paul is God's judgment of all human unrighteousness (injustice) and ungodliness. The latter describe sinful behavior but the real meaning of such behavior is explained only at the end of the argument (**Sin** as power, 3:9).

The entire text unit is basically an OT prophetic and Jewish apocalyptic indictment of humanity's perversion of God's created order and Jewish disobedience of the law. The center of the argument is God as the impartial judge of this perversion and disobedience. Equally noteworthy is Paul's repeated use of the Hebrew Scriptures: Psalms 106 and Jeremiah 2 in 1:23, Deuteronomy 28 in 2:11, Psalms 115:2 and 50:6 in 3:4, Psalms 14:1-3, 5:10, 139:4, 10:7, and 35:2 in 3:10-18, and Psalms 143:2 in 3:20. Paul's argument is designed for an audience that reads the Jewish Scriptures.

The Impartial Judgment of God on All Peoples

Romans 1:18–2:11

PREVIEW

The first supporting argument emphasizes the impartial revelation of God's wrath and judgment. The theme is the just retribution of God. The unit of 1:18-2:11 has a very distinctive and unifying "ring-composition."

1:16 to everyone believing, to the Jew first and also the Greek
  1:18a revelation of wrath
    1:18b upon all ungodliness . . . of people the ones
      1:18 wrath, unrighteousness, truth
        1:20 without excuse
        2:1 without excuse
      2:5 revelation, wrath
    2:8 truth, unrighteousness, wrath
  2:9 wrath upon every soul of people who
2:10 to everyone working good, to the Jew first and also the Greek

Notice the repetitions that tie the text together, *to the Jews and also to the Greeks* in 1:16 and 2:9 and 10; the revelation of the wrath of God in 1:18 and 2:5; to be without excuse in 1:20 and 2:1; and God's wrath against unrighteousness and untruth in 1:18 and 2:8.

The text also is unified by common words and themes. *All (pas)* is found in the key verses throughout 1:16–2:11, but is absent from 2:12-29. Key words in 2:12-29—law, circumcision-uncircumcision—are missing in 1:16–2:11. The idea of retribution dominates 1:18–2:11, but is missing in the 2:12-29 treatment of judgment.

In addition, the earliest known textual interpretations indicate a break in the argument at 2:12 rather than 2:1. The fourth-century manuscript Vaticanus contains paragraph divisions which define 1:18–2:11 as a paragraph. This division is supported by Greek and Latin chapter lists, aids that were developed to facilitate finding texts in codex (roll) form. These chapter lists report new headings for 1:18 and 2:12.

OUTLINE

The Thesis, 1:18

The Elaboration, 1:19–2:10
- 1:19-21 The inexcusability of humanity
- 1:22–2:3 The just retribution of God
- 2:4-5 The revelation of God's righteous judgment
- 2:6-10 The judgment according to works

The Conclusion, 2:11

EXPLANATORY NOTES

The Thesis 1:18

Verse 18, which was part of the letter's thesis statement, also states the theme of the text unit. The idea of the wrath of God is developed by repeating the retribution formula, *he gave them up* in vv. 24, 26, 28. The same idea is found in 2:1-11. *Wrath* in vv. 5 and 8 and *who will render* in v. 8 mirrors the theme of *God gave them up. The judgment of God* in vv. 2 and 3 or his *righteous judgment* in v. 5 recalls *the wrath of God* from 1:18.

The Elaboration 1:19–2:10

1:19-21 The Inexcusability of Humanity

The foundation of Paul's argument is the revelation of God. God is known through a self-revelation—"manifest" (*phaneroō*) takes up the "revelation" (*apokalyptō*) of v. 18. Two times in v. 19 Paul emphasizes God's initiative in revealing knowledge to humanity—*the knowable of God is manifest among them; God has shown it to them.* That knowledge has been available since the creation of the universe. Paul here shares the perspective of Wisdom 13:5 that one can know the Creator from the greatness and beauty of creation. Knowledge of God is implicit rather than explicit—the Hebrew Scriptures and Jewish literature reflect a deep conviction that God is not directly or explicitly knowable (e.g., Exod. 33:20; Deut. 4:12; Sir. 43:31; Sib. Or. 3:17;

Philo, *Som.* 1:65-66, 68-69; Josephus, *J.W.* 7:346). The nature of the knowledge disclosed through the creative actions—literally, "the things done"—is that God is divine and powerful.

The purpose of the revelation of knowledge about God is *so they are without excuse* (literally, "without apologetics" that is, without a defense). This phrase is the key to vv. 19-21. Paul is not making the case for a natural theology, that men and women can reason their way to God from nature (the argument from below to above), but asserts that humanity has no excuse because it has continuous access to knowledge of God [*Essay: Natural Theology*].

The sin of humanity is that men and women did not glorify God or give thanks. Humanity knew God, but did not recognize or honor God. The fundamental human perversion is rejection of God.

Two things here are important and foundational for Romans. First, the language is covenantal. *Glorify* and *give thanks* are relational terms that come from the OT. Creation establishes a bond between Creator and creature, but humanity rejects the bond. Second, the language used to reject the relationship is "honor-shame" [*Essay: Honor-Shame*]. *To glorify* is *to honor* and *to give thanks* is to express gratitude for a relationship.

The judgment for refusing to be in covenant with God is that human beings became "empty-headed" in thinking and unperceptive in discernment. Humanity loses touch with reality, does not think clearly, when it rejects God. The refusal to acknowledge God has consequences for knowledge and understanding (epistemology).

1:22–2:3 The Just Retribution of God

This section has a distinctive structure that uses the logic of the Jewish scheme of just judgment (*ius talionis*): crime, judgment, and punishment. The scheme is repeated four times: 1:22-24; 1:25-27; 1:28-31; 1:32–2:3.

Crime	**God's Reaction**	**Moral Consequences**
v. 22—asserting to be wise, they exchanged (*allassō*)	v. 24—therefore (*dio*) God gave them up	v. 24—impurity, dishonoring of bodies
v. 25—who (*hoitenes*) exchanged (*metallassō*)	v. 26—therefore (*dio*) God gave them up	vv. 26-7—sexual perversion
v. 28—they not thinking fit to know God	v. 28—just as (*kathōs*) God gave them up	vv. 28-31—unthinking mind, social vice

v. 32—who (*hoitenes*)
know the just judgment
of God   2:1—therefore (*dio*)   2:1-3—judge yourself,
                                no excuse   judgment of God

The issue in vv. 22-24 is idolatry; humanity exchanges the glory of God for a form of humanity and animals. Verse 23 refers to Israel's worship of the golden calf at Sinai by citing Psalms 106:20 and Jeremiah 2:11. *God gave them up*—the language involves an act of divine judgment—to impurity and the dishonoring of the human body. The most patent manifestation of both is sexual immorality. Linking idolatry and sexual immorality is common in the OT and Judaism. Idolatry, the root human sin in Jewish thinking and in Paul, leads to all other sins. But the logic of "idolatry leads to immorality" is usually applied to the Gentiles. The surprise here is that Paul uses the unfaithfulness of Israel itself, not the Gentiles, to document idolatry.

The key idea is "exchange" in vv. 25-27. Humanity exchanges the truth and worship of God for self-worship. The creature is substituted for the Creator. The judgment is specifically sexual immorality, the exchange of homosexuality for heterosexuality (associating idolatry and homosexuality as the primary example of sexual immorality was common in Jewish literature) [*Essay: Homosexuality*]. The text has striking parallels with the Wisdom of Solomon (esp. chs. 13-14), a first century B.C. apocryphal work. Both assume human beings can know God through creation (1:20-21; Wis. 13:1-5); both find human failure to know God inexcusable (1:21; Wis. 13:6-9); both associate idolatry and immoral behavior (1:24-31; Wis. 14:12-14, 27) and especially "unnatural sexual relations" (1:26-27; Wis. 14:26); both list a catalogue of vices (1:29-31; Wis. 14:23-27); and both believe sin results in the "darkening" of the mind (1:21; Wis. 11:15).

The sin in v. 28 is the refusal to acknowledge God (literally, *not think fit*). The judgment is *unthinking minds* (a play on the word "mind," *nous*) and social misconduct. The punishment is growing social vice and chaos. It is significant that the word heading the list of behaviors characterizing this chaos is *unrighteousness* (*adikia*).

In v. 32 the sin is the rejection of the just judgment of God, the refusal to accept God's just decree that the people who practice sin deserve God's end-time judgment (death). In fact, they actively approve wrongdoing. A dialogue form, known as the diatribe, is introduced in 2:1. An imaginary opponent or questioner raises a question or states an objection, which Paul answers [*Essay: Diatribe*]. The imaginary person here hypocritically condemns those who commit the acts described in 1:18-32, but does "the same things." People who judge others for wrongdoing but do wrong themselves are really judging themselves. Their punishment is the end-time judgment of God (*to krima tou theou* in *2:2*). The issue is the discrepancy between the imaginary questioner's claim to a higher morality and actual practice. The condemnation will serve as a precedent when Paul moves on in 2:17-29 to use the diatribe again to condemn the same kind of discrepancy among Jews who claim to know the law, but do not observe it.

The last unit, 1:32-2:3, is seen as the fourth part of the sequence, despite the change of tone and the form of the direct address in 2:1, for four reasons: 1) the form of the argument, introduced by "whoever" in v. 32, followed by the identification of the sin in v. 32, and the declaration of the judgment with *therefore*; 2) the content of the argument is that God recompenses according to people's actions; 3) the heavy use of "doing" words—"the ones doing such things," "doing them," and "those doing" in 1:32, "the same things doing" in 2:1, *the ones doing such things* in 2:2, 3, and *doing these things* in 2:3; 4) the prominence of judgment (*krin*) words—seven times in 2:1-3. The introduction of the "diatribe form" or the direct address in 2:1 does not necessitate the beginning of a new argument, but serves to concretize and sharpen the indictment of 1:18-32 (see Stowers, 1981).

Several things are noteworthy in this section. First, the critical human sin is the rejection of God: not give glory to God in v. 21, reject the glory of God in v. 23, deny the truth of God in v. 25, reject knowledge of God in v. 28. Second, broken relationships with God lead to broken relationships with fellow human beings. As in Genesis, man and woman reject God, and then each other. Third, the language of God's judgment is covenantal. God responds to human failure by turning away. Humanity rebels against God, who then abandons humanity and does not protect humans against themselves. Fourth, Paul reverses the normal understanding of cause and consequence. Moral perversion is the result of God's wrath, not the reason for it. Fifth, the consequences of rebellion against God are social and relational rather than religious. Perverted relationships and chaos in the social order result from rejecting God. Sixth, people become like what they worship. Substituting the creature for the Creator means that people become more creaturely, more animal-like, even bestial.

The language throughout is "honor-shame" [*Essay: Honor-Shame*]. The *impiety* (*asebeian*), the *unrighteous behavior* (*adikia*) and the *suppression of the truth* (*aletheian en adikia*) in 1:18 result in *uncleanness* (*akatharsia*) in 1:24, *dishonor* (*atimazesthai* and *atimia*) in 1:24 and 26, and *indecency* (*aschemosune*) in 1:27. All describe relationships in honor-shame categories—honor is replaced by its negation. Human rejection of God's honor by shameful actions constitutes an offense, which God judges by letting men and women become so shameless in their behavior that social order disintegrates.

Finally, there is a stylistic intensification through the passage. The portrayal of guilt tends to become shorter, and the description of the corruption more extensive. The manifestation of God's wrath, like the revelation of God's righteousness, does not remain in the private moral sphere. It leads from the inner misperception of reality to public chaos to eschatological judgment.

2:4-5 The Revelation of God's Righteous Judgment

The judgment of God is inevitable for unrepentant sinners. It cannot be escaped. A future day is coming which will reveal *the righteous judgment of God.* Therefore, men and women should not presume upon God's justice, as do the people who judge others while living unjustly.

2:6-10 The Judgment According to Works

Verse 6 states the principle of God's judgment: *to each according to his/her works.* It is a direct quote from Psalms 62:12 and Proverbs 24:12, and represents the classic statement of the Jewish doctrine of corresponding retribution [*Essay: Salvation-Judgment by Works*]. "To everyone" (*ekastō*) reaffirms the inclusiveness of all people.

Verses 7-10 outline the principle in an ABBA chiasm:

A Reward—for good works

       stress *works* of v. 6

 B Punishment—for bad works

 B Punishment—for bad works

       stress *to each* of v. 6

A Reward-for good works

The good and bad works again are described in largely relational and honor-shame language. The *to the Jew first and also the Greek* in both vv. 9 and 10 reinforces the universal thrust of *to each* and underlines the impartial judgment of God on all the people who receive the revelation of God's righteousness (1:16). The terms of judgment are precisely the same for all people.

The Conclusion 2:11

The section concludes with a summary statement that underlines the impartiality of God. The phrase "God does not show the face" is a classic Hebrew assertion of God's impartiality. "To show the face" to one person, but not another, is to show partiality. God does not show the face to anyone.

Comments and Observations

The opening argument of Romans is bracketed with a statement about impartiality. There is salvation, righteousness, glory, honor, and peace to all who believe (*faith* and/or *do good*) both Jew and Gentile (1:16 and 2:10). There is wrath and judgment against all unrighteousness, both Jew and Gentile (1:18 and 2:9). God disregards group distinctions in salvation and judgment. Verse 2:11 is a terse summary of the entire text unit.

We do not know who the specific addressees are in this text. While the argument is similar to Jewish polemics against the Gentiles, Paul does not identify Gentiles explicitly here. Moreover, while 2:1ff. reads like a typical Jewish criticism of fellow-Jews, Paul does not specify the audience. He stresses the impartiality of God, hence the recurrence of "all" throughout the text—salvation to *everyone*, wrath against *all*, *all* who judge hypocritically are without excuse, distress for everyone who does evil, glory and honor and peace for *everyone* who does good.

The focus of 1:18–2:11 is on God, not humanity or the sin of humanity. God is righteous and impartial.

Several other themes introduced in this text resurface later in Romans. First, the ideas that "God is impartial" or there is "no distinction between people" are used again at the conclusion of ch. 11, *God has consigned all people to disobedience in order that he may be merciful to all* (11:32). The argument of 1:16 through 11:36 is bracketed by the theme of "no distinction between people" before God in salvation or judgment.

Second, the creation theme of 1:19f. reappears in ch. 8. Paul introduces the creation story from Genesis to underline the covenantal character of relationships. God is knowable in and through creation. Human sinfulness consists in breaking covenantal relationships, with God first and then with fellow human-beings. Paul returns to the creation theme in 8:9-39 where creation is subjected to frustration and suffering because of humanity's rebellion. Human beings are central to the problem of creation as well as to its redemption. When humanity is redeemed by God, the creation is released and restored.

Third, the opening and closing arguments of Romans are concerned with the wrong judgment of people against each other (see Meeks, 1987). The middle of the first argument asserts that God judges people who hypocritically judge fellow human beings. The letter concludes (14:1–15:13) with an exhortation that Christians are not to judge fellow Christians who are different, but are to welcome each other. A distinct literary form, known as an inclusio (or parentheses), reminds the Roman Christians that there is no ground for passing judgment on one another.

THE TEXT IN BIBLICAL CONTEXT
The Impartiality of God

The impartiality of God is an important, though neglected, theme in the Bible. The OT makes four explicit statements along this line. Deuteronomy 10:17 asserts God's impartiality in order to exhort obedience to the law, and to emphasize God's justice for the marginalized, specifically orphans, widows, and resident aliens. 2 Chronicles 19:7 points to God's impartiality as a model for human judges to follow with Israel. Job 34:19 grounds divine impartiality in creation, and applies it to the equal treatment for rich and poor. In Psalms 82:1-4 God judges the gods of the nations for partiality, and calls for justice that stands with the marginalized.

The theme continues in intertestamental literature where impartiality is a basic attribute of God. But a new development occurs, as well. Impartiality moves from the law court to a future eschatological context. In the face of Israel's oppression, God's impartiality is affirmed to assure hope and guarantee future vindication. Israel's oppressors will not escape God's judgment, and Israel will not fail to receive her ultimate reward.

Paul's adds a new perspective in Romans. God's impartiality means there is no distinction between people. This opening argument in Romans provides the critical background to develop the idea of God's making right all people (3:21ff.). The doctrine of justification by faith for all people is based on the principle of "no distinction between people."

The impartiality of God is used in Acts 10:34-35 to help Peter understand that God accepts people across ethnic boundaries (*truly I perceive that God shows no partiality*). The gift of the Holy Spirit to Gentile Christians, just as it was given to Jewish Christians, confirms this impartiality. Therefore, Peter baptized and incorporated them into the church (cf. also 15:7-10).

The impartiality of God becomes the basis for ethical behavior in other NT writings. In Ephesians 6:9 it is the ground for masters treating their slaves well. Colossians 3:22-25 uses it to make exactly the opposite point. Slaves should work obediently for their masters, because God is impartial; justice will be done in the future judgment. First Peter 1:17 characterizes God as the impartial judge (literally, "the non-face showing judge") to exhort holy living.

Impartiality is the ground for God's righteousness. Because this righteousness excludes partiality, God judges all people and makes righteous all people "without distinction." Therefore, people are called to live justly without regard for the ethnic identity or social status of others.

TEXT IN THE LIFE OF THE CHURCH

Becoming What We Worship

Romans 1:18–2:11 is bad news. When human beings reject God, they commit themselves to other gods, to idols. The heart of the human crisis is idolatry, substituting someone or something for God as lord (Mammon, erotic sex, blood and soil, are some recent examples). When men and women do that, they become what they worship.

The news gets even worse. The punishment for idolatry is sin and more sin, perversion and more perversion, chaos and more chaos. The judgment of God matches the unrighteous actions of humans. This match underscores the appropriateness and the justice of the judgment. There is a direct relationship between deed and consequences. That, of course, is not new; Genesis 3-11 makes the same point. But it is frightening news.

Paul is describing alienation and dehumanization. The more people reject God for other gods, the more alienated and dehumanized they become. The idolization of "me" or "my people" results in total enslavement and perversion. The permissiveness of a culture that has "come of age" is the freedom to become even more permissive. Note also that the "abuses" that result from idolatry all concern relationships between human beings. The more people reject God the more dehumanized, the more fractured, the more abusive relationships become. The end is total social chaos.

God lets people become what they worship. The only question now is: who will we as human beings worship? The question is not, will we worship? We will. Rather, the question is, who will we worship? Whoever it is, we will become like our gods or like God.

To read Romans is worrisome. Paul's description of the human predicament that results from rejecting God is profound. It is bad news in any age.

The Challenge of Homosexuality

The issue of homosexuality is one of the most difficult issues facing the church in the twenty-first century. Paul's discussion of homosexuality in vv. 25-27 is the most extensive in the NT, and thus is very much at the center of the debate in the church, both then and now [*Essay: Homosexuality*]. He clearly rejects homosexuality; it reflects humanity's rebellion against God.

Paul's stance here is a theological one. How would Paul deal with homosexual people in the Roman churches? We have no direct evidence; he does not address the issue pastorally.

But the way he deals with the food and holy days issues in the Roman churches (chs. 14-15) gives us some clues to his pastoral strategies regarding divisive interpretive issues. The questions involve deeply held convictions about how to interpret the Scriptures and about purity standards in the churches. People are divided into different groups, which are engaged in name calling. They are trying to persuade others to "convert" to their point of view, and people are being hurt in the church.

Paul's overall pastoral counsel is that the different groups are *to welcome one another* just as Christ embraced them. The reason is that people with different theologies and practices are to be accepted in the churches. Diversity of behavior and practice is not to cause contempt or judgment among Christians if it is based on personal conviction, if it honors the Lord, if it takes place *in the Lord*, if it recognizes Christ as Lord. The center of the faith—the relation to Jesus as Lord—means that Christians are not to judge one another for differences that are not central. God is the only judge of acceptable behavior (see the discussion of chs. 14–15 for a more detailed exegesis).

How might Paul use this overall counsel to address the challenge of homosexuality in the church today? We can only suggest some possibilities that must be tested in the church. First, quite clearly Paul would say gay and lesbian people can be Christians. They are sinners saved by the grace and power of God, just like any sinner.

Second, I think Paul would say that gay and lesbian people can be members of the church. Paul knew better than most that members of the church are deeply flawed and sinful people who live by God's grace. Nearly all of the sins identified in his letters are practiced by members of the church. There are no perfect people in the church. If gays and lesbians cannot be part of the church, none of us can.

Third, I think Paul would say that sexual intercourse is intended for men and women in a monogamous heterosexual relationship. The creation accounts, he would say, assert that heterosexual relationships are the normative context for intimate sexual love. Paul, following Jesus, understood the creation accounts to mean that the "one flesh" of marriage and sexuality is limited to the relationship of a man and a woman. Sexual intercourse is not the definition of wholeness as human beings. Celibate people can be fully human and whole. Sexual intercourse is a definition of what it means to be married, not what it means to be human.

In all probability, Paul would say that gay and lesbian people should not be sexually active just as single heterosexual people should not be sexually active. He would say "no" to homosexual behavior. He would call people who have a same-sex orientation or preference to the celibate life, just like he called single heterosexual people to the celibate life. The celibate life is a high and noble calling in the church. Paul, would go on, I think, to say that the church, having said "no" and having called these Christians to celibacy, should be loving, caring, compassionate, and just in dealing with practicing homosexual people, just like it is in dealing with people guilty of other sexual sins (see Swartley, 2003, for an extensive discussion of homosexuality and the church).

If my reading of Paul's counsel is anywhere close to correct, what should we do with it in the church today? I think we should take it seriously. But, I also think, the church needs to keep thinking theologically about what it means that all people are fallen. Because we are fallen, we do not live up to the ideals and normative models taught in the Scriptures. The church understands that divorce and remarriage violates the normative model of a monogamous marital relationship. But the church has learned to be forgiving and inclusive of divorced and remarried people. What does that mean for the way the church deals with committed gay and lesbian couples? In addition, the church also needs to think about the reality of alternative marital arrangements in the biblical tradition, which go beyond the model of a monogamous relationship of one man and one woman (e.g., the practice of polygamy in Israel). Are some patterns of relationship so pervasive in a culture that the church must learn to live with them for a time even if they fall short of the normative pattern? These are questions, I suggest, the church should talk about in the spirit of Romans 14–15: not judging, but "bearing" one another, focusing on the center, and continuing to discern together the boundaries in fidelity to Scripture and the Spirit's leading.

The Impartiality of God

Romans 1:18–2:11 is good news. God is impartial and judges all unrighteousness without distinction for people. God does not reveal wrath to some and righteousness to others. God's wrath does not belong to one age (a bygone one at that) and righteousness to another. The point of the impartiality is that God does not have two faces that succeed each other. God, in fact, shows no face.

For Paul, the righteousness of God and the judgment of God are flip sides of the same coin. Both concern the nature of God as the impartial and just God, and the Lordship of God, the proper relationship of the creature to the Creator. One cannot have the righteousness of God, and its accompanying "making righteous," without the judgment of God.

The Equality of Gentiles and Jews Before God's Judgment

Romans 2:12-29

PREVIEW

The preceding emphasis on God's impartial judgment on all people raises questions for Jews and Jewish Christians. The critical question is: what about the law? Surely having privileged access to God's will gives the Jew an advantage at God's judgment.

The larger unit of 2:12–3:20 deals with the question of the law, the Torah of God given to Israel. The issue really amounts to, what about God's election of Israel? The principle about the law is stated in vv. 12-16. Having or not having the law decides the standard by which one is judged. This principle cuts across the Jewish picture of the Gentiles as condemned en masse at the final judgment. The law neither puts the Gentiles at a disadvantage, nor guarantees advantage for the Jews.

Verses 17-24 again use the diatribe form [*Essay: Diatribe*]. The dialogue is with an imaginary Jewish teacher who argues that the law gives the Jewish people a special relationship to God and a special position as guide and light to the Gentiles. Paul counters that the teacher's sin, and Jewish sin, contradicts this self-perception.

Verses 25-29 address a second question about Israel's privilege, what about circumcision? The answer is that breaking the law neutralizes both privilege and circumcision.

Verses 12-29, therefore, constitute a clear text unit. It is tied together by the repeated use of the word "law" (*nomos*, 19 times in 16 verses, nine times in vv. 12-16; "without law," *anomos*, twice, and the only times in the NT). Law dominates the argument until v. 25, where it is linked with "circumcision/uncircumcision." Neither law nor circumcision are mentioned prior to 2:12 and are dropped after 2:29. Law does not appear again until 3:19. A second word chain that unites the text is "secret," "the secrets of human beings" (v. 16), "the Jew in secret" (v. 29).

OUTLINE

The General Statement, 2:12-13
> The principle of impartiality is stated in two different forms: 1) Two parallel "whoever" clauses in v. 12, *whoever sinned outside the law . . . whoever sinned in the law . . .*; 2) a "not . . . but" clause in v. 13, *not the hearers, but the doers.*

The Test Cases, 2:14-27
> The principle of vv. 12-13 is tested with four cases, each introduced by a conditional sentence ("if . . . then"). The order is chiastic, ABBA:
> A Gentiles, vv. 14-16
>   B Jews, vv. 17-24
>   B Jews, v. 25
> A Gentiles, vv. 26-27

The General Statement, 2:28-29

EXPLANATORY NOTES

The General Principle—The Equality of Judgment in Relation to the Law 2:12-13

The notion that the Jew and Gentile would be rewarded or punished equally according to the things they did, and that they equally deserved God's judgment, requires explanation. The immediate Jewish response is a question about the law. Israel is marked off from the rest of the world by God's gift of the law. It is the symbol of her election, and thus introduces an element of favoritism. (The favoritism issue was a sensitive one in Judaism. Jewish leaders addressed it by saying God gave the law to all the nations, but only Israel accepted it.) Paul addresses the issue by focusing on what is ultimately effective in the final judgment. He now applies the doctrine of retribution to a norm, whose function is different for the Jew and the Gentile. In 2:4-10 his argument depended on performance. The norm for judgment was the same for Jew and Gentile. Paul now sharpens the argument.

Performance is still the issue, but the norm is different.

Paul emphasizes the impartiality of God's judgment by the parallelism of the sentence in v. 12. God judges both groups because both sinned. Those who sin in ignorance of the law (*anomos* = without the law) will be condemned in the final judgment. Those who sinned knowing the law (*en nomo* = in the law) will be judged according to the standard of the law. There is no distinction in the consequences of disobedience; both groups will be judged.

The statement of impartial judgment is expanded in v. 13 to include the idea of impartial reward. The contrast is between hearers and doers of the law. In the OT and Judaism hearing normally means doing; "hearing" and "doing" are synonyms in the daily Shema prayer of the Jews (Deut. 6:4-5). The hearing referred to here clearly is not real hearing as it falls short of obeying. Hearers who disobey will not be made righteous, but those who do the law will be made righteous. That sounds shocking to Protestants, but it is very Jewish and Christian. Paul is not articulating a doctrine of salvation, or justification by faith; rather, he is making the case for God's justice in judgment. Possessing and hearing the law, which Jews did at every synagogue service, does not exempt the Jews from God's judgment. Performance of the norm is the decisive factor [*Essay: Salvation-Judgment by Works*].

The First Case of the Gentiles 2:14-16

Verse 13 introduced a provocative idea. The case of the Gentiles who do not know the law is treated first. Verses 14-16 constitute one long sentence in Greek. Paul emphasizes two things: 1) the Gentiles *do not* have the law; 2) Gentiles *have* the ability to keep the law. The effect is to eliminate the law as a specific advantage of the Jews. Verse 13 established performance, not possession, as the decisive factor. Gentiles can meet this criterion as well as the Jews.

The label "Gentiles" designates Gentiles in general, not Gentile Christians, as often interpreted since Augustine. A reference to Gentile Christians would call into question God's impartial justice. The phrase *by nature do not have the law* is meaningless, if the reference is to Christians who have the law through the Scriptures. Furthermore, except for the reference to Christ's role in the final judgment in v. 16, there is nothing specifically Christian in the entire section. The issue is God's justice in treating Jews and Gentiles equally and impartially.

These Gentiles do not have the law *by nature*. Most translations connect by nature with what follows, and read *Gentiles who do not have the law do by nature what the law requires.* These translations then interpret Paul as saying that the Gentiles do the things required by God's law as a result of their possession of natural law. It is preferable, however, to connect *by nature* to the preceding phrase, and read *Gentiles who do not have the law by nature occasionally do what the law requires* (*nature* is associated with words that precede rather than follow in Paul's letters). The Gentiles do not possess the law by nature, that is, by virtue of their birth into a community that has the Mosaic Law. But they occasionally live consistently with the teachings of the law (the genitive is a partitive, they obey part of the law part of the time). The Gentiles know the law and can perform it. In fact, they demonstrate that *the work of the law is written in their hearts. Works of the law* (plural) are always negative in Paul [*Essay: Works of the Law*]. The singular *work of the law* refers to the essential unity of the law's requirements. This *work of the law* occurs in the inner person. The phrase explains how the Gentiles are "a law to themselves," even though they do not possess the law. They have a deep and wholehearted desire to do the essentials of the law.

Paul's first point about the Gentiles is that they have access to the essential moral requirement of the law and they occasionally do the law. Put a period at the end of v. 15a. The law gives the Jews no special advantage. In addition, Paul credits the Gentiles with conscience; they are aware of the wrongness of what they have done. Paul pictures them at the final judgment as people who try to avoid actions that would arouse their conscience. Their conflicting thoughts about good and evil as they face judgment is evidence of moral sensitivity. The language in vv. 15b-16 is legal. The scene is the final judgment, where Jews claimed they would have special advantages, because they had two advocates, the Torah and the commandments, to speak in their behalf. Paul argues that the Gentiles also have two advocates, the law and conscience. Jews and Gentiles are equal in the final judgment when God will disclose the secrets of all people's hearts. The measure of that final judgment will be Messiah Jesus, not Enoch, Melchizedek, or other heroic figures in Jewish speculation about who would assist God in the final judgment.

The First Case of the Jews 2:17-24

The Jews are mentioned specifically for the first time in v. 17. The concluding statements in vv. 28-29, *for he is not a real Jew . . . but he is a Jew,* form an inclusio [*Essay: Inclusio*]. The focus is Jewish identity and advantage. The form is a diatribe [*Essay: Diatribe*]. The dialogue partner is an imaginary Jewish teacher who seeks to instruct

Gentiles in the moral contents of the law. The text consists of two halves, vv. 17-20 and 21-23, with v. 24 providing a conclusion. The text is structured into groups of five components:

Jewish Privilege	**Role for Others**

The Claim: and if you are sure you are

[1] if you call yourself a Jew	[1] a guide to the blind
[2] and rely upon the law	[2] a light for those in darkness
[3] and boast in God	[3] an instructor of the foolish
[4] and know his will	[4] a teacher of little ones
[5] and discern good and evil taught by the law	[5] having the embodiment of knowledge and truth in the law

The "Reality"

[1] you teach others	[1] do you fail to teach yourself?
[2] you who preach not to steal	[2] do you not steal?
[3] you say not to commit adultery	[3] do you not commit adultery?
[4] you who despise idols	[4] do you rob temples?
[5] you who boast in the law	[5] do you not dishonor God by breaking the law?

"For, as it is written, 'The name of God is blasphemed among the Gentiles because of you.'"

The text begins with a list of Jewish privileges and claims. The second list outlines what the Jew hopes to be and do for others because of those claims. The qualities and roles in the lists have scriptural antecedents and parallels in contemporary Jewish literature. The final list pictures the gap between the self-understanding and the practice. The final or fifth element in the lists mentions the law. Who is "a Jew"? Paul says he/she is a person defined by the law—mentioned four times: *resting upon the law* (v. 17), *instructed from the law* (v. 18), *having the embodiment of knowledge and truth in the law* (v. 20), *you boast in the law* (v. 23). The law is the symbol of privileged status over against the Gentiles. Because of it, Jews *boast in God*. "Boasting" is negative, because it involves nationalistic exclusiveness that says God is exclusively the God of the people of the law, the Jews (cf. 3:27-29).

The accusing questions in vv. 21-23 stand in the prophetic tradition of rebuke and exhortation. The striking similarity of the specific charges with accusations against Jews in contemporary Jewish literature (e.g., *Pss. Sol.* 8:8-13; *T. Levi* 14; CD 4:12-17; 8:4-10; Philo *Conf.* 163) suggests that Paul is using an established rhetorical form. He is not saying anything new or anti-Jewish. The Jews break the very law in which they boast. The problem is discrepancy between profession and practice. Paul's point is not that the law is unfulfillable, or that the Jews are uniquely culpable, but that they are accountable to God for disobeying the law.

The emphasis on Israel's role in leading and proselytizing the nations forms the background for the climactic charge in v. 24 (the quotation is from Isa. 52:5 and Ezek. 36:20). The actual behavior of the Jews causes God's name to be blasphemed among the Gentiles. The mission of Judaism is to glorify God's name among the nations, but the combination of knowledge without practice results in alienating the Gentiles.

The contrast is between national pride in possessing the law, the sure and certain sign of God's favor, and transgression of the law, which dishonors God before the Gentiles. The law confers no special advantage to those who merely possess it. The Jews are as guilty as the Gentiles.

The Second Case of the Jews 2:25

The focus narrows in vv. 25-27 to circumcision, the critical symbol of Jewish identity in the first century. It is the great sign of election as God's people, the distinguishing boundary line that divides Jews from Gentiles.

Circumcision is defined strictly in terms of obedience to the law. It is of great value for Jews who obey the law. But if they break the law, as vv. 17-24 argue, then the value of circumcision is annulled, and they are no longer members of the covenant people. Thus, the Jews cannot claim circumcision as an advantage without obedience.

The Second Case of the Gentiles 2:26-27

If Gentiles keep the law, as vv. 14-16 asserted they can and do, then circumcision (God's election) is attributed to them. Not only do uncircumcised but law-obedient Gentiles become God's elect, they also become witnesses for the divine prosecution against the Jews in the final judgment; their obedience will be evidence of what the Jews should have been but were not.

There is evidence that "circumcision" and "uncircumcision," more literally, "circumcised penis" and "uncircumcised penis," were nicknames that were used against people in Rome (see Marcus, 1989). More than half the occurrences of "uncircumcised" in the NT occur in

Romans (11 out of 19 in Paul, 20 in the NT). Paul addresses the controversy by arguing that Gentiles who keep the law are also circumcised persons. Name-calling based on physical circumcision is inappropriate. Obedience is what counts.

Paul draws on earlier arguments in the four test cases to establish the equality of Jews and Gentiles. Both law and circumcision have been defined too narrowly as badges of national identity, which end up preventing the fulfillment of God's purpose in the law. Both are redefined strictly in terms of performance, obedience, which eliminates them as the special privilege of the Jews. Gentiles can and do meet this criterion.

The General Principle—The Relation of Circumcision and Obedience 2:28-29

Although Paul has eliminated the law and circumcision, he still considers them as defining criteria for the Jew. Therefore, Paul outlines a concept of the Jew in vv. 28-29 based on the same criteria.

Paul returns to the contrasting form of the opening general principle in v. 13: "for not . . . but." The true Jew is defined in terms of hidden criteria. Circumcision is of the heart and results from keeping the law. "Circumcision of the heart" is a phrase familiar in Judaism. It means the removal of any obstacles to the full obedience of the law. It cannot be read as advocating the cessation of physical circumcision. Rather, it describes an internalizing of the external act to achieve obedience. Real Jewish identity is defined as hidden, of the heart, by the Spirit. The truly obedient Jew will receive God's praise.

Paul makes a series of distinctions to which he will return in 7:6 and 8:4:

Public ("in the open")	Private ("in secret")
Fleshly circumcision	Heart circumcision
Written	Spiritual

If "Jewishness" is defined as a matter of the heart, of the Spirit, then Gentiles can be God's people too.

Comments and Observations

Paul extends the argument of the impartiality of God's justice. The Jews have no advantage over the Gentiles in the judgment despite the law and circumcision. Both are equal before God.

The argument of 2:12-29 parallels 2:1-11. The problem is the discrepancy between moral claim and actual behavior. The parallelism of the two diatribes expounds the meaning of the theological assertions in 2:6 and 11, God judges actual performance impartially. Human beings who judge others and Jews, who fail to live by the law they claim as the special mark of their identity, stand on equal ground. God judges all people impartially on the basis of their behavior, not their theology or their ethical claims.

Two things are noteworthy in this discussion. First, there is no parallel between 1:18-31 and 2:12-29. The first critiques human culture and religiosity in general for its idolatrous center. The worship of God requires a real conversion, a turning away from idolatry—cultural and religious—to center life in God. The critique of the Jew is much narrower. The problem is the failure to observe the law, the center of Jewish religion and culture. Paul upholds and affirms the validity and significance of the Jewish law for Jewish faith.

It is important, secondly, to note what Paul does and does not say about Jews and Judaism in this critique. Paul's basic charge against the Jews of his day is that of boasting about an identity they are not living. The Jews boast in God (v. 17), claiming God as the God of the Jews and not the Gentiles. They boast in the law (v. 23), not because they keep it, but because they believe possessing it marks them out as the chosen. This Jewish self-perception is reaffirmed and critiqued again in 3:27f. in light of the revelation of the righteousness of God through Messiah Jesus.

Boasting is a claim for honor over other people on the basis of status. The issue thus is competition for status. The category of the discussion again is honor-shame language. The Jews, specifically the Jewish-Christians in the Roman churches, are claiming precedence over other people on the basis of their knowledge of God. The reality, Paul charges, is shame before other people. Ultimate questions of honor and shame, he points out, will be decided by God, and there will be some surprise role reversals in that final judgment.

Paul's critique is not against Jewish legalism, but against the sin of breaking the law. Paul says nothing negative about the law; it remains, as in ch. 7, God's law, containing knowledge and truth. The problem for Paul is not the law, but its misuse. The critical problem is not legalism but "ethnic righteousness," the attempt to use the fact that God has entrusted the Jews with the law (3:2) as the foundation for permanent and automatic superiority over other people. Paul's critique of Jewish trust in the law and circumcision as badges of ethnic privilege does not abolish the idea of the "true circumcision," which keeps the law from the heart. Genuine Jewish identity, based on obedience of the law and inner circumcision, remains the calling of the Jews.

Paul's argument is both old and new. The problem of Jewish disobedience of the law is a long-term concern of the law's teachers and the Scriptures. "Circumcision of the heart" is a scriptural theme, as well, found also in contemporary Jewish literature. Even the notion that disobedient Jews will be judged by Gentiles who keep the law occurs in contemporary Judaism.

At the same time, Paul makes some radical moves. Circumcision is more than the equivalent of law observance in Judaism. It is the distinctive physical sign of belonging to Abraham's family. To assert that Gentiles could be counted as circumcised by keeping the law is an astonishing claim. Even more radical is Paul's transformation of the "both . . . and" of v. 25 (circumcision and law observance) to the "not . . . but" of vv. 28-29, (not "fleshly circumcision" but "heart circumcision"). While the latter does not exclude the former, the importance of fleshly circumcision as a distinctive marker of theological and sociological identity becomes less important. The threefold antitheses in vv. 28-29 further redefine circumcision as that which God effects by the Spirit rather than as a physical marking of identity.

Paul is not making a case against the law or Judaism, but for the impartiality of God with all people. But he also argues theologically for removing age-old distinctions that gave Israel an exclusive and exalted status with God. And socially Paul rejects the identity and boundary markers that separated Israel from the nations, Jewish Christians from Gentile Christians. The argument raises questions about circumcision and Jewish identity, which are discussed in 3:1-8.

The Objections of the Jews

Romans 3:1-20

PREVIEW

The dominant scholarly interpretation treats 3:1-8 as a digression. Paul is believed to get ahead of himself, briefly raising issues he will treat more fully in chs. 6-7 and 9-11. Read that way, however, the passage lacks unity and coherence. Most commentators see Paul addressing Jewish objections in vv. 1-4, and replying to charges of libertinism in vv. 5-8. Verses 9-20 complete the proof that all have sinned.

An alternative interpretation, proposed here, views the argument as the logical extension of the preceding unit. The discussion so far easily leads to the conclusion that Israel's sin has made the gifts of the law and circumcision ineffective. The result is that, if God is righteous as the impartial judge, God cannot also be righteous as the covenant savior of Israel. The Jew is no better off than the Gentile; election and covenant are meaningless. This conclusion raises profound questions about God for Jews, Jewish Christians and Gentiles sympathetic with the Jewish faith.

Paul uses the diatribe form to engage an imaginary partner with questions concerning God. Paul addresses two seemingly inconsistent ideas: 1) God's impartiality to Jews and Gentiles; 2) God's faithfulness to the covenant promises to Israel. The first point questions the advantage of being Jewish. To answer the question negatively would be bad politics; it would offend Jewish nationalism, which is part of the background of the letter. But even more important, a negative answer would be bad theology, for it would question the truthfulness of the Jewish Scriptures and the faithfulness of God. The issue is how can the doctrine of God's impartiality be reconciled with the scriptural proclamation of God's faithfulness to the covenant promises?

Furthermore, if God is faithful to the promises, does the Jew not have an advantage after all? Paul seeks to demonstrate from the law that Jews as a people are sinners (the language concerns peoplehood or people groups, not individuals), and thereby demonstrate that the law does not separate them from Gentile sinners. The law places both groups, in fact, the whole world, under the judgment of God. Jewish security, based on the possession of the law, is undermined. The Jew has no advantage in respect to judgment, because all—Jew and Gentile—are "under sin." The string of Scripture citations proves this. The "those in the law" (*tois en tō nomō*) in v. 19 applies to Israel. The guilty Jew is added to the guilty Gentile (whom the Jews know are guilty), and the whole world is arraigned before God.

OUTLINE

The Diatribe, 3:1-9

The Scriptural Warrant, 3:10-18

The Conclusion, 3:19-20

EXPLANATORY NOTES

The Diatribe 3:1-9

Paul uses the socratic method of asking and answering questions to

lead his imaginary partner to correct answers to real questions that follow from 2:17-29. Five questions and answers are given in the dialogue:

> Question: v. 1—What, then, is the advantage of being a Jew? Or,
> what is the benefit of circumcision?
> Response: v. 2—Much in every way! First, they were entrusted
> with the oracles of God.
> Question: v. 3—What now: If some were disobedient, does their
> unfaithfulness nullify the faithfulness of God?
> Response: v. 4—Absolutely not! Let God be true and every per-
> son a liar, as it is written, 'so that you may be justified
> in your words, and prevail in your judging.'
> Question: v. 5—But if our unrighteousness serves to show God's
> justice (i.e., our unrighteousness gives God an oppor-
> tunity to be merciful), what shall we say? That God is
> unrighteous to inflict wrath? I speak like a human.
> Response: v. 6—Absolutely not! How in that case could God
> judge the world?
> Question: vv. 7-8b—If God's truth abounds all the more to his
> glory because of my falsehood, why am I still con-
> demned as a sinner? And why are we blasphemed, and
> some accuse us of saying, 'let us do evil in order that
> good may come?'
> Response: v. 8c—The condemnation of such is just!
> Question: v. 9a—What, then, do we plead as a defense?
> Response: v. 9b—Nothing at all. For we already know that Jew
> and also Gentile are all under the power of **sin**.

The questions of v. 1 confirm the linkage of Jewish identity and circumcision. They give voice to the Jewish and Jewish-Christian conclusion, if Paul's argument is correct, that Israel's sin has nullified
God's covenant with Israel. God has broken faith, and, therefore, cannot be righteous.

Paul responds that there is great advantage in being Jewish. The
Jews have been entrusted with "the words of God," the Scriptures. To
be "entrusted" means to be in covenant; entrustment commits God to
Israel, and places Israel under obligation to faithfulness. No one else
in the world enjoys such an advantage. But note, the advantage is
entirely the initiative of God, not the goodness of the Jewish people.

The second question, v. 3, makes explicit the real issue, the faithfulness of God. Does Jewish unfaithfulness nullify God's faithfulness?

In ordinary covenants a betrayed partner might consider him/herself released from obligation, if the other party proved unfaithful. Will that happen with God's covenant with Israel?

Paul answers with the strongest possible denial in the Greek language, "Absolutely no" (*mē genoito*)! The denial is followed by an imperative, *Let God be true and every person a liar*. The command is declaratory; we confess that God is true. The suggestion that God could be unfaithful is so horrifying that Paul uses mostly Scripture to formulate his answer. The imperative uses the language of Psalm 116:11 and a quotation from Psalms 51:4. The Scriptures show that the sin of the sinner actually demonstrates God's righteousness as judge. Sin justifies God in punishing Israel because the people have broken the terms of the covenant.

It is important that this second exchange of the dialogue introduces "righteousness" language for the first time since the theme statement in 1:16-18. The word-cradle (the surrounding words that help define the meaning of the term) for "righteousness" is significant. A series of words are used to characterize God in contrast to the Jewish people:

The Jews	**God**
3:3 the faithlessness of them	the faithfulness of God
3:4 every person a liar	the God of truth
3:5 the unrighteousness of us	the righteousness of God
3:7 my falsehood	the truth of God

The parallel statements about God function as interchangeable synonyms. God has integrity; God keeps faith. The righteousness of God is God's faithfulness and truthfulness. God keeps covenant by saving and judging activity. The character of God stands in contrast to human behavior, which is unfaithful, untruthful, and unrighteous.

The righteousness language describes and defends God. It is introduced in Romans to answer questions about God, not to explain the salvation of human beings. A world that fails to honor God, and a people that claim special privilege from God raise questions about God that require response.

The citations from the Psalms lead to two further questions, dealt with in reverse order. The first question, vv. 5-6, comes from the Psalm 51 quote. It concerns God's justice in judging. If God's righteousness is established by Jewish unrighteousness, is God not unjust? If God gains from Israel's sin, is it fair to punish Israel?

Paul again answers forcefully, *absolutely not!* If God cannot judge sin that violates the covenant, God cannot judge the world, which Jews affirm. The Jew is caught. God must judge Israel for covenant unfaithfulness if God is to judge the world. The one side of God's righteousness, grace toward Israel, does not negate the other side, the right to judge sin. If God demonstrates "cheap grace" to Israel then God's role as righteous judge of the whole world is compromised and ineffective.

The fourth set of questions, the second to follow from the Psalms citations, concerns the ethical consequences of God's truthfulness in relation to human falsehood, vv. 7-8b. Paul poses the problem in the first person, a form of reducing the issue to its most personal and absurd level (*reductio ad absurdum*). Why am I judged a sinner, if my untruthfulness serves God's glory by showing God to be righteous? Could we as Jews not help God out by really sinning? Paul explicitly mentions that some people blasphemously claim that this in fact is his teaching, e.g., sin that God's grace may abound.

Paul dismisses the charge out of hand, God's judgment of such people is well deserved. The argument is morally absurd. All people, including the Jews, are fully responsible to God for what they do.

The final question, v. 9a, sums up the previous issues in a modified form, *what, then, do we plead as a defense?* If the conclusion of vv. 1-8 is that Israel's sin means God can be righteous as the eschatological judge, does that mean the Jew is really no better off than the Gentile at the judgment? What defense does the Jew make before God?

The answer is *nothing at all*. There is no defense against unfaithfulness. Furthermore, Paul asserts, we already know something, a reference to the argument from 1:18–2:29. Paul makes explicit what he has hinted at in the argument. What we know is *that Jews and Gentiles are all under the power of **Sin***. Paul repeats the catch phrase, *Jew and also Gentile*, but this time omits the word *first* thus emphasizing the exact equality.

Paul introduces the noun "**Sin**" (*hamartia*) for the first time in Romans. **Sin**, singular, in Paul is a power; sins, plural, refer to deeds. **Sin** is personified (throughout this commentary, put in bold to highlight Paul's unique understanding of it). It is a power, a magnetic field that draws all created reality into its force field [*Essay: Sin in Romans*]. In Romans, **Sin** forms a significant statement about Paul's view of the world (cosmology). **Sin** as power dominates all people.

Jews and Gentiles are equally under the power of **Sin**. Both are enslaved within its magnetic field. The Jews, of course, knew that about the Gentiles. But Paul's argument now includes them within **Sin's** reign.

The diatribe does not represent a digression in Romans, but a continuation of the discussion of God's impartiality. Paul correlates God's impartiality with God's faithfulness and righteousness in relationship to Israel even in judgment. The covenantal language affirms that God remains faithful to the promises to Israel despite her unfaithfulness and despite God's just judgment for this unfaithfulness.

The Scriptural Warrant 3:10-18

Paul supports his argument with a chain of seven biblical quotations, in sequence: Eccl. 7:20; Ps. 14:1-3 [=53:2-4]; 5:10; 139:4; 10:7; Isa. 59:7-8; Ps. 35:2. The string is constructed with artistry and unity out of excerpts from different texts. The Scriptures confirm the charge that all people, including Jews, are under **Sin**.

The opening line, v. 10, states the theme of the warrant: *no one is righteous, not even one. Righteous* is the key word. The closing line, v. 18, balances the first. *There is no fear of God*.

Verses 11-12 make the point that all humans without exception are sinners. The fourfold repetition of *no one is* emphasizes the point. Verses 13-14 use different images of human organs of speech to assert that all human speech is corrupted, lacking truth and integrity. Verses 15-17 focus attention on the violent character of human conduct. There is a steady progression from a lack of understanding and absence of seeking after God to deception and violence, the same progression present in 1:18ff.

The citation picks up themes and language from 1:18ff.: *there is no one who seeks after God* in 3:11 recalls 1:19-21. The lack of understanding of God sums up the claim of 1:22; the turning away of 3:12 uses similar language to 1:23; and the evil deeds of the third strophe are similar to the actions narrated in 1:30.

The chain of quotations forms a fitting illustration of the third thesis statement, 1:18, and the opening line of the first argument of the letter, the wrath of God is now being revealed. God is righteous. No human being is righteous. God, therefore, judges the world impartially and justly.

The Conclusion 3:19-20

Paul concludes the text unit, 3:1-20, and the first major argument of the letter, 1:18–3:20, by making two basic points. First, all human beings are accountable to God. The framework of the concluding argument is clear: *all are under* **Sin** (3:9). . . *no one is righteous* [*dikaios*] (3:10). . . *every mouth is stopped and the whole world is liable to judgment before God* (3:19) [*hupodikos, liable to judgment* in v. 19 comes from the same root as *dikaios, righteous,* in

v. 10]. The impartial and righteous God judges all unrighteousness irrespective of the identity of people. All people will be "speechless" in the dock. All are *without excuse* (1:20; 2:1).

Second, the Jewish people specifically are accountable to God's judgment. The conclusion speaks to the Jews and God-fearers who knew the law through the synagogue. "We know that whatsoever the law says" refers to the quotations in vv. 10-18. "To the ones in the law it speaks" identifies those who possess the law. The *in the law* (*en tō nomō*) is the same as in 2:12. *In the law* brackets the whole discussion from 2:12 through 3:19 to underline that the Jew and Gentile sympathizer with Judaism is being addressed throughout this section. Paul does not have to prove that Gentiles are sinners; that is axiomatic. Therefore, he emphasizes that the Jews have no advantage over Gentiles in God's judgment. The Jews are sinners by the very law on which they establish their privileged relationship with God. That law is an advantage (3:1-2), because it articulates the will of God. The law spares the Jews the perversions of the Gentiles. But when it comes to God's judgment, there is no favored people. Each people—remember, Paul is taking about groups, about Jews and Gentiles, not about individuals—is under **Sin** in its own way.

Verse 20 is added to confirm the focus on the Jews. The confirmation is another word of Scripture, Psalm 143:2b, *no person will be made righteous before God.* But the Psalm is introduced with an important Pauline modification, the phrase, *out of works of law* (*ex ergōn nomou*). Until the discovery of the Dead Sea Scrolls the phrase appeared only in the Pauline letters, and primarily in Romans and Galatians. It is clear from the context here that *works of law* are different than doing the law (2:13-14), or fulfilling the law (2:27), or the *work of the law written in the heart* (2:15), or *the circumcision of the heart* (2:29). The phrase is used in the summary of an argument against the Jewish assumption that God's covenant gives Israel special status and a special defense in the final judgment. It must refer to the attitude attacked in ch. 2, particularly circumcision.

The *works of law* is Paul's special phrase for identifying the heart of Jewish pride in the law and election, especially those symbols of the law that mark Jews as distinct from the nations. Circumcision, food and sabbath laws served that function in first-century Judaism. *Works of law* is thus a summary phrase for "ethnic righteousness," or the distinctive boundary markers that differentiate Jews from the world [*Essay: Works of the Law*]. The point of the Scripture reference is that Jewish identity, as symbolized by the law and circumcision, will not make any person righteous. That is the case, Paul adds, because contrary to typical Jewish thinking, the law does not protect against the power of **Sin**, but rather raises consciousness of **Sin**. The law was not intended to provide a sense of divine distinctiveness and security, but rather to make the Jewish people profoundly aware of their dependence on the grace of God.

Comments and Observations

Paul's purpose in 3:1-20 is to establish that God is just in the judgment of the Jew, and thus of the world. The primary means for making that case is the diatribe and the citation of Scripture. Paul refutes the idea that God is unjust (*adikos*) (v. 5). The refutation asserts that the Jew is guilty and without excuse in at least three different ways: 1) "under the power of **Sin**" (v. 9); 2) "no one is righteous" (vv. 10-18); 3) "the whole world is accountable to God" (v. 19). The Jew deserves God's judgment, just as the Gentile.

If Paul's language and argument seems very direct, even harsh, remember that he is arguing in prophetic mode. The dialogue is not one faith-family putting down a different faith-family; it is a dialogue within the family.

Conclusion of the First Argument

Paul has been arguing in his first thesis (1:18–3:20) that God is revealing righteous wrath against all unrighteousness. He supports his thesis with two primary points: 1) God is impartial; God's justice is evenhanded (1:18–2:29); 2) God's judgment is righteous; it is consistent with the covenant with the Jewish people (3:1-20). They are under the power of **Sin** just like the Gentiles, and, therefore, similarly subject to God's judgment. The impartial and just judgment of God over both Gentiles and Jews is the necessary presupposition to the contention that all are "under the power of **Sin**."

This reading of Romans is quite different than the traditional Protestant interpretation. That reading can be summarized as follows: 1) The gospel reveals the power of God and the gift of God. 2) The first argument outlines the need for the gift. The need is human sinfulness and the ineffectiveness of the law. The interpretation proposed in this commentary also begins with the gospel. The gospel reveals God's power, righteousness, and wrath. The first argument makes the case that the wrath of God is impartial and just. The first major point of Romans is not about human need, but about the nature of God. Paul begins by asserting the righteousness of God. The first line of evidence is the impartiality and justice of God in judgment. The second line of evidence will be the universal salvation of God through Messiah

Jesus (3:21f.). The Psalm 143 citation in 3:20 is a significant clue to the shape of this argument. It both affirms the unrighteousness of human beings before God and appeals to God to exercise righteousness for salvation. The Psalm thus provides a fitting conclusion to the first argument, and introduces the second thesis that Paul will develop (see Hays, 1980, 1989a).

The theological foundation Paul lays in this first argument is important for the larger argument of Romans. The righteousness of God, which the gospel reveals in a new and powerful way, can be challenged on three grounds: 1) not all unrighteous and evil people are brought to account before God. Paul shows in 1:18–3:20 that God takes all unrighteousness seriously, both Gentile and Jewish, and holds all people accountable. 2) God abandons the helpless—those powerless people whom God championed in the OT and whose rescue demonstrated righteousness—in favor of a special or privileged elite, the Jewish people. Paul in 2:12–3:20 demonstrates that there is no special or elite Jewish people, but that all "are under **Sin**" and in need of redemption. 3) God's impartial and just judgment of all people, including the Jews, means God has abandoned the covenant with Israel. Paul answers in 3:1-20 that God's judgment of the Jews is just precisely within the terms of the covenant. This theological foundation is necessary for the next argument that God demonstrates righteousness equally in the salvation of all people through Messiah Jesus.

The questions Paul answers in the dialogue and exposition of 3:1-20 shape the rest of the letter. The fear that Paul denies Israel's historic privilege is addressed in chs. 9-11. The charge that Paul's God is unfaithful and has no right to judge people is answered in 3:21–4:25. The accusation that Paul's gospel for Gentiles is all grace but without moral content—"do evil that good may come"—is refuted in chs. 5-8. The text unit, in other words, both summarizes the first major argument of the letter, and also outlines the agenda for the next three arguments.

TEXT IN BIBLICAL CONTEXT

The Picture of God

The central affirmations in Romans 2:11–3:20 are about God. In treating people the same, God is just and righteous. The three characterizations of God in 3:3-5 are especially important. God is faithful, despite human unfaithfulness. The formulation "the faithfulness of God" (*tēn pistin tou theou*) comes out of the OT. God is faithful in all actions (Ps. 33:4; Hos. 2:20; cf. also Ps. 98:2-3, 9); righteousness and justice are associated in both texts. The righteous live out of God's faithfulness (Hab. 2:4), and praise God for *great is your faithfulness* (Lam. 3:23). The language means "firmness," "reliability." God is steady, constant, and reliable. Paul affirms God's faithfulness at this point in Romans to stress the continuity of purpose in the covenant with the Jewish people.

"The faithfulness of God" becomes a formula in Paul (*pistos ho theos*). God is the faithful one who calls people into the family of God through Christ (1 Cor. 1:9; 1 Thess. 5:25), who enables and strengthens Christians in times of testing (1 Cor. 10:13; 2 Thess. 3:3), who says "yes" to humanity in the gospel of Jesus Christ (2 Cor. 1:18).

The first reference to faith after the theme statement in 1:16-17 is a word about God. *The righteousness of God is revealed out of faith*, and the faith is God's not Israel's or the Gentiles'. God, Paul asserts, is the reliable one who does not change course or break covenant because human beings are fickle or fail in covenant.

Paul makes the same point in different language when he states that "God is true" (*ho theos alēthēs*). The Hebrew word for truth is *emunah*, usually translated into Greek as "faith" (*pistis*). But it is translated as "truth" (*alētheia*) consistently in the Psalms to denote God's covenant faithfulness to Israel (cf. Pss. 33:4; 89:1, 2, 5, 8, 14, 24, 33, 49; 98:3).

The faithfulness and truthfulness of God help explain the meaning of the righteousness of God, another term with deep scriptural roots. The faithful and truthful God is righteous, and the righteous God is faithful and true [see explanation of 1:17, and *Essays: Righteousness* and *The Righteousness of God*]. Paul is at pains to emphasize that God is faithful, true, and righteous in relation to Israel, even a faithless and undeserving Israel. Such a God is foundational for the gospel Paul preaches, a gospel of universal salvation for all people.

The Family Debate

The language Paul uses in 2:12 through 3:20 to critique the self-understanding of his own people seems harsh, even offensive, when read at the distance of two thousand years. It is important to remember that his language comes from within his own faith community and from his Scriptures. It is the language of the Hebrew prophetic tradition, members of the community speaking to fellow members of the family. One of the most remarkable things about the Hebrew Scriptures is the minimal language of self-glorification, on the one hand, and the intense language of self-criticism, on the other hand. The historians and prophets of Israel portray a people who do not walk in the ways of God, break the covenant, and do not remember the mercy of God. The writers assume God's point of view rather than Israel's, and picture a people characterized by idolatry, injustice, duplicity, and failure. There are no heroes in the Hebrew Bible, no moral paragons, only failures; Moses, David, and Solomon, as examples, come under the judgment of God.

The language used in this self-criticism is harsh—"sinful nation," "offspring of evildoers," "rebellious people," "sons of the sorceress," "harlot," "stiff necked," "lying sons," "offspring of the adulterer and the harlot," "children of transgression," and "uncircumcised in heart" (see Isa. 1:21; 30:9-11; 57:3-5; Jer. 3:6; 7:25-26; 9:26; 11:7-8; Hos. 1:2). Isaiah and Jeremiah implore God not to forgive Israel (Isa. 2:9; Jer. 18:23). Jeremiah asks God to deliver Israel to famine, even to *give them over to the power of the sword . . . May their men meet death by pestilence, their youths be slain by the sword in battle* (RSV, 18:21).

The same language is found in the Dead Sea Scrolls. Fellow Israelites are called "hypocrites," "prophets of falsehood," "seers of deceit," "preacher of lies," "men of the Pit," "wicked priest," "perverse men" who "devise plans of Satan against" God's true teacher (see 1QH 4:6-8, 9-11, 13-14; 1QS 5:10-13; 9:16-18; 1QpHab 8:8; 9:9; 10:9; 11:4; 12:2). Again, there are prayers that enemies not be forgiven (1QS 2:4-9, 21-22). Similarly, Josephus uses harsh language that "far outstrips anything found in the New Testament" (Evans, 1993:8).

What must be understood is that this is the language of an intrafamily debate. It is language intended to undermine the self-understanding of the majority of the people, a theology that sees Israel's election as a source of security. This prophetic language is delivered by individuals deeply embedded in and part of the Israelite community, for the purpose of shocking the people out of a deeply flawed theology of "blessed assurance." It is the language of profound love and suffering for fellow-members of the family; it is not language directed toward outsiders and enemies.

TEXT IN THE LIFE OF THE CHURCH
The Faithfulness of God

The message of Romans 2:12–3:20 is good news. God is faithful, true, and righteous despite human unfaithfulness. God's faithfulness has been demonstrated in the history of Israel, and will be demonstrated again in Romans in the next text unit through Jesus Christ.

We can and do fail God, and each other. God holds us accountable. There is judgment; there are consequences within history and beyond. But God does not become like us, unfaithful, dishonest, and unjust.

History and experience raise questions about God. Why do great natural tragedies happen? Why is there human suffering and injustice? Do not history and experience show that God is unreliable? Paul's answer is "absolutely not!" God is faithful, true, and righteous with all people in all times.

The flip side of God's faithfulness and righteousness is that people are responsible for their actions. When Israel broke covenant, the people experienced the judgment of God. The story of Israel's judgment teaches all people that there is no special privilege or status that absolves them of obedience to God, of responsibility for their actions, of accountability for who they are and what they do.

The Language of Criticism

My children speak with a directness and candor to me that they do not use with other people, even with their mother. They learned such language from me, and they have earned the right to speak that way from living with me. Our direct, even blunt, language is a familial way of talking with each other. Some people are surprised, maybe even shocked, at how direct we are with each other (the same was true of the way my two brothers and I spoke with our father). To talk with other people the way we talk with each other in the family would be problematic. They would think we were unkind, even angry.

When familial language, which is bathed in deep, long-term, and loving relationships, is used with outsiders and in totally different contexts, the potential for misunderstanding and harm is great. And when such language is used to describe and judge one's enemies, it is completely inappropriate and offensive.

The blunt and candid language Paul uses in Romans 2-3 is familial language. It is used to challenge and correct a problematic self-understanding within Paul's community. When it is used by Christians to describe Jews, as has happened so often in Christian history, it becomes offensive and hurtful. It is then not language intended to renew but to judge.

The same is true in the church. Much hurt occurs because people use language to judge fellow-Christians when they have not earned the right to use such language through deep and loving relationships. We need to learn the difference between language of correction and renewal and language of judgment.

Romans 3:21-26

The Revelation of the Righteousness of God

The argument shifts in 3:21 to the second thesis of the letter: the gospel reveals the righteousness of God. The key words from 1:16-17—righteousness and faith—reemerge. The text begins and closes with God's righteousness. While the argument changes, themes from 1:18–3:20 continue: the relation of God's righteousness to the law (2:12-29; 3:10-20; 3:21), the impartiality of God (2:6-11; 3:19; 3:22), the universality of human sin (3:9, 19; 3:23), and the vindication of God (3:1-8; 3:25-26).

The second thesis sets up the argument for the remainder of the letter, especially the central section of Romans, chs. 4-11. God's righteousness is world transforming—it makes peace (5:1-11), it defeats the power of **Sin** (5:12-21), it renews people and creation (6:1-8:36), it incorporates Gentiles into God's people (9:6-29), and it assures the salvation of Israel (11:1-36).

PREVIEW

Two different interpretations of this text are possible. The traditional Protestant interpretation sees its thrust as God's gracious gift of salvation through faith in Christ. The righteousness of God is effective through faith in Christ. Christians are being justified by grace through God's action in Christ. Terms like "redemption" and "propitiation," together with the reference to "blood," show that the cross is the means of atonement. The point of the text, according to this view, is that the cross enables God to justify sinners on the basis of faith without compromising divine righteousness. The text highlights what humans get, the status of righteousness or justification before God, on the basis of human faith.

An alternative interpretation sees the thrust of the text as the revelation of God's end-time righteousness, which is effected through the faithfulness of Messiah Jesus. The faith theme is two-sided, the faithfulness of Jesus and the faith response of believers. The "without distinction" theme equalizes Jews and Gentiles (remember—"all" is polemical language in Romans). There is no distinction between classes of people. God's saving action—redemption and propitiation—through Jesus' faithfulness has a double effect. It demonstrates the righteousness of God, and it forms the basis for the redemption of all people. The point of the text is to prove the righteousness of God through the faithfulness of Jesus. It highlights the character of God as the Righteous One who redeems humanity and the world through the faithfulness of Messiah Jesus. The importance of God's righteousness for human salvation is assumed, but it is not the centerpiece of the argument.

The alternative interpretation is the preferred reading. The issue of God's integrity and righteousness now comes onto center stage in Romans. Paul's concern has less to do with the salvation of humans than with the righteousness of the saving God. Piling up three purpose clauses, all focused on the demonstration of the righteousness of God, shows just how central the vindication of God is in Romans and how important this issue must have been in the Roman churches.

The critical issue facing those churches was, how can God be trusted—is God righteous? If all humans are really "under the power of **Sin**," is this not evidence that God is unrighteous and cannot be trusted? If Gentiles can be incorporated into God's people without the central symbols of Jewish faith—keeping the law—is God not compromising divine righteousness and justice? Is God not abandoning special promises made to Israel?

The text is one long, complex sentence that is very carefully and tightly organized. It is centered in a double announcement that the righteousness of God has been revealed (vv. 21, 22a). The means of the revelation is explained in three "through" (*dia*) clauses (vv. 22b, 24b, 25a). The discussion of the means is interrupted by a parenthesis that represents a postponed conclusion from the previous argument (22c-24a). The unit concludes with three purpose clauses that all focus on the righteousness of God (25b-26). The text is framed by God's righteousness, its revelation (21-22b) and demonstration (25b-26).

OUTLINE (with author's translation)

The Revelation, 3:21-22a

But now apart from the law *the righteousness of God* has been and continues to be revealed, being witnessed to by the law and the prophets, *the righteousness of God,*

The Means, 3:22b-25a

through (dia) the faithfulness of Messiah Jesus to all the ones believing
Parenthesis—delayed conclusion, 22b-24a
(for there is no distinction,
for all have sinned and fallen short of the glory of God,
being made righteous freely by his grace)
through (dia) the redemption the one in Messiah Jesus, whom God purposed as a sacrificial offering
through (dia) the faithfulness *[of Jesus]* by means of his blood,

The Purpose, 3:25b-26

to (eis) demonstrate *his righteousness* through the forgiveness of previously committed sins in the forbearance of God,
to (pros) demonstrate *his righteousness* in the present (literally, "now") time,
to (eis) be himself righteous even in making righteous the one living out of the faithfulness of Jesus.

EXPLANATORY NOTES

The Revelation 3:21-22a

But now marks a turning point in the argument. Paul is going to explain the revelation of the righteousness of God.

The exposition is framed by a contrast of two "law" phrases. The first phrase, "apart from the law," points both backward and forward—back to "the ones in the law" and to "out of works of law" in the previous argument, and forward to *a person . . . is made righteous apart from the works of law* in v. 28. *Apart (chōris) from law,* standing between *by works of law* in v. 20 and *apart (chōris) from works of law* in v. 28 refers to the law as a boundary marker of Jewish identity. "Law" also points forward to the witness of the Scripture, *the law and the prophets* in the next phrase. Paul contrasts two different functions of the same Scriptures. The law as the boundary marker of Judaism plays no part in effecting the new manifestation of God's righteousness. God is now revealing the divine

righteousness without this hallmark of Jewish identity. The new revelation, however, is not an abandonment of the old, but is in continuity with God's previous actions and words with Israel.

Paul's second thesis begins with a revolutionary notion. The focal
point of God's end-time, world-transforming salvation has shifted away
from the Torah. Paul will announce the new center in a moment. But
first, he must qualify the idea of a new action of God independent of
the identity marker of Judaism. The Scriptures do testify to God's new
saving righteousness. Paul again anchors the new in the old, as in 1:2
and in his repeated use of Scripture to support his argument.

The new reality is that "the righteousness of God has been and
continues to be revealed." The double announcement of "the righteousness of God" makes the focus clear. Paul is talking about the end-
time saving and right-making power of God to transform the universe
[*Essay: Righteousness of God*]. This end-time power is being
revealed (*phaneroun* is a synonym for *apokalyptein* in 1:17). The
verb form (perfect tense) means the revelation is continuous; it has
taken place and continues to take place.

Paul's announcement is dramatic and transformative. He has just
argued that Jews and Gentiles stand equally before the righteous judgment of God because both are trapped in the magnetic power and structures of **Sin**. But now, a radically new reality exists. God's sovereign and
triumphant faithfulness to the covenant and creation is being revealed.

The Means 3:22b-25a

The means of the revelation of God's end-time righteousness is
Messiah Jesus. Paul argues this with three "through" clauses. The first
clause asserts that the revelation occurs "through the faithfulness of
Messiah Jesus." The preposition "through" is followed by the genitive
form of "faith" which in turn is followed by "Messiah Jesus." The genitive may be translated "faith in Jesus" (an objective genitive) or the
"faith of Messiah Jesus" (a subjective genitive). The phrase is interpreted here as referring to the faith, or better, the faithfulness of
Messiah Jesus (see The "Faith of Jesus" in Paul, below under Text in
Biblical Context). God is revealing end-time, saving righteousness
through the faithfulness of Jesus, not through human faith in Jesus.

The object of the revelation is explained in a purpose clause, "to
all the ones believing." It is for all people—Jews and Gentiles—who
respond faithfully [*Essay: Faith in Romans*]. The phrase emphasizes
the universal outreach of God's saving purpose. The clear emphasis
on the importance and necessity of human response makes the "faith
in Jesus" interpretation (objective genitive) nonsensical. The repetition

is unnatural and unnecessary. God reveals end-time righteousness in the world through the faithfulness of Jesus in order to call all people to be faithful to this revelation.

The Parenthesis 3:22b-24a

Paul interrupts the flow of the argument. *For there is no distinction* elaborates the meaning of *all* in *to all the ones believing*, and shifts the focus of the argument. Paul occasionally employs a stylistic device called "postponed conclusion." He intentionally creates a parenthesis in the discussion. A new argument is started before the previous one is summarized (see same in Rom. 10:17; 2 Cor. 5:21). *There is no distinction* points back to God's impartiality in 1:18–2:29. *All have sinned and fallen short of the glory of God* repeats the charge of 3:9-20. But the parenthesis is more than simply a summary of what has been written. It also moves the argument forward.

The parenthesis asserts three things, two looking backward and one looking forward. First, there is no distinction between groups of people—Jew and Gentile—before God, either in relationship to righteousness (just mentioned) or **Sin** (to follow).

Second, the parenthesis states that all people are trapped by the power of **Sin**; all exist in the kingdom of **Sin's** power (v. 23). The phrase *all have sinned is further explained as falling short of the glory of God*. *Glory* pictures the divine brightness that radiates from the presence of God. Humanity possessed this glory before the fall, according to Jewish thought. It was to be restored in the eschatological future. Being trapped by the power of **Sin** means being removed, alienated, from the presence of God. The loss of glory here recalls the previous reference to glory, humanity's exchange of God's glory for idolatry (1:23).

Verse 23 functions as a twist in the argument. One would expect an expansion of "are made righteous by faith without distinction." Paul rather refers to another universality, the pervasiveness of the power of **Sin**. Human solidarity in **Sin** requires a universal solution.

Third, the parenthesis advances Paul's argument with a counter-point. Paul elaborates "no distinction" in a positive direction, *being made righteous by grace*, v. 24a. The verb for "make righteous" (*dikaioō*), usually translated "justify," is used here for the first time in reference to the theme of Romans [*Essay: Righteousness*]. It declares that people are made righteous by God without distinction. "Gift" (*dorean*) describes the manner of "making righteous;" it is done freely, gratis. The means of making people righteous is *by his grace*. Grace is a dynamic word like righteousness. It describes the unconditional character of God's powerful action in Jesus independent of origin or race [*Essay: Grace in Romans*]. God makes righteous human beings by grace without distinction through the faithfulness of Messiah Jesus.

Back to the Main Argument

The second prepositional phrase that describes the means of God's revelation in Jesus is *through the redemption the one in Messiah Jesus* (v. 24b). The word "redemption" (*apolutrōsis*) denotes deliverance from slavery, freedom from an oppressive existence through someone's liberating action. Many in Paul's audience were slaves or ex-slaves, who understood the power of the imagery. The word is also full of covenant meaning, describing God's redemption of Israel in the Exodus and from Babylonian captivity. The enslaving or oppressive power here is **Sin** (v. 23).

The phrase "the one in Messiah Jesus" is the first occurrence in Romans of a common Pauline expression (over 80 times). It most often refers to the risen Christ as the sphere or domain in whom believers experience redemption or salvation. Christians have been freed from the force field of **Sin**, because Jesus entered into their state and transferred them to his domain.

Paul elaborates the nature of the redemption in Messiah Jesus with the relative clause, *whom God purposed a sacrificial offering*. The action is entirely God's. God takes the initiative—"put forward" or "purposed"—to effect redemption. The word translated *sacrificial offering* (*hilastērion*) is best understood as a divinely ordered sacrifice for **Sin**, rather than as a reference to propitiation in general. God is the subject of a gracious action; therefore, God cannot be pictured as appeasing or placating God's own wrath. The word pictures Jesus as God's intended atonement sacrifice in analogy to the Jewish festival of atonement, the day on which God "wiped away" the accumulated sins of the people for the previous year. God purposed Christ as the sacrificial offering to liberate Jews and Gentiles from **Sin**. Paul's thought here has much in common with Jewish martyr theology (see 2 Macc. 7:30-38; *4 Macc.* 6:27-29; 17:20-22) and the Jewish theology of the binding of Isaac, where the death of a martyr could atone for the sins of Israel. Paul universalizes this theology. Jesus is the ultimate martyr; he is God's Messiah whose faithfulness to death atones for the sin of all people.

The first two prepositional phrases use two metaphors to interpret Christ as the means of the revelation of the saving righteousness of God, faithfulness and atoning sacrifice. The third prepositional phrase combines the two metaphors into one final summary statement, *through the faithfulness by means of his blood.* The phrase has troubled scholars and translators. The NT, and certainly Paul, does not speak of faith in the blood of Jesus. Therefore, most scholars do one of two things: 1) eliminate the words "by faith" as a late addition to the text, and read "expiation in his blood"; or 2) put the words "by faith" at the end of the phrase instead of at the beginning as in the Greek, and translate *by his blood, to be received by faith* (e.g., the NRSV puts it: *by his blood, effective through faith*). There is no textual evidence to delete "by faith" or to place it after "in his blood." Although it is less convenient for translators, the phrase should be interpreted as found in the text, *through faithfulness by means of his blood.* The faith described is Jesus', not humanity's. Jesus demonstrated his faithfulness by giving his life as a sacrificial offering for **Sin**. The anchor for God's liberation from **Sin** is the faithfulness of Jesus, not faith in Jesus. Faith in Jesus is indeed necessary for people to appropriate the redemption in Christ—e.g., to all the ones believing in v. 22 (cf. Rom. 10:9-10)—but that is not the main point Paul is making here.

The Purpose 3:25b-26

The purpose of the revelation of the righteousness of God through Messiah Jesus is stated in two parallel purpose clauses followed by a concluding purpose statement. Except for a different introductory preposition, the two parallel clauses are virtually identical, *to (eis) demonstrate his righteousness* and *to (pros) demonstrate his righteousness.* The repetition underscores a singular purpose.

Each clause addresses a different issue involved in the demonstration. The first gives the reason for the demonstration, "because of the passing over of previously committed sins in the forbearance of God." The word translated "pass over" (*paresin*) can also mean "leave unpunished." It concerns sins committed earlier in history which were not judged due to the restraint of God. The phrase is a negative one from a Jewish perspective. The language points to outsiders. God's patience with the sins of the Gentiles, with the sins of Israel's oppressors, is the problem. The Jews fear that divine patience allows these sins to go unpunished (Isa. 41:14; 63:15; 64:10-12; *Pss. Sol.*; *4 Ezra*; *2 Bar.*; 2 Macc. 6:14). This fear reflects a widespread tradition, in which God's patience is conceived negatively as restraint that allows the sins of the Gentiles to accumulate.

The first purpose clause asserts that God has acted justly in relation to the sins of the Gentiles. They too now have access to a sacrificial offering that forgives sins, as the Jews had for generations through the sacrificial system and the Day of Atonement. God purposed Christ as a means of forgiveness in order to make right the divine relationship to the Gentiles as well as their relationship to the Jews. In other words, the first purpose clause refers specifically to God's new relationship to the Gentiles. It does not make sense if it refers to the Jews; they already had a means of atonement. The point of the phrase is that God now has taken decisive action to establish divine justice in relationship to all people and between all people. All sin has been "wiped away" in Messiah Jesus, who is the sign, the evidence, of the righteousness of God.

The second purpose clause states that the righteousness of God is a present reality; it functions "in the present time."

Paul's final purpose clause offers a ringing conclusion, *to be himself righteous even in making righteous the one living out of the faithfulness of Jesus*. The first phrase indicates that what is at stake is God's being righteous. The final reference to Jesus, again in the genitive, refers to the faithfulness of Jesus rather than human faith in Jesus. The basis of the Christian life is the faithfulness of Jesus. Believers are people who live out of that faithfulness.

This final clause offers an insight into the meaning of the atonement language in the text. For God to forgive humanity's sin lightly—a cheap forgiveness—would be unrighteous, a violation of God's integrity. The purpose of Christ's faithfulness and atoning sacrifice was to achieve a divine forgiveness that is worthy of God and consonant with divine righteousness.

Comments and Observations

The passage is dominated grammatically and thematically by the righteousness of God. It announces that God's long-awaited salvation is present through one person, Messiah Jesus. Two thousand years of Christian proclamation has removed the scandal within the church of the announcement that Jesus is the singular means of God's saving righteousness. But for Paul before the Damascus road encounter, and for his Jewish-Christian readers in Rome, this was a very startling proposition that needed much explanation and defense.

In addition to this singular focus of the text, a series of things is noteworthy. First, the text repeats convictions stated earlier: Paul's gospel is the fulfillment of Jewish Scriptures (1:2 and 1:17), the emphasis on faith (1:5, 16-17), the inclusion of the Gentiles within the scope of the gospel (1:5, 16), and the impartiality of God (2:11).

Second, the emphasis on faith centers uniquely on the faith of Messiah Jesus—mentioned three times. This christological interpretation of faith follows from Paul's messianic reading of Habakkuk 2:4 in

1:17. The faith of believers is mentioned once (v. 22b); such faith is important, but is not the critical point of this text. There are three subjects of faith, Christ's (the faith of Jesus), the believer's (to all the ones believing), and God's (the revelation of God's saving righteousness). Jesus is the focal point where the divine and human meet. His faithfulness is the supreme expression of faith in God and the embodiment of God's covenant and saving faithfulness to the world. Believers "faith"—mimic the faithfulness—the faithfulness of Jesus as God's act of salvation, just as Jesus "faithed" God. To focus on the faith of believers would hardly be new or startling; such faith is central to Jewish theology and practice. It certainly would not be grounds for the revelation of the end-time, world-transforming righteousness of God in the world. More importantly, it certainly would not be the basis for eliminating the distinction between Jews and Gentiles, which faith in 1:5, 1:16, and this text does.

Third, Paul articulates a theology of the cross in relation to Jesus. Jesus' death makes people right ("justified"), atones for sins, especially the sins of the Gentiles, and redeems people out of enslavement to **Sin**. God has acted in Jesus to put things right between Godself and the world enslaved to **Sin**. Jesus' death was a sacrificial offering; it was a *hilastērion,* a word that recalls both the Day of Atonement and the death of Jewish martyrs. Jesus' death liberates (*ransoms*) from enslavement. The death of Jesus is effective; it forgives previously committed sins and frees from enslavement. This death is to be "received by faith" without recourse to the cult. But it is much more important yet than liberating people from the power of **Sin**, which Paul will reaffirm in 8:3. It is the means of revealing the righteousness of God in the world. Jesus' death (and resurrection) introduce a new state of affairs in the world, a new age, a new creation. Paul will elaborate this later in chapters 5-8. What is clear is that Paul interprets the death of Jesus in Jewish apocalyptic terms; it defeats the power of **Sin** and signals a shift of the ages.

Fourth, the language of the text is uniquely Jewish—righteousness of God, glory of God, faith, redemption, sacrificial offering, by means of blood, make righteous. The language is covenantal. Paul is announcing the renewal of the covenant, in which God offers humanity a new exodus in order to maintain and uphold the covenant relationship established with Abraham. God's righteousness means action appropriate to the covenant, the salvation of all the children of Abraham, both Jews and Gentiles.

God is doing something radically new through the faithfulness of Messiah Jesus—revealing divine righteousness and redemption for all humans equally. God is renewing the covenant for Jews and Gentiles alike and equally. This refocusing of the text should not overlook the important subtheme of human faith and redemption. God is doing a new thing "for all the ones believing" in order to make righteous human beings so that they may once again see the glory of God.

TEXT IN BIBLICAL CONTEXT

One phrase makes a major difference in the interpretation of this text, "through the faith of Messiah Jesus" or "through the faith in Messiah Jesus" (*dia pisteōs Iesou Christou*, v. 22), and "the one out of the faith of Jesus" or "the one out of faith in Jesus" (*ton ek pisteōs Iesou*, v. 26). Grammatically, the phrase can be translated either as "the faith of . . ." or "the faith in . . ." The issue is the meaning of the genitive construction (the case denoting possession). Is it a subjective genitive ("of," speaking about the subject of the action) or an objective genitive ("in," speaking about the object of the action)?

The "Faith of Jesus" in Paul

The same phrase is used eight (or nine) times in the Pauline letters, four (or five) before the writing of Romans (Gal. 2:16 [two times]; 2:20; 3:22; maybe 3:26 [a question of an early and important textual variant]); and two following (Phil. 3:9; Eph. 3:12). In each case the translation makes an important difference in the interpretation of the text.

The "faith of" interpretation (subjective genitive) is preferred in all of these passages for a number of reasons. The first is usage of this language prior to Paul. The use of "faith" (*pistis*) with the objective genitive is unknown in classical and Hellenistic Greek (the dictionaries for this literature, Liddell-Scott-Jones and Moulton and Milligan, do not cite a single case). "Faith" with the objective genitive also is not found in Hellenistic Jewish literature; no such usage is found in the Septuagint, the Greek Pseudepigrapha, Philo (116 occurrences of faith), or Josephus (93 times). When writers in this literature use "faith" with an object, they use a form of the preposition "to," not "of." George Howard, following a careful study of usage, concludes that "faith" followed by a personal genitive describes the "faith of" the person rather than "faith in" (it is always subjective) (1973-74; see also 1967).

The second reason for preferring the "faith of" reading is usage within the New Testament. "Faith" followed by the personal genitive occurs 28 times outside of the Pauline letters. In 24 instances the genitive is clearly nonobjective, and in the remaining four it is not clear. Not counting the *faith of Christ* passages, faith with the personal genitive occurs 24 times in the Pauline letters. In every case the genitive is nonobjective. When Paul wishes to specify an object of human faith he does so with the preposition "to" (*pros* or *eis*). The use of "faith" language in the ancient world, as well as in the New Testament, overwhelmingly favors a "faith of" reading (subjective genitive) when "faith" is used with the genitive.

A third reason for preferring the "faith of Jesus" reading is that all the early translations of the New Testament translate the phrase in the eight Pauline texts as *the faith of Jesus*—the Syriac (Peshitta), the Sahidic Coptic, the Latin Vulgate. Wycliff and Erasmus, prior to Martin Luther, translated it as "the faith of Jesus." Until Luther translated it "faith in Jesus" it was consistently understood to mean "the faith of Christ." But even after Luther, the KJV translates it as *the faith of Jesus* (except for Rom. 3:26 and Gal. 3:26, based on the variant Greek reading).

A fourth reason is stylistic. To translate our phrase as "faith in Jesus" is repetitious and awkward in most of the texts. For example, Romans 3:22 reads "the righteousness of God through faith in Jesus Christ to all the ones believing." The human response of faith is mentioned twice. Or, Galatians 2:16 reads *we know that a person is not made righteous by works of law but through faith in Messiah Jesus, and we into Christ have believed, in order that we might be made righteous by faith in Christ and not out of works of law because out of works of law no flesh is made righteous.* The human response of faith is mentioned three times. In each text the sentence reads more smoothly if the phrase in question is understood as *the faith of Jesus.* The awkwardness of the sentence is removed, the critical role of Jesus in salvation is clarified, and the importance of the human response of faith is mentioned.

The case for a "faith of" reading is so compelling that a growing number of scholars are interpreting all of these texts as references to "the faith of Christ," rather than "faith in Christ." In fact, the case is so strong, asserts Leander Keck, that the burden of proof rests with the defenders of the traditional view (1989; see also B. Dodd, 1995; Harrisville, 1994; Hays, 1983, 1997, and 2002:xxi-lii; Hooker, 1989; L. Johnson, 1982; R. N. Longenecker, 1974; Pryor, 1983; Stowers, 1994; Wallis, 1995; Williams, 1987; Dunn, 1997a; Matlock, 2002; see also Dunn's and Hays' essays from their memorable SBL exchange on this issue in Hays, 2002:249-97).

But the real test of an interpretation is in the persuasiveness of the view in the exposition of texts. We examine each text briefly before returning to Romans 3:22 and 26.

In Galatians 2:16 (two occurrences) Paul is addressing the issue of how a person is made righteous. The options are (1) by works of law or (2) through the "faith of Jesus" or (3) through "faith in Jesus." To anchor the event and the means of God making humans righteous via Jesus' faithfulness is theologically more appropriate than it is to do so via the human response of faith. Furthermore, the human response is required in the text, *we into Messiah Jesus believed.*

The issue in Galatians 2:20 is the nature of the Christian life. *The life I now live in the flesh*: is it "by faith in the son of God" or "by the faith of the son of God?" If the former, the following phrase *the one loving me and giving himself in behalf of me* does not contribute to the logic of the sentence. But if Paul is writing about "the faith of the Son," the christological clause explains the meaning of "Christ's faith" as his loving and self-giving. Paul says the context of his life is the Christ event, the sacrificial life and death of Jesus. The following reference to nullifying the death of Christ supports such a reading.

Galatians 3:22 concerns the fulfillment of the promises of God, especially to Abraham. What was the basis of the promise? The "faith of Jesus" surely provides a firmer basis for the fulfillment of the promise. Furthermore, the purpose of the fulfillment is *that the promise might be given to those who believe.* Human faith is not unimportant. The question here is the foundation for that faith.

Galatians 3:26 reads *for in Messiah Jesus you are all children of God, through faith.* There is strong manuscript evidence that reads the last phrase as "through the faith of Jesus" (P[46], the earliest papyrus from around A.D. 200, and Alexandrinus, a codex manuscript from around A.D. 400). People are made children of God by the action of Jesus.

The issue in Philippians 3:9 is the ground of righteousness. Paul hopes to be found as not having a *righteousness based on the law,* but *the righteousness of faith in Christ* or *the righteousness of the faithfulness of Christ.* Whichever it is, it is "the righteousness of God which depends on faith." The ground for the righteousness of God must certainly be the faithfulness of Christ that does require a response of faith. Both the theology and the style make better sense if the reference is to "the faith of Christ."

Ephesians 3:12 concerns the basis of boldness and access with confidence to God. The grandeur of God and the plan of God described in the preceding verses would suggest grounding in Christ rather than in human faith.

The "Faith of Jesus" in Romans

With the broader NT picture in mind, we now return to Romans. Is the end-time righteousness of God manifested in the world "through the faithfulness of Christ" or "through faith in Christ" in v. 22? It is "for all the ones believing" in any case. Again, the theology and the style favor a "faith of" reading. God's end-time righteousness and faithfulness is revealed in the world through Jesus. The human response is necessary and important, but it is not the center.

The case for a "faith of" reading in v. 26 seems even clearer. The point of the last phrase is "to prove he is righteous even makes righteous" (literal translation). How is God righteous and how does God make righteous? Furthermore, the phrase in 3:26 has an exact parallel in 4:16. All translations render the latter as *the faith of Abraham.* Why not the same translation in 3:26? It grounds the righteous nature and righteous-making activity of God in Christ, rather than in humans.

Several things are noteworthy about the texts we have reviewed. First, all make reference to Jesus. Paul is concerned not only with "life in Christ," but with the activity of the earthly Jesus. Second, all the texts concern the ground or the basis of Christian existence. Third, all but one of the passages have to do with righteousness. Is righteousness based on human activity, e.g., works of law, or "the faith of Jesus" or "our faith in Jesus"? The logical and most effective antithesis to human activity is not more human activity, but divine activity, not our faith, but the faith of Jesus. The exception, Ephesians 3:12, concerns the ground for access to God, and there a christological anchoring seems more appropriate than a human one.

Messiah Jesus, rather than the human response of faith, is what matters regarding righteousness. The issue in Romans 3:21-26 is the end-time, world-transforming revelation of the righteousness of God for all humanity and all creation to overcome the power of **SIN**. The means of that revelation is "the faithfulness of Messiah Jesus."

Such a reading of Romans 3:21-26 is consistent with the messianic interpretation of the Habakkuk quotation in 1:17 and with Paul's interpretation of Christ in 5:12-21. The Habakkuk citation in 1:17, we saw, refers to the faithfulness of Messiah Jesus. Jesus is the one who lived "out of God's faith" to make possible the human response of faith. In 5:18-19 Paul will present Jesus as the obedient one who reverses the disobedience of Adam. The obedience of Jesus interprets his faithfulness in 1:17 and 3:22 and 26. Romans 3:22 and 26 are located between 1:17 and 5:18-19; they illumine each and must be interpreted in light of each.

TEXT IN THE LIFE OF THE CHURCH
The Righteousness of God

Martin Luther introduced a trend; he translated 3:22 as "through faith in Jesus Christ." His interpretation went almost unchallenged for 400 years. Except for the early English translations—Tyndale (1534), Cranmer (1539), King James Version (1611)—which translated "through the faith of Jesus Christ," all modern translations followed Luther. Only a few, e.g., NRSV, even provide a footnote that acknowledges an alternative translation. Luther's interpretation fundamentally changed the meaning of the text from "the faith of Christ" to "our faith in Christ." That interpretation was in line with Luther's emphasis on justification "by faith alone" (**sola fide**). The central question addressed by the text shifted from how does a righteous God deal with **Sin**, to how do individual men and women get saved? Luther's answer was "by faith," "by faith in Jesus Christ." The contrast in the text is "our believing" versus "our works." The nature of the gospel was profoundly changed; it was individualized and subjectivized. What became important was how "I" respond to the gospel "as the power of God for salvation." "I" can only respond "by faith," by believing in Jesus. When "I" do that, "I" am saved, "I" am accepted by the gracious God.

Romans 3:21-26 is not about how "I" get saved. It does not answer the question, "how do I find a gracious God." It is a statement about the righteousness of God. It answers the question, how can God be righteous in accepting ungodly people into the covenant people of God. The text is a defense of the justice of God, who deals righteously with human unrighteousness through the gospel, and in the process fulfills the promises to and the covenant with Israel. God is righteous with all humanity, Jew and Gentile, through the faithfulness of Messiah Jesus.

Paul is interpreting the meaning of Messiah Jesus in apocalyptic terms. Messiah Jesus represents the change of the ages, a change from wrath to salvation. Such a change is due to an act of God, not to any human action.

Messiah Jesus as the means of the revelation of the righteousness of God is the source of salvation for all humanity. He is the only one who matters in "justification," or "making righteous." Justification is by faith, but it is "the faith of the Messiah" prior to and the enabling basis and power of the faith response of humans. Justification requires the profoundest christology to be effective and to be just.

The structure of faith in Romans 3:21-26 is in concentric circles. Paul deliberately distinguishes the faith of Jesus from the faith of the believer. Both are necessary, but one is prior and the other responds.

One is corporate—it is for all humanity, Jews and Gentiles; the other is individualistic—it is "my" response to what is prior to and greater than "my faith." The circumference of the circle is dependent on the center, but the center is not dependent on the circumference; the faith of Christ continues to manifest the righteousness of God in the world and to redeem human beings even if I choose not to respond in faith.

Romans 3:21-26 is about gift, the gift of God's end-time, world-transforming righteousness to all humanity. It is not primarily about reception; only one phrase concerns reception, "to all the ones believing." God in Christ is graciously, freely, making righteous all people apart from any ethnic identity and its symbols of peoplehood.

David Ingles wrote a song in 1976 entitled "The Faith of Jesus." The lyrics read:

> I live by the faith of the Son of God, justified by the faith of Jesus. Looking from above with his eyes full of love is the way our Father sees us. But he only takes the view of me and you through the righteousness of Jesus, redeemed by the faith of the son of God, justified by the faith of Jesus.

That is what Romans 3:21-26 is about.

And finally, so what? Salvation is assured by God, not by me. Salvation is an objective reality, because of what God has done. I must appropriate it by responding in faith and obedience. But the possibility and assurance of salvation does not depend on my action.

Salvation Effects Change

The sixteenth-century Anabaptists did not make much of this text, but they should have. It provides the strongest possible theological foundation for their argument with the mainline reformers that "justification" does more than give people a right status with God. It transforms the nature of believers. God effects a change of being (ontological change), which Anabaptists taught concerning "the new birth," or conversion. That change of being is the basis for the life of discipleship, for a life of faithful obedience to Jesus and the teachings of the New Testament.

The gospel is the good news that God is doing a completely new thing in Jesus—demonstrating divine righteousness, making people right in relationship to God and each other, forgiving sins, liberating from the prison of **Sin**.

Such a gospel frees from guilt—actions that break covenant with God—and overcomes shame—makes right the broken relationships that put people down and make them angry. God's salvation restores shalom.

Romans 3:27–4:25

One God Makes Righteous All People on the Basis of Faith

PREVIEW

The traditional interpretation of 3:27-31 assumes that these verses are part of the 3:21-31 text unit, and that they outline the implications of justification by faith. Two basic arguments are presented: 1) justification by faith excludes boasting in works of law (e.g., works that seek to earn salvation); 2) justification by faith is demanded by Jewish belief in one God. All of ch. 4 then is read as a separate text unit that offers scriptural proof for the doctrine of justification by faith, by expounding the nature of faith.

This commentary reads 3:27–4:25 as one text divided into two sections: 3:27–4:2 is a dialogue on boasting; 4:3-25 is a biblical exposition of Genesis 15:6. Paul has shown in 3:21-26 that God is righteous in dealing with humanity through the faithfulness of Jesus and that this new revelation of God's righteousness includes the Gentiles. But Paul knows that people in his audience will have some questions about Israel's special status with God and about Israel's election in Abraham. Therefore, Paul engages once again in a conversation with his socratic dialogue partner.

The text argues that making righteous (*justify* in most translations) on the basis of faith, Christ's and the believer's, completes the purpose of God in the election of and the promise to Abraham. Thus, it establishes the law (3:31), and makes both Jews and Gentiles heirs of the promise.

OUTLINE

The Dialogue, 3:27–4:2

Question What then becomes of boasting? 3:27a

Paul   It is excluded. 3:27b

Question By what sort of law? Of works? 3:27c

Paul   No, but through the law of faithfulness. For we consider that a person is made righteous by faith apart from works of law. Or, is God the God of the Jews only? Is he not the God of the Gentiles also? 3:27d-29b

Question Yes, of the Gentiles also. 3:29c

Paul   Indeed God is one who makes righteous the circumcised out of faithfulness, and also the circumcised through faithfulness. 3:30

Question Do we make the law inoperative through the faithfulness? 3:31a

Paul   Absolutely not! But, on the contrary, we establish the law. 3:31b-c

Question What then shall we say? Have we found Abraham to be our ancestor ("forefather") according to the flesh? For if Abraham was justified by works, he has something to boast about. 4:1-2b

Paul   But not before God. 4:2c (JET)

(The question and answer translation of the dialogue is my attempt to show the dynamics of the conversation. It should not be read as a literal dialogue between Paul and his dialogue partner.)

The Exposition of Scripture, 4:3-25

Verses 3-25 are an exposition of Genesis 15:6 with an application for Christians. The exposition is clearly defined by the citation of Genesis 15:6 at the beginning, v. 3, and the close, v. 22; it is an inclusio [*Essay: Inclusio*].

A The text, 4:3

   B The meaning of *reckon*, 4:4-8

      the nature of God's reckoning, 4:4-5

      the support of Psalm 32:1-2; 4:6-8

   B The meaning of *faith*, 4:9-21

      the order of events in Abraham's life, 4:9-12

      the relationship between faith and promise, 4:13-16

      the nature of Abraham's faith, 4:17-21

A The text, 4:22

The meaning for Christians, 4:23-25

EXPLANATORY NOTES

The Dialogue 3:27–4:2

Then (oun) in v. 27 is drawing an inference from the previous argument. We could paraphrase like this, "Now, in light of what has just been said, what happens to boasting?"

Paul has presented a view of God and God's peoplehood that raises questions about Israel's special status. Boasting represents how the Jew has misunderstood the meaning of election, and the gift of the law that symbolized it in 2:17-24. In other words, the reference to boasting here concludes and summarizes a critique of Jewish self-understanding that Paul has been addressing since 2:17. This self-understanding involves three terms, calling oneself a Jew, relying on the law, and boasting before God. All three terms are central to the dialogue in 3:27–4:2. Boasting then refers to the Jewish confidence in a privileged status with God based on the possession of the law.

Paul already rejected such boasting once. In 2:17–3:20 he argued that Jews may not boast in the law because they do not keep it. In fact, the law stops every mouth by showing the reality of falsehood and the enslavement of all people to the power of **Sin** (3:19).

Paul rejects boasting here for a second time; "it is excluded" for one reason supported by two warrants. The reason boasting is excluded is a law. It is not the law of *works* but the *law of faith*. "Law" in the context of 2:12 through 4:25 must refer to the Torah. "Law of faith" or "faithfulness" is a paradoxical piece of word-play that combines "torah" and "faith," the key metaphors in Jewish, Jewish-Christian, and Pauline teaching. The question concerns the nature of the Torah. Is it a law that is characterized by faith or by works? Boasting is excluded by the law of faith, Paul asserts, Christ's faith and the believers's faith, identified in 3:21-26 as the basis for the revelation of the righteousness of God.

Paul's reason for rejecting boasting introduces a style of argument that characterizes this whole text unit. He argues throughout 3:27–4:25 by stating opposites. Here it is *not . . . but* (*ouki, alla*); so also in 3:31 (*mē, alla*), and 4:4, 13, and 20 (*ou alla*). Other forms are *not . . . also* (*ouki kai*) in 3:29, *but* (*alla*) in 4:2 and 5 (*de*); *not only . . . but* (*ouk monon alla*) in 4:12; *not only . . . but also* (*ou monon alla kai*) in 4:16 and 23; *or* (*ē*) in 4:9; *or* and *but* (*ē . . . alla*) in 4:10. Paul states an idea that is reasonable and current, and then rejects it for an alternative understanding.

Paul explains the *law of faith* with two different statements, one an early gospel teaching which summarizes 3:21-26 and the second a Jewish conviction. The gospel teaching, which Paul holds in common with other Jesus followers (*we reckon that*), is that a person is made righteous by faith, not by works of the law. The law of faith says that faith, not markers of Jewish identity, is the basis on which God makes people righteous. Paul is making a pun on law. The Jews have been thinking of God's revelation only in terms of the law, but God has now revealed divine righteousness *apart from the law* (v. 21a). The only law in the new situation of God's revelation through Messiah Jesus is the law of faith

The second explanation of the *law of faith* is the Jewish doctrine of monotheism, which holds that one God is the God of all peoples. One God, the Creator of the universe, does not have two faces toward the different peoples (remember the earlier argument for the impartiality of God, 2:11). Jews and Christians hold this conviction in common. In fact, the Jews in the Diaspora used the One God doctrine to defend incorporating Gentile proselytes into Judaism. Paul radicalizes this conviction by arguing that the one God makes righteous circumcised and uncircumcised people on the same basis, by faith. Gentiles do not have to become Jews to become part of the Messiah's people.

Jewish boasting is ended, because the one God of all people has revealed divine righteousness in Jesus. The question of people's relationship to God is moved to a different ground. It is now based on the free revelation of God's righteousness through the faithfulness of Jesus and the human response of faith.

But, another question is raised if Gentiles do not have to become Jews to be made righteous. Is the law not destroyed by the teaching of righteousness "through the faithfulness" (lit.)? The issue is the status of the law as the symbol of God's election of Israel. Is not the law, and thus Israel's covenant with God, wiped out by Paul's teaching? Paul decisively rejects the conclusion, *absolutely not* (v. 31)! Instead, the opposite is true. Paul claims that his teaching establishes the law, literally "lifts it up." Paul makes a provocative claim. He will elaborate in the interpretation of the story of Abraham.

For some Jewish Christians this discussion is getting out of hand. There is historical proof for being made righteous by works of law and for boasting. The evidence is Abraham, the father of the Jewish nation. Therefore, the questions in 4:1, *what then shall we say? Have we found Abraham our forefather according to the flesh?* This translation reads very differently than most English translations, e.g., NRSV (*what then are we to say was gained by Abraham . . .*), or NIV (*What then shall we say that Abraham . . . discovered in this matter?*). What these translations have in common is the translation of v. 1 as one sentence, and the omission of a very important phrase, *to find* (*heurēkenai*). Verse 1 actually consists of two questions. First, *what then shall we say?* is a complete sentence which introduces a false inference (see 3:5; 6:1; 7:7; 8:31; 9:14, 30 for the other uses of the same type of question in Romans).

The second question is, *to have found Abraham* . . . . The *have [we] found* question is a common Jewish expression for "we have found on the basis of Scripture." Furthermore, and even more significantly, the phrase *to find* is used with Abraham in Jewish literature to say that Abraham was made righteous because God found him faithful in the testing of the sacrifice of Isaac (see Sir. 44:20; 1 Macc. 2:52). In other words, the phrase Paul introduced here is used to interpret Genesis 15:6 through Genesis 22.

The first thing the Scriptures make clear is that Abraham is *the ancestor* of the Jews *according to the flesh.* The Jews are special and have a special relationship to God. Second, according to Jewish interpretation, Abraham abandoned idolatry at age 14 and put his faith in the One God who created all things, and was made righteous by works of law. Abraham, it was believed, kept the law perfectly even before it was given. Because he was faithful to God, even willing to sacrifice Isaac in obedience to God, God *reckoned him righteous.* Paul summarizes this teaching in a contrary to fact sentence, *if it is true that Abraham was made righteous by works*—which we all know is not the case—*then he has ground for boasting.*

By mentioning boasting, Paul returns to the previous discussion of 3:27. Verse 2 links three ideas, being ancestor according to the flesh, being made righteous by works of law, and boasting. The reference to boasting is a clue to the issue. If Abraham had ground for boasting, that would separate him from those who are made righteous by faith, and make him a witness for the Jewish idea of Israel's election (2:17-20). If Abraham had ground for boasting, he would be a witness against *the law of faith* (3:27-28). If Abraham had ground for boasting, God distinguished Israel from all other people as a special people with special privilege.

Paul answers the challenge in two ways. First, he agrees with his dialogue partner. Abraham did have ground for boasting if he was made righteous by works of law. The problem is that it did not help him in relation to God; it was *not before God.* Paul's second response is an exposition of Genesis 15:6.

Comments and Observations

The dialogue makes the point that boasting in special national privilege is ended by the revelation of the righteousness of God through the faithfulness of Jesus. Gentiles are now included in the one people the One God is creating in the world on the basis of faith, and this inclusion of the Gentiles is fulfilling God's covenant with Israel.

It is important to note two things about the dialogue. First, the language again is honor-shame language. Paul rejects a particular claim to honor that shames one people by giving special status and worth to another people. The universality of God—one God who makes righteous all people on the same basis—has radical social consequences. It includes all people of faith without distinction.

Second, the dialogue sets up the agenda for the biblical exposition to follow. Two questions are raised and answered very briefly at the end of the dialogue, the relationship of faith to the law (3:31) and the meaning of Abraham (4:1-2). Paul addresses these questions in reverse order in 4:3ff., first the meaning of Abraham (4:2-8) and then the relationship of faith and law (4:9-17).

The Exposition of Scripture 4:3-25

4:3, 22 The Text

The provocative *not before God* in v. 2 is interpreted by *for the Scripture says*. Romans 4:3-22 is an exposition of Genesis 15:6. The text is cited in full in v. 3 and the last half is cited again in v. 22. Verses 3-22 are bracketed by Genesis 15:6. In addition, parts of Genesis 15:6 are cited or alluded to in the body of the exposition, the *to reckon righteousness* phrase in vv. 5, 6, 9, and 11, the *he believed* phrase in vv. 17 and 18. The second half, *he reckoned to him righteousness* (Gen. 15:6b), is cited six times compared to three references to the first half, *Abraham believed* (Gen. 15:6a). That is a clue to something significant. Paul stresses the second half of the statement, *he reckoned to him righteousness*. The dominant contemporary Jewish interpretation emphasized the first half of the verse, and understood Abraham's faith as his faithfulness to God. The pattern of citation suggests that Paul wants to underline that "making righteous" is an act of God independent of any work or merit by Abraham.

Paul cites Genesis 15:6 because, as indicated above, Abraham was viewed as the model Jew whom God rewarded with righteousness. That is, there exists an interpretation of Abraham that directly challenges Paul's assertion that the gospel of righteousness by faith is rooted in the law. If Paul cannot offer an alternative interpretation of Genesis 15:6, he has lost the argument.

The text is normally read as A B B A, in chiastic parallelism:

Abraham (A) believed God (B),
and he [God] (B) reckoned Abraham (A) as righteous.

The emphasis is on the faith of Abraham. But that reading comes close to reading faith as a work, and God's *reckoning to Abraham righteousness* as a reward for the good work. That is exactly what Paul is rejecting. An alternative reading is possible. Genesis 15:6 is a Hebrew parallelism and can be read as an A B A B:

Abraham (A) believed God (B),
and Abraham (A) reckoned to him [God] (B) righteousness.

The subject and the object are parallel, not different. There is a long minority tradition in Jewish interpretation of understanding Genesis 15:6 in this way. Christians by and large have not known about this interpretation. Abraham, in this tradition, was not rewarded for any work or merit. Genesis 15:6, in this reading, centers on the righteousness of God. Abraham trusted God to be righteous. God made Abraham righteous.

Two words are critical to Paul's interpretation, *reckoned* (or, counted as a credit) and "*faithed*" (usually translated as *believed* or *trusted*). The verb form of faith is translated quite literally as "faithed" to communicate that the same word is used—the language is not about "faith" and "believing," but about "faith" and "faithing."

4:4-8 The Meaning of "Reckoned"

The exposition expounds *reckon* by stressing the work of God through a contrast of work/grace and of faith/works. Paul uses an example from the common experience of work to make his point. Reward for work done is not *according to grace* (*kata charin*). Paul and Judaism agree that Abraham was *reckoned righteous* on the basis of faith, but *faith* was understood differently. Jewish interpreters meant Abraham acted faithfully by keeping the law. Paul defines faith as absolute trust in God—Abraham "*faithed*," that is, intentionally committed himself to God. What distinguishes Paul's argument is that the *reckoning righteous* was undeserved, it was an act of God *according to grace*, not a reward for Abraham's faithful actions.

The contrast of works and faith makes the same point. God makes righteous the ungodly who "*faith*." God makes righteous the wicked, the lawless, the Gentiles who are outside the covenant when they intentionally commit themselves to God. God *reckons righteous* the human who "*faiths*" the God who graciously does the unacceptable.

Paul explains God's action in behalf of Abraham via David. David and his kingdom were seen in Judaism as proof of the blessings the descendants of Abraham were capable of receiving. Paul uses a familiar Jewish method of interpretation (*gezerah shawah*), the interpretation of one text via another text with the same key word, *reckoned*. The text is Psalm 32:1-2, a text applied only to Israel in Jewish literature. David pronounces a blessing. The subject of the action is God, not Abraham. God *reckons* a person righteous. Paul explains that God makes righteous *apart from works*, apart from any obedience to the law of the covenant. The emphasis is on the act of God. What God *reckoning righteous* means is defined as *forgiving lawlessness, covering sins,* and *not reckoning sins.* God grants salvation to those who have no claim on God.

What does Abraham mean? God made righteous the ungodly Abraham. Abraham has no ground for boasting. God *makes righteous, forgives* those outside the covenant, who exercise *faith* in God. Abraham is a witness for the *law of faith*, the fact that God makes righteous those who trust in the faithfulness of the divine.

4:9-21 The Meaning of "Faithed"

Verses 3-8 emphasized who made Abraham righteous. The issue shifts in v. 9 to Abraham as the father of Jews and Gentiles. The concern is when Abraham received the blessing of righteousness. Was it before or after the circumcision that defines Jewish identity?

The question is answered in two ways. First, Genesis 15:6b is cited again, *the faith to righteousness was reckoned to Abraham*. *Reckoned* again is important. It was reckoned to Abraham by God. Second, it was done to Abraham while he was uncircumcised. The point is hammered home with the repeated circumcision/uncircumcision contrast (vv. 9a, 10a, 10b, 11). Genesis 15, God reckoning Abraham righteous, was prior to Genesis 17, God making covenant with Abraham and decreeing circumcision as the sign of the covenant. Paul does not deny the significance of circumcision, but he reinterprets it. Circumcision was a sign and a seal, very covenantal language, but now the righteousness of faith was reckoned to Abraham while he was still a Gentile. The terms of the covenant are defined by faith.

The importance of the time sequence—reckoned righteous prior to circumcision—is stated in a purpose clause, which is chiastically arranged:

"In order that he should be
A Father of all the ones believing through uncircumcision so that they all might be reckoned righteous (Gen. 15:6b again),
B And father of the circumcised,
B Not only to the ones out of circumcision,
A But also to the ones marching in the footsteps of the faith, the faith in uncircumcision, of our father Abraham." (JET)

The purpose clause gives Paul's theological interpretation of the life of Abraham. Abraham is the "forefather" *according to faith*" (*kata pistin*), not *according to flesh*" (*kata sarka*), as in v. 1. He is the father of Gentiles and Jews. Abraham is identified as "father" six times (vv. 11, 12 [two], 16, 17, 18). He is the universal father, the foundation figure, the basis of unity.

Abraham defines the identity of his children. Hellenistic Jewish literature linked the one God formula and Abraham to legitimize the inclusion of Gentile proselytes in the Jewish community. Paul uses Abraham to argue an even more radical point. Gentile Christians are the children of Abraham without circumcision, without becoming proselytes, just as Abraham was reckoned righteous before circumcision. As the first Gentile convert, Abraham is the father of Gentiles, who, like him, trust God apart from the Jewish law, and of Jews, who do the law as an expression of faith just as Abraham did.

The discussion of the children of Abraham continues in vv. 13-22, but the contrasts change. They now are promise/law and law/faith. *Promise* and *inheritance* are the new words; promise occurs five times (vv. 13, 14, 16, 20, 21). The promise is the inheritance of the world and many descendants in Genesis 17:5 (also vv. 13, 17). From the beginning both terms, promise and inheritance, meant "the land" (Gen. 15:7) but over time they expanded to include "the whole world" and even "the world to come." The idea of "inheritance of the world" was the way the promise to Abraham was understood in Judaism. It reflects Jewish self-consciousness as God's covenant people who were chosen from among the nations of the world for the world.

Paul undercuts this nationalistic self-understanding by unhooking the promise and the inheritance from the law; they are not based on the law (*dia nomou*), but on *the righteousness of faith*" (*dia dikaiosunē pisteōs*). The expression *righteousness of faith* refers either to the faithfulness of God or of Christ in 3:21-26, not Abraham. Two reasons are given. First, the law limits the promise to one group, "those out of the law." It thereby nullifies "the faith" and "the promise" by making it exclusive rather than universal. Furthermore, the law works wrath. It defines sin, and results in judgment. The promise cannot be based on the law, and thus on Jewish identity. Second, faith alone is the basis of the promise because it is solely "according to grace" (*kata charin*, v. 16, NRSV, "*may rest on grace*"). God's grace defines faith for the second time (v. 4 was the first time). The reason is stated in a purpose clause: *to guarantee the promise to all seed.* The object of the guarantee is stated in another *not only-but also* clause, *not only to the one out of the law, but also*

to the one out of the faith of Abraham who is the father of us all . . . .
Faith defined as grace is inclusive; it is *to all.* By grace Abraham
becomes *the father of us all* (Jews and Gentiles) rather than *our
ancestor according to the flesh* (Jews only as in v. 1) [*Essay: Grace
in Romans*].

Everything hinges on God's gracious initiative. The evidence of God's
grace is regenerative and creative power (e.g., making alive the dead and
calling into being the not being). God, the Creator of life, continues to
create new life. The children of Abraham are the children of promise by
faith through the grace of the God who makes alive the dead.

Verses 9-21 elaborate the meaning of faith but little is said about
the quality of human faith until v. 17. Abraham's faith is mentioned in
v. 17 via an allusion to Genesis 15:6, "he believed God." Verses 18-
21 explain the nature of Abraham's faith, which is characterized as
trust in God to do the impossible (v. 17), as hoping against hope (v. 18),
as the conviction that God is able to do what is promised
(v. 21). It is defined three times as trusting God to make alive the dead,
to fulfill a promise against earthly realities that make impossible the
fulfillment of that promise. The opposite of faith is "be weak in faith"
(v. 19), "doubt" (v. 20), "unfaith" (v. 20).

Two things are amazing about the reference to Abraham's faith.
The first is that so little is said about it. The emphasis is not on the
quality of Abraham's faith, nor is there any explicit appeal to imitate
it. What the text does say is that Abraham's unconditional trust *gave
glory to God* (v. 20). By acknowledging his total dependence on God,
Abraham did what the "creature" in 1:21 refused to do, and what
boasting in *works of law* sought to deny (3:27). Second, more is said
about God than about Abraham's faith. The character of the God
"*faithed*" determines the character of the faith exercised. The point of
the text is that the fulfillment of the promise is based on the power of
God. Even more important than Abraham's faith is God's faithfulness.

What does faith mean? Faith is defined as much by God as by
Abraham. The promise is based on *the righteousness of faith* and on
grace. The exposition of Genesis 15:6 closes by focusing on God,
God reckoned him righteous (v. 22). The only appropriate response
to God's faith and grace is human faith as trust in the faithfulness of
God, even against all the odds. That is what Abraham did, and he
gave glory to God.

4:23-25 The Meaning for Christians

Paul applies the meaning of his exposition immediately. He assumes,
in continuity with contemporary Judaism, that the Scripture is written

for present believers as well as the original readers. The application is that Abraham is a paradigm for Christians. Three elements in Abraham are important for Christians: 1) *God will reckon righteous* 2) *those who faith God* precisely as 3) the *God who gives life to the dead* (lit., *the God who raises the dead*).

The Jesus whom God raised is described on the model of Isaiah 53. He was given over to death for human sin. The death of Christ is the basis of redemption. But, he also was raised to make righteous believers. The linkage of resurrection and make righteous is unusual, but significant. Normally Paul associates the death of Christ with making righteous, as in 3:21-26. Here it is connected with the resurrection because to make righteous and to make alive are parallel ways of describing the miracle of giving life to the dead.

Comments and Observations

Romans 4:3-25 is an exposition of Genesis 15:6 to support the theological claims of 3:21–4:2, especially the claim that the revelation of the righteousness of the one God for all people equally through faith alone, Christ's and the believer's, is consistent with the law. The Genesis text is cited at the beginning and end of the exposition, and at the close of every paragraph in it. But the exposition also advances the argument.

Romans 4 reinterprets of the significance of Abraham. Three motifs of Jewish ethnic religious self-understanding are rejected—righteousness by works of law, circumcision, and physical descent from Abraham. Paul does not reject his Jewish heritage, but he redefines it by reinterpreting the meaning of Abraham.

The exposition of the Abraham story centers in God, who is one, not many, and who makes Abraham righteous. This one God deals impartially with all people, Jews and Gentiles. They are all made righteous on the basis of faith *according to grace*, through God's gift rather than by any human works. Paul interprets Abraham as a vindication of God, who keeps promises, is faithful, and gifts people with righteousness *according to grace*.

The focus on God is bolstered by the faith references. Faith is exclusively in God. The God who is trusted does the miraculous—e.g., makes righteous the ungodly (v. 5), raises the dead (v. 17), does what is promised (v. 21), raises Jesus from the dead (v. 24). More is said about God in this "faith chapter" than is said about the character of faith. And even faith is interpreted as an act of God, *according to grace*.

The central thesis of the exposition is that Abraham is the father of both Gentiles and Jews. Abraham is a representative figure. Paul uses the Abraham story to explain the Jewish theology of the "merits of the fathers" (the works of the fathers are accumulated and meritorious for subsequent generations). But with a difference. The blessing of Abraham is not only for Jews, but also for the Gentiles. Abraham is not simply an example of Christian faith prior to Jesus. He is the father of all the people of God, which is now a worldwide people. God's answer to the sin of Adam is the people of Abraham.

This reinterpretation of Abraham becomes even more significant when the story is read in the context of the whole letter. Not only does Abraham's *gave glory to God* (4:20) answer humanity's refusal to glorify God (1:20), but Abraham as an "ungodly" (*asebē*) person, whom God makes righteous (4:5) contrasts with the "ungodly" (*asebeian*) who experience God's wrath (1:18). The "power" (*dunamis*) of God, which effects salvation (1:16) and is manifested in creation (1:20), is precisely the power Abraham faiths as capable of fulfilling what God has promised. The Creator God of 1:20 and 25 is the same God who calls "into existence the nonexistent" (4:17b). Abraham is the paradigmatic answer to the human problem.

Abraham also has a direct bearing on the divisions in the Roman churches. Jewish Christians must welcome Gentile Christians because both have the same father (15:7). That is a new development. While Abraham was used in Hellenistic Judaism to legitimize Gentile proselytes, these proselytes were not permitted to call him "our father"; when the Jews said "our father" the Gentile converts had to say "your father." But now in Rome, Paul says, Abraham is "our father" for Jews and Gentiles. Gentile Christians cannot write off the Jewish past as of no account; they share the same past and the same father.

In addition, both peoples are made righteous by God on the same basis, faith. Abraham is used to address the problems of faith in Rome. When Paul says Abraham was not weak but strong in faith, he uses the same language as in the conflict in Rome, "weak in faith" and "strong in faith." Abraham does not doubt (4:20, 21), while Roman Christians do (14:23). Abraham is fully convinced (4:21), while Roman Christians are not (14:5). Abraham's faith resulted in giving glory to God, which is precisely the outcome of Gentile faith (15:9).

Abraham, the father of all believers, is also the model believer who shows the Roman Christians what it means to be people of faith. His faith prefigures the faith of Christians, and also the faith of Christ. Both Abraham's and Christ's faith have "saving" significance; they both create a people. Abraham is the biblical precedent for the idea that the faithfulness of a single individual brings blessing on the many. Abraham is a type of Jesus. After all, the Abraham story is located between 3:21-26 and 5:12-21, the great expositions of the meaning of Christ in Romans.

THE TEXT IN BIBLICAL CONTEXT

Abraham

Abraham is a popular and important figure in Judaism. He is the father of the Jews, the model Jew, the one who forsook idolatry as a youth and placed his trust in the One Creator God and obeyed this God perfectly even before the giving of the law. To be a child of Abraham is the source of great pride.

Abraham is also important in the NT; he is mentioned 72 times. Nineteen of these references occur in Paul's letters, 18 in Romans and Galatians (the other one is 2 Cor. 11:22). All but four of them (Rom. 9:7; 11:1; 2 Cor. 11:22; Gal. 4:22) are found in Romans 4 and Galatians 3. The discussion of Abraham in these chapters has a high concentration of important theological words, e.g., faith, righteousness/make right (17), law (19), promise (12), works (seven), seed (six), nations/gentiles (four).

The Romans and Galatians discussions of Abraham center in an exposition of Genesis 15:6. Both letters of Paul appeal to Abraham as a scriptural demonstration. Each case follows a very important theological statement (Gal. 2:15-21; Rom. 3:21-26). Between this theological assertion and the exposition of the Abraham story there is a short dialogue paragraph (Gal. 3:1-5; Rom. 3:27–4:2) that raises practical questions related to the readers. Paul uses Abraham in both letters to discuss the basis for being in right relationship to God, and in both, he contrasts works with faith. Both assert that Gentile Christians are children of Abraham by faith just as Jews are children of Abraham.

There are also important differences between the Romans and Galatians interpretations of Abraham. There is a much greater focus on "the faith" in Romans 4 (vv. 3, 11, 12, 13, 16, 17, 18, 19, 20, 22). And "the faith" in Romans is God centered, not Christ centered as in Galatians. In fact, Christ is not mentioned until the end of the chapter, and then as the object of God's resurrection power, not the faith of Christians. Righteousness is nuanced differently in Galatians than in Romans. In Galatians it is synonymous with the Gentiles being blessed in Abraham (3:8) and receiving the Spirit (3:14). In Romans it concerns "making righteous" the ungodly (4:6), and is equated with forgiveness and covering of sins (4:7-8). Galatians pictures Christ as Abraham's singular seed; Romans 4 portrays all who believe, Jews and Gentiles, as Abraham's seed. In Galatians 3, the content of the promise is Christ; in Romans 4 it is Gentile inclusion in the people of God. Galatians stresses more discontinuity between God's promise and law while Romans stresses greater continuity.

The differences are due to the different audiences being addressed. In Galatians Paul is fighting rival Jewish Christian teachers who used Abraham to argue that circumcision and law observance are necessary to Christian faith. Paul responds by distancing Abraham from the law, arguing that he was made righteous through faith apart from the law. Gentile Christians are children of Abraham because of faith, not because of circumcision or law observance. God is fulfilling the promise to Abraham to include the nations of the world in the divine family by incorporating of Gentiles through faith. In Romans Paul is defending the proposal that his gospel of the righteousness of God for all people through the faithfulness of Jesus vindicates the faithfulness of God and fulfills God's covenant with Israel. Paul's goal is the unity of Jews and Gentiles in the Christian churches.

What is clear in both letters is that the Abraham story is used to address questions of the identity of the Christian community, the coexistence together of both Jews and non-Jews. Abraham, the first Gentile convert to God, represents the inclusion of Gentiles in the people of God without circumcision or law observance. This interpretation of Abraham is similar to the one offered by Luke-Acts. Luke uses Abraham to argue for God's saving inclusion of the outcast, people previously excluded because of their socio-religious status, e.g., their sins, their uncleanness due to illness or poverty, their Gentileness. Paul's emphasis on the inclusion of Gentiles does not, however, mean the exclusion of Jews from God's people, as he will emphasize in Romans 9-11. In these chapters Paul will appeal to Abraham again, now to emphasize God's continued election of and faithfulness to the Jewish people. Abraham legitimates both Jews and Gentiles. He is both the symbol and the reality of unity, not division, for the people of God.

Abraham means the inclusion of Gentiles in Romans and Galatians because inclusion is based on faith, not ethnic-religious identity symbolized by the law and works of the law. Abraham is the great representative of faith in God, and the theological as well as sociological equalizing power of salvation by faith. Salvation by faith means that all people have equal access to salvation and are included in the family of God. Abraham is the father of all peoples of faith because he was a person of faith. Hebrews 11 offers another example of this understanding of Abraham.

The apparent exception to Abraham as a person of faith is James

2:20-24. James seems to contradict Paul. Paul states that *a person is made righteous by faith apart from works of law* (Rom. 3:28). James asserts that *a person is justified out of works and not out of faith only* (2:24). James cites Abraham to support his position, and interprets Genesis 15:6 via Genesis 22 on the model of contemporary Jewish interpretation.

A careful study of James reveals there is no contradiction. The "field of battle" is different. Paul is speaking against ethnic pride that excludes some people from God's people. James is arguing against an orthodoxy that separates faith and good works, that says "faith alone." The language James uses is different than Paul's. "Faith" signifies intellectual acceptance of monotheism (even the devil has this faith), not trust in God to do the impossible. "Works" refer to acts of Christian love that fulfill the "perfect law of liberty" (1:25) and "the royal law" (2:8); James does not use the phrase "works of law," and does not define "works" as specific Mosaic commands that define ethnic identity. "Make righteous" for James means the recognition of what is good, helpful, and kind, not God's end-time power that "makes right" people and the cosmos. What matters for James is that faith find expression in specific deeds of love and kindness. He signals that clearly in the chiastic structure of v. 22:

> *The faith* is energized
> by *the works*, and
> out of (by) *the works*
> *the faith* is completed.

And that chiasm is at the center of a larger chiasm in vv. 20-24. The issues in the chiasm are clearly identified in the opening lines, vv. 20 and 24:

> you want to know . . .
> that *faith* apart from *works* is useless
> you see
> that a person is made righteous out of *works* and not out of *faith* only.

The text is a deliberate crosswise (ABBA)—

> the faith . . . works
> the works . . . the faith—

that makes one point: faith acts through works. Passive faith is no faith at all. Faith leads to works and is completed in works. That is thoroughly Jewish and thoroughly Pauline. Paul says in Romans 4 that Abraham's faith led to action, to covenant faithfulness with God which included circumcision.

TEXT IN THE LIFE OF THE CHURCH
Abraham Is Our Father

Romans 4 is the great faith chapter in Romans, and, together with Hebrews 11, within the NT. Since the Reformation, Abraham is presented as the model of salvation by faith, over against salvation by works. Faith in this paradigm is individual and concerns salvation—Abraham is a type of the person who through faith is saved. For example, Ernst Käsemann uses Abraham in Romans 4 to state the classical interpretation, "faith in Paul . . . is the act and decision of the individual person, and is thus an anthropological and not primarily an ecclesiological concept" (1980:109).

But all ancient interpreters of Paul through Augustine understood the reference to Abraham as corporate, not individual. Abraham as the father of faith is the representative figure of all human beings; he is inclusive of both Gentiles and Jews of faith. Romans 4 concerns the nature of the people of God. The Abraham story supports the claim that the revelation of the righteousness of God through the faithfulness of Jesus includes both Gentiles and Jews in God's people in fulfillment of God's covenant with Israel. Gentiles do not have to become Jews, that is, be circumcised, to be children of Abraham, to become members of God's people.

Because Abraham is our father, all members of God's people stand on the same level playing field. We become members of God's people on the same basis, by faith and obedience, as all other believers. Children who have the same God (3:27-31) and the same father (Abraham) should make peace with each other rather than fight each other as in chs. 14-15.

Abraham Faiths God to Do the Impossible

The object of faith in Romans 4 is God, not Jesus. Abraham trusted the God who makes righteous the ungodly and who makes alive the dead. Christians are called to trust the God who raised Jesus from the dead. There is no "believe in" formula (*pisteuein eis Christus or pistis en Christō*) in Romans 4, or for that matter in Paul (Christ is the object of confession, e.g., that Jesus is Lord, but not of faith). The focus is God. The object of faith is God.

God as the object of faith is defined in direct relationship to the condition of Abraham (and Sarah). Abraham is ungodly and his body is incapable of human reproduction (e.g., it is dead). Abraham trusted God to reverse the human condition, that is, to perform a miracle. This trust in God was not easy—Abraham did not weaken in faith (v. 19), he did not doubt the promise of God in unbelief (v. 20). Faith in God is a struggle—nothing is harder in life than to trust God above the reality of circumstances. But that is what Abraham did. He lived "out of faith" (*ek pisteōs*); his children are people who live "out of faith" in God. God made him the father of all people of faith so that God's people are people of faith rather than of genes. Abraham is the father of those who trust God ("out of faith," *ek pisteōs*) in confidence that they are included in the community of God's people. Such trusting obedience *gives glory to God* (4:20), what fallen humanity failed to do in 1:21ff. and what those made righteous by Jesus anticipate (5:2).

Summarizing the Argument

Chapters 1-4

Paul opens the letter by linking his vocational identity with the *gospel* 1) *of God*, 2) the fulfillment of Scripture, and 3) God's son (1:1-4). Paul announces at the outset that the central focus of his letter is God.

The opening four chapters begin with God, a God whose redemption is through Jesus Christ, is active in the impartial judgment of all peoples, and ends with God making righteous all people through the death and resurrection of "Jesus our Lord." The God who is the source of Paul's gospel is clearly the God of Abraham, of Israel, of the Scriptures. But this God is also the God of all human beings and of the creation.

Romans 1-4 argues for the righteousness of God in judgment and salvation. God, who is impartial, judges all people equally and makes righteous all people on the same basis. The heart of the argument is that God has disclosed end-time righteousness in and through Messiah Jesus. This revelation has created a new reality, salvation and righteousness that deals with God's wrath, overcomes the power of **Sin**, and incorporates Gentiles into the people of God in fulfillment of the promises of God.

The argument presupposes the election of Israel as God's people and the salvation and incorporation of Gentiles into the people of God through Christ. Paul demonstrates that neither Israel's election nor the salvation of Gentiles in any way compromises God's righteousness and integrity. God is impartial to all people. Jews and Gentiles are equally accountable to God, and are made righteous on the same basis. What God requires of Jews and Gentiles is unconditional trust, faith, in the divine power to fulfill the promises to Abraham. Each major point in the argument is confirmed by an appeal to Scripture, Habakkuk 2:4 in 1:17, an extended citation of Scriptures in 3:10-18, the exposition of the Abraham story in 4:3-25.

The argument of 1:16–4:25 is directed especially at the Jewish Christians and their Gentile supporters in the Roman churches. It is designed to effect a change in their thinking and attitudes toward Gentile Christians. God is righteous in extending end-time righteousness to Gentiles through Messiah Jesus. Gentile Christians are true children of Abraham because faith, the Messiah's and the believers, is the determining factor in salvation and in identifying Abraham's true children. God's fulfillment of the covenant with Abraham through the incorporation of Gentiles into God's people does not invalidate Israel's election but confirms it.

Paul's argument so far centers the views of the Gentile Christians. He gives them a sense of solidarity with Jewish identity and history. He shows them that "being made righteous" and "strong faith" are found first in Abraham. Paul thus reminds both Jews and Gentiles that the gospel is *to the Jew first and also to the Gentile.* Trusting Gentiles are one with trusting Jews in Abraham, because of the new revelation of the righteousness of God through Messiah Jesus. But Paul also lays the foundation for his subsequent exhortation to the Gentile Christians in chs. 9-11. Ethnic Israel will not be excluded from God's salvation, because *as regards election they are beloved for the sake of their ancestors* (11:28).

Romans 5:1–8:39

The Meaning of the Revelation of the Righteousnes of God

Romans 5–8 is the third argument within the second section of the letter, 3:21–11:36. Paul has explained the revelation of the righteousness of God through Jesus Christ for all people, 3:21-26, and the inclusion of all people in the family of Abraham, 3:27–4:25. He now describes its meaning for followers of Jesus, both Jewish and Gentile. The revelation does something: it confers on all believers the blessings promised to Israel.

The change of subject matter involves a change of style and language. Chapters 1:18–4:25 were in the third person, except for the concluding comments in 4:22-25. Chapters 5-8 are in the first or second person, except for 5:12-21. Paul addresses the Roman Christians directly in chs. 5-8. As the chart indicates, the predominant language shifts from "faith" to "life," "death," and "sin:"

	Chs. 1-4	Chs. 5-8	Chs. 9-11
Faith	31	3	14
Righteousness	30	23	11
Life	2	24	3
Death	0	43	0
Sin	4	41	1

Chapters 1–4 spoke much about Jews and Gentiles. In chs. 5–8, there is no such talk, though Paul returns to this theme in chs. 9–11. The *righteousness of God* is not mentioned in chs. 5–8. The OT is cited 21 times in chs. 1–4, 32 times in chs. 9–11, but only twice briefly in chs. 5–8 (7:7; 8:36). Exegetical arguments like those in chs. 3–4 drop out until chs. 9–11. In addition to the heavy use of *life death*, and *sin* language, Paul introduces other new terms—e.g., *enmity, reconciliation, slavery, freedom, adoption, peace, God's love,* and *Holy Spirit.* A final stylistic difference is that each chapter closes with an *our Lord* formula, *through Jesus Christ our Lord,* or *in Jesus Christ our Lord* (5:21; 6:23; 7:25; 8:39).

But, there also is continuity. Law continues as a subtheme in the letter, mentioned in 5:20-21 and receiving detailed discussion in 7:1-25. The references to boasting in 5:2-3, 11 indicate that Paul is continuing the argument from chs. 2–4. "Salvation" is reintroduced for the first time since 1:16. Chapters 5–8 discuss the meaning of Christ's death (3:22-26) from several different perspectives. The death of Christ *for our trespasses* and his resurrection *for our being made righteous* (4:25) changes reality; it means a new understanding and reordering of life.

While explicit Jew-Gentile language is absent in chs. 5–8, the agenda remains implicit. The continued discussion of "Jewish" issues (e.g., the law), makes this clear. Equally important is Paul's significant exposition of the universal relevance of Messiah Jesus and the Holy Spirit in chs. 5, 6, 8, and the use of cherished Jewish language to describe the new people God is creating in the world.

Chapters 5–8 are defined clearly as a text unit by a double inclusio. The first is the beginning and ending of the text unit with the christological formula *our Lord Jesus Christ* (5:1; 8:39). The second is the chiastic structure of chs. 5–8:

> A Peace with God, 5:1-11
> > B Victory over **Sin** via Christ, 5:12-21
> > > C Death of the Old Humanity, 6:1–7:6
> > B Victory over the Flesh via the Spirit, 7:7–8:11
> A Sonship with God, 8:12-39

The chiastic structure suggests a specially close parallel between 5:1-11 and 8:12-39. Both sections indicate that the consequences of being made righteous are peace with God and hope. Both stress the theological and christological basis for this peace and hope; it is the result of the love of God expressed in the gift of Messiah Jesus poured *into our hearts through the Holy Spirit.* Hope in both sections confronts and overcomes suffering because the love of God "will not let us go" (5:3-4, 6, 8, 9, 10; 8:17-18, 32, 35-39).

Chapter 5:1-11 introduces the themes that are developed more fully in ch. 8, especially 8:12-39. Chapter 5:12-21 outlines the christological victory over Adam that is the basis for the peace with God of 5:1-11 and 8:12-39. Chapters 6–8:11 answer questions which can be raised concerning **Sin** (6:1–7:6) and the law (7:7–8:11). These questions were hinted at earlier (3:8; 3:31; 4:13-15), but were not answered.

Peace with God

Romans 5:1-11

PREVIEW

Chapter 5:1-11 is a clearly defined text unit. Chapter 4:24-25 serves as a solemn conclusion to the discussion of 3:27–4:22. Chapter 5:1-11 is distinct from what follows in 5:12f. The first person style of 4:24-25 is continued in 5:1-11, while 5:12-21 shifts to the third person. The subject matter also is different from what precedes and what follows. The first and last verses of 5:1-11 form an inclusio, both concern peace/reconciliation with God, both contain the formula, *through our Lord Jesus Christ.*

Ch. 5:1-11 is also a transitional passage. Chapter 4:23-25 asserts that Abraham was "for our sake also," the "our" being defined as "the ones faithing the resurrection of Jesus our Lord out of the dead." Chapter 5:1-11 begins to explain what the death and resurrection of Christ means for "the ones faithing."

The text unit enumerates the benefits or blessings that flow from the revelation of the righteousness of God through the faithfulness of Christ to those being faithful. The use of point-in-time action, past tense verbs, "having been made righteous" (*justified*, in vv. 1 and 9), indicates that the action mentioned is prior to the action of the verbs that follow. The fact of "being made righteous" is the basis for conclusions that can be drawn. Each statement of the basis is followed by a listing of benefits, peace and boasting, salvation and boasting. Paul exhorts acceptance of the benefits in the first list, and narrates the benefits as fact in the second list.

Two forms of reasoning are used in 5:1-11. First, the *not only, but also* argument is used in vv. 3a and 11a. Paul thus "exceeds" the statements made in vv. 1-2 and vv. 9-11 respectively. Secondly, the minor to major argument, *much more*, is used in vv. 9a and 10c. What applies in a lesser case will certainly apply in a greater one.

At the heart of the conclusions is the fact that there now exists a state of peace or reconciliation with God. The cause of the hostility has been removed at God's initiative. Therefore, boasting, which was excluded earlier, is now acceptable.

OUTLINE

The Basis, 5:1a
> Therefore, **having been made righteous** out of faithfulness

The Exhortations, 5:1b-8
> 5:1b-2b Peace with God
> 5:2c-4a Boasting in hope
> 5:4b-8 God's Love Poured Out

The Basis, 5:9a
> Therefore, much more **having been made righteous** now by means of his blood

The Benefits, 5:9b-11
> 5:9b-10 Salvation from wrath
> 5:11 Boasting in God

EXPLANATORY NOTES

The Basis 5:1a

Paul begins the new argument with a *therefore*, followed by a participial clause, *having been made righteous out of faithfulness*. He uses language that both summarizes what he has said and sets forth what is to follow (a technique called *transitio*).

Paul establishes the inauguration of "being made righteous" as a past fact. *Righteousness* here, as elsewhere in Romans, is clearly a relational term, defined by peace, access, and reconciliation. The opening participle could be translated as *having been established in right relationship with God*.

The source of "being made righteous" is defined by the unique phrase "out of faith" (*ek pisteōs*). The meaning here must be determined by the previous uses of the phrase in Romans. In 1:17 and 3:26

it referred to the "faithfulness of Messiah Jesus," in 3:30 it described the faith of Gentiles ("the uncircumcised"), and in 4:16 it is used twice, once to indicate that the source of righteousness is faith *in order that the promise may rest on grace*, and the second to describe Abraham's faith as the father of all people of faith. "Being made righteous" is a function of faith as trust and obedience, first the Messiah's faithfulness and then the followers of Abraham (4:16) and the Messiah (4:24). The parallel phrase in v. 9, *therefore, much more having been made righteous now by means of his blood*, suggests that the primary reference here is to the faithfulness of Christ. Peace with God and salvation from God's end-time wrath are grounded objectively in what God has done in Christ, rather than subjectively in human response.

The Exhortations 5:1b-8

Because people are made righteous through the faithfulness of Christ certain benefits are available. Formerly the preserve of Jews alone these benefits now are available for all believers equally. The two which Paul exhorts the believers to accept and enjoy are peace with God and boasting in the hope of the glory of God.

5:1b-2b Peace with God

Verse 1b has a textual problem. Most translations read *we have peace with God*, and then indicate an alternative reading in the footnote, *let us have peace with God*. The manuscript evidence (the external evidence) for the *let us have* reading (exhortative) is stronger than the more popular *we have* translation (indicative). The external evidence is supported by the structure of the argument. Verse 1b—*let us have peace . . .*—and v. 2c—*let us boast . . .*—are parallel imperative statements. Further, the logic of Paul's argument focuses on God's initiative and work. God, the Patron, has made peace and established reconciliation. What is called for now is for the clients, the followers of Jesus, to make peace with God and each other. Paul is saying, in effect, "now that God has put us in the right relationship, let us take advantage of what that means (i.e., peace)."

What Paul wants his readers to have is *peace with God*. Peace is the comprehensive description of the blessings of salvation in the OT. It is a relational term, not a subjective one. The word means fulfillment of wholeness, the completion of salvation. Peace defines holistic well-being, because the cause of alienation has been removed, "the enemiiness" (v. 10) has been ended. It has the same meaning here as "reconciliation" in v. 11.

In Jewish thought, peace and righteousness are complementary concepts; *the effect of righteousness will be peace* in Isaiah 32:17 (see also Pss. 35:27; 72:3; 85:10; Isa. 9:7; 48:18; 60:17). Peace is a covenant term (e.g., Num. 6:22-27; Ps. 55:18-19; Isa. 48:17-22; 54:10; Jer. 14:19-21; Sir. 47:13; 2 Macc. 1:2-4). Its full realization belongs to the eschatological age; *I will make a covenant of peace with them* (Ezek. 37:26; see also Isa. 9:6-7; 54:10; Ezek. 34:25-31; Mic. 4:5; Hag. 2:9; Zech. 8:12; 1 En. 5:7, 9; 10:17; 11:2). Paul both announces the fulfillment of this hope for all people, and exhorts the Roman Christians to accept its reality. He again links righteousness and peace in 14:17—*the kingdom of God is . . . righteousness and peace. . . .*

Paul's exhortation *to have peace with God* bears directly on problems in the Roman churches, conflict among different groups of Jesus followers. Believers who have been made right with God are to work for peace with God and with each other. Paul here anticipates his more specific exhortations to peaceful living among the Roman Christians in 12:18, and 14:17 and 19.

The evidence of *peace with God* is access *to this grace in which we stand*. The word *access* (*prosagōgē*) means "to be introduced." It is a word of privilege with either political or cultic overtones ("cultic" refers to religious observance/worship, e.g., sacrifice, Temple practices). As a political word, it describes the introduction of a commoner to royalty. It is also a cultic term that describes being conducted into the inner sanctuary of the Temple. The point is that followers of Jesus do not enter *righteousness* or *peace with God* on their own, but need an "introducer," namely Christ. Through Christ they are introduced to the gracious righteousness of God *in which we stand* already. Christians are already righteous, and thus at peace with God, as far as God is concerned, because of the faithfulness of Christ.

5:2c-4a Boasting in Hope

The second exhortation is that people made righteous should *boast in our hope of sharing the glory of God*, v. 2c. The word normally translated *rejoice* is the same word translated *boast* earlier in Romans. It should be translated as "let us boast" in parallel with the "let us have peace" in v. 1, rather than as the *we rejoice* in many translations (NRSV, however, reads *we also boast*). Boasting about a salvation and identity that excludes some people is rejected. Boasting about social status that honors some people and shames others is excluded. But boasting about end-time hope that depends entirely on the initiative and power of God is encouraged.

The object of boasting is *the glory of God*, the glory that describes the likeness and radiance of God, from which humanity was cut off by **Sin**. The ultimate eschatological hope for the Jews was the restoration of this likeness of God. In Christ the believer has the hope of seeing the end-time glory restored. In fact, in 8:30 Paul says glory is already a fact for the followers of Jesus. The notion of boasting in future glory affirms Paul's understanding of present end-time existence. The Christian life is not defined solely in terms of the past. The future has broken into the present and is the basis of Christian boasting.

The *not only, but also* phrase in v. 3 signals that Paul is going to extend and intensify the boasting claim of v. 2. He contradicts the natural tendency to be ashamed of and to bemoan tribulations by urging believers to boast in the midst of them. *Tribulation (thlipsis)* can mean any trouble, but it had definite end-time associations in Jewish apocalyptic literature and early Christian preaching (cf. Mark 13:19). It means the sufferings, literally "birth pangs," of the last days. The coming of the Messiah and the end-times, it was believed, would be associated with intense *tribulations*. The theme of enduring suffering was a prominent feature of Jewish martyr theology, of which Job was the model. Its theology was based on the idea of God's disciplinary chastisement of Israel (see Deut. 8:2-5; Prov. 3:11-12; Sir. 2:1-5; 4:17-18; 18:13-14; 23:1-3; Wis. 3:1-6; 11:9-10; 2 Macc. 6:12-16; 7:32-33; in the NT, 1 Cor. 11:32; Heb. 12:5-11; Rev. 3:19). Suffering due to faithfulness was evidence of Israel's covenant relationship with God. Why boast in suffering? Because it produces (lit., "works out") patient endurance which leads to a "quality of provenness," which in turn confirms hope.

5:4b-8 God's Love Poured Out

Suffering normally produces shame in an honor-shame culture, because the superior, the one holding honor, is humiliating the inferior. The end-time suffering in Rome that is associated with the reversal of the honor-shame code, that is, welcoming the inferior, does not produce shame (unfortunately, often translated as "not let us down") for Christians, because *God's love has been poured into our hearts.* "The love of God" refers to the character of God (a subjective genitive). God is love. "Poured out" (*ekkechutai*) is normally used with God's wrath (Ps. 79:6; Ezek. 7:8; Rev. 16, eight times), never with God's love. But, it is used with the coming of the Holy Spirit (Joel 2:28-29; Acts 2:17-18, 33; 10:45; Tit. 3:5-6), which explains its use here. The tense of the verb (perfect) suggests an ongoing state that is the result of a once-for-all event.

The coming of the Spirit is a mark of the end-time in Judaism (Isa.

32:15; 34:16; 44:3; Ezek. 11:19; 36:26-27; 37:4-14; Joel 2:28-32) and the early church; Paul speaks elsewhere of the Spirit as a "pledge" or "guarantee" (Rom. 8:23; 2 Cor. 1:22; 5:5). Jewish and Gentile Christians experience the love of God by means of the gift of the end-time Spirit. The proof that hope will not be shamed is that God loves by giving the Spirit to people of differing socio-economic groups. The presence of the Spirit is the first evidence of God's love. Followers of Jesus experience this love at the deepest center of their lives, "in their hearts," and as the fulfillment of the new covenant promises to Israel (Jer. 31:31-34).

The second evidence of the love of God is the death of Christ, vv. 6-8. He died "in behalf of . . ." (four times, vv. 6b, 7a, 7b, 8b); that is, his death was substitutionary. Christ did this for people described as *weak, ungodly*, and *sinners*. The first and last descriptors are made with a construction (genitive absolute) which indicates a permanent condition (lit. "weak being" and "sinners being"). "Ungodly" is the word used to characterize the people who did not worship God in ch. 1 and Abraham before God made him righteous in ch. 4. The language describes a reality that humans could not rectify on their own. They needed a divine initiative, which is exactly what the death of Jesus was. Human beings would not offer to die for another person even if he/she were completely upright before the law ("righteous"), although one might agree to die for a benefactor ("the good person") in Roman culture to whom one owed an honor, a personal and social obligation. But God, in this case the benefactor, was not obligated in any way to weak, ungodly, and sinful human beings. God personally and intentionally (the emphasis is very clear in Greek) demonstrated love in the death of Christ.

The language of weakness here is the same that is used in chs. 14–15 to describe one group of Christians in Rome. The use is probably deliberate. God took the initiative to honor the shamed via love. Followers of Jesus are asked to do the same; they are called to treat the weak the way God in Christ treated them.

The Basis 5:9a

The *much more* of v. 9 indicates that Paul is going to use a "lesser to greater" argument to outline the second round of benefits. He repeats the "having been made righteous" of v. 1, and then adds *now* and *by means of his blood*. The reference to blood uses sacrificial imagery that sealed the covenant between God and Israel. Christians have been made righteous in the present by the sacrificial death of Christ.

The Benefits 5:9b-11

To be made righteous by God is a great gift. But *much more* results from this event. The *much more* is defined as salvation from wrath and boasting in God. The first benefit links *being made righteous now* with future end-time salvation.

5:9b-11 Salvation from Wrath

To be made righteous is to be saved from God's end-time wrath. The means of salvation is reconciliation with God. Reconciliation describes a transformation of relationship. The word is determined by the word *enemies*. *While we were enemies* is the third in a series of phrases characterizing humanity, "being weak," "being sinners," and now "being enemies." Each term designates a more serious condition; "weak" is fairly gentle, "sinner" is more serious and severe, "enemy" is emotionally charged. "Enemy" has both an active and a passive sense; humans hate God and are hated by God. The relationship is fractured by mutual hostility. Reconciliation puts an end to enmity; the relationship is restored, access is reopened, oneness is reestablished. The means of reconciliation is "through the death of his son." Reconciliation is a completed action, a fact of God's initiative in Jesus Christ.

But that is not all. Paul uses his second *much more* argument in v. 10. God who has reconciled enemies through Christ will do even more. God will save in the future. The means of salvation is *by his life*. The death effects reconciliation, the resurrection effects salvation. Paul refers to two great moments in salvation history, the moment of God's reconciling activity in the present and the moment of God's saving activity in the future. Believers stand between these two great moments.

The repetition of *much more* and future salvation in vv. 9 and 10 indicate that these two verses are parallel statements. Verse 10 is a restatement of v. 9 in different language. Being made righteous and reconciliation are both relational terms that define each other as well as the nature of salvation.

5:11 Boasting in God

Paul uses the second *and not only, but also* argument to describe the second blessing and to conclude the text unit. Every term in v. 11 comes from earlier usage in this text, *boasting* from v. 3a, the formula *through our Lord Jesus Christ* repeats v. 1c, *now* recalls v. 9a, and *reconciliation* is taken from v. 10. The *and not only, but also* means

Paul is intensifying the previous statements. Being made righteous, being reconciled, being saved are great, but *much more we are boasting in God*. Boasting in one's ethnic or social status is excluded by Paul. The only legitimate boasting is "bragging" about what God has done in Christ.

Comments and Observations

Chapter 5:1-11 is a strategic bridge passage. It summarizes and builds on the arguments of 1:16–4:25 by interpreting the righteousness of God through the faithfulness of Christ. Being made righteous has consequences for "all the ones having faith"; they are reconciled, they boast, they are assured future salvation.

The outline of the benefits of being made righteous significantly advances the argument of the letter. Paul makes explicit his unity with the readers in this text unit. He referred to the readers in the introduction to the letter, 1:1-18, but the references are third person— e.g., apostle to the Gentiles, "the ones being in Rome" (1:6-7)—or at best second person—e.g., "among whom also you are called of Jesus Christ" (1:6-7), *I thank my God . . . for all of you* (1:8), *I am longing to see you* (1:11), *I am eager to preach the gospel to you* (1:15). The emphases are on Paul as apostle and the readers as the object of his ministry. There is no real identification with the Christians in Rome until 4:24-25. The identification introduced at the end of ch. 4 is greatly expanded in 5:1-11. These verses contain 18 first person plural elements. Paul now speaks of the life that he and the Roman believers share as followers of Jesus. The inclusive but impersonal *all* believers of 1:16–4:23 becomes us. Paul and the Roman Christians share the same faith in God and the same life in Christ. Except for 5:12-21 this personal identification continues through ch. 8.

As part of this identification of himself with the readers in Rome, Paul introduces more personal, relational language to describe the results of the revelation of the righteousness of God, *peace, access, love of God, reconciliation*. This relational interpretation of righteousness will build through the following chapters until it reaches a climax in 8:31-39 where the "union" with God is asserted to be unbreakable.

Paul so far has made the case for the righteousness of God and for the importance of faith, Christ's and the believers. Now for the first time he describes the life of faith. He does so by picturing God and believing humans as bonded to each other by the event of "making righteous out of faith." They are in relationship—they are at peace, they have access, they share God's love, they share the Spirit of God, they are reconciled. The Christian life is defined as a life of relationship with God, of solidarity with God. This is the foundation for the subsequent exhortations to solidarity, to welcoming and loving relationships among fellow Christians in Rome (chs. 12–16).

The christological emphasis of chs. 5–8 with its different vocabulary and themes, has always raised questions of its relationship to the rest of Romans. The older Protestant interpretations read Romans 1–8 as a progression from justification in chs. 1–4 to sanctification in chs. 5–8. The History of Religions interpretation during the first part of the twentieth century argued that chs. 1–5 contained Paul's dialogue with Jews, while in chs. 6–8 his real position emerged, a position deeply influenced by Hellenistic rather than Jewish thought. Chs. 9–11 were always the problem in these interpretations, and were often either ignored or treated as an appendix to the real center of Paul's thought. More recent interpreters have seen the continuity of chs. 1–4 and 9–11. Given the apparent link between chs. 1–4 and 9–11, chs. 5–8 now become the problem, because they seem discontinuous with these surrounding chapters.

The interpretation outlined here reads chs. 5–8 as continuous with chs. 1–4. Chapter 5:1-11 anticipates the conclusion of 8:31-39. The Creator God who acted in behalf of Israel while they were sinners has acted again to deliver all human beings. The reason for both actions is the love of God, a theme as covenantal as righteousness. The fruits of being made righteous—peace with God (the great eschatological hope of the prophets; e.g., Isa. 32, 54, 59; Jer. 8; Ezek. 34, 37); access to God (the goal of Temple worship); the coming of the Spirit (the hope of Isa. 11 and 61; and Ezek. 11, 18, 36, 37, 39); boasting in the hope of the glory of God (which Adam lost and is to be restored)—all articulate the dreams and eschatological hopes of Israel. Those hopes are now fulfilled, Paul asserts, in Messiah Jesus and in the people of faith—Jews and Gentiles.

Paul pictures the current experience of followers of Jesus as the end-time fulfillment of the promises and prophecies for Israel. Even the theme of current suffering stands within the story line of Israel's experience and hope. The people of Israel suffer as they await the final vindication of God. The suffering of the people is transferred to the Messiah in some branches of Jewish thought. The death of innocent martyrs is believed to turn away the wrath of God (2 Macc. 7; 4 Macc. 17). The only difference in Paul is that the people rescued are not the nation of Israel, but the Jew-Gentile family of Abraham from 3:21–4:25. The result is that boasting, which was disallowed to the nation of Israel, is restored to the children of Abraham who are made righteous out of faith because this people boasts in the salvation of God that extends the blessings for Israel to all people. At every point in the opening argument of chs. 5–8, what is ascribed to those "made righteous out of faith" is what had been defined as the privilege of Israel. Paul is advancing a singular argument—the revelation of the righteousness of God to all humanity—not digressing from it.

The text is a bridge in another very important way. It pictures God as the Patron who freely gives new status and privileges to the client, humanity. God the Patron is clearly the superior person in the narrative. God is righteous and loving. God is the person of honor. Humanity, the client, is a weak, ungodly, sinful enemy. Humanity represents the dishonorable, the shameful.

God as the honorable Patron acts against all social convention and honors the shameful client. God gives the client a new status—righteousness. This gifts the client with enormous privileges—peace with God, access to God, hope of sharing the glory of God, recipient of God's love, reconciliation with God, future salvation from the wrath due the dishonorable client (1:18f.).

God the Patron gives all of this to humanity, the client, freely and without obligation, through the death of Christ. Paul elaborates the meaning of Christ's death as gracious gift (3:24) through the metaphor of the dominant social system of the day, patron-client, and the dominant social value, honor-shame. The patron, not the client, takes all the initiative to establish a relationship of honor that overcomes the distance between them and replaces shame with honor. God the Patron is a model of how patrons, the strong in the church, should relate to clients, the weak.

THE TEXT IN BIBLICAL CONTEXT

Romans 5:1-11 contains two important and related themes that recur in Paul, boasting and reconciliation.

Boasting

There is a negative and a positive boasting in Romans. Boasting in exclusive Jewish identity and salvation is excluded (2:17, 23; 3:27; 4:2). Boasting in God (5:2, 11), in suffering (5:3), and in the fruits of Christian mission (15:17) are affirmed. What is clear is that the statement in 3:27—boasting is excluded—is not Paul's central thesis about boasting. Boasting in Romans is not fundamentally about human pride and arrogance, which is the opposite of faith; it is not reliance upon oneself rather than upon God, as in so much Protestant interpretation (see Bultmann, 1951:281, for a classic Protestant interpretation). Paul does not prohibit boasting itself. He rejects only boasting of special status as a Jew. Boasting that affirms God and the work of God is encouraged.

Paul's interpretation of boasting in Romans is consistent with his use in other letters. "Boasting in the Lord" is exhorted twice with the citation of Jeremiah 9:22 (1 Cor. 1:31; 2 Cor. 10:17). Boasting in Christ is affirmed (1 Cor. 15:31; Gal. 6:14; Phil. 1:26; 3:3). Boasting in weakness is appropriate (2 Cor. 11:30; 12:5, 9). The most characteristic form of boasting in Paul is in the fruits of his mission (e.g., 2 Cor. 7:4, 14; 8:24; 9:2, 3; 10:8; 11:10, 12; 1 Thess. 2:19). Paul boasts in the results of his missionary work both to encourage the churches he has established and to oppose other missionary efforts that seek to undermine his work. He consistently rejects two kinds of boasting, boasting in exclusive Jewish identity (Gal. 6:13; Eph. 2:9), and "boasting in the flesh" (e.g., 1 Cor. 1:29; 3:21; 5:6; 13:3; 2 Cor. 11:18; Phil. 3:3). The "boasting in the flesh" comes closest to the dominant interpretation of boasting in Paul; it involves the rejection of God and the work of God. But it is important to note that it is only one boasting theme in Paul, and that it serves a very specific function. The rejection of "boasting in the flesh" is certainly not Paul's dominant boasting theme, and is not present at all in Romans. Paul has more positive things to say about right boasting than negative things to say about wrong boasting.

Reconciliation

Boasting in God is specifically linked in Romans to reconciliation with God (5:11). Reconciliation language is used 13 times in Paul's writings (the verb *katallassō* occurs six times—Rom. 5:10 [twice]; 1 Cor. 7:11; 2 Cor. 5:18, 19, 20; the noun *katallagē* is used four times—Rom. 5:11; 11:15; 2 Cor. 5:18, 19; the verb *apokatallassō* occurs three times—Eph. 2:16; Col. 1:20, 22). The two critical texts are Romans 5:10-11 and 2 Corinthians 5:18-21. In the first, we have seen, reconciliation is an act of God prior to and independent of any human response—humans were reconciled to God while enemies (10a), they have been reconciled (10b), they have received reconciliation (11c). God initiates reconciliation; humans receive it. 2 Corinthians 5 makes the same point. God reconciles "us" and "the world" through Jesus Christ. Therefore, followers of Jesus exhort people *be reconciled to God*. The effect of God's initiative is to make Christians "the righteousness of God." The Colossians 1:15-20 hymn asserts that God reconciles *to himself all things . . . making peace by the blood of the cross*. And in Ephesians 2 God reconciles Jews and Gentiles to each other and to God through Christ.

God is the subject of the action in reconciliation, humans and the world are the objects. God acts to remove the alienation that stands between the divine and the human. Humans and the world were destined for God's wrath, because of **Sin**/sin. Now God and humans, yes even the cosmos, can enjoy reconciliation, peace, because God has acted in the death of Christ. That is cause for such joy that Paul uses the word "boasting" as the best way to express the appropriate response.

THE TEXT IN THE LIFE OF THE CHURCH
The Problem of Suffering

Romans 5:1-11 confronts the church with a dilemma, the relationship of the greatness of God's salvation and the problem of suffering. The death and resurrection of Christ results in a fundamental transformation of existence for Christians: we are made righteous, vv. 1, 9; we have access to God's gracious and righteous presence, v. 2; God's love has been poured into our hearts, v. 5; the Holy Spirit has been given to us, v. 5; we are reconciled with God, vv. 10-11. A new reality exists. The great promises of God to Israel, the long-term dreams of God's people, are an experiential reality for people of faith.

But suffering, weakness, and sin continue as well. Suffering always troubles the people of God. It seems to contradict the transformed reality of *being made righteous, reconciliation with God, the love of God in our hearts*. Suffering raises questions about God. Why suffering? And, in this text, why the absurd exhortation to boast in suffering? Or, elsewhere in Paul, boasting in weakness? Something seems out of sync.

The language of the text itself offers guidance for struggling with the dilemma. First, the text distinguishes the objective reality of salvation and the subjective experience of it. Having established that believers are made righteous out of faithfulness—the fact, the objective reality—Paul exhorts *let us have peace with God*. The reality of God's salvation must be accepted, appropriated by faith and by living peacefully. That appropriation must move from the edge of life to the center of life for each person and the entire community of God's people.

Second, the text distinguishes present reality from future hope. The reality of being made righteous, being reconciled, the love of God poured into our hearts is balanced by the future tense of salvation, *we shall be saved* through Christ from future wrath (v. 9), *we shall be saved by means of his life* (v. 10). Christians live between the "already"—made righteous, reconciliation—and the "not yet"—we shall be saved. Salvation is primarily future in Paul; it awaits completion.

Therefore, *we hope for the glory of God* (v. 2). The past work of
God in Christ and the present experience of God's grace leads to the
future. Hope of completed salvation arises from the experience of
future salvation now already in present experience. Salvation is ultimately future, eschatological, and cosmic (as ch. 8 makes clear).

Faithfulness is no guarantee against suffering between the times.
Therefore, Paul exhorts the reframing of suffering, especially suffering
for faithfulness. Christians are to boast in suffering, thus declaring
their dependence on God and confessing that testing reinforces hope.
Suffering between the times does not contradict the experience of
God's grace, but complements it by strengthening the character of
grace and faith.

Reframing the Meaning of Christ's Death

The Romans 5:1-11 text is instructive for the church in another sense.
It shows how Paul reinterprets the death of Christ via the dominant
social structures and values of the culture. The death of Christ does
forgive the guilt of a guilt-forgiveness structured culture. But, it also
reconciles enemies in an honor-shame culture by overcoming the
shame of being the inferior person. Christ wipes away sin to absolve
guilt, but he also gives new status and privilege to honor the shameful. He lifts up the shamed and gives them a new identity, which they
can respect.

Paul's creative theological thinking frees the church to ask how it
should interpret the meaning of salvation through Christ in ways that
address the deep questions and values of cultures in new times and
places. Minorities, women, post-modern men and women are searching desperately for metaphors of salvation that are as transformative
in these times as the "forgiveness of guilt" model was in earlier times.
Removing shame, and the deep anger which accompanies it, is one
such image.

Salvation from Guilt and Shame

The manifestation of sin as guilt and shame involve quite different subjective and objective realities. Guilt is a function of an act, a deed,
which breaks a law. A person experiences guilt when he/she is disobedient, transgresses a clearly defined boundary, either intentionally
or unintentionally. Shame focuses on the self in relation to an other;
a person does not meet an expectation, of the group, the deity (e.g.,
"fall short of the glory of God"), or the self. The group and the person are disappointed. The person has not made a mistake, but is a
mistake. A person who sins by breaking a law is a violator, whereas a

person who sins by not meeting an expectation is unworthy, unclean, dirty, and thus excluded from the group.

The subjective consequence of breaking a law is a feeling of guilt and remorse. The person is self-accusatory and fears punishment for the disobedience. The person is angry at the lawgiver and the self for violating the law. Hostility characterizes the person. The subjective consequence of not meeting an expectation is shame, feeling disgraced and exposed before one's primary community. The person has lost face, has lost worth. He/she depreciates the self and fears abandonment. The person experiences a profound feeling of embarrassment, is filled with rage, and feels alienated from the community.

The objective consequence of disobedience is that the person is accused or charged with the violation. A sentence is rendered, which includes restitution for the wrong where possible. The objective consequence of not meeting an expectation, individual or group, is disapproval and rejection. The person is held in contempt, ridiculed before the group. Relationships are broken, and the person is excluded from the community. He/she is separated, "put outside the camp." The individual needs to go to a new place and build a new identity.

The remedy, salvation, for guilt is expiation, forgiveness, pardon, and restitution where possible. Salvation is fairly simple and straightforward. The remedy for shame is complex and difficult. The center of salvation is reconciliation. The person must be re-honored by being reaccepted and reincorporated into relationships and the community. The social disgrace must be removed, the exclusion overcome, and the person given a new identity and personal worth in the community.

The church in the West has focused almost entirely on salvation from guilt. Jesus on the cross expiates for disobedience, he forgives the guilt of violating the law. God puts people in the right, "justifies," because Jesus "took my place in the court room," "paid the price of my sentence." But salvation as expiation, justification, or forgiveness does not begin to address the problem of shame. It does not "save face," give people a new identity, re-honor them as people of worth, reincorporate them into a community. Dealing with shame requires quite a different soteriology. God "makes peace" (*we have peace with God*, Rom. 5:1), love is extended (*God shows his love for us*, Rom. 5:8), reconciliation occurs (*while we were enemies we were reconciled to God . . . we are reconciled and saved by his life*, Rom. 5:10), a new identity is given (*we are children of God*, Rom. 8:16, who have been adopted as sons and daughters, Rom. 8:23). The saving message is not that "you are forgiven," but that "you are in Christ" (in

Christ's body), that "God is for us" and that nothing, nothing *will be able to separate us from the love of God in Christ Jesus our Lord.* Jesus on the cross re-honors people by taking on their shame, by removing the alienation that separates them from God and others, and thereby reincorporating them into God's people.

The affirmative, sometimes very emotional, response from women and minority groups, in the writer's experience, to the distinction between sin as guilt and sin as shame, and the teaching of different forms of salvation for different experiences of sin, suggests that church must become much more sensitive to the diversity of peoples experience of sin, and to the need for different experiences of salvation, different understandings and experiences of the grace of God through Jesus Christ to transform broken and sinful men and women.

	Guilt/Forgiveness	Shame/Honor
Focus	act/deed	self in relation
Nature	disobedience broke a law made a mistake	not meet expectation disappointed am a mistake
State	violator	unclean, dirty
Subjective	remorse self accusation fear of punishment anger depression hostility	shame–disgrace–exposed self-depreciation fear of abandonment rage embarrassment alienation
Objective	accused charged condemn—sentence	disapproval ridiculed—hold in contempt exclude—separate— relations broken—go to a new place to build a new identity
Remedy	expiation—forgiveness pardon restitution	reconciliation re-honor—restore face reacceptance, reincorporation

(The chart is based on materials in Kraus, 1987; Green and Baker, 2000.)

The Politics of Peace

The exhortation *let us have peace with God through our Lord Jesus Christ*, followed by the assurances of reconciliation and salvation, are politically subversive statements. Peace, reconciliation, and salvation is *through our Lord Jesus Christ* (twice, vv. 1, 11), not through Caesar. The peace of God is different than the "peace of Rome" (*pax Romana*). The first comes because God showed love by embracing the weak, the sinful, and the enemy in Messiah Jesus. The latter is a function of the exercise of power, overwhelming power. God makes peace by reconciling enemies. Caesar, and his kind, makes peace by smashing enemies. Can the church, which is always tempted by the peace of power (e.g., the politics of land and blood, or the politics of one version of the faith over another), live only by the peace of God, making peace by reconciling enemies?

P. M. Friesen was a distinguished Russian Mennonite leader who risked his life in the early-twentieth century to make peace between the Russian majority and the Jewish minority in Sevastopol. Russia had just lost the Russo-Japanese war and there was much dissatisfaction with the government. Some blamed the Jews for the defeat. The press fanned the hostility with inflammatory articles. Speeches inciting violence against the Jews were frequent at public rallies.

Friesen was ill and confined to bed. But one day he asked his wife Susanna to bring him his clothes because he had an assignment from God. He rushed to the market place where a crowd of several thousand was gathered to hear inflammatory speeches. Before arriving he wrote his name and address on two cards and put one each in a coat and pant pocket. He feared that he might be killed for what he planned to do and wanted identification so that his family could be notified.

Once at the market place Friesen forced his way through the crowds to the center. He climbed to the top of the vehicle that was serving as the podium and began to address the crowd. He reminded the people that they called themselves Christians, and that Christ had come in love giving his life for all people. Through Christ's death all humans had become brothers and sisters. Therefore, none of the people present wanted to soil their hands with the blood of their brother's or sisters. Seeing one of the dirty Russian workers standing nearby, he pulled him up on the truck and kissed him on both cheeks in Russian style. Then he called out, "now we will all go home to our work." The crowd obeyed. Jews were no longer molested in Sevastopol. Friesen made peace by standing with the weak at the risk of his own life.

The Victory of Christ Over Sin

Romans 5:12-21

PREVIEW

Verses 12-21 of chapter 5 shift from the first person to the third, signaling a change of subject from what precedes and what follows. The text is an extended comparison between Christ and Adam. Both are viewed as representative figures whose actions affect all humanity. The comparison makes one basic point: Christ is greater than Adam, and, therefore, the result of his life—righteousness and life—is greater than the result of Adam's—sin and death. The fundamental comparison is straightforward:

Adam	⟶	Sin	⟶	Death
Christ	⟶	Righteousness	⟶	Life

But this single point is made in a complex way, as Paul explains the basic comparison repeatedly with different words. The arguments of the comparative statements are not always easy to follow. The resulting complexity is the source of both great theological richness and debate.

The focus of interpretation since Augustine has been Adam, especially the sin of Adam. But that is not the focus of Paul. His central concern is christology. This text is the second most important presentation of Christ so far in Romans; the first was 3:21-26. Adam is introduced as a foil for Christ, to draw attention to the cosmic significance of Christ and the salvation he effects. The purpose is to ground the hope Paul expressed in 5:1-11—peace with God, salvation from God's wrath, reconciliation with God—in christology.

The comparison/contrast nature of the argument is clear from the language Paul uses. He continues the *much-more* method of comparison from vv. 1-11 (see vv. 15 and 17). To that he adds *just as . . . so also*, and *not as . . . so also* comparisons. The comparisons look like this:

just as . . . so also   v. 12

not as . . . so also	v. 15
for if . . . how much more	v. 15
not as . . . (so also)	v. 16
for if . . . how much more	v. 17
(just) as . . . so also	v. 18
just as . . . so also	v. 19
just as . . . so also	v. 21

The contrasts made by these comparisons are:

the one—the many	vv. 15, 19
trespass—free gift	v. 15
trespass—grace of God	v. 15
judgment—free gift	v. 16
condemnation—righteousness	v. 16
trespass—righteous act	v. 18
disobedience—obedience	v. 19
sin—grace	vv. 19-20

The central themes Paul wishes to address through these contrasts are indicated by the repeated use of key terms: *one man* (12 times), *grace/free gift* (seven times), *human being* (six times), *sin* (six times), *trespass* (six times), *righteous (dik)* words (six times), *reign* (five times), *many* (five times), *all* (four times), *abound* (three times).

OUTLINE

The Origin of **DEATH**, 5:12-14
    5:12   Thesis
    5:13-14 Supporting Argument

The Comparison of Adam and Christ, 5:15-21
        5:15-17 Contrast: Trespass and Gift
        5:18-21 Four Comparisons
            Trespass and Condemnation with Righteous Act and
                Righteousness
            Disobedience with Obedience
            Sin with Grace
            Death with Life

PERSPECTIVES FOR INTERPRETING THIS UNIT

Background—Adam in the First Century

At the heart of the comparison in this unit is a contrast between Christ and Adam. To understand the contrast, and especially the radical nature of what Paul does, we need to know something about how Adam was understood in first-century Judaism. Adam was the subject of considerable discussion and speculation. Most of what Paul says about him is found in various strands of Jewish tradition. While the themes about Adam are diverse, and certainly not systematized anywhere in the literature, two basic pictures of Adam are current.

First, he is the cause and the explanation of sin. He introduced sin into the world by disobeying the law (Torah). Adam is the first sinner. The effects of his sin were death and the corruption of the world.

Second, and very different, Adam is pictured as the first Israelite, the first patriarch of the Jewish people. Many different images are used to characterize him in this stream of thought (e.g., he was born circumcised, he was pious, he was a high priest and dressed in the garments of the high priest, he was buried with Abraham, Isaac, and Jacob). The message of these images is that Adam as the first Jew was the image of the humanity God intended in creation. The real subject in this stream of thought is not Adam as the representative of humanity, but Adam as the representative of the people of God. This form of Adam theology advances a claim about the place of Israel in the purposes of God. Israel is God's true humanity, who will overcome the power of sin in the world. This Adam theology is transposed into nationalist theology during the Maccabean period, 163 B.C. and later. Israel alone is God's true humanity to undo the power of sin. The origin of sin in this scenario is ascribed to Eve, Satan, or the angels cohabiting with women in Genesis 6 (see Dunn, 1998; Scroggs, 1966; Levison, 1988; Wright, 1983, 1991, for more background on Adam in Jewish thought).

Background—Apocalyptic Theologies of Sin

One other stream of Jewish thought lies behind the comparisons Paul makes, Jewish apocalyptic theology (see discussion in the Introduction, the Larger Thought World of Romans). This theology existed in two forms, cosmic apocalyptic eschatology and forensic (legal) apocalyptic eschatology. In the cosmic form this age is under the dominion of evil, angelic powers. These powers have usurped control of the world from God, and are responsible for evil in the world, including human sinfulness and its consequence, death. God, it is believed, will invade the world very soon, overthrow these evil powers, and establish divine rule and righteousness in the world.

The forensic mode of apocalyptic thought paints a quite different picture. Evil is due to human responsibility, not cosmic evil powers. Human beings are free persons, and they make wrong choices, they reject God; they are responsible for sin. God has provided the law as a remedy for this situation. The law is God's great gift to help people overcome sin; it gives people a second chance. God will hold people accountable in the Last Judgment for their obedience or disobedience to the law. God will give eternal life to those who live in obedience to the law, eternal death to those who disobey the law. The origin of sin in this scenario is the result of a human fall, the disobedience of Adam and Eve.

In some literature, the two forms of thought are married. In the Qumran community, which produced the Dead Sea Scrolls, for example, the two theologies are merged. There the law functions also as God's powerful weapon against the cosmic evil powers. Through the law God enables "the righteous community" to resist and overcome the power of demonic forces. As one scholar says, "in Jewish apocalyptic eschatology, God's Law provides a ticket, the only ticket, on a through train from this world to the next" (de Boer, 1988:90; also de Boer, 1989).

Paul interprets the victory of Christ over sin by a very creative theological interaction with the Jewish Adam theology and apocalyptic eschatology just outlined.

EXPLANATORY NOTES
Diagrammatic Flow of Thought

Paul again uses a sustained logical series of points (one contrast and four comparisons) to make his basic point that Christ's benefits surpass Adam's legacy: salvation trumps sin in Christ. To perceive the intricacy of Paul's argument, we diagram the thought-flow, as follows (JET):

The Origin of **DEATH**, 5:12-14
>   Therefore,
>>   Thesis, v. 12
>>>   12a just as through one person **Sin** entered the world,
>>>   12b and through **Sin Death**
>>>   12c so also **Death** spread to all people
>>>   12d because all sinned.

Supporting Argument—The Relation of **Sin** (Adam) and Law (Moses), vv. 13-14

13a   For **Sin** was in the world prior to the law,

13b   but **Sin** was not registered because there was no law.

14a   But **Death** reigned from Adam to Moses

14b   even over those who did not sin in the likeness of the transgression of Adam,

14c   who is a type of the coming one.

The Comparison of Adam and Christ, 5:15-21

The Contrast (**Trespass** and **Gift**), vv. 15-17

First Thesis

15a   But not as the trespass, so also the gracious gift,

Supporting Argument, v. 15b-c

15b   for if by the trespass of one person, the many died,

15c   how much more the grace of God even the free gift in the grace of the one person Jesus Christ abounded to the many.

Second Thesis, v. 16a

16a   And not as through one who sinned [so also] the gift.

Supporting Argument

16b   For the judgment out of one [trespass] to condemnation,

16c   but the gracious gift out of many trespasses to righteousness.

17a   For if by means of one trespass **Death** reigned through one person,

17b   how much more those who receive the abundance of grace even the gift of righteousness shall reign in life through the one Jesus Christ.

The Comparison (Trespass and Condemnation with Righteous Act and Righteousness, Disobedience with Obedience, **Sin** with Grace, Death with Life), vv. 18-21

Thesis, v. 18

18a   So then, just as through one trespass [there is] condemnation for all human beings,

18b   so also through one righteous act [there is] righteousness of life for all human beings.

Supporting Argument, vv. 19-21
19a   For just as through the disobedience of one person the
       many were made sinners,
19b   so also through the obedience of one the many will be
       made righteous people.
20a   And law came in alongside with the result that trespass
       would increase,
20b   but where **Sin** increased the Grace super-abounded,
21a   in order that just as **Sin** reigned in death,
21b   so also the Grace might reign through righteousness to
       eternal life
21c   through Jesus Christ our Lord.

The Frame—The Beginning and the End 5:12 and 21

A clear correspondence and supersession in thought exists between
the beginning and the end of the unit, vv. 12a-b and 21a-b. The text
unit begins with the entry of sin into the world and ends with the triumphant reign of grace.

The beginning of v. 12, "because of this" in the Greek text indicates that Paul is completing the argument he has made so far,
1:18–5:11, with its concluding assertion of peace and reconciliation
between God and humanity, 5:1-11. That is a very bold claim. Paul
grounds that claim in vv. 12-21.

Verse 12 personifies **Sin** (set in **bold** to make this clear). **Sin** is
singular. It is **Sin** as power, as reign, as magnetic field [*Essay: Sin in
Romans*]. **Sin**'s entry into the world meant the entry of **Death**, also
personified [*Essay: Death in Romans*].

Sin as power strode onto the stage of human history through one
person. The one person is not identified in the text, but reference to
Adam is unmistakable for Paul and his Jewish-Christian audience, as
v. 14 indicates. **Sin** and **Death** entered the world as the legacy from
Adam seen as the universal patriarch. Adam is the inaugurator of solidarity in **Sin** and **Death**.

Paul's opening statement presupposes the Jewish apocalyptic worldview. The reality of the present world is that it is ruled by the evil powers of **Sin** and **Death**. Where **Sin** came from Paul never discusses. He
is interested only in the fact of Sin, not its origin. Nor does he discuss
how **Sin** and **Death** became linked. He and fellow Jews just assume on
the basis of Genesis 2-3 that Death is the consequence of **Sin**.

Verse 21 restates v. 12a-b and answers it. Verse 21 is introduced
as a purpose clause, "in order that." This clause follows from what
Paul has just said about the relationship of **Sin**, law and **Grace**. But

it also answers v. 12a-b. The "in order that" is followed by a comparison that begins with *just as*, exactly as in v. 12. *Just as* **Sin** *reigned in* **Death** summarizes v. 12, *so also* **Grace** *might reign through righteousness to eternal life* responds to v. 12. The rulership of **Sin** is answered by the rulership of **Grace** [*Essay: Grace in Romans*]. **Grace** also rules, and it dispossesses the rulership of **Sin**. The nature of **Sin**'s rule is characterized by one phrase, *in death*. The more powerful rulership of **Grace** is characterized by two phrases, *through righteousness* and *to eternal life*. The means of **Grace**'s rule is the end-time and powerful righteousness of God. God's **Grace** overcomes **Sin** because *the righteousness of God is being manifested in the world through the faithfulness of Jesus Christ*. The consequence of the rule of **Grace** is eternal life, the answer to **Death**.

There is one final comparison that frames the passage. If we look at v. 12, it begins with *through one man*. By contrast, v. 21 ends with *through Jesus Christ our Lord*. One person, Jesus Christ, answers one person, Adam.

The frame of the passage looks like this:

through one person
　　Sin came into the world and through **Sin Death**
　　Grace reigns through **righteousness** to **eternal life**
through Jesus Christ our Lord.

This frame defines the comparison being made throughout the passage. The categories of the comparison are cosmic apocalyptic. It involves two people and two powers of universal significance. The point of the comparison is that the second person, Christ, triumphs over the first person, Adam, and because of that the rulership of **Sin** and **Death** is replaced by the rulership of **Grace** and **Eternal life**.

The frame of the comparison helps interpret the remainder of v. 12. Verse 12c-d elaborate the meaning of the entry of **Sin** into the world in 12a-b. **Death** is universal because **Sin** is universal, v. 12c. **Sin** is universal in v. 12 for two reasons. First, it entered the world as power; it controls the world. Second, Paul adds in v. 12d *because all have sinned*. This last phrase in v. 12 has been one of the most controversial in the NT; it is the basis for the doctrine called "original sin." There is now general agreement that it means *because all have sinned* rather than "in whom all have sinned" [*Essay: Original Sin*].

Paul, in agreement with Jewish apocalyptic eschatology, affirms both "corporate destiny"—**Sin** because of one and personal responsibility—all sin. Adam is a representative personality, a paradigm.

Everyone chooses to live within that paradigm.

Death is universal because of the introduction of **Sin** by Adam and because all sin. **Death** dominates humanity because of one primal act and because human beings continue the practice of acting sinfully. The relationship of the one act of Adam and the continued acts of human beings is not addressed by Paul; it is only stated. Speculation about the transmission of Adam's sin is only that—speculation.

This reading of v. 12 treats it as a complete sentence. The traditional interpretation states that Paul begins a thought in v. 12, and interrupts it. He is then said to complete it either in v. 15 or v. 18, depending on which commentary one reads. In the interpretation just outlined, the sentence expresses a complete thought. The thought is simple and direct:

one person	$\longrightarrow$	**Sin**
Sin	$\longrightarrow$	**Death**
Death	$\longrightarrow$	all people

The Relation of Sin (Adam) and Law (Moses) 5:13-14

Verses 13-14 are not a digression, but the next logical step in Paul's train of thought. The point of v. 12, **Death** as the consequence of **Sin**, is now applied to the time prior to the law. The thesis of vv. 13-14 is that ***Death*** *reigned from Adam to Moses*, because ***Sin*** *was in the world*. Paul uses the metaphor of a ruling monarch. The evidence of the presence of **Sin** in the world is that **Death** ruled over all people even prior to the giving of the law. The **Sin** could not be tracked or counted, because there was no accounting system, which is what the law provides. But clearly **Sin** existed, because people suffered the consequences of **Sin**, the sentence of **Death**'s rule.

Paul makes this point by distinguishing **Sin** from *transgression* (*parabasis*). *Transgression* means a willful breaking (literally, "a stepping over") of a law. People before Moses did not commit sinful acts by breaking the law, because there was no law. But they still died. Two things are noteworthy in the distinction Paul makes. First, what entered the world with Adam's *trangression* was not "transgression," but **Sin**. Universal sinfulness was not "personal sin." Second, **Death** is conceived primarily as punishment for submission to **Sin**. People from Adam to Moses did not sin as Adam did, by transgressing a divine commandment. Paul is referring to the Jewish teaching that Adam was the first sinner, and his sin was against God's law. "The likeness of the sin of Adam" is identical with the later sin against the law given to Moses. **Sin** entered the world before Adam and caused him to transgress, and subjected all people to the rule of **Death** even when they did not transgress a law.

Paul's explanation of the relation of **Sin** and law makes some very important claims. First, Paul defends the law. **Sin** is not a function of the law. Every human being came under the power of **Sin** before the giving of the law. The law functions to define the shape of **Sin**, but does not cause it. The law reveals what **Sin** looks like (i.e., the rejection of God). That, of course, means that it is only in the presence of the law, only in Israel and the church, that **Sin** is really understood. Second, v. 14 describes the similarity of Adam and Moses. Both were under the law. All other people between them were not under the law, and thus did not "transgress" the way both of them did. Adam as "a type of the coming one" is a reference to Moses rather than to Christ, as in traditional interpretation. **Death** reigned between Adam and Moses, the great models of law, even though all people were not under the law. Third, Paul's interpretation of the relation of **Sin** and law is clearly within the cosmic apocalyptic framework. The problem in the world is **Sin** as power. Humanity exists in a corporate solidarity in **Sin** even apart from personal sin as transgression. The law does not rescue people from that power, but rather helps define the nature of **Sin**.

The Comparison of Adam and Christ 5:15-21

Verses 15-21 compare Christ and Adam in two different ways, by contrast in vv. 15-17 and then by comparison in vv. 18-21.

The Contrast, vv. 15-17

Two negative contrasts with parallel structures are outlined:

> not as, vv. 15a, 16a
> so also, vv. 15a, 16a [implied]
> for if, vv. 15b, 17a
> how much more, vv. 15c, 17b.

The first contrast, v. 15, focuses on the effect produced by Adam and Christ as the two representatives of humanity. The central contrast is *trespass* (*paraptōma*) and *free gift* (*charisma*). The free gift affects all humans in the same way as the *trespass* did. Paul uses a third word for sin, *trespass* (earlier **Sin**, *hamartia*, and transgression, *parabasis*). The word used here means "to fall away or from," in this case from God. The sin of Adam was to reject God. The effect of this one action was that *the many*, that is, all, died. The contrast uses the *much more* argument from vv. 9 and 10. The "one person Jesus Christ" effected *the grace of God even* [rather than *and*] *the free gift in grace* (JET). The double use of grace—*the grace of God* and *in grace*—is amplified by the word *free gift* to underline the gracious gift nature of Christ's work. The gift in this context is righteousness, *the free gift of righteousness* in v. 17, *unto righteousness of life* in v. 18, *will be made righteous* in v. 19, *through righteousness* in v. 21. The free gift of righteousness is not only to *the many*, a reference to those beyond the Jewish people, so as to equal Adam's sin, but *abounded for the many*. It went far beyond what was needed to correct the consequences of Adam's trespass. The correspondence between Adam and Christ is that both have consequences for all humans. The difference is that the grace of God through Christ is more abundant than the sin of Adam.

The second contrast, vv. 16-17, focuses on the agents who produce the universal effects. The contrast also radicalizes the consequences of each agent's action by interpreting it apocalyptically. The key word is the repeated "one person" (*henos, one man*, NRSV). The "sin of one person" is set directly against "the gift of one person." The one trespass produced condemnation, eschatological judgment. The gift is greater than "the one person's sin" and its consequences because it responds to "many sins" and results in righteousness. The contrast looks like this:

one sin $\longrightarrow$ judgment $\longrightarrow$ condemnation

many sins $\longrightarrow$ divine gift $\longrightarrow$ righteousness.

Christ did not simply begin where Adam began. He began where Adam left off by taking on the whole trail of sin that Adam initiated, the "many sins" of all Adam's descendants.

The contrast is interpreted apocalyptically in v. 17. The one trespass, which in v. 15 resulted in the death of the many, here results in the reign of **Death**. One person's trespass introduces the rule of **Death**, total end-time separation from God. Again, Paul uses the "much more" argument to provide the counterpoint. *The ones who receive the abundance of grace even the gift of righteousness shall reign in life through the one Jesus Christ.* The recipients of grace are liberated from the power of **Death**; they rule in life. An eschatological reversal takes place. Verse 17, in addition to intensifying the contrast to the *not as . . . so also* argument of v. 16, also interprets v. 15:

v. 15 by the trespass the many died	the free gift abounded for the many
|	|
v. 17 by one trespass death reigned	those who receive the abundance of grace shall reign in life.

The gift is quantitatively and qualitatively greater than the trespass. Ruling in life is much greater than being defeated in **Death**. The gift of **Grace** will not merely replace the reign of **Death** with the reign of life, but will make the recipients "grace kings." Paul uses a Jewish apocalyptic idea, the reign of the saints, to express the superiority of **Grace** over **Sin**.

5:18-21 Four Comparisons

Paul then makes a series of comparisons in vv. 18-21. The first in vv. 18-19 is structured in two parallel statements (see translation above). The first, v. 18, has two axes, *trespass* (*paratōma*) and *condemnation* (*katakrima*), and *righteous act* (*dikaiōma*) and *the realization of righteousness* (*dikaiōsis*). One trespass results in the condemnation of all. One righteous act produces "righteousness of life" for all. The second comparison in v. 19 returns to the *just as* language of v. 12, and sums up the entire passage so far. The disobedience of one person made the many sinners. The obedience of one will make the many righteous. Verse 19 interprets v. 18:

v. 18 through one trespass condemnation for all	through one righteous act righteousness of life for all
|	|
v. 19 through the disobedience of one the many are made sinners	through the obedience of one the many will be made righteous.

Jesus is the basis of righteousness. His obedience is God's way of making humans righteous and overcoming the **Sin** of Adam. Paul is elaborating the "faith of Jesus" in 3:21-26.

Two humans, Adam and Christ, by their two acts brought about two results. The two acts are disobedience (*parakoe*) and obedience (*hupakoē*). The one was unfaithful to God, the other faithful. What makes the second person so amazing is that he is able to undo the disastrous outcome of the first person's disobedience. The faithfulness of Christ reverses the unfaithfulness of Adam and assures righteousness for all who faithfully commit themselves to God (*who receive the abundance of grace even* [rather than *and*] *the free gift of righteousness*, (JET) v. 17).

Paul follows through the implications of Christ's replacement of Adam by addressing the law's role in bounding sin in v. 20. He pictures the law as standing "alongside," which is widely interpreted as a negative comment about the law. But that is not the case at all. It refers to the law standing alongside as a helper to bound sin. The real question concerns the role of the law "standing alongside." Is the purpose of the law to increase sin? Verse 20b is usually interpreted as a purpose clause. If it is a purpose clause, then God gave the law to increase human sinfulness. That would be a very problematic understanding from the Jewish perspective. The law is God's revelation; it is God's gift of grace to help the people of God bound and overcome sin. In forensic apocalyptic, the law is the God-given solution to the sentence of death that results from the fall of Adam and Eve. In the Dead Sea Scrolls the law is also God's powerful instrument to help the elect overcome evil cosmic powers.

The phrase translated "to increase sin" can be either a purpose or a result clause. If it is a result clause, it describes what in fact the law does. As such, it would then be translated, *the law came alongside with the result that sin increased* (JET). The law shows human sinfulness up for what it really is. The fault is not the law, but human sinfulness. Chapter 7:7ff., which is a commentary on v. 20a, favors interpreting the phrase as a result clause. The problem is **Sin**, not sinful deeds. The law was not able to bound **Sin** as power, but could only show how sinful **Sin** is. The law intensified and solidified the reign of **Death**, because it was not able to overcome the power of **Sin**. The law was not able to be part of the solution, but in a strange way became part of the problem by showing how sinful people were under the power of **Sin**. Paul's understanding of the law here hinges on his understanding of **Sin** and **Death** as cosmic powers. The law helped bound sins, as the Jews believed, but it was not a powerful enough antidote for **Sin**.

The good news is that God's **Grace** is greater than **Sin**. Therefore, the conclusion in v. 21 that "grace reigns through righteousness to eternal life" is the answer to the entrance and reign of **Death** in v. 12.

Comments and Observations

This text is about "one person." "One person" is the most frequent word (12 times); "through one" is the most dominant phrase (10 times). "One person" does something for "the many." There are two "ones" in this text, Adam and Christ. Each is a representative figure. The action of each has universal consequences and introduces cosmic powers that far transcend the one act: **Sin** and **Death** by the one, **Grace** and **Life** by the other. Each has a cosmic legacy. Each creates and represents a people who live with the effects of each one's action. There is an Adam people and a Christ people. The concern is the big picture, the large canvas, not the individual trees.

The focus of the text is Christ and Christ's people, not Adam and Adam's people. The text is about good news, not bad news. It is more about the greatness of Christ's salvation than about the greatness of Adam's sin. That is clear in the structure of the text. In every comparison made between Adam and Christ, every phrase that refers to Adam (vv. 15b, 16b, 17a, 18a, 19a, 21a) is more than counterbalanced by a phrase devoted to Christ (vv. 15c, 16c, 17b, 18b, 19b, 21b). Furthermore, Christ is mentioned in the main clauses, while Adam is relegated to subordinate clauses. Paul's argumentation is from the minor (Adam) to the major (Christ). The "much more" argument is the critical logic. Adam is a problem, a serious problem, but Christ is "much more." Christ corrects not only Adam's sin, but also the sins of all Adam's descendants. Paul is explaining the ground for hope and reconciliation (5:1-11), not the origin and terrible tragedy of **Sin**.

The "much more" argument is even more specific than that Christ is greater than Adam. Paul's real point is that **Life** replaces **Death**. **Sin** produces **Death**, cosmic **Death**. The salvation that Christ offers must be more than the forgiveness of sins; the NRSV translation of v. 18 "one man's act of righteousness leads to justification and life for all men" represents a serious misinterpretation that tries to maintain the old "sin-forgiveness" typology. The text reads literally, "*through one righteous act righteousness of life to all people.*" The traditional "sin-forgiveness" interpretation of Christ's victory—Christ's sacrificial death results in the forgiveness of a person's sin—is replaced by the deeper **Death-Life** interpretation. The ultimate consequence of Adam's sin is apocalyptic **Death**. God's grace that offers no more than forgiveness of sins is no solution for this terminal condition. **Life** is needed to overcome **Death**. Paul pictures the victory of Christ as an apocalyptic event, not merely as an act of sacrificial love. The victory of Christ addresses **Sin** and **Death** as cosmic powers and slave masters.

The way in which Paul develops this story line of Adam and Christ is profoundly Jewish, and much more radical than usually thought. Paul adopts the one Jewish interpretation of Adam as the first and great sinner, but he rejects the second one of Adam as the first patriarch or as the paradigm of salvation and hope. Christ for Paul is the first patriarch, the paradigm of salvation and hope. Christ replaces Adam. Christ is both the Last Adam, the reality of end-time humanity, and the means by which the new humanity is attained, a feature in Jewish theology not ascribed to Adam.

The uniqueness of Paul's Adam-Christ comparison lies in the shift from Adam and his people Israel to Christ and his people—Jews and Gentiles. The role assigned to Israel, in one tradition of Jewish interpretation, has been taken by Messiah Jesus. It is not Israel's obedience that functions to undo **Sin** and **Death**, but the obedience of Jesus. That means the role of the law also changes; it does not bound **Sin** but ends up intensifying it by showing the power and pervasiveness of **Sin** among the people of the law. **Sin** can be overcome and the "lost glory" (3:23) regained, but only through Messiah Jesus. Paul presents Jesus as the climax of the Jewish story, because only he introduces an end-time power strong enough to overcome the power of **Sin** and **Death**.

The magnitude of Christ's victory over **Sin** and **Death** creates a problem for many. If Adam's sin means universal **Sin** and **Death**, then Christ's victory must mean universal salvation. If all are sinners and die because of Adam, then all must be saved because of Christ's "much more" salvation. Paul affirms both universality and individual responsibility. **Sin** is universal—it is a cosmic power—and salvation is universal—it is greater than **Sin** and reverses the consequences of **Sin**. But sin is also personal—"because all sinned" (v. 12)—and salvation is personal—"all who receive" (v. 17) [*Essay: Universalism*].

TEXT IN BIBLICAL CONTEXT

Adam and Christ in 1 Corinthians

The Adam-Christ comparison is used only one other time in the NT, 1 Corinthians 15. Paul compares Adam and Christ twice in 1 Corinthians 15, vv. 21-22 and 45-49.

The comparison in vv. 21-22 is in answer to a Corinthian teaching *that there is no resurrection of the dead* (v. 12). Paul answers in v. 20 by asserting that Christ's resurrection from the dead is a *first fruits* event. That is, Christ is the first evidence of the harvest that guarantees the full harvest, in this case the end-time resurrection from the dead. Verses 21-22 explain the metaphor of *first fruits* in a perfect double parallelism:

for (explaining Christ as the first fruit)
   since through a human being,   death,
   so also through a human being,   resurrection of the dead;
for (explaining how so)
   just as in Adam   all die,
   so also in Christ   all will be made alive.

Paul's concern, as in Romans 5, is Adam as the cause of death and the cosmic consequences of Adam's death, "all die." Adam again is a foil for Christ, this time as the first fruits. Christ answers Adam's death and "all dying" with resurrection and with future "making alive." Paul interprets Adam and Christ in apocalyptic terms. Both are cosmic figures who effect cosmic consequences. Just as Adam determined human destiny, so Christ as first fruits does. The inevitable process of death initiated by Adam will be reversed. Such a reversal is necessitated by Christ's resurrection as the first of the coming end-time resurrection (recall Rom. 1:4).

The agenda shifts from the resurrection of the dead to the nature of the resurrection body in v. 35. Verses 45-49 are part of Paul's answer that different modes of existence involve different kinds of bodies. The Adam-Christ comparison, picked up from vv. 21-22, is used to assert that earthly humanity is like Adam's body, and heavenly humanity will be like Christ's resurrected body. Believers who presently share Adam's body will be transformed in the future to share Christ's resurrected body. Paul makes this point by quoting and interpreting Genesis 2:7 twice (vv. 45, 47). The first contrasts Adam as a living soul and Christ as *a making-alive spirit.* The contrast is not "living soul" and "living spirit," but *making-alive spirit.* The contrast is sharpened even further, by calling Christ *the last Adam* and *the second man.* Christ is both the goal—the paradigmatic person—and the transforming agent—the one who makes alive.

Christ in 1 Corinthians 15 initiates Israel's longed-for resurrection and end-time transformation. The resurrection of Christ guarantees the future resurrection of his people. Christ does this as the *first fruits,* but also as the ruler of the cosmos, who will defeat all enemies, including **Death** (vv. 24-28, 51-57). Jesus replaces Adam, realizes the hope of Israel, and is the focal point and source of **Life** for God's people. *Death is swallowed up in victory . . . thanks be to God who gives us the victory through our Lord Jesus Christ* (vv. 54, 57).

Both Romans 5 and 1 Corinthians 15 view death as a superhuman cosmic power, as **Death.** Both also declare Christ's victory over **Death.** The transformative language Paul uses in Romans 5 and

1 Corinthians 15—Christ defeats **Sin** and **Death**—is expounded else-where in Paul with other "new creation" images. Christ is the *first born of a new family* in Romans 8:29. In 2 Corinthians 3:18 *we all are being changed (metamorphized) into his image from glory to glory.* And in 2 Corinthians 5:17 to be *in Christ* means to participate in a *new creation* in which *the old has passed away* and *the new has come.* Christ effects a cosmic transformation—he replaces **Sin** and **Death** with **Life** and new creation. Christ inaugurates a new age.

TEXT IN THE LIFE OF THE CHURCH

The Preoccupation with Sin

The central focus of this text is Christ and his victory over **Sin** and **Death**. But the church has been primarily concerned about sin in this text. A review of commentaries makes this evident. For example, Luther (1515-16), C. H. Dodd (1932), Leenhardt (1957), Morris (1988), and Edwards (1992) devote more space to discussing the question of sin in v. 12 than anything else in the text. Furthermore, much of the discussion has been shaped by the concept of "original sin" [*Essay: Original Sin*]. Luther and Calvin, following Augustine, have set the agenda. Luther asserts that v. 12 concerns "original and not actual sin." Calvin claims that Adam "corrupted, vitiated, depraved, and ruined our nature . . . he could not have generated seed but what was like himself . . . we are all imbued with natural corruption." Adam's disobedience, it is claimed, fundamentally changed human nature, and this corrupted human nature is passed from gen-eration to generation through biological reproduction. In addition, sin is individualized, as in Luther. Sin is personal, not cosmic or structur-al. Such views are not limited to theologians of the past. They are common today.

Three observations are necessary in response to such interpreta-tions. First, the text says nothing about the corruption of human nature, about sinful tendencies, or about how Adam's sin was passed on in the world. All such interpretations represent theologies that are read into the text, not explanations of what is written in the text. In addition, they both either minimize or struggle with human responsi-bility (therefore, the debate about the relationship of v. 12a and 12d), and God's call for repentance, for moral change. Second, one of the most serious problems of this traditional interpretation is that it mini-mizes and individualizes the nature of **Sin**. The real point that Paul is making about sin is that it is **Sin**. Adam let loose a cosmic power that overwhelms everything and rules history and nature [*Essay: Sin in Romans*]. **Sin** is a cosmic and powerful magnetic force that seeks to pull everything into its field. Nothing can control or bound it, not even God's good and revealed gift of the law. **Sin** is so powerful that *all sin*, all submit to the rule of **Sin** (well, almost all). Third, v. 12 is really more concerned with the consequence of **Sin** than **Sin** itself. **Sin** introduced **Death**, and all die. Paul's starting point is not a theoretical discussion of **Sin**, but the all-pervasive and fearful reality of **Death**. The empirical problem for all people is the coming of the "grim reaper," and that must be changed for God to save humanity and the world. **Death** is a function of sin. That is why Paul narrates the entrance of **Sin** into the world. But Paul does not discuss the origin of **Sin** or explore how **Death** resulted from Adam's disobedience; he simply makes assertions.

The Good News

Romans 5:12-21 is really about good news, not about sin or **Sin**. It announces that the miracle of God's **Grace**, *the free gift of righteousness* has invaded the cosmos in *the righteous act* of one human being, Jesus Christ our Lord. **Sin** did not conquer one person (remember the "almost all" in the last paragraph). Jesus chose not to submit to the rule of **Sin** but to obey God, and thus reveal and release the end-time, transforming righteousness of God in the world. The power of that revelation of God's righteousness "makes righteous," not only "reckons righteous." Paul here is describing the saving power of God that "makes right," that straightens out, the world thrown out of alignment by **Sin**. **Sin** causes people to "miss the mark" or to "step off the road" and thus produces **Death**. Christ puts people "on target" or "back on the road" that leads to **Life**. **Life** replaces **Death**. No, much more than that, the **reign of Life** replaces the **reign of Death**. Christ does not simply return humanity to its original state, but raises humanity to a new level of reality and experience, to the rule of **Life**.

If Augustine, Luther, and Calvin, and their theological children, underestimated the nature and power of **Sin** so do most modern commentators and preachers. **Sin** has been humanized and individualized again, but in a different way. Sin today is defined as moral lapse—a mistake, a flaw, a slip, an abuse. Salvation today calls for therapy, but not for the appropriation and experience of Jesus' victory over the power of **Sin**. God did not send Jesus to overcome individual moral failures, but to take on the power of **Sin** and to conquer the ultimate consequence of **Sin**, **Death**. **Life** is the gift of God *through Jesus Christ our Lord*, not the fruit of my own self-discovery whether alone or with the help of a professional healer.

This reading of Romans 5 should come as no surprise to people in the Anabaptist tradition of the church. The text was central to the debate between the Anabaptists and the Reformers in the sixteenth century. The Anabaptists consistently rejected Augustine and Luther's notion of "original sin." They, therefore, also rejected infant baptism as the means of washing away original sin. Children are born innocent; they inherit no sin that must be cleansed by baptism. Sin, in this tradition, is a function of adults making wrong choices, disobeying God. Though children are inclined to sin, not until they are capable as adults of repenting from sin and accepting by faith God's grace and salvation through Jesus Christ are they morally accountable (see Friedmann, 1973:61-67; 1959:79-82). Friedmann quotes numerous Anabaptist writers in support of this view. Sebastian Franck, in his *Chronica* (1531) puts it this way:

> Nearly all Anabaptists consider children to be of pure and innocent blood and they do not consider original sin as a sin which of itself condemns both children and adults. They also claim that it does not make anyone unclean except the one who *accepts* this sin, makes it his own and is unwilling to part with it. For they claim that foreign sin does not condemn anyone, and in this they refer back to the Eighteenth Chapter of Ezekiel. (fol. 446) (Friedmann, 1973:63)

Not all Anabaptist scholars agree with this representation of the early Anabaptism on original sin. The issue continues to be debated both by the historians of Anabaptism and also in the beliefs of the heirs of the tradition. The 1995 *Confession of Faith in a Mennonite Perspective* says:

> Sin is part of the human condition; we participate in it. The sin of Adam and Eve affects all (Rom. 5:12, 19); at the same time, we are held accountable for our own behavior. As the Anabaptist leader Pilgram Marpeck wrote, any heritage we have received from our first parents does not deprive us of our own final responsibility before God (Ezek. 18). Although human beings have free will, choice is limited. By the grace of God, we have been given the freedom to choose the bond of covenant relationship with God or to choose bondage to sin (Rom. 6:16-18), which leads to final separation from God. (Art. 7.4, p. 33)

These Anabaptists also taught that Christ's victory over sin fundamentally changes human nature (it effects an ontological or metaphysical change). Salvation effects more than a change of status—the gift of "right standing" before God—but in fact makes people righteous. Followers of Jesus are "born again," transformed into new creatures. Therefore, the believers church calls for a life of discipleship in community consistent with the new nature of the Christian (see Friedmann, 1952, 1994; van der Zijpp, 1959; Weingart, 1994).

The Death of the Old Humanity

Romans 6:1-7:6

PREVIEW

Romans chapters 6–8 develop the theme of life in Christ in light of his victory over **Sin**. This triumph means that the followers of Jesus are freed to live a new kind of life, a life that realizes Israel's dreams for the future. These chapters offer one of Paul's great statements on Christian ethics. Because Christians have died to **Sin**, they are to live out the **Grace**, **Righteousness**, and **Life** which they have in Christ. They do not "live out" their salvation by their own strength—**Sin** is too powerful to permit that even with the help of the law—but by the power of Christ, the community of Christ (the church), and the Spirit. Paul urges in these chapters that Roman Christians live out what they are, that they "walk the talk."

Paul describes the new life in Christ by asking and answering three questions in 6:1-8:11: 1) Should we sin so that grace may abound? (6:1); 2) May we sin because we are not under the law? (6:15); 3) Is the law sinful? (7:7). All three questions explore the implications of his radical assertions in 5:20 that the law results in the increase of **Sin**, and that where **Sin** increases **Grace** increases much more. Paul treats the issues in reverse order of the sequence in 5:20: the relationship of **Sin** and **Grace** in 6:1–7:6, the relationship of law and **Sin** in 7:7–8:11. He also reverses the order of treating the subjects in 6:15–7:6. The sequence in vv. 14-15 is law and grace. He first explains "under grace" in 6:16-23 and then "under law" in 7:1-6.

The structure of the argument from 6:1–8:11 is an inverted chiasm:

A Radical claim re the law: *law* increased **Sin** (5:20)
  B Radical claim re **Sin**: where **Sin** increased **Grace**
     increased even more (5:20)
  B Question re **Sin**: Are we to continue in sin . . .? (6:1)
     C Question re **sinning**: are we to sin because we are *not*
        under law? (6:15)
        D Question re **sinning**: are we to sin because we are
           under grace? (6:15)
        D Elaboration on being **under grace** (6:16-23)

    C Elaboration on not being *under law* (7:1-6)
  A Question re law: is the *law* **Sin**? (7:7)

Paul answers the first two questions, 6:1 and 15, by narrating the death of the old humanity and the emergence of a new humanity. The central agenda is the relationship of **Grace**, law, and **Sin**. The thesis is stated in 6:2, Christians have died to **Sin**. Paul makes a principle statement in 6:3-14 that explains the thesis statement, and then illustrates the thesis in two different ways, slavery in 6:15-23 and marriage in 7:1-6.

OUTLINE

The outline is determined by the three questions in 6:1 and 15, and 7:1 (the first two are in the chiasm, the third question elaborates on the second):

Question—shall we continue in sin? 6:1
    6:2 Answer—thesis statement
        Elaboration of the thesis, 6:3-10
            6:3-4 Baptism into Christ
            6:5-7 Grafted into Christ
            6:8-10 Death/life with Christ
        Conclusion—restatement of thesis, 6:11

    6:12-14 Exhortations based on thesis

Question—shall we actively sin because we are not under law but under grace? 6:15
    6:15c-16 Answer—thesis statement
    6:17-23 Explanation of the thesis
        The contrast of "then" and "now," 6:17-19
        The contrast of results/ends, 6:20-23

Question—do you not know that the law is binding only during life? 7:1
    7:2-3 The example of marriage
    7:4 Thesis statement
    7:5-6 The changed ages

EXPLANATORY NOTES

Several things are noteworthy in this outline of the section. First, the initial text unit, 6:1-14, is structured into two concentric inclusios:

Sin, law, **Grace**, 5:20-21—reference of 6:1 question
    Death, **Sin**, 6:2—statement of thesis
    Dead, **Sin**, 6:11—restatement of thesis
Sin, law, **Grace**, 6:14—conclusion

Second, there is a parallel structure between 6:1-3 and 15-16. Both contain a what question, a second question that states the issue, a strong denial to the second question, and a third question which calls attention to the reader's knowledge.

6:1-3		**6:15-16**	
1a	What then shall we say?	15a	What then?
1b	Shall we continue?	15b	Are we to sin?
2a	Absolutely not!	15c	Absolutely not!
3a	Do you not know?	16a	Do you not know?

Sin That Grace May Abound 6:1-11

6:1 First Question: Shall We Continue in Sin

Paul returns to the dialogue style. The opening question, *what then shall we say?* introduces a false inference which Paul recognizes could be drawn from what he has just said. The second question, *shall we continue in sin that grace may abound?* states the false inference. Paul asserted in 5:20 that where there is an abundance of **Sin** there is a superabundance of **Grace**. The question in 6:2 changes the meaning of Paul's statement of fact (*where*) into a causal relationship (*because*).

Why this question? The traditional answer is that some people could twist the logic of 5:20 into a "libertine" justification for continued sinning, that one should actively persist in sin in order to enjoy a greater amount of God's grace.

It is better to read the objection and answer in light of the Jewish understanding of the relation of sin, law, and grace. *What then* questions in Romans always involve Jewish issues and perspectives (3:1, 3, 5, 9; 4:1; 6:1; 7:7; 9:14, 30; 11:17). Jewish theology correlates grace and law. God gave Israel the law so that the covenant people could live by grace. The law is the means of grace to bound sin; it is the mid-point between grace and sin to control and limit sin (grace—law—sin). No one in Judaism taught that righteousness is by the law rather than by grace. No one posed grace and law as alternatives; Jews saw the law as the gift of grace to overcome sin.

Paul in Romans breaks the correlation of grace and law because it limits grace to Israel, the people of the law. The Jewish grace-law correlation runs counter to Paul's gospel that God's promises, and thus God's grace, includes all people, Jews with the law and Gentiles without the law. So, Paul set **Grace** and **Sin** in antithesis in 5:20. He also takes the bold step of linking the law with the **Sin** side of the antithesis, rather than the grace side or even the midpoint between grace and sin (grace——law——sin instead of grace—law—sin, as above). Instead of saying the law controls or overcomes **Sin**, Paul says it is inadequate to deal with **Sin** (see 8:2). The law ends up increasing **Sin**, not decreasing it. To the Jewish affirmation of the law as the means provided by God to deal with sins, Paul's response is heretical.

The question now becomes, if you remove the law as the middle term between grace and **Sin**, in what relation do they stand? Still worse, if you set God's law on the side of **Sin**, are you not saying that **Sin** promotes grace? If grace no longer gives the law to control **Sin**, are you not encouraging **Sin** so that grace may be experienced? The inference here is similar to the slanderous charge Paul mentioned and rejected in 3:8.

It is important to see v. 1 in the light of Paul's apocalyptic argument in 5:12-21. **Sin** is both a ruler and a kingdom, which dominates humanity; Paul is not talking about "sins." The thesis of the false inference is that, since the law no longer functions to control **Sin**, people should remain in the old kingdom of **Sin** in order that the rule of **Grace** should increase.

6:2 Answer—Thesis

Paul rejects the false inference with *absolutely not*! He explains that rejection with a question that emphasizes the present reality of Christian existence. How can people who have died to **Sin** still live in the kingdom of **Sin** (*live in it* refers back to **Sin**)? Paul expects his readers to answer that it is impossible for Christians to live under the rule of **Sin** because they have died to it. The phrase "we have died to **Sin**" is the thesis that Paul now expounds.

Elaboration of the Thesis 6:3-10

Paul explains the thesis statement with three metaphors.

6:3-4 Baptism into Christ

The first metaphor is drawn from baptism. Paul explains Christian death to **Sin** by linking baptism and Christ's death. He does this by interpreting both death and baptism as religious ritual events [*Essay: Death/Baptism as Ritual Events*].

Verse 3 is a chiasm that joins the baptismal formula *into Christ* and the concept of baptism into Christ's death:

A   have been baptized
  B   into Messiah Jesus
  B   into his death
A   have been baptized.

The intentional construction of this chiasm is clear when it is compared with the other baptismal formulae in Paul's letters (translated literally to highlight the change):

into the name of Paul you were baptized (1 Cor. 1:13);
not into my name you were baptized (1 Cor. 1:15);
all into Moses were baptized (1 Cor. 10:2);
all into one body were baptized (1 Cor. 12:13);
into Christ you were baptized (Gal. 3:27).

Paul has altered the normal baptismal formula from *into Christ you were baptized* (Gal. 3:27 is probably the earliest form) to *you were baptized into Christ Jesus* for theological reasons. This text and Galatians 3:27 are the only times Paul associates the name "Jesus" with the baptismal formula. Paul has structured the chiasm to highlight the close association between Christian baptism and Christ's death. The past event of Christ's death is indissolubly linked with the past event of Christian baptism.

The *do you not know* phrase in v. 3 (together with other references to *knowing* in vv. 6, 8, 9, 16) has led many to conclude that Paul is referring to a common early Christian teaching about baptism. The problem with such an assumption is that Romans 6 is the only text that connects baptism and Christ's death (the Col. 2:12 *you were buried with him in baptism* is later than Romans and is linked to the *putting on/off* theme rather than death to **Sin**). Paul often uses *you know that* to introduce an element from tradition which he modifies or expands (e.g., Rom. 6:16; 7:1; 1 Cor. 5:6; 6:15). What the Christians in Rome do know is that baptism is a ritual death and that they were baptized *into Christ* (*into*, i.e., *eis*, was part of the most common baptismal formula in early Christianity for the first two centuries). Paul begins with what the Christians know and adds a new element, baptism into Christ means baptism into Christ's death.

Baptism into Christ has been interpreted in one of two ways. The more popular and traditional interpretation reads it as an abbreviation of "baptism into the name of Jesus." It understands baptism as effecting a mystical (older view) or a personal (more recent view) relationship with Christ. But Paul never speaks of "baptism into the name of Christ," only of *baptism into Christ*. His only reference to baptism into a name is the negative one that no one was baptized into his name (1 Cor. 1:13, 15). The second view is that *into Christ* has a "local meaning." *In* or *into* denotes a place, boundaries, or restrictions. *Baptism into Christ* refers to incorporation into Christ as the inclusive person or into the body of which Christ is the head.

The second view is preferable for several reasons. First, baptism was practiced widely in the ancient world, including in Judaism, as an act of death to a past community and way of life and as incorporation into the life of a new religious community. Baptism by definition means to transfer a person from one religious community to another. The identity of the community can be symbolized by the leader. Second, the context is concerned with corporate entities and realities—Adam as a representative figure, **Sin**, old man, body of sin, slaves of sin, versus Christ as a representative figure, **Grace**, *living in God,* slaves of righteousness, slaves of God. The burden of this text unit is the relationship of Christians to two kingdoms and two lords—both kingdoms and lords by definition involve a community of people. In *baptism into Christ* believers have been transferred from one kingdom into another.

Third, the *with* compound words that are used to interpret the meaning of baptism in the context—*buried with* (v. 4), *grafted together with* (v. 5), *crucified with* (v. 6), *died with* (v. 8), *live with* (v. 8)—all picture an inclusion or incorporation rather than a relationship. Fourth, the parallel baptism texts in Paul all deal in corporate categories. To be baptized into Christ in Galatians 3 means to *put on Christ* and to become part of a new community that changes the way people relate to each other. In 1 Corinthians 10 Israel's *baptism into Moses* pictures an incorporation into the Israelite community being redeemed from Egypt, of which Moses is the representative; it does not describe the establishment of a personal relationship between individual Israelites and Moses. Baptism *into one body* in 1 Corinthians 12 is defined as creating one sociological and spiritual people. Finally, parallel *in* phrases, *in sin* and *in the law*, picture a people under the control of **Sin** or law. People living "in" exist in a domain that is ruled by a master who controls them. Thus, to be *baptized into Christ* means to be transferred from one order of life to another, to be liberated from **Sin's** power and incorporated into the new community of which Christ is the inclusive representative [*Essay: Into/With Christ*].

Paul defines *baptism into Christ* as baptism into his death. Verse 4 adds *were buried with him*. The goal of the burial via baptism is *to the death*. In the ancient world death and burial were one event; a person was not considered to be fully dead until buried [*Essay: Death/Baptism as Ritual Event*]. The point of *baptism into death* is that baptism negates **Sin**. A baptism-sin connection was common in the early church. John the Baptist and the early church baptized *for the forgiveness of sins* (e.g., Mark 1:4; Luke 3:3; John 1:29; Acts 2:38; 22:16; Col. 2:13). Paul is building on a Jewish and early Christian tradition that links atonement and baptism with cleansing from sin. But he does not associate baptism with repentance (*metanonia*), or forgiveness (*aphesis*), or sins (*hamartiai*). Paul's theology of baptism is a combination of baptism as ritual death and as apocalyptic event. Because **Sin** is a power that rules, baptism involves the negation of **Sin**, liberation from **Sin**, and transference to the power and rule of another lord, rather than forgiveness of sins.

Baptism into Christ defined as *baptism into Christ's death* means that the Christian has been incorporated into Christ as an inclusive and corporate person who represents a new kingdom. Christians are people who have made a radical break, they have died to **Sin**; they have been transferred from one ruler and his people to another ruler and his people.

Verse 4 concludes with a purpose clause that is jarring. Paul has just linked Christians with Christ's death. The *just as* Christ was raised out of the dead through the glory of the Father should be followed by *so also* we were raised with him by baptism. The *just as—so also* parallelism really requires it, as does the *through the glory of the Father*. The Christian's death through baptism represents a power event, a death to **Sin**, and should be answered by another power event. The resurrection of Jesus is a power event in Paul (see 1:3-4; 4:24-25). *Glory* is a power word; it describes the power of God gloriously exercised. The phrase *through the glory of the Father* describes a power play, God using power to raise Jesus. The next power play should be to raise Christians with Jesus, but it is not. Rather, it is that Christians may live differently in this life. Instead of claiming that Christians are raised in baptism, Paul compares Christ's being raised with the new moral life of Jesus followers. *Newness* (*kainos*) denotes end-time renewal whereby Christians have a new quality of life here and now.

Christians cannot actively continue in **Sin**, because baptism into Christ means the end of life in the kingdom of **Sin**, and is intended to create lives characterized by Kingdom morality in daily experience. Christ and the body of Christ, the church, have become the middle ground between grace and sin, and God's answer to **Sin**.

6:5-7 Grafted into Christ
The second metaphor comes from the world of medicine. *To be united with* describes the practice of grafting skin over a wound or setting broken bones. It unites two things into one for healing and growth. The metaphor again is corporate. Paul is talking community language, different realities grow into one.

The structure of this second analogy, vv. 5-7, is parallel to the third in vv. 8-10:

vv. 5-7	**vv. 8-10**
"if" question	
if we united to the likeness of his death (v. 5a)	if we died with Christ (v. 8a)
then answer	
but also we shall be resurrected (v. 5b)	we shall live with him, (v. 8b)
explanation and consequences	
knowing that our old humanity was crucified so that the body of sin might be destroyed in order that we no longer be slaves of sin, (v. 6)	knowing that Christ having been raised from the dead, he will never die, death no longer rules over him, (v. 9)
basis and result	
he who has died is made righteous from sin (v. 7)	he died to sin once-for-all ... he lives to God (v. 10)

The *growth together with* is Christ's death. Verse 5 motivates v. 4c; it asserts that Christians should walk in newness of life because they have died a death that is a copy of Christ's death. And since that is the case, Christians also will be united with Christ in a resurrection like his. The first action, death, is past with ongoing effects (perfect tense). The second action, resurrection, is future.

Paul elaborates his understanding of the Christian's death in v. 6 with a chiasm:

A the old humanity
   B has been co-crucified
   B to be completely disabled
A the body of sin.

The *old humanity* and the *body of sin* are parallel and define each other. Both are corporate terms (see Eph. 4:22-24 and Col. 3:9-10 for a similar corporate understanding of *old* humanity). The *old humanity* refers to the people of Adam, the descendants of the one person of 5:12-21 who live under the rule of **Sin**. The *body of sin* is singular with an article in contrast to the personal *in your body* in v. 12. It defines the *old humanity* as the people under the power of **Sin**. The result of the Christian's death with Christ is *the crucifixion of the old humanity*. The peoplehood of the old kingdom has been put to death for two purposes. First, *in order that the body belonging to **Sin*** might be completely disabled. Death with Christ is to make the old enslaved kingdom so dysfunctional that it is not a viable community. The second purpose is that Christians would be freed from slavery to **Sin** (lit., *not to be slaves to sin*, v. 6). The reason is that a person who has died has been released from the reign of **Sin** (lit., *made righteous from sin*, v. 7).

The second metaphor reinforces the thesis of v. 2. Christians have died to **Sin** by being grafted into Christ's death. They have been freed from **Sin's** rule, and entered a new community and mode of life.

6:8-10 Death/Life with Christ

The third metaphor is dying and living with Christ. Verse 8 relates the believer to Christ, but then the focus shifts entirely to Christ. If Christians have died with Christ, which they have, then they also will live with him [*Essay: Into/With Christ*]. The basis for that "trust" (lit., *we believe that*) is the resurrection of Christ, which is a triumph over **Death**. Christ died a unique, a once-for-all death to **Sin**. Christ's resurrection is an end-time event. He was not raised like Lazarus to an extension of natural life, which would once-more-end in death. He will not die again.

The emphasis is upon the finality of Christ's death. Paul underlines this theme with two negatives, not die and not rule and the *once-for-all* phrase. This christology is important because it grounds the anthropology of v. 6, *you shall not be slaves to sin*. Because death no longer rules Christ, Christians who have died with Christ shall not be slaves of **Sin**.

Conclusion 11

The mood shifts from declaring what is (the indicative) to command (the imperative). Because Christians have died to **Sin**, they must continuously choose to think differently about themselves (*logizesthe* is present tense). The new self-understanding is that what is true of Christ (v. 10) is true of them. Christians are not only dead to **Sin**, they are living with God. Christians are living to God *in Messiah Jesus*, in the sphere of the corporate body that Christ represents in the world [*Essay: Into/With Christ*]. *In Christ Jesus* must still be understood in light of the Adam-Christ parallel. It means to live in the kingdom of Christ rather than the kingdom of **Sin**. Verse 11 shows why it is impossible to *live in Sin* (v. 2). Christians cannot simultaneously be ruled by **Sin** and by Christ. Through baptism-death they have been separated from one kingdom community and incorporated into a different kingdom community.

Exhortations Based on the Thesis 6:12-14

Verses 12-14 exhort Christians to resistance, to fight the rule of Sin in their moral lives. The structure is an ABBA chiasm:

> A do not let **Sin** reign, v. 12
> > B do not present your members, v. 13a
> > B present yourselves and your members, v. 13b
> A **Sin** will not reign over you, 14a.

It is important to note that the subject in AA is **Sin**, not the Roman Christians (contrary to many English translations). The subject in BB is the Roman Christians. The first imperative in A is in the third person. It is really a prayer as in the second and third petitions of the Lord's Prayer (Matt. 6:9-10 // Luke 11:2—*let your name be sanctified, let your kingdom come*). Paul brackets the exhortations to Christians with a prayer for God to overthrow the reign of **Sin** and a promise that **Sin** will not reign over them. A paraphrase of this first exhortation might read, "let God arise and end the reign of **Sin**. . ." The purpose is that Christians will not obey the desires of their inner selves (lit., *passions*) to rebel against God. If they do **Sin** will reestablish its rule.

The BB in v. 13 consists of two parallel commands, a negative and a positive:

do not present (or yield)
>   your members
>>   as weapons belonging to unrighteousness
>>>   to **Sin**

but present (or yield)
>   yourselves
>>   to God
>   and your members
>>   as weapons of righteousness
>>>   to God.

The negative imperative is present tense: *do not continue to place yourselves at the disposal of.* Your members (*mele*), *yourselves,* and *bodies* are synonyms. *Weapons belonging to and used by unrighteousness* (*instruments of wickedness,* NRSV and NIV) is military language. Christians are exhorted to stop reporting for the military duty of unrighteousness or injustice. Instead, they are to report to God and to become weapons for doing righteousness. The righteousness here is the righteousness of God, the end-time power of God to make the world right. The language comes from Israel's holy war tradition. Two powers are at war, **Sin** and God. Christians are commanded to resist **Sin**, while presenting arms to God and righteousness (see 12:21 and 13:11-14 for a similar theme in Romans. See also Eph. 6:11-17).

The reason for the promise in v. 14, **Sin** *will not rule over you,* is that *you are not under law but under grace.* Paul comes full circle to 5:20-21 and 6:1. Christians do not live *under the law,* which results in the increase of **Sin**. Rather, they live *under* **Grace,** the counter power to **Sin** that empowers Christians to live within the rule of **Righteousness** and **Life** [*Essay: Grace in Romans*]. In v. 1 *grace* was the problem. Now it is the solution. The problem now is not grace but the law, an assertion that will require further explanation.

Practice Sin to Enjoy Grace 6:15-23

Second Question: Shall We Actively Sin ... under Grace? 6:15a-b

The statement about the relationship of law and grace in v. 14 leads to the questions in v. 15. Do Christians actively practice sin because they are under grace instead of under law? The question continues to pursue the relation of grace, law, and sin.

The way the issue is defined, *under law,* is a problem. The phrase *under* law (*hupo nomon*) is not used in Jewish literature to describe the relation of Jews to the law. It is used only by Paul, and primarily in Galatians and Romans (1 Cor. 9:20 is the exception). In Galatians the phrase appears to be an expression of Paul's opponents to which he responds. It is used to describe the relation of Gentile Christians to the law. To be *under law* is linked to obeying the total law. That requirement in Judaism is especially for Gentile proselytes. Gentile converts to Judaism show that they have broken with their pagan past by *obeying the total law*, by taking on *the yoke of the law*. The specific reference to *my brothers* and *to those who know the law* in the discussion of what it means to be *under the law* in 7:1-6 suggests that Paul does not limit the phrase to Gentile Christians in Romans.

The question of v. 15 is a Jewish one. If the law is not paramount among Christians, then **Sin** is rampant. The law is the barrier to the reign of **Sin**. That is why Christians must keep the law. To now live *under grace* instead of *under law* must mean the power of **Sin** is out of control.

Paul answers with two analogies, one from slavery that applies especially to Gentile Christians, and one from marriage that applies especially to Jewish Christians. The point of each in a different way is that the follower of Jesus is freed from the control of **Sin**. The law does not bound Sin. Something and someone else is needed to overcome its reign.

6:15c-16 Answer—Thesis

Paul answers in two ways. First, he issues a forceful denial, "absolutely not!" Second, he asks a question which at the same time provides an answer. The question is, "do you not know that you are slaves?" The analogy is important. Verses 15-23 are about slavery. The notion of freedom is present only as a contrast to slavery, not as the fundamental point of the argument. The human condition is defined as enslavement. A slave is a person who is owned by someone, who is not free, but must obey the owner.

Clarity about the central argument is important. Paul is not contrasting a good, freedom, and an evil, slavery. He is contrasting two slaveries. The question outlines the alternative slaveries in the starkest terms. The options are **Sin** or OBEDIENCE. Each demands obedience. Each has consequences, death for obedience to **Sin**, righteousness for OBEDIENCE.

6:17-23 Explanation of the Thesis

Paul elaborates the meaning of slavery by contrasting the options of what the Christians were before they became Christians, "then," and what they are "now."

Then	**Now**
slaves of sin, v. 17	obedient out of the heart, v. 17
	freed from sin, v. 18
	slaves of righteousness, v. 18
yielded members to	yielded members to righteousness,
impurity, v. 19	v. 19
lawlessness, v. 19	
slaves of sin, v. 20	
free from righteousness, v. 20	
ashamed, v. 21	freed from sin, v. 22
	slaves of God, v. 22

Paul also contrasts the results of these two options:

to death, v. 16	to righteousness, v. 16
	to type of teaching, v. 17
to lawlessness, v. 19	to holiness, v. 19
to death, v. 21	to holiness, v. 22
	to eternal life, v. 22

Several things about this comparison are noteworthy. First, the fundamental contrast is **Sin** and **Righteousness**. Both are presented as powers that govern a kingdom and that demand obedience from the slaves. **Sin** is described in different ways: as uncleanness (*akatharsia*), v. 19, as lawlessness (*anomia*), v. 19, as things to be ashamed of (*hois epaichunesthe*), v. 21. **Sin** expresses itself in sexual immorality, in violation of the law, in inappropriate behavior. The language used to define **Sin** is very Jewish; it expresses especially Jewish concerns about the sins of Gentiles (see 1:24 and 27 for the use of the same language). **Righteousness** is a synonym for God, v. 22, and clearly has the same connotation as earlier in Romans, the saving power of God to make the world right. But righteousness also is defined by obedience, freedom, slavery, yieldedness or presentation for service, holiness (twice), and eternal life. This word cradle for righteousness indicates that, in addition to referring to God's right making power, the term also has a strong ethical quality. **Righteousness** describes the character of life for those baptized into Christ. It is a life of obedience and enslavement to God, and of freedom from **Sin**. The double reference to holiness introduces new and significant language in Romans. Holiness was both a goal of Israelite life and a claim Israel made for itself in light of her election. Both Israel's claim and goal is a reality for those baptized into Christ.

Second, the categories of the discussion are consistently corporate. The issue is lordship, which by definition involves a community of people, in this case slave communities that have a different ethos and live by different ethics. Third, there is only one imperative in the text unit. Verse 19 concludes the *then-now* contrast with a *just as—so also* argument. Just as Christians once reported for service to uncleanness and lawlessness, so now they must report as servants to righteousness.

The analogy concludes with a final comparison in v. 23. The provisions of **Sin** are death. The word normally translated "wages" really means "provision." Slaves were not paid wages (*opsonion*, provisions, is not *misthos*, wages). Slaves are given goods to sustain them. The provisions of the master, **Sin**, are deadly; they are poisonous, and produce death when consumed. Christians receive a free gift, eternal life. The means and context of the gift is Jesus Christ as Lord.

The point of the argument is that baptism means a change of ownership and a change of community. Followers of Jesus, especially Gentile Christians, have been transferred from the ownership of **Sin** to **Righteousness** (GOD). Transference does not mean freedom. Rather, it means the transfer from one lord and his community to a new lord and his community. The one explicit exhortation, and the implicit exhortation throughout the analogy, is that followers of Messiah Jesus must live by the rules of the new lord and his community. Verse 17 identifies those new rules as a new "pattern of teaching" to which Christians were handed over. Christians were made captive to a new teaching, i.e., the gospel and its ethical claims, through the catechismal instruction they received as new members of the church. Christians as slaves are to live obediently to the new teaching of the new lord, freed from sin, slaves of **Righteousness** and of GOD.

To Those Under the Law 7:1-6

Third Question: Do you not know the Law is binding only during life? 7:1

The third question picks up the *under the law* phrase from 6:14-15. Chapter 7:1-6 is the final text unit of 6:1–7:6 rather than the opening text of 7:7–8:11. The linkage to what precedes is signaled by two things. First, the parallel thematic structure belongs to 6:1ff. and underscores the continuity of theme:

Ch. 6		**7:1-6**	
6:1	Sin	7:1	Law
6:2	We died to sin	7:4	You died to the law
6:4	Walk in newness of life	7:6	Serve in the new life of the Spirit
6:7	He who died is free from sin	7:6	We are discharged from the law, dead to what held us captive
6:18	Set free from sin	7:3	Free from the law

Second, the language of 7:1-6 flows out of 6:1ff., e.g., reigning (*kurieuei*, v. 1; trans. *binding* in RSV and NRSV), the continued treatment of death, the idea of *freed from* (6:6; 7:2, 6), the metaphor of *fruitbearing* (vv. 4-5), and *slavery* (v. 6).

The question is directed primarily to Jewish Christians and their supporters. The readers *know the law*, and are called *my brothers* in v. 4, a designation that Paul elsewhere uses for his Jewish kinspeople (9:3). The question asks if the readers do not know that death means release from the law and its claims, even for Jews.

7:2-3 The Example of Marriage
Paul illustrates the answer to the question with the example of marriage before explicitly stating the answer.

> Married woman——First husband
> dies
> Second husband

The point of the analogy is clear: death puts an end to the legal marriage and frees the wife to *marry another*. The details of the example, the identity of the wife and the husband, are much debated. The most common interpretation says the wife represents the Christian, the first husband is the Mosaic Law, the second husband is Christ. In addition to assuming a very negative view of the law, this interpretation ignores the fact that Paul explicitly says he is addressing Jewish Christians about a very Jewish issue, the role of the law.

An alternative interpretation suggests that the woman represents Israel and the first husband corresponds to the *old man* of 6:6, to which Christians died in baptism. Israel was bound by the law to a solidarity with Adam, *the old man*. Paul is still working out the meaning of Adam and Christ from 5:12-21, especially the relationship of sin, law, and grace from 5:20-21. The law, as Paul has suggested earlier

(3:20; 5:20) and will develop in 7:7ff., has not alleviated the plight of Adamic humanity, but rather made it worse. Therefore, Israel is bound more closely to **Sin** by the law rather than liberated from it. Through Messiah Jesus Jewish Christians have been freed from the solidarity, which bound them to Adam and have entered a new life in Christ.

7:4 The Thesis Statement

Paul answers the question of v. 1 and interprets the meaning of the marriage analogy in v. 4. The argument is particular; it concerns Jewish Christians (*my brethren*). The answer involves a negative and a positive, just as the marriage analogy does. Negatively, the Jewish Christians have been freed from the law because a death has taken place. The means of the death is *through the body of Christ*, through incorporation into the community of which Christ is the head. The positive answer involves a remarriage to the resurrected Messiah. A transfer of reigns and dominion has occurred. Jewish Christians have exchanged the reign of **Sin**, 5:21a, for the reign of **Grace**, 5:21b. They no longer belong to Adam and his people but to Christ and his people. They are not *under law but under grace* so that they may *bear fruit for God*.

7:5-6 The Change of the Ages

Paul explains the thesis statement by elaborating both the negative and the positive assertions of v. 4. The structure of the explanation is a *then-now* analysis. The contrast is the two apocalyptic ages. The double contrast in v. 6—old/new, letter/Spirit—signals the radical nature of the shift of ages.

Then	**Now**
living in the flesh	discharged from the law
sinful passions aroused by the law	dead to what held us captive
work to bear fruit of death	
serve under old letter	serve in new life of the Spirit

The "then" analysis elaborates 5:20, the reign of **Sin**. People "then" lived in the force field of the flesh; the *in the flesh* is clearly the negative counter to *in Christ*. It is the equivalent of *in Adam, the old humanity, the sinful body* [*Essay: Flesh in Romans*]. The law energized **Sin**, fostered its growth rather than bounded it. It linked Jews to Adam and resulted in the intensification of **Sin**. It is the code of an old era.

Two things are noteworthy about Paul's analysis of the "then."
First, he links *flesh* and *letter* for the first time since 2:28-29. There
it refers to external circumcision apart from inner obedience to the
law. It reflects the problem of Jewish boasting in the law for purposes of national salvation. The *death to the law* here is a narrower
notion than usually thought; it is a death to the law as letter, to the law
as the boundary marker between Jews and non-Jews rather than to
the law as the revelation of the will of God. Second, Paul is reintroducing the question of the law's relationship to grace and **Sin**, and
again linking the law to the **Sin** side of the continuum. The implications are so radical, and the potential misunderstandings so extensive,
that Paul will both qualify and elaborate this theme in 7:7–8:11.

The "now" analysis elaborates 5:20b, 5:21b, 6:14-15. The transference of baptism has terminated the power of the flesh, which the
law unsuccessfully sought to control, and inaugurated a new era. The
Jewish Christian does not sin because he/she has died to the law's
power to intensify **Sin**. To be freed from *under the law* does not
mean freedom to sin, but freedom to be slaves of the Spirit. He/she
has been remarried, and now lives with a new partner in a new environment. The Jew is now living in the new, end-time, life of the Spirit.
The new boundary marker is Christ and the Spirit, not the law. This
means a new ethic, which leads away from **Sin** to the fulfillment of
the law through the power of the Spirit. Paul will elaborate this theme
in 8:1-11.

Comments and Observations

Romans 6:1–7:6 argues that the cross-resurrection of Messiah Jesus
fundamentally reorients the world. Christ effects a change of the ages.
That change is the foundation of Christian morality. Followers of
Jesus have died to the old age in the cross of Christ. They belong to
a different people and therefore live differently than people still living
in the old age. They are assured of resurrection with Christ and eternal life in the future. The past, the present, and the future have
changed because of Messiah Jesus.

The change means there are now two kingdoms and two kingly
powers. All reality—cosmic, historical, sociological, theological—
exists in one of these two kingdoms and under the rulership of one of
these powers. The structure of the world looks like this:

Adam	**Christ**
Sin	**Righteousness**/God
In it	In Christ
Old humanity	Grace
Body belonging to **Sin**	
Death	Life
Flesh	Spirit
Law	

Paul's theology in Romans 6:1–7:6 is apocalyptic. The categories are cosmic and corporate, not individual. Human history is the stage for holy war (see also 12:21; 13:11-14; Eph. 6:11-17). Each kingdom makes a total claim on human beings; each lord demands total subservience. Men and women are slaves of one lord or the other.

The foundation of Christian ethics for Paul is that followers of Jesus have died to **Sin** in baptism into Christ. Baptism effects a transfer from one world to another, and together with the faith decision that accompanies it, frees people from one kingdom and incorporates them into another. The new lord, like the old one, makes a total claim for obedience.

Baptism effects a transfer of kingdoms, because it is an eschatological christological event (see Gal. 1:4 and Col. 1:20 for similar "transfer of kingdoms" imagery). It does not have independent power. It is significant and effective precisely, and only, because it is incorporation into Christ's death and resurrection, and into the people God is creating through Christ.

Throughout this text unit death initiates life as the center of new life. **Death** is the ultimate manifestation of the reign of **Sin**, and, therefore, the point at which **Sin** is dethroned and eventually destroyed. The transference from the kingdom of **Sin** to the kingdom of **Righteousness** or from life in the flesh to life in the Spirit requires death. Death effects the change to life not as the realization of human action or potential, but solely as the gift of God in Jesus Christ, as **Grace**. Precisely because the **Grace** is costly—it necessitates death, Christ's and the believer's—its demands are high, total enslavement and obedience.

"Shame" language reappears in this text. It is one of the marks of the non-Christian life, where people were ashamed of their behavior. The opposite of shame is not honor here, but righteousness and holiness. Behavior that is righteous and holy results in honor, lifting people up in chs. 12–15 rather than tearing them down.

The language of this text has some interesting and suggestive links with 14:1–15:13. To be *enslaved* in ch. 6—either not enslaved to **Sin** (7:6) or enslaved to **Righteousness** and God (6:18, 22)—in 14:18 means enslaved to Christ in order not to offend the *weak* in faith. The exhortation to *present* members to service in 6:13, 16, 19 reappears as the command *to present your bodies as a living sacrifice* in 12:1 and as a warning in 14:10 not to judge fellow Christians *because we will be presented to the judgment seat of God*. Paul admonishes the *strong* in 14:17 that the kingdom of God is not about food and drink, but about *righteousness and peace and joy in the Holy Spirit* because righteousness concerns right ethical behavior in 6:13, 16, 18, 19, 20. The theme of *living to/for the Lord* in 14:8 recalls the *living for God* in 6:10-11. The issue of lordship, so prominent in 6:1–7:6 (6:9, 14; 7:1), reappears in 14:9. Because the purpose of Christ's death and resurrection is *that he might be lord of both the dead and the living*, followers of Jesus must remember that they do not live for themselves and therefore they should not judge fellow believers. Paul's argument for Christian morality in 6:1–7:6 is laying the foundation for some practical ethical exhortations in 14:1–15:13.

TEXT IN BIBLICAL CONTEXT

Two themes in Romans 6:1–7:6 appear elsewhere in the New Testament, especially in the other Pauline writings. One is baptism, and the other is dying and rising with Christ.

Baptism

While baptism is referred to often in the narrative writings of the New Testament (e.g., gospels and Acts), the interpretation of its meaning is found in the various letters. Eleven different texts interpret the meaning of baptism; all in the Pauline writings except Hebrews 10:22 and 1 Peter 3:21. Space does not permit a study of all the texts. Attention is drawn only to those with thematic parallels to Romans 6.

The context for the interpretation of baptism in Galatians 3:27 is the change of the ages—*before the coming of the faith* (v. 23) people were under the tutorial restraint of the law, but *now that the faith has come* (v. 25) they are no longer under custodial care. Therefore, *all are children of God through the faithfulness of Christ* (the P[46] reading, the earliest manuscript containing the Pauline letters, is preferred to the *faith in Christ Jesus* reading). People have become children of God because *having been baptized into Christ, you have clothed yourselves with Christ. To be clothed with* is to become a new person, to take on the character, virtues, and intentions of the person. The result is unity, the elimination of privilege based on human distinctions, which divide people in the old age, e.g., race, gender, class. Baptism highlights the new reality of Christian faith, and the resultant new status of oneness and equality among all believers.

In 1 Corinthians 12 Paul is instructing the Corinthians about the relationship of the gifts of the Spirit and the unity of the church as the body of Christ. He grounds the diversity of gifts in the oneness of the body of Christ (v. 12). The *just as—so also* clause (12d) indicates that Christ as the body of the community is the foundation for the unity of the church. Baptism undergirds this unity because diverse people are baptized *by means of one Spirit* into the one body.

Paul makes the same point in 1 Corinthians 1:10-17. Divisions in the church are inappropriate because Christians were baptized into Christ, not into various leaders in the church. Again baptism unifies rather than divides people because it incorporates people into Christ.

The baptismal reference in 1 Corinthians 10:1-13 makes a quite different point. Paul interprets Israel's deliverance from Egypt through the Red Sea as a baptism (*into Moses*) and the gift of manna in the wilderness as the Lord's Supper. The purpose is to warn the Corinthians against immoral behavior. Christians are people living between the ages (*to whom the end of the ages has come*, v. 11). Participation in baptism and the Lord's Supper does not guarantee the reality of end-time salvation if the behavior negates the reality of salvation. The Corinthians are in danger of negating their salvation through misconduct, just as their forebearers did. New reality demands new conduct.

Paul consistently interprets baptism in apocalyptic categories. Baptism negates a past life and incorporates people into a new reality that transforms existing relationships. In Galatians it transcends privileges based on human distinctions, while in 1 Corinthians 12 it unifies diversity. Baptism effects a unity of Christian people. The new quality of life in Christ's kingdom community also necessitates a lifestyle that is consistent with the death of the old age and the realities of the new age (slavery to righteousness, life with God, being clothed with Christ, participating in the bread and drink of the Lord's Table).

Dying and Rising with Christ

Dying and rising with Christ in Romans 6:1-7:6 is an apocalyptic event that is associated with baptism. It means a past death to the old Adamic humanity and the promise of resurrection in the future. Death and resurrection with Christ means the transfer from one dominion and its ruling power to another kingdom and its ruling power.

The apocalyptic theme continues in Galatians, but without any association to baptism. Paul's crucifixion with Christ in Galatians 2 interprets *died to the law in order that I might live with God* (v. 19). The context is the argument that Gentiles and Jews are made righteous by the faithfulness of Christ rather than the works of the law (2:15-21). To be *crucified with Christ* is explained as *Christ lives in me,... and the life I now live in the flesh I live by the faith of the Son of God who loved me and gave himself for me* (2:20). The picture describes a change of dominions and masters again. *Those who belong to Christ* in 5:24 have *crucified the flesh* and live by the Spirit. The struggle between the powers of the flesh and the Spirit, described in 5:16-26, is resolved by Christians through crucifixion with Christ. In 6:11-16 Paul contrasts himself with opponents who boast. His only boast is in the cross of Christ through which he has been crucified to the world and the world to him. Paul's death with Christ is interpreted as a cosmic, end-time event. He has died to the world's value structure and now lives in the context of *a new creation (kainē ktisis)* which transcends the central values and symbols of the old world (v. 15).

Paul's defense of his apostolic ministry in 2 Corinthians 5:11-21 has some significant similarities with the Galatians 6 description of dying with Christ. In contrast to his opponents, who *boast in appearances*, Paul's ministry is motivated by *the love of Christ*. The reason for this motivation is *he that died in behalf of all, and, therefore, all died* (v. 14). The purpose of these two deaths, Christ's and the believers', is *that the ones living might no longer live to themselves* but to Christ. The result is a new world order, *a new creation* (the only other use of the phrase *kainē ktisis* in the NT), in which the old has passed and the new has come. The world has changed so dramatically for Christians that even their worldview is changed, *from the now time we do not know one thing according to the flesh* (v. 16). God effects (v. 18) a profound and fundamental reorientation for people who die with Christ (see further Shillington, 1998:128-41).

Colossians 2:8-15 links dying and rising with baptism. Baptism involves a *burial with him [Christ]* and a resurrection. The death and resurrection with Christ is *through the faithfulness of the working of God, the one who raised him from the dead* (v. 12). The *dying with* is described *as the stripping off of the body of flesh* (v. 11). The result is that Christians now experience *completion* in Christ, who is defined earlier as the one in whom dwells *the total fullness of deity* (v. 9). Christians have already been made alive with God, which is defined as the *free forgiveness of all the transgressions* (v. 13) (see further Martin, 1989:110-17).

Other *dying and rising with Christ* texts could be studied (e.g., Phil. 3:21; Eph. 2:5f.; Rom. 8:17, 29f.; 2 Tim. 2:11f.). All make the same basic point that Christians *die with Christ* and are *raised with him*. Sometimes this death is linked to baptism, but at other times it is not. What is clear is that a real death to a past world occurs and Christians are transferred to a new world order. The language is corporate and cosmic. A change of ages, of world systems, and of rulers is being described. Usually resurrection is promised as the completion point of this transference, although in Colossians 2 that completion is already a present experience. This *dying and rising with Christ* is an eschatological event that is already being experienced by Christians.

To *die and rise with Christ* means the powers of the old age no longer enslave (Rom. 6:2f., 7:1f.; Gal. 2:19; 5:24). Christians are no longer bound by the values of the old world system (Gal. 6:14; 2 Cor. 5:14f.). Christ now lives in Christians (Gal. 2:20), who live by the Spirit (Gal. 5:25) and are part of a new creation. (Gal. 6:15; 2 Cor. 5:17). The structure of human existence has been fundamentally altered by *dying and rising with Christ*. Therefore, these Pauline texts call the followers of Jesus to live differently and to walk the talk.

TEXT IN THE LIFE OF THE CHURCH

The Problem of Sin in the Church

The media is full of "sin" stories among Christians, sins of physical and sexual abuse, sexual unfaithfulness, financial corruption, personal and financial selfishness and greed, lack of integrity in relationships in homes and in the church. Romans 6 is about these sins.

Do Christians live in **Sin**? Paul's answer is, "absolutely not!" It is impossible because they have died to **Sin** and entered a new kingdom community; they have become slaves in the new kingdom. As citizens of a new kingdom, they live differently, present themselves for battle against **Sin**, obey **Righteousness**, and they live out the teachings of the gospel.

What do we do with the gap in the church between Romans 6 and the prevalence of sin in our communities and lives? Is the problem that becoming a Christian no longer involves a fundamental transformation for so many in the church? Is it possible that incorporation into the church is no longer linked with death, with a deep-seated change of allegiance?

The sixteenth-century Anabaptists consistently believed that *being made righteous* effected a real death and a real transformation in people. "The heart" of a believer, Menno Simons said, "is renewed, converted, justified, becomes pious, peaceable, and joyous, is born a child of God." (in Wenger, 1955:115). Salvation renews the divine image in people and makes the believer a participant in the divine nature. Therefore, this tradition especially calls for walking the talk, for living the new life of the new being.

The Anabaptists did not understand such transformation to lead to "perfectionism," to the notion that believers do not and cannot sin. They recognized that Paul speaks of two deaths in Romans 6, a past dying and a present dying with Christ. The two do not contradict each other. Paul is addressing two important and related issues: 1) a decisive event in the past that changes the nature of reality and people, 2) the continued existence of the old world and its magnetic pull for all human beings. If the first is weakened, there is nothing essentially new about the Christian's situation in the world. If the second is forgotten, Christianity degenerates into the kind of spiritualism that Paul battled in the Corinthian churches. Past death and daily present death belong together. There is no complete redemption of humanity until the total transformation of the cosmos. For the present Christians still live in the body and in the world. They continue to be the point of the battle between God and **Sin**. It is still possible for Christians to be slaves of **Sin** by acts of sin. Paul's exhortations are aimed at this possibility.

Christians are active participants in a cosmic struggle with **Sin**. They engage in that struggle as people who have been released from the former slavery, and who have been enslaved to a new master. A new power in a new kingdom now determines their lives. But the power of the old kingdom must never be underestimated. The enslavement of the Christians to the reign of **Grace** must be renewed daily in death to **Sin** and obedience to God. Human beings are saved, become Christians, only because they have a new lord. **Grace** is a new lordship. Therefore, Paul exhorts to remain in this new lordship, and to manifest this new lordship in will and actions every day.

The Challenge of Baptism

Baptism has become a rite of passage in many churches within the believers church tradition. It is what happens in the transition from childhood to adulthood. Baptism for Paul is a rite of passage, but from an old life in solidarity with Adam and **Sin** to a new life in Christ and the Spirit. Might the problem of sin in the church be a function of a low doctrine of baptism? What is baptism a death to in the church today? Baptism is usually not expected to effect much of a change these days. What if baptism became as important in the church today as it was for the sixteenth-century Anabaptists? For them it marked a deep and profound commitment to leave the ways of sin and the world and to follow Jesus even unto death. Baptism in water and the Spirit meant a willingness to accept the baptism in blood, death for obedience to Jesus.

A Narrative Spirituality

Paul conceives of the Christian life as one modeled on Jesus—death with Christ, buried with Christ, to be resurrected with Christ. The believer's life corresponds to the life of Jesus—obedience to God, death, burial, and resurrection. To be a Christian is to be like Jesus, to relive the life Jesus lived. This co-Jesus life suggests a narrative spirituality, a living with and dying with Jesus, which challenges most modern and post-modern spiritualities. Living like Jesus, rather than pursuing self-fulfillment, might also address the problem of sin in the church.

This narrative spirituality says that the modern gospel that "God accepts us the way we are" is nothing less than heresy. God calls Christians to change—to become slaves of Jesus as Lord, to live in God's kingdom, and to become soldiers of righteousness in the battle with evil.

Victory Over the Flesh/Sin Through Christ and the Spirit

Romans 7:7–8:11

PREVIEW

The question in 7:7, *is the law* **Sin***(ful)*, is the third of the questions in 6:1–8:11 that discuss the implications of Paul's statements in 5:20. Paul's concluding comments in the previous text unit (6:15–7:6)—*you have died to the law* (7:4), *our sinful passions energized by the law* (7:5), *but now we are liberated from the law . . . so that we are serving in the newness of the Spirit and not the antiquated code of the letter* (7:6)—require explanation. Does the logic of 5:20 and 7:4-6 not imply that the law itself is **Sin**(ful)?

The problem is clearly the law. The questions of 7:7 and 7:13 define the issue as the relationship of the law and **Sin**—*is the law* **Sin***?* and *does the good thing (law) produce death in me?* The resolution in 8:1-11 again centers on the law, Christ and the Spirit *doing* *what the law could not do.* Paul in 7:7–8:11 explains the meaning of 7:5 and 6. Ch. 7:7–25 elaborates the meaning of the relationship of law with flesh and **Sin**—all the key words of 7:5 recur (law, flesh, **Sin**, passion, members, death). Ch. 8:1-11 interprets the meaning of *discharged from the law* and serving *in the new life of the Spirit*—the key words from 7:6 are explained (law and death, Spirit and new life).

The contrast of the ages—the "then-now" of 7:5 and 6—is also played out—the *I am fleshly, sold under **Sin*** as the "then" is contrasted with *now there is no condemnation in Christ Jesus.* In addition to this structural continuity, there is verbal continuity which binds 7:7–8:11 together. The dominant word from 7:7 through 8:11 is *law* (*nomos*), 20 occurrences in 30 verses plus six uses of *commandment* (*entolē*). The specific reference *to the law of God* in 8:7 picks up the identical phrase from 7:22 and 25. The *dwelling within* theme of 7:18 and 20 reappears in 8:9-11. The "liberation" motif in 8:2 answers the question of 7:24, *who will rescue me.* Two other phrases bind the whole together—*freed from the law* in 8:2 picks up *freed from the law* in 7:3, and *in Christ* in 8:1-2 picks up the *in Christ* phrase from 6:23.

OUTLINE

The Weakness of the Law Due to the Flesh/Sin, 7:7-25

7:7a-b	First Question: What shall we say? Is the law **Sin**?
7:7c-d	Thesis

        Explanation of the thesis, 7:7e-11

7e-8a	First explanation
8b-10	Second explanation
11	Third explanation

        Conclusion, 7:12

7:13a	Second Question: did the good [the law] work death in me?
7:13b-d	Thesis

        Explanation of the thesis, 7:14-25

14-17	First explanation
18-20	Second explanation
21-25	Third explanation

The Fulfillment of the Law Through the Victory of Christ and the Spirit, 8:1-11

Basic Conclusion, 8:1

Basic Explanation, 8:2

First Elaboration, 8:3-4

3a	The state of the law
3b	The sending formula

4a   The fulfillment of the law
4b   The manner of the law's fulfillment
Second Elaboration, 8:5-10
5   The two power spheres,
6   The consequences of the two powers
7-8   The two powers in relation to God and the law
9-10   The state of the Roman Christians
Second Conclusion, 8:11

PERSPECTIVES FOR INTERPRETING THIS UNIT

Several topics and issues present perspectives that permeate the commentary on this portion of Romans. These are both prefatory to, inherent in, and crucial to the commentary below:

A Defense of the Law

Romans 7:7–8:11 is a defense of the law. But why? It is required by two things in Paul's logic. The first is what he has said about the law so far in Romans. He has drawn a series of contrasts, especially in 5:20–7:6, in which the law is consistently linked with **Sin** or evil rather than with the grace and righteousness of God:

Law	**Grace**
Sin	God
lawlessness	righteousness
wickedness	obedience
impurity	holiness
death	eternal life
in flesh	new life of Spirit
old written code	

Such an analysis is very problematic for a Jew. The law is the great revelation and gift of God, so how can it consistently be linked with **Sin**? How can Paul include the law among the powers arousing **Sin** and leading to sin and death? How is it possible to avoid the blasphemous conclusion that the law itself is **Sin**? Moreover, lurking behind that implication is a question about God. If the law is **Sin**(ful), then God is a fraud who tricked Israel by giving her evil in the name of good. Paul must respond to the implications of his analysis. Romans 7:7–8:11 is his response; it is his explanation of 5:20-21 and 7:5-6.

Second, Paul is making the larger case for Christ as the only power strong enough to overcome the power of **Sin** and the consequences of Adam. The law, he has argued, is not able to do that, in fact it results in the increase of **Sin**. He must explain why. Paul does that in 7:13 with two purpose clauses (*hina*), *in order that **Sin** might be seen* and *in order that **Sin** might become exceedingly sinful*. In 5:20 he says the law is very important in God's plan. Rather than bounding and freeing from **Sin**, it serves to focus and concentrate **Sin** in one place, in Israel. Why? So that Christ can deal with it and fulfill the law (8:3-4).

Romans 7:7–8:11 is about God's vindication of the law in establishing a new covenant, which renews the one made with Israel in the flesh and enables the fulfillment of the law in the Spirit. The law itself is not **Sin**(ful). It is God's good gift, but the gift has been subverted by the powers of the **Sin** and the **Flesh**. God's victory over **Sin** and the **Flesh** in Christ and the Spirit makes possible the fulfillment of the law. Romans 7 is not about human experience, Paul's or anyone else's, but about God's law.

The pattern of the argument is from plight (7:7-25)—**Sin** exploiting the law which leads to death rather than life—to solution (7:25–8:11)—Christ and the Spirit overcoming the power of **Sin**. An inclusio—slavery in 7:6 and 7:25—defines the plight and the solution, **slavery** to a written code which cannot overcome **Sin**, and **slavery** to the law of God which equals life in the Spirit of the new covenant and empowers to fulfill the law.

The Meaning of "Law"

Not everyone will share this interpretation of Romans 7:7–8:11. The text unit has been the center of debate since the early church. Two issues are central. The first is the meaning of the word *law*. It has several possible meanings: 1) the covenant law of God, the Torah; 2) a specific law or commandment (e.g., the marriage contract in 7:1-3), the tenth commandment on coveting in 7:8; 3) law as a principle or order; 4) an anti-law, law which expresses the will of **Sin**. The question in 7:7f. is whether Paul is talking about the covenant law of God throughout the text unit. Or, does he also talk about law as a principle of order or even about an anti-law when he talks about the *other law, the law of **Sin***, and *the law of **Sin** and death*? The explanatory notes will show that Paul here talks about the law as the covenant law of God and as an anti-law.

The Meaning of the "I"

The second issue, and the most hotly debated one, is the meaning of the repeated "I" (*egō*). That question is complicated because Paul speaks of the "I" in the past tense in vv. 7-13, and in the present tense in vv. 14-25. Four major proposals have been argued in the history of the church: 1) Paul is speaking autobiographically about himself (the debate then is whether he is speaking of his pre- or post-Christian life); 2) Paul is speaking about every human being; 3) Paul is speaking about Adam; 4) Paul is speaking about Israel. The first interprets the "I" as personal, while options 2-4 interpret it as a rhetorical form.

There is a growing consensus today that Paul is not speaking auto-biographically. A pre-Christian autobiographical interpretation not only is at variance with every description of first-century Jewish life, but also contradicts Paul's own statements about his life as a Jew in Galatians 1:13f. and Philippians 3:4f. A post-Christian autobiographical reading results in a very contradictory picture of the Christian life within a short space in Romans—died to **Sin** in ch. 6, *I am fleshly, sold under **Sin*** in 7:14, *captive to the law of **Sin** which dwells in my members* in 7:23, no condemnation in 8:1. These dissimilar emphases, coming so close together, may confuse readers, leading one to wonder if Paul was confused. But this is not so, as explained below.

The majority opinion favors a reference to every person. It is the nature of the human condition to struggle with law, expectation, and demand. A universal reference to human experience is hardly conceivable, however. The text unit is defined by the use of the diatribe, which, as noted earlier, introduces Jewish agenda. Here the specific issue is the status of the covenant law, hardly a universal concern of men and women outside of Judaism.

An influential minority with growing support in recent years argues for a reference to Adam. Romans 7 does use the language of Genesis 3—*commandment* could be a reference to the command in the Garden not to eat of the tree of knowledge. Jewish tradition defines the sin of Adam and Eve as lust or covetousness; the word *deceived me* in 7:11 is the word used in Genesis 3:13 (it also is used in 2 Cor. 11:3 and 1 Tim. 2:14 in association with the fall). The sequence in Genesis and Romans 7 is the same (innocence, commandment, desire, transgression, death). The motif of knowledge, including knowledge of good and evil, is prominent in both Genesis 3 and Romans 7. **Sin** is personified in both passages, the serpent in Genesis, a power in Romans. The linkages to the story of Adam's fall in Genesis are so strong that one major commentator has argued that the "I" can refer to Adam and only to Adam (Käsemann, 1980). On this model, v. 9a (*apart from the law*) refers to the period between Adam and Moses, vv. 9b-24 to the time from Moses to Christ, v. 25a to the period initiated by Christ.

An even smaller minority, but one that goes back to Chrysostom in the early church (fourth century A.D.), sees a reference to Israel. Romans 7:7-25 is about the law, Israel's unique possession (2:12, 17-24; 3:2; 9:4) and that which distinguishes her from the Gentiles (2:12, 14). The citation of the tenth commandment from the Sinai Covenant in v. 7, understood in contemporary Judaism as a summary of the entire law, underlines the focus upon Israel. This covenant and this law are for Israel, not for anyone else, and certainly not for the Gentiles or every human being. The key verb, "covet" (*epithymein*), is used in OT accounts of the giving of the law on Sinai and Israel's subsequent fall in the wilderness (e.g., Ps. 105:14 LXX; Paul also uses this text to interpret Israel's experience in 1 Cor. 10). Verses 8b-9 interpret 5:13-14—*apart from the law sin lies dead . . .* as referring to the period between Adam and Moses as a time *without the law* when **Sin** was not tracked, and *when the commandment came, sin revived and I died* interprets the meaning of the giving of the Sinai Covenant.

A few scholars recently have suggested that the Adam and Israel interpretation really belong together. Israel, upon receipt of the Torah, acts out the fall of Adam. Therefore, the text combines the language of Genesis 3 and explicit references to the Sinai Covenant. What is being asserted is that law had the same effect upon Israel that the commandment in the Garden had on Adam. Such an interpretation is very much in line with the analysis in 5:12-21 about Adam as the first Jewish patriarch, and Paul's linkage of Adam's and Israel's sin. The discussion in 7:7-25 is Israel specific. Israel, after all, was the nation of the law. The problem is not Adam in every human being, but Adam in Israel and Israel in Adam.

A collective understanding of the "I" is not without parallel in the OT and Jewish literature. The prophets of Israel identify themselves with the nation (Jer. 10:19-20; Mic. 7:7-10; Lam. 1:9-22). The prayers of confession (Ezra 9:5-15; Neh. 9:6-31; Dan. 9:4-19; Bar. 1:15–3:8) and psalms of lament (Psalms, Jeremiah, Lamentations and Qumran) use the personal pronoun to express anguish over Israel's repeated disobedience of the law.

An even more significant factor favoring such a rhetorical and collective understanding of the "I" is the diatribe form of the 7:7-25 text. The rhetorical "I" is used several times by Paul in diatribe exchanges—e.g., Rom. 3:1-8; Gal. 2:15-21. In each case a rhetorical question opens the exchange and is followed by a categorical rejection, *absolutely not.* The diatribe in 7:7-25 personifies the abstract—Adam/Israel, law, **Sin**—to explain the law's inability to overcome **Sin**.

The change of tenses between vv. 7-12 and 14-25 does not argue against such an interpretation. Verb tenses can indicate time, but also aspect or condition. Verses 7-12 narrate an event in the past; vv. 14-25 describe a condition or state. Part one narrates the arrival of the law as an event in the life of Israel. Part two describes the continuing state of Israel living under the Torah. Israel first acts out the fall of Adam and then the death of Adam. Again, such descriptions of both event and ongoing state are not unusual in Jewish prayer and confessional literature (e.g., Isa. 63:5-12; Jer. 3:22b-25; Ezra 9:5-15; *Jos. Asen.* 12:1-13; Tob. 3:1-6; Bar. 1:15–3:8; 1QH 1:21-27; 3:19-29; 11:9-10).

EXPLANATORY NOTES

The Weakness of the Law due to the Flesh/Sin 7:7-25

Paul asks and answers two questions: is the law to be identified with **Sin** (v. 7) and is the law responsible for death (v. 13)? Each question is answered with the powerful negative, *absolutely not*, followed by an explanation of the reason for the negative answer.

7:7a-b First Question

Paul opens the text with the diatribe style. What shall be said about the law in light of 7:5-6? Is the law of God itself **Sin**?

7:7c-d Thesis

Paul's first answer is emphatic, *absolutely not*! Paul explains with a "but" answer. The law is not **Sin**, but it does have some relation to **Sin**, as Paul asserted in 3:20 and 5:13, 20. The law functions to make **Sin** known, or to define **Sin** in categories that people understand and experience. The word for "know" (*ginōskō*) tends to mean personal or experiential knowledge. Paul's thesis is that without the law there is no experience of **Sin** because there is no definition of what constitutes **Sin**.

Explanation of the Thesis, 7:7e-11.

The explanation has a repetitious quality. The opposition of death and life (vv. 9, 10) and **Sin** using the law as an *opportunity* (vv. 8, 11) are repeated twice. The repetition intensifies both the argument and **Sin's** use of the law.

7e-8a First Explanation

Paul illustrates the thesis by citing the tenth commandment against coveting (Exod. 20:17; Deut. 5:21); he quotes only the verb and omits the object (*what belongs to another*). The nature of **Sin** is defined as *covet* or *desire (epithymia)*. This understanding of **Sin** was consistent with a widespread notion in the ancient world that desire was the root of all evil. As noted already, such a summation of the law was current in Judaism (see *4 Macc.* 2:6; Philo, *Decal.*, 142ff.). One word can say so much because the term used for covet covers more territory than the English word. It includes idolatry, sexual sin, tempting God, and murmuring (see Paul's definition of it in relation to Israel in 1 Cor. 10:6-10). Covetousness was the form of **Sin** for Satan and Adam in the Garden, and for Israel in its history with God. The law exposes **Sin** by defining boundaries for human life. It gives **Sin** a military base of operations from which to attack people and nurture covetousness. **Sin** and law are differentiated, but also related. **Sin** is able to make an ally of what was intended as its enemy.

8b-10 Second Explanation
The second explanation is structured as a chiasm:

    A   dead
       B   law
       B   commandment
    A   died
       B   commandment
    A   death

The explanation begins with a thesis statement interpreted by the description of an event. The thesis is that **Sin** is dead without the law. Paul began by asserting that **Sin** is not known without the law (v. 7). Now he makes a more radical assertion. **Sin** does not even exist without the law. The thesis is interpreted by the story of the coming of the law. Israel as the children of Adam were alive without the law until the time of Moses. **Sin** was present, but sleeping. But with the arrival of the law at Sinai, **Sin** was defined and came alive. The law was intended to give life, but it turned life to death by empowering **Sin**.

11 Third Explanation
The third explanation repeats v. 8 with a variation. In v. 8 **Sin**, finding opportunity in the commandment, created desire. Here **Sin**, finding opportunity in the commandment, deceives and kills. Again, the repetition represents intensification. The language comes from Genesis 3, with **Sin** replacing Satan. In Genesis Satan used the commandment to seduce Eve. Here **Sin** uses the law to seduce Israel. The law in both cases was designed to nurture life, and its violation brought death.

Paul's explanations of his opening answer clearly qualify his statements about the law in 7:5-6. The law "energizing our **Sin**(ful) passions" is explained as the law making **Sin** known and **Sin** using the law as a base for military operations. The word *aphormē* in vv. 8 and 11 (*opportunity* in most translations) pictures the law as a military base—scouts and troops are sent out from this base to spy on and conquer people. The law itself now does not energize **Sin** but is used by **Sin** to activate sinful behavior and thus *enslave* people.

Conclusion 7:12

So that (*hōste*) introduces a conclusion. Paul has differentiated **Sin** and the law. The problem is **Sin**, not the law. The law was not able to give Israel a realm where the power of **Sin** could not operate. In Eden and at Sinai the law provided **Sin** a leverage with which to push every Israelite into the force field of **Sin**. The conclusion, and the answer to the question in v. 7, is that the law is absolved of any responsibility for **Sin**. The law is not **Sin**. Rather, it is holy; it comes from God. Paul could hardly use a stronger theological word to affirm the law. It participates in the very nature of God, and is what Israel is to be before God. And the imperative quality of the law, the commandments, share the attributes of the law. They are holy in origin, righteous in nature, and good in their effects. The law in whole and in part reflects the character of God. It is the opposite of **Sin**. The problem is that **Sin** is able to use it against its nature.

7:13a Second Question: Did the Good (the Law) Work Death in Me?

Paul's affirmation of the law creates a problem. The law is good, but it leads to death. Paul frames the problem with the last words of the previous three sentences, *to death* (v. 10), *to kill* (v. 11), *the good* (v. 12). Does the good, that is, the law, produce death; that is, does the law kill? Does good create evil?

7:13b-d Thesis

Absolutely not is Paul's first answer. As in v. 7, Paul follows up with a "but" answer. *But* **Sin** serves a purpose, which is explained in two purpose clauses with "through" or "by means of" phrases. The first purpose is that **Sin** *might be revealed through the good working death in me.* The good, which is the law, unmasks **Sin** and gives it clearly defined boundaries. The result is that the law *works* death, because people are pulled across the boundaries by **Sin**. *Works*, as a verb (*katergazomai*), first used in v. 8, is the thematic verb of this section (vv. 13, 15,

17, 18, 20). It means to *create* or *produce*. The law creates death by drawing boundaries which people cross. The second purpose of the law intensifies the first. The law serves *to make **Sin** sinful to an extraordinary degree*. It demonstrates the real character of **Sin** and its consequences, death. At precisely the time that **Sin** appears to have conquered the law, the law proclaims God's will. It fulfills the divine purpose by revealing the radical sinfulness and awful result of **Sin**.

Explanation of the Thesis 7:14-25

Paul elaborates the thesis in three arguments, carefully constructed in parallel fashion. Each begins with a statement of self-knowledge, moves to a description of behavior, and ends with confession that confirms the knowledge admitted at the beginning of the argument.

vv. 14-17	vv. 18-20	vv. 21-25
For I know that the law is spiritual, but I am fleshly, sold under **Sin**. For what I do, I do not understand.	For I know that good does not dwell in me that is, in my flesh.	Therefore I find that when I wish to do the law, the good, that evil lies close by.
	The good I wish lies close by, but not doing the good.	
For what I do not wish this I do.	For the good I wish, I do not do.	I delight in the law of God in the inner being.
But what I hate, this I do. I do.	But the bad I do not wish, this I do.	But I see another law in my members warring against the law of my mind, and taking me prisoner to the law of **Sin** that exists in my members.
And if not what I wish this I do,	And if not what I wish this I do,	
I agree that the law is good.		
		Wretched person I am! Who will rescue me out of the body of this death?

		Thanks to God through Jesus Christ our Lord.
Now not I working it, but the **Sin** living in me.	not I working it, but the **Sin** living in me.	Therefore, then I, I serve the law of God in my mind, and in the flesh the law of **Sin**.

The argument is clearly repetitive. The first two explanations conclude with the same phrase, *I do not do it, but the **Sin** living in me.* There is progress and intensification within the repetition.

14-17 First Explanation

Paul's first explanation builds on an imbalance of being (ontology). He affirms the Jewish axiom of v. 12. The law is *spiritual (pneumatikos)*, it comes from and embodies the Spirit of God. Israel, which is *fleshly (sarkinos)*, exists in sharp contrast. Israel belongs to the realm of the flesh, and is determined by the flesh [*Essay: Flesh in Romans*]; she is living in and for the world. Israel's fleshly nature is further defined as *sold under **Sin***. The word sold comes from the world of slavery. Israel has sold itself into the slavery of **Sin**.

The split between the law and Israel produces a divided being. The Jewish people as a people do not practice what they wish, but do what they hate. They are caught in the contradiction between willing and doing (remember 2:17-24). This split reveals that Israel acknowledges the law as good, and that the problem is **Sin** dwelling within.

18-20 Second Explanation

The second explanation begins with the confession of the first explanation. **Sin** living within means that the good (the law) does not dwell within, that is, in the flesh. The focus shifts from the law entirely to the "I." The split between wishing and doing is total; the difference is intensified by the characterization of behavior as "good" and "evil." The "I" is completely impotent to do the good which lies close by; instead, it does the evil. The resulting confession repeats the lament of the first explanation (v. 17), **Sin** living within produces disobedience. The problem is no longer the "I," but **Sin**, an internal power which controls actions. Paul's apology for the law has now advanced significantly beyond the initial argument—the law is good. To this affirmation he has added two arguments: 1) Israel is equally blameless because it agrees with the law and condemns sinful behavior; 2) **Sin**, residing in Israel and dominating the flesh, is responsible for evil.

21-25 Third Explanation

The final part of Paul's explanation involves a complex wordplay on the word law (*nomos*). It introduces a startling new metaphor, an anti-law. The "I" finds that when it wishes to do the law, which is defined as good, evil lies close at hand. The good law in v. 21 refers to the Torah. Paul is summarizing the central arguments of the preceding explanations by rephrasing v. 10 and by using the good and the evil contrast of vv. 18-19.

v. 10: I found in me the commandment   to life   to death
v. 21: I find the law   the good   the evil

All the references here denote the Torah. Apart from a clear signal that a different kind of law is being introduced, such as Paul gives in vv. 22f., a Torah reference is required by his prior references in Romans to the law as the Torah of God. Paul returns to an explicit defense of the law following the implicit defense of the divided "I." Israel wills to do the covenant law, but finds that evil stands in the way. Paul explains why the law is inadequate as a means of grace to bound **Sin**. The law informs the will of Israel, but is not able to empower the doing. The law is too much the tool of evil to be able to overcome **Sin**.

Paul further explains the weakness of the law by contrasting two laws. The contrast is sharpened by another use of the opposites *the good* and *the evil*. The one law, the law of God, is good, and "a different law" or an anti-law is evil. Here two different laws are clearly under discussion [*Essay: Law in Romans*].

the good   **the evil**
law of God, v. 22   different law, v. 23
law of my mind, v. 23   law of Sin, v. 23
law of God, v. 25   law of Sin, v. 25

The law of God cannot be evil (7:7). The "different law" is other than and standing over against the law of God; as evil, it cannot be the law of God.

Israel prefers the law of God. The *inner self* (lit., the inner person, that is the inner center of thinking and willing) and *the mind* are synonyms for the "I." It *delights in the law*, one of the highest expressions of piety in the Psalms (e.g., 1, 119) and the goal of every good Jew. The problem is that a war is waging within (*in my members*) that takes Israel captive to the law of **Sin** that also exists *in my members*. The language is provocative. Israel has been defeated in war. The crisis of the defeated and broken self, at war and enslaved, is deepened by **Sin's** creation of an anti-law. **Sin** living within has created its own law that takes Israel captive against its will. The *captivity* of the law in 7:6 has been qualified radically and redefined as captivity to the law of **Sin**. The verbs for *captivity* in 7:6, *hold down*, and 7:23, *speared down*, offer dramatic pictures of the reinterpretation of 7:6 in 7:23.

Israel's situation is desperate. The future is death (*the body of this death*). Therefore, the anguished confession and cry of v. 24. A dramatic and powerful rescue operation is Israel's only hope. The word for rescue (*hruomai*) consistently has an eschatological nuance in the NT. It describes a deliverance from the powers of this age, here **Sin** living in the flesh. Paul thanks God for the victory through Christ. He will interpret the nature and meaning of the victory in 8:1-11.

Paul returns from the brief anticipation of future salvation in vv. 24b-25a to define the terms of Israel's condition. The emphatic "I" (lit., "I, I") *serves the Torah of God in my mind and in the flesh the law of* **sin**. Israel recognizes that its last hope, the law of God, to which she wishes to be enslaved rather than to **Sin**, is incapable of delivering her. The presumed agent of deliverance has been overpowered and perverted by **Sin**.

While vv. 24-25 conclude the first part of the argument in 7:7–8:11, they are also transitional. Verses 24a and 25b summarize the argument Paul has been making in 7:7-25. Verses 24b-25a anticipate the argument Paul will make in 8:1-11.

The Importance of the Verbs

The explanation is dominated by three kinds of verbs, knowing, willing, and practicing. The "knowing" verbs are: *we know* (v. 14), *I understand* (v. 15), *I agree* (v. 16), *I know* (v. 18), and *I find* (v. 21). Two phrases with verbs of "knowing" plus an object, *I delight in the law of God* (v. 22) and *I see another law* (v. 23), intensify the emphasis on knowledge. Four things are known: the law of God, the reality of disobedience, the power of the flesh, the existence of an anti-law. The verb "to will" is used five times, vv. 15b, 16a, 18b, 20a, 21a; "to hate," another volitional word, is used in v. 15b. The "I" wills to obey the law and do the good. Verbs of doing—creating (*katergazomai*, vv. 13, 15, 17, 18, 20), doing (*prassō*, vv. 15, 19, and *poieō*, vv. 15, 16, 19, 20, 21)—are used 12 times. The "I" has the will; the volition is strong and on target. But the practice has been defeated in war and taken captive. It languishes in the chains of **Sin** in the flesh. The knowledge is informed, the will is active and strong, but the practice is mortally wounded.

Comments and Observations

Paul makes a vigorous and provocative defense of the law. The subject of Israel's plight is never the law, but always **Sin**. The law is
involved, but as a passive instrument. It was intended as a counter-
weight to **Sin** but has been neutralized, or *weakened* as 8:3 says. The
law is and remains the covenant law of God; holy, righteous, good,
and spiritual.

The problem is **Sin** as personified power. **Sin** is not a transgression or a misstep. Rather it is a power that conquers and rules the cosmos and every human being. Even worse, **Sin** is a tyrannical power
that lives within Israel. **Sin** as power resides in the domain of the flesh,
the force field operating through the body and linking people with the
world system of the old age. The flesh and the Spirit are competing
force fields. **Sin** as power dominates the force field of the flesh.

Israel never hears the law at ground zero, as neutral, free to practice the obedience the law calls for. **Sin** is prior to the law. Only Jews
already involved with **Sin** hear the law. **Sin** is more powerful than
even the holy law of God because **Sin** rules and resides within; it is
already present and operating when the law is first heard. Israel, and
only Israel in a primary sense because only she possesses God's
unique gift of the Torah, is victimized before the arrival of the law.
Vis-à-vis this situation no law, not even God's law, can liberate the Jew.

But why this overwhelming concentration of **Sin** in Israel? Why a law
from God that cannot deal with the power of **Sin**? Paul's defense of the
law again raises profound questions about God. Has God given Israel a
gift that only traps her deeper and deeper in **Sin**? If the primary function
of the law is to reveal the "extraordinary" nature of **Sin** as power, has
God not created unredeemable evil? Is not God the source of evil?

Paul's defense of the law has been misunderstood by many.
Romans 7:7–8:11 may well be his most important teaching about the
law. The gift of the law serves to focus and concentrate **Sin**/sin. The
law magnifies **Sin**/sin within Israel. It could not do that anywhere else
because no other people had the law. Where there is no law, there is
no sin. The law results in the increase of sin (5:20), and is, in fact,
intended to reveal the enormity and the indescribable tragedy of
Sin/sin (7:13). The incredible drawing together and concentration of
Sin/sin in Israel, the people of God, is intentional, Paul argues. The
reason is explained in 8:1-11, so that **Sin** can be dealt with and
defeated by Israel's representative, Messiah Jesus [*Essay: Law in
Romans*]. The law is associated with the **Sin** side of the **Sin—Grace**
continuum—it is connected to flesh, lawlessness, impurity, letter,
death—to make possible **Grace**. Universal **Sin** is particularized,

brought together in one people and one place, to make possible particular salvation for all, salvation through one person in one place for the cosmos and all human beings.

The Fulfillment of the Law Through the Victory of Christ and the Spirit 8:1-11

The nature of the argument shifts from the diatribe to assertion. Paul moves from asking and answering questions to proclaiming and exhorting. The argument is a syllogism, a form of reasoning that consists of three propositions: 1) a major premise, 2) a minor premise, 3) a conclusion. The truth of the conclusion depends on the truth of the premises. The conclusion here precedes the minor premise:

1) major premise—the problem is **Sin** and death operating through the law, 7:7-25;
3) conclusion—there is no condemnation for those in Christ, 8:1;
2) minor premise—God has overcome the problem, 8:2-11.

Three other features of the text are important. First, 8:1-11 is interpreting 7:6, life in the Spirit. Therefore, Spirit language dominates the text. Spirit has been referred to only five times so far in Romans, but occurs 21 times in 8:1-39, 11 times in vv. 1-11 alone. Almost always *spirit* (*pneuma*) refers to the Spirit of God (the human spirit is mentioned only in vv. 15 and 16).

Second, the text is about opposites, Spirit and **Sin** in v. 2, and Spirit and flesh in vv. 4-11. The first half of the text unit, 7:7-25, pictures Israel suffering under **Sin** and the flesh; the second half presents the Spirit overcoming **Sin** and the flesh. The relationship of the two parts of the text is the "once-now" structure of Paul's theology, **once** under the power of **Sin** and flesh, which used the law against itself for death, but **now** in Christ and the Spirit fulfilling the law and experiencing life.

Third, 8:1-11 also picks up and builds on 5:12-21. The key word of Paul's conclusion in v. 1, "condemnation" was last used in 5:18 to compare Adam and Christ. In 5:18, which is the climax of the vv. 12-19 comparison of Christ and Adam, "condemnation" is the result of Adam. It also appears just prior to the radical assertion in 5:20 that the law is linked to **Sin**. Paul now shows how the linkage is overcome.

Basic Conclusion 8:1

Paul asserts his conclusion, *therefore, now there is not one condemnation to the ones in Christ Jesus.* The previous sentence,

7:25b, began with *therefore, then* (*ara oun*), and ended with *I serve the law of* **Sin** *in the flesh*. The counter is *therefore, now* (*ara nun*). Paul offers an eschatological contrast; "now" describes the reality of the eschatological future in the present time. "Now" there is *not one condemnation*, no end-time judgment. Such judgment has been eliminated *for the ones in Christ Jesus*, for those in the body of Christ, the church. The end-time judgment which Israel deserved for enslavement to **Sin**, and service to the law of **Sin**, has been removed.

Basic Explanation 8:2

Verse 2 is explanatory (*for*). It offers the principle explanation for the conclusion stated in v. 1. There is no condemnation because there is freedom. The nature of the freedom is clearly defined. One law has freed from another law, *the law of the Spirit of life in Messiah Jesus* has freed *from the law of* **Sin** *and death*. The two laws of 7:22-25, the law of God and the anti-law, appear once more. Both are described in the language of 7:7-25. The first one is *the law of the Spirit of life*; the terms come from 7:14 (the law is spiritual) and 7:10 (*the commandment is to life*). The law that comes from God is the law of the Spirit of God, and that law produces life. The *other law* is *the law of* **Sin** (7:23, 25) that produces death (7:24). The law is defined in terms of two power structures—the law of the Spirit and the law of **Sin**. The law of the Spirit is stronger and frees from the law of **Sin**. This liberation is effected in and through Messiah Jesus. The phrase *in Messiah Jesus* is placed before the verb *freed* in Greek to emphasize the means of the freedom.

There is no end-time condemnation for those in Messiah Jesus, because the Torah of God has been liberated for its intended goal of life by the Spirit and Christ. Law, Spirit, Christ, and life are linked positively. "What we have here," Tom Wright says correctly, "is Pentecost-theology; as the Jews celebrate the giving of Torah, so the church celebrates the giving of the Spirit, not to abolish but to fulfill the earlier gift and its final intention" (1991:209).

First Elaboration 8:3-4

Paul's explanation (v. 2) of his conclusion (v. 1) is so provocative that he must interpret what he has just said. Verse 3a restates premise a), the problem is **Sin** operating through the law. The problem is that *the law was powerless because it was weakened through the flesh*. The NRSV translation, *what the law could not do*, is misleading. The NIV rendering, *what the law was powerless to do*, is more accurate. The word used for power (*dunamis*) is the same one used to describe the power of the gospel in 1:16, only here a prefix is added which changes power into powerlessness. The power loss was due to *weakness*, more literally *illness*, which was caused by the power domain of the flesh. The problem is not the law, but the flesh; it injected a virus that produced illness.

God mounted a rescue operation. *God sending his own son* is "a sending formula" used in the early church to formulate a christology. The point of the christology is that God sends the son *in the likeness of sinful flesh* to effect redemption. Messiah Jesus identified fully with the human condition. Two terms are critical. *Likeness* describes a completely adequate expression of a reality. *Flesh* means solidarity with humanity and a power or sphere of power [*Essay: Flesh in Romans*]. Christ fully identified with the power of **Sin** in the power sphere of the flesh (see 2 Cor. 5:21 for a similar statement of Christ's radical identification with the human condition).

The form of the redemption effected by Christ is defined as "a sin offering" (*peri hamartias*). The language has Old Testament sacrificial associations. A sin offering is an offering for "sins of ignorance," sins that the Israelite did not wish to commit, which is precisely the problem described in 7:7-25. The crisis of 7:7f. is that people delight in the law of God, but find themselves unable to do it. Paul says that Jesus resolves that problem. The result of the sin offering is that Messiah Jesus *condemned* **Sin** *in the flesh*, dealing with the problem of **Sin** in its domain, its own force field. God breaks the power of **Sin** by Jesus who liberates the law from **Sin** and death. A great reversal is effected by the son in the flesh.

Verse 4 states the purpose of the son's sending and redemptive action. It is *in order that the righteous requirement of the law might be fulfilled*. The term *righteous requirement of the law* (*to dikaiōma tou nomou*) is singular, describing the righteous requirement of the law as a whole or as a unity. It is "fulfilled" (the verb is passive) "among us" (*en*), not "by us" (*dia*). Something is accomplished for followers of Jesus. The righteous requirement of the law, precisely what the law of God required in 7:14-25 and which the "I" willed to fulfill, has been fulfilled by Messiah Jesus. Law fulfillment is not something done by followers of Jesus, Jew or Gentile, but by the faithfulness of Jesus. There is no end-time condemnation in Christ (v. 1), because the law is fulfilled and because **Sin** is condemned in the flesh (v. 4).

To the one not walking according to the flesh but according to the Spirit indicates the manner of the law's fulfillment. *Walk* is a metaphor for ethics; it describes life that is conducted according to a standard. The standard is defined as *according to the flesh* or *accord-*

ing to the Spirit. Two rules or force fields of power are pictured. The old power structure of the flesh/**Sin** has been displaced by the new power structure of the Spirit, which is the Spirit of Christ (vv. 2, 9). Followers of Jesus walking in the power field of the Spirit fulfill the law. The fulfillment of the just requirement of the law is not the goal of Christian doing, but its basis and context. The law is not fulfilled because it has been internalized (Jer. 31 is not the background), but because the Spirit has been internalized. The Spirit now lives where **Sin** once lived. Therefore, the law is fulfilled.

The Second Elaboration 8:5-10

The author's use of *for* multiple times in 5a, 6a, and 7 (twice) and *because* in v. 7 indicate that Paul now explains the meaning of the *flesh—Spirit* contrast at the end of v. 4.

To *live* or *be according to something* is to obey it, and hence to live within its power structure. People, Paul says, live in one of two kingdoms or under one of two rulers, flesh or Spirit. The kingdom determines the thought pattern or the worldview. "The things of the flesh thinking" describes more than simply "thinking about fleshly things," just as "the things of the Spirit" is talking about more than spirituality. Paul is describing a fundamental value system, a moral center or compass, which shapes how people live. The options are the rule of a worldview determined by the flesh or the rule of a worldview determined by the Spirit.

The consequence of the flesh worldview is death, complete separation from God (v. 6). The consequence of the Spirit worldview is life and peace. The great goals of the Jewish people and the Hebrew Scriptures, life and well-being, are obtainable through the rule of the Spirit.

The reason the worldview of the flesh is so fatal is grounded in its view of God (vv. 7-8). This worldview is characterized by a state of eneminess to God; it is actively hostile to God. It is further defined as a refusal to submit to God's law. The law of God is a good thing (7:7-25); it reveals the will of God. To choose to submit or obey that law (lit., *to order oneself by it*) is the mandate for the Jewish people. But people with a fleshly worldview do not; in fact, they are powerless to do that (the same word used to characterize the law as powerless in v. 3). The fundamental problem of the fleshly worldview is that it does not give people the power to please God. The implication, though not stated, is that the people living *according to the Spirit* fulfill the law and thus please God. Paul again emphasizes that the flesh is the problem of the law, and that the Spirit is God's answer to that problem. Paul's alternatives can be schematized like this:

Flesh Worldview	**Spirit Worldview**
hostility to God	peace with God
disobey the law	fulfill the law
death	life

Paul addresses his Roman audience directly in vv. 9-10. He personalizes the more abstract worldview discussion with "you," and in the process offers one of his clearest statements on the nature of the Christian life. Followers of Jesus live under the rule of the Spirit, not the rule of the flesh, if the Spirit of God dwells in them, which the Spirit does. Paul makes an assertion, a statement of fact (the "if clause," or conditional sentence, is a fulfilled condition). Followers of Jesus are people of the Spirit, people who live in the worldview and power sphere of the Spirit. Paul adds, a person who does not have the Spirit of Christ does not belong to Christ, that is, is not a Christian.

The result of having the Spirit, and thus being a follower of Jesus, is stated in v. 10. *If Christ is in you (which he is), the body [is] dead because of* **Sin** *and the Spirit [is] life because of righteousness.* Paul's opening, *Christ in you,* is unusual. He normally talks about *believers in Christ* (the only comparable phrase is *Christ lives in me* in Gal. 2:20). *Christ in you* is synonymous with *you in the Spirit, Spirit of God dwells in you,* and *Spirit of Christ has* in v. 9. The Spirit is defined as *the Spirit of God* and the *Spirit of Christ.* The context of the Spirit is described as *in you* (plural), or with the possessive *have.* The two references to the Spirit and the *Christ in you* phrase are synonymous descriptions of the Spirit worldview or power sphere. The equation of three different terms to describe the reality of the Spirit is characteristic of Paul. For Paul, Messiah Jesus is the fullest manifestation of God. The Spirit is the Spirit of God and of Jesus. The church is the body of Christ and the fellowship of the Spirit. The one Spirit constituted one body, one community of those who received the Spirit. The followers of Jesus, Jew and Gentile, at one and the same time are the body of Christ, possess the Spirit of God, and have Christ present in the community. Thus, *Christ in you* is not primarily an individual experience. It was always an experience *in Christ,* that is, within the body of Christ. To be *in Christ* is to share in the surge of charismatic life which flowed from the Spirit and within the Christian community. It was essentially a social rather than an individualistic phenomenon.

To live *according to the Spirit* is to live within the community of the Spirit that is shaped by the Spirit worldview given by God. The result of living in the power sphere of the Spirit is life. The quality of that life is described as *the body is dead because of **Sin** and the Spirit is life because of righteousness.* Paul is talking here about the life in the Spirit. He is not contrasting two forms of life, life in the flesh and life in the Spirit. Therefore, *the body is dead because of **Sin*** is a reference to the death to **Sin** of the Spirit led, Christ possessed, people (a summary of ch. 6). The people in whom Christ is present have died to **Sin**, and thus are released from its controlling power. They also experience the life-giving quality of the Spirit because of the righteousness of God revealed in the world through Messiah Jesus. Righteousness language, reintroduced for the first time since 6:20, is presented as the antithesis to **Sin** as in ch. 6. The Spirit gives life, because the righteousness of God has overcome **Sin**.

Second Conclusion 8:11

Paul's first conclusion asserted that there is no condemnation in the present time. The second conclusion expands the life-giving quality of the Spirit's presence (vv. 2, 10). *If the Spirit of the one [God] who raised Jesus from the dead dwells in you, which he does,* then *God will give life to your mortal bodies through his Spirit which dwells in you.* The indwelling of the Spirit is the guarantee of a life-giving process, which in the future will transform (*will give life* is a future tense) even the mortal body that is now destined for death. The life the Spirit gives leads to resurrection, the ultimate vindication of God's people. The old dualism of flesh and spirit is overcome in a new unity. Condemnation is replaced by life for *those in Christ* and for the people of the Spirit. But note, there is a close connection between the power of the Spirit and the life, death, and resurrection of Christ. Paul will develop that connection in the next section.

Comments and Observations

Paul's logic in this text unit is both clear and complex. **Sin** caused death, and so prevented the law from giving life. The law exposed **Sin**, and so caused it to be focused and concentrated in one people and one place. **Sin**, collected in this one place, is dealt a decisive death-blow through God's sending the Son in the likeness of sinful flesh. When God condemns **Sin** in the flesh of Christ on the cross, **Sin** is rendered powerless. The Spirit, of God and of Christ, becomes the power that makes possible law-fulfillment and gives new life.

The power of **Sin** and flesh, which crippled the law as the mid-point between **Grace** and **Sin**, is overcome by the new mid-point, Christ and the Spirit. Liberation from **Sin** is possible, but not via the law. Rather, liberation is a function of Christ and the Spirit.

The structure of thought and the language is profoundly covenantal. The law is part of a covenant that was intended to give righteousness and life (Deut. 30:15). Messiah Jesus, the representative of Israel, fully identifies with humanity and fulfills the covenant; he does and completes *the righteous requirement of the law* (v. 4). Those in Christ and the Spirit, i.e., those who have covenant membership in the new covenant community, receive life and righteousness, literally, *life because of righteousness* (v. 10). The linkage of the gift of life to resurrection assures the ultimate vindication and hope of Israel. Those in whom Christ and the Spirit are present constitute the covenant people of God.

The view of the law is exceedingly positive. The questions of 7:7 and 7:13 are answered. The law is the law of God; it is holy, righteous, good, and spiritual. It is the covenant law for God's people. The law is fulfilled through Christ and the Spirit. The new covenant people are the people whom the law fits. Paul really does *build up the law* (3:31).

The law is fulfilled and morality is possible, even necessary, through Christ and the Spirit. The questions of 6:1 and 6:15 are answered by life in Christ and the Spirit. The new covenant given in Christ and the Spirit does not nullify the call of God for people to bound **Sin** and to be holy. On the contrary, the law is fulfilled and **Sin** and the flesh are defeated as people live in the power domain of the Spirit.

"As people live" is critical to the logic of Paul's argument. Living *according to the flesh* is still a possibility. But it is not necessary because **Sin** *dwelling in me* is now replaced by Christ and the Spirit *dwelling in me* (three times, vv. 9, 10, 11). Choices have to be made—live in the worldview of the flesh or live in the Spirit. These choices have consequences—disobeying the law means death, fulfilling the law means life/peace.

Finally, the flesh/Spirit dualism extends the Adam/Christ contrast. Two opposing kingdoms are waging war. The language is apocalyptic, and comes specifically from Israel's "holy war" tradition. Two representatives of the opposing armies face each other in behalf of their respective armies. The victor's army is declared the winner in the war. Because Messiah Jesus condemned **Sin** in the flesh and the Spirit triumphs over the flesh, those in Christ and the Spirit share the victory.

TEXT IN BIBLICAL CONTEXT

The critical parallel texts to Romans 7:7–8:11 are found in Paul's letter to the Galatians. There he also discusses the purpose of the law (3:19-23), the redemptive role of Messiah Jesus in relationship to the law (4:1-7), the contrast of flesh and Spirit and the fulfillment of the law through the Spirit (5:16-26).

Following an extended discussion of the relationship of the law to Christian experience, faith, and promise, Paul asks in 3:19, *why the law?* He gives one answer in two different forms. The basic answer is that the purpose of the law is to deal with sin. The first form of the answer is that the law provided a way to deal with acts of sin until Christ came (it *was added because of transgressions*, v. 19). God gave the law for a specific time period, *until Christ came*, to define and concentrate deeds of sin, on the one hand, and to bound and restrain sinful behavior, on the other. The law in this role is inferior to the promise (v. 21), and is not the source of a living and righteous relationship with God (v. 21). The second form of the answer intensifies the first by the use of apocalyptic theology. The function of the law is to confine all things—all created reality —under **Sin**. The law focuses and concentrates **Sin** as power and restricts it. The purpose of this function of the law *is in order that the promise might be given through the faithfulness of Messiah Jesus to all the ones believing* (v. 22). The law brings **Sin** together in one place and confines it so that God can deal with it through Messiah Jesus.

Verses 23-25 explain the temporal role of the law. The law served to put the Jewish people ("we") in protective custody in the present evil age (v. 23). It served as a custodian, one who guards and protects children, until the apocalyptic revelation of the faithfulness of Christ. The intent is again defined by a purpose clause, that Israel would be made righteous out of the faithfulness of Christ (*the faith* and *the faith to be revealed* in v. 23 refer back to *the faithfulness of Jesus Christ* in v. 22; and the *out of faith* in v. 24 refers back to the previous *out of faith*, which referred to Jesus). Now that Messiah Jesus has come, and makes people righteous by his faithfulness, that is, deals with **Sin**, the protective role of the law is ended (v. 25).

The relationship of the law to **Sin** and sins is very similar to that expressed in Romans. The law serves a positive function, to concentrate and restrain **Sin** and sins, until God deals with **Sin** in and through Messiah Jesus.

The way God deals with **Sin** through Christ is defined in Galatians 4:4-5 in terms that are structurally and linguistically parallel to Romans 8:3-4.

Galatians	**Romans**
when the fullness of time came	what the law was unable to do
God sent his son	God sent his Son
born of a woman	in the likeness of sinful flesh
under the law	as a sin offering,
	and condemned sin in the flesh

in order that he might	in order that the righteous
redeem	requirement of the law
those under the law	might be fulfilled in us

God deals with **Sin** by sending Messiah Jesus, who identifies fully with the human condition and redeems from that condition. In both Romans and Galatians the redemption in Christ does something to the law, fulfills the law in Romans, redeems those confined by the law in Galatians. In both letters this description of Christ's redemption is followed immediately by a discussion of the role of the Spirit in making followers of Jesus, Jew and Gentile, children of God who pray the distinctive Christian prayer, *Abba! Father!* (See the exposition of 8:12-30 for a further discussion of this parallel.) The structure of salvation in both letters looks like this:

God sends the son;
the son redeems;
redeemed people live in the Spirit.

The *life in the Spirit* theme is developed in parallel ways in both letters. The Spirit is the power that overcomes the flesh and that makes possible the fulfillment of the law in Galatians 5:16-26, just as in Romans 8:4-11. The flesh and the Spirit are opposites; the singular *fruit of the Spirit* stands over against the many *works of the flesh*. Those who *belong to Christ* (lit., *are of Christ*) crucify the flesh and order their lives by the Spirit. People who walk in the Spirit and exhibit the fruit of the Spirit fulfill the law. Law and Spirit belong together, in contrast to the opposition of Spirit and flesh, because people empowered by the Spirit live the law.

TEXT IN THE LIFE OF THE CHURCH

Romans 7:7–8:11 is primarily about God and the goodness of God. It is not about schizoid and frustrated humanity. This text is about theology rather than anthropology.

The Glasses of the Past

Ever since Augustine, the focus of interpretation in this text has been anthropological, the internal struggle of individual men and women. The struggle is either pre-Christian people trying to meet the oppressive demands of the law outside of grace, or, more likely, Christians struggling with sin in the context of grace. Augustine turned the attention of the Western Church inward, to the introspective conscience. He wrote an autobiography, his *Confessions*, in which he reported his own inner struggle with life and faith. Augustine read his experience into the language of Romans 7. Paul as a Christian struggled with the law and with the flesh, just as Augustine did. So convinced of this was Augustine that he made Romans 7 the key to the rest of the letter. Romans is about the interplay of law and grace. It describes the inner conflict between the flesh and the Spirit that Paul makes theologically explicit in 8:5-8. Augustine's *Confessions* were the first in a long history of "tell-all" stories that have profoundly shaped the way Christians in the West think about the Christian faith.

Luther captured the essence of the struggle with his famous statement that the Christian is "justified and sinner at the same time" (*simul justus ac peccator*). The Christian self is profoundly divided; it wants to live under and by grace, by the Spirit rather than by the flesh, but it cannot, because sin and the flesh activated by the law are so compelling. Grace and law are opposing realities that pull Christians apart. The Christian life is a struggle, and then we die. Augustine and Luther also legitimated the telling of these stories of struggle. It is part of true Christian humility and self-knowledge to share the conflict within. The more intense the conflict the greater the evidence of the grace of God (and, in the modern world, the greater the bank account).

All of the Augustinian and Lutheran interpretations share three things in common. First, they interpret the language of 7:14, "spiritual" (*pneumatikos*) and "fleshly" (*sarkinos*), to mean that humanity is divided into two basic groups, Christian and pagan. Only Christian people, these interpretations assume, could struggle with the law as described in Romans 7. Philip Melanchthon, Luther's successor and one of his chief interpreters, says it forthrightly: "Paul is speaking here of the sort of person he was after his conversion. For before his conversion that conflict did not exist since an ungodly person does not will from the heart what the law admonishes" (*Römerbrief-Kommentar* 1532:224). Time and distance from the sixteenth century has not changed this perspective. One of the magisterial commentaries of the twentieth century is by C. E. B. Cranfield, who asserts that "a struggle as serious as that which is here described can only take place where the Spirit of God is present and active" (1975 [vol. 1]:346).

The second shared assumption, and closely related to the first, is that the law in Judaism and law in general is negative. The law makes demands, it limits freedom. It cannot be obeyed or fulfilled. The chief role of the law is to increase sin in order to lead people to grace. But even within the context of grace, the law still permits sin and the flesh to tempt human beings, to lead them into sin, or equally bad, to permit them to think that their obedience fulfills the will of God and makes them righteous. Men and women struggle with the law before grace, and after grace.

Third, Augustine, Luther, Cranfield, and people of like mind, are interpreting Romans 7 for "Christianized societies." Their worldview is Constantinian. Such a worldview must explain the problem of massive sin and disobedience in the church and in the "Christian culture." The language of inner struggle and the divided self helps justify the reality of "fallenness" in the church and the culture.

A Different Reading

All of this is far removed from Paul and first-century Judaism. Gone is the deeply held conviction in Judaism that the law is God's good gift of grace to protect people from sin. "Delight in the law," whether Psalm 119 or Romans 7, is incomprehensible. In fact, in this scheme Jews, including Paul and the apostles, are ungodly people before becoming Christians who could not delight in the law and who could not do the law.

Paul himself, let alone volumes of Jewish literature, paints a very different picture. He has a robust conscience, rather than a tortured conscience victimized by guilt. He is proud and confident of his Jewish heritage and faith; it is a good thing (Phil. 3). The law is God's good law, which he seeks to do as a Jew and which Christ brings to fulfillment for Christians who live in the Spirit. Nothing in Paul's letters reflects a personal struggle in his Christian life. Romans 7 certainly says nothing about life in Christ, let alone about a struggle in the faith. The Christian faith is eschatological good news. Paul did not leave Judaism because he was frustrated and unfulfilled. Rather, Paul argues that Messiah Jesus brings Judaism and its quest for life through the law to fulfillment.

Romans 7 is about God, not the struggle of men and women with God. The agenda is defined clearly as the law by the questions in 7:7 and 13, and by the fulfilment of the law in Christ and the Spirit (8:1-11). Paul offers a ringing affirmation of the law. The law, even in its function of defining and intensifying **Sin**, serves the purpose of concentrating **Sin** in one place and one people so that God can deal with it. The law serves the purpose of God by enabling God to defeat **Sin** once and for all through Jesus. Messiah Jesus brings the law to fulfillment by doing what the law was not able to do, condemning **Sin** in its force field, and placing Jewish and Gentile believers in the power field of the Spirit.

Romans is the good news that there is a moral compass in the world—the holy, righteous, good, and spiritual law of God—and that Christ makes possible life according to that compass through the defeat of **Sin** and life within the community of the Spirit.

Such a reading of Romans 7:7–8:11 is a long way from Augustine and Luther, but much closer to first-century Judaism and Christianity. Paul and his fellow-Christians had not turned inward, nor were they trying to make sense of the failure of people in the culture to "walk according to the Spirit." They were building communities of mixed ethnic people who were trying to understand the purposes of God through Messiah Jesus in a changing world. An ongoing agenda in their thinking was the role of the law of God in relation to God's purpose in history and in the new covenant communities called the church. That law, and its moral content, was not abolished by Christ. Quite the contrary, Christ and the Spirit enabled the minority communities of Jesus followers to embody the morality of the law by "walking according to the Spirit."

The Gift of the Law

The law is good. It should be embraced as the moral compass for people and communities caught in the moral vacuum and relativism of post-modern meaninglessness. The demands of the law—honor God, honor parents, do not covet, do not steal, do not commit adultery— are designed for the well being of the believing community and the world. The love of God and neighbor leads to the highest good within the Christian community and in the larger society. The church would do well to emphasize the law in its teaching and practice, the law as presented in the OT, the law as interpreted and reinterpreted by Jesus and the apostles.

The sixteenth-century Anabaptists understood the law in such positive terms. The law was more than "demand." The law was a guide to righteousness, as well as a definer of sin. Menno Simons presents Jesus as a new Lawgiver and the commands of the gospels as an integral part of the gospel. Obedience to the commands of the NT represents the true way of receiving Christ by faith.

The Gift of the Spirit

But law must be interpreted and practiced post-Messiah Jesus within the context of Spirit empowerment and Christian community. Messiah Jesus has given the Spirit to dwell within and to enable the fulfilment of the law. The context for faith and law fulfilment is life in the Spirit. Every follower of Jesus has the Spirit; the Spirit defines what it means to be Christian. The presence of the Spirit empowers obedience and gives life and peace.

Romans 8 was one of the most used texts in the sixteenth-century Anabaptist movement. People empowered by the Spirit were new kinds of people. They, therefore, rejected Luther's notion of "justified and sinner at the same time." Christians were made righteous, they were different people who lived differently, who fulfilled the law in a life of radical discipleship, because they experienced the life transforming power of the Spirit.

The charismatic renewal of the church in the twentieth century is teaching the church again that life in the Spirit genuinely transforms people and the church. The closer linkage of this renewal with the ethics of the Spirit would represent a genuine Pauline recovery. The Spirit in Paul makes a difference in how followers of Jesus live, more than how they feel.

The Challenge of Worldviews

We all live with a worldview, a set of assumptions and perspectives that shape the way we see and interpret life and reality. We talk easily about a "western worldview," by which we mean a view of the world from the perspective of modern and post-modern European and American cultures.

Paul challenges us with two worldviews, the worldview of the flesh versus the worldview of the Spirit. The worldview of the flesh is centered in me, in what serves and pleases me and my interests. The worldview of the Spirit is centered in God, in what serves and pleases God and God's mission in the world. Paul's contrast of two different worldviews is part of a larger doctrine of "two ways," two alternative ways of thinking and living that was common in the first century (see 1QS 3:17-26; Rom. 1-2; 1 Cor. 6:9-10; Gal. 5:19-23; Eph. 2:11-12; 4:17-19; Col. 3:12; 1 Tim. 6:2-11; *Did.* 1-5; *Ep. Barn.* 18-20).

What would it mean for the church to focus more on the question of worldviews? On the deep assumptions and perspectives that shape our values and relationships? What would Paul's particular contrast, worldview of the flesh and Spirit, look like in the church today? What does it mean for the church to be shaped by the worldview of the Spirit? What does it mean to understand following Jesus as living in a state of war against the kingdom of the flesh?

Children of God

Romans 8:12-39

PREVIEW

Chapters 5–8 are bounded by the reality of a new relationship with God. As noted earlier, there is a thematic and verbal similarity between 5:1-11 and 8:12-39. A key term is hope based on being made righteous, which creates a confidence of salvation from eternal death. The new relationship is described as peace with God (5:1; 8:31-34), endurance of suffering (5:2ff.; 8:18-39), and the love of God (5:5-8; 8:35-39).

The text is unified by the theme of Jesus' followers being the children of God (vv. 14, 15, 16, 17, 19, 21, 23, 29). As so often in Paul's letters, his concluding thought in one section provides the bridge to the next text unit. Verses 12-17 constitute an elaboration of v. 9, *the Spirit dwelling in you*, and vv. 18-30 explain the meaning of vv. 10-11, the Spirit *will give life*.

The themes of the letter are drawn together into a new argument that is cosmic in its vision. The covenant purpose of God is fulfilled in Christ and the Spirit. Christ's people are the children of God, the title of Israel going back to the Exodus and the eschatological hope of the Jews. All creation will be renewed with the revelation of the new character of redeemed people. Suffering is part of this identity and revelation, just as it was for the Jews. The center of this cosmic transformation is Christ. He is the first-born among many believers, and the one who will guarantee the triumph of God over all suffering and all powers. The vision is grand. The destiny of Israel is fulfilled in Messiah Jesus and the new family who become the heirs of God with him.

OUTLINE

The Spirit and Family Relationships, 8:12-17
    8:12-13   Summary
    8:14   Thesis
    8:15-17   Elaboration of the thesis

The Triumph of Glory Over Suffering, 8:18-30
    8:18   Thesis

EXPLANATORY NOTES

The Spirit and Family Relationships 8:12-17

12-13 Summary

Paul addresses the Roman Christians directly with a summary of 8:4-11. The summary draws a conclusion, *therefore, then*, which also is an exhortation. As in ch. 6, the sharp alternatives of what Christians already are or are not (in vv. 4-11) get blurred in life; the indicatives are qualified by imperatives. The conclusion-exhortation is both negative and positive. Verses 12-13a state the negative. Followers of Jesus living in the flesh are not under obligation to live according to the worldview of the flesh. The clear implication is that Christians can still live *according to the flesh.* The boundaries between the worldview of the Spirit and of the flesh do not run simply between believers and nonbelievers; they run through the believing community and through believers. The consequences of living the fleshly worldview is death.

The positive conclusion, v. 13b, sums up the results of living the Spirit worldview. The result is end-time life. But that result requires the continuous action of putting to death *the actions of the body,* the behaviors that grow out of a fleshly worldview. Real moral discipline and effort is called for, but it is a moral effort *by the Spirit.* The moral effort Paul exhorts is not very different from contemporary Judaism, only there it was defined as observing the law. What is distinctive here is that the moral discipline is maintained only in and by the Spirit who enables fulfillment of the law and energizes the moral will (vv. 4-11). The good news of the conclusion is that this is the way Christians are living. Verse 13b is a fulfilled conditional sentence; *if by the Spirit you are putting to death the actions of the body, which you are, you will live.*

Paul sums up the ethical argument he has been making since 6:1 with stark alternatives—"you will die" or "you will live." The choice confronting Christians is reminiscent of the options Moses gave Israel in Deuteronomy 30:15-20. Jesus followers must choose between life in the flesh and life in the Spirit. Only the latter fulfills the law and gives life. With this summary Paul concludes his discussion of ethical concerns arising from the greatness of Christ's salvation that began with 6:1. He now returns to the magnitude of salvation in Christ, the subject of ch. 5.

14 Thesis

Paul expands the reference to the Spirit by stating the thesis that articulates the real point of the text unit. *As many as permit themselves to be led by the Spirit of God are children of God.* He again summarizes the previous descriptions of life in the Spirit. *To be led by the Spirit* is a synonym for *to walk according to the Spirit, to have the worldview of the Spirit, to be in the Spirit, to have the Spirit* (vv. 4-13). Paul's provocative thesis is that people who choose to live in the Spirit are incorporated into the family of God as sons and daughters.

Paul's thesis introduces language that dominates and unifies 8:12-39. Several different terms and one phrase are used to describe Christians as members of God's family, *sons of God* in the Greek and RSV (vv. 14, 19), *children of God* (vv. 16, 17, 21), *adoption as children* (vv. 15, 23), *conformed to the image of his son* (v. 29), *many brothers/sisters* (v. 29). This family terminology is significant for Paul's audience. To be *children of God* is the unique privilege of Israel in the OT and Judaism (see, e.g., Exod. 4:22-23; Deut. 14:1; 32:5-6; Isa. 1:2-4; 30:9; 63:8; Hos. 1:10; 11:1; Wis. 12:7, 21; 16:10, 21, 26; 18:13; 19:6; Sir. 36:17; 1 *En.* 62:11; *Jub.* 1:24-25; 2:20; *Pss. Sol.* 17:30; *As. Mos.* 10:3, 4; *Sib. Or.* 3:702; 5:202; 3 *Macc.* 6:28). This status, linked to election and calling, is what distinguished Israel from the nations. *Children of God* is synonymous with *people of God.* The language applied especially to Jews in apocalyptic literature. *Sonship* became synonymous with righteous. The ones made righteous are the children of God, and the children of God are the righteous ones. Furthermore, it is associated in apocalyptic literature with rescue from humiliation, oppression, destruction, and death. The rescue is this-worldly in literature that pictures redemption as a historical process, and other-worldly in literature that anticipates a meta-historical redemption. The point is that the status of *children of God* preserves this people through suffering of all kinds. Even the greatest oppressors in the cosmos cannot invalidate this family status.

Paul's thesis is that all, Jew and Gentile, who choose to live in the Spirit are children of God. Their status is defined by the Spirit, not by faithfulness to the law or certain symbols of the law (e.g., works of law). Followers of Jesus who live in the Spirit, which fulfills the law

(vv. 4-11), enter into the historic and eschatological privileges of Israel. Together with v. 9, Paul is defining the Christian life in terms of life in the Spirit and the new status of a family relationship with God.

15-17 Elaboration of the Thesis

Verses 15-16 explain the meaning of being children of God. Verse 17 draws a critical conclusion from vv. 15-16.

Paul elaborates v. 14 both negatively and positively. Christians *did not receive a spirit of slavery to be fearful people again*. The *did not receive* is a point action verb (aorist); it points to a specific experience, baptism and the reception of the Spirit, which constituted the beginning of the Christian life. A slave is not in control of life, but lives at the mercy, and thus fear, of someone else. *To be fearful again* points to a contrast. Paul's language has epochal connotations, the old epoch of "slavery to the flesh," versus the new epoch of "slavery to the Spirit." To be a child of God means to be free from the slavery of the flesh, from the fear of bondage to **Sin**.

The positive meaning, the radical contrast, is that *you received the Spirit of adoption*, that is, "the Spirit which effects adoption" as children. The Spirit, which to this point has been called the Spirit of life (v. 2), the Spirit of God (vv. 9, 14), the Spirit of Jesus (v. 9), and the Spirit of the one raising Jesus from the dead (v. 11) is now called the *Spirit of adoption*. Adoption is a unique Pauline term (see 8:23; 9:4; Gal. 4:5; Eph. 1:5). It defines a legal change of status. "Slavery" and "adoption" emphasize a gulf, one characterized by fear of the master, the other by the intimacy of a family. Believers now are legally children with the same status, security, and privileges as birth children.

The evidence of the new status is that *in the Spirit we cry Abba Father*. The prayer is an intense and deeply emotional cry of exultation. *Abba Father* was the distinctive prayer of Jesus that defined God in intimate parental terms. It was given the disciples by Jesus as a sign of their identity. All believers are children of God because in the Spirit they pray the same prayer as Jesus. The covenant of Abraham has been extended to all who are children of God in the Spirit (Rom. 4; Gal. 3).

The Spirit who effects the adoption also witnesses with the human spirit of the believer that *we are the children of God* rather than slaves. In Judaism, two witnesses were needed to establish something. Here the two witnesses are the Spirit of God and the spirit of believers.

The conclusion of the explanation, v. 17, is that as children of God believers are heirs and recipients of God's estate. The language is distinctively Jewish. Jews as the children of God are the heirs of the promises to Abraham. In fact, a recurrent theme in Jewish literature is that Israel itself is God's inheritance. Paul's point is that the inheritance has been redefined. All believers, Jews and Gentiles, are now heirs of God, but only because Christ is an heir, and they are fellow heirs with him. Christ is what believers become. Christians do not become heirs independent of Christ.

Paul adds a shocker in v. 17b. The glory of the inheritance is qualified by a strong "if" clause (lit., "if indeed"). The *if indeed we suffer with in order that we may be glorified with* takes up an established link between child status and suffering in Judaism, and applies it to Christians. Jews know that they suffer because of their unique relationship to God. Paul asserts that the reality of suffering goes with the privileged inheritance of being a child of God. The term *to suffer with* means to suffer the same thing as. Just as Christians die with Christ in baptism (ch. 6), so also they participate in the suffering that characterizes the current age of the rule of **Sin**. Furthermore, the suffering is life-long (the verb is present tense). The purpose of the suffering is defined by a purpose clause, *in order that we may be glorified with*. Suffering with Christ is not optional; no suffering, no future glory. The future glory describes the radiance of God. It characterizes God's original creation, which was lost by Adam and will be restored in the end-time through Messiah Jesus.

The Triumph of Glory Over Suffering 8:18-30

The abrupt conclusion to v. 17 introduces the theme of vv. 18-30. Glory brackets the text unit, *the coming glory to be revealed* in v. 18 and *those he made righteous he also glorified* in v. 30. Paul discusses the relationship of suffering and glory by using earlier language from ch. 8: liberation from slavery (vv. 2, 21), resurrection (vv. 11, 23), children of God and adoption (vv. 14-17, 19, 21, 23), the role of the Spirit (vv. 6, 27; 11, 23; 15, 23; 15-16, 26). Paul is clearly building to the climax of an argument.

But he also is framing a climax to chs. 6–8. He presents the cosmic outworking of salvation in Adam categories. He paints a picture that describes the reversal of Adam's sin and the restoration of creation. The verbal links to 1:18-30 are multiple: creation (1:20, 25 // 8:20-22), futility or emptiness (1:21 // 8:20), bestow glory (1:21 // 8:30), glory (1:23 // 8:18, 21), image (1:23 // 8:29), degraded body/redeemed body (1:24 // 8:29).

Paul confronts the reality of suffering among Christians and transforms it by linking it to the salvation of creation, via a thoroughly apocalyptic theology. The language is poetic—nonhuman reality or creation is personified. Creation and humans share a common fate and destiny—they suffer together, they are renewed or *saved* and transformed or *glorified* together, all common themes in the Jewish Scriptures and apocalyptic literature (Isa. 11:6-9; 43:19-21; 55:12-13; Ezek. 34:25-31; Hos. 2:18; Zech. 8:12; 1 En. 45:4-5; 51:4-5; 4 Ezra 8:51-54; 2 Bar. 29:1-8; Sib. Or. 3:777-95).

18 Thesis

Paul introduces the thesis by setting in confrontation the present reality of suffering and future glory. The suffering Christians experience in the present age (lit., "the now time") cannot be compared with the end-time glory to be revealed.

Paul explains the thesis in three subunits that deal with creation (vv. 19-22), Christians (*we*, vv. 23-25), and the Spirit (vv. 26-30). Recurring words and themes run through these sections: groaning (vv. 22, 23, 26), hope (vv. 20, 24, 25), expectation (vv. 19, 23, 25), children of God (vv. 19, 21, 23, 29). The whole is tied together by the keyword *groaning* (*stenazein*). Each subunit has its own theme: freedom versus slavery (vv. 19-22), eager expectation sustained by hope (vv. 23-25), the intercession of the Spirit for the Christian (vv. 26-30).

The Groaning of Creation 19-22

The whole creation expects redemption with intense eagerness (lit., "the eager expectation of creation is awaited eagerly"). The focus is the end-time revelation of the new family of God. *The revelation of the children of God* in v. 19 is parallel to the glory that is going to be revealed in us in v. 18. That glory is the end-time family of God that includes all peoples.

The created order awaits redemption so eagerly because creation is caught up in humanity's futility. "Futility," used elsewhere only in 1:21, refers to something that does not function according to design. Creation was drawn into the consequences of Adam's sin against its will (lit., "not willingly"). Creation was subjected, or more literally "ordered under" (the verb is used twice in v. 20 for emphasis), by God to the conditions of Adam's fall. The result is that creation is enslaved, which is further defined as the decay of mortality. Paul is interpreting Genesis 3, and together with Judaism holds to the intimate unity of humanity and creation.

Creation longs for redemption because it was subjected *in hope* (v. 20). The redemption of creation is defined as freedom from slavery to the mortality of decay. This redemption is further specified as *the freedom of the glory of the children of God*. Paul's reference here is probably to the apocalyptic notion of God's elect appearing with the Messiah. The redemption of creation will be mediated through the glorification of the family of God at the parousia. So eager is the intense expectation of creation for this redemption that it is likened to childbirth. The created order is in the birth pains of being pushed out into redemption. The imagery comes from Jewish apocalyptic. The created order is going through the "messianic woes," the tribulations ending the present age and introducing the age to come (see Dan. 7:21-22, 25-27; 12:1-3; *4 Ezra* 5:1-13; 6:13-24; 9:1-3; *2 Bar.* 25:2-3; 27:1-15; 48:30-41; 70:2-10; Rev. 6:12-17; *1 En.* 62:4; 1QH 3:7-18; *4 Ezra* 10:6-16; Mark 13:8 // Matt. 24:8; John 16:21). Suffering is linked to hope and to new life in the transition between the ages. The suffering of God's children *with Christ* is a function of human submission to **Sin**, and part of a cosmic quest for redemption. The healing of the peoples through the adoption of Gentiles as the children of God results in the healing of creation.

The end-time appearance of the family of God is the decisive event that creation awaits. It will reverse the rebellion of humanity against God and the loss of the glory of God (ch. 1).

The Groaning of Christians 23-25

The *not only but also* at the beginning of v. 23 indicates a close parallelism between the experience of creation and of believers. Cosmic redemption is the context for the believer's eager desire for end-time salvation. The *intense waiting* (used two times here) is defined by the repeated use of *hope* (five times).

Two decisive moments characterize the redemption of followers of Jesus. The first is the reception of the Spirit. Paul returns to the definition of the Christian as one who has the Spirit (v. 9). The reception is a *first fruits* event. The image comes from the Jewish practice of bringing a "first fruits" of the grain harvest as offering to the Temple. The offering is the beginning of the full harvest, and the guarantee that the whole process will be completed. The harvest toward which the first fruits of the Spirit point is the resurrection of the body, the second decisive moment of redemption. The Spirit begins a process of redemption that leads to a new embodiment. Redemption cannot be complete with the gift of the Spirit or within the present creation, it requires an "adoption" to a new family in a new created order. Creation looks for the revelation of the children of God; believers look for their own adoption as God's children, which is defined as the redemption of the body. The current status of family relations is incomplete; it requires a new creation.

The time between the two moments of receiving the Spirit and the resurrection of the body is a time of groaning. Christians, because of the Spirit, groan in longing for complete redemption. Spirit possession does not distance Christians from creation, but rather intensifies the solidarity with creation both in suffering and in hope for full salvation.

The Groaning of the Spirit 26-30

The opening of v. 26, *in the same way also*, together with the repeat of the "groaning" theme indicates that a parallelism with the previous comparisons is intended. The situation of the Christian between the ages is one of weakness. The weakness is defined as a problem of prayer, specifically not knowing what to pray. The not praying *as we ought* in v. 26 is further explained as *according to God's ordering* or will in v. 27. On the one hand, Christians pray *Abba, Father*, but, on the other hand, their ability to pray is seriously limited by inadequate knowledge about God's design for what is intended.

The good news is that God's Spirit shoulders the weakness (lit., "lends a hand"). The Spirit is pictured as present and assisting believers in the depths of human crisis, their inability to communicate with the intimate *Abba, Father*. The Spirit intercedes with *wordless groans*, without the speech which distinguishes humans from animals in the ancient world. The image pictures "depth" communication, which is below ordinary human consciousness. Such communication is possible, Paul assures his readers, because God *is the Searcher of the human heart*, an intriguing picture of God from biblical and Jewish tradition (1 Sam. 16:7; 1 Kings 8:39; Pss. 7:9; 17:3; 26:2; 44:21; 139:1-2, 23; Jer. 17:10; Wis. 1:6; Sir. 42:18; *Bib. Ant.* 50:4). God alone knows the deep center of people. God knows *the mind of the Spirit*, a repeat of the phrase from v. 6 where it stands over against *mind of the flesh* and gives life and peace.

Paul reverses the normal understanding of the Spirit as the one who *searches everything, even the depths of God* (1 Cor. 2:10-11). The Spirit, present in the depth of human creatureliness, here is known to God and does what Christians cannot do for themselves, intercedes for them according to the will of God. In 8:34 Paul pictures Christ as interceding at the right hand of God. The idea of humans needing intercession before the throne of God, either by angels or distinguished leaders (e.g., patriarchs, prophets), was common in Judaism (Job 33:23-26; Tob. 12:15; *1 En.* 9:3; 15:2; 99:3; 104:1; *T. Levi* 3:5-6; 5:6; *T. Dan.* 6:2). What is remarkable here is that it is the eschatological Spirit and the risen Christ who do the interceding.

The ongoing crisis of faith, or the depth of Christian groaning together with the created order, could hardly be pictured more graphically. Believers have the status of being children in a new intimate family relationship with God, but they are not able to communicate properly with God. The experience of contradiction living between the ages is profound. Christians are totally dependent on the help of the Spirit and Christ.

The fact that the Spirit prays according to God's will means that *we know* something. What is known is described in two "that" clauses, the first in v. 28 and the second in vv. 29-30. The first thing that believers know is that *God works all things to the good to the ones loving God.* As the footnotes in most Bibles indicate, v. 28 has some serious text critical problems. The translation just given favors the longer reading of the earliest manuscripts (P[46], A, B). *God* is the subject of the action, and *all things* the object. In the midst of the uncertainty, even the crisis caused by suffering and by inadequate communication, Paul assures his readers that God can be trusted and that God wills and works the good for the members of the family. The children of the family are defined as *the ones loving God* and *the ones called according to purpose.* The verb "to love" is used here for the first time to characterize the response of believers to God. *Those who love God,* usually combined with *and keep his commandments,* is a characteristic description of pious people in Judaism (Deut. 7:9; Ps. 145:20; Tob. 13:12, 14; Sir. 1:10; 2:15, 16; *Pss. Sol.* 4:25; 10:3; 14:1; 4QpPs. 3:4-5). Paul both identifies with this understanding and breaks with it by using only the first half. The second description is equally Jewish. God's purpose and election (calling) are two sides of the same coin. The heritage of Israel is used to characterize believers, Jewish and Gentile. Christians are people who love God and who are elected according to God's purpose.

The second thing that Christians know is *that those whom God foreknew God predestined to be conformed to the image of his Son* (v. 29). Paul uses five verbs heavy with scriptural and Jewish meaning—foreknowledge, preordained (or predestined), called, made righteous, glorified—to describe the activity of God in behalf of believers. "Foreknowledge" does not just mean advance knowledge, but the choice (really "election") that accompanies such knowledge. Preordain or "predestine" adds that God has a plan for the elect. The Christian community is defined as God's elect people; Paul is not talking here about the election of individual human beings (more on this topic in the discussion of ch. 9). The election and the plan is to be conformed to the being of the Son, to become like the reality the Son embodies.

The intent of the plan is defined by a purpose clause, that he may be the firstborn among many brothers/sisters. The purpose is to make Christ the firstborn of the new race of end-time people. The closest parallel text is Hebrews 2:6-10; Jesus completes the original purpose of Adam in order that he might bring many sons and daughters to glory. Christ replaces Adam, the firstborn of the human race, and Israel, the firstborn of God's children (Exod. 4:22; Sir. 31:9; *Pss. Sol.* 18:4). Earlier Christ was conformed to the reality of sinful humanity (8:3). Here God's plan is to conform humanity to the reality of Christ as the corporate representative of God's elect people in the world.

The brothers and sisters God elected in Christ are called, made righteous, and glorified. *Called* picks up the *the ones called according to God's purpose* from v. 28. "Calling" and "sonship" are frequently associated in Jewish literature. God's making righteous—putting people in the right and declaring them right—recalls 1:16 and 5:1. Paul concludes the paragraph with the concept used at the beginning, glorified. Salvation is a process of being glorified. In 1:21 humanity refused to glorify God. Here God glorifies human beings. God reverses human sin and restores humanity to its intended status.

The agony of groaning—for creation, Christians, and the Spirit—is answered with the assurance of glorification. The shape of the glory is described in three different forms: the revelation of the children of God for creation, the redemption of the body for Christians, and the conformity of Christians to the image of the Son for the Spirit.

Suffering is part of the cosmic reality. Christians participate in that suffering. Here it is a function of growth, growth toward God's glorification. It is part of the transformation process of being adopted as the children of God. Suffering does not lead to despair for Christians because God is working out a plan that moves through adoption as children and through suffering to glorification.

The Triumph of God in Christ 8:31-39

Paul concludes every major section of the letter with a carefully phrased confessional or hymnic statement. The first major argument, 1:18–4:25, concluded with a confessional statement in 4:24-25. The third major argument, chs. 9–11, concludes with a grand poem in 11:33-36. Paul concludes his second major argument in a similar way. Verses 31-39 are a carefully crafted summary statement, really a "victory song of salvation." With much repetition, the summary makes one basic assertion: God is on our side. That summary, which functions to conclude 8:1-11 and 12-30, therefore, has many links with the preceding discussion: vv. 31-32 take up *God's sending the son* from v. 3; the assurance of no condemnation in v. 34 repeats v. 1; the *with him* in v. 32 gathers up the "with" words in v. 17; the *intercedes* in v. 34 repeats the same word from vv. 26-27. But the summary also concludes the second argument, chs. 5–8. The theme and mood of this text are parallel with 5:1-11, as noted earlier. The victory song serves as a summary conclusion to the letter so far, 1:18–4:25 and 5:1–8:39.

The structure of the summary is question and answer. Paul asks six questions, in two different sequences. The main theme of the text is framed in the first three questions, vv. 31-32. The second question, v. 31b, states the theme. The third question, v. 32, provides the proof: God has given us the Son. The second set of questions, vv. 33-39, repeat the first set of questions and expand the theme. There is a progression in the length of the questions throughout the series. In the first series, question two is longer than one, and three is longer than two. The same pattern holds in the second series. Paul is clinching an argument by repetition upon repetition. Let no one forget, let no one doubt, God is for us.

31-32 First Questions

The first question, *what then shall we say about these things?* clearly introduces a conclusion. It is the same question we have encountered earlier in Romans in a slightly different form. The *these things* refers to what Paul has been saying in chs. 5–8, and in 8:12-30.

The second question states the theme of the text, and of Paul's gospel, "if God is for us, who can be against us?" If the one God of the universe—the basic assumption behind the question is Jewish monotheism—is for us, which God is, nothing can prevail against us. History is ambiguous, as the reality of suffering indicates, but the outcome is not, because *God is for us.* Paul's confidence is that of Isaiah (40ff.) and the Psalms (23, 56, 118).

The evidence that God is for us, and the basis of the third question, is that *God did not spare his own son but gave him up in behalf of us all* (v. 32). The *gave him up* (*paredōken*) clause reflects an early Christian understanding of Jesus' death; it was a vicariously representative and sacrificial death. God's giving up Christ for salvation here answers God's giving up human beings in ch. 1 for rebellion. The *of all* is inclusive of Jews and Gentiles, as are so many of the "all" modifiers in Romans. The *not spare* theme may be a reference to Abraham's sacrifice of Isaac in Genesis 22:16 (the same words are used). In contemporary Judaism, Abraham's offering was important evidence of his faithfulness to God (see explanation in ch. 4). If Paul's reference is to the same event, his point is different. His focus is the faithfulness of God. Precisely because God is faithful, as evidenced in the *not sparing* and *giving up* Jesus, Paul asks the third question, *how shall he not also with him give us all things?* The *all things* (*ta panta*) refers to all created reality. God through Christ gives everything to all the sons and daughters in the family (see also 4:13—the descendants of Abraham *inherit the world*).

33-39 Second Questions

Paul follows up the first three questions with three more. The first question, v. 33, asks *who will bring charges against the elect of God?* The scene is the final judgment. "To charge" is legal language for making a formal accusation against someone. The people charged are God's elect. *The elect of God*, the central concept of Jewish self-understanding which excludes all other people, here is inclusive of all the children of God, Jews and Gentiles. The question is answered immediately. It is absurd because God, repeated for emphasis (*the elect of God—God*), is the one making righteous. No one can charge God's children because, as Paul has argued throughout Romans, God makes people righteous in and through Messiah Jesus.

The second question repeats the first in different form, *who can condemn?* (v. 34). Who is in a position to condemn God's children in the final judgment? No one can because Jesus died, and even more important, was raised from the dead. Furthermore, this Jesus is now the prime minister of God, which is what *seated at the right hand* means. Paul here is responding to contemporary Jewish speculation about who sat on and controlled the thrones of the heavens—was it Adam, Enoch, Melchizedek, or the Messiah? Paul's answer is that Messiah Jesus, the crucified and risen one, alone is the prime minister who controls the eschatological court room. Further, as the chief officer in charge of God's reign, Christ makes the case (lit., *intercedes*) *in behalf of us*.

Paul's thesis is that God is for us. The best evidence is Jesus. Therefore, the third and final question, *is there anyone who can separate us from the love of Christ* (v. 35)? The tribulation list that follows uses the language of religious persecution (*suffering, anguish, persecution*) and end-time suffering and deprivation (*famine, nakedness, danger, sword*). The list is supported by the quotation of Psalm 44:22, a text that was also used by Jewish leaders to interpret the deaths of the Maccabean martyrs *for the sake of the law*. The people of God suffer, are killed and slaughtered for God's sake. But God's children triumph, literally *win a glorious victory*, through the enablement of the one loving them. The one loving them is Christ in v. 35 and God in v. 39. Jesus as the Messiah embodies the covenant love of God so that the two can be cited as synonyms of the divine love for the children of God. Paul *has been and is persuaded* (perfect tense) that none of the powers of the cosmos will be able to separate God's children from *the love of God*. The paired list of powers is formidable— *death/life* as definitions of the human condition in chs. 5–8; *angels/rulers* as supernatural intermediaries in the heavens and political leaders on earth in the governance of the nations and Israel; *things present—things to come* as all dimensions of time; *powers* as powerful supernatural beings; *height/depth* as symbols of heavenly and subterranean realities; *any other creature* to cover anything else in the cosmos. None of these powers—visible or invisible, heavenly or political—will be able to drive a wedge between the people of God and the love of God. Whatever power these powers may use *against us* (v. 31), the love of God is greater.

Paul summarizes his argument with the confident assertion that *God is for us*. The election and the love of God, two sides of the same coin in Jewish thought, are linked in a ringing affirmation of God's commitment. To be children of God means preservation and victory despite the struggles and suffering of living in history.

Comments and Observations

Paul makes a series of important assertions in this text unit. First of all, he both explains and illustrates the power of God for salvation, which triumphs over all opposition and evil and transforms all relationships. All people, not just a few, can become the *children of God*. Insiders and outsiders are now honored; shame is overcome. If suffering seems to contradict this honor by inflicting shame on Christians, their vindication and honor will be confirmed by God in the eschatological judgment of the world. Paul is not ashamed of the gospel (1:16), because it overcomes all the powers in the cosmos.

Second, the Christian life is defined here, as in 8:1-11, as life in the Spirit. Christians are people who are led and empowered by the Spirit. And precisely because of that they are children of God who enjoy an intimate relationship with God and live in the confidence that God protects and saves even in the midst of suffering and persecution. What is surprising about this definition of the Christian life is that nothing is said about faith. Paul does not say here that Christians are people who believe or trust in Christ, but people who live in the Spirit.

Third, the theme of reversal is prominent. In 1:18-31 humans sought autonomy from God, and in the process enslaved creation as well. The glory of God was exchanged for the image of the mortal human being. All this is reversed in 8:12-39. Believers recognize God; they are led by the Spirit of God. They are to be revealed as the children of God. And when that happens all creation will be liberated. God, however, not humans, effects the reversal. God in Christ replaces fear, creation in travail, decay, frustration, groaning, and suffering with the revelation of the children of God, liberation from bondage and decay, glorification.

Finally, all the blessings promised to Israel are now given to "those in Christ." The ideas and themes that have characterized Israel's self-understanding as the people of God are applied without any kind of qualification to Gentiles as well as Jews. In fact, Paul's use of historic Jewish categories is so complete that it creates a serious problem. If Paul is correct, what happens to Israel? The question 8:12-39 raises becomes the subject of the next major section of the letter, chs. 9–11. As so often in Paul, the conclusion of one argument sets up the agenda for the next.

TEXT IN BIBLICAL CONTEXT

The central theme of 8:12-39—being children of God—is linked to a sending formula in Romans 8 and the role of the Holy Spirit that Paul uses to interpret the meaning of Jesus and the Christian life. The structure of the text is parallel to Galatians 4:4-7.

<u>Romans 8</u>	<u>Galatians 4</u>
	v. 4 But when the fullness of time came,
v. 3 God sent his son in the form of sinful flesh and he condemned sin in the flesh,	God sent his son born of a woman, subject to the law
v. 4 that the righteous requirement of the law might be fulfilled in us, who walk not according to the flesh, but according to the Spirit.	**v. 5** that he might redeem those under the law, that we might achieve acceptance as sons.
v. 14 For as many as are led by the Spirit are sons of God, **v. 15** for you have not received the Spirit of slavery	**v. 6** But because you are sons.

to fear again, but you received
the Spirit of adoption as sons
in whom we cry,
"Abba! Father!"
v. 16 This Spirit bears witness
with our spirit
that we are children of God.
v. 17 And if children,
also heirs, heirs of God,
and co-heirs with Christ . . .

God has sent the Spirit
of his son into our hearts,
crying
"Abba! Father!"
v. 7 So you are no longer
a slave,
but a son,
and if a son also an heir
through God.

The theology of the two texts is structurally similar, as well:

<u>**Romans**</u>	<u>**Galatians**</u>
The sending of the son	The sending of God's son
Saving result re law	Saving result re law
Life by the Spirit	Adoptions as children
Adoption as children	Presence of the Spirit
Abba! Father! prayer	Abba! Father! prayer
Heirs	Heirs

In both texts, Jesus liberates from enslavement that is linked with the law (the fulfillment of the law in Romans 8, the redemption of those under the law in Galatians 4), mediates adoption as children of God through the Spirit, initiates believers into the same intimate relationship with God that characterizes his life (the "Abba" prayer; M. M. Thompson, 2000b:21-34), and makes believers heirs to the promises of God. The adoption as children in Galatians is explicitly reminiscent of Israel's liberation from Egypt in the Exodus event; Israel's experience is a type of the eschatological redemption of believers. The adoption in Romans has future components that are not found in Galatians. The revelation of believers as the children of God is the moment of liberation for which all creation longs (v. 19). That revelation is associated with the "redemption of our bodies" (v. 23), which in turn is defined as *being conformed to the image of his Son, in order that he might be the firstborn among many brothers* (v. 29). To be conformed to the Son means to become co-rulers of the cosmos with him (v. 32). The goal and the end of this adoption process is glorification with Christ (vv. 17, 30). That is why believers yearn so deeply for the actual fulfillment of their adoption (v. 23).

Both Romans 8 and Galatians 4 reflect a significant Pauline reinterpretation of an important Jewish understanding of 2 Samuel 7:14.

The promise to David that a descendant *will be a son to me* was interpreted as an "adoption formula" in later Jewish writings, and interpreted eschatologically. The "adoption as a son" was applied to the Messiah (4QFlor. 1:11), to Israel as the people of God (Jub. 1:24), and to both the Messiah and Israel (*T. Jud.* 24:3). The context in all three texts is the restoration of Israel to a new covenant relationship with God. This restoration is associated with deliverance from Israel's enemies, the advent of the Messiah, the coming and work of the Spirit, divine adoption as children, the fulfillment of the law, and the kingship of Yahweh.

Paul reinterprets the 2 Samuel 7:14 tradition to apply to Christians. All of the themes of the Jewish eschatological expectation associated with this text are applied to Jewish and Gentile believers: deliverance, role of the Spirit, adoption, fulfillment of the law, kingship of God. God in Christ has restored the covenant of Israel. Those in Christ and the Spirit are now the children of God, and in the future will inherit all God's promises to Israel.

Paul's promise and claim is radical, so radical, in fact, that it raises profound questions about God and about Israel which Paul must address. Chapters 9–11 deal with these questions.

TEXT IN THE LIFE OF THE CHURCH
The New Family of God

This text has been the focus of many subthemes—the intimate connection between humanity and creation, the problem of suffering, the nature of hope, the doctrine of predestination. While important themes, the central one is that God through Christ and the Spirit makes all people members of the divine family. God is the subject, people are the objects.

God in Christ is doing a new thing, creating one people composed of Jews and Gentiles. That people is defined by life in the Spirit and as the children of God.

Everything that is said about the various subthemes is said first and foremost for and about this family of God. Creation groans for the liberation that will come with the revelation of this family; it is not the end-time coming of Christ, but the coming of God's family that creation anticipates. The people of God suffer with the rest of creation, but they suffer in hope because they know "God is for us," and will conform them to what Jesus is at God's right hand.

Paul does not outline a theology of creation here, but rather an ecclesiology of creation that is due to God's sending Jesus and the work of the Spirit to create the family of God. Suffering is a serious problem in history, which Paul answers with the end-time transformation of God's people into the likeness of Christ. The antidote to suffering is the glorification of God's people.

The centrality of the children of God is underlined once more by the repeated "all" in the concluding phrases of ch. 8: *God works all things to the good to the ones loving God* (v. 28); *God gave up the son in behalf of us all* (v. 32); *God will give us all things with him* (v. 32); *We are more than conquerors in all these things through the one having loved us* (v. 37); *not one thing in all creation will be able to separate us from the love of God* (v. 39).

The gospel is the power of God for salvation (1:16). It demonstrates that God reveals end-time righteousness, which is defined here as *God for us.* The "us" describes the family of God, composed of Jews and Gentiles, which will be blessed by God in ways that will transform history and creation.

The inclusiveness of the family of God—Jews and Gentiles in the first century—calls for a new sociology of the church in the twenty-first century: Christians of wealthy and poor nations, Christians of the west and the east, Christians of the north and the south. If God is for **all** followers of Jesus, as God is, then the transforming power of the gospel must be expressed in an inclusiveness that transcends western upper and middle class ideologies and values. The profound suffering of many Christians and churches in the world—Western and non-Western—must become a passionate concern and cause of the church of Messiah Jesus and the Spirit.

Living in the Spirit

Paul is usually interpreted as defining the Christian life as a life of faith. Faith is certainly important for Paul, the faith of Christ and the faith of Jesus' followers. A response of faith and obedience is foundational to being made righteous, to appropriating God's salvation in Christ. But Paul does not define the Christian life in Romans as much as a life of faith as life in the Spirit and the community of the Spirit. To be a Christian is to have the Spirit "dwelling within," to live in the Spirit, to be an integral part of the community of the Spirit.

There is something profoundly Pauline about the charismatic renewal in the church. The Christian—corporately and individually—is centered in and energized by the Spirit of God. What would happen if the church understood itself as the community of the Spirit rather than the community of faith?

The Church and Creation

Paul's ecclesiology of creation is linked to the renewal of creation. Humanity is an integral part of the created order; it is not independent of or set apart from nature. Humans are made of dust and return to dust. The fall of humans due to **Sin** "subjected" creation "to futility." Similarly, the salvation and re-creation of humans involves the "liberation" of creation.

Paul's vision for the future salvation of the world has profound implications for the church. The role of the new family of God in the redemption of creation calls the church to an engagement with nature and the environment. The "healing" of nations and creation—the realization of Isaiah's vision of the peaceable kingdom (Isa. 11:1-9)—involves a moral claim in the present—the reconciliation of people with God, each other, and nature. The stewardship of creation, the renewal of the environment, must be high on the churches agenda, albeit in the full recognition that "the liberation of creation" will be a re-creative act of God.

The Mystery of Suffering

Few experiences in life are as troubling and mysterious as suffering. In this text suffering is a function of growth toward God's future, rather than a discipline for sin. It has a messianic quality—Christians suffer with Messiah Jesus as fellow-heirs in order to be perfected (glorified). In other words, suffering has a redemptive quality—that is part of the mystery of suffering. But the salvific quality of suffering must be interpreted with great caution, as many women have pointed out in recent decades. Such interpretations must come from the people who actually suffer—minorities, women, churches experiencing persecution in many countries of the world—not from males in powerful and comfortable positions who benefit from such counsel.

The sixteenth-century Anabaptists were a people who suffered much for their faith. They saw themselves as co-sufferers with Christ, and went to their deaths with confidence and hope. They took great comfort from the assurance that nothing would separate them from the love of God. The same is true for many Christians in different parts of the world today. Indeed, there has been more suffering and more martyrs for the Christian faith in the twentieth century than in all history heretofore. [See commentary and stories in Waltner, 1999, especially 1 Peter 2:11–4:19].

Summarizing the Argument

Chapters 1–8

Paul's thesis statement made three assertions: 1) the gospel is the power of God for the salvation of all; 2) the righteousness of God is revealed in the gospel; 3) the wrath of God is revealed in the gospel. Paul developed the last statement first. In 1:18–3:20 he explained that the wrath of God is revealed impartially and justly. From 3:21 he has been expounding the second thesis that the righteousness of God is revealed for all humanity through the faithfulness of Jesus Christ, 3:21-26. The revelation means salvation for all people, 5:1–8:39.

The nature of the universal salvation in Christ is described in three broad categories: 1) a new relationship with God in 5:1-11 and 8:12-39—peace with God and a new family relationship—brackets the entire discussion; 2) victory over the power of **Sin** via Jesus (5:12-21) and baptism into the church of which Christ is the head (6:1–7:6); 3) victory over the flesh/**Sin** through Christ and the Spirit (7:7–8:39).

The effect of the second argument so far is to assert that the gospel is the power of God for salvation. The gospel effects salvation, deliverance, liberation from the power of **Sin**. It creates a new domain, a new kingdom, a new people. Salvation fulfills the covenant purposes of God and will renew the total creation. The Christ and the Spirit-people are the children of God, the historic title for Israel. The destiny of Israel has devolved first on Messiah Jesus, and then on the people of Jesus and the Spirit. Therefore, the new family composed of Jews and Gentiles in whom the Spirit is present and who are led by the Spirit inherit all the promises of God to Israel.

The righteousness of God has been defined as the love of God, profoundly relational and covenantal definitions of God. The righteousness and the love of God mean that *God is for us*, and will both save and protect believers despite all forms of hostility, opposition, and oppression. God's impartiality in judgment is balanced by God's impartial commitment to the new family in personal, collective, and cosmic salvation.

But a critical question remains. If God's faithfulness effects such a powerful salvation, why the unbelief of Israel? Does not Israel's unbelief call into question the righteousness and love of God? If God cannot save Israel, can God save anyone and/or anything? That is the question Paul must now resolve.

Romans 9:1–11:36

The Faithfulness of God to Jews and Gentiles

The tone and content of Romans 9 is dramatically different from that in ch. 8. The resounding confidence and optimism of ch. 8—God will triumph over all the powers, and nothing will separate believers from God's love—is gone. Paul is in anguish—he is willing to be cut off from Messiah Jesus, and he struggles theologically with profound questions about God—has the word of God failed, has God rejected Israel?

Chapters 9–11 constitute the fourth major argument in 3:21–11:36. These chapters are a clearly defined text unit. The argument begins with a distinct introduction, 9:1-5, and concludes with another doxology, 11:33-36.

Paul's gospel was *to the Jew first and also to the Gentiles*. His experience is more like "to the Gentiles first and also to a few Jews." Gentiles responded positively. Some Jews responded positively, but most rejected the gospel. The church was becoming a Gentile community—that is a serious problem among the Roman house churches. Gentile Christians were boasting that God had rejected Israel, and that the Gentile-Christian church had replaced Israel (11:17-24). This raised profound theological questions. Is God not powerful enough to redeem the Jews? Is God not keeping faith with the covenant, not being true to the word and the promises given to Israel? The subject matter is God, not Israel. Can God be trusted or not? If God is not faithful with Israel, how can Gentile Christians trust this God? Only a God who keeps covenants and promises can be a righteous God who makes the world righteous.

237

The connections with what has preceded are many and critical. Chapter 8 describes Jesus followers as "adopted children" (v. 15) who look forward to eschatological adoption (v. 23). Chapter 9 lists such adoption as the first privilege of Israel (v. 4). Chapter 8 calls Christians children of God (*sons* and *children*, vv. 14, 16f., 19, 21). Chapter 9 speaks of Israelites as *children* (v. 8) and *sons* (v. 26). Both chapters link adoption as children with the calling of God (8:28, 30; 9:7, 12, 24, 25, 26); both see the elective purposes of God at work (8:28; 9:11); both present glory as the goal of God's plan (8:18, 21, 29; 9:23). In short, both chs. 8 and 9 have in common the language traditionally used to describe the privileges and identity of Israel; one uses the language to describe the scope and magnitude of God's salvation, the other to defend God's integrity in relation to Israel. The latter is necessary because of the former. The problem of God in ch. 9 is a function of the eschatological blessings of God on all people in ch. 8. The "divine design" seems to have collapsed because God is giving others what was promised to Israel.

The connections within Romans go even deeper than ch. 8. Chapters 9–11 return to the questions and themes of ch. 3; they really exposit the meaning of ch. 3. Notice the parallels:

3:1-2	9:1-5	The privileges of Israel
3:3-4	9:6-13	The unfaithfulness of Israel does not mean the unfaithfulness of God
3:5-6	9:14-18	God's judgment of some does not mean the injustice of God
3:7-8	9:19-29	It is not unfair for God to find fault—judge
3:9-20	9:30–10:3	Works of the law do not save the Jews
3:21-26	10:4-21	Christ fulfills God's righteousness
3:27-31	11:1-36	God is the God of Jews and Gentiles, and will save both

The central theme of chs. 9–11 is the faithfulness of God. That theme is stated clearly in a thesis statement in 9:6—the word of God has not failed, and the rhetorical question in 11:1—has God rejected his people? The answer is developed in two ways. First, Paul resumes the diatribe style of question and answer. He knows that his opening defence of the reliability of God in 9:6-13 will raise objections. Therefore, he uses the diatribe style to pose questions that will determine his overall argument. The major questions are clearly indicated by the use of introductory formulas. The first two in 9:14 and 9:30—*is there injustice with God?* and *why* are the Gentiles attaining a righteousness they did not pursue while the Jews are not fulfilling the law they are pursuing?—are introduced by *what, therefore, shall we say?* The other questions in chs. 9 and 10–9:19, 20-21, 22-23, 32; 10:14-15, 18-19 are clearly second-order questions. The third and fourth major questions in 11:1 and 11:11—*has God rejected his people?* and have the Jews *stumbled so as to fall?*—are introduced by *I, therefore, say . . .* Three of the four major questions are denied by the *absolutely not!* answer, while none of the other questions are negated. Secondly, Paul shapes his answer by the exposition of Scripture—35 of the 90 verses in chs. 9–11 contain direct quotations of biblical texts (the 39% citation rate is higher than any place else in Paul's writings; the next is 28% in Rom. 4, and 25% in Gal. 3). Chapters 9–11 offer an interpretation of Israel's Scripture. If the question is *has the word of God failed?* then the answer must come from an explanation of the word of God. That is what Paul offers throughout Romans 9–11.

At a structural level, this reinterpretation of Israel's Scriptures retells Israel's story from Abraham (9:6f.) through the Messiah's fulfillment of that story (10:4) to Paul's own mission to Israel and the world (10:14-21). It is at the same time a retelling of the story narrated by Paul already in 7:7–8:11. God's gift of the Torah became an occasion for stumbling (7:7-25 and 9:30–10:3). God again brings the Torah to fulfillment through Messiah Jesus (8:3-4 and 10:4).

The argument of chs. 9–11 is introduced with Paul's personal lament about Israel's state, 9:1-5. It is the first of four times Paul interjects himself into the discussion in these chapters, each at an important turning point in the argument. In 10:1-2 he prays for Israel's salvation and bears witness that she has a zeal for God, albeit an ignorant zeal. There is evidence in 11:1 that God has not rejected Israel because he has called a remnant. In 11:13-14 he defines his own ministry to the Gentiles as a means *to make my fellow Jews jealous, and thus save some of them.* Paul's story is an integral part of Israel's story.

The thesis of chs. 9–11 is stated in 9:6, the word of God has not failed. Everything that follows in chs. 9–11 is designed to support the opening assertion that God is faithful and can be trusted. The argument proceeds in three main sections:

9:6-29   God's word has not failed;
9:30–10:21 Christ is the fulfillment of the Word of God;
11:1-32   God has not rejected Israel.

A doxology concludes the argument, 11:33-36.

There is a parallelism between the first and the third arguments both in style and content. Both argue against a misunderstanding of God. Both treat similar subjects:

9:6b-29	**11:1-32**
Abraham, v. 7	Abraham, v. 1
(Isaac) our ancestor, v. 10	Their ancestors, v. 28
Jacob, v. 13	Jacob, v. 26
Call, vv. 11, 24, 25, 26	Call, v. 29
Election, v. 11	Election, vv. 5, 7, 28
Harden, v. 18	Harden, vv. 7, 25
Have mercy, v. 23	Have mercy, vv. 30, 31, 32
The mercy, v. 23	The mercy, v. 31
To love, vv. 13, 25 (2 times)	To love, v. 28
A remnant, v. 27	A remnant, v. 5
Will be saved, v. 27	*Will be saved,* v. 26

The middle argument clearly has a different form. The three arguments form an ABA chiasm. Each argument in turn is developed by three sub-arguments.

For many centuries, interpreters, especially Protestants, thought Romans 9–11 was marginal in the letter. The chapters were either an excursus or a sermon that Paul had preached elsewhere and, for reasons that are not clear, inserted into the letter between chs. 8 and 12. Romans, on this view, really should be read by moving from ch. 8 to 12. More recent interpretation sees chs. 9–11 as the climax of the letter. They offer the solution to deep theological questions about God that are raised in chs. 1–8, but not addressed until here.

The Lament of Paul for Israel

Romans 9:1-5

PREVIEW

Paul begins with a lament, an emotional statement of his own feelings and desires. It is designed to evoke compassion for the Jews from the Gentile Christians, and to help them embrace his deep desire that they fulfill their destiny in the plan of God.

The pathos Paul feels is increased by the sequence of double expressions in vv. 1-3:

I am telling the truth	I am not lying
my conscience bears witness	in the Holy Spirit
great sorrow	continual pain
accursed	from Christ
my brothers	my kinspeople by race.

Paul identifies deeply with his own people. The issue of Israel's destiny is very personal, as the repeat of his concern in 10:1 indicates.

OUTLINE

The Oath, 9:1-2

The Wish, 9:3

The Privileges, 9:4-5

EXPLANATORY NOTES

The Oath 9:1-2

Paul opens his lament for Israel with an oath that he is telling the truth. The strong statement may well reflect criticism that he is answering. Elsewhere he uses the denial form, *I am not lying*, to respond to actual criticism. Some Christians, probably Jewish Christians, thought he had turned his back on his own people with his mission to the Gentiles. Paul, therefore, calls in a double witness to validate his truth claim, *in Christ* and *in the Holy Spirit*.

What is Paul telling the truth about? He is in a state of deep personal anguish about his people. Both the form and the content of his lament is common in Jewish apocalyptic literature, especially in relation to the destruction of Jerusalem.

The Wish 9:3

Paul's burden is so profound that he wishes he could be cursed by God (lit., *damned*) for the sake of *his people, his relatives according to the flesh* (genetic descent, not race). He pictures himself as a "salvation history" figure willing to offer himself as a vicarious sacrifice on the model of Moses (Exod. 32:32), the Suffering Servant (Isa. 53:5-6), or the Maccabean brothers (4 Macc. 17:22). The implication is that the Jewish people are accursed, and Paul wishes to take their place.

The Privileges 9:4-5

Paul identifies his people as *Israelites*. "Israel" was the favorite name of the Jewish people; it characterizes their self-understanding and identifies them as God's elect, covenant people. Other people called them "Jews," as Paul did earlier in Romans (nine times in chs. 1–3). In chapters 9-11, however he speaks as an insider: 12 of the 19 uses of "Israel" in his letters occur in Romans 9–11; "Jew" is used only twice (9:24; 10:12). Paul uses the family name to talk about family identity and destiny.

Paul further defines his people with three "who" clauses. The first lists six feminine nouns with similar sounding endings:

adoption as children (*hiothesia*)	glory (*doxa*)	covenants (*diathēkai*)
giving of law (*nomothesia*)	worship (*latreia*)	promises (*epangeliai*)

The rhythmical quality indicates that the meaning lies in the whole list rather than in the separate terms. The Israelites are God's children, who know the glory of God (probably a reference to God's special appearances or theophanies to Israel, e.g., Exod. 16, 24, 40; Lev. 9; Num. 14), who live in a covenant relationship with God, who have the law of God, who worship God, and who are heirs of the promises of God. The identity of the Jewish people could hardly be described more fully.

The second identifying "who" clause (5a, *on*) states that Israelites are the children of *the fathers*, an obvious reference to the patriarchs.

The climactic privilege of the Israelites is that they are the people of the Messiah. The qualification of Messiah with *the one according to the flesh* indicates there is more to the Messiah than this. The more is defined in the next phrase, *who is over all*, that is Lord of all things. This Messiah, Paul will say in the next reference to him, brings the law to fulfillment for the purpose of righteousness (10:4). Paul's lament contains a very provocative idea that he will develop. At the center of Jewish privilege there is an eschatological person who fulfills Israel's destiny and is God's means of salvation for her and for the whole world.

There is one startling feature in the list of privileges. It is precisely the privileges that Paul earlier has transferred to Messiah Jesus and those *in him*: adoption as children (8:15), glory (5:2; 8:18, 21), covenants (4:13, and the references to election in 8:30, 33), the fulfillment of the law (8:2, 4), worship (the redemptive sacrifice in 3:25), the promises (4:13f.), the fathers (Abraham in 4:11f.), the Messiah (1:3-4; 1:16-18; 3:22-26; 6:1f.; 8:1f.). Paul's gospel is the good news that Israel's unique heritage and status have become God's gift to the people of the world in Messiah Jesus. That gift, however, does not deny the ongoing validity of these privileges to Israel. But Israel's rejection of the climactic privilege, the Messiah and the fulfillment he brings, raises the questions that trouble Paul so deeply and that he addresses in chs. 9–11.

The lament closes with a doxology whose punctuation is much debated. There are three options. The first punctuates after Christ in the translation (*flesh* in Greek, since the word order is *"Christ according to the flesh"*), and refers the whole passage to Christ (so the NIV, *of Christ, who is God over all, forever praised! Amen*). It is then a doxology to Christ. The second option also punctuates after Christ (so NEB and TEV). But while Christ *may* be designated as the Lord of all, both NEB and TEV connect the praise phrase to God. The doxology then praises God as the one to be blessed. A third option is taken by the KJV, NASB, JB and NRSV, with the latter rendering it: *comes the Messiah, who is over all, God blessed forever, Amen*. This third option leaves the meaning a bit ambiguous, suggesting perhaps that both Christ and God are to be linked with *who is over all*, and both are recipients of the doxological praise. In light of the parallel doxologies in chs. 9 and 11, the second option is preferable since it parallels 11:33-36. God is the one praised for the incomparable privileges granted to Israel. The focus on God is reinforced then by the concluding doxology in 11:33-36, which clearly is a doxology to God rather than Christ.

God's Word Has Not Failed

Romans 9:6-29

PREVIEW

Paul states the thesis of chs. 9–11 and the first argument, 9:6-29, in 9:6a: God's word has not failed. The argument is framed as an inclusio by the word *seed* (*sperma*) in vv. 7 and 29 (*descendants* and *children* in most translations). Both verses are scriptural citations, Genesis 21:12 in v. 7, and Isaiah 1:9 in v. 29. Two other key words are used to unify the text and the various other scriptural citations. First, the word *son* (*huios*) is used in v. 9 in the citation from Genesis 18:10 and in vv. 26-27 in quotes from Hosea 1:10 and Isaiah 10:22-23. Second, the word *called* (*kaleō*) in the Genesis 21:12 citation in v. 7 is used again in vv. 25-26 from Hosea 2:23 and 1:10. Other texts cited in the exposition of Scripture do not contain one of the key words, but the words are found in the immediate context of the original citation.

A study of the key words used suggests a chiastic structure for the argument:

    A   9:6-9   word, Israel, called, seed, children (of God)
        B   9:10-13   called, loved
            C   9:14-18   mercy, willing
            C   9:19-23   willing, mercy
        B   9:24-25   called, loved
    A   9:26-29   called, children (of God), Israel, word, seed

The key words indicate the subject of the argument. God calls a people. The pattern of this calling is consistent with God's purposes. The argument consists essentially of a citation of Scripture and a brief commentary. For example, in the first argument, vv. 6-13, Paul supports his main argument (vv. 6-7a) with four Scripture citations (vv. 7b, 9, 10b-11a, 12-13) interpreted by two scriptural commentaries (vv. 8, 11b). The pattern is repeated throughout the text.

OUTLINE

Paul supports his opening thesis statement about the reliability of God with three parallel assertions that determine the outline of the text.

Thesis Statement, 9:6a
Statement 1—God's call rather than birth determines Jewish ancestry, 9:6b-13
    9:6b-7a   Argument
    9:7b   Scriptural proof
    9:8   Scriptural commentary
              Supporting Scripture citation 9:9
              Supporting scriptural story 9:10-11a
              Supporting scriptural commentary 9:11b
              Supporting scriptural citations 9:12-13

Statement 2—God's sovereignty is just and serves God's purposes of wrath and mercy, 9:14-21

9:14a First question
9:14b Denial
9:15 Scripture citation
       Scripture commentary 9:16
9:17 Scripture citation
       Scripture commentary 9:18
9:19 Further questions
       Counter questions 9:20
       Scriptural example 9:21

Statement 3—God's election purposes a new people, 9:22-29
    9:22-23 Question
    9:24   Thesis
    9:25-26 Scripture citations
    9:27-28 Scripture citations
    9:29   Scripture citation

EXPLANATORY NOTES
God's Call 9:6-13
Thesis Statement 9:6a

Paul's thesis is simple and direct. The word of God has not failed, literally, not *fallen off* as flowers from a stem. The thesis presents God as a defendant in court. Paul is the defense attorney who will argue that God is trustworthy.

The Priority of God's Call 9:6b-13

The thesis is supported by an argument that makes a distinction within Israel. God's word has not failed because *not all those descended from Israel are Israel.* Paul distinguishes between ethnic Israel and true Israel on the basis of the Abraham story. Not all of Abraham's children are *seed,* as God's promise did not mean the "salvation" of all his descendants. The scriptural proof is Genesis 21:12, *in Isaac shall your seed be called.* Paul's point here is the reverse of 4:13-18, where he argued that Abraham's seed was more extensive than his physical descendants. But the central point is similar. The true children of Abraham are not defined by physical descent or ethnic origin.

Verses 8-13 interpret and support the argument of vv. 6-7. Verse 8 offers a commentary on the Genesis citation in v. 7b. The commentary makes a negative and a positive statement. First, the children of the flesh (e.g., Ishmael and his descendants) are not the children of God. The positive assertion is that the children of promise (e.g., Isaac and his descendants) are *reckoned* as seed. The commentary is supported with another Scripture citation, Genesis 18:10. The son born to Sarah is a gift of divine promise and initiative, *I will come.*

Paul's first point is that from the beginning God has made a differentiation within Israel:

Ethnic Israel	**True Israel**
the ones not out of Israel	Israel
Abraham's children	seed
the children of the flesh	the children of God
	the children of promise
	seed
	son

God has a commitment only to the second group. While many Jewish contemporaries linked descent from Abraham with covenant salvation, some distinguished a "true Israel" from the larger group (CD 4:2-12; 4QFlor. 1:14-19; *1 En.* 1:8-9). Paul uses the distinction to argue that God's salvation and blessing is based solely on God's choice and promise.

Paul adds another scriptural story for support. Ishmael and Isaac were the children of two different mothers and two different sex acts. But Rebekah got pregnant with twins through one sex act with one man (Gen. 25:21). And even here God made a choice before they were born, before they could do any works that deserved being selected.

Verse 11b offers the second commentary. The choice of Jacob over Esau is interpreted with a purpose clause, *in order that the freedom of election in God's purpose might remain not out of works but out of calling.* The commentary is supported by two scriptural citations, Genesis 25:23 and Malachi 1:2-3, representing the Law and the Prophets. The first speaks of the two children as two nations. The second was interpreted in contemporary Judaism to say God hated Esau because of his "bad deeds." Paul rejects that interpretation by using the text to assert that God made the choice before birth, and thus before any performance of deeds.

Several things are noteworthy about Paul's first argument. The distinction between ethnic Israel and true Israel is based on the principle of selection. God made choices from the beginning, as illustrated in the history of the patriarchs. In seven verses Paul has introduced the central patriarchs of Israel's story—Abraham, Isaac, and Jacob—to ground divine election solely in the call of God, not on people's deeds. This call theme is repeated throughout 9:6-29 (see vv. 24, 25, 26, in addition to vv. 7 and 11). Second, Paul has reintroduced one of the critical phrases in the letter, *out of works*. It is an important phrase in the developing argument (e.g., 9:32, 11:6). *Out of works* is contrasted here with *out of calling*, not with *out of faith* as earlier in the letter. The issue is the calling of God, not making righteous by faith. Paul rejects both salvation by birth (Isaac), and salvation by works (Jacob). Election (i.e., salvation) is based solely on God's call, and has been so from the beginning of Israel's story. Third, election language here is corporate language, not individual. Paul is talking in salvation history terms: God chose a people through Isaac rather than Ishmael and through Jacob rather than Esau to be the people of the covenant and of promise.

Paul's point is clear. Salvation is based exclusively on the call of God. God never promised to save all ethnic Israel, so the rejection of Messiah Jesus by the majority of Jews does not undermine the integrity of God's word. Paul's argument suggests that this rejection is a sign that Israel stands outside the Abrahamic covenant and thus the people of God. Israel now stands where Ishmael and Esau once stood.

God's Sovereignty 9:14-21

Paul's opening argument for election independent of human involvement, even prior to the birth of the people involved, raises questions about the justice of God. Is God not arbitrary and thus unrighteous? The question both echoes 3:5 and is different from it. There the question was God's justice in judgment, while here the issue is God's justice in election. Paul rejects the suggestion of God's injustice in the strongest possible terms, *absolutely not!* The question is profoundly Jewish. The question is not, "is election unjust?" Jews believed in election; God had elected them as a people. Rather, the question is, is God unrighteous to the covenant by electing some within Israel and not all?

Paul grounds the denial in an exposition of the nature of God's mercy in vv. 15-18. Mercy is the key term in vv. 15, 16, and 18; vv. 15 and 18 are structurally parallel (*I will have mercy on whom I will have mercy* and *he has mercy upon whomever he wills*). The key to interpreting God's mercy, and to answering the question about God's righteousness, is the citation of Exodus 33:19b. There the context is Moses' intercession to save the people of Israel following the idolatry of the Golden Calf. The issue is the glory and the name of God. In the fullest self-disclosure of God prior to Jesus, God is revealed as merciful and compassionate. God's election and preservation of Israel is due solely to mercy and compassion, not the goodness of Israel. The critical issue in election is the purpose of God—to create a people that brings glory to the name—and the nature of God—merciful and compassionate.

The commentary in v. 16 interprets God's mercy by contrasting human effort and divine mercy. God's election is righteous because it means that "chosenness" is based exclusively on divine mercy, not upon human effort (lit., *willing and running*). Paul emphasizes that election is based solely on the nature and purpose of God. A second Scripture citation, Exodus 9:16 in v. 17, further explains the righteousness of God. Pharaoh, who wished to destroy God's people, is another example of God's mercy. Pharaoh's intent served God's sovereign purpose of electing Israel. God demonstrated the divine, saving power of God (as in 1:16) so that the divine name would be proclaimed in the world. The focus here is not on the judgment of Pharaoh, but on God's mercy toward Israel. God saved Israel from Pharaoh and in the process demonstrated saving power. The commentary in v. 18 reaffirms that God is a God of mercy; God has mercy on whom God chooses, in this case Israel.

The flip side of God's mercy is judgment; God hardens whom God chooses, in this case Pharaoh (but earlier Esau). God's righteousness is manifest in divine mercy, which by definition cannot be claimed or earned. Even the opponents demonstrate God's mercy, because they serve to reveal God's power and name. Paul's defense of God also lays the groundwork for what follows. The contrast between Esau and Pharaoh, on the one hand, and Israel, on the other, in the electing purposes of God could mean that Israel as a people could become like Esau or Pharaoh.

Paul's emphasis on divine initiative in election resurrects a previous objection from 3:7. If God alone is responsible in election, and if God even uses human unfaithfulness to further the divine design, is God not unjust to find fault with human beings (v. 19)? Is election not in conflict with judgment? If God's power is totally effective in achieving the divine purposes, is there any room left for human responsibility? Paul lets the objection be heard, but his concern is the freedom of God rather than the freedom of human beings.

Paul responds to the questions with a series of counter questions that include a scriptural citation (v. 20) and illustration (v. 21). The first counter question in v. 20 states an intentional contrast between humanity and God—*O man, who are you to answer back to God?* The second question uses the words of Isaiah 29:16 but changes a statement into a question. What right does the creature have to demand from the Creator an explanation for how it was made? The question raises the problem of 1:18-32, the creature rebelling against the Creator. Paul's language here is nuanced; the word for *made* or *shaped* (*plassō*) is one that is used in the OT of God's election of Israel (Deut. 32:6; Isa. 43:1, 7; 44:2, 21, 24; 49:5, 8; 53:11).

The illustration of the potter is a popular image of God in Judaism (see Ps. 2:9; Isa. 29:16; 41:25; 45:9; Jer. 18:1-6; Sir. 33:13; *T. Naph.* 2:2, 4; 1QS 11:22). Paul's use of it is clear. The potter can make a beautiful piece of artwork and a chamber pot (a potty) from the same lump of clay. The potter is creative; he makes pottery for different purposes, or he may remake something that looks like a failure. The clear implication is that the creature must submit to the Creator, even if and when the Creator changes plans and determines to make something different. Both the OT texts and Paul's use of the potter image make it clear that he is talking about the fate of Israel as a people, not about the fate of individual human beings. The example here prepares the way for the resolution of the problem of Jewish unbelief in ch. 11—God will save all Israel for the sake of the promises to the patriarchs.

The lead question was about the justice of God, v. 14. It is important to note that the question of God's justice for Paul is quite different from modern concerns about theodicy. Modern theodicy focuses primarily on the unjust suffering of innocent people. Paul believes that all human beings are sinners who deserve judgment (3:9, 10, 19). His question is, why does a righteous God leave sinners unpunished? Paul's answer is the mercy of God. God restrains judging human sin because of divine mercy, because of a desire to see all humans redeemed (3:25). Pharaoh and Israel should have been destroyed, but God exercised mercy and used both to achieve a larger divine purpose. God is righteous because God is merciful, because God causes even evil to work for good. And because God is just, God is free to elect.

The first two assertions in 9:6f. argue two aspects of the same point: God's promise and call are based on divine sovereignty and are unrelated to human descent or activity. So far Paul has not said anything with which a Jew would disagree. Even 9:6 is within the realm of traditional Jewish understanding. Jews know that not all Abraham's descendants are his heirs. Any Jew would affirm Paul's claim that God elected Isaac and not Ishmael, Jacob rather than Esau. It was common knowledge that Pharaoh's hardening was for God's glory and Israel's ultimate good. The scriptural citations and illustrations all make the same point: God endures or permits Israel's enemies for Israel's sake. The argument so far says nothing unusual, but it does lay the groundwork for something startling.

God's Election Purposes a New People 9:22-29

Verses 22-23 constitute one long question. The question begins a new paragraph, *but what if God wishing to demonstrate his wrath and to make known his power* . . . (most translations do not translate the *but*). Paul is making a new point, his first distinctively Christian argument so far in chs. 9–11.

The question asks the readers to consider a possible way to understand God's purpose. What if the Creator God, who wishes to exercise end-time judgment (*show his wrath*) and thus demonstrate divine power, has tempered deserved judgment with patience. Evil, here the rebellion of the creature against the Creator, deserves God's judgment. The objects of the judgment are *vessels of wrath made for destruction.* In the context these vessels would be Esau and Pharaoh. What if God withholds judgment *in order to make known the riches of his glory for the vessels of mercy, which he prepared before hand for glory?* In the context, and in Jewish theology, the vessels of mercy would be Israel. While the Jewish Christians in Paul's audience would be nervous about postponing divine judgment on enemies like Pharaoh, they would certainly affirm their election, and God's intention to make known the riches of divine glory through them. The question plays directly into Jewish national theology.

In v. 24 Paul turns the tables. More accurately, he drops a fragmentation bomb. The *vessels of mercy* are not the Jews, but *us whom God has called not only out of the Jews but also out of the Gentiles.* The bomb fragments fly in many different directions. This new people is *called,* one of the main thematic emphases in the argument of 9:6ff. Second, the composition of this new people is defined by the familiar *Jew/Gentile* phrase from earlier in the letter (1:16; 2:9, 10; 3:9) and the *not only/but also* argument of 3:29 and 4:12, 16. Third, the nature of this new people is in fulfillment of Israel's Scripture. God's calling this new people is a demonstration that the word of God has not failed. Fourth, just as the *vessels of mercy* are redefined, so also the *vessels of wrath* are redefined. The *vessels of wrath* are now suddenly unbelieving Jews, rather than Esau and Pharaoh.

Verse 24 rearranges the preceding argument. Verses 22-23 are suddenly parallel with v. 17. Verses 14-18 illustrated the impartiality of God. God makes equal use of vessels of mercy and vessels of wrath. Moses was an example of mercy and Pharaoh of wrath. God did not liquidate Pharaoh, but used him to demonstrate divine power and to proclaim the divine name in all the earth. The same is happening again, only now Israel represents the vessels of wrath. And again, God is not destroying Israel but using her unbelief to demonstrate divine wrath and to proclaim glory to all the nations. The point that the concentration of wrath in one people serves the purposes of God builds on Paul's earlier suggestion that God called Israel to be the people where **Sin** would be focused so that it could be condemned and defeated in one place by one person (5:20; 7:13-8:2).

The radically new element that changes everything is the inclusion of the Gentiles. Paul has not excluded the Jews; that issue does not arise until 9:30f. and is not explicitly asked until 11:1. Paul simply redefines God's people by including believing Gentiles. God's merciful calling of Gentiles is no different than God's merciful call of Israel.

Paul's astounding claim requires biblical proof, which is supplied in vv. 25-29 in a chiasm that builds on v. 24:

    A v. 24a Jews
        B v. 24b Gentiles
        B vv. 25-26 Gentiles
    A vv. 27-29 Jews

Paul reapplies Hosea 2:1 and 2:25 from Israel to the Gentiles. His substitution of *called* for *will say* reinforces the *call* language in the argument. The point of contrast is *not my people/my people, not my beloved/my beloved*, and *not my people/children of the living God*. It may also be that the phrase *in the place where I said to them*, which originally referred to Palestine, is here intended to evoke the image of the end-time pilgrimage of the Gentiles to Zion, but that is not the central point of the citation. Gentiles, who were not the people of God, are now the people of God, not because of their ethnic or moral claims, but because of the call of God. Gentiles are now the children of the *living God*, a characteristic Jewish definition of God that contrasts the God of Israel with the *dead idols* of the Gentiles. The "innovative boldness" of Paul's hermeneutic in reinterpreting the Hosea texts is hard to imagine.

Verses 27b-28 contain a mixed quotation from Hosea 1:10 and Isaiah 10:22-23, and v. 29 is a verbatim quote from Isaiah 1:9. God's call of Israel has in no way been abrogated by the call of the Gentiles. Isaiah shows that a remnant of Israel has been saved. God has retained a seed (*sperma*), v. 29, which recalls Abraham's seed in v. 7. The survival of a seed is a sign of God's grace. The presence of a remnant in the new vessel is a sign of mercy, not of failure or injustice.

At the center of these biblical proofs stands the claim of 9:6, God's word has not failed, but is being accomplished. God's electing will has not collapsed for two reasons: it was never intended to apply to Israel alone, and the inclusion of the Gentiles has been on precisely the same grounds as Israel's election. Furthermore, God is just toward ethnic Israel. Not only does her unbelief deserve judgment, but this judgment was foretold by the prophets. In fact, Isaiah predicted it would be so severe that only a remnant would be saved. And, as in the past, God is using Israel's current unbelief to show mercy to others.

Comments and Observations

Paul essentially retells the story of Israel in ch. 9. He narrates the holy history about the patriarchs in vv. 7-13, the exodus and wilderness wanderings in vv. 14-18, and the exile and return of a remnant in vv. 24-29. Such retellings of Israel's story were common in Jewish literature, e.g., Jubilees. The point of this retelling is that at each critical stage God chooses one person or group and not another.

Romans 9:6-29 is a coherent argument, which asserts that God's past relationship with Israel is consistent with current realities. God graciously continues to elect a people, and does so impartially. The entire argument is for Israel's place in salvation history. Except for one element the argument would be acceptable to the Jewish Christians and Jews in Paul's audience. Paul clearly insists on the validity of Israel's claim to be God's people. He affirms the basic premise of Israel's theology, God's free election of Israel. He also reasserts the mercy of God toward Israel: God created Israel, God bestowed privilege on Israel, God judges Israel for sin. The only new element is that the Gentiles are now included in God's mercy. Paul does not say that the Gentiles displace Israel, but are included in Israel. Chapter 9 is an argument for Israel, not against Israel. But it also raises the question, what happens to Israel, ethnic Israel according to the flesh? Paul picks up that question in 9:30f.

TEXT IN BIBLICAL CONTEXT

Paul uses *election* (*eklogē*) language to describe the purposes of God in Romans 9. Four of the seven NT references, four out of five uses of "election" in Paul, are found in Romans 9–11 (9:11; 11:5, 7, 28). Paul supports election language in ch. 9 in two ways: 1) he frames the text unit with *called* language (vv. 7 and 25-26), and 2) he cites Scriptures that speak of God's election. Most of the citations describe God making choices, e.g., Isaac over Ishmael, Jacob over Esau, the hardening of Pharaoh, *not my people* becoming *my people* and even *sons of the living God*, the remnant over the whole.

Election and Jewish Identity

"Election" is OT language that has been seriously misunderstood in the history of the Christian church. It is God and peoplehood language. Israel exists as a people because of God's choice. Election was the call of God to serve God by bringing light and salvation to all people (Isa. 2:1-4; 49:5f.; 51:4f.). Election is first and foremost an act of God, God creating a people by calling. Second, election is primarily a corporate concept. God calls a people, Abraham and his descendants, Isaac and his children, Jacob and his family.

Corporate election does not mean that all people in the group are elect. People who violated the covenant could be cut off (Exod. 12:19; Num. 19:13). The individual members of this elect people had to decide if they wished to accept and live by the terms of the election. For example, God elected a tribe, the Levites, to be the priests of the people. They were chosen as a category or group of people. That did not mean that all individual Levites were priests; some individuals were disqualified for a variety of reasons, e.g., gender, deformity or illness, guilt for sins. Individual disqualification did not negate the election of the group.

Election language in the OT makes the astounding assertion that God has chosen a people to serve and represent God in the world. But this election does not guarantee that all Israelites are elect.

Election, together with monotheism and eschatological hope, constituted the center of Jewish faith in the first century. The Jewish people lived by the deep conviction that they alone had been chosen to be the people of God. God chose Abraham and his children to be the means of undoing evil in the world, of reversing the sin of Adam. The problem from Paul's perspective was the exclusivity of "only this people." Election was nationalized in Judaism during the intertestamental period and became synonymous with Jewish identity. Non-Jews were not elect; they could become elect only by becoming Jews.

Paul's Perspective on Election

Paul challenges Jewish and Jewish-Christian views of election. He uses the patriarchal stories to reaffirm that "not all out of Israel are Israel" (v. 6). The equation of election and Jewish identity is wrong. Second, Paul uses the prophets, especially Hosea, to assert that non-Jews are being elect as the people of God.

The central point of Paul's election language in Romans 9 is that God, and only God, elects—it is by divine calling and mercy, not because of anything the elect are or do. The object of this divine electing is a people, a corporate entity—children, sons, seed, vessels, a people are all plural. God is electing a new people composed of Jews and Gentiles in creating a new vessel.

Paul's continued discussion of election in ch. 11 reinforces the themes of ch. 9, but also reaffirms the faithfulness of God to the election of Israel. Election of a remnant to represent the whole is by grace, not works (vv. 5-6). Israel as a whole failed to attain that election (v. 7) because it pursued its own national righteousness rather than the righteousness of God (10:3f.). But, God will yet save Israel as a people. Why? Because Israel as a people is elect; *as regards election they are beloved for the sake of their forefathers for the gift and the call of God are irrevocable* (11:28b-29).

Election language in the Bible is about God—God's choosing and faithfulness—and about peoplehood. God is the one who elects. A people is created by election, first Israel and then the church composed of Jews and Gentiles.

TEXT IN THE LIFE OF THE CHURCH

Romans 9:6-29 is about the faithfulness of God to the covenant and promises to Israel despite Israel's rejection of Messiah Jesus. The Christian church has made this a text about the church's displacement of Israel, about the foreknowledge of God in election, and about God's election of some individuals to salvation and some to damnation (double predestination). The latter two interpretations led to endless debates about the relationship of divine sovereignty and human free will.

Displacement Theology

By the second-century Gentile Christians lost interest in the questions of God raised by Jewish rejection of Jesus. As Paul's burden for the salvation of the Jewish people became increasingly foreign to the church, the meaning of the text was turned on its head. The dominant interpretation from the second century onward became the "substitution model," the church replaced Israel, the church is the new Israel. Election became a message about God's rejection of the Jews and the selection of the Gentiles. The destruction of Jerusalem was the key evidence that God had judged the Jews for the crucifixion of Jesus. They were now a people without land, temple, altar, sacrifices, prophets, priests; and none of these would ever be restored again. The God who blesses faithful Jews and judges unfaithful Jews but always remains loyal and faithful to this people in Romans 9 was changed into a God who has withdrawn loyalty from them forever, and now blesses good Christians and judges bad ones. The Jews served only as examples of God's election or predestination to judgment.

The substitution theory has persisted. Romans 9 is read as an apology for the church as "the true Israel," as the actual bearers in the present and the future of the blessings of God promised to historic Israel. Gentile Christians are the true children of Abraham and the only remnant of historic Israel elected to salvation. The central characteristic of this interpretation is to set the church into radical contrast to Judaism: Judaism is a religion of salvation by works and Christianity is a religion of salvation by faith.

Theology of Predestination

Beginning with Origen in the third century A.D., a second theme emerged—the relationship of the sovereignty of God to individual human free will. As outlined by Origen, God foreknew the behavior of persons, and elected them to salvation or damnation accordingly. God's election of people was based on their intention and actual behavior.

The concern for God's foreknowledge in the Greek fathers hardened into a theology of predestination with Augustine, early-fifth century, and in Latin theology. The leading interpretation of Romans 9 in the West asserted that this text is about the predestination of some to grace and others to damnation. Jewish unbelief was simply an example of the latter. The purpose of Romans 9, then, is to underline divine sovereignty in the age of grace without regard for human works or will. Human free will is totally enslaved by sin, and thus under the judgment of God. Protestant interpreters, led by Luther and Calvin, built on this tradition.

The fundamental assumption underlying the Augustinian and Protestant interpretation of Romans 9 is that Paul's primary concern is the eternal salvation or damnation of individual persons. The Jewish people are nothing more than examples of people damned because of unbelief. It is hard to imagine a more radical reinterpretation of Paul's meaning in Romans 9, or a more dangerous and damaging interpretation in the history of the church. This interpretation resulted in a long history of hostility toward the Jewish people that reached its apex in the Nazi Holocaust.

God's Election of Jewish and Gentile Peoples

Romans 9 is pro-Israel; it makes the case for the faithfulness of God to the covenant and promises to Israel. The climax of this argument is yet to come in Romans 11. Paul's theology of election is corporate.

He is not talking about God's election of individual men and women, but of a people, first the Jewish people, and then Jews and Gentiles. God elects a particular people to bring salvation to the world. In Jesus Christ God narrows the focus of election even further. As Paul argued earlier in Romans, God in Christ elects all humanity to be the people of God (5:12-21) and desires them to become children of God in Jesus. That does not mean that all humans are saved, just as God's election of Israel did not mean that all Jews were saved. Paul is clear that only those human beings who exercise faith in Christ and have the Spirit enjoy the saving blessings of God's election (see 3:22-26; ch. 4; 9:30-32; 10:9, 16, 20-21).

Election in Romans 9 is an affirmation of God's faithfulness. God remains faithful to election, to the choices made in history. But Romans 9 also indicates that the boundaries of election have been opened up beyond the Jewish people to include Gentiles. That is a word of divine grace and mercy for both Jews and Gentiles; it is not a word of judgment on the Jewish people.

Election Is About God's Love and Mercy

But Romans is also a word about God's love, mercy, and lordship in history. God loved Jacob. God's election of some is grounded in mercy and compassion. God's election and plan for a people and for humanity is not cancelled because of human unfaithfulness. God uses even human rebellion to proclaim the divine name and *to make known the riches of his glory* in all the earth.

The idea of divine rejection, *Esau I hated* and *he hardens the heart of whomever he wills*, is a corollary to the main point, but not the principal claim. Furthermore, Paul's purpose in describing God's election of some and not others is to critique a Jewish doctrine of pre-destination, which is presumptuous. The Jews think they are elect, and Esau and Pharaoh are the ones excluded from election. Paul's point is that Israel now stands where Esau and Pharaoh stood, because Israel has become disobedient and hard of heart, while Esau and Pharaoh as symbols for the Gentiles are now included in the elect. Election is based on God's call, not on ethnicity. That is a word of grace and hope, not of rejection and arbitrariness.

It is also important to remember that the emphasis on divine initiative in Romans 9 is both very Jewish and very relevant to Paul's audience. Paul puts the emphasis in election where the Jews put it, God's freedom to be God, to be the potter who creates and recreates. Human responsibility is not the agenda in Jewish "potter theology" nor in Romans 9; human responsibility is not addressed in any form until 9:30ff. Gentiles in the ancient world were dominated by a fear of fate, the inevitability of impersonal forces in the cosmos. No one can escape his/her appointed position and destiny in life. Determinism is a pervasive belief in the ancient world. That is why astrology was so popular. Paul's emphasis on divine initiative in election is not offensive. In fact, Paul's theology is good news. History is determined by the Creator God who makes and remakes, who makes *not my people my people*. History is not determined by fate, but by the God who calls, who knows my name, and the God who transforms *not my people into the sons of the living God* (2 Cor. 6:18 includes *and daughters*).

Pervasive misinterpretation of Romans 9 over the centuries has made it almost impossible for preachers to preach on this text. However, with the first-century understanding of election in mind, post-modern preachers can once again proclaim the good news of Romans. Namely, reinforcing the overriding theme of Romans, this chapter stresses that God is in charge; God is the One who calls a people, because of love, mercy, and compassion.

Christ Is the Fulfillment of the Word of God

Romans 9:30–10:21

PREVIEW

The second argument in chs. 9–11 proceeds from the conclusion just drawn, that election of a new vessel of Jews and Gentiles demonstrates God's faithfulness. That conclusion raises a question about Gentile inclusion and Jewish exclusion. If God is creating a new vessel, why are Gentiles responding affirmatively to this new reality, but the Jews as a people are rejecting it?

The form of the argument at the beginning (9:30-33) and the end (10:14-21) is the diatribe. The answers to the questions, as well as the central section of the unit, involve extensive Scripture citation and interpretation.

The argument is framed by an inclusio—Gentile inclusion in 9:30 and 10:20, Jewish exclusion in 9:31 and 10:21. The use of two quotes from Isaiah to complete the inclusio in 10:20-21 highlights the importance of the issue. The contemporary reality—the Gentiles finding the prize even though they are not in the race, while the Jews have not reached the finish line even though they have run hard—is a fulfillment of God's word.

The explanation of the current dilemma is further framed by the use of language from earlier in the letter—righteousness, law, faith, works. The use of this language in Romans can be plotted like this:

	1:16-18	3:20-5:21	6–8	9	9:30-10	11	12–16
righteousness	1	14	6	0	11	0	1
faith (noun)	3	20	0	0	5	1	7
faith (verb)	1	7	1	0	8	0	3
law	0	17	30	0	4	0	2
works	0	5	0	1	1	1	1

Paul uses a series of contrasts—Gentile/Jew, out of faith/out of works, righteousness of God/own righteousness—to argue that there is a right and a wrong righteousness, and a right and a wrong practice of the law. Israel is excluded from the new peoplehood because she has chosen both the wrong righteousness and the wrong practice of the law.

The frame—Israel's refusal to trust God—points to central theme, Christ is the fulfillment of the law and the plan of God. The correct righteousness and understanding of the law is found in Messiah Jesus. He is the fulfillment of the goal in the race for Gentiles and Jews. He is the good news for all people who will hear and obey.

OUTLINE

Diatribe—Israel pursued the law and righteousness incorrectly, 9:30–10:3
> 9:30a   First question
>> First answer 9:30b
>> Second answer 9:31
>
> 9:32a   Second question
>> First answer 9:32b-33
>> Personal lament 10:1
>> Second answer 10:2-3

Thesis—Christ is the goal for Jew and Gentile, 10:4-13
> 10:4   Thesis statement
>> Scripture citation 10:5-6a
>> Scripture interpretation 10:6b

EXPLANATORY NOTES

Israel Pursued the Law and Righteousness Incorrectly 9:30–10:3

The opening question in v. 30, *what then shall we say?* is a typical Pauline introduction to a new argument (see 4:1; 6:1; 7:7). The question is followed by the first of the parallel contrasting statements: the Gentiles did not pursue a goal but achieved it; the Jews pursued a goal but failed to achieve it. The imagery is athletic. What follows must be understood as a metaphor of a footrace. The Gentiles were not in the race but won the prize. The Jews were running very hard but failed to win.

What is striking is that the goal of the race is defined differently. Righteousness is used three times in four words to define the goal for the Gentiles; v. 30 literally reads, *the Gentiles not pursuing righteousness attained righteousness, righteousness out of faith.* Paul is clearly recalling the thesis of 1:16-17. The language is covenantal. Because Gentiles were outside the covenant, they were not seeking a right relationship with God, that is, they were not interested in the saving power of God that puts people right within the covenant. But once they learned about God's righteousness, the Gentiles experienced its saving power because they accepted it by faith.

In contrast, Israel *raced with all its might* after *the righteous law* (*nomon dikaiosunē*). The goal is the law, not *the righteousness of the law* as in most translations (that would require *dikaiosunē nomou*). The law is defined as righteous in 7:12 (*nomon dikaiosunē* is a subjective genitive—lit., *law of righteousness* or *the law which is righteous*); it is the standard which defines what God requires of the covenant people. Israel's goal was the law, but it did not win the race and get the prize (lit., *to the law not it attained*). The double mention of the law as the goal—law of righteousness and law as the goal—is deliberate. Israel did not pursue righteousness, but the law. The fact that Israel's not reaching the goal of the law is parallel to the Gentiles attaining righteousness indicates that for Paul both goals are closely related. They are parallel, not opposed to each other as in much Protestant interpretation.

The startling contrast between Gentiles and Israel and the shocking analysis of Israel's failure raises the second question (v. 32a), *why* (lit., *on account of what?*). The question is, why did the Jews not reach the goal of the law? Paul offers two answers, 9:32b-33 and 10:2-3, each involving a contrast. The answers are interrupted by a personal lament for Israel's failure (10:1).

The first answer for Israel's failure is *because not out of faith but out of works* (v. 32b). The contrast is the earlier *out of faith/out of works of law*. Israel's problem is not the goal, the law, but the means of pursuing the goal. Paul does not disparage the law. Israel raced after a good goal in the wrong way, by means of Jewish ethnocentrism [*Essay: Works of Law*], which excluded the Gentiles instead of by faith (or faithfulness) which is an option for all peoples (some manuscripts read *works of law* rather than simply *works*). Paul explains Israel's failure by another race metaphor, she stumbled on a stone. The stumbling image is interpreted by a mixed Scripture citation from Isaiah 28:16 (*behold, I lay in Zion a stone of stumbling and a stone of offense*) and 8:14 (*and the one faithing it [or him] will not be ashamed*).

The stone image and the Isaiah citations have historically been interpreted to mean Israel's rejection of the Messiah. But the reference is the law, not the Messiah. There is no discussion of the Messiah in the context; he has not been mentioned since 9:5 and is not mentioned until 10:4. Paul is discussing Israel's failure to achieve the goal of the law. The *stone* image carries multiple meanings in the OT and Judaism—the word of Yahweh, the law, the righteous community (Qumran), the messiah (Targums), the Temple (Rabbis), the universe (Rabbis). While 1 Peter 1:6 uses the stone image messianically, Paul here is using it in its OT sense as the law. The *in him* phrase from

Isaiah 8:14 can also be translated as *in it* (*ep autō* can be either a dative masculine, *in him*, or neuter, *in it*). The only antecedent is either the law or the word of Yahweh; it cannot be Christ, because Christ has not yet been mentioned. While the same phrase refers to God in 10:11 and to the Messiah in 1 Peter 2:6, the context in each case helps determine the meaning. Here the context is Israel's failure to attain the law because she did not pursue it out of faith. Just as Israel refused to trust the word of God in the face of the Assyrian threat (Isa. 28), so now she stumbles over the law in faith. It is "by faith alone" which is the stone of stumbling because it is inclusive of all people. The Jews rejected the inclusive way of faith for the exclusiveness of Jewish nationalism.

Paul's comments about the law again are very positive. The law is righteous. Israel's problem is not that the law was bad or unfulfillable, but that Israel raced after the good goal in the wrong way. Paul's first explanation of Israel's failure recalls his earlier indictment of the Jews in 2:17-29 and 3:20, 27-30.

Paul is so overwhelmed by Israel's failure to attain the law that he interrupts his argument with another personal lament, 10:1. His deep desire and prayer is for the salvation of Israel. The phrase *to salvation* echoes the thesis of 1:16, and would be entirely consistent with Israel's pursuit of the law *out of faith* as Paul demonstrated in the story of Abraham (ch. 4).

Paul's second answer for Israel's failure uses different language. The problem now is not her relationship to the law but to the righteousness of God. The fundamental contrast, *the righteousness of God/own righteousness*, is intensified by one other, *zeal/ignorance*. Israel is a people characterized by *zeal for God*, a technical phrase for Jewish piety passionate to do God's will. It became a synonym for *zeal for the law* during the Maccabean period, and took for its models Simeon and Levi (Jth. 9:4; *Jub.* 30:5-20), Phinehas (Num. 25:10-13; Sir. 45:23-24; 1 Macc. 2:54; 4 Macc. 18:12), Elijah (Sir. 48:2; 1 Macc. 2:58), and Mattathias (1 Macc. 2:19-26; Jos. *Ant.* 12:271). A key component of this zeal was the exclusion of all non-Jews and non-Jewish things from the covenant community. Acts confirms that such zeal was present in the Jerusalem churches (21:20), and Paul himself modeled it in his persecution of the church (Gal. 1:13-14; Phil. 3:6). The problem with Israel's zeal is that it is *without knowledge* and *ignorant*, which literally means lacking discernment, the ability to differentiate the true nature of reality. The language is full of irony. In its zeal for God Israel misunderstands the very criterion by which zeal is to be evaluated, true knowledge of the will of God.

The object of knowledge, or the point of ignorance, is righteousness. The contrast is the righteousness of God (the language of 1:16-17 and 3:21-26) and *their own righteousness*, the saving power of God to make the world right versus the exclusive ethnic righteousness of Israel. The subject is Israel as a people, not individual Jewish people. "Their own" (*idios*) contrasts "*ours*" with "*others.*" The Israelites *are seeking to establish* their own national righteousness, which excludes all other people. The word for *establish* (*stēsai*) is normally used in the OT for God's establishment of the covenant. Israel here seeks to do God's business. The problem of this *seeking* is defined by one further contrast, *not submitting* (lit., *ordering* or *standing under*). The issue is voluntary subordination rather than seeking. Israel as a people is ignorant because it seeks its own exclusive righteousness by refusing to submit to the righteousness of God.

Christ Is the Goal for Jew and Gentile 10:4-13

Paul makes a thesis statement in v. 4 that summarizes what he has said so far—the *for* means that v. 4 builds on what has just been said—and pushes the issue one step further. The thesis statement introduces Christ into the discussion of Israel's destiny for the first time, and links him to both the law and righteousness for the first time in chs. 9–11. The phrase *fulfillment of the law* (*telos nomou*) is placed first in the sentence to give it the critical emphasis. The thesis statement is about the fulfillment or the completion of the law defined in reference to the Messiah.

The much debated *telos nomou* means fulfillment rather than end of the law for two reasons: 1) that is its normal meaning in the OT and in Paul (see Badenas, 1985); 2) the expressly goal-oriented nature of the preceding race track language and the following *to righteousness* phrase requires the sense of *reaching the goal* or *winning the prize*. Paul's opening assertion is that the law reaches its goal or its fulfillment in the Messiah. This opening thesis statement is modified by *to righteousness to all the ones believing*. The law is fulfilled by Messiah Jesus in relationship to righteousness for all who exercise faith. The law's relationship to righteousness is fundamentally changed by Christ. Paul's thesis here is a restatement of 8:4, Messiah Jesus did what the law was not able to do and thus fulfilled the objective of the law. Christ does that for all people who trust; the universalism of the gospel, for all people (see 1:16), replaces the particularity and exclusiveness of Jewish nationalism. Christ, law, righteousness, and faith, all key terms in Romans, are bound together in a provocative interpretation. The law is a good thing that Christ brings to the goal of God's righteousness for all people of faith.

Paul supports the thesis statement of v. 4 with another round of scriptural citations and interpretation. The first two, Leviticus 18:5 and Deuteronomy 30:11-14, have been the center of much debate. Traditionally these two passages have been interpreted to say contradictory things: Accordingly, Leviticus affirms righteousness by works of the law, while Deuteronomy rejects such a teaching for righteousness out of faith. In other words, Paul is thought to use Scripture against Scripture.

Such a reading is not necessary. The *for* at the beginning of v. 5 indicates that what follows is intended as a further clarification of what Paul has just said about the law being fulfilled in Christ for the purpose of righteousness. The Levitical citation is introduced by a phrase that is not found in Leviticus, *the righteousness out of the law*. The placement of this phrase at the beginning of the sentence (the emphatic position) means it is the central idea Paul is expounding. What does Paul say about *the righteousness out of the law*? He cites a modified form of Leviticus 18:5, *the person who does it [the righteousness of the law] will live by it [the righteousness of the law]* (This translation assumes a text-critical decision that the pronoun following "by" [*en*] is "it" [*autē*] rather than "them" [*autois*]). This reading is supported by the more reliable manuscripts and is the more difficult reading). This citation of Leviticus 18:5 is very different from that in Galatians 3:12 (*whoever does them shall live in them*). The concern in Romans 10:5 is doing the righteousness of the law, not doing the law as in Galatians. Furthermore, the addition of *the person* (*ho anthrōpos*) as the subject of the citation in Romans universalizes the Leviticus quote in continuity with a similar modification of this text in contemporary Judaism. That is, the quote is now talking about any person, Jew or Gentile, not just a Jew. The Leviticus 18:5 citation combines two critical words from v. 4, law and righteousness, to promise life to those who do the righteousness of the law that Christ brings to fulfillment. Paul's point is very similar to his earlier assertion in 8:3-8 that the law is fulfilled by those who walk according to the Spirit.

The Deuteronomy 30 quotation in vv. 6-8 is continuous with and builds on v. 5. The usual translation of *but* in v. 6 should rather read *and*. The citation is unusual in three respects. First, Paul introduces it as a word of *the righteousness out of faith*. Second, he is selective in the parts of the text he uses. Paul omits any reference to *doing the law* (Deut. 30:12, 13, 14). Third, he offers a running commentary on the meaning of the text for his readers.

The source of the citation in v. 6 is said to be *the righteousness of faith*, not Moses or Scriptures. The entire phrase should be read as

a description of the righteous faithfulness of God (a subjective genitive—lit., *the righteousness of faithfulness*), rather than human righteousness based on faith (an objective genitive). It is not the human
experience of righteousness by faith, which says that any person can
fulfill the righteousness of the law by faith, but the faithful and righteous God. The citation itself is divided into two sections by the *but
what does it say* at the beginning of v. 8. Verses 6 and 7 present the
negative, that which is not necessary. Verse 8 spells out the positive,
all that is necessary, which is explained in vv. 9ff. The point of vv. 6
and 7 is that human beings do not face a difficult task.

The opening citation from Deuteronomy 8:17 and 9:4, *do not
say in your heart*, recalls God's salvation of Israel from Egypt and
warns against self-reliance and complacency in the Promised Land.
God's covenant is a function of gracious election, not Israel's righteousness. This opening line is followed by the picture of people exert-
ing superhuman effort, looking high and low for Christ. *Heaven* and
abyss are symbols of the inaccessible. Because Christ is the fulfillment
of the law who offers life, people are pictured as looking everywhere
for him. But Christ has already come down from heaven, and been
raised from the dead. The interpretive center of the citation and commentary is the nearness of the word in v. 8. It explains why human
effort is of no value. Searching for Christ is unnecessary, Paul asserts,
because he is present. Christ is present in *the near word*, which is no
longer the law but *the word of faith* preached by Paul.

Paul reads the Deuteronomy text as a summons not to do the law
but to hear the true content of the word of God, which is now the
word about Christ. The text that originally proclaimed the nearness of
the law now proclaims the nearness of Christ. Israel's pursuit of the
law by works (9:32) and her attempt to establish righteousness by
human effort (10:3) is futile because both the law and righteousness
are now present and fulfilled in Jesus and available by faith.

Paul reinterprets the Deuteronomy text to say that just as Moses
disclosed and made accessible the Torah of God, so Christ has made
accessible righteousness to all who exercise faith. What Israel could
not do through *works* or her *own seeking* God has done. *Christ is
the goal of the law for righteousness to all who trust.*

Paul's provocative reinterpretation is made even clearer in his
expansion of each key term of Deuteronomy 30:14 in vv. 8b-9:

Deuteronomy	**Romans**
The *word* is near you	the *word* of faith which we preach. If you confess

in your *mouth*	with your *mouth*
	that Jesus is Lord,
	and if you believe
and in your *heart*	in your *heart*
	that God raised him from the dead
	you will be saved.

The real meaning of Deuteronomy 30 is to be found in Christian preaching, and the confession that Jesus Christ is Lord.

Paul's interpretation of the Leviticus and Deuteronomy texts in explanation of v. 4 is making a very bold claim. He is asserting that Israel's exile has ended in Messiah Jesus and that the covenant has been renewed. The Deuteronomy text was so understood in Judaism [see "Text in Biblical Context"]. Israel's story—the giving of the law, disobedience, judgment, and exile—has been fulfilled in Messiah Jesus. He is the goal of the law, which gives righteousness and life to all people who confess Jesus as Messiah and Lord. God, as promised, is renewing the covenant through him.

The nature of the Christian confession, which is linked into the text of Deuteronomy 30, is laid out in a chiasm in vv. 9-10:

A If you confess with your mouth that Jesus is Lord,
  B and believe in your heart that God raised him from the dead, you will be saved.
  B For one believes with the heart to righteousness,
A and one confesses with the mouth to salvation.

The confession has two components: confession of Jesus as Lord and trust in God's resurrection of him from the dead. The first means acknowledging Jesus Christ as Lord of the world and the church. A transfer of allegiance and ownership is announced publicly. The second calls for trust in the faithfulness of God, as the reference to God's resurrection of Jesus and the second use of Isaiah 28:16 indicates. The goal of the confession and faith is righteousness (confession to righteousness) and salvation (trust to salvation) used here as synonyms. The triple use of *salvation* in vv. 9, 10, and 13 in connection with *confession* and *calling on the name of the Lord* emphasize that Jesus is the Lord through whom God grants salvation to all people who confess and call on him. The linkage of the key concepts of the letter and of the argument in 9:30f. in this chiastic formula—faith, righteousness, salvation—underline Paul's emphasis on righteousness by faith alone for all people irrespective of ethnic heritage (9:31-32; 10:4).

Paul reinforces the argument of righteousness by faith through the citation of Isaiah 28:16b in exactly the same form as quoted earlier in 9:33 except for the substitution of *all* (*pas*) at the beginning of the verse. Paul inserts his own commentary into the body of the text to strengthen the theme of universality. The *all* in v. 11 is the equivalent to *there is no distinction* in v. 12 and the *all* of Joel 3:5 in v. 13. The decisive concept, however, is *trust* (*pisteuōn*). The one trusting God will not be put to shame. The antecedent of *upon him* (*ep' autō*) here is God in contrast to *law* in 9:33. *God* in v. 9b is the nearest antecedent rather than *Lord Jesus* in 9a (as in most commentaries). In 9:33 the Jews who related to the law *out of faith* rather than *out of works* would not stumble or be put to shame. Here the people who live *out of faith* in the God who raised Jesus from the dead and made him *Lord* need never fear. Paul again clinches an argument by a creative use of Scripture that now calls all people, not only Jews, to a life of trust in God. *The everyone who trusts* phrase is a throwback to the theme of Romans, *to all the ones trusting* (1:16). The *I am not ashamed"* of 1:16 and the *not be put to shame* of 10:11 come from the same root (*ischuō*). But even more important, the "faith formula" here is expositing the *to all the ones trusting* of 10:4, and the ones trusting of vv. 9 and 10. All people who put their trust in God via Messiah Jesus for salvation, Paul asserts, will never be *let down*.

The universal implications of *to all the ones trusting* and the *all* are spelled out by *there is no distinction between Jew and Greek* (v. 12). The *no distinction phrase* was used by Paul in 3:22 to reject any distinction between Jews and Gentiles regarding **Sin**. Here he states the positive, Jews and Gentiles both can trust God and be made righteous. The reason is simple. As monotheism was the reason God made righteous Jews and Gentiles through faith in 3:29-30, here the argument is derived from lordship. All have the same Lord and all enjoy the rich resources of divine grace. The universality of righteousness by faith in Christ abolishes any distinctions between people. Paul sums up his argument with a quotation of Joel 3:5. *All* is used for the fourth time in vv. 11-13. The one who is *Lord of all* and *the name of the Lord* refers to God rather than Christ. The subject from v. 9 on is God. Lord of all is a title for God, and the *calling upon the name of the Lord* is a technical term for calling upon God (it is used six out of eight times in the NT in reference to God; twice to Jesus). The people who call upon God in faith, whether Jew or Gentile, experience the gift of salvation that God is offering the world in Christ.

Paul emphasizes the unification of all nations before God on the basis of faith in vv. 9-13. Messiah Jesus is the fulfillment of the law to everyone who trusts because the goal of the Torah is that all nations become one before God. *Out of faith* removes all distinction and special privilege. God grants salvation to all who confess Jesus as Lord and who call upon the name of God. Paul again affirms that the word of God has not failed. It is fulfilled in Messiah Jesus.

The Gospel Is for All Who Hear 10:14-21

Paul continues the pattern of argument supported by scriptural citation. In vv. 18-21 the Scriptures actually become the argument rather than the support for it. The sequence of Scripture citations concludes the entire argument on the same model as the conclusion of 9:6-29 where vv. 24-29 offer a series of quotations. The citations are framed to repeat the opening claims in 9:30-31, Gentiles become God's people while the Jews are excluded. At the center is a very important verbal sequence that is missed in English because different words are used to translate a similar root in Greek: *obedience* in v. 16 (*hupakoē*, lit., *hearing under*, that is, hearing that obeys what is heard), *heard* in v. 16 (*akoē*), *heard* in v. 17 (*akouō*). This *obey-heard* language is framed by two quotes from Isaiah that are critical to Paul's argument. Both citations are interpreted in contemporary Judaism and the early church in ways that help Paul make his point. The Isaiah 52:7 citation in v. 15 speaks of a plurality of preachers of the good news, although both the Hebrew and Greek texts speak only of a single messenger. Paul's citation is in line with current Jewish exposition, which uses both Isaiah 40:9 and 52:7 to picture a great number of people announcing the beginning of the reign of God (Isa. 52:7c). For Paul this eschatological hour has already begun because Jesus inaugurates God's reign. Paul interprets the failure of Israel to respond to the gospel with Isaiah 53:1 (v. 16), the Servant Song that describes the suffering, death, and exaltation of the Servant of God. Both the Markan Jesus and Paul interpreted the death of Jesus in light of this song (Mark 10:45 parallel; 1 Cor. 15:3-5; 2 Cor. 5:21; Rom. 4:25). Paul uses it here to argue that Israel's rejection of the gospel was announced in the Scriptures, thus it is in fulfillment of the word of God.

The text unit opens with a series of rhetorical questions that build on the Joel citation in v. 13. The *calling on the Lord* theme permits Paul to explain the rejection of Israel in the most explicit terms so far, and also to offer an interpretation of the Christian mission to the world. Christian confession requires trust, which necessitates hearing, which cannot occur without preaching, which presupposes the commissioning of the preacher. The sending forth of many proclaimers is a magnificent end-time event, as prophesied by Isaiah (52:7).

The great tragedy of history is that *not all obeyed the gospel*. *Not all* here stands in contrast to *all* in vv. 11-13. The gospel is for *all* without distinction, but *not all* obey. *Obedience* is defined as the appropriate response to the gospel in continuity with the letter's opening and closing call for the *obedience of faith*. The unbelief of many is not surprising; Isaiah predicted it in describing the destiny of the Suffering Servant. Verse 17 introduces a conclusion (therefore) which summarizes the gospel. The source of trust is hearing, and what is heard is *the word about the Messiah*.

Verse 18 poses the second critical question. Is the disobedience of many due to not hearing the gospel? The negative answer is supported with a citation of Scripture (Ps. 19:4). The Christian mission has taken the gospel to the world. The third question, v. 19, becomes people specific. Paul has not named Israel so far in this discussion of disobedience to the gospel. As in 9:31, he now specifically names Israel. The issue is who constitutes the new people of God? If the gospel has gone to the world, is the problem of Jewish rejection due to Israel not understanding? Paul answers with three Scripture citations.

The first is Deuteronomy 32:21. God is provoking Israel to jealousy and anger by being gracious to people who are *not a people* and *foolish people*. The citation is exceedingly provocative. In the OT it is usually Israel who provokes God to wrath. Paul uses the one text that speaks of God provoking Israel. The word for *provoke* (*parazeloō*) comes from the root for *zeal* (*zeloō*). Israel has a zeal for God (10:2) that is now reversed by God's zeal against Israel. Together with the preceding and following verses, Deuteronomy 32 contains important terms in Romans, wrath (vv. 19, 21), children (vv. 19, 20) and the only occurrence of *faith* (*pistis*) in the Torah (v. 20). In addition, the Deuteronomy quote sets up the argument of ch. 11; God is extending eschatological salvation and peoplehood to the Gentiles to make Israel jealous. In typical Jewish style, the citation from the Torah is followed by a word from the prophets. Isaiah 61:1 repeats the opening line of 9:30; God has found a people who were not seeking or asking for God (i.e., the Gentiles). The final citation from Isaiah (61:2) repeats the claim of 9:31. Israel stands in contrast to the Gentiles; she is a disobedient and rebellious people.

The concluding three citations all involve direct speech of God. The emphasis is on divine initiative. The opening question of 9:31, why Israel is not part of the new vessel God is creating, has been answered in two ways. First, Israel is a disobedient people; she pursues the law incorrectly, she seeks to establish her own righteousness to the exclusion of other peoples, she does not submit to God's righteousness, she has not accepted the Messiah as the fulfillment of the law, she is rebellious against the will of God. Second, God is fulfilling a purpose in history. God has chosen to remake the people of God by "calling" other people (9:14-29; 10:18-21). In ch. 9 the "call of God" constitutes the true Israel. Here, the people "calling on God" meet the requirement to become members of God's people irrespective of their ethnicity.

The passage provides a unique insight into Paul's understanding of his mission. His use of Isaiah in vv. 15 (Isa. 51:7) and 16 (Isa. 53:1) suggests that he understands his mission as in continuity with Isaiah's. The *feet* (plural rather than singular as in Isaiah) of those proclaiming the good news are now Paul and his associates. The *from us* in v. 16 refers to Paul and his associates. The word of Christ in v. 17 is Paul's preaching of the gospel of Messiah Jesus. Paul sees himself as a co-worker with Isaiah in preaching the good news of God's salvation for Jews and Gentiles.

TEXT IN BIBLICAL CONTEXT

Two quotes from the OT are central in interpreting this text, Leviticus 18:5 in 10:5 and Deuteronomy 30:11-14 in 10:6-8. Interpreters usually contrast these two texts: Leviticus describes righteousness by works of the law and Deuteronomy describes righteousness by faith. Galatians 3:12, where Paul also cites Leviticus 18:5, is used to sharpen the contrast even more. The one who does the law is justified, but no one can fulfill the law, because its demands are beyond fulfillment. In other words, Paul, it is claimed, uses the Leviticus text to summarize the principle of salvation through works of the law in order to demonstrate through the Deuteronomy text that what the law says is impossible and wrong.

Leviticus 18

Leviticus 18:5 comes from a context in which Yahweh's claims upon Israel are being asserted in parallel form to Exodus 20:1-17 and Deuteronomy 5:6-21. The preface in vv. 2b and 4b, *I am the Lord your God*, and the conclusion in 5b, *I am the Lord*, are covenantal in form and content. Israel is called to observe the law because Yahweh is Israel's God. Israel is asked to live out its covenant-faith with Yahweh. For such faithfulness Israel will live. Leviticus 18:5 is about faithful obedience to the redeeming and covenanting God, not about flawless obedience as a means of salvation.

Leviticus 18:5 is used four times in the OT, Ezekiel 20:11, 13, 21 and Nehemiah 9:29. Ezekiel uses the text in a judgment speech to characterize the law as the great gift of life and deliverance, which set Israel's life on a new foundation. Israel is condemned for not following the good will of God. In Nehemiah 9:29 the Leviticus text is cited in a prayer, which describes Israel's covenant relationship with God and the promise of life which God gives.

The Leviticus text is cited with some frequency in Jewish literature, and always to make a positive statement about God and the law. One theme stresses the life giving quality of the law. For example, the law can be set aside during times of persecution or war to preserve life. Thus, the Sabbath law is set aside during the Maccabean wars. A second theme teaches that even Gentiles can study and obey the Torah, and therefore share its promises. A third theme emphasizes how easy it is to obey the law.

Leviticus 18:5 is not used in the OT or Jewish literature to teach perfect obedience to the law or salvation by means of doing the law. Rather it is used to call Israel to faithfulness to its covenant relationship to Yahweh and to affirm the promise of life which follows such obedience. Paul's use of Leviticus 18:5 in Galatians 3:12 cannot be used to determine its interpretation here. The context is very different. We know that Paul can use the same citation for different purposes in different settings, as his use of Psalm 142:2 in Galatians 2:16 and Romans 3:20 demonstrates. But even more significant, Paul alters the text of Leviticus 18:5 so much that he clearly does not intend to use it in the same way as in Galatians. Different words, let alone the same words, in different context mean different things. Furthermore, the traditional interpretation does not fit the Romans context where Paul has been arguing that righteousness by works is precisely Israel's problem. To suddenly affirm what Paul has been denying makes nonsense of the theology Paul has been developing from 9:30ff.

Deuteronomy 30

The Deuteronomy 30 text comes from a similar context. Chapters 29–30 describe the renewal of the covenant. Yahweh has acted to redeem Israel, and promises to circumcise her heart (30:6). Deuteronomy 30:11-14 emphasize that the word of Yahweh is ultimate and all-sufficing. It requires no human effort because Yahweh has done all, even placing it on Israel's lips and in her heart. The command of Yahweh is easy to obey.

Deuteronomy 30:11-14 was subject to considerable reflection in

Judaism. The text is consistently handled freely, as freely as Paul's citation. Baruch 3:29-30 uses it to equate Wisdom, a mediator between God and Israel, with the law and to proclaim the nearness of the Torah through Wisdom. Philo, a contemporary of Paul, uses it to teach that the good and righteous life is not hard to pursue because God has placed it in the heart and mouth. A third interpretation emphasizes that the Torah is fully revealed to Israel and is understandable. A recently discovered text among the Dead Sea Scrolls reflects a fourth theme (4QMMT). Law observance is to be intensified when God ends Israel's exile in the imminent end of time. A fifth, probably later than the NT writings, uses it to teach that the law was given once and for all through Moses.

The Baruch and 4QMMT texts are particularly relevant to Paul's interpretation. Both point to the time when God will restore Israel—bring Israel's exile under pagan oppressors to an end. Baruch urges the quest for Wisdom while 4QMMT urges the observance of specific ritual laws in the Temple as the means of Israel's salvation.

Paul takes a rather popular text and interprets it christologically to demonstrate that the law itself witnesses to the possibility of doing its righteousness by faith in Christ. Christ replaces the law in these texts. The *righteousness of faith* announces that God's end-time salvation is near and available to those who trust in Messiah Jesus. He brings the law and Israel's story to fulfillment by renewing the covenant.

The two texts, Leviticus 18 and Deuteronomy 30, do not oppose each other in Judaism or in Paul. The apostle does not use Scripture to straighten out Scripture. Rather, he invokes two quotations as witnesses to Christ as the fulfillment of the law and the covenant. They reveal how the righteousness manifested in Christ is that to which the Torah pointed. The promise is fulfilled, just as the word of God taught.

TEXT IN THE LIFE OF THE CHURCH

The Church's Historic Grid

Two dominant themes have been developed from this text since the Reformation: 1) human responsibility; and/or 2) criticism of Jewish faith and practice. In the first theme the failure of the Jews to respond positively to the gospel of Messiah Jesus is a paradigm of human failure to exercise faith. Men and women insist on working out their own salvation through works; they pursue their own righteousness rather than accepting the righteousness of God. In the second theme the Jewish people stand condemned and rejected for failure to accept Jesus as the Messiah. Therefore, the law (really their religion) has been ended, even abolished.

Jesus Fulfills the Law and God's Promises

Romans 9:30–10:21 is not primarily about human responsibility or the criticism of Jewish faith. It does address the question of Israel's rejection of Jesus as Messiah. But that is not its central issue. The critical and creative center of this text is the fulfillment of the law, and thus Jewish hopes, in Jesus. It describes how through Messiah Jesus Israel is transformed from an ethnic people into a worldwide family in fulfillment of the promises of God.

This text focuses much of the argument of Romans. Messiah Jesus is the goal of the law; he brings to fulfillment the plan of God that was given in the covenants with Abraham and with Israel at Sinai. The Torah itself was given to facilitate this goal. What was the goal? It was a worldwide people of faith living out of and in the righteousness of God. Jesus is the climax who makes this goal near and accessible for all people, Jews and Gentiles.

Jesus' fulfillment of the goal of the law means two paradoxical things. First, he brings to an end the process of concentrating **Sin** in Israel. Messiah Jesus on the cross takes on and defeats **Sin** once and for all. Israel especially, but also all humanity, can be freed from **Sin's** oppressive reign. Secondly, Messiah Jesus fulfills the purpose of Israel to bring light and salvation to the nations. Christ fulfills the covenant with Israel and creates a new covenant between God and humanity. Israel is vindicated. God is bringing salvation to the nations through her in fulfillment of the promises to *the fathers. All people*—the *all who believe* in 10:4 is critical—can now be members of this new covenant.

Israel's sin in the face of this grand covenant climax is national righteousness. Israel wants to confine the grace and righteousness of God to herself; therefore, she pursues the law by works that distinguish her from other people, and seeks to establish her own national righteousness rather than submit to God's cosmic saving power.

The law is not an evil that Christ must bring to an end. The law is good—it is *the righteous law* (9:31)—which God gave Israel at Sinai to guide her in being a righteous people and being a witness to the nations. Israel's problem was not the law, but the way she pursued it. The law is a good goal as long as the race is *by faith* rather than *by works*.

Paul's view of the law here is very much in continuity with 3:21–4:25 and 7:7–8:11. In each of these texts the righteousness witnessed to and promised by the law is fulfilled in Christ. The 3:21–4:25 text and this one support Paul's fundamental claim about the positive witness of the law to righteousness by faith with OT citations, Genesis 15 in ch. 4 and Deuteronomy 30 here. Two contrasting perspectives on the practice of the law, by faith or by works, are described. The law in faith *establishes the law* in 3:31 and leads to the goal of the race in 9:31. All link righteousness, faith, and law positively and constructively with Christ. Christ, the fulfillment of the law, brings the word of God to its goal. That is good news for Israel and for the world.

Preaching the Good News

The good news of the gospel of Messiah Jesus is to be preached. It is still true that people cannot respond to the good news if they do not hear, and they cannot obey if they do not hear. The "lived witness" of the Believers Church tradition is an important form of witness. But it cannot and must not replace the preaching of the good news, the verbal declaration that Jesus is Messiah and Lord, he fulfills God's plan for humanity and he alone is Lord of the world.

Obedient Hearing

The evidence of faith is "obedient hearing." The response to preaching must be more than "faith." It must be faith that expresses itself in obedience. Israel, Paul claims, heard but did not obey. What does it mean for the new people of God, the church of Jews and Gentiles, to "obediently hear" the Word of God in postmodern times? Might Paul be critical of the church today for its much talk, but highly selective obedience? Would he see the church as "a disobedient and contrary people"?

God Has Not Rejected Israel

Romans 11:1-36

PREVIEW

Chapter 11 is the climax of Paul's argument in chs. 9–11. The rhetorical question in v. 1 states the central problem he has been addressing, *has God rejected his people?* Verses 1-10 summarize important elements of what he has been saying and set the stage for the final argument. Paul reaffirms the faithfulness of God by reusing important terms from earlier in the letter, e.g., remnant, by grace and not works, the rest are rejected by God. Verses 11-32 make the case for the future salvation of Israel and the importance of this salvation for the world. The mercy of God in saving Israel and the world in faithfulness to the divine word is so grand that a doxology is required, vv. 33-36.

The diatribe form of the argument that characterizes chs. 9–10 continues, a question answered by Scripture and interpretation. Paul is reinterpreting Israel's Scripture to affirm the faithfulness of God. But there is also a change of emphasis. Chapters 9–10 interpreted Israel's past and present. Chapter 11 looks to the future. This change is evident already in the form of Paul's questions. Instead of *what then shall we say?* in 9:14 and 30, we now have *I say* . . . (11:1, 11). Paul shifts from the plural to the singular.

One more stylistic feature is worthy of note. Paul returns to the "much more" argument which he used in ch. 5. The second argument, vv. 11-24, is framed by the "much more" logic (vv. 12 and 24). The argument without the "much more" language also is used in v. 15. If Israel's current disobedience already means the salvation of Gentiles, how "much more" will her future salvation mean for the world?

OUTLINE

Diatribe—The remnant and the rest, 11:1-10
    11:1a First question
           11:1b   Denial
           11:1c   Autobiographical confirmation
           11:2-4   Scriptural citations
           11:5-6   Interpretation
    11:7a Second question
           11:7b   Thesis
           11:8-10   Scriptural citation

Diatribe—The importance of Israel's future salvation, 11:11-24
    11:11a   The question
    11:11b   Denial
    11:11c-12 Thesis
    11:13-16   Explanation
    11:17-24   Exhortation

Assertion—The mystery of salvation for Jews and Gentiles, 11:25-32
    11:25a   Introductory statement
    11:25b-26a Thesis
    11:26b-27 Scriptural citation
    11:28-32   Explanation

Doxology, 11:33-36

EXPLANATORY NOTES

The Remnant and the Rest 11:1-10

The opening question puts the critical issue on the table. *Has God rejected his people?* is not a new question. It was asked often in the OT, especially during and after times of severe national crisis (e.g., Judg. 6:13; 2 Kings 23:27; Pss. 44:9, 23; 60:1, 10; 74:1; 78:60, 67; 108:11; Jer. 7:29; 31:37; Lam. 2:7; 5:22; Ezek. 5:11; 11:16; Hos. 9:17). The designation of God's people as *the laos of him* (lit.) denotes Israel as marked out from the other nations (*ethnē*). Has the prophetic fear of God rejecting Israel happened now because Israel rejected God's Messiah and God's new people composed of Jews and Gentiles? Paul answers with his brisk denial, *absolutely not!*

Paul supports the denial with two answers, the first autobiographical and the second scriptural. Paul is an insider, an Israelite *out of the seed of Abraham* (he meets the qualifications of 4:13-18 and 9:7-8). He also is from one of the favored tribes, Benjamin. He is an authentic member and representative of God's people. He symbolizes God's ongoing faithfulness to the whole people.

The scriptural answer uses and interprets three texts. The real answer to the question of v. 1 uses the same words as the question, which are the words of 1 Samuel 12:22 and Psalm 94:14. The promise is particularly reassuring because it follows Israel's sin in 1 Samuel and comes despite God's discipline in Psalms. Paul adds an interpretive comment, *whom he foreknew*. He uses the language of election (see 8:29) to affirm that God knew this people before choosing them, and, therefore, will not reject them now just like he did not in the past. The second text introduces Elijah's complaint against Israel (1 Kings 19:10, 14). The third text gives God's reply to Elijah (1 Kings 19:18). God's response is presented as a divine decree. The text cited is modified to emphasize God's initiative, *I have kept for myself*. Despite Israel's unfaithfulness God has kept a remnant, a common theme in the OT (see Isa. 10:22; 11:11-12, 16; 37:31; 2 Kings 19:30-31; Mic. 2:12; 4:7; 5:7-8; Zech. 8:12) and Judaism (see the Dead Sea Scrolls, esp. 1QH 2:12; 6:8; 7:10, 12; 1QpHab. 10:13; 4QpPs. 37). It could serve as a symbol of judgment (see 9:27 where Paul cited Isa. 10:22 to say that God's judgment is so severe that only a remnant will be left), or as a symbol of hope (see Isa. 11), which is how it is used here. In remnant theology the part represents the whole. That theme is underlined by the number 7,000, a symbol of completeness. The remnant is a promise of a larger whole to come. The movement toward v. 26 is set in motion at the outset of the argument.

In vv. 5-6 Paul offers a significant interpretation of remnant theology. He uses three connectives—*thus, therefore, also*—to explain that a remnant remains to the present (Paul is making an important point because nowhere else does he use three connectives in succession). The present remnant obviously refers to Paul and the Jewish Christians. But more than that, this is a remnant *chosen according to grace.* For the first time since 6:15 Paul reintroduces the word grace; it is clearly a very critical term in his argument, because he uses it four times in two verses. Election, the key term in Israel's self understanding, and grace, a key term in Paul's theology of salvation and peoplehood, are linked for the first time in Romans. Grace and works are contrasted for the first time in Romans. The elect remnant exists only by an act of God's free and unconditional choice. God did not elect Israel or the remnant because of who they were or what they did. Specifically, grace excludes works, the definition of election that marks Jewish identity. Paul is summarizing his entire argument in these verses—salvation, whether called righteousness or election, is by God's grace (3:24-6:15). That is why salvation cannot be restricted to Israel (3:20, 27-28; 9:32).

Paul's theology of the remnant raises the question of the remainder of Israel, *the rest,* which he addresses in vv. 7-10. The question is brief, *what then?* The first phrase of Paul's answer recalls 9:31, Israel did not find what it sought. In contrast, *the elect attained it,* an echo of 9:30. The elect are a group within Israel, namely, the Jewish Christians. What they attained is not stated explicitly, although the larger context suggests inclusion in the end-time people God is creating. *The rest (hoi loipoi),* that is, the majority of the Jews *were hardened* (lit., *petrified*). Paul explains what he hinted at in 9:22, 23, 33; Israel's failure is by divine design. Israel apart from the remnant became dead-like. Paul's thesis is provocative, and requires biblical support, which he offers with two citations.

The first Scripture is from Deuteronomy 29:4 with an introductory phrase from Isaiah 29:10 (*spirit of stupor*). Israel is blind once again by divine action. Now, as in the past, the elect people are prevented by God from seeing the nature and direction of God's purposes. The catchword for the second citation from Psalm 69:22-23 is *unseeing eyes.* The Psalm was originally a prayer for judgment on David's enemies. As in 3:10-18, Paul turns David's petition against his own people. Israel is now in the position David sought for his enemies, trapped in a snare, blind, backs bent in slavery. As God hardened Pharaoh in ch. 9, so now God hardens Israel. The great majority of Jewish people are under the judgment of God. The law, the prophets, and the writings, the entire Jewish Scriptures bear witness to this judgment. But the judgment has very important limits. Paul breaks off the citation just before the Psalmist says *let them be blotted out of the book of the living.* The hardening of the Jews did not lead to their destruction.

The Importance of Israel's Future Salvation 11:11-24

The second argument appears repetitive because it picks up themes from previous arguments. Verses 11-12 recall Paul's talk of Israel's stumbling in 9:32-33 and 11:9-10, and the divine jealousy in 10:19. The apparent digression in vv. 13-14 elaborates the idea of *jealousy* from 10:19 and 11:11. Verse 11 intensifies the argument by reintroducing the lesser to the greater logic from ch. 5 (*much more*). This form of argument is repeated again in v. 24. Verse 15 reformulates v. 12 without using the "much more" formula. A peculiarity that characterizes this section is the omission of Scripture references. This is the only major argument in chs. 9-11 that does not refer to and interpret Scripture.

The allusion to Israel's fall in v. 9 raises the question, did Israel fall so badly that it is eliminated from the race? Paul denies the possibility, *absolutely not!* The fall of the Jews did not lead to their elimination, but to the mission to the Gentiles. *Their trespass* is not defined here, but must be understood in light of Paul's previous argument that the Jews pursued righteousness out of works and rejected Jesus as the messianic fulfillment of the law for righteousness. The mission to the Gentiles serves a very distinct purpose, *to provoke them [the Jews] to jealousy.* The idea of divine provocation again uses the unusual language of Deuteronomy 32:21 from 10:19. Paul interprets the purpose of the Gentile mission in terms of the divine intention to provoke the Jews. Verse 12 outlines the consequences of Israel's positive response in parallel lines:

But if

Jews	World/Gentiles
their trespass	riches for the world
their failure	riches for the Gentiles
	how much more will their fullness mean?

The contrast is between Israel's current situation—defined as trespass and failure—and the current Gentile experience—defined as riches or abundance. The contrast points to an even greater wealth when Israel does respond affirmatively to the gospel ("much more").

Paul's thesis in the second argument is that Israel's hardening or falling is temporary and redemptive. Here, as in relation to Pharaoh in ch. 9, it serves a redemptive function; there Israel sees deliverance as an act of God and the Egyptians know that *I am Yahweh*, here the mission to the Gentiles provokes the Jews to jealousy. Paul elaborates this thesis in direct address to the Gentile Christians in Rome; the you in v. 13 is emphatic. Paul defines his own ministry in terms of the divine *jealousy* theme of v. 11 (and 10:19), saving some out of his own people. Even as an apostle for the incorporation of Gentiles into God's people, he is God's agent to effect the divine judgment of Deuteronomy 32:21 on Israel and thus help prepare this people for future salvation. The *some out of them* designates the remnant of Jews who now believe. Paul's passion for the Jews is critical because the salvation of the Gentiles and the world ultimately depends upon the salvation of Israel. While the structure of v. 15 is the same as v. 12, the language in v. 15 is more positive and defining. If Israel's current "rejection" of the gospel already means reconciliation for the world, which it does as demonstrated in the Gentile mission and churches, then the acceptance of the gospel by Israel as a people will mean the eschatological resurrection from the dead. The redemption of the world depends on the salvation of Israel.

Paul concludes his explanation of the thesis in vv. 11c-12 with two metaphors that both summarize what he has been saying and explain the critical role of the remnant for all Israel for the salvation of the world (v. 16). The remnant of Jewish Christians is the first fruit (*first fruit* here, as in Rom. 16:5 and 1 Cor. 16:15, refers to the first Christians in a region or group). If the first fruit is set apart for God (which is what *holy* means), then the whole people represented by this fruit is as well. The logic is the part to the whole. And, if the root is separated to God, then so are the branches, the rest of the Jewish people. The logic is the root to the plant. The *branches* reference here can hardly be to Gentile Christians because that is a different point Paul will make in the exhortation to follow.

Paul, it would appear, has fundamentally changed the normal pattern of Jewish eschatological expectation. That expectation believed the end-time sequence would be as follows: the coming of the Messiah, the affirmative response of the Jews to the Messiah, the affirmative response of many Gentiles to the Messiah and their pilgrimage to Zion, the salvation of the world. Paul has changed the pattern: the coming of the Messiah, the affirmative response of a remnant of Jews, the affirmative response of many Gentiles, the affirmative response of the Jews as a people, the salvation of the world. The response of the Jews and the Gentiles has been reversed, but the central place of Israel in this salvation has not been displaced. The end-time salvation of Israel will mean eschatological life for all people. While Israel as a people is now hardened, there is still a future which will mean salvation for her and the world.

Paul's second argument reframes an important theme that he has been developing since ch. 5. Israel is the means of the world's salvation by being the place where **Sin** is focused, gathered, and concentrated. The election of Israel means that she carries the burden of **Sin** for a season to bring salvation to all people. Here the form of that argument is that Israel's unbelief, or fall, or hardening, is one phase in God's plan. This phase is temporary; it does not mean that Israel is excluded from salvation forever. Her present "hardness" serves the purpose of salvation for the Gentiles. The grandeur of that salvation cannot be compared with the "much greater" grandeur of what God will do for humanity and the world when Israel will be saved. The obverse side of that argument, of course, means that the salvation of the Gentiles now also is but one part of God's plan, namely, the salvation of the nations through Israel. The Gentiles are not a new and independent people of God; they are being incorporated into God's people Israel.

Paul breaks into the argument with an exhortation directed to the Gentile Christians in Rome. The address is very direct—you in vv. 17, 18, 20, 21, 22, 24. The problem is the presumptuous boasting of the Gentile Christians. The earlier "ethnic righteousness" of the Jews, which Paul rebuked, has now been turned on its head. The Gentile believers are looking down on the Jews in their hardened state, and saying that God has turned away from them once and for all. The Gentile Christians have displaced the Jews; the salvation of the Gentiles is now the crowning work of God. The problem created by Gentile boasting is just as serious as Jewish boasting in ethnic righteousness. In both cases one group within God's inclusive people is saying we are "the elect," "the saved," and "what we have you cannot have."

Paul addresses Gentile boasting by extending the root-plant metaphor from v. 16 to a specific plant, the olive tree. The metaphor has historic roots; Israel is an olive tree (Jer. 11:16; Hos. 14:6). The issue here is the relationship of different branches to the tree itself. The root is clearly Jews and Jewish Christians, the cut branches the Jews who rejected the gospel of Messiah Jesus, and the wild branches the Gentiles who have accepted the gospel. Olive trees were the most widely cultivated fruit trees in the Mediterranean. Farmers

renewed old olive trees by grafting in wild olive branches. Paul is using
a metaphor that would be familiar to his readers. The purpose of the
grafting here is to make the wild olive branches *partners* (lit., fellow
sharers) *in the rich root of the olive tree* (v. 17). The point of the
metaphor is not the cutting down of the tree and replacing it; that is
precisely what Paul rejects. The point is cutting off branches and grafting in new ones to make it more fruitful. The tree remains, and
receives new life through new branches.

The purpose of the metaphor is to admonish Gentile Christians.
Two commands center the admonition: *do not keep on boasting
over the branches* (v. 18), and *do not think thoughts of pride, but
of fear* (v. 20). The first imperative uses the same word for boasting
that Paul used to indict the Jews in ch. 2. Boasting denies dependence
on God by making a claim, by insisting on a right to privilege. The second admonition refers to the presumption identified in v. 19, God has
cut off Israel and replaced her with the Gentiles. Only the fear of God,
the beginning of wisdom in Jewish piety (e.g., Ps. 2:11; Prov. 1:7;
3:7; Sir. 1:11-14), can keep faith from turning into arrogance.

The admonitions are supported by three arguments. First, the
Gentiles depend on the Jewish roots (v. 18b). God has not turned the
tree upside down so that the Gentile branches now support the root.
A Gentile church without Jewish roots is not the church of God.
Gentile Christians remain dependent on the rich Jewish root that goes
back to Abraham. That is true, Paul argues in diatribe fashion with an
objector, even though God did judge the branches for *unfaithfulness*
(also used in 3:3 of Israel). Israel's judgment for *unfaithfulness* is a
reminder that the Gentiles are now "in" only because of faith, not
because of rights.

Second, Gentiles who fall into the same error as the unfaithful
Jews will share the same fate (vv. 19-22). If the promises of God to
Israel did not spare the Jews from being cut off, then Gentile
Christians should not assume they are exempt from the same judgment. Any believers, Jew or Gentile, can be cut off by becoming
unfaithful, that is, by becoming presumptuous or arrogant about
God's grace. God is by definition severe (*apotōmian theou*) toward
those who *fall*;" God cuts them off, but is good (*chrēstotēs theou*)
toward those who *remain in that goodness*.

Third, Jews can more easily be reinstated into the tree (e.g., God's
plan), than can Gentiles (vv. 23-24). The *power of God*, the same
power as in the power of the gospel (1:16) and the power which is
able to fulfill the promises to Abraham (4:21), can rejuvenate with-
ered, cut off branches and graft them back into the tree. In fact, by

using the "much more" argument again, Paul says God can graft natural branches *much more* easily than wild branches. God, of course, will do that only if the Jews respond in faith (lit., *if they not remain in unfaithfulness*).

The point of Paul's admonition is clear. Presumption, whether Jewish or Gentile, is fatal. Paul has turned the tables. Earlier the problem was Jewish and Jewish Christian presumption, now it is Gentile Christian. Inclusion in God's salvation and peoplehood depends entirely on continuous faithfulness, on trust in the grace and goodness of God. Presumption is "unfaith;" it replaces dependence on the grace of God with claims on God. Undergirding these admonitions is an affirmation of the priority of the Jews. They are the root and their identity is inviolate. God has not replaced the Jewish tree with a Gentile Christian one. Gentile Christians are dependent on the Jewish root. The Jewish root receives new life through the Gentile Christian graft, but is not dependent on the graft. As Paul said in the thesis statement of the letter, *the gospel is the power of God to salvation . . . to the Jew first and also to the Gentile* (1:16). There is a Jewish priority—both temporal and theological—in the gospel. Verses 25-32 explain why.

The Divine Mystery of Salvation for Jews and Gentiles 11:25-32

Paul's introductory disclosure formula, *I do not want you to be ignorant*, emphasizes the importance of what he is going to assert (see 1:13 for a similar statement). Paul wants his readers to understand a *mystery*, a Jewish apocalyptic word that denotes divine secrets revealed by God, usually concerning knowledge about the end-time fulfillment of God's plan. In the Pauline letters the mystery always involves God's intention to include the Gentiles with the Jews in salvation (see Eph. 1:9-10; 3:3-6; Col. 1:26-27; 2:2; 4:3). The purpose of disclosing the mystery here is *in order that you may not think too highly of yourselves*. Paul is still addressing the incorrect Gentile Christian attitudes of v. 20.

The mystery contains three parts. First, a hardening has come upon a part of Israel (v. 25c), that is, *the rest* of vv. 7-9. The hardening is God's work. The emphasis is not on the guilt of Israel, but on the work of God.

Second, the hardening is temporally limited, *until the fullness of the Gentiles has come in* (v. 25d). *Fullness* (plērōma) here is the same word for the final salvation of the Jews in v. 12. It indicates the complete number of Gentiles determined by God for end-time salvation. The use of the same word suggests an equivalency of Jewish and Gentile end-time salvation; there will be a *fullness* of both peoples. *Gentiles* is a collective term; not every Gentile is meant. *Come in* denotes entrance into a community of people, here clearly into Israel. It is the equivalent to *being grafted in* in vv. 17, 19, 24. The Gentiles are now being incorporated into Israel. The shift from exclusion to inclusion of the Gentiles began in 9:22, and was developed in 9:30–10:13. Paul does not say that Israel must become part of the church, but that the Gentiles will be brought into Israel. He may well be alluding to the OT and Jewish vision of the eschatological pilgrimage of the Gentiles to Jerusalem. The sobering warning for Gentiles is that the time for their salvation is limited, their opportunity for inclusion will come to an end just as the time of Israel's hardening will be terminated. That will be the time for Israel's salvation.

Third, *and so all Israel will be saved*. *All Israel* means Israel as a corporate people, not every Israelite. *All Israel* stands in contrast to *the remnant* in v. 5, *some* in v. 17, and *from a part* in v. 25. When the *full number* of the Gentiles are converted, all Israel will be saved. The difference between *fullness of the Gentiles* and *all Israel* is significant. Not "all Gentiles" but a *fullness*, an unknown number of Gentiles, contrasts with *all Israel*, Israel as a people.

The three elements of the mystery are interdependent. Paul links the salvation of the Gentiles with the salvation of the Jews. The restoration of Israel is a consequence of the salvation of the Gentiles, and the salvation of Israel is necessary for the salvation of the Gentiles. The Gentiles first and then the Jews for Paul represents universality, the fulfillment of God's plan to reconcile Jew and Gentile into a single Israel.

Scripture validates the mystery and indicates the manner of its fulfillment (lit., *in this manner*). The quotation combines lines from Isaiah 27:9 and 59:20-21:

> *The Deliverer will come from Zion,*
> *he will banish ungodliness from Jacob* (Isa. 59:20)
> *and this will be my covenant with them* (Isa. 59:21a),
> *when I take away their sins* (Isa. 27:9).

The Redeemer will come from Zion (*ek*), rather than *for the sake of Zion* (*eneken*, LXX). The Redeemer in the context of chs. 9-11 is Messiah Jesus rather than Yahweh as in Isaiah. The Redeemer will do two things. First, he will reverse the *ungodliness* (*asebeia*) of 1:18 (the ungodliness and unrighteousness of people) and demonstrate the reality of 4:5 (God makes righteous the ungodly) by taking it away.

The ungodliness that originally caused the breach between God and Israel, and thus the judgment of God, will be removed. Secondly, God will renew the covenant with Israel and express it by *take away their sins*. Israel's hope for the renewal of the covenant and the forgiveness of sins will be fulfilled (Isa. 4:4; Jer. 31:33; Jub. 22:14-15; *Pss. Sol.* 18:5). Israel's eschatological salvation will be the fulfillment of her historic faith and covenant, not her conversion to another religion.

Paul's language is clear and deliberate. He uses "covenant" in Romans only in association with Israel; it is God's covenant with the Jewish people. "Forgiveness of sins" is not normal Pauline language; he speaks rather of victory over the power of **Sin**. But here Paul is talking about the salvation of Israel in fulfillment of God's promises, which means renewing the covenant and forgiving Israel's disobedience of the terms of the covenant. But the sequence is also important. Renewal and forgiveness do not happen, contrary to most first-century Jewish expectation, in nationalist terms or against the Gentiles, but with and following the salvation of the Gentiles. The progression is from the Jews to all peoples, not to the Jews. God's plan of salvation has always been inclusive and universal, just as Scripture promised.

Paul's explanation of the mystery of God's salvation is structured with a series of contrasts. The language—election, call, mercy—and the contrasts offer a summary of Paul's argument in chs. 9–11, and of the entire letter so far.

With respect to the gospel	they are enemies for you;
with respect to election	they are beloved on account of the fathers.
	For the gifts and the call of God are irrevocable.
Just as you once were disobedient to God	
	but now have received mercy by their disobedience
so also they have now been disobedient for your mercy in order that	
	they also now they might receive mercy.

God has consigned all to disobedience in order to have mercy on all.
The first two contrasts, *with respect to the gospel* and *with respect
to election*, denote two distinguishing characteristics of God's plan of
salvation. *The gospel* is Paul's key term for the period introduced by
Christ, which also happens to be the time of Gentile acceptance and
Jewish disobedience. *Election* defines God's relation to Israel which,
Paul has argued throughout chs. 9–11, has not changed.

The second contrast could hardly be sharper, *enemies/beloved*.
Israel is currently an enemy of God because of her hostility to God's
Messiah and the inclusion of Gentile people. But the hostility serves a
purpose, it is for the sake of the Gentiles. "Eneminess" (being in the
enemy category), however, is a temporary characteristic. Why?
Because God's election of Israel is irrevocable; the gospel of God's
Messiah for Israel and all the nations does not change Israel's election.
Israel's election is inviolable for two reasons. First, *because of the
fathers*, that is, the promises to Abraham, Isaac, and Jacob. Second,
God is faithful and reliable. God's gifts—certainly the list in 9:4-5—and
call are unchangeable. God does not give and then take back.

The third set uses the *just as—so also* formula of ch. 5 to contrast
disobedience and mercy. The period of disobedience (Adam in ch. 5)
clearly includes Israel just like the era of mercy (Christ in ch. 5)
includes Israel. The *then-now* contrast pictures two eras in salvation
history, Gentile disobedience followed by Jewish disobedience. To
maintain the balance, the now time is divided into two epochs: mercy
to the Gentiles followed by mercy to the Jews. The disobedience of all
theme (*apeitheō*, twice) rephrases 5:12-21, all are under the power
of **Sin**. Although the characterization of God's salvation as mercy
underlines the covenantal nature of God's actions, Paul's argument is
provocative. Gentile disobedience did not disqualify them from mercy
while Jewish disobedience did qualify the Gentiles. Jewish assumptions about God are turned on their head.

Paul concludes the argument in v. 32 with a summary of the theology of Romans. God judges all **Sin** by "imprisoning" people in their
disobedience, a summary of 1:18–3:20. The purpose of God's judgment is salvation for all, here defined again as mercy, a summary of
3:21–11:32. The gospel is for all, Jew and Gentile. God's mercy and
Israel's covenant privilege has been extended to all, Jew and Gentile.

Doxology 11:33-36

We have noted earlier that Paul concludes major arguments with a
doxology. He has been making the case for God's inclusive and universal salvation. Verse 32 is his final formulation of the central thesis

of the letter. Worship is the only appropriate response to the grandeur of God's work of salvation. Paul breaks out in a hymn of praise to God.

The doxology is a nine line poem. It is framed by a three member opening line—the riches, wisdom, knowledge of God—and by a three member concluding line—from him, through him, to him. The middle section consists of three double lines which comment in reverse order on the first three characteristics of God identified in the opening line. Each opening line contains a parallel clause that further describes the attribute praised in the first line. The lines are formulated as rhetorical questions. The expected answer for each question is "no one."

The hymn is profoundly theological; it is a poem of praise to God. There is no reference to Christ in the hymn. Paul has just outlined and analyzed the history of salvation effected by God. He now praises God the author and creator of this salvation history.

The opening line praises God's inexhaustible depths of character. God is profound, not superficial. The riches of God are limitless (lit., *a treasury without a bottom*). The wisdom of God is incomparable. The knowledge of God is without boundaries. The affirmation of God's wisdom and knowledge in creation, revelation, and redemption is a common theme in the OT and Jewish literature.

The first middle pair borrows themes from Job to focus on the justice and ways of God. They are beyond human comprehension (lit., *inscrutable and untraceable*). The second pair, v. 34, is a quotation from Isaiah 40:13 (similar thoughts are expressed in Job 15:8; Isa. 55:8-9; Jer. 23:18). No human being can know or understand the mind of God, or offer God advice. The third pair quotes Job 41:11. God is rich. God owes no one anything for anything.

God is the creator, the sustainer, and the goal of all creation (lit., *all things*). All created reality comes from, is maintained by, and moves toward God. Therefore, the common benediction in Paul and the NT, *to him the glory for the ages, amen.*

The first major argument of Romans began with the rebellion of the creature against the Creator (1:18ff.) The second major argument closes with a poetic acclamation of God. The God who is righteous, who elects a people and remains faithful to that people despite their disobedience, who effects salvation in Messiah Jesus for all people and for the creation, is worthy of praise.

TEXT IN BIBLICAL CONTEXT

The Prophecies of Isaiah

Paul's use of the Isaiah prophecy about the redemption of Israel (vv. 26b-27) refers to one of the great eschatological traditions of the

OT and first-century Judaism. Isaiah 27 and 59 are among the most significant biblical pictures of the future of Israel. The scenario outlined in Isaiah 59:12—63:7 is parallel to that found in Isaiah 26:7—27:13. While the details in the pictures differ, both portray God as a military commander who comes to rescue Israel from captivity and oppression (cf. Yoder Neufeld, 2002:308-10). Both speak of the forgiveness of Israel's sins, the subjection and judgment of her enemies, the renewal of the covenant between God and Israel, and the return of the dispersed Israelites from the nations of the world. The triumph of God and the restoration of Israel is followed by the pilgrimage of the nations to Zion to submit to the rule of God and to worship God. God fulfills all the dreams and aspirations of Israel—e.g., peace, security, prosperity, the rule of justice and righteousness, honor and tribute from the nations of the world, the visible presence of God among the people (see also Isa. 10:12-12:6; 29:1-8; 33:1-35; 41:2-28; 49:1-13; 54:1–55:5; 56:3-8).

The various scenarios and the details are developed further in the literature of Judaism (see 1 En. 91:7-17; Bar. 4:21–5:9; Sir. 37:1-17; Ps. Sol. 17:21-32; speeches in the Test. XII Patr., e.g., T. Zeb. 9:7-8, T. Dan. 5:9-13, T. Naph. 8:2-3; Test. of Mos. 10:1-10; the War Scroll of Qumran, 1QM). What is common in all these portraits is that God will move out from Zion to free and restore Israel and to judge the nations of the world. Paul's interpretation of this action as *all Israel will be saved* is no different than *all Israel will be gathered to the Lord* in the Testament of Benjamin 10:11 and *all Israel has a share in the coming world* in Sanhedrin 10:1. That is, Paul shares a common vision with his contemporaries for the future salvation of Israel as a people.

In some of the Jewish literature a messianic figure from David's lineage plays a role in the end-time salvation of Israel. In most of the literature, the saving action is God's alone. Where the Messiah plays a critical redeeming role, he not only triumphs over Israel's enemies but also brings salvation and gathers all Israel from the nations (see 4 Ezra 13:35; 4QFlor. 1:12).

In some, but not all, of these scenarios the nations come to Zion to worship and obey the laws of God. Five different expectations about the Gentiles may be discerned in Jewish literature: 1) the wealth of the nations will flow into Zion; 2) the Gentile rulers and nations will serve Israel; 3) Israel will be the light to the nations, and her salvation will extend to all peoples; 4) the Gentiles will be destroyed; 5) the Gentiles will be judged, and not dwell in Israel. The assumption behind the belief in the salvation of the Gentiles is that Judaism is the one true religion that will become the universal religion of all people. What is clear in the literature outlining such expectations is that the salvation of the Gentiles is a by-product of the restoration and salvation of the Jews, and will come to the Gentiles only with their conversion to the Jewish religion. The salvation of the Gentiles is linked to their becoming Jews.

Isaiah in Paul's Interpretation

Paul holds in common with many Jews of the first century a vision for the salvation of Israel that also will benefit the Gentiles. But he also breaks with critical elements of the Jewish vision. First of all, Paul says nothing about the regathering of the Jews or about their restoration to the land of Palestine. He breaks apart the almost universal linkage of Jewish eschatology, the salvation and the restoration of Israel. Second, Paul introduces a limiting or qualifying factor in God's intervention to save Israel, a factor that stands entirely outside of Jewish history, *until the fullness of the Gentiles come in*. Something is prior to God's salvation of the Jews, namely, the salvation of the nations. Jews and Gentiles stand on an equal footing before God. God is now saving the Gentiles, and will in the future save Israel. That is a radical revision of Jewish understandings of salvation history. Third, God's salvation is the same for Jews and Gentiles; it is based only and totally on God's mercy. While the Jews are loved and elect because of the "forefathers," their future salvation will be based exclusively on God's mercy, not on ethnic or national privilege.

What Paul does not say may be as important as what he says. He says nothing that would clarify the meaning of *the fullness of the Gentiles*. He says nothing about the nature of Israel's salvation except that it will involve a radical change in its attitude to the gospel. He gives no hint about the time of Israel's salvation. Most scholars argue that it will be an end-time event that will precede the parousia of Messiah Jesus, but they cannot base that on the text of Romans 11. Paul is confident that God will save all Israel, but he does not specify when. His accent falls rather on the inclusion of the Gentiles and the unity of Jews and Gentiles in God's salvation promise and covenant.

TEXT IN THE LIFE OF THE CHURCH
Supersessionism

Romans 11 has been the center of two very problematic interpretations in the history of the church, one ancient and the other modern. The first, known as supersessionism, teaches that God is finished with the Jews and that the church is the new Israel which has replaced (superseded) ethnic Israel. Already in the second century Justin Martyr argued that the church is Rachel, the loved wife, who has displaced Leah, the first wife, and is the sole inheritor of the name and possessions of Israel. Cyprian in the third century A.D. taught that the Gentiles instead of the Jews would attain the kingdom of heaven. John Calvin, and most of his theological descendants, argue that "all Israel" in Romans 11:26 means the church. In a variety of different ways theologians since the second century have argued that the church is the New Israel that has replaced historic Israel as the people of God because Israel rejected God's Messiah, and, in fact, crucified him.

A teaching could hardly be further from Paul's intent than supersessionism. The target of Paul's exhortations in ch. 11 is precisely Gentiles who hold an early version of that view. He is talking about the Jewish people to Gentiles who boast that God has set Israel aside (11:17-24). His opening line in Romans 11 is that God has not rejected Israel (11:1). The rejection of Israel is only temporary (11:25), and even in this interim time Israel is a means of riches for the world (11:12). The gifts and call of God are irrevocable (11:29). The church depends on Israel for its life and mission; Israel is the root that sustains the church, not vice versa (11:18). Chapter 11 says nothing about a curse on the Jews because of their rejection of Christ, nor does the rest of the NT. Chapter 9:30–10:21 speaks of stumbling by Israel, but 11:11 explicitly asserts that this stumbling does not mean a fatal fall. The harsh statement in 1 Thessalonians 2:15 is aimed at Jews who are persecuting the church, not at the Jewish people as a whole. Supersessionism is a theology that strikes right at the heart of Paul's gospel, *to the Jew first and also to the Gentile*. Without the Jews there is no Christian church.

Two Covenant Theology

The ultimate historic tragedy of supersessionism in Nazi Germany has led to the reverse, the argument for two distinct covenants and ways of salvation for the Jews and the Gentiles. Commonly referred to as two covenant theology, this modern interpretation makes the case for two people of God. Salvation is through the Torah for the Jews and through Jesus Christ for the Gentiles. In other words, the Jews will be saved by God apart from Messiah Jesus. Furthermore, each covenant should be respected in its own right without people from one group trying to convert people from the other.

Two covenant theology represents a serious problem. First, it essentially clings to a system of ethnic religion, one for Jews and a different one for Gentiles. It teaches precisely what Paul argues against in Romans, that Christian faith and the church is exclusively for one people, Jews or Gentiles. Second, Paul has argued throughout Romans that the Jewish doctrine of one God means that this one God saves all people on the same basis in fulfillment of the promises to the patriarchs and the covenants. Two covenant theology challenges Jewish and Pauline monotheism. Third, the gospel, Paul also argues, is the good news that God has now offered righteousness, end-time salvation through one person, Messiah Jesus, who fulfills the promises of God and the mission of Israel to bring salvation to all people and the cosmos. When the deliverer of 11:26 is said to turn away godlessness from unbelieving Israel and forgive their sins, the most obvious meaning is that sin is their unbelief and that Israel will come to believe in the Messiah.

Finally, throughout Romans and especially in chapter 11, Paul makes the case that God is creating one end-time people in the world, not two. In 11:11-14 he outlines his expectation that all Israel will become incorporated into the community of faith. The analogy of the olive tree (vv. 17-24) indicates that the broken off branches will be grafted back. Paradoxically, in this one people the Jews have a priority based on the promises of God. That priority means that both people will be redeemed on the same basis, that both people need each other to experience the real grandeur of God's salvation, and that the Gentiles will join the Jews, not the reverse, in the renewal and unification of the eschatological people of God.

Paul's burden in Romans is that one God is creating one people through one person. Any theology that breaks apart this unity, whether to raise one group above the other (supersessionism) or to distinguish the one people from the other (two covenant theology), misunderstands the central passion of Paul.

The Rejection of Anti-Judaism

Romans 11 calls the church to repudiate anti-Judaism in every form. The Jewish people are critical and foundational to the church. The church's story is part of the larger story of Israel as the people of God. Christians worship the God of Israel, the God of Abraham, Isaac, Jacob, Ruth, Mary, Jesus, and Paul. Jesus is the Messiah of this God, who brings to fulfillment the promises of this God. Any claim to obscure or reject the church's worship of the God of Israel, YHWH, casts doubt on the trustworthiness of the God the church proclaims. If God does not keep faith with Israel, how and why can this God be trusted to keep faith with any other peoples? The church's place within God's covenant is secure only if the Jewish people remain part of the covenant. The Jews are the trunk, the Gentiles the branches. Without the God of Israel and the Jewish people, there is no Messiah and no Christian church.

The Jewish faith is not simply one more religion among the other religious traditions (e.g., Hinduism or Buddhism). The Jewish people are half brothers/sisters of Christian people—they come from the same parents chosen to be the people of God in the world. They continue to be God's people despite their refusal to believe that Jesus is the Messiah. God's grace toward Israel persists despite the fact that it rejects this grace for the present time. The Christian mission to the Jewish people, which continues the mission of Peter and Paul, is to call this people to the fulfillment of its faith in Messiah Jesus, not to the conversion to a different God and a different faith.

The Jewish-Christian Schism and Contemporary Response

While many in the Believers Churches may reflect the larger views of Protestantism in which the schism between Jews and Christians that begun in the second centuries is assumed as normative, some noteworthy efforts to rethink the relationship have occurred. Jacob J. Enz enumerates numerous ways Mennonites have sought significant relationships with Jews, with some giving most of their careers to establishing relationships with Jewish people (469-70). Frits Kuiper, a Mennonite theologian in the Netherlands helped begin a Christian kibbutz in Galilee, *Nes Ammin*, an "ensign to/for the peoples" (469), with the hope that here a Jewish-Christian witness might be given to the world.

John Howard Yoder lectured and wrote significantly on the Jewish-Christian schism, provocatively challenging settled conceptions and exploring new ways of thinking on this matter. Ten incisive essays by Yoder on this issue have been edited and published posthumously by Michael G. Cartwright and Peter Ochs, Christian and Jewish scholars respectively (2003). Both Cartwright and Ochs introduce the volume by respective essays on what Yoder's work means to current efforts among scholars shaping post-Shoah (Holocaust) Rabbinic Judaism (Ochs) and post-Christendom Christian witness, in which the relationship between Jews and Christians is special (Cartwright). Yoder's first essay is entitled, "'It Did Not Have to Be.'" Yoder argues that most of the first-century Christians (the "Nazarenes" or followers of the Jesus Way) were part of the pluriform nature of emerging Judaism. Many continued to worship with Jews in synagogues and continued to varying degrees practices of ritual and moral purity laws.

Yoder contends that Christianity in the first three centuries and Judaism for most of the last 2500 years bear witness to a Jeremiah-type existence: make your home and witness in the circumstance of diaspora. Only when Christianity became a state church under Constantine and regained establishment and whithin the empire did it seal its cleavage with Judaism, and then also resorted to persecution of Jews. But for heirs of the radical reformation, this is not normative, nor is it so in post-Christendom free church models. Indeed, Yoder calls for radical changes in thinking and relationships, in which the church must repent of its negativity toward Judaism, let alone its persecution of Jews, and thus consider what restitution might mean for the church on this matter.

The book includes a lengthy Appendix that narrates a 53-year history (1949-2002) of Mennonite efforts in the Middle East (among Jews and Palestinians) as two significant contexts for the development of Yoder's thought on this topic. The thrust of Yoder's essays, fully grasped, leads us not only to rethink the schism but also to lament the loss of the solidarity between Jews and Christians that Paul expresses in Romans 9–11. Even more, these essays urge that the past enmities between the two faith communities cease and a new engagement occur.

A practical effort to engage cooperatively in being God's people is represented by the Mennonite church planting effort in Boston. Together two congregations, one Mennonite and the other, messianic Jewish, purchased land and built a building that would serve both communities, one on Saturday Sabbath, and the other on Sunday Lord's Day. Might this too be seen as an ensign to the world?

Summarizing the Argument

Chapters 9–11

Chapters 9–11 are a critical component in the argument of the entire letter. The question of the relation of Gentiles to Jewish Christian and Jewish people in the plan of salvation underlies the whole argument of Romans from the statement of its theme in 1:16. The gospel is the power of God for salvation to everyone who trusts. . . . But the gospel is also "to the Jew first and also to the Greek." God's faithfulness to

Israel as the elect people is not negated by including the Gentiles, but
is rather affirmed by it. The God who makes righteous the ungodly,
both Jewish and Gentile, is the God who may be trusted to keep the
promises to Israel.

The Abraham references in chs. 4 and 9–11 (9:5, 7; 11:1, 28)
underline the overarching unity of Paul's argument. The case for the
thesis of the second major argument of the letter, the revelation of the
righteousness of God to all people in 3:21-26, is framed by discussions of Abraham, ch. 4 and 9:5, 7 and 11:28. In ch. 4 Abraham is
the father of Gentile Christians as people of faith. In ch. 9 Abraham
is the father of the children of promise. In ch. 11 Abraham is the
ground for the election of unbelieving Jews. Abraham demonstrates
the legitimacy of Gentile inclusion in the people of God in ch. 4 and
of God's ongoing election of Israel in chs. 9–11. Abraham is the basis
for arguing both the centrality of faith in Messiah Jesus and the
integrity of God's covenant faithfulness. Abraham is the father of all
the people of God. Therefore, he is the basis for exhorting Jewish
Christians in ch. 4 to accept Gentile Christians who trust God in
Christ apart from works of law. In ch. 11 he is the basis for rejecting
Gentile Christian arrogance toward the Jews and for exhorting their
humble recognition of the ongoing priority of Israel in God's plan.

Chapters 9–11 are a single sustained argument that explains both
Jewish unbelief and Gentile faith. The question that elicits Paul's argument is not only, has God's faithfulness to Israel been nullified by
Jewish unbelief, but also, has God ceased to be impartial by calling
primarily Gentiles to faith in the present time? Divine faithfulness and
impartiality are in dynamic tension in all three stages of the argument.
The first argument, 9:6-29, demonstrates how God elects both Israel
and the Gentiles on the same basis, mercy without regard for human
behavior or worthiness. The second argument, 9:30–10:21, shows
that Christ is the goal for both Jew and Gentile, and that the impartial proclamation of the gospel functions to harden Israel so that the
Gentiles can be reached. The third argument, 11:1-32, indicates that
Israel's hardening is temporary, destined to be removed by the fullness
of Gentile faith. The mystery revealed in 11:25-27 makes explicit
what has implicitly driven the argument since 9:6—the interrelated-
ness of Jew and Gentile in salvation history. God's back-and-forth
dealings with Israel and the nations are the concrete manifestation of
Paul's dual claim that God is both faithful and impartial.

Chapter 11 is a key to this larger argument. It makes the case that
Jews can (vv. 1c-6) and will be saved (vv. 11-32) even though a temporary hardening prevents most from responding positively in the

present time (vv. 7-10, 26). In fact, it is in the interests of the Gentiles that the Jews be saved, because the grandeur of God's salvation will be geometrically increased. Verses 28-32 make clear that God's word has not failed. God's plan is the temporary casting away of Israel for the sake of saving the world. Thus, God is both righteous and impartial to all people. While this theology was developed earlier to critique Jewish arrogance, in ch. 11 it is aimed at Gentile arrogance. Paul makes it clear that Gentile Christians have not replaced Israel as the true people of God, but depend upon Israel and her salvation. That is a very important point because two issues are at stake: first monotheism, one God of Jews and Gentiles, and secondly ecclesiology, one church composed of Jews and Gentiles.

The whole argument is about the covenant faithfulness of God. Paul interprets and reinterprets the covenant history of Israel—from Abraham, Isaac, and Jacob to Moses and the Exodus in ch. 9 to Deuteronomy 30 in ch. 10, to the covenant renewal prophecies of Isaiah and Jeremiah in ch. 11—to make the case for the righteousness and faithfulness of God in salvation history. God has been narrowing Israel down, choosing this son and not that one, choosing some of the wilderness generation and not others, making Israel the vessel of wrath to demonstrate God's riches to the vessels of mercy, hardening Israel to save the world. Israel's vocation is to be the people of God for the salvation of the world. That is the theme Paul drives so hard in ch. 11 as the climax of the history: *through their trespass salvation has come to the Gentiles* (v. 11); *their trespass means the riches for the world, and their failure riches for the Gentiles* (v. 12); *their rejection means the reconciliation of the world* (v. 15); *you . . . now have received mercy because of their disobedience* (v. 30); *they have now been disobedient in order that . . . you may receive mercy . . .* (v. 31).

God's plan for Israel was to make her the people for saving the world. While that vocation was distorted by Israel's presumption that election meant national status and privilege, her role has been restored in Messiah Jesus. God brings salvation by triumphing over **Sin** in Messiah Jesus. To do that **Sin** needed to be focused and concentrated, literally piled up, in one place. Part of Israel's salvation history vocation was to be that place, to be hardened for the world, to become the vessels of wrath, in order that God could deal with **Sin** in one place, in one people, and ultimately in one person, the Messiah. God in Messiah Jesus has triumphed over **Sin**, 3:21-26 and 5:12-21, in order to save the world. God has put forward the *hilastērion through faithfulness by means of his [Jesus'] blood to demonstrate that . . . he is righteous even making righteous.* Christ fulfilled the

special role of Israel by fulfilling the law for the purpose of righteousness to all people of faith. Israel's vocation of being the place where
Sin was gathered was never intended by God to be permanent, but
as a temporary means for the salvation of all people.

The Gentile mission fits precisely into this plan of God. It is the
positive result of Israel's vocation of hardening and wrath, and in turn
is to be the means of calling Israel to the full salvation that God
intends. The privileges and blessings of those *in Christ* (chs. 5-8) were
those belonging to Israel. In Messiah Jesus they have been given to
Jewish and Gentile people of faith in order to make the nonbelieving
Jews jealous of their inheritance, and thus open to the new and final
end-time revelation of God's righteousness.

God's plan of salvation for the world means that Gentiles cannot
be arrogant—there is no church apart from Israel—and that God will
keep the promise to *save all Israel* for the sake of the salvation of the
world.

Romans 12:1–15:13

The Living Sacrifice of the Righteous Community

The final argument of Romans is contained in 12:1–15:33. Paul has redefined the people of God in chs. 1–11. The righteous and merciful God is creating one unified people of Jews and Gentiles. God's salvation always requires a way of life that is consistent with the salvation experienced. The Jews called this response *halacha*, walk, while later Christians called it ethics, the way to live. The form of such ethical teaching in Paul's day was moral instruction through exhortation.

Paul has already indicated in chs. 6 and 8 that being made righteous requires a transformed life and *service of righteousness* (6:18). In chs. 12–15 Paul outlines in greater detail the ethics for the Roman Christians that should follow from God's salvation. In other words, chs. 12–15 exhort the righteous community to the shape of its lifestyle. The lifestyle is defined at the outset as a sacrifice (the atonement metaphor from 3:21-26), that is, as a life of sacrificial thanksgiving to the mercies of God. It is further defined as a transformational ethic. The center of the transformed life is remaking the intellect so that Christians can test the good and the true. The foundation for ethics is to think differently. In the missionary situation, new Christian communities in the context of a pagan world, intellectual transformation in light of what God is doing is critical. Without a different worldview that transforms the basic categories of thinking and appropriate behavior there will not be a different style of living.

The final section of the letter is carefully crafted and argued. It is framed by a parallel structure, *the I exhort you* formula (*parakaleō*) in 12:1 and 15:30. Each "exhortation formula" is associated with the metaphor of sacrifice, a living sacrifice in 12:1-2 and the sacrifice rendered by the Gentiles in 15:14-19. The double exhortation in the closing argument is unusual in Paul. He usually uses one "exhortation formula" that is linked to the opening "thanksgiving," and thus says something about the purpose of the letter. The double "exhortation formula" in Romans is linked to the thanksgiving, mutual encouragement, and a visit to Rome, and thus also says something about the purpose of the letter (more on that later).

The frame brackets four specific exhortations that are ordered in an ABAB pattern.

A 12:1a The Exhortation (*Parakaleō*) Formula
  B 12:1b-2   The Living Sacrifice
    A 12:3-16   The Renewal of the Mind
      B 12:17–13:10 Repay Only the Good
    A 13:11-14   The Renewal of the Mind
      B 14:1–15:13 Welcome Differences
  B 15:14-29   The Sacrifice by the Gentiles
A 15:30-33   The Exhortation (*Parakaleō*) Formula

The unity suggested by the frame is intensified by the repetition of key words. The dominant words that link the parts are *one another* (10 times—2:5, 10 [two], 16; 13:8; 14:13, 19; 15:5, 7, 14), *think* (nine times—12:3 [four], 16; 13:14; 14:6; 15:5), *the good* (eight times—12:2, 9, 21; 13:3 [two], 4; 14:16; 15:2), *love* (six times—12:9; 13:8, 10 [two]; 14:15; 15:30), *please* (six times—12:1, 2; 14:18; 15:1, 2, 3). Other words that are repeated at key points include: *mercy* (12:1, 8; 15:9), *repay* (12:17; 13:7-8), *discern* (12:2; 14:18, 22). The repeated words suggest the shape of the ethic that Paul exhorts: think differently about people, do good for and love people, please God and neighbor rather than oneself.

The Living Sacrifice

Romans 12:1-2

PREVIEW

Paul lays the foundation for a series of exhortations to the Roman Christians by moving backward, *therefore, I exhort you . . .* because of what God has done, e.g., *the mercies of God*. God has done something. Therefore, Paul issues a principled exhortation and a series of commands that follow. To be made righteous by God and to become a member of God's people requires resocialization; it affects the most fundamental relationships, perceptions of reality, understandings of the self. Earlier in Romans Paul has spoken about this transformation as dying and rising with Christ (ch. 6), as living in the Spirit (ch. 8), or as adoption into the family of God (ch. 8). The metaphors speak of a radical break with the past and the beginning of a new way of life. The radical nature of the resocialization process for the Roman Christians is restated with a new set of metaphors—*sacrifice to God, nonconformity to this world, transformation* (literally, metamorphosis) *of the mind*. What these metaphors require is detailed in chs. 12–15.

OUTLINE

The Exhortation Formula, 12:1a
The Living Sacrifice, 12:1b-2
    12:1c-d   The First Command
           The Command 12:1c
           The Reason 12:1d
    12:2   The Second Command
           The Negative Command 12:2a
           The Positive Command 12:2b
           The Purpose 12:2c

EXPLANATORY NOTES

The Exhortation Formula 12:1a

Verses 1-2 serve as a "headline" for the whole section. It begins with a very specific exhortation formula that is used often by Paul when he shifts to the ethical sections of his letters (e.g., 1 Thess. 4:1; Phil. 4:2).

The exhortation is a direct appeal, *I exhort you*, coupled with the familial form of address, *brothers/sisters*. The exhortation carries a strong imperative force, e.g., "I command you to. . . ."

The exhortation is grounded in the past—*therefore, through the mercies of God*. It is difficult to know if the *therefore* links this exhortation to the immediate preceding argument (chs. 9–11, esp. 11:30-32 with the threefold reference to God's mercy) or to the larger argument for God's saving righteousness of all people (chs. 3:21–11:36). The same is true of *the mercies of God*. Is Paul referring to the immediate context or to the larger argument of the letter? The difference is not significant. Two things are clear. The plural *mercies of God* reflects the Hebrew plural (e.g., 2 Sam. 24:14; 1 Chron. 21:13; Pss. 25:6; 40:11; 51:1; Isa. 63:15), and refers to God's merciful treatment of sinners by making them righteous (4:5) and showing compassion to them (9:18; 11:32). Secondly, the phrase establishes the ground for what Paul will exhort. The basis for his exhortation is the merciful actions of God to the Christians in Rome.

The Living Sacrifice 12:1b-2

The exhortation is stated in two sentences that are parallel in form and consecutive in sequence. The first, v. 1b-d, deals with "the body" or the corporate life of the church. It is concerned with the nature of the religious life, the cultic sacrifice of the body to God. The second, v. 2, focuses on the mind or the intellectual aspect of the Christian life, the renewal of the mind to discern the will of God.

The metaphor of the first command is radical. The Christians are exhorted *to present your bodies as a sacrifice . . . to God*. The language of sacrifice was common in the ancient world. No institution was more important in the Jewish world than the Temple, and the central act of Temple worship was sacrifice. Many, if not most, other ancient religions also practiced it. The ritual involved sacrificing a victim, usually an animal but occasionally another person, in the place of the one making the sacrifice. Such a sacrifice had multiple meanings. It was an act of thanksgiving to God, or the gods, for a gift (e.g., salvation, health, rescue, a child, a benefit). It also put a person or people in contact with the transcendent world. In the awesome moment when the victim's life ascended to God and its body lay on the altar as a gift, the patron shared in the total consecration of the victim and vicariously crossed the boundary into the presence of God. Sacrifice was the connecting point of two worlds, the human and the divine, the historical and the transcendent.

Christians are asked to give up their individual (bodies as plural)

and corporate (sacrifice as singular) life in total consecration to God.
Nothing could be more startling or demanding. Furthermore, the sacrifice is to be living and ritually pure. It encompasses the entire new
life of the Christian; it is transferred from a one-time cultic act to a living consecration to God. And it must be *holy*, that is, specially set
apart for God, and *pleasing to God*, that is, acceptable to God. The
latter phrase is rare in the Greek Bible; it is used to describe the lives
of Enoch (Gen. 5:22, 24), Noah (Gen. 6:9), and Abraham (Gen.
17:1). The words that describe the sacrifice are standard qualities in
Judaism and the ancient world.

Paul cannot be accused of cheap grace, a gospel of easy forgiveness with no demand. The gift of God's mercy requires total consecration, and *the rational service* of the Christian community. The
word normally translated "spiritual" is the word for "logic," for straight
thinking. The "right thinking" Christian community will think that the
appropriate response to the *mercies of God* is total consecration of
life to God. Paul is not talking about a spiritual service or disposition;
rather, he is talking about the mind. He is concerned here with the
head, a concern that is reinforced by the repeated references to the
mind in the exhortations that follow.

The second command focuses the "thinking" component of the
sacrifice in the first command. The first part of the command is negative, Christians and the church *are to continuously stop being conformed to this age*. The church is actively and continuously to engage
(present imperative) in mental resistance to outside pressure to conform to *this age*, to the worldview of the present world. *This age* is
apocalyptic language. Paul is thinking of the present evil age in contrast to the age to come. The root word for *nonconformity (schēma)*
means "scheme," or "form." It refers to the world's underlying value
system. Paul recognizes the power of the dominant social groups, the
culture, and institutions of *this age* to shape the thinking and behavior of people. He therefore exhorts the church to engage in active
resistance to such socialization.

The second part of the command is positive, *but continuously be
transformed through the renewal of your intellect*. The church is
actively and continuously to be changed, literally metamorphosed
from one stage of understanding to a higher one through the renewal of the intellect. Paul's word for renewal means to make new, now
from the eschatological perspective of what God is doing in the world
through Christ.

The reason for this active engagement in intellectual transformation *is in order that you may test what is the will of God, the good,*

well-pleasing, and complete. The word for *test* means to determine what is valid or genuine, to distinguish the authentic from the sham. Non-transformed Christians cannot discern or test the direction God wishes. The capacity for Christians to test or discern appropriate mental and moral judgment and action depends on *not conforming but being transformed through the renewal of the mind.* The will of God is defined as that which is good (what is intellectually and morally consistent with the righteousness of God), the well-pleasing (what is acceptable to God), and complete (what moves toward wholeness).

Comments and Observations

Paul's opening frame is absolutely startling in its demand and scope. It would be difficult to think of a more radical foundation for ethical conduct in the church. Ethics in Romans is grounded in total self-sacrifice and total intellectual transformation, the surrender of the self and the reformation of the mind.

But, more than that, the ethical foundation outlined here is startling for four other reasons. First, it is God-centered, grounded in the mercies of God, the well-pleasing to God, the will of God. Life in the Christian community must be reshaped by who God is, by what God has done (made people right), by what is acceptable to God (living sacrifice, set apart to and for God, rational service), and by what is consistent with the will of God (good and whole).

Second, the opening frame builds on what Paul said earlier in the letter and ties the ethical foundations to the theological convictions he has outlined. The *sacrifice to God* here answers the wrong service of 1:18ff. (the same word as in 1:25), the failure to honor and thank God (1:21), the exchange of the glory of God for idols (1:23), the worship of the creature rather than the Creator (1:25). The sacrifice of the body replaces the dishonoring of the body in impurity, unnatural passions, and destructive social behavior (1:24-32). The renewal of the mind answers the darkened mind that rejects the truth and fails to discern the knowledge of God (1:21, 22, 25, 28, 32). The contrast between non-Christian people and the Christian community is dramatic:

1:18-32	**12:1-2**
the wrath of God	the mercies of God
refuse to glorify God	thankful sacrifice
dishonor the body	offer the body
idolatrous service	reasonable service
mindless mind	renewed mind
reject the just will of God	discern the will of God

Not only does Paul answer ch. 1 in the opening frame of ch. 12, he also builds on what he said in chs. 6 and 8. The verb *to present* was used five times in ch. 6 (vv. 13, 16 and 19 twice each time) and in close connection with *body* (vv. 12-13). Christians are not to present their members to sin as instruments of unrighteousness, but rather to present themselves to God in ch. 6. In ch. 12 they are to present their bodies a sacrifice to God. The first imperative of the letter, *think of yourselves as dead to sin and living to God* (6:12) is picked up in the idea of a *living sacrifice to God. The slaves of God . . . to sanctification (or holiness)* is similar to the offering to God that is *holy.* Paul's emphasis on the mind in ch. 12 builds on chs. 7 and 8. The *mind* agrees with the law in 7:23 but is frustrated by *captivity of the law of* **Sin**." The *mind of the flesh* is hostile to God and results in death, while the mind that is determined by the Spirit is capable of pleasing God in ch. 8. The new identity of Christians is centered in the presentation of the self to God and the transformation of the mind in chs. 6, 7, 8 and 12.

The third striking feature of the opening frame is the emphasis on the mind, on thinking. The transformed mind is critical to Christian behavior. Paul says more about the mind in chs. 12–15 than in any other passage in his letters. He is concerned with the head, with the intellect. Correct thinking is critical to right living. The church over the centuries has been much more concerned with the heart than with the head. It does not talk about "converting or sharpening your brain for Jesus' sake," but that is what Paul says in the opening frame and in the exposition of that headline in 12:3f. The church cannot reshape its identity without a transformation of the mind of individuals and of the collective body.

Finally, the opening frame is critical because it defines a new group identity for the church. Christians are people with a new ritual. Participation in ritual marks the incorporation of people into a group and its identity. The central ritual of the church is not the sacrifice of something to God, but the sacrificial giving of the self to God and the community. Christians are people with a new worldview, a new way of thinking that enables them to discern the will of God. Knowing and doing God's will was a very important goal in Judaism; the echo of 2:18 (*knowing the will of God and instructing others*) is hardly accidental. Christians are people who can do that because their minds think the things of the Spirit (ch. 8).

The Renewal of the Mind

Romans 12:3-16

PREVIEW

Paul has just identified the transformation of the mind as a critical imperative for Christians. He now explains the meaning of such renewed thinking. The text unit is clearly defined by a play on the word *think* in vv. 3 and 16. *Correct thinking* is the frame or inclusio. It means: 1) that Christians are members of a body that simultaneously is characterized by great diversity and great unity (vv. 4-8), and 2) that Christians are to love without hypocrisy (vv. 9-15).

OUTLINE

    A The Frame—think correctly, 12:3
       B To live as the body of Christ, 12:4-8
       B To love without hypocrisy, 12:9-15
    A The Frame—think correctly, 12:16

EXPLANATORY NOTES

The Frame 12:3 and 16

Paul introduces the text unit with the authority of a teacher; he speaks on the basis of a grace that has been given to him. The concern for correct thinking is not his, but God's, which Paul passes on: the Christians in Rome (*to all the ones being among you*) must learn to think differently about themselves. Translated literally, the opening words in v. 3 read: *not to think more highly [hyperphronein] than it is necessary to think [phronein] but to think in order to be sound in thinking [sōphronein].* Verse 16 is similar: *the same thing thinking [phronountes] among one another, not proud things thinking [phronountes] but associating with the lowly ones. Not become smart-headed [phronimoi] according to yourself.*

Paul contrasts two kinds of thinking, "thinking beyond the proper bounds" or hubris thinking (*hyperphronein*) and modest or reasonable thinking (*sōphronein*). The first describes arrogant and ambitious thinking, the second pictures self-controlled thinking. Both kinds are used in political contexts to describe the relationship between people.

The first creates conflict and destroys community, the second controls ambition for the welfare of the community.

The concern for "right thinking" opposed to "wrong thinking" picks up the language from elsewhere in the letter—the critique of "arrogant thinking" in 11:20 and the rejection of "conceited thinking" in 11:25, and introduces a phrase which will be repeated in 15:5, *the same thing thinking among one another*.

The problem among Christians in Rome is ambitious thinking, *thinking arrogantly* in v. 3 and *proud things thinking* in v. 16. The antidote to this communal poison is *to think reasonable thinking* in v. 3 and to associate with *the lowly ones* and *not become wise according to yourself* in v. 16. Correct thinking in v. 3 is based on a mean outside of the self, *to each as God has measured a measure of faith*. The gift of God to each person, not personal ambition, is the standard for self-assessment. The goal is defined in v. 16 as *the same thing thinking among one another*. The means is more radical than in v. 3; it is not keeping within the limits of what God has given, but the total reversal of *associating with the lowly ones*. The antithesis to *the proud* in v. 16 is *the lowly*, the people who lack honor and instead are characterized by shame. People in the church can *think the same thing among one another* only when the people of status and power associate with *the shamed*, the people with no honor and status. The unity of the community is threatened by arrogant thinking. The renewal of the mind calls for subversive thinking and behavior, choosing to give up power and status to become one with the lowly.

Paul can call for status reversal with integrity, because he practices it in his own ministry. He does not preach *with eloquent wisdom lest the cross of Christ be emptied of its power* (1 Cor. 1:17); he surrenders all his rights in the gospel for the welfare of his churches (1 Cor. 9:15-18); he refuses to boast except in his weakness because *when I am weak, then I am strong* (2 Cor. 12:10); he willingly suffers the loss of all privilege for the sake of *gaining Christ* (Phil. 3:4-11). Paul practices status reversal and calls Jesus followers to such a value commitment and lifestyle because that is how Jesus lived. Jesus surrendered status for the weak and the lowly (2 Cor. 8:9).

To Live as the Body of Christ 12:4-8

Paul illustrates the exhortation to correct thinking by referring to the community as a body, a common metaphor in ancient political thought. A community or a city was compared with the human body to encourage cooperation and unity.

The first line of the metaphor speaks of diversity, many different members with different functions. The second line centers the diversity—*the many are one body in Christ*, which is further defined as *members one of another*. The third line exhorts the use of the different gifts given by God to each member. Seven gifts are identified. Prophecy denotes the spiritually inspired but rational ability to discern and declare God's workings in the community and God's will for the church. The value of the gift is determined by its origin in faith and by its capacity to strengthen faith (*the measure of faith* refers to the source of the prophetic word, i.e., a word from God, and to the results of the measurement). The gift of service provides acts of service to the community. *The one who teaches* passes on and interprets the teachings of the faith. *The one who exhorts* nurtures the practice of the ethical implications of the faith. The gift of charity from one's own resources must be exercised with simplicity. *The patron* who provides financial support for those in need must demonstrate earnest dedication. The gift of mercy must be bathed in a cheerful spirit. Each gift is to be exercised faithfully for the benefit of the whole community (see 1 Cor. 12 and Eph. 4 for other gift lists with similar concerns for unity in diversity).

The point of the metaphor is that the sum is greater than the parts; the Roman Christians must learn to see themselves as interdependent parts of a larger whole. All parts are important and needed for the well-being of the whole. No part should think arrogantly about its importance or role. Thinking too highly of oneself is inappropriate, because each gift is defined by *being members one of another*. The churches are composed of interdependent people.

To Love without Hypocrisy 12:9-15

The second form of correct thinking is defined by the opening phrase of v. 9, *love without hypocrisy*, which serves as the headline of the text unit. The linkage of *love* with *unhypocritical* is a uniquely Pauline phrase (used only here and in 2 Cor. 6:6 in the NT). Christians are to live authentically loving lives. They are not to be two-faced, e.g., talk one line and live a different one.

Paul spells out the content of love in two different ways. The first characterization of the life of love is detailed in a carefully constructed poem (a ring composition):

A Abhorring the evil
   sticking to the good
   B with brotherly love loving one another
     with honor giving the lead
     with zeal not timid

> C in spirit zealous
> > in the Lord serving
> B in hope rejoicing
> > in tribulation bearing up
> > in prayer remaining constant
> A to the needs of the saints partnering
> > the love of strangers pursuing (usually translated as
> > "hospitality pursuing").

The translation is intentionally literal. It shows the heavy use of participles and prepositions to tie the whole together. The point of the poem is very clear—be active in loving in a variety of ways, e.g., shrinking from evil with horror, persisting in good, honoring, standing with, being partners with Christians in need, actively loving strangers. The unity of the church is built as people exercise love to each other in the spirit and in the Lord; the "C" at the center is clearly important as the ground to enable active loving.

The first "A" introduces a theme Paul will develop in the next text unit, 12:17–13:10, resist evil in all forms by pursuing the good and loving. To *love without hypocrisy* involves moral judgment, distinguishing good from evil and then pursuing the good. The discernment of the good here and in 12:17–13:10 expands on the same theme from 12:2. The transformed mind seeks the good. True love, like the will of God, involves discriminating moral choices.

The second characterization of the life of love is given in vv. 14-15. The construction changes abruptly from participles to imperatives—bless, bless, do not curse. The meaning of the previous poem is radicalized by means of two words—bless and pursue. *To bless* in biblical tradition means to call down God's gracious power on someone, including prayers for leniency, or forgiveness, or salvation. The term *pursue* (*diōkontes*)—can also mean "persecute"—*bless the ones persecuting* ("you" is not in the best manuscripts). The *love of strangers* and *blessing the one pursuing* is a play on words (*diōko* in both phrases). Intentionally and actively loving strangers and blessing the ones pursuing or persecuting believers are flip sides of the same coin. Verse 14 may be a Pauline commentary on the words of Jesus about loving the enemy and praying for the persecutor (Matt. 5:44) or blessing the persecutor (Luke 6:28). The language and sentiment were also common in the OT (Ps. 36:22; Prov. 3:33; 30:10) and Judaism (Ecclus. 21:26-7; 33:12) so that Paul could be quoting a word of wisdom. To love means to ask God to bless even people who persecute; it certainly excludes the opposite, cursing the oppressors. Love means solidarity with people whether in joy or sorrow.

Comments and Observations

The transformed mind that Paul calls for involves a radical resocial-ization of the dominant mind set. The honor-shame code of Roman society is turned on its head. Christians are people who think differ-ently about themselves and about others. They think honestly about themselves and give priority to the needs and well being of other peo-ple. Everyone is valued and loved as members of the same family. The less honorable, or the shamed, are lifted up and honored. Even per-secutors or oppressors are blessed. Such counterculture behavior can occur only if the mind has been changed at its deepest center because of the mercies of God (12:1) and the service of Christ (12:11).

Many commentators suggest the audience shifts in v. 14 from peo-ple inside the church to those outside. The frame of vv. 3 and 16 hardly supports such a neat distinction. Christians can be persecuted and oppressed by fellow-Christians, especially in communities of diverse ethnic composition and socioeconomic distinctions, as well as by non-Christians in the society. The transformed mind must learn to treat fellow Christians of different ethnic origin and of high and low status as brothers and sisters. At the same time, as the next text unit indicates, distinct lines between "inside" and "outside" cannot be drawn. Loving behavior promotes the good and resists evil both with-in and outside the believing community.

TEXT IN BIBLICAL CONTEXT

Paul's concern for the mind in this text is not out of character. He is the one early Christian writer who carries a concern for the mindset or worldview of his churches. Twenty of the 24 references to "mind" (*nous*) in the NT are found in the Pauline letters, 23 out of 26 refer-ences to "thinking" (*phroneō*) are Pauline. Paul is uniquely a pastor of the mind.

Importance of Renewed Mind

The mind and thinking are not neutral for Paul. They reflect a larger life reality that has consequences. People can have an *unfit mind* that is incapable of discernment, or minds that are *hardened* (2 Cor. 3:14), or *blinded minds* (2 Cor. 4:4), or thoughts that lead them *astray* (2 Cor. 11:3), or they can *be futile in their thinking* (Eph. 4:17). To let one's mind be shaped by the value system of *the flesh* (Rom. 8:5) or *earthly things* (Phil. 3:19; Col. 3:2) displeases God and leads to death. In contrast, to let one's mind be shaped by *the Spirit* (Rom. 8:5) or *the things above* (Col. 3:2) pleases God and leads to life. To think *as a child* reflects an immaturity that needs to be outgrown. The mind can be shaped by the *thoughts of Satan* (2 Cor. 2:11) or it can know *the mind of the Lord* (Rom. 11:34; 1 Cor. 2:16).

Renewed Mind and Relationships

Paul's concern for the thought life of Christians and the church focuses on two issues. First, the way one thinks determines self-perception and thus relationship to others. The contrasts are *thinking too highly* or *arrogantly* versus *thinking soundly* or *sensibly* (Rom. 11:20; 12:3, 16; Col. 2:18). Paul's concern here is honest self-assessment between different groups of people and between people of different socioeconomic strata in the church. The critical value at stake is the quest for honor in an honor-shame culture.

The use of the contrast *thinking too highly* (*hyperpronein*) and *thinking soundly* (*sōphronein*) is common in ancient philosophy related to issues of conflict within communities. It is political language designed to reduce strife and to help restore harmony and balance. "Thinking soundly" is the individual or corporate virtue which overcomes the vice of pride (hubris) that underlies the conflict. Hubris thinking is arrogance that leads to the violation of appropriate personal and social limits. It is caused most commonly by pride due to strength and wealth. Such thinking is especially tempting to people in power. "*Thinking soundly*" outlines a middle way to balance conflicting interests that disrupt the community.

The language is used in this classical sense in the New Testament. "*Thinking soundly*" is the antidote to individual and group pride. The image of the body and its members in Romans and church divisions in 1 Corinthians indicates relations between individuals and groups in the community. The specific call to solidarity with the humble in Romans 12:16 indicates the political nature of the language in Romans. The identification of the gospel with the foolish, the weak, and the despised in 1 Corinthians makes a similar point. The same themes are found in Philippians 2:5-11—the unity of mind, brotherly love, not to seek glory for oneself but instead to give more glory to others. The call for "*thinking soundly*" in the pastoral letters is concerned with building the community of faith rather than the control of individual appetites and desires, as in most interpretations. Young men and women, older men and women, church leaders are called to "*think soundly*" for the well-being of the entire Christian community (Tit. 1:8; 2:2, 4, 5, 6, 12; 1 Tim. 2:9, 15; 3:2; 2 Tim. 1:7). The demoniac of the Gerasenes is able to participate in community life—sit attentively in a group—after Jesus casts out the demons and the man is *in his right mind* (Mark 5:15; Luke 8:35). Paul and other early Christian leaders link thinking and a subversive political order. Those with status are to seek out the lowly and lift them up, give them honor. The welfare of the whole is more important than the individual. Such subversive behavior can occur only if people's thinking or worldview has been radically changed.

Common Mind

Paul's second concern for the thought life is even more radical. He calls Christians to "a common mind," *the same thing thinking among one another* (v. 16a). It is one thing to call for a worldview that reverses the basic patterns of thought and behavior in a given culture. It is quite another to ask that the Christians and the churches agree on such a radically new way of thinking and acting. But that is the meaning of the phrase *to be of the same mind*. Paul uses the motif of "one mind" six times (Rom. 12:16; 15:5; Gal. 5:10; 2 Cor. 13:11; Phil. 2:2; 4:2). These exhortations all call for "a unified mind," especially among church leaders, when the church supports *the weak* (Rom. 12:16; 15:5-6) and when the church is torn by conflict (2 Cor. 13:11; Gal. 5:10; Phil. 2:2; 4:2). Unity is tested most severely when the church must deal with the weakness or shame of fellow-Christians and when there are differences of opinion. Paul exhorts unity in the church by calling people to discern a common direction, to agree about basic ideas and strategies, to have unity of mind. The model for developing such unity of thought is Jesus. It is possible only if people act like Jesus did, giving up personal ideas, preferences, and positions for the welfare of others and for the sake of the whole.

Paul's focus on "the mind" of individual Christians and the church is ultimately a concern for community solidarity. *Thinking soundly* and unity of mind are indispensable for the unity of the Christian community.

TEXT IN THE LIFE OF THE CHURCH
A Radical and Concrete Ethic

The interpretation of Romans 12:1-16 (usually through 12:21) in the church is dominated by two themes: 1) Paul is outlining his ethics more systematically than in any other letter; 2) His ethic is an ethic of love. Luther opens his interpretation of this section with the sentence, "the apostle is about to teach a Christian ethic" (Luther, 1961). C. H. Dodd, 400 years later, suggests that Paul comes closer to "giving a systematic treatment" of Christian ethics in Romans 12–15 than anywhere else and that love is the center of that ethic (1932:197). Paul

Achtemeier in a popular commentary for preachers focuses on love as the solution to problems of pride and overinflated egos (1985). This way of defining the theology of the text, of course, leads to struggles with the relationship of grace and ethics for many Protestant interpreters. Teachers in the church like Luther, Nygren, and Achtemeier go out of their way to emphasize that the concern for ethics here does not constitute a new law. Grace and ethical instructions are not incompatible, they assure us.

The dominant modes of interpreting this text make two problematic assumptions: 1) Paul is outlining a systematic ethic rather than giving instructions for specific issues in the house churches in Rome; 2) His ethical instructions are grounded in love. Romans 12 is simply a less poetic version of 1 Corinthians 13.

A more historical and radical reading of the text is required. Paul is addressing a specific set of values and behaviors among the Roman Christians. Further, he is calling for much more than love. He is talking about the mind, not the heart. He is arguing for a change of worldview, a fundamental shift of values. Love of the other and of the oppressor is an example of what this new worldview and value system looks like in actual church life. Paul is exhorting a resocialization of the Christian community that will make possible a love that will honor rather than shame Christians who are different.

A New Value System

The real challenge of this text for the church is to construct a worldview, a value system, which incarnates the gospel in ways that build unity and nurture solidarity among Christians of different racial, class, gender, and socioeconomic status groups. The call for thinking patterns that are consistent with the gospel and for "one mindedness" in the church, especially unity of mind among leaders, is far more radical than any love ethic. But such a radical sacrifice is precisely what Paul suggests constitutes the renewal of the mind so that individual Christians and the church can please God and discern the divine will.

What would a genuinely equalitarian worldview and value system look like in the church? How can the church "rehonor" people who have been shamed by powerful white male dominated structures, especially women and minority groups? Is it possible for church leaders to give up the quest for power and status for unity of thinking and action in the church? Paul calls for a real revolution in the church, one which is much more radical than "a love ethic."

Repay Only the Good
Romans 12:17–13:10

PREVIEW

Paul develops two themes introduced in vv. 9 and 14, hate evil and do the good (v. 9) and reject revenge against opponents or enemies (v. 14). A series of key words define the text unit—repay (12:17 and 13:7), obligation or owe (13:7, 8), evil and good (12:17, 21; 13:3, 4, 8), love (13:8, 10). The unit is tied together by the theme of obligation or repayment in relationship to evil and good. In a society where Christians are persecuted by fellow Christians and non-Christians, should they practice revenge? In a society where Christians are overtaxed and taxed unfairly, should they resist the taxing function of the state? Should Christians repay evil with evil? Paul's answer to every question is "no." Instead, he argues, Christians should repay evil with good, pay taxes, and love the neighbor. Paul makes his case with three commands.

The Pauline exhortations are principled and politically realistic at the same time. Paul does believe that Christians should do good and hate evil, that revenge should be left to God, that Christians should live by love. But he also knows he is addressing a minority group in a hostile environment. Any kind of explicitly revolutionary or culturally subversive activity by these people would be political and social suicide. To argue for non-retaliation, for payment of taxes, for life governed by peace and love is good political realism for a new and small group of Christians trying to live out the gospel in an alien context.

OUTLINE

The First Imperative—Do not repay (apodidōmi) evil but overcome evil, 12:17-21

    A 12:17a Do not repay evil (kakon)
        B 12:17a   For evil (kakou)
              12:17b   Think the honorable before <u>all people</u>
              12:18   Live peacefully with <u>all people</u>
              12:19   Do not avenge yourselves
                            Scriptural confirmation 12:20
        B 12:21a   Do not be overcome by evil (kakou)
    A 12:21b but overcome evil (kakon) with the good.

The Second Imperative—Be subject to the governing authorities, 13:1-7
  13:1a   Thesis—Command: be subject
                   Theological reasons 13:1b-2
                   Practical reasons 13:3-4
                   Restatement of thesis 13:5
  13:6-7   Application, specific commands
                   Specific—pay taxes 13:6
                   General—repay (*apodidōmi*) everyone the obligation
                   (*opheile*) 13:7

The Third Imperative—Be <u>obligated</u> (*opheilete*) to no one except to love, 13:8-10
  13:8a Thesis—Owe (*opheilō*) to no one except <u>to love</u> (*agape*)
    A 13:8b Reason—<u>loving</u> the other <u>fulfills the law</u>
                   Scriptural confirmation 13:9a-e
                   Scriptural interpretation 13:9f
    A 13:10 Reason—the love (*agape*) to neighbor not works evil
                   (*kakon*)
                   —<u>love</u> (*agape*) is <u>the fulfillment of the law</u>

EXPLANATORY NOTES

Do Not Repay Evil but Overcome Evil with Good 12:17-21

The text unit has one theme—actively reject retribution in any form. The theme is stated three times, at the beginning, in the middle, and at the end: 1) *repay no one evil for evil* (v. 17), 2) *never avenge yourselves* (v. 19), 3) *do not be overcome by evil, but overcome evil with good* (v. 21). Paul rejects the moral code of the ancient world which justified paying back harm done to oneself or to loved ones (the *lex talionis*).

Paul exhorts more than rejection of retribution. He also counsels behavior that assumes a new world view or a new set of values: 1) *take thought for what is noble in the sight of all people* (v. 17), 2) *if you are capable, live peaceably with all people* (v. 18), 3) *if your enemy is hungry, feed him, if he is thirsty, give him drink* (v. 20), 4) *overcome evil with good* (v. 21). The first counteraction picks up the idea of right thinking, literally, *thinking beforehand.* Instead of retaliation give forethought to behavior that is *beautiful* and *good* before all people and act on the basis of these values.

The second counteraction picks up the peacemaking theme of Jesus (Matthew 5:9), actively engage in peacemaking or be a peacemaker. The qualification *if you are capable* (lit., *if you have the power*) recognizes that peaceful living takes two sides. In a context of oppression and persecution it may not be possible, or it may not lie within your power, to live peaceably. The verbal form (*eirēneuontes*) requires the supplying of a helping word in English, living, pursuing, building, and so forth. Making peace a verb, not available in English, connotes a dynamic element often missed in current discussions on peace.

The third counteraction is a quote from Proverbs 25:21-22. Do not respond to hostility only with passivity—leaving it to God—but with concrete acts of kindness. Such action Paul explains with the strategic metaphor of *burning coals upon his head*, signifying that it will confuse the opponent. It is not clear whether the metaphor connotes judgment in keeping with numerous OT precedents (Zerbe, 1992:182-84, 196-201), symbolizes contrition and repentance, as in such a custom in ancient Egyptian penitence and reconciliation ritual (Klassen, 1962:337-50), or fire-starting coals that are a friendship gift (Isaak, 2003:37). But the exhortation to act kindly is clear. Responding to evil with hospitality and kindness has a positive effect-it unsettles the enemy. The final counteraction uses the imagery of a Christian standing in the middle of a battle with the evil of the present age. Do not respond to the power of evil by using the means of evil, hostility or retaliation, but with the power of good.

The theological reason for the exhortation is given in the middle, *leave it to the wrath of God* (v. 19), supported by a word of Scripture, *vengeance is mine, I will repay, says the Lord* (Deut. 32:35). The people of God are not to retaliate for evil done to them, because judgment is God's business. Retaliation against the enemies of God's people was both advocated and practiced by the Jewish Zealots in Paul's day. The Zealot option may well have been a factor among Roman Jews and Jewish Christians (see the introduction to the commentary "The Pastoral Context of the Churches in Rome"). Paul, in agreement with a series of Jewish teachers (*T. Gad* 6:7; 1QS 10:17-18; CD 9:2-5; 2 *En.* 50:4), rejects revenge against opponents whether outside or inside the boundaries of God's people, because such action must be left to God.

Comments and Observations

Several things are striking about this text. The first is the emphasis on public behavior—*all people* is repeated twice (vv. 17 and 18). The way Christians deal with oppression and persecution is observable and observed. The second is the pervasive teaching and spirit of the Sermon on the Mount. Evil is to be countered publicly with goodness and loving action.

Paul's exhortation to overcome evil with good links this text to what precedes and follows. This entire section of Romans begins with the need to make choices between the ages. The text unit that follows anchors the call to live out of a different worldview in eschatology, in reality that *the night is far gone, the day is at hand.*

Many commentators suggest that Paul is addressing persecution by non-Christians or people outside the Christian churches. He may even be addressing the beginnings of the persecution of Christians by the government which resulted in the mid-60s persecution by the emperor Nero. Evidence within the text supports such a reading: 1) *the one another language* from 12:3-16 and 13:8-10 fades and is replaced by *all* language. In 1 Thessalonians 5:15 and 3:12 and Romans 13:7 "all" language refers to outsiders. 2) The word for persecution, *diōkein*, normally refers in Paul to hostility from outside the Christian community. 3) The placement of 13:1-7 within this context suggests relations with the larger culture. 4) The use of apocalyptic language—overcoming evil with good—is especially appropriate for relations between insiders and outsiders. On the other hand, the emphasis on public action (*all people*) and positive acts of kindness toward persecutors can fit internal tension between different ethnic and socioeconomic church groups as well. As the history of the church has demonstrated only too often and too well, persecution of Christians by fellow Christians can be as intense and brutal as persecution by non-Christians and/or the state. Whatever the source of persecution, Paul rejects retaliation and exhorts the counteraction of loving kindness.

Be Subject to the Governing Authorities 13:1-7

The second argument, controversial and much debated in church history, consists of a simple command followed by reasons and a specific application. The language is closely linked to the prior text unit: good and evil (12:17, 21; 13:3-4); wrath (12:19; 13:4-5); vengeance/executor of justice (the same basic word stem in 12:19 and 13:4); all people/all (12:17-18; 13:1, 7), obligation (12:17; 13:7). My approach to this text is indebted to John H. Yoder's groundbreaking contribution in *The Politics of Jesus* (1994:193-211).

13:1a The Command

The command is *every person be subject to the governing powers.* The call for *submission* (lit., lining up properly) is not a call for obedience (lit., bending one will to the will of another). Submission means to accept the claims of, to be subject to, to be properly lined up or ordered; the opposite is to resist or disrupt proper ordering, not dis-

obedience. The command requires the moral choice to line up properly rather than to resist or oppose. While the *every person* may be
universal in scope—all people—its reference here is to Paul's
Christian readers. The *governing powers* refer to the officers of the
government rather than to invisible angelic, even demonic, powers
who stand behind and empower the state government. The language
used is that of Hellenistic administration. In addition, the very specific
reference to government officials in v. 3 and vv. 6-7 defines the meaning as human beings who work in the government. Paul never tells his
readers to submit to angelic powers; in chapter 8 the Roman
Christians are told to resist and oppose the angelic powers who seek
to separate them from Christ (vv. 37-9; see also 1 Cor. 15:24-27;
Gal. 4:8-11; Col. 2:15).

Paul gives two reasons for his command, one theological (vv. 1b-
2) and the second practical (vv. 3-4). Each reason is given in two parts.

13:1b-2 Theological Reasons

The theological reasons are: 1) the governing powers are given their
authority by God and ordered by God. 2) Whoever resists them is
resisting God's ordered power and is thus liable to judgment. The first
theological reason reflects a general biblical understanding—all
authority in the world comes from God and is to serve the purpose of
ordering nature and society. This first reason is grounded in the
Jewish Scriptures (e.g., Prov. 8:15f.; Isa. 41:2-4; 45:1-7; Jer. 21:7,
10; 27:5-6; Dan. 4:17) and reflects a widespread teaching in first-century Judaism (Ecclus. 10:4; 17:17; Wis. 6:3; *Ep. Arist.* 224).
Josephus, a contemporary of Paul's, wrote "no ruler attains his office
save by the will of God" (*J. W.*, 2:140).

The second theological reason states the logical consequence of
the first. Literally it begins with *so that*. Resisting or opposing the governing powers makes people liable to judgment.

Paul's language here is very precise and nuanced. Verses 1-2 are
dominated by "ordered" language. A literal translation makes this
clear:

> Every person let be subject (*hypotassō*, lit., ordered under) to the gov-
> erning powers (*exousia*). For not there is power (*exousia*) except
> from God, and the ones being from God have been ordered
> (*tassō*). So that the one being disorderly (*antitassō* = standing
> against order) to the power (*exousia*) ordered (*diatassō*) by God is
> standing over against (*anthistēmi*), and the ones standing over
> against (*anthistēmi*) will receive to themselves judgment.

The critical word is "ordered" (*tassō*). Paul does not talk about the powers being "ordained" or "appointed," that is, somehow specially blessed by God, as in most translations. Rather, he talks about the powers being ordered, or literally lined up like troops for battle, and about people's relationship to the powers as either *properly ordered*—lined up in proper order—or *standing over against*—intentionally lined up improperly. The role of the governing powers is described as an ordering one, and the relationship of people to the powers also is described as an ordering one.

The judgment for those who resist this ordering function—that is, *stand over against*—probably refers to divine judgment rather than the judgment of the governing powers. While the second theological reason in vv. 3-4 is often interpreted to mean the judging role of the powers, there are good reasons to think it means God's judgment. The word for judgment in v. 2 (*krima*) is usually used by Paul to describe the judgment of God (10 out of 11 uses in the Pauline letters, and all five of the other uses in Romans—2:2, 3; 3:8; 5:16; 11:33—refer to the divine). Furthermore, the language of judgment in vv. 3-4 is not *krima* of v. 2, but wrath (*orgē*) which consistently refers to the "wrath of God." It seems Paul is saying that the consequence of resisting the governing power is the end-time judgment of God.

12:3-4 Practical Reasons

The second set of reasons for submitting to the governing powers are practical (vv. 3-4): 1) governing authorities are to control evil; and 2) governing powers are ministers of God for the purpose of doing good. These reasons introduce a new idea into the argument, the positive role of the governing powers. Paul reintroduces the theme of doing good rather than evil. Governmental officials are not a terror to people who do good, but only to those who do *the bad*. The role of government is to reward good and punish evil. Paul, despite his own mistreatment by Roman officials (e.g., 2 Cor. 6:5; 11:23-25; Acts 16:22-24), sees the governing powers as serving a positive force. Therefore, he says *if you do not want to fear the powers, do good and you will be approved* (v. 3c). His positive view of the governing powers is even more explicit in the second practical reason (v. 4). The governing powers are *ministers of God* to the Christians for the purpose of the good. The evidence of this "ministry" is that the governing powers carry the sword, both the symbol and the reality for the execution of God's wrath on *the one doing the bad*.

The metaphor of *the sword* has many meanings in Greek literature. It can be a symbol of authority. For example, the police soldiers who accompanied Roman tax collectors were often called "sword bearers" to legitimate the tax collecting function. But it also was an instrument of capital punishment. The practical reasons for submitting to the governing powers offers a positive view of these powers, and outline criteria for evaluating the powers. They are to promote the good, which is defined as doing justice and controlling evil.

13:5 Restatement of the Thesis

In v. 5 Paul restates the thesis of v. 1—*therefore, it is necessary to be subject* (same verb as v. 1). The language suggests that the ordering structures of society are divinely given, and, therefore, *being subject* is required. Two reasons are given: 1) because of the judgment of evil (lit., *because of wrath*—"God" is not in the original text though most translations read "the wrath of God"), which summarizes the theological reasons of vv. 2-4; 2) *on account of conscience*, a new reason. The word *conscience* refers to the ability to reflect critically on what is appropriate. While it usually refers to past action, here it clearly refers to future action. If one thinks critically about the state of affairs in the world in light of God's ordering of governing structures, Paul says, it is wise and prudent to submit to the governing powers.

13:6-7 Application

On account of this introduces the conclusion of the text unit and the point toward which Paul has been driving. The phrase normally looks both backwards and forwards. Paul has exhorted *be subject to the governing powers* to address a specific issue, the payment of taxes. That is the backward perspective. The forward one is that the people collecting taxes *are ministers of God who constantly attend to this very thing.* The actual practice of the Roman Christians is *that you are in fact paying taxes* (the verb describes an ongoing activity rather than a command). The reality for the Roman Christians is that they are paying taxes in order to *be subject to the governing powers* and in recognition of the fact that *the governing powers* are *ministers of God* in performing their task.

Many commentators suggest that the practice of paying taxes among the early Christians was due to the teaching of Jesus found in Mark 12:13-17 and parallels (Paul's language is closest to Luke's account) the practice of Jesus recorded in Matthew 17:24-27. While Paul does not explicitly quote Jesus here, the similar teaching in 1 Peter 2:13-17; 1 Timothy 2:1-2 and Titus 3:1 could be a function of such teaching.

The final exhortation is an imperative: *keep on giving to everyone what is owed*, or more literally, *continuously pay to everyone the obligations.* The phrase involves a conventional expression for financial or social indebtedness. The goal is to be free of all debt to anyone. Four specific examples are cited to define the obligations: direct taxes (*phoron*), indirect or custom taxes (*telos*), fear (*phobon*), and honor (*time*). The list has parallelism and rhyme: *phoron, telos, phobon, time* in Greek. This poetic structure suggests that one should not give precise definitions to the terms. Thus the frequent attempt to interpret *fear* as a reference to the governing powers and *honor* as a reference to God is overdone. The phrase illustrates the nature of the obligation to the governing authorities as ministers of God. Christians are to meet all their obligations so that they are free of the control of others, especially governing authorities, and are free to devote themselves to their new obligations.

Comments and observations

Several things are striking about this text. The first is its straight logic. Three roles are contrasted: the authorities, submitting to (standing under—*hyper* language), resisting (standing over against—*anti* language). The authorities are legitimate agents of God. Submitting or "standing under" is affirmed as the proper relationship for the Roman Christians. Resisting or "standing over against" is rejected as improper.

The second is the intended audience. The people addressed are subjects, not the governing authorities. The third person is used in vv. 1-2, *every person be subject*. In vv. 3-7 the second person is used, e.g., *you not fear, you do what is good*. Paul's concern is the practice of Christians as subjects. He is exhorting specific behavior for a small, local group of Christians. He is not outlining a theology of the state or a balanced view of civic responsibilities.

The third is the style of the passage. Two things are noteworthy. The seven verses are built with seven uses of the connector word *for* (1b, 3a, 4a, 4c, 4d, 6a, 6b) and the repetition of words. *Fear* is used four times (3a, 4b, 7d [two times]). Several words are used three times ("power," 1a, 1b, 3a; *phoros* tax, 6a, 7b [two times]; good, 3a, 3d, 4a; bad, 3b [two times], 3c). Five words are used twice (subject, 1a, 5a; servant, 4a, 4c; wrath, 4c, 5b; *telos* tax, 6c; honor, 6e). In addition, the practical reasons for submission consist of an opening declaration followed by a series of "if . . . then" conditional sentences which are answered by declarative statements:

> v. 3b—*if you not wishing to fear the powers, then the good do* . . .
> v. 4a—declaration: *for servant of God he [governing official] is to you for the purpose of good*
> v. 4b—*if you the bad may do, then fear*

v. 4c-d—declaration: *for not in vain the sword he wears. For he is a servant of God, an executioner of justice . . .*

The repetition and dialogue in the central section has led some scholars to see a piece of early Christian catechism here. If this is correct, the text outlines early teaching about the relation of Christians and the earliest churches to the state.

The fourth striking feature is the description of government authorities as servants/ministers of God three times (vv. 3, 4, 6). The first two use the word *diakonos* (our word "deacon" comes from it), the same word used in 15:8 to describe Christ as a servant of Israel, and in 16:1 to describe Phoebe as a servant of the church. The third term (*leitourgia*) refers to public servants in Hellenistic society, but it is a word that has distinct priestly and cultic connotations in Jewish and Christian literature. Paul's use of the term here suggests he may be ascribing some kind of sacred character to government officials, and he does so specifically in relation to collecting taxes (*to this very thing*). This language, when combined with the positive assertions Paul makes about governmental officials, reflects an amazingly high view of public office.

A fifth observation is that the singular command *to be subject* seems to be driven by one issue in particular—the payment of taxes. We do know there was growing resistance to the taxation system in Rome at the time Paul wrote the letter. The protest became so widespread that Nero reformed the tax system in A.D. 58 to prevent a revolt. Both forms of taxation in Rome are mentioned in v. 6, direct taxation or tribute (*phoros*) and indirect taxation and customs (*telos*). The latter was collected by tax farmers, and was infamous for over-collection, extortion, and exploitation. Paul's strong encouragement to pay taxes suggests the Christians in Rome were tempted by the tax revolt movement, a protest that would have been nurtured by any Zealot sentiments against Rome among the Jewish Christians in the churches.

Sixth, the text supports Paul's anti-imperial stance in the letter. Despite the high view of governmental office, it constitutes a clear rejection of self-divinizing Caesars. The rulers are established by God for the purpose of promoting justice and order. The clear implication is that they will be held accountable by the God who established them.

A final comment concerns the theological centering of the text. There is no christology here; it is all theology. God is the one who establishes and orders the powers. Governing officials are servants of God. It is God who judges the resisters.

Be Obligated to No One Except to Love 13:8-10

The third command returns the entire discussion to the theme of love introduced in v. 9. It consists of a simple and direct exhortation. The command is linked to the second exhortation by the word "obligation" (*opheilō*). The *pay to everyone the obligations* of v. 6 is interpreted here to mean the only *obligation* Christians have is to love one another. A further link with the preceding is the theme of not doing evil (12:17, 20, 21; 13:3, 4). The opposite of *not doing evil is loving the neighbor*.

The command is expounded by an ABBA poetic structure of 8b and 10b:

A   the one loving (*ho agapōn*)
   B   the law has fulfilled (*nomon peplēroken*)
   B   the fulfillment of the law (*plērōma nomou*)
A   is the love (*hē agapē*)

This larger poetic structure is supported by another ABBA structure in v. 10:

A   the love (*hē agapē*)
   B   does not work evil to the neighbor
   B   the fulfillment of the law
A   the love (*hē agapē*)

The reason for the exhortation to *be obligated to no one except to love* is that love fulfills the law. And that love does not do evil to the neighbor.

The neighbor is defined in the first "A" as *the one who is different or the other* (*ton heteron*). The reference here must be defined by what has preceded in the entire text unit, the one who persecutes and thus evokes the desire for revenge, and the governing powers that tax unjustly and thus tempt the possibility of active resistance.

The reason for the exhortation is supported with scriptural confirmation and interpretation. Paul cites four of the five commandments from the second table of "The Ten Commandments"—do not commit adultery, do not kill, do not steal, do not covet (see Exod. 20:13-17; Deut. 5:17-21). The interpretation is anchored with an interpretive comment, *the law is summed up in this word*, and another citation of Scripture, *you shall love your neighbor as yourself* (Lev. 19:18).

Comments and Observations

Some commentators have suggested that Paul's exhortation here is dependent on Jesus' double command to love God and neighbor (Mark 12:28-34 par). While the gospel saying and Paul both cite Leviticus 19:18b, *love the neighbor as yourself*, the love exhortation in Romans as in Galatians 5:14 is the single command to love one's neighbor, not the double command. The different nature of the exhortations makes it difficult to argue Pauline dependence on the words of Jesus.

The definition of love with specific commandments from the Torah reflects a larger theme in Paul and in Romans. Love is not an undefined ideal. Its practice is measured by the observance of specific commandments. It is not possible to love and also commit adultery, kill, steal, or covet. Soon Paul will add other specifics; e.g., welcome the other, greet the other.

The specification of love as *the love* twice in v. 10, at the beginning and end of the poetic structure, may suggest that Paul is referring to "the love meal" or the observance of what is later called the Lord's Supper. The love feast is inconsistent with doing any form of harm to a fellow believer in the house churches of Rome. As chapters 14–15 will illustrate, the greatest barrier to the practice of such love in these churches was "welcoming" Christians who were different, who insisted on conformity to various Jewish laws. Christians were shaming one another at the love feasts. Paul exhorts living up to the commandment of love, and thus fulfilling the whole law, before getting to the specific social issues in the churches.

TEXT IN BIBLICAL CONTEXT

The dominant themes in this text—non-retaliation and submission to the governing authorities—stand in a long tradition of biblical interpretation.

Non-retaliation

Paul is not introducing a new ethic when he commands non-retaliation against evil. Rather he is reaffirming a widespread teaching of Scripture and Jewish exhortation. Non-retaliation is specifically taught in Leviticus 19:18, Deuteronomy 32:35-36, and Proverbs 20:22, and practiced in Exodus 23:4-5 and 2 Chronicles 28:8-15. Similar teachings are found in other Jewish literature (e.g., *T. Gad* 6:1-3; *T. Jos.* 18:2; *T. Benj.* 4:2-3; *Jos. Asen.* 23:9; 28:5, 10, 14; 29:3), and in the sayings of Jesus (Matt. 5:38-48 // Luke 6:27-36). Joseph was the model of such non-retaliation in Judaism (*T. Jos.* 17-18), Jesus in the early church.

Even more striking is the similarity of themes found in this text and extrabiblical Jewish literature. Paul uses six different themes in the argument of v. 14-21:

1) bless or do good to those who wrong you (vv. 14a, 20, 21b);
2) do not curse oppressors/persecutors or repay evil for evil
   (vv. 14b, 17a, 21b);
3) maintain solidarity, harmony, peace (vv. 15, 16, 18);
4) consider what is "noble in the sight of all" (v. 17b);
5) do not avenge yourselves (v. 19a);
6) leave vengeance to God (vv. 19bc).

Each of these themes is repeated in Jewish literature. For example, the Damascus Document from the Qumran community uses Leviticus 19:18 to assert that vengeance is a divine prerogative. Therefore, members are warned not to act vengefully to a fellow member of the community. Or, the Manual of Discipline, also from the Qumran community, exhorts repaying evil with goodness because judgment belongs to God (see also *2 En.* 50:3-4; *T. Gad* 6-7; *Jos. Asen.* 29:10, 14). Doing good and avoiding vengeful behavior toward insiders and outsiders is a common motif in the Jewish literature of Paul's day. Members of the various communities are to make every effort to maintain solidarity, peace, and love with opponents and persecutors.

Paul's first exhortation—do not repay evil but overcome evil—affirms a common scriptural and Jewish teaching to reject retaliation in favor of behavior that builds peace. The social context is provided in the texts which precede and follow, disagreements about the payment of taxes to the state, differences about appropriate food, refusal to welcome people who are different.

Submission to the Authorities

Paul's second command—*be subject to the governing authorities* —was also well known. From Jeremiah's exhortation *to seek the welfare of the city where I have sent you into exile, and pray to the Lord on its behalf, for in its welfare you will find your welfare* (29:7), to Proverbs' charge to *fear the Lord and the King, and do not disobey either of them, for disaster comes from them suddenly . . ."* (24:21-22), the Jewish people were encouraged to submit to governmental leaders. The Pauline warrant for such submission—God gives the rulers their authority—is a common theme. Think only of Proverbs 8:15-16—*By me kings reign, and rulers decree what is just, by me rulers rule, and nobles, all who govern rightly*—or Daniel 2:21—*God deposes and sets up kings*—or Daniel 4:17—*the Most High is sovereign over the kingdom of mortals; he gives it to whom he will . . .* (see also 4:25, 32; 5:21)—or the Wisdom of Solomon 6:3-4—*For power is a gift to you from the Lord, sovereignty is from the Most High*—or Ecclesiasticus (Sirach) 17:17—*over each nation he has set a governor"*—or the pseudepigraphic *Letter of Aristeas* 224—*God assigns glory and greatness of wealth to kings . . . no king is independent. All of them wish to share this glory, but they cannot—it is a gift of God* (see also 219).

The exhortation to be subject to the governing authorities is both similar to and different from three other texts in the New Testament. First Peter 2:13-17 uses the same "stand under" term to exhort submission (v. 13). But the submission is less explicit than in Romans—it is *to every human creation for the Lord's sake whether the king as supreme or to the governors as having been sent by him . . .* (vv. 13b-14a). There is no word about the divine ordering of the kings; the governing authorities are ordered by the king, not God. Furthermore, and very significantly, the entire exhortation is framed by *to every human creation* (v. 13) and *to all people* (v. 17). Kings and governors are subsets of all people. The purpose of the governing authorities is similar to Romans, *punishing evil doers and praising those doing good* (v. 14b). The primary motive for submission in both Romans and 1 Peter is *the will of God*, but the secondary motives are different: escaping fear and gaining praise in Romans (v. 3), disproving false accusations against Christians in 1 Peter (v. 15). There is no reference to taxes in 1 Peter, no idea of the governing authorities as servants of God, and no suggestion that resisting governing authorities equals opposition to God. Both texts conclude by using *fear* and *honor* in the same order, but the use is quite different. The reference in Romans is general, *to whom fear the fear, to whom honor the honor*. In 1 Peter God is the object of fear and the king the object of honor. But the honor due the king is qualified by the chiasm in which it is placed:

Honor all people
  Love the brotherhood
  Fear God
Honor the king.

Honoring all people and honoring the king are parallel. Honoring the king does not involve notions of divine status or authority (see further on 1 Peter in Waltner:86-89).

Titus 3:1-3 also exhorts submission to the rulers and authorities. But the emphasis is quite different. The exhortation is in the form of a reminder of behaviors that are to characterize Christian conduct. *Submission to the rulers and authorities* is the first behavior listed. It is followed by *to be obedient, to be ready to take any honest work, not to slander anyone, not to be quarrelsome, to be considerate, to show gentleness to all people.* The list would suggest that the concern is with disorderly and perhaps subversive behavior. Nothing is said about the nature of the ruling authorities or submission to them. The motivation for proper conduct is Christian experience (v. 3). The lives of Christians used to be characterized by the opposite behaviors, but God *saved us . . .* (vv. 4-7).

The third text, 1 Timothy 2:1-3, is very different from the others. Chapter 2 is the first of a series of exhortations to Timothy to direct his offensive against false teachers in the church (ch. 1). The theme of the initial exhortation is the gospel for all people (*all people*, v. 1; *all people*, v. 4; *all*, v. 6). The specific command in v. 1 is to offer prayers of various kinds for all people, including *kings and all in high positions* (v. 2a). The motivation is *that we may lead a quiet life in all godliness and dignity* (v. 2b). Such a life is *good and acceptable before God our Savior who wishes all people to be saved* (vv. 3-4).

Several things are striking in these "parallel" texts. First, none of them say anything about the divine authority of the governing authorities even though each in a different way exhorts submission to and respect for them. Second, each in a different way invokes the will of God as a motivation for submission and respect. Third, all are optimistic about the government's role to punish evil and reward good (Rom. and 1 Pet.), to enable Christians to silence their accusers by right public conduct (1 Pet.), and to make possible a good life that facilitates the proclamation of the gospel (1 Tim.). Neither Romans nor the three parallel texts believe the governing authorities will become the enemies of the church, even though Romans and 1 Peter at least were written to people who had experienced their disruptive force. All of these texts believe that the governing authorities will practice and promote justice. None anticipates a conflict between loyalty to God and support of the authorities. In other words, the parallel texts stand very much in the tradition of Romans 13, even though all are more muted than Romans. All stand at considerable remove from the book of Revelation, where the Roman Empire is seen as the beast, as the enemy of the people of God. Here loyalty to God conflicts with loyalty to the emperor, who claims divine status and persecutes and kills believers (see discussion of John Yeatts, *Revelation*, who notes illustrations of the church's critique of government injustice, suffering amid persecution, and triumphing through all this with vibrant worship, especially 235-37, 257-60, 415-34). This Pauline tradition also differs from the "critical distancing" from the governing officials by Jesus and his disciples as portrayed in the Synoptic gospels, most starkly in Mark 10:42-45 (see Pilgrim 1999:41-124, especially 60-61).

One other comment should be noted about this biblical tradition of the governing authorities in Paul. It belongs to the genre of wisdom teaching. It assumes the existence of governing structures and authorities for the ordering of human society, specifically the control of evil and the promotion of the common good. These texts are not intended to legitimate governing structures and authorities nor to offer a prophetic critique of them. The governing structures and authorities are seen as necessary for the welfare of the human community. Therefore, they should be respected, honored, and submitted to. Resistance is not wise or good.

THE TEXT IN THE LIFE OF THE CHURCH
Living Nonviolently

The Believers Church tradition is known for its pacifist teachings and practices. But abuse—power, gender, sexual—is a major problem in these churches, as in most churches. Passive-aggressive behavior is common. Is that not a form of retaliation?

What does it mean to live peaceably in the family? In the Church? What does it mean to reject revenge in the family? In the church? In the culture?

Might it be that the peace churches give such priority to peace teachings and conflict resolution seminars, because there is so much unresolved conflict in these communities? Why is there such a fear of candid discussion of the real issues in the church? They are discussed in coffee shops. Can real and deep conflicts be resolved without open conversation that facilitates understanding, growing trust, and finally resolution?

Church and State

Few texts have been as controversial in church history as Romans 13:1-7. The central debate is the relationship between the church and the state. Specifically, how does the church read Romans 13 when it disagrees with the policies and actions of the government of the time?

The critical issue is the linkage of God and the powers. This connection has been interpreted in two ways. The authorities are sanctioned in the first as instituted by God, and, therefore, to be obeyed. They are sanctioned but relativized in the second by their accountability to God. In other words, the text can be read in diametrically opposing ways from within the text itself. The first insists on the "divine right" of the authorities and the obligation to obey them. The second relativizes their power by making them accountable to God, and then qualifying the obedience of the subjects by various criteria. The same text is given either an affirmative or a critical reading. The choice of reading depends almost entirely on the life setting and expectations of the readers. An "innocent reading" of the text does not appear possible.

The affirmative reading assumes that the text outlines Paul's basic political theory for all times, places, and peoples. It offers the fundamental theology for defining the relation between church and state, subject and authority.

The critical reading uses very different strategies to relativize the authorities and the seeming unqualified call for obedience to them. First, Romans 13 is relativized by reading it in the wider context of the letter, especially 12:1-21 and 13:8-10, as well as other texts of the New Testament, which prioritize obedience to God rather than "men" (Acts), or which show the demonic side of the state (Revelation). A second strategy is to introduce criteria for differentiating between good and bad governments—authority is accountable to God and only those who demonstrate such accountability should be obeyed, or only authorities who are servants who serve the common good (13:4) are worthy of obedience. The third strategy is to restrict the scope of Romans 13 to a specific situation or problem in the Roman churches of the first century A.D., e.g., the need to bound charismatic enthusiasm, or the need to control Jewish revolutionary zeal against the Roman government.

Both readings can be found in almost every era of Christian history and in every denominational tradition, including the historic peace churches. When the church coexists in a happy marriage with the state or when the church and the state face a common enemy, Romans 13 is read affirmatively. But when the church finds itself in tension with the state, or when it is an oppressed minority, or when it is persecuted by the state, Romans 13 is read with a critical strategy.

Faithful to God and Subject to Government

Stories of faithful Christians who followed the way of Jesus Christ and encountered opposition from government abound. In some cases governments changed policies, because of the faithful witness of Christian believers. These stories illustrate how Romans 12:17-21, 13:8-10, and the exhortation in 13:1-7, all fit into the same ethic and life of the believer. Cornelia Lehn's collection of over 50 such stories from the first century to the twentieth century, in *Peace Be With You*, illustrates the breadth and power of such faithful witness. Second-century Roman soldier Servitor, having just become a Christian before he was sent off to the army front, risked his life to cross the river and give food to the starving enemy army of barbarians from the north. He was caught by a Roman sentry and consequently sentenced to death by emperor Marcus Aurelius, who mocked Servitor's testimony, "I obey my Master, Jesus Christ. He is Lord of heaven and earth, and he has commanded us to love our enemies. That means feeding them when they are hungry" (Lehn:20-21).

Or, Maximilianus' testimony before the North African proconsul, Dion, in his refusal to take up arms, "I cannot serve as a soldier. I cannot do evil." His father, Fabius, a recruiter for the army, refused Dion's command to persuade his son to recant. Fabius became pale and replied, "No, even if I could change his mind, I would not. I am proud of my son." Fabius walked the streets lamenting his son's imminent death and he had not long to wait. Maximilianus was executed the next morning (Lehn:22-23).

Early Anabaptists witnessed to government leaders to call them to the standards implicit in Romans 13:1-7. Hear what Menno Simons says in several of his writings:

> That the office of the magistrate is of God and His ordinance I freely grant. But him who is a Christian and wants to be one and then does not follow his Prince, Head, and Leader Christ, but covers and clothes his unrighteousness, wickedness, pomp and pride, avarice, plunder, and tyranny with the name of magistrate, I hate. For he who is a Christian must follow the Spirit, Word, and example of Christ, no matter whether he be emperor, king, or whatever he be. (in Wenger, 921-22)

> Be pleased, in godly fear, to ponder what it is that God requires of your Highnesses. It is that without any respect of persons you judge between a man and his neighbor, protect the wronged from him who does him wrong, even as the Lord declares, Execute judgment and justice, Assist, against the violent, him that is robbed, Abuse not the stranger, the widow, the orphan, Do violence to no man, and shed no innocent blood, so that your despised servants and unhappy subjects, having escaped the mouth of the lion, may in your domain and under your paternal care and gracious protection, serve the Lord in quietness and peace, and piously earn their bread, as the Scripture requires. (Wenger:526)

Surrounded by a cloud of faithful witnesses, we today face the challenge of being faithful to Jesus Christ in owing no one anything but love and being subject also to the authorities that rule the respective countries where we Christians live.

The Renewal of the Mind
Romans 13:11-14

PREVIEW

This text represents the apocalyptic counterpart to 12:1-2; it provides the eschatological foundation for the exhortations just completed and those to follow. The imminence of salvation's completion is the ground for renewing the mind and conduct of believers. In 12:1-2 the renewal was characterized by "nonconformity" and "transformation." Here it is pictured in the more dramatic and concrete language of baptism into the Christian community—undressing and dressing, walking in light rather than darkness. But the goal is similar, the renewal of the mind, specifically *not to give prior thought to the things of the flesh to fulfill its desires* (v. 14).

The text begins with the reason for renewed Christian moral conduct and then gives three commands about the shape of such conduct. The similar language and content in other Pauline texts (e.g., 1 Thess. 5:1-11; Col. 3:1-11; Eph. 5:8-20) suggests Paul is drawing on a common formula which may have been part of the baptismal liturgy of the early church.

OUTLINE

The Reason, 13:11-12a—the opportune time

The Imperatives, 13:12b-14—*let us . . .*
    13:12b   Put off the works of darkness and put on the armour of light
    13:13   Walk properly as in the day
    13:14   Put on the Lord Jesus

EXPLANATORY NOTES

The Reason: Knowing the Opportune Time 13:11-12a

The opening phrase, *and this, knowing the opportune time*, both gathers up what has been said and lays the foundation for what is to follow. The reason is an opportune "kairos" moment well known to the Christians in Rome as a unique time filled with divine saving and renewing potential.

This kairos time is described with a striking mixture of metaphors—it is time to wake up, the end-time salvation is very near, the night is ending and the day is approaching. All of the images are familiar Jewish word pictures for the great day of salvation and liberation. The moment for the completion of salvation is much closer than when the Christians first believed and were baptized (at most 20 years for the oldest believers). Day and night are contrasting concepts describing good and evil. *The day* is parallel to *the salvation* which is near. Sleep is a negative image symbolizing the inactivity of the mind, even the complete abandonment of thinking. *Wake up* language means to be mentally alert, to be ready for the day of the Lord. Night and day combined with sleep and wakefulness picture life either far from God or in the presence of God.

It is important to note that the night has not ended, but is far advanced. The light of day has not yet come, but soon will. Believers in Rome live at the edge of the great change between this age and the age to come, on the cusp of the tension between what is and what shall be.

The Imperatives 13:12b-14

In light of the kairos moment, Paul issues three exhortations.

13:12b Put off the works of darkness and put on the armor of light.

Paul introduces the familiar imagery of *taking off* and *putting on* clothes (see also Eph. 4:22, 25; Col. 3:8; James 1:21; 1 Pet. 2:1; Job 29:14; Pss. 93:1; 132:9, 16; Prov. 31:25; Isa. 51:9; 61:10). These are word pictures for abandoning vices and replacing them with virtues and for discontinuing immoral conduct and pursuing moral conduct. The language is that of baptismal instruction in which new converts are urged to get rid of past values and practices and adopt ones appropriate to their new way of life. The context suggests two kinds of change of clothing, night to day, and clothing with the gear of war. The stronger the eschatological urgency, the more appropriate the imagery of preparation for war. The negative half of the contrast exhorts getting rid of works of darkness, the values and conduct of a tired and inactive mind. The positive half of the exhortation—*put on the armour of light*—indicates that preparation for warfare is very much on Paul's mind. He is not simply calling for a new set of clothes, but for preparing for a war that must be won. He does not detail the armour of light here, but in a parallel passage in 1 Thessalonians 5:8 it consists of faith, love, and hope. Baptism for

Paul means enlistment in the army of a new commander and engagement in the battle against the evils of darkness.

13:13 Walk properly as in the day.

The second imperative sheds some "light" on what it means to live in the daylight. Proper Christian conduct abandons sexual orgies, drunkenness, debauchery, rivalry, and jealousy. Such behavior was common in Roman taverns at night. While Paul details only the negative behavior to be avoided at night, the counter behaviour would be sobriety, mental alertness, and solidarity.

13:14 Put on the Lord Jesus.

The final command uses the put on image for the second time, *put on the armour of the Lord Jesus Christ*, and with this new clothing avoid the drives of the flesh. To put on Christ is to live under his lordship and within his community (see 6:1f.).

Comments and Observations

Between major exhortations to repay evil with good (12:17–13:10) and to welcome people who are different (14:1–15:13), Paul reminds the Roman believers that they must think differently than their neighbors. Baptism into Christ and the Christian church called for a different life, which is defined by two kinds of images: 1) temporal—the eschatological hour is far advanced; 2) counterpoint—sleep/wake, night/day, put off/put on, darkness/light. Christians are confronted by the eschatological moment with a sharp either/or. The pull of the larger culture to fall asleep or to enjoy the night must be resisted daily by the light of the new day that is dawning.

The call of 13:11-14 to think and live differently parallels the opening of the final argument in 12:1-2. *To not be conformed to this age* here becomes *wake from sleep* because *the night is far gone*. The exhortation *to be transformed by the renewal of your mind* becomes *cast off the works of darkness* and *put on the armour of light* and *walk in the day by putting on Christ*.

One other parallel, which is rooted in eschatological thinking, is "the combat" motif. In 12:21 the Christians are urged to *conquer evil with good*. Here they are to battle darkness and immoral conduct with light and Christ. The first use of the combat motif is followed by a series of exhortations to non-retaliation. The second follows the exhortation *to love one another* and is followed by a series of commands to *welcome the other*.

Eschatology motivates new thinking and behavior. But the eschatological teaching itself is minimal. The present age is passing away. The hour of salvation is very near, but still future. The kairos moment in which Christians live requires critical thinking and living which is informed by light rather than darkness.

THE TEXT IN BIBLICAL CONTEXT

The dark and light metaphor is common in Jewish and early Christian teaching. In Jewish tradition, light comes from God but has been withdrawn from the earth and humanity because of sin. People, including Jews, therefore wander in darkness. A future time is coming when the darkness will end and the light be restored.

In between "the times" light and darkness are largely religious-ethical categories. Jewish people have access to the light in God's revelation, the law. People can choose to walk in the light by obeying the law. Jews must choose whether they want to be children of light or children of darkness. In the Dead Sea Scrolls this theme is associated with the coming eschatological battle. The children of light are exhorted to prepare for a battle against the children of darkness or Belial. They prepare for it in the confidence that the forces of light will triumph and destroy darkness. The children of light—also referred to as the righteous, or the wise, or the enlightened—will live in happiness and glory.

The major themes of the Romans text are found throughout the New Testament. Exhortations to wakefulness are common in the Synoptic Gospels and are associated with expectation and preparedness (see Mark 13:34-36; Matt. 24:36-44; 25:1-13; Luke 12:35-40; 21:34-36). The night in these texts is associated with the present age. Followers of Christ face numerous temptations—worldly cares, the false glamour of wealth, all kinds of evil desires—and must "keep awake." Similar exhortations to wakefulness are found in the letters (1 Thess. 5:1-11; Eph. 5:8-14; 6:10-20; Col. 4:2; 1 Pet. 5:8). The call to wakefulness is consistently grounded eschatologically. The light and darkness motif is a recurring theme (see esp. John 1:1-18; 12:46; Matt. 4:16; Acts 26:18; 2 Cor. 4:6; 6:14; Eph. 5:18; Col. 1:12-14; 1 Pet. 2:9). The light in Judaism was embodied in the law while in the early Christian writings it refers to Christ. A third theme running through these texts is the importance of armour and the reality of warfare (see 1 Thess. 5:6-8; 1 Cor. 16:13; Eph. 6:10-20; 1 Pet. 5:8-11). This reference to *weapons* and eschatological conflict is consonant with parallel images in Paul, *weapons of righteousness* (Rom. 6:13; 2 Cor. 6:7), weapons of divine power (2 Cor. 10:3-4), *the breastplate of faith and love* and *the helmet of hope, the armour of God* (Eph. 6:10-20; see also Yoder Neufeld, 2002:290-316). The linkage of wakefulness and prayer found in the Gethsemane account (Mark 14:38 par., Luke 21:36) and in Ephesians (6:18) and Colossians (4:2) is not present in Romans.

TEXT IN THE LIFE OF THE CHURCH

In Paul's letters the purpose of eschatological teaching about the end of history is ethical exhortation. It is not speculation about the time of the end. Paul displays no interest in calculating the time of the end. It is simply near or imminent (see Geddert, 2001:324-25; Elias, 1995:211-13, for similar understandings).

Baptism as Enlistment

The association of eschatology with the *cast off/put on* imagery of baptism is a reminder that baptism is more than "the outward sign of an inward reality." Baptism into the Christian community means "enlistment," signing up, for the battle of light against darkness, morality against immorality, and righteousness/justice against injustice (see Yoder Neufeld, 2002:316 for a similar understanding of baptism).

The church of Messiah Jesus would do well to redefine baptism as "enlistment" in the army of God rather than as a rite of passage to adulthood in the Christian community. It is a sign of "coming of age" only to the extent that it says that one is old enough and responsible enough to join the army, the army of God's people to do battle with darkness in light of the imminent approach of the end.

Call to Faithfulness

The prospect of the eschaton, the end, is a motivation to live faithfully—in this text to live in the light rather than the dark, to live with public integrity, to be armed for battle with the forces of evil and injustice. To be awake, to put on Jesus Christ, to walk in the light means the church is continually being nonconformed by the dominant values of the prevailing culture and is being transformed by the renewal of its thinking.

The imminence of the end calls the church to the practice of moral discernment. What are the "works of darkness" in various cultures? The growing HIV/AIDS epidemic suggests that Paul's concerns for sexual promiscuity and drug abuse ("drunkenness") are still profound manifestations of darkness. Jealousy seems not to have gone away in twenty centuries. What other works of darkness does the church struggle with?

Might greed and conspicuous consumption be evidences of darkness in many churches in the West? What about racism or sexism?

What does it mean for the church to conquer evil with good and to welcome the "other," because it believes the eschaton is nearer today than yesterday? The texts that precede and follow this one suggest that for Paul it means to love the other inside and outside the church, to live justly, to live peacefully, to welcome a diversity of people in the church (12:1–13:10, 14:1-13). The church would do well to follow the example of Paul.

Welcome Differences

Romans 14:1–15:13

PREVIEW

Paul's concluding exhortations address very concrete and critical problems among the Roman house churches: differences, name calling, and alienation over the specific Jewish practices of eating and observing special days. Both practices had become central to Jewish identity since the middle-second century B.C.; they were boundary markers which defined Jewish particularity over against other people. The observance of these customs became disruptive among believers in the Roman churches. Paul exhorts tolerance and outlines the theological basis for it. Four commands structure the contents of the exhortation.

The argument is clearly connected to earlier sections of Romans. The structural parallel with ch. 2 is striking—exhortation against judging others (2:1-3; 14:3-4, 10) followed by the reminder that all must face the judgment of God (2:16; 14:10-12). Three themes from the introduction to the larger text unit, 12:1-2, are picked up again. The way one "thinks" shapes action even when done *in the Lord* (14:6). Because of that, Paul prays that God will grant the Christians a common mind (15:5). Doing what is *pleasing to God* translates into the strong not pleasing themselves (15:1), but rather their neighbor (15:2) just as Christ did not please himself (15:3). The theme of discerning God's will is picked up in 14:22—the one who does not judge himself on what he has discerned is blessed.

OUTLINE

First Imperative—Continually welcome the one weak in faith, 14:1-12
    14:1   The Command
    14:2-4   Example 1—Eating
               The problem, 14:2
               The mutual obligations, 14:3
               The critical question, 14:4
    14:5a   Example 2—Observing days
    14:5b-9   The Critical Criteria
               Personal conviction, 14:5b
               Honor the Lord, 14:6
               Live to the Lord, 14:7-8
               Christ is Lord, 14:9
    14:10-12   The Critical Questions

Second Imperative—Do not judge one another, 14:13-23
    14:13b-15 First Command—do not put a stumbling block in the way of a brother
    14:16-18   Second Command—do not let the good be blasphemed
    14:19-23   Third Command—pursue peace and mutual upbuilding

Third Imperative—The strong ought to bear the weaknesses of the weak, 15:1-6
    15:1a   The Command
    15:1b-2   The Explanation
    15:3   The Model
    15:4   The Scriptural Confirmation
    15:5-6   The Prayer-Wish

Fourth Imperative—Welcome one another, 15:7-13
    15:7a   The Command
    15:7b-12   The Ground
                   The Christological Ground, 15:7b-9a
                   The Scriptural Ground, 15:9b-12
    15:13   The Prayer-Wish

EXPLANATORY NOTES

Welcome the Weak One 14:1-12

14:1 The Command

The command which opens the first and last paragraph of the text unit brackets the closing exhortation—*welcome* one another (14:1 and 15:7). The word for *welcome* means to accept into one's home, into one's circle of friends, or here, into the community of believers who meet in one's tenement apartment or house. The social setting is intimate, the space and the people one calls family.

The object of such warm embrace is *people who are weak in faith*. The description is pejorative—it is a nickname used to shame another group. The other group is not named here; *the strong* are not identified until 15:1. The *in faith* is critical. Some believers cannot trust God completely; they need to qualify their faith with additional props or requirements (detailed in vv. 2 and 5).

The command *to welcome* the weak is reinforced with a pastoral concern, do not welcome the weak in faith for the purpose of subjecting them to discussions (lit., "debates" or "arguments") about issues over which there is disagreement. The dominant group should not embrace the weak in order to pressure them to accept its views and practices. In other words, a diversity of views and practices should be accepted in the churches.

Paul follows up the command to welcome people with different theologies and practices with two examples.

14:2-4 Example 1—Eating

The faith of the one group permits them to eat *all things*, specifically meat, while the weak in faith eat only vegetables. The subsequent discussion about *unclean* and *clean* foods (14:14, 20), as well as the concern for festivals in v. 5, indicates that the issue here is Jewish dietary laws which had become the badge of Jewish identity (see, for example, Dan. 1:3-16; 10:3; Tobit 1:10-12; Jth. 12:2; 1 Macc. 1:62-63; *Jos. Asen.* 7:1; 8:5). The kosher laws that distinguish Jews and Jewish sympathizers from non-Jews are the concern. Jews living in the Diaspora often could not certify that food was kosher, that is, "clean." This was especially true when eating with Gentiles who were not sensitive to Jewish purity concerns. While meat offered to idols may be included (as in 1 Cor. 8–10)—such meat would be "unclean"—that is not identified as the central concern here.

But more than food is at stake. Food and theology are often linked, especially in ethnic-religious groups. The meat eaters despise (lit., *hold in contempt*) the nonmeat eaters. The language is strong—the meat eaters think they are so superior that they look down on and shame the nonmeat eaters. Conversely, those who abstain from eating meat judge the meat eaters as so unfaithful theologically that they merit divine judgment.

Paul rebukes both groups. The meat eaters should not despise *the weak* and the latter should not pass judgment on the former. He adds two reasons for rebuking *the weak* for their judgmentalism. First, using the same word as in v. 1, he asserts that God has embraced and accepted the meat eater. Secondly, Paul uses the master-slave relationship to assert that one master cannot judge the slave of another master. Each master determines if his slave will stand, that is, be acceptable, in the judgment. The point is that God, as the master of the meat eaters, is the sole judge of acceptable behavior.

14:2 Example 2—Observing Days

Paul outlines the second example in exact parallelism to the first. The issue now is observance of days. While the precise nature of the dispute is not identified, it clearly involves the observance of Jewish feast days, especially the Sabbath. Sabbath observance was another boundary marker in Judaism, especially Diaspora Judaism (see Josephus, *Ant.* 14:241-46; Philo, *Legat.* 155-58). Some Roman believers want to maintain the Jewish practices of Sabbath observance, while others treat all days the same. The issue of Sunday versus Sabbath was not yet an issue in the early church, and did not become a matter of dispute for several centuries. The linkage of food and Sabbath was not uncommon in Judaism (CD 6:17-18; Jos., *Ant.* 11:346).

14:5b-9 The Critical Criteria

Paul seeks to modulate the disagreements among the Roman Christians by outlining a series of criteria by which to evaluate differing practices. The first criterion is personal conviction, v. 5b. What one eats and the observance of days should be based on intellectual conviction (*convinced in his own mind*). The second is honoring the Lord and giving thanks to God. The third is living in the Lord. The fourth is recognizing that Christ is Lord of all of life. Diversity of behavior and practice should not cause contempt or judgment among Christians if it is based on personal conviction, if it honors the Lord, if it takes place *in the Lord* rather than on strictly personal grounds, and if it recognizes Christ as Lord. Christians can disagree with fellow Christians on a range of issues and practices if there is agreement and faithfulness at the center.

14:10-12 The Critical Question

Why would believers despise or judge fellow believers? The obvious answer is that there is no good reason for such attitudes and behaviors. After all, every (emphatic) believer will be publicly accountable before the judgment seat of God when the behind-the-back shaming of one group by another will be exposed. The biblical foundation is Isaiah 45:23. Therefore, every individual will give personal account to God; no one will be exempted and no one will give account for the other person or group.

The exposition of "welcoming one another" as not judging Christians who are different in vv. 3-12 is reinforced by the chiasm which structures the argument:

    A vv. 3-4b   Do not judge
      B v. 4c   Relation to the Lord
      B vv. 8-9   Relation to the Lord
    A vv. 10-11 Do not judge

The center of the faith—the relation to the Lord—means that Christians are not to judge one another for differences that are not central, even if the differences are as important for some people as eating and "holy days."

Do Not Judge One Another 14:13-23

"Judging" was the activity of the strong in the first imperative. The second paragraph focuses especially on the "judging" attitudes of the strong. The theme is stated in v. 13a, *therefore, let us not judge one another*. This command is elaborated in three additional bluntly stated negative imperatives, vv. 13b, 16, 19. The entire paragraph concludes with another reference to "judging," v. 22. In between the opening and closing references to "judging," Paul repeats the three themes of the paragraph—1) do not cause stumbling, vv. 13b and 21; 2) all food is clean rather than unclean, vv. 14 and 20b; 3) do not hurt a fellow believer because of food, vv. 15 and 20a.

The first explanation of what *not judging one another* means is *but rather determine* (a play on the word judging) *not to place a stumbling block or a scandal before a brother* (v. 13b). Before Paul names the *stumbling block* he states his own personal conviction, *nothing is unclean in itself*. He makes his own stance as emphatic as possible by a triple assertion—*I know, I am persuaded, in the Lord*. The word for *unclean* (*koinos*) was a very important term in first-century Judaism to denote ritual impurity (see Jth. 12:7; *Jub.* 3:8-14; 1 Macc. 1:47, 62; *Pss. Sol.* 8:12, 22; 1QS 3:5; CD 12:19-20; Mark 7:2, 5; Acts 10:14; 11:8). Ritual purity is one boundary marker that many cultures establish to differentiate "their" culture from another, and it was distinctively so in first-century Judaism. The difference between "clean" and "unclean" food defined the difference between "holy" and "unholy." It marked the line between what was acceptable and unacceptable for members of God's people. Paul's assertion that *nothing is unclean* is thus very bold, even heretical, for Jews and Jewish Christians who believed ritual purity was critical for the identity of God's people. Paul's agreement with the theology of the strong seems to remove any distinction between the people of God and all other people.

But Paul immediately qualifies his statement by acknowledging that perception is reality: food is unclean for the person who thinks it is ritually impure. He thus agrees with the strong theologically, but emphasizes the importance of recognizing the validity of the beliefs and practices of the weak. Paul, in effect, shifts the point of the dispute from a boundary marker distinguishing different groups in the churches to an affirmation of diversity of perspectives among the churches. Therefore, he argues that the strong (*you*) are not walking in love if they grieve or offend the weak (*your brother*) by what they eat. The strong must not cause the *ruin*, by which Paul obviously means spiritual and theological upheaval, of the weak by what they eat. After all, Christ died for the weak as well as the strong, and his death demonstrated what it means to walk by love.

The last time Paul used *stumbling block* and *scandal* (9:32-33) he was referring to the misuse of the law (by works instead of by faith). Here he again uses them to identify a misinterpretation of the law, using a specific law to differentiate groups of people. Paul's absolute rejection of the Jewish food laws may well be based on the equally emphatic statement by Jesus in Mark 7:15. The theme of *walking by love* links this section with one of the important themes in the entire last argument, *let love be genuine*, (12:9), *love fulfills the law* (13:8-10).

The second explanation of *not judging one another* is *do not let your good be blasphemed*, v. 16. The strong are not to give the good of the faith, the gospel of salvation and righteousness, a bad name in Rome because of disputes among the churches. The reason is that the reign of God is not defined by *eating and drinking*, but by *righteousness* (the right making power of God), *peace* (God-given wholeness and harmony), and *joy* (God's gracious gift of delight) which comes in and with the presence and power of the Spirit of God. Paul uses the phrase *the reign of God* rarely (14 times compared with 105 uses in the Synoptic Gospels), but his use here is strategic. Just as Jesus' proclamation of the reign of God broke open the practice of table fellowship, so the reign of God means the loving acceptance of people in the churches who disagree about eating ritually clean or unclean foods. The ethics of the kingdom eliminates the need to judge people before God and each other.

Therefore, Paul asserts in his third explanation *let us pursue peace and the things that serve to build up one another*, v. 19. The strong are actively to work for the well being of the church as a whole rather than pursue their own ideological interests. *Building up* imagery is important for Paul (1 Cor. 8, 10, 14; 1 Thess. 5:11; Eph. 2:19-21; 4:12, 16, 29). It is a metaphor for encouraging mutual interdependence and harmonious relationships among Christians who find it easy to shame each other, that is, to put each other down. Paul explains precisely what he means with another imperative and another explanation. The command is *do not destroy the work of God for the sake of food* (v. 20). The word *destroy* is the opposite of *building up*. The *work of God* refers to the churches. The first part of the explanation repeats v. 14—everything is clean, that is, ritually pure—and the second part repeats v. 15—it is wrong to cause fellow Christians to stumble theologically and spiritually by the food other believers eat.

Paul amplifies the explanation with three principles for Christian living. First, it is good to abstain from eating meat (ritually impure food) and drinking wine (offered to the Roman gods before being sold) occasionally (the verb is point action, in a specific instance) or anything else which causes a fellow Christian to stumble. Second, the strong should keep their more expansive trust in God—a trust which frees them from the beliefs and practices of more restrictive fellow believers—between themselves and God. Strong Christians should not need to display their faith in public if it creates problems for weak Christians. Christians who do not need to judge themselves for what they discern as correct are *blessed*, Paul asserts. The third principle is that everything that is not *out of faith* is sin, everything that does not have its source in the faithfulness of Jesus is flawed by human enslavement to the power of **Sin**. That is why those who eat ritually impure food when they doubt if it is permissible (lit., is *of two minds*) condemn themselves because they are not acting *out of faith*.

Paul's second exhortation is finely nuanced and balanced. Nothing is ritually unclean by itself. Old lines for demarcating the holy and the unholy, and thus those who are "in" from those who are "out," no longer apply. The more expansive believers can and should rejoice in their theological and spiritual freedom. True faith means freedom, and freedom involves diversity. But the exercise of freedom must be conditioned by love, by the effect the freedom has on believers whose faith is less expansive and can be injured or even ruined by the public display of freedom by others.

The Strong Bear the Weak 15:1-6

15:1a The Command

Paul reinforces the point of the second imperative by repeating and reframing the central exhortation. The strong, identified here for the first time by name, are defined as powerful people who can dominate others. Paul includes himself among the strong, further solidifying his identification with this group (see Rom. 14:14). The strong people in the churches have an obligation *to bear up the weaknesses of the weak*. The weak are defined as the people without power who lack the capacity to make things happen. The obligation of the strong is not merely to affirm the weak in their weakness, but literally to *lift up and carry* the ongoing consequences of their weaknesses.

15:1b-2 The Explanation

Paul immediately explains what he means. The strong are to desist from doing what comes natural to them, to please themselves. Instead, he elaborates by means of another exhortation, *let each one of us please our neighbor for the good* (not "his good," as in many translations). Every strong person in the church is to seek the welfare of the neighbor, which 13:10 defined as *loving* and doing *nothing bad*. The use of the language from ch. 13 is probably intentional. Such action does two things, it serves *the good*, the same phrase 13:4 uses to describe the role of governing authorities, and it builds up the whole (not "edify him," as in many translations). The strong are to build up the community by carrying the weaknesses of the powerless. The exhortation turns the expected behavior of an honor-shame culture on its head. The strong do not further weaken the weak by shaming them, but rather lift them up and carry them.

15:3 The Model

The ground for Paul's radical command is Jesus. The Messiah did not please himself, but modeled serving others. Paul explains what that meant for Christ by quoting Psalm 69:9, one of the most quoted Psalms in the early church, to interpret the meaning of Jesus' suffering and death. The citation is significant for two reasons. First, the believer laments his/her affliction by enemies and his/her own people (see vv. 8, 28). Second, the citation uses "honor-shame" language; it translates literally as *the insults of the ones continually insulting you fell on me.* Christ models how to handle insults; he absorbs and carries them on behalf of others.

15:4 The Scriptural Confirmation

Paul has just made a very radical assertion. The strong people in the church shall act like Messiah Jesus, they shall absorb and carry the shame of the weak. To make sure they take his biblical interpretation seriously, Paul adds that the Scriptures (here specifically Ps. 69:9) were written *before hand* for the instruction of contemporary believers. The purpose of this teaching is defined by two "through" clauses, in order that *through endurance* (the kind of endurance modeled by Christ) and through the *encouragement derived from the Scriptures we might have hope.* The Scriptures nurture hope by showing that God works through weakness and suffering to do the good and build the whole.

15:5-6 The Prayer-Wish

Paul concludes his third imperative with a prayer-wish that *the God of endurance and encouragement* (the same two words used in v. 4 to describe the purpose of scriptural teaching) will enable the believers in Rome *to think the same thing among one another.* The phrase is the same one Paul used in 12:16 at the conclusion of his discussion of "correct thinking." Here the phrase is defined further by *according to Messiah Jesus.* The example of Messiah Jesus cited in v. 3 shows that to please others rather than oneself is the way to achieve a common mind in the church. The purpose is *that with one mind and with one voice you may glorify the God and father of our Lord Jesus Christ.* The word for "common mind" is a political word that pictures the unanimity of a group (it is used 10 times in Acts). Genuine worship of God requires a common mind and voice—mind and mouth must be in harmony. When that happens the failure of people to worship God (1:21) is reversed. Paul's prayer-wish is that the honor-shame divisions in the church can be overcome so that the church can worship God.

Welcome One Another 15:7-13

The structure of vv. 7-13 follows that of vv. 1-6: exhortation, ground (example of Christ, Scripture), prayer-wish.

Paul returns to the opening imperative, *welcome*, but now broadens it (v. 7a). In 14:1 the imperative was to welcome the weak person. Here it is to welcome one another. Paul broadens his exhortation to include everyone. Christians are to practice mutual acceptance of people with different theologies and values, specifically those who eat different foods and observe different holy days.

Paul grounds his command in two things, the model of Jesus and the teachings of the Scriptures (vv. 7b-12). *Just as Christ accepted you* indicates the manner of Christ's embrace of different people (in 14:3 God's welcome was the ground for the exhortation). Christ, the Jewish Messiah, lived and died for all people, Jews and Gentiles, *for the glory of God*.

Paul elaborates the meaning of Jesus' example by returning to the major themes of the letter. Christ welcomed Jew and Gentile by becoming a servant of the circumcised (the Jews). This is the only place where Paul calls Christ a *servant* (*diakonos* = deacon), a servant for a people distinguished by circumcision (one of the three boundary markers of the Jews).

Christ became a servant of the Jews for two reasons. The first is *in behalf of the truthfulness of God in order to demonstrate the reliability of the promises to the fathers.* The reference to *the truthfulness of God* returns to a description used in 3:4 and 7. There and here it emphasizes the covenant faithfulness of God. Through Messiah Jesus, God keeps faith with the promises made to the Jews. Second, Christ became a servant of the circumcision *in behalf of the Gentiles in order that they might glorify God for his mercy.* Paul again picks up earlier themes in the letter. The Gentiles is used for the first time since 11:25, and recalls the argument of chs. 2–4 and 9–11. It is used six more times in the next four verses to emphasize the importance of including the Gentiles in the people of God. Mercy recalls one of the major motifs of chs. 9—11, while *to glorify God* reverses the indictment of humanity in 1:21 and recalls the previous closing statements in 8:30 and 15:6. The linkage of the fulfillment of the promises to Israel and the inclusion of the Gentiles recalls the discussion of Abraham in ch. 4 as the *heir of the world* and the *father of many nations* in fulfillment of God's word.

Paul closes his final exhortation for mutual acceptance by summarizing the central argument he has been making in the letter. He reaffirms the priority of the Jews and the inclusion of the Gentiles in the church through Messiah Jesus as the fulfillment of the promises of God.

Paul confirms his summary with a sequence of four scriptural citations from the law, the writings, and the prophets which are united in their reference to the Gentiles. One word links all four quotations, *the nations* (also *Gentiles*). Verse 9b is a verbatim quote from Psalm 18:49. David, the messianic prefigure, will praise God among *the nations*. Verse 10 cites Deuteronomy 32:43, the last verse of the song of Moses. The great founder of Israel exhorts *the Gentiles* to praise God with Israel. Verse 11 quotes Psalm 117:1 to exhort the Gentiles to praise God. The reason given in verse 2 of the Psalm is the steadfast love ("mercy" in Greek) and faithfulness ("truthfulness" in Greek) of God. Paul concludes the citations with a word from his favorite writer, Isaiah 11:10. *The root of Jesse* was a title for the Messiah in Judaism (Isa. 11:1-5; Ecclus. 47:22; 11QPat 3-4; 4QFlor 1:11), which Paul uses to present Jesus as the ruler of and the source of hope for *the Gentiles*. The Messiah from the Jews is the hope of all people, Jews and Gentiles.

Paul concludes the last argument and the main body of the letter with a prayer centered in God and in hope: *the God of hope . . . in hope by means of the power of the Holy Spirit* (v. 13). The wish is that this God will fill believers with joy and peace and make them abound in hope, all qualities that will help them fulfill the prayer-wish of vv. 4-5 *to think the same thing among one another.*

Romans 15:7-13 has been called the climax of the letter, the conclusion of its theological and ethical argument. Just as 1:16-18 opened the main argument of the letter so 15:7-13 concludes it. The gospel as the power of God for the salvation of Jews and Gentiles results in a unified community of Jews and Gentiles who with one mind and one voice glorify God. The problem of *not honoring* God (1:21) or *dishonoring God* (2:23) is overcome by a unified people honoring God. The christological grounding of this new community in universal praise of God is made clear by the letter's opening confession of the Davidic Messiah (1:2-4) and the closing reference to the *root of Jesse* (15:12). Romans is framed by a christological confession about Jesus as the Jewish Messiah who brings salvation and hope to Jews and Gentiles.

Comments and Observations

The language Paul uses for the rival groups in the churches, "weak" and "strong," had clear sociological meaning in first-century Rome. The terms are standard descriptions of social hierarchy. The "strong" are people with social power, property, influence, and material resources. They are Roman citizens or foreign-born who have been acculturated as Romans. The strong exercise power over those below them. The "weak," in contrast, are people of low social standing. The word initially was used to describe the servile classes. Over time it came to mean people with no financial resources, that is, "the poor," and people who could not defend themselves because they have no authority. It also was associated with the practice of foreign religion. "The weak" are generally people without Roman citizenship. In short, the language of Romans 14–15 describes primarily status groups. The "strong" had the power to force the "weak" into patterns of behavior the weak would otherwise shun.

Read in light of this sociological understanding, Paul's exhortations are very radical. The *welcome one another* means do not use the culture's standard honor categories to differentiate and shame fellow Christians, but rather elevate people of low status by accepting them as equals. The command against forcing the "weak" to consume food considered forbidden means the "strong" are not to use their social power to force the "weak" to follow the eating patterns of the "strong." The "weak" are prohibited from judging (14:4a, 10a), but only the "strong" are exhorted to change their actual behavior (14:13, 19, 21; 15:1) because they alone have the power to do that.

Differences in status are usually maintained by different rituals. Therefore, each group had distinct ritual practices, e.g., observed different days and thanked God for the opposite acts of eating and abstaining. Such ritual differences are usually based on different theologies and values, here eating meat and drinking wine is central to Christian life in the new age, versus such food is not acceptable in any setting.

Different status groups with distinct rituals often define ethnic identities. The scorn of the strong (14:3, 10) fits Roman attitudes toward foreigners. Roman citizens were ethnocentric; they resented the influx of foreigners and looked down on their ethnic distinctives. Ethnic differences also are usually associated with different diets and eating habits. Paul's use of "clean/unclean" language indicates a strong Jewish ethnic component to the tensions over food.

Eating habits function as boundary markers. Food encodes social and religious values. Differences in food easily lead to social conflict. The problem in Rome is complicated by two factors. First, meat in first-century Roman culture, as in many cultures today, is considered food for special occasions and special people. Second, there are hints of eating excesses among the "strong" (13:13; 14:2, 17, 21) which would fit their higher economic status.

In a similar way, observance of days is a boundary marker. The calendar defines the value of time. Designating certain days as special or holy gives a group a sense of order and distinguishes it from others.

Control of the calendar also is a symbol of power. The controversy over days in Rome indicates a struggle for social control in the church. Making others observe certain days confirms one's influence over them.

These cultural differences thus represent much deeper issues in the Roman churches. Groups are shaming and condemning each other, even calling each other names, because status and power are at stake. Paul's exhortations call for such a radical sociological and theological reorientation that they are almost nonsensical in Roman culture. For the strong to accept the weak makes them equals and thus shames the strong. Paul wants to break accepted boundaries of the dominant culture and bring in a new code of honor for the Christian community.

The radical new Christian code of honor is grounded theologically. Paul gives a series of reasons for the new sociology. First, God has welcomed believers (14:3) and alone is judge (14:11-12). Second, Jesus' example is normative; as he became a servant of all people, so believers must become servants of different classes and ethnic groups (15:3, 7). Third, all Christians are the Lord's (14:8-9) and are equally obligated to honor the Lord (14:6). Fourth, the personal conviction and faith of believers is important (14:5, 22-23); Christians must respect the faith commitments of fellow believers even when they lead to different ethical conclusions. Finally, Christians must not offend fellow believers (14:13, 15, 20-21), especially the more vulnerable believers, by behavior they know will cause anguish and pain.

The closing exhortation to unity in 15:7-13 is structurally a very important text unit. It is an inclusio for two larger arguments in the letter. The entire ethical argument of Romans 12:1-15:13 is framed by a call for the unity of the Christian community—the unity of the one body in 12:3-8 and the unity of Jewish and Gentile Christians in 15:7-13. The meaning of the opening exhortation in 12:1-2—*present your bodies . . . do not be conformed*—is now clear. Romans 12:1–15:13 concerns the oneness of the Christian churches in their internal life and in their relationship to the larger culture.

The closing set of exhortations in Romans also frames the entire argument of the letter. Romans, as was pointed out in "The Framing 1:1-15 and 15:14-33" and "Summary for 1:18–2:11," is framed by two inclusio's: 1) the opening and closing travel-mission narrative, and 2) the *do not judge* because all people are equal before God arguments. The do not judge and impartiality arguments are reaffirmed here and then radicalized by the outlining of the social implications. *Do not judge* and all people are equal before God means that people of different socioeconomic status and ethnic identity are to embrace one another as brothers and sisters. Judging and shaming fellow Christians contradicts the universal righteousness and judgment of the one God. The profound theology, christology, and sociology of Romans is intended to instruct Christians how to be gracious neighbors to fellow believers who are different. The theological argument of Romans is designed to provide a basis for the exhortation to the unity of diverse people groups in the church.

One other frame is important. Romans begins with the announcement that Jesus is the son of God (1:2-4) and that salvation and righteousness come through the gospel of this Messiah, not through Caesar (1:16-17). The letter concludes with the assertion that *the ruler of the Gentiles* and *the hope* of the Gentiles is from *the root of Jesse*, that is from Messiah Jesus (15:15). Romans is an anti-imperial tract. It begins and ends by asserting that Jesus is Lord, Caesar is not.

The theology of food and days which Paul articulates raises profound questions about his interpretation of the Jewish Scriptures and his claim to *lift up the law* (3:31). When he says that *all food is clean* he is contradicting clear scriptural teachings and laws about clean and unclean foods, and thus about what constitutes holiness before God. Paul in practice is relativizing or even undermining the law. In a real sense he is being "unbiblical"—he is saying that certain teachings of Scripture are no longer valid because they create divisions and disunity in the one inclusive people God is creating in Messiah Jesus. Paul radically reinterprets Jewish Scripture and theology because of a new theological insight and conviction—the unity of the Christian community God is calling forth at the dawn of the new age [*Essay: Law in Romans*].

TEXT IN BIBLICAL CONTEXT

Food is an important issue in the early church. What and with whom one eats is freighted with great meaning. The issue is addressed in the Synoptic Gospels (in Mark, in chs. 2, 7, 11 and Luke 5, 7, 14), in Acts (chs. 10, 15), and in three letters of Paul (Rom. 14–15, 1 Cor. 8–11, Gal. 2).

Clean or Unclean?

Two different issues are involved in these texts—what one eats and with whom one eats. Is the food "clean" or "unclean" (kosher food and/or food not offered to idols), and are the people with whom one eats clean or unclean? These are significant issues in the ancient world generally, and especially in Judaism. The foods identified in Leviticus 11 as unclean cause defilement. That is, they disqualify people for worship, and at a deep personal level they stain the inner conscience, thereby creating barriers between the individual, the corporate community, and God. In short, the dietary laws mean "you are what you eat." Holy people eat only holy food.

Jesus' (in Mark) and Paul's assertions that all foods are clean or "holy" represent a break with Jewish theology, values, and practice on this issue. Their affirmation of all foods as clean creates conflict for people with more restrictive theological and moral sensitivities. Some Christians are liberated, others are horrified and offended.

With whom one eats is equally important, because "like eats with like." Food is more than biological sustenance; it also is social language. It helps define one's relationship to other people. It defines who belongs to a group and thus who is welcome. It defines group boundaries—whether Jewish Christian-Gentile Christian (Gal. 2; Rom. 14–15), Christian-pagan (1 Cor. 8–10), or rich-poor (1 Cor. 11).

Paul consistently argues that: 1) all food is clean; 2) food does not define group identity in the church; 3) the liberated and/or the wealthy must exercise their freedom and affluence cautiously and lovingly in order not to offend the more restrictive or poorer and in order to build the whole Christian community. The theological and social meaning of food is redefined as inclusive rather than exclusive. Everyone who confesses Jesus as Lord or who "is in the Lord" belongs to the Christian community irrespective of what or with whom he/she eats.

Food and Community

Food is a social language about relationships among Christians. The ethic of relationships which Paul advocates consistently can be summarized as follows. First, the welfare and "up-building" of the whole takes priority over the welfare of the part or the individual. The community is prior to and more important than the individual. Second, the example of Jesus "who did not please himself" but served others is the paradigm for relationships. Concern for the other takes precedence over concern for the self. Third, diversity within the community is a manifestation of the Spirit and should be welcomed and embraced as a gift. The rejection or condemnation or shaming of believers who are different denies the work of God's Spirit. Fourth, love, the will and the emotion to embrace, is to be the dominant ethic in the church. That ethic is not soft or "fuzzy," but intentional and truthful, including "truthing in love." Fifth, freedom is exercised within the context of responsibility, both for the unity of the whole and for the well-being of the vulnerable and the marginalized.

THE TEXT IN THE LIFE OF THE CHURCH
Boundary Maintenance

All branches of the Christian church, and especially those from the radical or believers church tradition, have historical tendencies to be boundary oriented. The mindset is either/or. One is either on this side of the boundary and thus in, or on the other side of the boundary and thus out. The boundaries are not drawn on matters essential to the Christian faith—the oneness of God, the Lordship of Jesus Christ, the presence of the Holy Spirit in the church and in individual Christians, the saving power and effectiveness of Jesus' life, death, and resurrection—but on issues of ethical practice which help differentiate Christian groups from the larger culture and from one another (the latter is often more important than the former, at least since the Protestant Reformation). Numerous church divisions have taken place on boundary issues, such as food, dress, hair covering, or mode of baptism. Many people have been excluded from Christian communities because they eat the wrong food, associated with or married the wrong people, participated in a forbidden activity, or wore inappropriate clothes.

Rebuilding the Center

An alternative to this "bounded set" approach to faith and life is what is called "centered set." The dominant concern is with a clearly defined center and the relationship of people to that center. The question asked is not has someone crossed the boundary, but is a person moving toward the center or away from it. The center, not the boundaries, defines what it means to be Christian and a member of the Christian church.

The critical need of the church in the postmodern world is to become thoroughly "center set" in its orientation and commitment. The center of the faith has eroded, some even say collapsed, under the pressures of modernity and postmodernity. People in the church lack clarity about and deep commitments to the center. The renewal of the center is imperative if the church is to be viable and vital in the twenty-first century.

Criteria for Inclusion

What would happen if the Pauline warrants—God's welcome, Christ's example of inclusion, honor the Lord, in the Lord, personal conviction/faith—became the church's criteria for inclusion and exclusion? Can the marginalized in the church be embraced? Can the powerless be welcomed and lifted up by the powerful? That is what Paul advocated in the first century because of who God is—righteous—and because of what God has done through the faithfulness of Messiah Jesus—made righteous. Can the church in very different times and places model such practices for the same reasons?

The Politics of Paul

Romans is framed by a political message—it begins and ends by asserting that Jesus, rather than Caesar, is Lord. Jesus is the Son of God who brings salvation, righteousness, and peace to all people (1:2-4, 16-17). He is *the ruler of the Gentiles* and the hope of the nations. But more than that, Jesus is *Lord both of the dead and of the living* (14:9). Paul challenges the lordship of Caesar with the Lordship of Jesus. Paul's gospel is good news for all people—Jews and Gentiles—but bad news for Caesar. Romans challenges the fundamental assumption of Roman imperial rule, that Caesar is divine and lord.

Romans challenges another pervasive assumption in Roman culture, namely, that some people are better than others, e.g., that Romans are wise and cultured compared to "the foolish" and barbarian people of other ethnic origins. That is, he undermines the ideology of "land and blood" that was used by the Romans to justify their imperial order and rule, just as it has been used by empires and rulers since then to legitimize the oppression of one people by another as well as the "ethnic cleansing" of one people by another. Paul's gospel calls for one unified community of diverse people who welcome "the other," the people who are different, because that is what Messiah Jesus models as the intention of God for all people and nations.

Within this overarching anti-imperial rhetoric, Paul exhorts submission to governing officials in order to maintain social order and peace (13:1-7). Followers of Jesus have an obligation to reject vengeance, to repay evil with good, to support the structures of order (e.g., taxes), to practice love within the believing community and in the larger social order (*owe nothing except love*). The governing officials are *servants of God*, and thus accountable to God, who are ordered by God to promote good work and restrict bad work (13:3).

The politics of Paul is finely balanced—challenge the macro assumptions and structures while supporting the micro structures that provide order and stability.

What does the politics of Paul look like in the twenty-first century, in the democratic west? What are the fundamental macro assumptions which the gospel should and must challenge? What does the Lordship of Jesus mean in democratic cultures? Does the Lordship of Jesus have any relevance in a culture that separates the public and the private on the pervasive assumption that the latter is the domain of the church while the latter is completely off limits? What does the Lordship of Jesus mean in a unipolar world, a world dominated by one super power which raps itself in the flag of the "good" and the "Christian faith"? What does the Lordship of Jesus mean in totalitarian and oppressive cultures?

What about the politics of land and blood? Few institutions have supported this ideology more than the church. Can the church be genuinely transformed into a community that "embraces the other" just as Jesus embraced us?

Romans 15:14–16:27

Conclusion

PREVIEW

Paul concludes the letter by returning to his mission to the Gentiles, to his travel plans, and to his concerns for the obedience of faith among the Roman Christians. The themes of the introduction and the conclusion are similar (see "The Framing of the Introduction and Conclusion" for the details). Romans is bracketed by an apostolic presence (*parousia*), as there outlined on pp. 45-46. The letter ends the way it began, by Paul talking about his apostolic presence and mission.

OUTLINE

Paul's Mission, 15:14-21
15:14	Paul's Confidence
15:15a	Paul's Letter
15:15b-17	Paul's Ministry
15:18-20	Paul's Strategy
15:21	Scriptural Confirmation

Paul's Plans, 15:22-29
15:22-24	Paul's Hope
15:25-27	Paul's Immediate Mission
15:28-29	Paul's Hope

Paul's Request for Prayer, 15:30-32

Letter Closing, 15:33–16:27

EXPLANATORY NOTES

Paul's Mission 15:14-21

Paul begins his conclusion with personal warmth and emphasis—*My brothers and sisters, I myself am persuaded concerning you yourselves.* The subject of his deep confidence in the Roman Christians is *that you yourselves are full of goodness, are filled with all knowledge, being empowered also to stand up mentally to one another.* In v. 13 Paul prayed that the believers would be *filled with joy* and peace. Here he believes they are filled with the knowledge of God's saving purposes, as he has outlined them in the letter (Paul really did not have to teach them all the things he has written). The *being empowered to stand up mentally to one another* picks up key language from the letter—*power* from 1:16 and *the powerful* (the strong) in chs. 14–15 while *stand up mentally* echoes Paul's concern for correct thinking (chs. 12–15). Here correct thinking specifically means able to correct or admonish one another; the Roman Christians are capable of holding each other accountable for the mindset and behavior Paul has just advocated.

Despite his strong affirmation of the Roman Christians' character and abilities, Paul has written *you rather bluntly in part as a way of reminding you.* The *rather bluntly* certainly refers to the specific exhortations in 12:1–15:13, but it may well refer to the entire body of the letter. Paul's "straight talk" is cushioned by the very diplomatic assertion that he is only reminding them of what they already know. He has said "nothing new."

The reason Paul has written so candidly is that he has been graced by God to be a minister of Messiah Jesus to the Gentiles (vv. 15b-16). Nowhere does he outline his missionary self-understanding more clearly than here. Paul defines his ministry with two purpose clauses: *in order to be an officiating priest of Jesus Christ to the Gentiles serving the gospel of God as a priest* (v. 16a-b) and *in order that the sacrificial offering rendered by the Gentiles might be acceptable [to God] having been set apart by the Holy Spirit* (v. 16c-d). The concentration of Jewish cultic language is striking—*an officiating priest, serving as a priest, sacrificial offering, acceptable, set apart*. Paul is a priest, the offering is one that the Gentiles make through the mediation of his priestly service (the *he prosphora ton ethnon* is a subjective genitive, *the offering that the Gentiles make*, rather than a genitive of apposition, *the offering consisting of the Gentiles*, as in most translations). The offering is acceptable to God because the Holy Spirit has set it apart or made it holy for that purpose. Paul's ministry is defined exclusively in scriptural and Jewish language. He is fulfilling the mission of Israel—he is being a priest to the nations and enabling them to make an offering to God.

Even more startling, his mission breaks down the old cultic barriers between Jews and Gentiles which kept the Gentiles out of the holy space of the Temple. The Gentiles present the offering—they are in the most sacred space and they have been made acceptable to God by the Holy Spirit. Paul's ministry makes the unclean clean, holy, and acceptable, and thus redefines the boundaries of group identity. He understands this ministry to be so significant that he boasts before God (v. 17). Boasting is rejected if it excludes some people from God (3:27 and 4:2), but grace which includes all people is grounds for boasting.

Paul knows that boasting is dangerous. He immediately qualifies his boasting, therefore, by asserting that *he does not dare to speak about anything except what Christ has accomplished through me* (v. 18). Paul is only an agent for doing the work of Christ. The goal of that work is *the obedience of the Gentiles in word and work*. In 1:5 the goal was *the faithful obedience of the Gentiles*, here it is the holistic obedience (speech and behavior) of the Gentiles. Paul has worked toward that goal *in power*" . . . *by means of the power of the Holy Spirit* (v. 19a). The gospel is the power of God (1:16) and Paul has served that gospel in *power*. The evidence of that power is *signs and wonders*, Jewish language for describing the miracles of Israel's exodus from Egypt. The significance of Paul's mission is parallel to the Exodus event—just as Moses led Israel from slavery in Egypt into the freedom of the promised land so Paul has led the Gentiles from slavery in **Sin** and exclusion from God's people into the eschatological people of God.

The result of Paul's "exodus mission" among the Gentiles is that he has completed preaching the gospel in an arc (literally, a circle) from Jerusalem to Illyricum (present day Serbia/Albania). He started in the center of Judaism—the gospel is to the Jews first and also to the Gentiles—and has now moved halfway around the northern arc of the Mediterranean basin. Paul is painting with a broad brush. He has not literally preached in every community between Jerusalem and Illyricum, but he has planted the flag of the gospel, young churches, in the major centers along the arc. From these the gospel is moving into the surrounding communities and peoples. Paul was a strategic thinker and actor. He "intentionally aspired" to move into virgin territories and preach the gospel where the name of Christ was unknown. Contrary to many of his opponents who sought to claim his territory (Gal. 1:6-9; 2 Cor. 10:16, 11:4), Paul did not wish to minister in areas where others had preached Christ and started churches.

Paul confirms his understanding of his mission with a quotation from the Servant Song in Isaiah 52:15 (v. 21). The point of the Scripture is the impact of the Servant upon the nations. Paul sees his mission in similar terms, as completing the mission of the Servant by taking the gospel to the nations. Paul interprets his ministry in salvation-historical terms.

Paul's Plans 15:22-29

Paul's plans are twofold. First, he wants to visit the churches in Rome on the way to Spain, vv. 22-24 and 28-29. The language he uses to describe this dream repeats what he said in 1:10-15: a series of hindrances prevented him from coming (v. 22, 1:13), the long-term dream to visit Rome (v. 23b, 1:10-11), the desire for mutual encouragement and renewal (vv. 24, 29, 1:11-12). Second, before Paul can come to Rome he must go to Jerusalem on an urgent strategic mission (vv. 25-27).

Verses 22-23 must be read together with vv. 18-19. They indicate that Paul was hindered from coming to Rome earlier, because he was so busy completing his mission in the East. *This is the reason* at the beginning of v. 22 looks backward. *But now no longer place having in these regions* (v. 23) reaffirms Paul's strategic sense of mission. He has completed his work from *Jerusalem to Illyricum*, and now wants to move west in fulfillment of his long dream. He is very diplomatic in outlining his plans. He just wants *to pass through* on the way to Spain (twice in vv. 24 and 28). Paul is not coming to Rome to "take charge." He will not violate his commitment to not build on another's foundation (v. 20). Paul does hope to receive some help for the journey to

Spain and he wants to enjoy and be renewed (lit., *filled up personally*) by the company of the Roman Christians. The word used for *help for the journey* is almost a technical term for the provisions local churches made to support missionaries—funds, supplies, companions (Acts 15:3; 20:38; 21:5; 1 Cor. 16:6, 11; 2 Cor. 1:16; Titus 3:13; 3 John 6).

The reasons Paul wants to go to Spain are not clear. Spain represented the western end of the Mediterranean and thus would complete the arc from Jerusalem over the northern half of the Mediterranean. In other words, the goal of Spain may be part of Paul's larger missionary vision, but nowhere does he say that. Christian tradition is divided over whether he reached his destination. The available evidence does not indicate any churches in Spain until the second century A.D. What is clear is that achieving the goal would be difficult. No substantial Jewish population existed in Spain until the third and fourth centuries A.D. Any mission to Spain would be a genuine pioneer venture—there were few Jews and few if any synagogues to serve as a base. At best there were a few God-fearers or proselytes. Such a mission would require a level of planning and support that would be very different from Paul's earlier work. The support of Rome would be critical.

But before Paul can move west he must complete his mission in the east. The *but now* at the beginning of v. 25 repeats the *but now* at the beginning of v. 23. *But now* there is no longer a place in the east, *but now I am going to Jerusalem.* The phrase indicates an important transition. Paul must round off his mission in the east by delivering a collection from the churches of Macedonia and Achaia *to the poor among the holy ones (or, the saints) in Jerusalem.*

The description of the Jerusalem Christians may denote actual economic poverty, but it may also reflect a self-understanding of the Jewish Christians there that flowed from a broader Jewish view of the significance of Jerusalem as the city of both "the holy" and "the oppressed (the poor)." Paul mentions only the churches closest to Rome even though other churches also contributed (e.g., Galatia—1 Cor. 16:1, Asia—Acts 20:4), and he emphasizes that the churches of these regions decided to raise the money (*they resolved,* v. 26). The language used to describe the offering is theologically weighted—it was an *act of service* (lit., *deaconing*), an *act of fellowshipping* or mutual sharing (the same word for sharing the blood and body of Christ in 1 Cor. 10:16; the Holy Spirit in 2 Cor. 13:13, 14, Phil. 2:1; the gospel in Phil. 1:5; Christ's sufferings in Phil. 3:10; the faith in Philem. 6), a moral *obligation*, a *priestly or cultic service*, and a *fruit*.

The freight of this language and symbolism is increased by the contrast of *spiritually sharing* and *fleshly obligation*. The Gentiles are under moral obligation to offer the Jews in Jerusalem the *priestly service* of their fleshly means because the Gentiles *have shared in the spiritual blessings* of the Jews. Paul underscores the priority of the Jews and the dependence of the Gentiles upon the Jewish heritage. His language also indicates the erosion of the boundary between the sacred and the profane—the "fleshly" contribution of the Gentiles is a priestly service rendered for a spiritual blessing. It may well be that Paul views this priestly service of the offering as a fulfillment of scriptural promises of the Gentiles turning to Zion (Isa. 2:3; Mic. 4:4) and the nations streaming back to the city of God (Isa. 60:5f.) (see Shillington:170f., 261-62 for a more detailed discussion of the collection).

Paul's Request for Prayer 15:30-32

The strategic importance of the mission to Jerusalem is signaled by the way Paul describes the deliverance of the offering in v. 28—*when I have completed this and have 'sealed over' to them this fruit*—and by his request for the prayers of the Roman Christians for the mission. The word for *sealed over* suggests the secure transfer of ownership; Paul will transfer the collection and the Jewish Christians will accept it. It is precisely "the transfer of ownership" that is so significant and at the same time filled with such great danger. Therefore, Paul appeals (the same word as in 12:1) to the churches *through our Lord Jesus Christ and through the love of the Holy Spirit to struggle intensely with me in prayers in my behalf to God* (v. 30). The language of the appeal is intense and personal. It calls for the disciplined activity of contesting, even struggling, through prayer with and for Paul's mission.

The purpose of the prayer is defined by two purpose clauses. The first has two parts which involve one critical problem (v. 31). Part one is that Paul be rescued or preserved from *the unbelievers* in Judea. *The unbelievers*, used only in Romans in Paul's letters, is his description of fellow Jews who reject the gospel of Messiah Jesus (see 10:21; 11:30-31). The deliverance of the offering is so important that Paul is risking his life. Part two is *and my service to Jerusalem be acceptable to the holy ones*. His mission is to Jerusalem, the center of Jewish faith and the location of the mother church of the Christian community. Paul fears that he will be rejected in Jerusalem and that the Jewish Christian churches will not accept the offering he brings. Nationalist zealotry is increasingly militant in Judea as developments progress toward the war of A.D. 66-70. Christians in Jerusalem were affected by this rising nationalist fervor. Any breach of Jewish group boundaries is under increasing threat. Paul's law-free gospel for Gentile Christians represents precisely such a breach which at least representatives of the Jerusalem churches have opposed in several different regions of the Pauline mission (e.g., Galatia, Philippi).

The more sharply the Jews of Jerusalem react to Paul's presence and offering the greater the likelihood that the Jewish Christians will feel pressure to reject him and the offering. We know from Josephus, a Jewish historian contemporary to Paul, that the Jews of Jerusalem become so suspicious of the offerings of Gentiles to the Temple that one of the first actions after the beginning of the war in A.D. 66 was to refuse any monies from non-Jews. Paul's mission is truly a high risk venture. His own life and his vision for a unified people of God composed of Jews and Gentiles is at risk. If the Jewish Christians reject the offering, do not find it "acceptable," a massive breach between the Jewish Christian and the Gentile Christian churches will have been opened, perhaps even an unreconcilable breach. Paul sees his mission to Jerusalem in salvation-history terms; it is a kairos event in the saving purposes of God.

The second purpose for prayer is *in order that I may come to you with joy through the will of God being refreshed by you* (v. 32). Only if Paul is delivered from the nonbelieving Jews in Jerusalem and the offering is acceptable to the Jewish Christians will he come to Rome with joy and be renewed.

Letter Closing 15:33–16:27

The "letter closing" in Paul's letters include a series of common features: a peace greeting, greetings, final exhortations, and a grace benediction. Paul follows that pattern in Romans although in a slightly altered order.

15:33 Peace Greeting

Paul begins with his favorite benediction—*may the God of peace be with you all.* Paul uses the description of God as *the God of peace* in three other benedictions (1 Thess. 5:23; 2 Thess. 3:16; Phil. 4:9). He also uses the picture of God as a God of peace in three words of assurance (16:20; 1 Cor. 14:33; 2 Cor. 13:11). The benediction is especially appropriate in this letter—the churches of Rome need the presence of *the God of peace* to empower peace in the relationships of the various house churches.

16:1-2 Letter of Recommendation

Letters of recommendation for traveling Christians and leaders was customary in early Christianity (e.g., 2 Cor. 3:1). Paul here recommends a Gentile woman by the name of Phoebe (the name is common in Greek mythology). The fact that she is named first is often taken as evidence that she was the bearer of the letter to Rome. The form of the recommendation is that the Roman Christians *stand with her*, that is, welcome ("roll out the red carpet") and support her. The identification of her as a *sister* (*adelphē*) is striking. Male members of religious groups were typically identified as "brothers" (*adelphoi*) in the ancient world, but the feminine form is seldom used to identify female members. The designation of believing women as "sisters" is a uniquely Christian practice (e.g., 1 Cor. 7:15; 9:5; Philem. 2; James 2:15; Ign. *Pol.* 5:1; *2 Clem.* 12:5; 19:1; 20:2) and indicates the inclusion of women in the definition of the Christian community as a family.

Paul indicates that Phoebe is a leader in the church in two different ways. First, she is a minister (*diakonos*) in the church of Cenchreae (near Corinth). The word designates a significant leadership role. It is used seven times to characterize Paul's ministry (1 Cor. 3:5; 2 Cor. 3:6, 6:4, 11:23; Eph. 3:7; Col. 1:23, 25), six times to characterize his male associates (1 Cor. 3:5; Eph. 6:21; Col. 1:7, 4:7; 1 Thess. 3:2 in some major manuscripts; 1 Tim. 4:6), twice of government officials (Rom. 13:4), three times of people who work together with *bishops* (*episcopoi*—Phil. 1:1; 1 Tim. 3:8, 12) in church leadership, once of false apostles (2 Cor. 11:15). The usual translation of the word here as *servant* (KJV, NASB, NIV) or even *deacon* (NRSV; *deaconess*, RSV) reflects a negative view of the leadership role of women in the early church, since in many of the texts cited above the translation is *minister*. Surprisingly, the Roman Catholic translations have been more generous (Douai-Rheims NT, *our sister, who is in the ministry*; New American, *our sister, who is [also] a minister*). Phoebe's role is defined by leadership language that Paul uses to define his role and that of his associates. Second, Phoebe is a *patroness of many and of myself*. The noun *prostatis* is common in the ancient world but is used only here in the NT. It pictures a benefactor who supports and protects others as well as provides leadership in the community. The verb form is used three times in the NT to describe leadership in the church (1 Thess. 5:12; 1 Tim. 3:4-5, 5:17). This person usually presided over the affairs of the church, including the common meals and observance of the Lord's Supper. About ten percent of the patrons in ancient Rome were women.

The letter of recommendation for Phoebe is both interesting and significant for the role of women in the early church. Women in antiquity were usually characterized by their relationship to men, e.g., daughter, wife, widow. Phoebe is defined by her church functions rather than her gender. She was clearly a person of means who provided leadership in the church.

16:3-16 First Greeting List

Paul greets 27 people—25 individuals by name, two by relationship (Rufus' mother and Nereus' sister)—and five groups (*the church in their house*, v. 5; *the family of Aristobulus*, v. 10; *the family of Narcissus*, v. 11; *the brethren who are with them*, v. 14; *all the saints who are with them*, v. 15). The groups represent five different house churches in Rome. The greetings are extended through 16 imperatives in the second person, *you greet.*

The list of greetings are usually passed over quickly as "boring." But they are full of information that tells us a great deal about the churches in Rome (see R. Finger's treatment of Romans from the perspective of the diversity evident among the house churches). The most important things we learn are the following.

First, Paul has a good number of personal acquaintances and co-workers in Rome—Prisca and Aquila, Epaenetus, Andronicus and Junia, Urbanus, Rufus and his mother. Prisca and Aquila are the most familiar. According to Acts 18:2 Paul met them in Corinth following their expulsion from Rome by Claudius in A.D. 49. Paul stayed with them and worked together in the tent making business. Later they traveled with him to Ephesus and stayed there for some time (Acts 18:18-19; 1 Cor. 16:19). Now they are back in Rome. They are affluent—they travel, they have a business, and they have a house large enough to serve as a house church. The fact that "all the churches of the Gentiles" are grateful to them suggests they have been generous in supporting the Pauline mission among the Gentiles and maybe also other Christian groups. Prisca is usually mentioned first (Acts 18:18, 26; Rom. 16:3) which suggests that she is a person of higher social status than Aquila. They are "fellow-workers" with Paul who have risked their lives for him. They are the hosts and thus also the leaders of a house church.

The most interesting of Paul's acquaintances are Andronicus and Junia. They are a husband and wife team, not two men as in most modern translations. The male name Junias is not found anywhere in ancient literature, whereas Junia is a common female name (found 250 times). The name was understood as a female name throughout the early history of the church—the major commentators on Romans in the ancient church interpreted the name as feminine, e.g., Origen, Jerome, John Chrysostom. It was not understood as a masculine name until Aegidius (1245-1316) interpreted the reference as "these honorable men." Martin Luther popularized the masculine reading of the name in 1515/16. The persistence of the masculine reading despite the overwhelming evidence to the contrary indicates the male bias in the translation and interpretation of the Scriptures from the Middle Ages onward. Andronicus and Junia are Jews (*my kinsmen*, RSV; *relatives*, NRSV) who became Christians before Paul, and thus probably Palestinian Jewish Christians. They spent time in prison with Paul. And *they are prominent among the apostles*, suggesting they belong to the large group of the apostles appointed by the risen Christ in 1 Corinthians 15:7. The language indicates they were important leaders among the earliest Christian churches who joined Paul's missionary enterprise among the Gentiles.

Epaenetus, a Gentile name, was an early convert of the Pauline mission in Asia who continued to enjoy a close personal relationship with Paul (*beloved*). Urbanus, a common Roman slave name, may well have belonged to the imperial household. He is a *fellow worker* together with Prisca and Aquila. Rufus, a familiar slave or freedman name, was *specially chosen* for a particular task (we are not told what). His mother served Paul as her own son.

Paul's acquaintances and co-workers in Rome include two prominent Jewish Christian couples in the early church, an early Gentile convert and three people of slave or freedman social status.

Second, women were prominent and important in the early Christian church and in the churches of Rome. Nine, or one third, of the 27 people greeted are women. With the addition of Phoebe, 10 women leaders in the church are identified. Even more interesting than the numbers are the functional roles attributed to them—Phoebe as minister and patron, Prisca as fellow worker and host of a house church, Junia as apostle, Mary, Tryphaena and Tryphosa (the common stem of their names indicates they are probably sisters) and Persis as hard-workers, Rufus' mother as mother. Of the 10 women only three have no role attributed to them. Women and men alike are described as fellow-workers, apostles, fellow-citizens, fellow-prisoners, beloved. Only women are called minister, patron, hard-workers, sister, mother. Only two descriptive terms are applied to men which are not applied to women—tested (Apelles, v. 10) and chosen (Asyncritus, v. 14). Romans 16 provides the best first-hand list of the variety and influential roles played by women in the early church. More dramatic and influential roles are attributed to the women, despite their smaller number, than to the men. Romans documents that men and women were equals in the leadership of the churches in the Pauline mission.

Romans also suggests the established patriarchal status in the household is not important in the churches. Prisca, Junia, and Julia are not identified as wives, nor are the other named women linked to fathers or husbands. Paul greets the women in Rome because of their commitment to the gospel and leadership in the church, not because of their family relationships.

Third, the names tell us a good deal about the ethnic and socio-economic composition of the churches in Rome. There are typical Jewish names in the list—Prisca and Aquila, Andronicus and Junia, Herodion, Aristobulus, Mary, and Rufus. Most of the names are Gentile, which may reflect the ethnic balance in the churches. Some of the people have economic resources—Prisca and Aquila, Andronicus and Junia, Epaenetus, Aristobulus, Narcissus—they can travel and have households. The majority of names were common among slaves, freedmen and freedwomen—Ampliatus, Urbanus, Stachys, Tryphaina, Tryphosa, Persis, Rufus, Asyncritus, Phlegon, Hermes, Patrobas, Hermas, Philologus and Julia (probably a husband and wife), Nereus. Many of the names were found among slaves of imperial households. The churches of Rome reflect a cross section of the lower half of the socioeconomic scale with the majority coming from the lower strata of Roman society.

Fourth, the Jewish-Christian names confirm that after Claudius' edict of expulsion of Jewish people was lifted, Jewish Christians did return to Rome again.

Finally, the greetings document that the Christians of Rome were organized into various house churches. There were distinct congregations rather than one single congregation. The Christians of Rome, as in the other parts of the Roman Empire, initially met in the homes of members who could afford large houses. Archaeological findings indicate that these homes had room for 40 to 80 people. The letter which Paul is concluding would thus be passed from house church to house church and read aloud and discussed anew each time.

Paul concludes the greetings with a final exhortation and a third person greeting. The formula, *greet one another with a holy kiss*, is used regularly in the Pauline letters (1 Cor. 16:20; 2 Cor. 13:12; 1 Thess. 5:26; also in 1 Pet. 5:14). Kissing (cheek to cheek) as a form of greeting reflects a widespread practice in the Orient. The addition of *holy* indicates it was an act of family bonding in the Christian community. *All the churches of Christ greet you* is unique in Paul.

Practically it must refer to the churches which Paul has founded. But that itself is significant. Paul speaks for all of the churches in his mission as he concludes his letter to the Roman Christians and heads for Jerusalem with the offering.

The greetings of Romans 16 are very inclusive—gender, ethnic identity, and socioeconomic status are not important. That is a very appropriate ending to a letter which has argued for the impartiality of God toward all people.

16:17-20 Final Exhortations

Paul interrupts his closing greetings with a sharp warning. This closing exhortation parallels similar warnings in Galatians 6:11-15 and Philippians 3:2-21, and may well be the final paragraph written in Paul's own hand (see 1 Cor. 16:21-24; Gal. 6:11-18; Col. 4:18; 2 Thess. 3:17). The *I appeal to you, brothers,"* is identical to 12:1 and 15:30; it is a strong call to action. The warning has two parts: 1) *to look out for those who create divisions and obstacles which are opposed (against) to the teaching you learned;* 2) *stay away* (lit., *bend away) from them.* The first warning calls for the critical examination of people who destabilize the equilibrium (the stasis) of the churches and who erect stumbling blocks which oppose the teaching the Roman Christians have received. Romans 6:17 and this text refer to a body of teaching passed on to the churches which has a normative quality, according to Paul. People who divide the churches by contradicting *this teaching* are to be avoided. The *stay away from them* phrase is characteristic of wisdom exhortations to avoid evil (e.g., Ps. 34:14; Prov. 1:15; 3:7).

The reason such people are to be avoided is that they serve their own interests (lit., belly as a symbol for that which is fleshly and evil; so also Phil. 3:19) rather than *our Lord Christ* (v. 18). This language was used elsewhere in contemporary Judaism to warn against false teaching. These *false teachers* deceive the *unsuspecting* (lit., *without evil minds* or *the simple*) by smooth speech and flattery.

In v. 19 Paul praises the Roman Christians. He is deeply grateful that their *obedience (faithfulness) is known by all* (lit., *has come to everyone's ear*). Therefore, he renews an earlier exhortation that the believers be wise to the good and innocent of evil (see 12:17–13:10).

Paul does not identify the people he is warning against. The "false teachers" are hardly the groups identified in chs. 14–15; he counts himself among the strong and his call to "welcome one another" would be contradicted by the strong words of this warning. It seems best to see the warning as a general one against people who seek to divide the churches and confuse Christians by their teachings. Paul knows from experience that such teachers are present in the churches and his knowledge of the issues dividing the Roman churches makes him only too aware of how susceptible they would be to "false teachers."

The peace benediction (v. 20a) is quite unlike his other peace benedictions which describe what God will do to the readers. This benediction rather outlines what God will do to Satan by means of the Christians in Rome. *The God of peace will crush Satan under your feet very soon.* The description of God as *the God of peace* repeats a phrase from 15:33. This God will crush Satan, the personification of evil, the adversary of God, the leader of the angelic armies opposed to God (other names for Satan in the first century include Beliar/Belial, the devil, Mastema Azazel, the angel of darkness). Genesis 3:15 nurtured an eschatological hope shared by Paul and other contemporary Jews for the final defeat of the demonic. That defeat is imminent and will be aided by the obedience of the Roman Christians (*under your feet*), Paul asserts. The obedience of the Roman believers and the end-time defeat of Satan are linked. The strong affirmation of the Roman Christians in the final warning and the peace benediction reiterates Paul's positive statements in the introduction to the letter and thus helps frame the letter in a way that endears him to his readers.

16:20b Grace Benediction

Paul gives his usual grace benediction in briefer form than is customary ("Christ" is not found in the better manuscripts).

16:21-23 Second Greeting List

Paul gives a second set of greetings, this time from other people. Timothy is one of Paul's closest associates; he is mentioned regularly at the beginning of Paul's letters (six times). Lucias, Jason, and Sosipater are fellow Jewish Christians (*kinsmen* in RSV; *relatives* in NRSV). All three could be different forms of names found elsewhere—e.g., Lucias as Luke (Col. 4:14; Philem. 24; 2 Tim. 4:11), Jason could be Paul's host in Thessalonica (Acts 17:5-7, 9), and Sosipater the Sopater of Acts 20:4—but we cannot be certain about this. Tertius, the secretary who wrote the actual letter, also sends greetings. Tertius is a common slave or freedman name. The precise role of Tertius in writing the letter is not known. Did he take dictation from Paul, or did Paul give him instructions about what to write and then he wrote drafts and revised them in light of Paul's feedback?

Two of the last three greetings indicate people of socioeconomic status. Gaius, almost certainly the man mentioned in 1 Corinthians 1:14, is host to Paul and to the whole church. The phrase *whole church* echoes a similar one in the Hebrew Bible which refers to the actual gathering of Israelite representatives for consultation or worship. It suggests either that the whole church in Corinth, that is, the various house churches, or that leaders from the entire Pauline mission were hosted by Gaius. Erastus is a financial officer in Corinth. He is certainly a person of influence within the financial sector of the city, and maybe a man of some wealth and status. Quartus is a common name among slaves and freedmen.

The benediction in v. 24 is not found in the earliest and best manuscripts of the letter.

16:25-27 Doxology

Paul ends the letter with praise to God. The structure of the doxology is poetical and liturgical.

> **to the** one powerful to strengthen you
> > **according** to my gospel
> > > and the preaching of Jesus Christ
> > **according** to the revelation of the mystery
> > > having been preserved in silence from eternity
> > > but now **having been made known**
> > > > through the writings of the prophets (the entire Scriptures)
> > **according** to the order (command) of the eternal God
> > > to the obedience of faith
> > > to all the nations
> > > **having been made known**
> **to the** only wise God
> > through Jesus Christ
> **to that** one be glory for the ages. Amen.

The doxology sums up the central themes of the letter and uses some of its significant language: the power of God (1:16/v. 25), the gospel and the preaching of Christ (1:3, 9 // v. 25; specifically, *according to my gospel* in 2:16 // v. 25), the revelation of the mystery (3:21; 11:24 // v. 25), the fulfillment of the Scriptures (1:2, 3:21, 15:4 // v. 26), the obedience of faith to all the nations (1:5; 15:18 // v. 26); the ascription of glory to God (11:36, 15:6-9 // v. 27).

Romans is about God. It begins and ends with God. The power of

God is a specific theme which Paul introduces at crucial points in the argument of the letter (1:16, 20; 4:21; 9:17, 22; 11:23; 14:4) to address the weakness and disobedience of human beings. This power is made known in Paul's gospel which reveals a mystery that fulfills an eternal order of God. The purpose of that order is the faithful obedience of the nations to the one God through Messiah Jesus.

The Theology of Romans

The theology of Romans concerns the gospel as God's salvation of all people as the foundation for inclusive community.

The Context

The theology of a writing answers a question(s). It addresses a reality or issue(s). Romans is a pastoral letter intended to reconcile differing groups of believers in the house churches of mid-first century Rome. Paul writes Romans to make the case for his gospel against two group theologies and their accompanying social practices, Jewish-Christian ethnocentrism which excluded Gentiles from the people of God, and Gentile Christian ethnocentrism which claimed that God had judged and rejected the Jewish people. The audience is primarily Gentile Christians with a Jewish history (God-fearers or proselytes), but also Jewish Christians, both of whom have questions about each other and about God. The letter answers a series of questions. What is required to be members of God's people? What about God's dealings with Israel? Underlining these questions is the most fundamental one of all, what kind of God is God? Is God righteous or not?

The Center

The theological center of Romans is the gospel of God's salvation for all people. The gospel is first and foremost about God. It reveals the righteousness of God, the faithful and true One who keeps faith with God's promises and word. The gospel as the revelation of the righteousness of God reveals eschatological judgment against all **Sin** and salvation from the power of **Sin**.

The gospel of God's apocalyptic salvation is revealed and effected in the world through the faithfulness of Messiah Jesus (3:21-26; 5:12-21). Salvation is a gift of God's grace through Messiah Jesus for all people. No human worth or work can effect it. Salvation is based on faith, first the faithful obedience of Jesus and then the faithful response of human beings, both Jews and Gentiles.

The gospel of God's salvation is universal; it is equally available and effective for all people irrespective of ethnic origin or race. It can change both the relationship between people and the foundational value system that shapes how they relate, e.g., the honor-shame code. God judges the sin of all people impartially, and saves impartially whether Jew or Gentile. This salvation of both Jewish and Gentile peoples does not invalidate the prior election of Israel. God will yet save Israel as a people just as God is now saving both Jews and Gentiles to constitute a new people of God.

The good news of God's apocalyptic salvation does more than save diverse peoples; it also effects cosmic salvation. All creation will be renewed through God's salvation of humanity in Messiah Jesus. Two great doxological statements at the conclusion of two important arguments in the letter, 8:31-39 and 11:33-36, assert that the salvation of God in Messiah Jesus is comprehensive. Nothing in the cosmos—death, life, angels, principalities, powers—can inhibit or limit the saving love of God in Messiah Jesus.

The gospel of God's salvation addresses the real problem in the world, the cosmic power of **Sin**, and alone offers the power to overcome this demonic and enslaving force. This cosmic power pervades everything and enslaves all reality, human, spiritual, material. The law, the revelation and gift of God to Israel, was not powerful enough to overcome the cosmic power of **Sin**. Rather, it served to concentrate **Sin** in one people and in one place so that God could deal with and overcome it. The gospel alone is more powerful than **Sin**. The victory of Messiah Jesus over the power of Adamic sin and the power of the Spirit over the power of the flesh alone is able to free human beings and creation from the power of **Sin** and **Death**.

The comprehensiveness and grandeur of God's salvation in Messiah Jesus means God is making all people—Gentile and Jew—righteous and giving them all the historic blessings of Israel, e.g., life, election, new covenant, hope. But precisely the universality of this salvation in Messiah Jesus raises questions about God's strange ways with Israel. Why are so few Jews responding affirmatively? Has God in fact abandoned the promises to Israel? Has God rejected Israel? Paul's answer is an emphatic and absolute "no." God is fulfilling the promises to Israel in the gospel of salvation for all people. God will also save Israel in fulfillment of these promises.

The Consequence

According to Romans, life is not lived in a neutral zone. Human life exists in power zones, either the power sphere of **Sin** or the power sphere of **God**. God's salvation in Messiah Jesus effects a transfer from the power sphere of **Sin** to the power sphere of the **Spirit**.

The powerful gospel of God's salvation calls for new life in the Spirit and obedience. To be made righteous by the gospel of God's salvation means a "slavery to righteousness" (6:15f.). It means to live in the Spirit. The Christian life in Romans is defined more as life in the Spirit than as a life of faith. The life of obedience to which the gospel calls is made possible because of the "indwelling" and empowerment of the Spirit. The evidence of the new obedience, of the new righteousness, is found in how the Christians in Rome deal with one another, how they resolve their tensions in the churches, how they "welcome one another" in love. Chapters 12–15 are the practical test case of the gospel of God's salvation. The center is a remade and transformed mind that thinks and lives like Christ, who welcomes everyone by not pleasing himself but rather taking on the dishonor of others for the fulfillment of the promises of God (15:3).

The Sum

The theology of Romans is theologically centered. God effects apocalyptic, end-time salvation. God does this through the faithfulness of Jesus. Everything God does, everything that matters for Paul, everything that believers are and hope for, pivots on Jesus "in whom" and "through whom" God effects salvation. Two prepositional phrases are critical in Romans, "through Christ" and "in Christ Jesus." Jesus is the agent through whom God has acted, is acting, and will act. Everything believers have is "in Christ": baptized into Christ" (6:3), dead to sin and alive to God (6:11), "no condemnation" (8:1), the life of the Spirit (8:9-11), the love of God (5:5, 8), union with God (8:39).

God effects salvation in Messiah Jesus by creating a new people, baptized into Christ, who live by the eschatological Spirit. God's salvation knows no favorite people, but it also keeps faith with the prior promises of God to Israel. God effects salvation so that people shall live differently now in the context of the church.

The theology of Romans makes the claim that God is righteous and acts righteously. God is righteous because God keeps faith. God acts righteously by making people and the cosmos righteous in and through Messiah Jesus. Precisely because God is and acts righteously in the gospel, Paul is not ashamed of this gospel; it overcomes the problem of shame in an honor-shame culture and the problem of ethnocentrism in which one group puts down another group. He knows that this gospel means that different ethnic groups do not need to and should not judge one another—a "do not judge" inclusio frames the letter (1:18–2:11 and 14:1–15:13). He argues that this gospel includes Jews and Gentiles made righteous by the faithfulness of Jesus and living harmoniously by the power of the Spirit. Paul thus does not reject the Jewish faith and people, but redefines it in light of the fulfillment of God's promises to the nations in Messiah Jesus. Therefore, all forms of ethnocentrism—Jewish and Gentile—are out. Diverse ethnic groups are to welcome each other as Christ welcomed them for the glory of God (15:7).

What does such a reading of Romans mean for the historic doctrine of justification by faith, which defined the theology of the letter for so many centuries? It means that the profound theology, christology, and soteriology, which is at the center of so much of the theology of Romans, is not designed to tell individual people how to find a gracious God, but to instruct people, who already have experienced the grace of God, how to be gracious neighbors to fellow believers who are different. The doctrine of justification by faith is grounded first and foremost in the faith of Jesus Christ who thus makes salvation possible. Derivatively then, the doctrine includes also the faith of those who believe. In Romans, Paul appropriates this doctrine to *address* primarily the matter of accepting fellow believers of different ethnic backgrounds and status as equals in the church. While Paul assumes throughout the letter that believers experience God's salvation by faith—i.e., by trusting God (so e.g., Rom. 10:9-10)—the concrete dimension of bringing diverse people into one community of faith is the principle concern (Rom. 10:12-13; v. 11 bridges the two points).

Paul's claim that God is effecting universal salvation, righteousness, peace through Messiah Jesus represents a subversive political statement. Paul frames Romans as a political manifesto—Jesus is the son of God and the only Lord worthy of confession. Caesar is not Lord, and Caesar does not bring real salvation, justice, and peace. But Jesus Christ does!

For further study see: Byrne, 2001; Grieb, 2002; Hay, 1995; Keck, 1989; Morris, 1970; Soderlund and Wright, 1999; Stuhlmacher, 1988; Wright, 1991.

Essays

CHIASMUS A chiasmus is a symmetrical structure involving some form of inversion, or the reversing of word order in parallel phrases, around a central idea. Several different forms of chiasm are used in the New Testament:

A *simple chiasm*: ABCBA. This chiasm involves a crossing point, as in,

A   B
   C
B   A

The "X" shape of the chiasm forms the Greek letter *chi*, from which we derive the word chiasm. Romans 8:9-11 is structured as a simple chiasm:

A You are not in the flesh but in the Spirit
    if indeed **the Spirit of God dwells in you**.
    B If anyone does not have the Spirit of Christ
        one does not belong to him [is not of him].
        C But if Christ is in you (plural),
            your body is dead because of sin
            but your spirit is alive because of righteousness.
    B If the Spirit of him who raised Jesus from the dead dwell in you,
A he who raised Christ from the dead
    will make your mortal bodies live
    through the **indwelling of his Spirit in you**.

The individual elements can parallel one another based on content or other characteristics in a positive or negative fashion. Thus, A-A are parallel and synonymous, and concern life through the indwelling of the Spirit of God; B-B are parallel but contrasting or antithetical, does not have the Spirit of Christ/has the Spirit of God; C is the pivot or center, body dead/spirit alive. C is clearly the center about which the other elements are arranged by direct or synonymous (A-A) and antithetical (B-B) parallelism.

Other forms of chiasmus are known as parallelisms, as in:
A direct parallelism: ABAB, where the second AB echoes the first AB.
An inverted parallelism: ABBA. This form of parallelism is common in
    Romans, as in 1:17-18; 2:7-10; 2:14-27.
An antithetical parallelism: ABAB, where the second AB presents an idea
    opposite that introduced in the first AB.
For more details, see Breck, 1982; Lund, 1942; Ellis, 1982.

THE IDENTITY OF CHRESTUS The traditional interpretation of
Suetonius' "disturbances at the instigation of Chrestus" as a reference to
Christian preaching in Rome is problematic for several reasons. 1) It assumes
that Suetonius is wrong and cannot be trusted as a historian. Not only did he
not know how to spell Christus correctly, but also he reports that Chrestus is
alive, present, and active in Rome in A.D. 49. It is clear that when Suetonius
introduces Christians into his work in connection with Nero's persecution, he
is discussing them for the first time. He would have recognized the importance
of their first appearance in Rome if it had been earlier. Suetonius' sources led
him to think that there was a person called Chrestus actually present in Rome
in A.D. 49. 2) The Jews possessed a strong lobby in Rome during the time of
Claudius and Nero that would have been able to set the record straight in the
literary treatment of their case. If Chrestus refers to Christus the Christian
Messiah, the Jewish lobby missed a unique opportunity to blame the
Christians. 3) It assumes that the Acts report regarding Rome is not reliable.
Acts 18:1-3 mentions that Aquila and Priscilla left Rome because of the expulsion of the Jews by Claudius. Luke knows of the expulsion, but does not connect it with Christian preaching. Furthermore, if the Roman Christians had
been the victims of Jewish-Christian rioting in Rome, Acts would have mentioned this because it would have provided "an effective prelude to the vindication of the Christians when the Jews sought Gallio's intervention against
them" in Acts 18:12-17. Suetonius and Acts agree that the action of A.D. 49
was against the Jews. 4) Finally, Luke reports that the Jewish leaders of Rome
were willing to listen to Paul around A.D. 60 because they knew little of
Christianity (Acts 28:17-30). These leaders' ignorance of the Christian message a decade after the expulsion of their community, "because of Christian
preaching," is hardly credible. The only reason the expulsion has been connected with Christian missionary activity is the occurrence of the name
Chrestus.

Chrestus was a fairly common Roman name in the first century, and a
name with special messianic connotations among the Jews. A series of scholars have proposed that it refers to a Jewish messianic agitator who incited the
Jews to rebellion in Rome in A.D. 49. This thesis seems more likely for the
following reasons.

1) It takes Suetonius seriously. Chrestus is a real person agitating among
the Jews in Rome. We do not have to say that Suetonius was confused.

2) It fits Jewish-Roman relations at mid-century. The years leading up to
A.D. 66-70 were filled with Jewish-Gentile clashes in different parts of the
empire and with various measures against Jewish excesses which had nothing
to do with the earliest Christian church. We know of 15 such clashes alone in
the 15 years preceding the edict of Claudius. These years, of course, were followed by the heightening tension that led to the war of A.D. 66-70. The activities of Chrestus must be placed within the framework of Jewish patriotism

and the growing conflict between the Jews and Rome that resulted from the increased influence of extremist movements in Judaism throughout this period. A mid-century tax revolt in Rome that was supported by the Jews reinforces this picture.

3) The Jewish messianic interpretation of Chrestus' agitation fits the patriotic nature of Roman Jewish relations with Jerusalem. From the outset, the Jews of Rome maintained close political and intellectual affiliation with Palestine and Jerusalem. Most of the Jewish residents in Rome originally came from Palestine as immigrants or captives. They paid the Temple Tax and went on pilgrimages to Jerusalem. Roman Jews followed events in Jerusalem and Palestine closely, and expressed national loyalties in public demonstrations. For example, following the death of Herod the Great in 4 B.C. his sons presented their case to Augustus. A delegation of 50 Palestinian Jews also came to Rome to plead with Augustus that Palestine be placed under a governor appointed by Rome, rather than under the Herodian family. Some 8000 Roman Jews supported the Palestinian delegation. The leaders of Palestinian Jewry, in turn, took great interest in the Roman communities and made frequent visits to Rome. The constant interchange between Palestinian and Roman Judaism is confirmed in Acts 28:21; the Jewish leaders in Rome say to Paul, "we have received no letter from Jerusalem about you." It is not difficult to imagine messianic agitations in Rome as relations between Rome and Jerusalem deteriorated during the 40s and 50s, and as relations between Roman Jews and the government remained fragile, even tense.

4) The Jewish messianic interpretation of Chrestus' agitation fits the contents and tone of a letter from Claudius to Alexandria in A.D. 43. The letter warns that Jews must not import political agitators from Syria and upper Egypt. If they do, Claudius will proceed against them with "righteous anger" and force.

The agitations of Chrestus in Rome in the late 40s look like what Claudius warned against in A.D. 43. Claudius responded by expelling the Jews from Rome. It was a local police action taken in the interests of peace. The cause was political agitation within the Roman Jewish community, an agitation that has all the appearances of "zealot" motivations and goals.

See Benko, 1969; Borg, 1972.

DEATH IN ROMANS Death is especially prominent in Romans 5–8. The noun form, *thanatos*, occurs 22 out of 47 times in Paul (120 in the NT). Only the Gospel of John shows a comparable interest in death (19 times). The verbal form, *to die* (*apothnēskō*), is used 23 out of 42 times in Paul (113 in the NT). Again, the only comparable writer is John with 28 uses. Twenty-one of the 22 references to death in Romans are found in chs. 5-8 (1:32—death as the judgment of God—is the exception). Seventeen of the 23 occurrences of *to die* are found in chs. 5–8 (the six occurrences outside these chapters are all in ch. 14: vv. 7, 8, 9, 15).

Death language in Romans indicates several things. First, the dominant association is **Sin** (5:12, 17, 21; 6:16, 21, 23; 7:5, 10, 13; 8:2). Death also is associated negatively with the law (7:10, 13) and flesh (8:6).

Second, death is a personal and cosmic power, just like **Sin** (cf. 1 Cor. 15 where it is one of the principalities and powers). It rules by itself (5:14, 17) and through **Sin** (5:21). Death is **Death**. **Sin** is the procreator of **Death**. **Sin** and **Death** are inseparable allies. They are the supreme powers of the old age which rule all human beings and creation. **Death**/death is a paradigm of all reality and existence; it is both a symbol and reality of a cosmos that is opposed to God and is ruled by opponents of God. This understanding of **Death** is framed through cosmic apocalyptic categories [see Notes on 5:12-21, as well as the Introduction to this commentary, "The Larger Thought World of Romans," and *Essay: Sin*].

Third, while the verbal form *to die* carries some of the same association as the noun, its use reflects a very significant shift of focus. *To die* is still associated with **Sin** (5:15), law (7:2, 3, 6, 10), and flesh (8:13). However, the verb form is associated much more with Christ and his work. Its primary usage is to describe the death of Christ as a saving event (5:6, 8; 6:9, 10; 8:34; 14:15). It also describes the death of Christians to **Sin** through union with Christ (6:2, 7, 8), and the reality of "death in Christ" at the time of physical death. Over against the negative association of dying, *to die* is linked positively with the grace of God (5:15), overcoming the rule of **Sin** and death (6:9), freedom from the law (7:2, 3), life in the Spirit (7:6; 8:13), the gift of life itself (8:13; 14:7).

Death has multiple meanings in Romans. At one level it refers to biological death (6:6; 7:2-3; 8:38; 14:7, 8). Second, death denotes punishment for sins—for transgression of the will of God (e.g., 1:32). Third, death refers to a sacrificial act, either Christ's atonement for sins (5:6, 8, 10) or a heroic death for another person (5:7). Fourth, it means eschatological **Death**, which in turn denotes different things: a) **Death** is a cosmic power and ruler (5:12, 14, 17, 21; 6:9) that b) results in separation from God (5:12, 14, 17, 21; 6:9, 16, 21, 23; 7:5, 10, 13; 8:6, 38). Alternatively, c) death can refer to Christ's victory over **Sin** and **Death** (5:15-19; 6:9, 10). Fifth, death refers to the Christian's death to **Sin** (6:3, 4, 5, 7, 8), or failure to die to **Sin** (8:2, 6, 13). This understanding results in a series of moral exhortations that Christians forsake **Sin** and sins, because they have already died to **Sin** and sins. Death here is a past event, which is a motive for Christian ethical behavior. Finally, and closely related to this moral understanding, **Death** is a punishment for enslavement to **Sin** and willful sinning (6:16-19; 7:7-25). **Sin** means existential estrangement from God, but, more significantly, eschatological separation from God, **Death**.

Paul's interpretation of death is profoundly Christological. In addition to the six verbal associations, the noun death is associated with Christ's death five times (5:10; 6:3, 4, 5, 9). Christ is the antidote to **Death** and death. He gives his life in death (5:6-10) and triumphs over **Death** (6:9, 10). The form of the antidote is the reign of grace (5:17, 21); life (5:21; 6:4, 5, 21, 23; 7:5; 8:2, 6), including Christ's being raised from the dead (6:9); righteousness (5:17; 6:16); the Spirit (7:5; 8:2, 6); peace (8:6). The triumph of Christ over **Death** guarantees Christians that they will not experience eschatological death—nothing, not even **Death**, will separate them from God (8:38).

Christ is the antidote to **Death** because his life, death, and resurrection effected a shift from *this age* to *the age to come*. That shift redefines **Death** by robbing it of its ultimate power to rule humanity and creation. The liberation of human beings and creation from the power of **Death** has already begun through the power of Christ's victory over **Death**.

Paul's interpretation of death is also profoundly moral. Mortality and morality are linked. **Death** is the tragic result of Adam's moral failure, and a punishment for the moral failure of all his descendants, except Jesus. When believers die with Christ they die to **Sin** and sins, and thus also to the power of **Death**. That results in morality, in lives that resist and triumph over **Sin**.

Paul's interpretation of death in Romans uses the language of cosmic apocalyptic, **Death**, much more than forensic apocalyptic, death. Death is primarily **Death**; it is a function of the rule of evil cosmic powers. Therefore, Paul interprets the meaning of Christ's death and resurrection as victory over **Sin** and **Death**. An atonement interpretation of Christ's death—death as forgiveness of sins—does not address **Death** due to **Sin**. Salvation language must always address the problem of **Sin**. **Sin** as **Sin** and **Death** must be triumphed over by death as defeat of the powers and resurrection as victory over the powers.

For further study, consult: Beker, 1990; Bailey, 1979; C. Black, 1984; de Boer, 1988; Keck, 1969.

DEATH/BAPTISM AS RITUAL EVENTS Death and baptism are very important religious ritual events in the ancient world. Paul builds on this understanding in Romans 6.

Death is a radical, separating boundary-line event. It is a rite-of-passage that fundamentally transforms the life of the individual and society. It separates an individual from an immediate past world, and transitions the person into another realm in all cultures that believe in some form of life after death (a common belief in the first-century Jewish and Greco-Roman world).

All cultures develop rituals designed to mark and interpret the transition that occurs in life crisis events (besides death, these include birth, puberty, marriage, and entrance into a religious community). The transformation that occurs in such events is commonly understood to involve three phases: separation, transition, and (re-) incorporation. The dominant symbols of these stages are death, change, resurrection or rebirth.

Death ends life in this world, and terminates all relationships in an individual's life world—marriage, family, religious affiliation, political status, and role. Mourning symbolizes the redefinition of all relationships. Burial, a very important ritual in the ancient world, initiates and transitions the deceased into "community of the dead." A person who is not buried has not died fully, that is, has not been transitioned into the next form of life, the company of the other dead. Death and burial in the ancient world usually occurred on the same day.

The rite of passage marks the transition from one status to another. The person involved is set apart from the rest of society. Normal structures no longer count, because this person is being transformed, has permanently left one community and has entered a new one. The dead person lives an existence which no longer has the destiny of death, but rather rebirth of some sort (however that is defined in the culture, i.e., the liberation of the soul from the body in much Greek thought).

Three other things are noteworthy about the language of death rituals in the ancient world. First, there is talk of new knowledge, a new ethic, a new manner of acting, which is appropriate to the new mode of existence. Second, there is talk of a future form of existence which is experienced partially and before the appropriate time (proleptically—the time frame for this experience varies in different cultures). The person who has died is "not-what-he/she-once-was" and "not-yet-what-he/she-shall-be." Third, the transition from this life to the new form of life is led by an initiator who has gone through the entire process of transformation. Total submission to this initiator is required to complete the process of change. Enslavement language is characteristically used to define the relationship to the initiator.

Baptism was a highly significant rite-of-passage event that was practiced by most religious communities. A person was separated from his/her past religious world, transitioned to a new religious community, and promised a new form of life in the future. Baptism had two meanings: 1) it cleansed the person from the pollution of evil (a ritual purification), and 2) it effected the death of the person (a ritual of death-burial). Both the cleansing and death-burial were understood to effect a separation from the previous life world, and to incorporate the person into a new world complete with new knowledge and a new ethic.

Paul uses death and baptism as rite-of-passage events in Romans 6 to interpret the meaning of Christian baptism into Christ's death. Paul argues that Christians have really died in baptism into Christ. A radical separation from the **Sin** structured world of the past has occurred (vv. 2, 6, 7, 11) and an incorporation into a new community of the redeemed has taken place (vv. 3, 4, 6). Life in the new mode of existence is different; it is characterized by walking in newness of life (v. 4), freedom from **Sin** (vv. 6, 7, 11), and living with God (v. 11). This transitional mode will be transformed in the future into a resurrection mode of existence (vv. 5, 8).

It must be emphasized that Paul's understanding of baptism was not uncommon in the ancient world. For example, baptism was required in Judaism for proselytes from paganism. The event was defined as a death and rebirth event that was so radical it changed all relationships; the husband-wife bond and the parent-child bonds were dissolved and needed to be reformed in the context of the new mode of life and community as "reborn" Jewish relationships.

What is new in Paul is the definition of the rite of passage events as "in Christ." Existing rituals are redefined messianically, e.g., baptism into Christ, death "in the Lord" (14:7-8).

See Carlson, 1993; Daube, 1981.

DIATRIBE A "diatribe" is an ancient literary form that narrates a dialogue, a conversation, between a teacher and an imaginary student. It is a form of the Socratic question-and-answer method of teaching. The intent is to raise questions or state objections the teacher knows the student will have with the argument just made. The purpose is to point out errors in thinking in order to persuade.

The context for a diatribe is instructional. The questioner is a student, not an enemy or opponent. The conversation is dialogical, not polemical.

Paul uses the diatribe more often in Romans than in any other letter. The form of the diatribe in ancient literature and in Paul varies. The most common forms used in Romans are: 1) a sudden turn to address an imaginary questioner (e.g., 2:1-5, 17-24; 9:19-21; 11:17-24; 14:4); 2) a response to an immediately preceding objection or false conclusion (e.g., 3:1-9, 31; 4:1-2a; 6:1, 15; 7:7, 13; 9:14, 19; 11:1, 11, 19); 3) a dialogical exchange (e.g., 3:27-4:25).

The use of the diatribe does not mean a change of subject or the beginning of a new argument, as often thought, but the sharpening of the issues raised and a concretizing of their meaning.

The best study of the diatribe form and its use in Romans is Stowers, 1981 and 1988.

FAITH IN ROMANS "Faith" is such a common word in Christian faith that its meaning is assumed. Faith is usually understood as "belief," i.e., the acceptance that something is true, or "trust" i.e., confidence in someone or something. The primary focus is subjective response, e.g., I believe, or I trust.

A series of studies have raised serious questions about these assumed meanings. These studies have shown that in the Greek language and in Greek Jewish literature (the translation of the OT into Greek, the Septuagint; the Apocrypha; the Pseudepigrapha; Philo; and Josephus) the commonly assumed meaning of *pistis* as "faith" or "trust" is in fact the minority meaning. The Septuagint never uses *pistis* as "faith" or "trust." It uses "faith" (*pistis*) to translate the Hebrew *emunah*, which means firmness, certainty, dependability. The dominant meanings of faith in the LXX are 1) pledge, reliability, or faithfulness, 2) proof or evidence. The focus is the ground for faith, the basis on which subjective trust or belief may be founded. This interpretation of faith in Greek Jewish literature is in continuity with the meaning of faith in classical Greek. Faith from the seventh century B.C. through the fourth century A.D. basically means two things: 1) trust in others which is evidenced in action or behavior; 2) persuasion of a thing, confidence, assurance (see Liddell and Scott). James Kinneavy concludes a comparison of faith in Greek rhetoric and the NT by asserting that "the *pistis* (faith) of the NT can almost always be interpreted as persuasion" (1987:147). With very few exceptions, he argues, the noun faith can be interpreted "persuasion" and the verb "believed" as "was persuaded."

Faith is a very important word in Romans. Its occurrence is the second highest of any writing in the NT, 62 times compared to 98 in the Gospel of John. The use of the verbal form ("to believe," *pisteuein*) is the third highest in the NT (John = 98, Acts = 37, Romans = 22), and the use of the noun form ("faith," *pistis*) is the highest in the NT, 40 times).

A study of the use of faith (*pistis*) in Romans reveals some very interesting things that are important clues to the meaning. First, the use of the word is clustered, as follows:

35 times in chs. 1-4
3 times in chs. 5-8
14 times in chs. 9-11
10 times in chs. 12-16

Within this clustering, there is a further narrowing of use. In chs. 1-4, 28 of the 35 uses, or 45% of the use in the entire letter, occur in chs. 3-4. And in chs. 9-11, 13 of the 14 uses, or 21% of the use in the letter, are found in chs. 9-10. Sixty-six percent of the faith vocabulary occurs in four chapters. All of these chapters are particularly concerned with issues of Jewish relationships to the gospel. Chs. 5-8, often viewed as the critical description of the Christian life in Romans, use faith only three times.

Second, Paul creates many unique faith phrases in Romans that are not found anywhere else in the NT. The letter opens and closes with *to the obedience of faith* (eis hypakoēn pisteōs) in 1:5 and 16:26. A form of *to all the ones believing* (panti to pisteuonti) from 1:16 is repeated in 3:22, 4:11, and 10:4. Paul speaks in other letters of *the ones believing*, but never of *all the ones believing*. *Out of faith to faith* (ek pisteōs eis pistin) in 1:17 is unique to Romans, as is the phrase *entrusted the words of God* in 3:2. Only in Romans does Paul write about *faith upon* (*epi*), 4:5, 18, 24; 9:33; 10:11. *Out of faith in order to grace* (*ek pisteōs hina kata charin*) in 4:16, and *how to call to whom not believed* (*eis hon ouk episteusan*) in 10:14 are found only in Romans.

In addition to these more general phrases, Paul creates a series of unique phrases in association with other key terms in Romans. Faith is linked to righteousness in four rather startling phrases: *his faith to righteousness* (*he pistis autou eis dikaisounēn*) in 4:5, *the faith to righteousness* (*he pistis eis dikaisunēn*) in 4:9, *through righteousness of faith* (*dia dikaiosunēs pisteōs*) in 4:13, and *believe to righteousness* (*pisteuontai eis dikaisounēn*) in 10:10. The law is defined by faith in 3:27, *through law of faith* (*dia nomou pisteōs*). Faith and circumcision/uncircumcision are connected in four distinctive phrases: *make righteous circumcised out of faith and uncircumcised through the faith* (*peritomen ek pisteōs kai akrobustian dia tes pisteōs*) in 3:30; *circumcision as a seal of the righteousness out of faith and the one in the uncircumcision* (*tēs pisteōs tēs en tē akrobustia*) in 4:11; *for the purpose that he may be the father of all the ones believing through uncircumcision"* (*pantōn tōn pisteuontōn di' akrobustias*) again in 4:11; and *to the ones being ordered in the footsteps of faith, the one in uncircumcision of our father Abraham* (*tēs en akrobustia pisteōs*) in 4:12.

Paul creates these phrases to make a special theological claim that addresses a specific set of problems and issues. Faith clearly has something to do with obedience, with all people, with righteousness, with the law, and with circumcision and uncircumcision. The Jewish nature of the agenda identified in the first point is strengthened.

Third, a study of the word cradle of faith—the words that cradle faith in the various texts or that are associated with it—are equally informative. The dominant words are: obedience, nations, Jew/Gentile, salvation, righteousness of God, righteous, circumcision/uncircumcision, no distinction, boasting, works of law, law, promise, Abraham, hearing, preaching, and eating.

Fourth, faith is often an antithesis word in Romans; it is used over against something else. The "something else" reveals something about the meaning of faith. The primary points of contrast are: Jewish unfaithfulness (3:3); boasting, law of works, works of law (3:27); Jew-Gentile, circumcision-uncircumcision (3:29-30); destroy the law (3:31); works (4:4-6); circumcised-uncircumcised (4:9-12); law-promise (4:13-16); dead body, weak, strong (4:19-20); works of law (9:32); righteousness out of the law (10:5-6); right/wrong thinking (12:3); doubting (14:22-23).

Fifth, faith is used very often in prepositional phrases, seven with "through" (*dia*), e.g., *through the faith of Christ, expiation through faith, the ones believing through uncircumcision* (3:22, 25, 27, 30, 31; 4:11, 13); 13 with *out of* (*ek*), e.g., *out of faith to faith, made righteous the circumcised out of faith, out of faith in order to grace* (1:17 [2x]; 3:26; 3:30; 4:16 [2x]; 5:1; 9:30, 32; 10:6, 17; 14:23 [2x]); seven with "to" (*eis*), e.g., *to obedience of faith, the faith to righteousness* (1:5, 17; 4:5, 9; 10:10, 14; 16:26); five with "upon" (*epi*), e.g., *faith upon the one making righteous the ungodly, everyone believing upon him shall not be ashamed* (4:5, 18, 24; 9:33; 10:11); three with "in" (*en*), e.g., *the faith the one in uncircumcision, believing in your heart that God . . .*" (4:12; 10:9; 15:13). The use of faith in these prepositional phrases needs much more study, including a comparison of the other prepositional phrases in the Pauline letters that use faith. What is immediately apparent is that Paul in Romans does not talk about *faith into Christ* (*eis*) as in Galatians 2:16 and Philippians 1:29, or *faith in Christ* as in Ephesians 1:13 or Colossians 1:4.

Concomitant with the absence of *faith in Christ* phrases, is a sixth observation. The primary object of faith in Romans is God (4:5, 17, 18, 24; 10:9, 11). Christ is the probable object of faith in 6:8. The law is the object in 9:33. There is something very God-centered about faith in Romans.

Finally, it is worth noting what is absent from faith language in Romans. Paul never speaks of "faith alone." James (2:24) is the only NT writer to use this phrase. And Paul never makes faith the subject of an imperative; he never issues a command "to faith."

Two other phenomena are significant. The first is the use of the phrase *out of faith* (*ek pisteōs*). Paul uses the phrase only in Romans and Galatians; 12 times in Romans, and nine in Galatians plus two uses with the word "hearing" (*out of the hearing of faith, ex akoēs pisteōs*, 3:2, 5). In Romans it is used seven times with righteousness words (1:17 [2x]; 3:26, 30; 5:1; 9:30; 10:6), three times with law (4:16 [2x]; 9:32), twice with doubt/sin (14:23). Galatians associates the phrase with righteousness five times (2:16; 3:8, 11, 24; 5:5), and once each with sons (3:7), blessing (3:9), promise (3:22), law (3:11), plus the 3:2, 5 uses of *out of hearing of faith* associated with the Spirit. Three times the phrase is used to contrast faith and law in Romans (4:16; 9:32; 10:5-6). The same contrast is found twice in Galatians (3:11; 5:4-5). *Out of faith* contrasts once with *works of law*, plus the 3:2, 5 contrast of *hearing of faith* with *works of law*. The phrase is concerned with the source or ground of righteousness or salvation. Righteousness, family relationship, promise, blessing are based on faith, Christ's, Abraham's, the Christian's. They are not grounded in the law or in works of the law.

Why the use of this distinctive phrase only in Romans and Galatians? Something peculiar to these letters must lie behind this use. The phrase is used only once in the LXX, in Habakkuk 2:4. That text is quoted twice by Paul, Romans (1:17) and Galatians (3:11). The *out of faith* phrase in Romans and Galatians is probably a direct function of Paul's citation of Habakkuk. The Habakkuk citation, we have seen, is a messianic reference; it speaks about the Messiah as the one who lives out of faith or faithfulness. The source of faith in Habakkuk, as understood by Paul, is Messiah Jesus.

The second significant phenomenon is the close correlation of "faith" and "obedience" in Romans. The letter is framed by the phrase the *obedience of faith*. The phrase is programmatic. Paul signals the closest possible relationship between faith and obedience. Faith is defined by obedience, and obedience is defined by faith. The German *Glaubensgehorsam*, "obedience in faith," comes close to Paul's meaning.

The problem of the Israelites in 10:16 is that they have not *obeyed the gospel* (*hupēkousan tō euangeliō*). Paul never combines faith with "the gospel" to mean acceptance of the gospel, but he here defines acceptance of the gospel as *obedience to the gospel*. He describes the goal of his mission in 15:18 as the *obedience of the Gentiles*. In 16:19 the obedience of the Roman Christians is known among Christians all over the world, while in 1:8 it was the faith of the Roman Christians that *was proclaimed in the whole world*. Faith and obedience are essential equivalents in Romans. The one cannot be understood apart from the other.

The close relationship of faith and obedience explains the relationship to righteousness in chs. 1–4 and chs. 6 and 10. Righteousness in chs. 1–4 describes God's character—God is righteous—and God's act—God makes righteous. Righteousness in Romans 6 is ethical; it describes the character and life-style of Christians. Christians submit to, offer themselves to, righteousness. "Obedience" describes the response of submission to righteousness. The unique phrase *faith to righteousness* (4:5, 9; 10:10) becomes *obedience to righteousness* (6:16). Christians are people who are *obedient out of the heart to the type of teaching you received* (6:16) to be *slaves of righteousness* (6:18); in 10:9 they are people *who believe in your heart to righteousness*.

The close relationship of faith and obedience sounds strange to Protestant ears. The sixteenth-century controversy over the nature of salvation drove a wedge between faith and obedience, between faith and works. The second was considered chronologically secondary, and not an integral part of faith. The event of becoming a Christian was defined by cognitive or intellectual (believe the truth of the gospel) and fiduciary (believe or trust in) understandings. Obedience was excluded from the definition of becoming and being a Christian. But Paul was not a sixteenth-century Protestant. He was a first century Jew. His thinking was shaped by the Hebrew scriptures and contemporary Jewish thinking. Faith and obedience belong together for him; both terms have covenantal meanings. Both talk about submitting to God's will and obeying God's teachings. And because obedience involves hearing, in fact comes from the same word as hearing, Paul formulates phrases like *the faith out of hearing* (10:17) or *out of the hearing of faith* (Gal. 3:2, 5), which are simply other ways of speaking of the *obedience of faith*. The relationship can be diagrammed as follows:

Reception	Response	Behavior
Faith	hear gospel be persuaded	trust in/commit to
Obedience	hear gospel submit	do/act

Faith and obedience belong together in Paul; they qualify each other reciprocally. There cannot be faith without obedience—faith without obedience is dead (James 2)—and there cannot be obedience without faith.

The structure of faith in Romans 4 underlines this close relation. It may be outlined as follows:

God's gift as grace
Acceptance of the gift through faith
The covenant of righteousness through the law
Obedience to the law as the way of faith

The call of God to Abraham is God's gift of salvation. Abraham responded through faith. The covenant through circumcision symbolized the core of the law. Abraham obeyed, and this was his way of faith. Faith and obedience are one action. Faith is demonstrated by obedience.

This structure of faith is grounded in the biblical story, first in the story of Abraham and then in the story of Israel as a people. God saved Israel out of Egypt (Exod. 20:2). Israel accepted this gift by following Moses. The covenant was contracted at Sinai. Keeping the law, symbolized by the Passover event, is obedience as the way of faith.

What is faith in Romans in light of this evidence? It involves three things. First, faith is evidence or pledge that provides the ground for trust. It concerns the basis for persuasion, for reliability, for dependability. The basis for faith in Romans is God and Jesus. God is the righteous one, the one who is faithful.

God is *faithful* when humans are unfaithful (3:3). The righteousness of God is revealed *out of faith* (1:17). The evidence is Jesus who reveals God's end-time faithfulness through his own faithfulness to God, *the faith of Jesus*. The unique *out of faith* phrase from the messianically interpreted Habakkuk citation articulates the ground of faith. Jesus is the basis of faith; he is the epistemological ground of faith. Christ is the pledge or assurance from God which grounds and makes possible human faith.

Second, faith involves commitment to, trust in God. Human beings must respond to the evidence of God's faithfulness, to the pledge of God's faithfulness in Christ. The nature of that trust, defined most clearly in Romans 4, is trust in God to do the impossible, "to hope against hope." The object of this trust in Romans is almost always God. Trust is God-centered. It is the persuasion that God is faithful, and can be counted on to keep promises.

Third, faith as trust is expressed in evidence or in pledge, called obedience in Romans. Doing the will of God, living as though the promise of God is a reality, whether that is Jesus (*the faith of Jesus*), or Abraham (*the faith of Abraham*), or a Christian believer (*to all the ones believing or acting from faith* when eating or not eating), is the evidence of trust. Faith is faithfulness. That is who God is, that is how Jesus lived, that is how Abraham lived, and that is how followers of Jesus are called to live.

This understanding of faith is very biblical. Paul is interpreting faith as understood in the Hebrew Scriptures, now refracted through Messiah Jesus as the evidence of God's faithfulness and through the inclusion of all peoples in God's people.

Faith as evidence and trust functions in a very specific way in Romans. First, faith equalizes all people and universalizes salvation. Faith involves *all the ones believing, no distinction*, Abraham, Jew and Gentile, circumcised and uncircumcised. Faith rejects all forms of particularity—e.g., law, works of law, circumcision, boasting—that exclude some people from incorporation into God's people—e.g., Gentiles, uncircumcised.

Second, faith assures God's end-time salvation for human beings. Different words for this salvation are used—righteousness, promise, reconciliation, son/daughtership, access to God. The point is that all people, irrespective of racial or religious heritage, may experience or participate in God's gift of salvation on the same basis—faith as trust in the evidence of God's faithfulness.

Third, faith linked to obedience serves to unify divided groups. *The obedience of faith* incorporates the code words of the various groups in Rome by reminding them that God's salvation calls for a response of trust that consists of obedience. Faith that does not submit to righteousness, that does not welcome "the other," is not faith.

For further reading, see: Bartsch, 1968; D. Campbell, 1992; Corsani, 1994; Du Toit, 1991; Hay, 1989; Howard, 1973-74; Kinneavy, 1987; Lindsay, 1993; O'Rourke, 1973; Stowers, 1989.

FLESH IN ROMANS "Flesh," *sarx*, is a distinctively Pauline term. It is used 91 times in the Pauline letters (out of 147 uses in the NT). The 26 occurrences in Romans represent the greatest use in Paul (and the NT). Galatians follows with 18 occurrences, 1 and 2 Corinthians with 11 each. In addition, Paul uses two "flesh" derivatives, both meaning "fleshly" in 7:14 (*sarkinos*) and in 15:27 (*sarkikois*).

Flesh in Paul has a wide spectrum of meaning. It can be a synonym for *human being* (the Ps. 143:2 citation in Rom. 3:20). The word can denote human weakness and moral-spiritual inadequacy (Rom. 6:19). Or, it can describe human descent or kinship (Rom. 1:3; 8:3; 9:3, 5; 11:14). The word also can have a negative meaning, an inferior mode of being and living, specifically a way of life controlled by a power that is opposed to God.

Flesh is essentially a contrast word in Romans, even a polemical term. That is, it is used primarily with negative connotations and in contrast to something better and superior. Flesh carries this "over against" meaning even in some of the uses that are normally more neutral, e.g., kinship relationships. Flesh in Romans stands most often in opposition to Spirit (*pneuma*).

The dominant use of flesh occurs in chs. 6–8; 17 of the 26 uses are found in the 33 verses between 6:19 and 8:13 (65% in Romans, 19% in the total Pauline corpus). An understanding of flesh must begin with this heavy concentration.

Flesh in Chs. 6–8

Apart from the reference to the moral-spiritual limitations of the Roman Christians in 6:19, flesh in chs. 6–8 is a negative, contrast term. The key meaning is stated in 7:5, which we noted in the explanatory notes is the introductory statement for 7:7-25. Life prior to "belonging to Christ" is characterized as life *in the flesh*, which in turn is defined as a life of sinful passions aroused by the law and producing death. The flesh is linked to sin, law, and death. To live in the flesh is to live in the old age rather than the age to come.

Paul explains what life *in the flesh* means in 7:14; it is to be subject to another power, *sold under Sin*. The contrast is the law. The law is spiritual, while the "I" is fleshly (*sarkinos*) because it is subject to **Sin**. Paul elaborates in vv. 18 and 25. No good dwells *in my flesh*, and *in the flesh* the "I" serves the *law of Sin* rather than the *law of God*. *In the flesh* characterizes life subject to **Sin**.

In 8:3 Paul offers the antidote to life *in the flesh* subject to **Sin**. The law could not overcome **Sin** because it was weakened *through the flesh*, through life controlled by **Sin**. But God sent the son *in the likeness of sinful flesh* for the purpose of condemning sin *in the flesh*. Christ defeated **Sin** in its domain, the flesh (see Explanatory Notes on 8:3).

Christ's defeat of **Sin** in the flesh sets up a power struggle between life *according to the flesh* (*kata sarka*) and life *according to the Spirit* (*kata pneuma*). Christians are not to "walk" according to the power of the flesh but according to the power of the Spirit (8:4). These two powers produce alternative worldviews (8:5-6). There is a fleshly worldview that stands opposed to a spiritual worldview. The fleshly one is hostile to God, cannot please God, and leads to death (8:7-8). The spiritual one submits to the law of God and leads to life and peace (8:6-7). Christians are people who do not live *in the flesh* but *in the Spirit* (8:9). They are under no obligation to live *in the flesh* or *according to the flesh* (8:12). They will die if they choose to live *according to the flesh*, and they will experience life if they choose to *live by the Spirit* (8:13).

The dualism Paul outlines here is profound. To live *in the flesh* is to live in the old age subject to **Sin** and thus opposed to God. Life *in the flesh* is not neutral. The flesh is the source of corruption due to the power of **Sin**. But the flesh is more than the source of human failure. The unique phrase *according to the flesh*" (*kata sarka*) points an independent power with its own world view that fundamentally stands opposed to all that God represents and desires, that opposes the power of God *according to the Spirit*.

Flesh in Chs. 1–4

The negative, contrast understanding of flesh in chs. 6–8 is evident already in Paul's earlier references. The context for the 2:28 reference is a critique of Jewish boasting *in the law* and *in circumcision*. Flesh refers to circumcision as a physical act *in the flesh* and stands in contrast to circumcision *in secret, a circumcision of the heart in the Spirit* (2:28). Flesh is linked with boasting and the letter of the law, and is juxtaposed to the Spirit.

Even the apparently neutral reference in 3:20 to *no flesh being made righteous through works of law* is probably more negative than thought. Paul's change of the Psalm 143:2 citation from *all life* to *all flesh* is significant. *All life* and *all flesh* both express universalism, that is, all people. But given the earlier linkage of "flesh" and circumcision, Paul seems to summarize 2:25-29 and answer the question about the advantage of circumcision raised in 3:1. Not only is no one justified by works of law, but specifically no circumcised flesh is justified by works of the law (e.g., circumcision).

Similarly, the apparently neutral description of Abraham as *our forefather according to the flesh* (4:1) is linked to *being made righteous by works* and *boasting*, and is juxtaposed *to God* (4:2). Kinship with Abraham is not all it was made out to be.

Christ "according to the flesh"

The one reference in chs. 1–4 to Christ as *descended from David according to the flesh* (1:3) is the first of three references to Christ in association with the flesh in Romans; the other two are 8:3 and 9:5. The 1:3 identification of Jesus as a Davidic descendant *according to the flesh* is a clear statement of kinship. But the contrast, *appointed son of God in power according to the Spirit of holiness*, indicates immediately that Jesus is more than according to the flesh.

The 8:3 reference to Jesus *in the likeness of sinful flesh* makes the point that Christ's mission was to defeat **Sin** in the flesh in order that the law of God could be fulfilled. The flesh is something Christ identifies with to overcome.

In 9:5 *out of whom the Christ, the one according to the flesh*, clearly denotes physical descent and kinship. But this "advantage" of the Jewish people is qualified in two ways. The first is by the little particle *to* in Greek before *according to the flesh*, which means something like insofar as he was according to the flesh. Again, the implication is that there is more to Christ than kinship with the Jewish people. The second qualification is the depreciation of Jewish kinship that follows immediately, and the contrast of *children of the flesh* with *children of promise*.

It would appear that even the association of Christ with flesh does not overcome the negative meanings of flesh. Christ is more than flesh.

Flesh in Chs. 9–11

Apart from the 9:5 reference to Christ *according to the flesh*, flesh in chs. 9–11 is used to define Jewish kinship. The Jews are Paul's people *according to the flesh* in 9:3. But they are not the real descendants of Abraham; the *children of promise* are (9:8). The *children of the flesh* are the recipients of God's hatred (9:13), and are vessels of wrath (9:22). In 11:14 Paul defines the purpose of his ministry as *making jealous the ones of my flesh* in order to save *some of them*.

Flesh in Chs. 12–16

Paul makes two references to flesh in the final chapters. The 13:14 exhortation to *make no provision for the flesh* is instructive for his understanding. The reference occurs in the context of eschatological contrasts—light and darkness, the old and the new aeons—and a listing of the evil deeds of the old age. It stands in contrast to *putting on* the armour of light in v. 12 and Messiah Jesus in v. 14. Flesh represents the darkness of the old age, which is to be rejected in favor of the light of the new age and Christ.

In 15:17 Paul urges the Roman Christians to share material things (lit., *fleshly things, sarkikois*) with the Christians in Jerusalem because they have received *spiritual things* from them. The "minor to major" argument again indicates the inferiority of *the things of the flesh* to *the things of the Spirit*.

Conclusion

Flesh in Romans is a profoundly negative force. It is a power that leads human beings into death, which subjects them to **Sin**. It is so powerful that the law is not able to control it. Flesh denotes humanity as belonging to the old age and determined by **Sin**. The flesh is inferior to the Spirit and normally stands over against the Spirit. The only antidotes powerful enough to overcome the power of the flesh are Christ and the Spirit.

The radical contrast of flesh and Spirit must be understood communally as well as individually. To live *according to the flesh* is to live within a realm, within a community with a worldview. The Jews as a people boast *in the flesh* (2:28). Paul's language is similar to the Dead Sea Scrolls, which contrast living in the society of the flesh or the community of the covenant. Paul's apocalyptic language pictures two distinct communities under the control of very different powers with distinct ways of life.

For further study, read: Dunn, 1973; Jewett, 1971:49-166; Thiselton, 1975.

GRACE IN ROMANS   Grace (*charis*) is an important theological term in Protestant Christianity. It is associated with two understandings: 1) salvation as free gift, in contrast to any human effort to earn it; and 2) grace in opposition to law, with law as the symbol for "works-salvation."

Grace is an important word in the NT (155 uses), and especially in the Pauline letters (100 of the 155 uses). Romans uses grace the most in the Pauline letters (24 times); 2 Corinthians is next (18 times). The related word "free gift" (*charisma*) is with one exception a Pauline term (17 times in the NT; six in Rom.; seven in 1 Cor.; 1 Pet. 4:10 is the one non-Pauline use).

The root word for grace, *char*, means well being (compare *shalom* in the OT). Many different meanings are derived from this root: grace, favor, beauty, thankfulness, gratitude, delight, kindness, and benefit. The precise meaning of grace must always be determined by the context in which it is used.

The use of grace in the OT (190 times in the LXX; 61 times as the translation of *chen*) provides some basic clues to background meaning. Grace denotes the action of a stronger person who voluntarily chooses to come to the aid of a weaker person. The stronger person often is God; God acts to supply grace to the weak or needy (e.g., Gen. 39:21; Exod. 3:21; 11:3; 12:36).

Grace is used in four different ways in Romans. First, it is used in Paul's greetings (1:7; 16:20) in association with "peace," another word for well being. Paul wishes his readers "well," always in God and Jesus Christ. Second, it means "thanks" (6:17; 7:25). Paul thanks God for the salvation of the Roman Christians from enslavement to **Sin** and from death. Third, grace is a word for ministry and for gifts of ministry. Paul's own ministry and mission is an act of grace (1:5; 12:3; 15:15). And the ministries of the church are free gifts (*charismata*) that are *according to grace* (*kata charis*). They are neither earned nor deserved, but are gifts that are to be exercised for the benefit of others. Fourth, grace means salvation, but with two quite different though related fields of meaning.

Grace means salvation as gift (3:24; 4:4, 16; 5:2; 11:5, 6). Salvation, defined by different metaphors (redemption in 3:24; righteousness in 5:2; election in 11:5), is something that God gives to human beings. Salvation as "grace-gift" is often defined over against another reality, **Sin** (3:24) or mode of attempted salvation, works (4:4; 11:6 where grace is used three times to emphasize the gift character).

But grace, as salvation, is more than gift. It also means salvation as power. In chs. 5 and 6 Paul consistently defines grace as **Grace**, as the power that defeats **Sin**. **Grace** is understood as an apocalyptic power. It abounds more than sin as trespass leading to **Death** (5:15) and **Sin** (5:20). **Grace** reigns over **Sin** and **Death** (5:17, 21; 6:1, 14, 15). **Grace** is the power of God that comes to the aid of weak, human beings enslaved in the magnetic field of **Sin** and **Death**, and pulls them into the new magnetic field of **Righteousness** and **Life**.

A "free gift" (*charismata*) is an effect of grace or a concrete manifestation of God's grace. Paul's use of the term follows the same pattern of meaning as grace. Twice it refers to ministry, Paul's (1:11) and the ministries given to the church *according to grace* (12:6). Four times it defines salvation as power (5:15, 16; 6:23; 11:29). In each of these references "free gift as power" stands over against something (acts of sin, either trespass in 5:15 or transgression in 5:16; **Sin** in 6:23; disobedience in 11:29).

Several things are noteworthy about Paul's grace language in Romans. First, when Paul uses grace as greetings, thanks, or ministry there is no juxtaposition. Grace is gift from God in whatever form it is given. Second, when grace is defined as "salvation as gift" it can stand over against something. Three of the six "salvation as gift" uses stand over against **Sin** (one) or works (two). Third, all of the "salvation as power" references are juxtaposed to **Sin** or sin (12 times with 3:24). The real enemy of God's salvation either as gift or power is **Sin**, not works as in most Protestant theology. Works is a problem, but a minor problem compared to **Sin**. Paul uses grace language primarily because humanity needs help; it is enslaved, not because most humans think they can work their way out of their dilemma. Fourth, grace stresses the gift character of God's salvation in whatever form it is given. It can only be received (5:17). Finally, Paul never juxtaposes grace and law in Romans. In the one text that has been used to juxtapose grace and law, 4:16, the contrast is faith and law rather than grace and law. Grace does not overcome the law, but **Sin**.

For further study see: Bassler, 2003:24-33; Doughty, 1973-74:163-180; Eastman, 1999; Nardoni, 1993:68-80.

HOMOSEXUALITY Romans 1:25-27 is the most crucial New Testament text on the question of homosexuality. It offers the most explicit theological condemnation of homosexual behavior in the NT. It also is the only passage in the entire Bible that refers to lesbian sexual relations.

Several things about the discussion of homosexuality in this text are important. First, Paul is diagnosing the human condition, not describing individual acts of homosexual behavior. The story of Romans 1:18f. is about the human fall—human rejection of God.

Second, Paul's description of homosexual behavior is illustrative of the main argument, human rebellion against the Creator. It is thus secondary to the main point Paul is making. But it is an illustration that Paul and his contemporaries understood. Homosexual behavior is a rejection of the sexual distinctions fundamental to God's creative design. The Genesis creation stories are clearly in the foreground of Paul's thinking—God as Creator (*God created . . .*), image (*God created humankind in his own image . . . male and female he created them*).

Third, the concept of "nature" (*physis*) introduced into the argument in v. 26 makes the point that homosexual behavior rejects the male/female complementarity of creation. Women and men exchanged the *natural use* (*kata physin*) for that which is *contrary to nature* (*para physin*). The repetition of the *natural use* in v. 27 makes clear that the phrase refers to heterosexual as opposed to homosexual intercourse. The latter is characterized as *contrary to nature*. There are many instances in Greco-Roman literature of the opposition between *natural* and *unnatural*. Actions *according to nature* (*kata physin*) are praised and actions *contrary to nature* (*para physin*) are condemned. The opposition is used to distinguish between heterosexual and homosexual behavior in the absence of a convenient Greek word for "heterosexual" and "homosexual." The rejection of homosexual behavior as *contrary to nature* also was a common one in Judaism. Josephus, a first century (A.D.) Jewish historian, writes, "the law recognizes no sexual connections except for the natural (*kata physin*) union of man and wife . . . it abhors the intercourse of males with males . . ." (*Ag. Ap.* 2:199). Philo, another contemporary of Paul, uses similar language (*Spec. Laws.* 3:37-42).

Fourth, the reference to both gay and lesbian sexual relations indicates that Paul is talking about more than the practice of pederasty, adult men engaging in sexual acts with boys. Paul is concerned with sexual behavior, which reflects a fundamental rejection of God's creative design.

Fifth, homosexuality is not the cause of the wrath of God, but the consequence of God's decision to "give up" rebellious creatures to follow their own futile thinking and desires. The deliberate repetition of the verb "exchange" forges the link between the rebellion against God and the *shameless acts* of v. 27. Both are evidence and consequence of the rebellion against God.

Homosexual behavior for Paul is an illustration of human rejection of God the Creator. It entails a violation of the creaturely nature of persons. It is against the nature of the female to have sexual relations with another female, and it is against the nature of the male to have sexual relations with another male.

The statements of Paul, and other Jewish writers, must be read against the background of a hierarchical worldview in which sexual intercourse of males with males was perceived as a higher form of sex than heterosexual intercourse. Because the male was viewed as superior to the female, as a higher form of life within the hierarchy, sex with another male was viewed by many as superior to sex with a female. Sex with the wife was for procreation. Sex with a female prostitute or another male was for pleasure. In short, homosexual practice in much of the ancient world was tied to a negative view of woman. Furthermore, homosexuality was practiced in the context of "sexual switch-hitting," wife and male friend, not as an exclusive form of sexual relationship. Paul views such ideology and its practice as sexually immoral, and as evidence of humanity's rebellion against God.

The recent attempt to distinguish sexual acts and sexual orientation is foreign to Paul. Thus, for example, the argument by some scholars that Paul's condemnation of homosexual behavior in this text applies only to homosexual acts committed by heterosexual persons, not to persons with a homosexual orientation, is to confuse exegesis and hermeneutical presupposition. Richard Hays counters correctly that "the fact is that Paul treats all homosexual activity as prima-facie evidence of humanity's tragic confusion and alienation from God the Creator" (1991:19).

Paul's condemnation of homosexual behavior must be qualified by several observations. First, Paul is not proscribing homosexual behavior in Romans 1, but using it as an illustration of rebellion against God. To use other words, Paul is not teaching sexual ethics, but analyzing the tragic human condition that follows from human rejection of God.

Second, homosexual behavior is not defined as more sinful or more reprehensible than the others forms of human rebellion against God listed in 1:28-31. It is a more vivid image of rebellion against God's creative intentions, but not a more serious sin.

See Balch, 2000; Boswell, 1980; Brooten, 1996; Gagnon, 2001; Hays, 1986; 1991; 1996:379-406; Seow, 1996; Scroggs, 1983; Swartley, 2003; Wink, 1999.

HONOR-SHAME Personality in the West is defined by individualism. A person is a bounded, unique, more or less integrated self. Persons are taught to be distinctive wholes and individuals, to stand on their own feet. They act singly and alone, and are responsible only for their own actions. The core value of this culture is personal freedom. Until post-modern times sin was defined as personal guilt. Guilt requires forgiveness, cleansing. More recently sin has become meaninglessness, which requires meaning or a sense of purpose. Such an understanding of personhood and salvation is a very peculiar idea in most cultures of the world. Guilt-forgiveness or meaninglessness-meaning cultures are relatively recent western developments.

Most ancient cultures, and many modern ones (e.g., African, Latino, Japanese) are honor-shame cultures. The group is prior to and more important than the individual. Groups are unique and distinct, not individuals. "Belonging" or being part of a group is the critical value. A person is someone whose self-awareness depends on being part of a group (being embedded). A person is who he/she is perceived to be by the significant others in the culture, e.g., family, patron, leaders of society, deity (ies). A person internalizes and makes his/her own what the significant others think and say. The focus of attention is away from the individual ego to the demands and expectations of the others who can grant or withhold reputation. The core social values of such a culture are honor-shame.

Honor is the value a person has in the eyes of the group. It is the claim to worth and the acknowledgment of worth by significant others. Such honor is either ascribed—the honor of family (genealogy), ethnicity or tribe, wealth—or acquired—the honor achieved by excelling over others.

Name and honor are the central concerns of people in every context of public action. They give purpose and meaning to people's lives. A good name and family honor are core values in the culture. Honor is intimately related to power and wealth. To interact with social, ethnic, or economic inferiors is to recognize them, to give them status and thus honor, and thereby to lose personal honor.

In such a culture every interaction outside the family involves the recognition of honor or the loss of honor. Every social contact is a contest for honor, e.g., gift giving, invitations to dinner, seating at dinners, debates, buying and selling, arranging marriages, business, mutual help.

Acceptance and respect from the significant others, from the primary group, overshadows all other considerations. Attempts to damage reputation are constantly made, and must be warded off or honor is lost. To be rejected by the significant others or the primary group is a death worse than physical death. People in such cultures go to any length to protect and enhance honor, and will do anything to avoid the loss of face.

The honorable person is the one who can maintain his/her social boundaries in the interaction of power and respect with others, including God or the gods. The shameless person is the one who does not observe and/or maintain social boundaries. When honor is violated, what is required is satisfaction, e.g., the restoration of honor in the eyes of the significant others.

People virtually without any honor in the NT world are marginalized people, such as lepers, the poor, women, slaves, Gentiles in the Jewish world, Jews in many parts of the Gentile world. Such people are constantly taken advantage of. They have no means to defend any sense of honor, let alone, to gain it. They are totally dependent on others, powerful and wealthy patrons to give them honor, or fathers or husbands in the case of women.

For further reading, see Malina, 1981; Moxnes, 1988a and 1988b; Neyrey, 1991; Peristiany, 1965; Pitt-Rivers, 1968.

INCLUSIO An "inclusio" quite literally means the beginning and the end correspond. A figure of speech, a word, a phrase, a formula, or a citation of a scripture is used to frame a text. Words or ideas from the beginning of a text unit are repeated at the end. A text is "included," that is, defined, by this literary technique.

Some examples of Paul's use of "inclusio" in Romans are as follows:

4:3-22—a scripture citation
    4:3—Genesis 15:6
    4:22—Genesis 15:6
chs. 5–8—a confessional formula
    5:1—our Lord Jesus Christ
    8:39—our Lord Jesus Christ
5:1-11—an idea
    5:1—peace with God through our Lord Jesus Christ
    5:11—reconciliation through our Lord Jesus Christ

INTO/WITH CHRIST Paul uses two phrases—*into Christ* (*en Christō*) and *with Christ* (*sun Christo*)—in ch. 6 that reflect much wider usage, and are full of meaning. In each case a preposition, either "in" (*en*) or "with" (*sun*), is combined with Christ to say something about the relationship of him and believers.

The preposition "in" normally has either a local (e.g., in the space or domain of), or an instrumental (e.g., by means of) meaning. "With" has associational meanings.

"In Christ" is used 170 times in the Pauline letters. It is often considered a formula saying, but its use is too diverse to be a fixed formula. The phrase is peculiarly Pauline. It is not found prior to Paul, and is used rarely outside the Pauline letters (e.g., 1 Pet. 3:16; 5:10, 14). The phrase *with Christ* is not used as often, only 14 times in the Pauline letters, although when the preposition "with" (*sun*) is combined with other words the usage increases considerably.

The *in Christ* phrase or its equivalent (*in the Lord, in the Lord Jesus*) is used 21 times in Romans. Ernest Best has modified the Albrecht Oepke typology of *in Christ* phrases in Paul to outline eight different uses and meanings. Of the eight, seven are used in Romans:

1) A is *in Christ*: 6:11; 8:1; 16:7, 8, 11. *In Christ* has a local meaning; it refers to the community *in Christ*. The references are all plural. The antitheses in 6:11 (dead to **Sin**) and 8:1 (*in flesh*) indicate realms of being. The ch. 16 references suggest living in the dominion of.

2) A does something to B *in Christ*: 9:1; 16:2, 3, 9. Christians are connected to each other and to a group because they are *in Christ*. The predominant meaning again is local. The context for truthfulness is in the community of Christ. Christians in ch. 16 live in the dominion of.

3) A does something in the Lord: 14:14; 15:17; 16:12b. The context for the "doing" is local, "in the realm of."

4) A is "X" in the Lord, with "X" representing some quality: 16:8, 10, 12a, 13, 22. The context for the ascribed quality is "in the community of."

5) God gives/does something *in Christ*: 6:23; 8:2. The gift is linked with salvation. *In Christ* preserves its local meaning, and implies the community in Christ. The antithesis of *in Christ* in 8:2 is the realm of **Sin** and **Death**.

6) The gift of God that is *in Christ*: 3:24; 8:39. Christ is the historical person in whom salvation is present. The 3:24 reference is instrumental, *by means of Jesus Christ*. But in 8:39 the meaning is local; Christians have security against all forces of opposition in the realm of Christ.

7) A,B,C . . . are one *in Christ*: 12:5. Different Christians form a unified community *in Christ*.

The only classification of the formula that is not used in Romans is the cosmic one, e.g., *in him all things were created . . . and in him all things hold together* (Col. 1:16, 17).

Three things are obvious in a study of these different uses in Romans. First, "in" has a strong local flavor. It describes the space or the domain in which Christians exist; they live *in Christ*, in the sphere or domain of Christ. Second, the phrase describes a relationship between Christians and Christ that at the same time involves a relationship with other Christians and all of the Christians together with Christ. That is, the phrase is social in meaning rather than individualistic. *In Christ* has meanings that are related to *the body of Christ*. Third, the formula is connected with God's salvation through Christ, e.g., redemption (3:24), eternal life (6:23), no condemnation (8:1), freedom (8:2). The phrase defines the salvation, which creates the in Christ relationship of Christians with Christ. *In Christ* characterizes both the salvation made possible through Christ and the "place" in which Christians exist.

Christ effects salvation. Christians enter a relationship with Christ that puts them into a relationship with other Christians. Christians are not alone in Christ, but are *in Christ* with others, which separates them from people who are not *in Christ*. The different Christians *in Christ* constitute a unified community, a body, a whole, that makes them "brothers/sisters" with each other even when they do not know each other. The "brothers/sisters" have unique obligations to each other as members of this one body, e.g., they speak the truth to one another (9:1), they think carefully and honestly about the gifts God has given them (12:5), they greet each other as people *in Christ* (ch. 16), they receive one another when they travel from one town to another (16:2), they provide for each other even when they have not known one another before (16:2).

The local or community meaning is reinforced by the parallel "in" phrases in Romans. *In the law* and *outside the law* denote a state or a community of people. The same is true of *in flesh* and *in Spirit*. To be "in" something or someone is to exist in a domain of reality, and to live within a community of people characterized by that reality.

The *with Christ* phrase is used only twice in Romans, 6:8 (*if we die with Christ*) and 8:32 (*he who did not spare his own son but gave him up for us all, will he not also give us all things with him?*). But compound words, "with" combined with another word, increase the emphasis. Four such compounds are used in Romans 6 (vv. 4, 5, 6, 8). The *with Christ* theme is used in four different ways. First, Romans 8:32 uses it without explicit reference to fellowship with Christ (God will give Christians *all things with him*). Second, the phrase is used to describe a death that Christians have died with Christ in the past. Romans 6:3-11 is the principal passage (see also Col. 2:13–3:5). Death with Christ is linked with baptism (so also in Col.), but there are other texts where the death of believers with Christ is mentioned without any reference to baptism (e.g., Gal. 2:19, 20; 6:14; 2 Tim. 2:11-12). Third, Paul speaks of a present suffering with Christ in Romans 8:17 (or present dying with him in 1 Cor. 15:31; cf. 2 Cor. 4:10-12; Phil. 3:10). Finally, there are texts that speak of a resurrection with Christ. In some the future life already is partially present (Rom. 6:4, 6; 7:4; cf. also Gal. 2:20; 2 Cor. 4:10, 11; 5:17). The resurrection with Christ is future in Romans 6:5, 8; 8:17 (cf. also 2 Cor. 4:14; 13:4; Phil. 3:21; 1 Thess. 4:14-17; Col. 3:4; it is a past event in Col. 2:12, 13).

The point of all the *with Christ* texts is that Christians are with Christ in Christ's experience, either death or resurrection. They are included in Christ; what happened to him happens to them. The formula is not concerned with how Christians experience what happened to Christ, but with the fact that they share in the historical events of his cross and resurrection. Because of Christ's death Christians have died to **Sin**. Because he was raised, Christians already experience some form of resurrection life or will enter into a new mode of life in the future. The "with" association is very one-sided; the believer is *with Christ*, not Christ with the believer. While the formula in Romans is used with the plural, it does not have the same social quality as the *in Christ* formula.

The two phrases are not equivalent, but they are linked. Those who are *in Christ* have died and risen *with him*. Those who are alive *with Christ* are *in him*. Both are used to make the case that the Christian life, "now," is different than the pre-Christian life, "then." The *with Christ* texts emphasize that it is Christ's life, death, and resurrection which Christians share; the *in Christ* texts picture the new life and the relationships which result from death and resurrection *with Christ*. *With Christ* describes the origin of the Christian life; *in Christ* defines its quality.

Both phrases picture the relationship of Christ and Christians in personal and organic terms. Behind both lies the idea that Christ is a person who includes believers. The older language used to describe this reality was corporate personality. Because of problems with that language, current language talks about solidarity or inclusive personality. Christ is an individual—e.g., Jesus, the Son of God, the Lord—but Christ is more than that. Christ is a representative figure, just as Abraham and Adam are. Believers in Christ exist in solidarity with him. The solidarity or representative aspect is defined cosmically and eschatologically in Paul rather than mystically. Christ is the first of a kind, just as Adam and Abraham were. Each is a progenitor, each initiates a community of people, each represents a whole world, an order of life and death.

Most of the *in Christ* and *with Christ* language occurs in two contexts in Romans—either as part of the interpretation of what Christ's victory over Adam and Sin means, chs. 6–8, or in the practical application of what Christ's salvation means for the way the Christians live in Rome. To be *in Christ* or to *die/live with Christ* must be interpreted in light of the other corporate images Paul uses to interpret the meaning of Christ's victory over Adam. *In Christ* or *with Christ* are in some sense synonyms for righteousness, grace, life, Spirit, all of which stand over against Adam, **Sin**, old humanity, body of sin, death, flesh. They describe what it means to be followers of Christ. Christians are people who exist in a relationship with Christ that "saves" them, that makes them participants in the death and resurrection of Jesus, and that relates them to other Christians in a new organic community in which Christ is the center and leader (the head) and which is different than other communities in the world.

See Beker, 1980:272-74; Best, 1955:1-64; Colijn, 1991; Cranfield, 1979, 2:833-35; Moule, 1977:54-69; Sanders, 1977:458-61; Wedderburn, 1985.

LAW IN ROMANS   The "law" (*nomos*) is a very important sub-theme in Romans. It is used 72 times out of a total of 119 uses in Paul's letters (compared to 32 uses in Gal., nine in 1 Cor., three in Phil.). Sixty percent of Paul's uses of "law" occur in Romans. In addition, the word "commandment" (*entolē*) is used seven times in Romans (a total of 14 uses in Paul's letters). Ten out of the sixteen chapters in Romans have something to say about the law—it is a subject in every chapter from two through 10, and is the central theme in two major sections of the letter, 2:12–3:20 (30 uses) and 7:1–8:11 (28 uses). Moreover, 10 out of 14 phrases in Paul which define the law by a genitive noun, e.g., the law of faith or the law of **Sin**, are found in Romans.

Usage alone indicates that Paul is preoccupied with the question of the law in Romans. The interpretation of this data has been the subject of much debate among scholars for centuries, a debate which remains very active to this day. The diversity of interpretations is so significant that the claim is made that the person who thinks he/she understands the meaning of the law in Paul has misunderstood Paul. Part of the problem is that Paul's use of law in Romans is read through the filter of other letters, especially Galatians.

What is Paul saying about the law in Romans (the relation to what he says in other letters is the subject of a different essay)?

The Reference of "Law"

Law has multiple connotations in Romans. Generally and most often it refers to the Mosaic Law, to the Torah of the Covenant which can be obeyed or disobeyed, done or transgressed, e.g., 2:12, 13; 5:13, 20; 7:7, 12; 13:8, 10.

But it also can be used in a more specific sense to refer to the Pentateuch, e.g., *the law and the prophets* (3:21), or it can be used more broadly to refer to the scriptures as a whole, e.g., *whatever the law says* in 3:19 as a summary category for the citations of wisdom and prophetic texts in vv. 10-18. Law also can refer to a specific commandment, e.g., marriage legislation in 7:2-3, the seventh commandment in 7:7. The law can be characterized by the use of genitive phrases, e.g., the law of God (7:25; 8:7) or of righteousness (9:31), which define the specific quality of the Mosaic Code—it comes from God and is righteous or just. But the same genitive construction also can be used to characterize a law which is against the law, e.g., *the law of **Sin*** (7:23, 25) or *the law of **Sin** and death* (8:2)—the law is linked to **Sin** and death rather than life. It is precisely these multiple references that stand behind the debate about the meaning of law in Romans and in Paul.

The Essence of the Law
Paul says some very positive things about the law in Romans. It is a special divine gift to Israel (9:4) that is holy, righteous, good, and spiritual (7:12, 14, 16; 9:31). With different terms Paul makes the claim that the essence or the character of the law is good. It comes from God and participates in the qualities that characterize God.

The Functions of the Law
The good law functions in different ways in the life of God's people.

1) *The law witnesses to the will of God.* The law is a great advantage for the Jewish people (3:2) because it discloses the will of God to Israel (2:18; 7:1-3). It helps them discern "what is really important" (2:18), because it teaches *knowledge and truth* (2:20) and testifies to the righteousness of God (3:21). Because the Jewish people have this witness—*the oracles of God* (3:2)—they have a great advantage over non-Jewish people; they know the will of God with a clarity that no other people enjoy.

2) *The law defines the identity of Israel.* The law sets the Jewish people apart from other people. In contrast to Gentiles who do not have the law by birth, they have the law by nature (2:12-14). Because of the law they call themselves "Jews" (2:17). They are a people who may be characterized as *in the law* (3:19) and *out of the law* (4:14, 16). The law defines who the Jewish people are—they are the people of the law, *resting upon the law* (2:17), instructed from the law (2:18), *having the embodiment of knowledge and truth in the law* (2:20). The law, in fact, is so defining that the Jewish people "boast" in it (2:23; 3:27) and in *the works of the law*, which mark them as distinct from "the Gentiles" [*Essay: Works of Law*]. The law is the goal that the Jewish people pursue with all of their energy (9:31), because it is their great advantage over all other people (3:2).

The law as a definer of a distinct people does not play a role in the universal revelation of God's righteousness in Messiah Jesus (3:21). That revelation is for all people—Jews and Gentiles. It, therefore, stands in continuity with the law as scripture—*the law and the prophets*—but not the law as boundary marker between peoples (3:21).

3) *The law is a contrast symbol.* The law is used in Romans to make a series of contrasts, law/promise, law/faith, law/grace (4:13-16). The promise to Abraham and "his seed" is not a function of the law but of faith. The law brings God's wrath because it defines **Sin** for the people who know the law. The law does not bring the promise. That is a function of God's grace, which is inclusive of all people. The law restricts—it is only for those who are *in the*

law—whereas faith and grace are inclusive—they are for all people.

4) *The law is a narrative of promise.* Paul reinterprets the Abraham story as a narrative of promise for all people. Abraham, the father of one of the key restricting symbols of the law (e.g., circumcision), becomes the father of faith that includes all people (3:27–4:25). Abraham's faith rather than his circumcision is the foundation of God's promise to the world. The scriptural narrative of the law redefined by faith upholds the gospel of the righteousness of God through the faithfulness of Messiah Jesus (3:31).

5) *The law defines sin.* A dominant theme in Paul's interpretation is that the law defines **Sin**—*through the law comes knowledge of* **Sin** (3:20), *where there is no law there is no transgression* (4:15), **Sin** *is not counted where there is no law* (5:13), *the law entered with the result that trespass increased* (5:20), *except for the law I would not have known* **Sin** (7:7), *apart from the law* **Sin** *lies dead* (7:8), *in order that* **Sin** *might be shown to be* **Sin***, and through the commandment might become sinful beyond measure* (7:13).

The law, because it discloses the will of God, functions to define **Sin**. It establishes boundaries, it builds a fence. To cross the boundary or to climb over the fence, that is, to transgress, is to violate the will of God, to break the law, and thus to sin. The law defines and exposes **Sin**/sin as the complete violation of the will of God.

The language of Paul is carefully nuanced. **Sin** as power is prior to the law. The law defines what **Sin** looks like in human and communal behavior, e.g., idolatry, covetousness, hatred, lust. The law does not cause **Sin**, but defines its shape as that which is exceedingly evil. **Sin** is understood and tracked as **Sin** only in light of the law (5:20 is interpreted as a result clause rather than a purpose clause—see commentary on 5:20). The law is linked to **Sin**/sin in Romans not as a causative factor, and, therefore, itself sinful, but as a definitive factor, as a definer of how sin is the manifestation of **Sin**.

The law as the definer of **Sin**/sin does stimulate sinning—*energizes the passions of sin* (7:5), provides "a military base" (opportunity) for **Sin** to attack people (7:8), revives sin (7:9). The creation of boundaries is used by **Sin** to stimulate the human imagination and will to "step over" and thus to sin. This pull of **Sin** to sin in turn "works" death (7:13).

6) *The law pronounces the judgment of God.* The effect of the law's definition of **Sin** is that it pronounces judgment upon all human sin. The *just decree of God* (1:32) demonstrates that people who transgress the law of God deserve to die. The law is a standard by which God judges people *in the law*, people who have the law (2:12). The citation of the scriptures in 3:10-18 uses texts that originally condemned the enemies of Israel but now document that all human beings—Jews and Gentiles—are under the power of **Sin** and thus accountable to judgment. *The law brings wrath*, that is the just judgment of God, on all who transgress (4:15). Only those *who are in Christ Jesus* are freed from this judgment (8:1).

7) *The law is a continuing standard for conduct.* Messiah Jesus fulfills the law (8:3-4; 10:4). God's answer to **Sin's** use of the law and its resulting judgment is a rescue mission by the Son (8:3) in which **Sin** in the power sphere of the flesh is condemned. The result is that the law weakened by the power of the flesh is overcome. The law is fulfilled in Messiah Jesus for the followers of Jesus (*among us*, 8:4). The standard of conduct in the law (the ethics of "walk" in 8:4) is fulfilled by the disciples of Jesus who live in the

power sphere of the Spirit, the power which overcomes the power of **Sin**/flesh. The Spirit enables the fulfillment of the standard of conduct in the law.

The precise shape of this fulfillment of the law is outlined in 13:8-10 as the love of the neighbor, the person in Rome who is different. Love of the neighbor does not hurt, literally, do evil to the neighbor—does not commit adultery, does not kill, does not steal, does not covet. Such love, empowered by the Spirit of Messiah Jesus (8:4), fulfills the law. The law fulfilled by Messiah Jesus continues to define the conduct of the community of Jesus followers.

The Problematic of the Law

The function of the law just outlined seems straightforward and non-controversial. The law is good and does good things, including defining the nature of **Sin**. The law makes it possible to know what **Sin** is and thus to avoid sinning. What is the problem? Why all the debate about the law in Romans?

The problematic of the law in Romans is a function of several things: 1) the linkage of the law with **Sin**, the placement of the law on the **Sin** side of the continuum of sin to grace, the definition of the law as under the control of **Sin** rather than the means of controlling **Sin**, the location of the law in the present evil age and not in the age to come. 2) The language of no longer being *under the law, died to the law, released from the law* in 6:15-7:6. 3) The defense of the law in Romans 7:7-8:11 with its notion of an anti-law, the law of **Sin** and death. 4) Closely related are the genitive descriptions of the law, e.g., the law of works, the law of faith, the works of the law. 5) The relativization of the practice of the law.

The Relation of the Law and Sin

The Judaism of Paul's day linked the law and sin in a positive way. The law was a means of grace to resist sin. Its function was to guard against sin and thus lead to deliverance and life. In contrast, Paul links the law and **Sin** negatively, and does so in a progressive fashion. At level one, the law defines **Sin**, energizes **Sin**, and results in the increase of sin (3:20; 4:15; 5:13, 20; 7:7, 8, 9, 13). At a more profound level, Paul links the law and **Sin** eschatologically. The law belongs to Adam's side of history rather than to Christ's. It is part of the present evil age introduced by the sin of Adam rather than the age of salvation introduced by Christ (5:12-21). The law's function of defining and energizing **Sin** is given eschatological validity by its connection to Adam. This validation is intensified by the linkage of the law to **Sin** rather than to grace. The law results in the increase of sin, not in the revelation or manifestation of God's grace, because Sin uses the law to nurture human transgression. The result is God's judgment and **Death** (see the exposition of 6:1f.).

The "under the law," "died to the law," and "released from the law" phrases in 6:15–7:6

Paul's discussion of the relation of **Sin**-law-**Grace** uses negative language about the law. Baptism into the community of Messiah Jesus means a transfer from the domain of the law to the domain of Grace. Membership in the community of Jesus' followers means no longer living "under the law," no longer obligated to obey all the requirements of the law.

But Paul goes even further. *My brethren*, which to him always means his Jewish kinspeople, *have died to the law* by becoming members of the body of Messiah Jesus (7:4), and *have been released from the law, having died to that which held them down* (7:6).

The Jewish followers of Messiah Jesus experience a fundamentally and, from a Jewish perspective, a radically transformed relation to the law. They are released from the obligation to obey the law's requirements because in the new domain of **Grace** they overcome **Sin** and obey the law in and through the eschatological Spirit. Paul's analysis of the law is simultaneously the most negative and the most positive in his letters. Jewish-Christians now are empowered by **Grace** and the Spirit to fulfill the law. The point is that Messiah Jesus changes their relationship to the law.

The defense of the law in chapter 7:7–8:1

Paul's defense of the law in 7:7–8:11 focuses its relation to **Sin** rather than grace. The law is good, but it is a captive of powerful eschatological forces, **Flesh** and **Sin**, which use the law to demonstrate the radical sinfulness of **Sin** and to work death rather than life. **Sin**, not the law, is responsible for evil because it uses the law against its nature and purpose and against the deep desire and intention of the Jewish people. **Sin**, in fact, as an eschatological power has created an anti-law, the law of **Sin** and death, to defeat the people of the law and deepen their captivity to **Sin**.

There is no hint in Romans of the law as a means of grace in either the Jewish sense—the law helps resist sin—or the Protestant sense—the law increases guilt to prepare the way for grace. The good law rather is used by **Sin** to document the Adamic quality of all human behavior and enslave all human beings to its power.

The law intensifies **Sin** in Israel so that God can defeat **Sin's** power through the rescue mission of the Son. The Son defeats **Sin** in its domain, the **Flesh**, to fulfill the law and to make possible its fulfillment through the Spirit, the eschatological power of God given to the followers of Messiah Jesus (see the explanation in 7:7–8:11).

The genitive descriptions of the law

The distinctive use of genitives to characterize the law in Romans (so also in Galatians)—*the law of works* (3:27), *the law of faith* (3:27), *the law of my mind* (7:23), *the law of sin* (7:23), *the law of the Spirit of life* (8:2), *the law of sin and death* (8:2), *the law of God* (8:7), *the law of righteousness* (9:31)—serve two functions. First, they make a series of contrasts:

law of works	law of faith
law of sin	law of my mind
law of sin and death	law of the Spirit of life.

The first contrast rejects any form of Jewish and Jewish-Christian boasting on two grounds: 1) the Christian affirmation that people are made righteous by faith and not works of law [*Essay: Works of Law*]; 2) the Jewish doctrine of monotheism (see the exposition of 3:27f.). The second set of contrasts (7:23–8:2) distinguish two laws, the good law of God with which the Jewish people agree, and the anti-law of **Sin**, which misuses the good law for evil (see the explanation of 7:7–8:11). The second set of genitive constructions—*law of God* and *law of righteousness*—define the quality of the law; it comes from God and is righteous.

These genitive constructions fit Paul's larger argument. The law is God's good revelation. But it is used by **Sin** to intensify the captivity of the Jewish people to the power of **Sin**.

The relativization of the practice of the law

One of the most puzzling features of Paul's interpretation is the paradox between his strong affirmation of the law and his relativization of its practice by Jewish Christian people. Circumcision is relativized by the tradition of the "circumcision of the heart" (2:25-29). Jewish food laws and Sabbath observance are relativized by the individualization of these practices—people may or may not choose to observe them (14:1f.). This principled subjectivization of law observance is significantly intensified by 1) Paul's own stance—he is on the side of the strong and is free to eat anything (14:2); 2) the patronizing characterization of people who observe the food laws as "weak"; 3) the clear assertion that food is not an important value which defines the boundaries of the Christian community (*the kingdom of God is not food and drink . . .* 14:17). While Paul legitimizes the observance of food laws in the Roman churches, he in effect relativizes the actual observance of precisely those laws which are central to first-century Jewish identity. Food laws, which are foundational for Jewish identity, are peripheral to the identity of Christian communities and thus matters of personal taste. The requirement that law observant followers of Jesus accept non-observant followers undermines the religious, social, and cultural integrity of Jewish-Christian identity.

While affirming the law as God's good revelation and insisting that he upholds the law (3:31), the effect of Paul's teaching on actual law observance is to challenge its theological foundations. He undermines the intellectual and cultural identity of Jewish Christian people by making it a matter of personal choice, a choice that must not create barriers in relationships between believers. The unity of the church—small house churches and the collectivity of churches in Rome—is more important than the observance of any food laws or holy days which define the Jewish-Christian identity of one group within the church. Paul, it would appear, affirms the law theologically but undermines it practically if its observance in any way threatens the sociological inclusiveness and unity of Christian communities. Word (theology) and deed (practice) are dissonant. If that sounds confusing in the twenty-first century, it was most problematic, even offensive and heretical, in first century Jewish and Jewish Christian communities. No wonder Paul was controversial then, and remains so now.

For further study see the following for the major literature and bibliographies to a large body of journal articles: Boyardin, 1994; Dunn, 1990a and 2001b; Hübner, 1984; Laato, 1995; Martin, 1989; Räisänen, 1983 and 1992; Sanders, 1983a; Schreiner, 1993b; Thielman, 1989 and 1994; Tomson, 1990; Westerholm, 1988.

LETTER FORM   Letter writing was a common form of communication in the ancient world. Its major function was to represent a form of "life-together" during a time of separation. That is, the letter was a substitute for actual presence; it turned absence into presence (*apousia* into *parousia*). It is not surprising, therefore, that many letters conclude with references to coming visits as a means to empower the relationship. The letter served two other functions: 1) to maintain personal contact, and 2) to impart information.

The letter had a common form—opening, body, closing. This three-part structure emerged as a substitute for spoken conversation in order to perform the three functions. The letter itself constituted presence. The opening and closing maintained personal contact. The body imparted the intended information.

Paul was the first Christian leader to popularize the letter as an authoritative form of communication within the early church. He thus exerted a primary influence in the formation of the NT apostolic letter tradition. The basic form that Paul used—opening, body, closing—followed the common letter pattern of the ancient world. His letters diverge from the common pattern at two important points. First, his letters are much longer than most and they are more extensive in all three divisions. Second, most are communal in nature. They are addressed to Christian house churches, intended to be read aloud in congregational meetings. Paul speaks to churches in his capacity as apostle, and most often as founding father. This setting and relationship helps explain some of the unusual epistolary features of his letters, e.g., the opening prayers of thanksgiving and the closing benedictions, the embedded hymns and confessions, the summarized doxologies, the appeals to scripture, the moral instructions, the combination of private opinion and official authority, the generally passionate mood.

The opening and closing of letters were fairly standardized. Paul follows the general pattern, but modifies it to suit his purposes. A comparison illustrates the similarity and the differences:

Greek Letter Openings	Paul's Openings
Prescript = introduction	Prescript
Author = superscription	Author
Addressee = ascription	Addressee
Greeting = salutation	Greeting
Health Wish	Thanksgiving
Prayer Formula	Prayer Formula
Disclosure Formula	Disclosure Formula

Apart from the length of the opening, Paul's major change is to substitute a thanksgiving section for the common "health wish." This probably reflects the influence of Hebrew letter form, which usually included a thanksgiving following the prescript.

Greek Letter Closing	Paul's Closing
Final Wish	Hortatory Remarks
Greetings	Peace Wish
Health Wish	Greetings
	Holy Kiss Greeting
	Grace Benediction

The bodies of Paul's letters are less stereotyped than the opening and closing patterns. This is expected in letters since the body conveys the specific message that the occasion requires. The one exception to this greater freedom is the form of the "body closing," the section of the body proper that concludes the body and precedes the closing. The standardized "body closing" has three parts: 1) a statement on the motivation for writing; 2) a responsibility clause outlining what is expected of the recipients; and 3) the promise of a visit. Paul modifies this "body closing" form by combining the motivation for writing and responsibility clauses, and inserts a "confidence formula," in which he expresses confidence in the reader's faith and ability to follow through on his teachings. He concludes the body-closing with the promise of a visit.

For further reading, see Aune, 1987; Gamble, 1977; Kennedy, 1984; Stowers, 1986; White, 1972; Yoder Neufeld: 351-53.

LIVING IN THE SPIRIT The life of the Jesus follower for Paul is primarily *life in the Spirit*. The Spirit is referred to 138 times in the Pauline letters (an additional seven times in the Pastoral Letters). The vast majority of these references are to the Holy Spirit, that is, the Spirit of God (125 out of 138). Romans and 1 Corinthians contain the most references, 31 and 36 respectively. Of the 31 references to the Spirit in Romans, 21 occur in chapter 8. This chapter, Romans 8, is one of Paul's clearest and most expansive statements on the Spirit, specifically on the Christian life as life in the Spirit.

The Spirit is the answer to the power of **Sin/Flesh** and the ensuing weakness of the law. That is, what the law was not powerful enough to do—overcome the power of **Sin/Flesh**—the Spirit makes possible. Paul characterizes life in the Spirit in five ways in Romans 8.

Liberation from Sin

The antidote to the *law of Sin and Death*, the personified powers of evil which make the law impotent and enslave Israel, is the *law of the Spirit of life in Messiah Jesus*. Both "laws" are constructs of Paul to interpret the meaning of the "two laws" in 7:7-12, the Torah of God and *the law of Sin*. The Torah of God gives the life intended by God for the law through the Spirit in the context of the people of Jesus. In addition, the Spirit liberates from the "law of **Sin** and **Death**."

One of the key understandings of God in Israel is that Yahweh is "the living God" in contrast to the dead idols of the nations. The "living God" of Israel gave the law to liberate Israel from evil. What the law was not able to do because of its enslavement by the cosmic power of **Sin** God does through another cosmic power, the **Spirit of God**. God gives life and freedom from **Sin** through the **Spirit** in the context of the believing community. Therefore, there is no eschatological judgment, *no condemnation for those in Messiah Jesus*.

In 8:10 Paul adds that those whom "Christ indwells" (*Spirit of God indwells* in v. 8) experience the Spirit of life *because of righteousness*. Because Christ has put followers of Jesus in a right relationship with God, they experience eschatological life, and that despite the fact that their bodies are dead *because of the power of Sin*. And in 8:13 the Spirit gives life by empowering believers to *put to death the practices of the body*.

Fulfillment of the Law

The Spirit enables the fulfillment of the Law. The law is the central focus of the long sentence in 8:3-4—it begins and ends with the law, *for the law weakened by the flesh . . . in order that the righteous requirement of the law . . . .* The problem of the weakness of the law is overcome by Jesus condemning **Sin** in the **Flesh**. The purpose of this redemptive action is *that the righteous requirement of the law might be fulfilled in us . . . who walk according to the Spirit*. The good and righteous law of God is fulfilled by the power of the Spirit, by those who live in the power domain of the Spirit. It is not fulfilled by those who observe the law—e.g., food and festival laws in ch. 14—but by the Spirit (see Gal. 5:13-25 for a similar claim).

Gordon Fee is correct to suggest that Paul interprets the law via a chiastic structure in 7:7-8:4:

A   The law is good, just, holy (7:13)—[the first law]
    B   The law is used by another law (7:14-24)—[the second law]
       C   The law of the Spirit of life (8:2a)—[the third law]
    B   The third law sets free from the second law (8:2b)
A   The third law fulfills the intent of the first law (8:3-4) (see Fee, 1994:525)

The effectiveness of the Spirit's enablement of law fulfillment is detailed in 8:5-8. The people who live *according to the Spirit* live out the goals of the law—submission to the law, life, peace, please God. The great aspirations of the Jewish people—to experience God's eschatological life in the present, to experience wholeness in all relationships, to please and honor God—by submitting to the good and holy law of God are achieved by living in the Spirit. Paul says the same thing in different words in 14:17—the *righteousness, peace, and joy* of the Kingdom of God, the goal of Jewish life and law observance, come from the Holy Spirit, not from observing Jewish food laws.

Fulfilling the law through living in the Spirit is contrasted with another way of living. Those who live *according to the flesh* achieve none of these goals—they do not submit to the law, they live in a relationship of hostility to God, and they are unable to please God. The law is fulfilled only through life in the Spirit. The expression of that fulfillment is love of neighbor (13:8).

New Identity

The Spirit who liberates from **Sin**, who gives life, and who enables the fulfillment of the law gives followers of Jesus a new identity. They are adopted as children of *God—they are sons of God* (8:14), they receive the *Spirit of sonship* of the eschatological kingdom which overcomes the *spirit of slavery* of the present evil age (8:15), they pray Jesus' prayer of familial intimacy with God, *Abba Father* (8:15), they experience the reality that they are children of God (8:16), they become *coheirs with Christ* of God's inheritance (8:17). The hopes and dreams of the Jewish people are experienced by those who live in the Spirit.

Divine Assistance and Future Hope

The Spirit who gives followers of Jesus a new identity assists them in the present by standing alongside to lighten the burden of weakness by facilitating communication with God that is consistent with the divine will.

The Spirit offers eschatological hope. The future is bright for those who live in the Spirit. They have the assurance that the Spirit will give life to their *dying bodies*, just as Jesus was given new life in the resurrection from the dead (8:11). The presence of the Spirit represents the *first fruits*, the guarantee, of the eschatological redemption of their bodies, that is, the resurrection from the dead (8:23). The new life of the Spirit now will be transformed into eschatological life.

Conclusion

The presence of the Spirit defines those who are followers of Jesus. Disciples of Jesus are people who live in the Spirit. The lives of believers are characterized by *living in the Spirit*. The believer's faith response is the means of appropriating "the redemption in Messiah Jesus, of appropriating the revelation of the righteousness of God through Messiah Jesus. The Christian life in Romans, however, is portrayed primarily as a life empowered by living in the Spirit.

See Fee, 1994:472-634, for the most comprehensive study of the Spirit in Paul, including Romans.

NATURAL THEOLOGY Romans 1:19-21 and 2:14-15 have been the classical center for arguing that Paul taught a natural theology (so especially Roman Catholic theology and much mainline Protestant thought). The argument is that Paul's thought here reflects either dependence on or similarity to Stoic natural theology as mediated through Hellenistic Judaism.

Stoicism was an ancient school of philosophy current with the early centuries of the church. Stoic cosmology (origin and nature of the world) taught that the creative and unifying principle of the world was a reality called one of many different names: spirit (*pneuma*), reason (*logos*), nature (*physis*), common law (*nomos*), god (*theos*). This "reason" or "nature," often called a natural law, is prior to creation and governs the universe. It may be discerned by the careful observation of nature. The goal of human beings is to live in conformity to "nature" or "reason." This law of nature is eternal and unchangeable. "Justice" is established by nature. The laws of human communities are valid to the degree they are in harmony with this natural law. Laws are needed for human communities because most people do not participate sufficiently in the "reason" to live in harmony with "nature." Wise men (the Stoics were very gender specific), however, are "self-sufficient," because they live in harmony with "nature," and thus do not need local laws. Cosmology and ethics are thus linked in a rigorous and closely reasoned ethical system.

A careful reading of Romans 1 and 2 indicates that Paul knows nothing of Stoic "natural theology." 1) Paul's focus is the judgment of God, not the creation of the universe. 2) He does not have an independent doctrine of creation. Creation theology in Paul is a function of theology proper, talk about God, and anthropology, talk about the creatureliness of humanity. 3) Paul makes no reference to the order of the universe (*dioikesis* or *taxis*) as a base for knowledge of God. Knowledge of God is not perceived as a problem, but is presupposed as self-evident for everyone. 4) Paul does not argue that God can be deduced from divine works, and, therefore, humanity should have deduced God, the form of the argument in Hellenistic Judaism. Rather, he asserts that humanity did know God. The problem is that human beings did not give glory and thanks. 5) Paul does not argue that people naturally do the will of God. The point of 2:14 is that the Gentiles do not have the law by nature of their birth and cultural-religious inheritance, not that they naturally do what the law requires. 6) The rhetoric in Romans is not philosophical (especially metaphysical) speculation, but prophetic accusation. The purpose is not to reason from below to above, but to assert the "excuselessness" of the creature before the Creator. Paul is not seeking to explain a point of contact with the divine, but to characterize God as powerful lord and humanity as in revolt against the known lord. The focus on the power and lordship of God is to emphasize the creatureliness of humanity. That creatureliness is evidence of God's lordship. As Guenther Bornkamm says so well, Paul does not "infer God's being from the world, but . . . the being of the world from God's revelation" (1969:59). 7) Paul knows nothing of "self-sufficient" human beings. All humans are creatures who worship a god or the God.

Natural theology is foreign to Paul. He knows only of revealed theology.

See Bornkamm, 1969:47-70; Käsemann, 1980:39-43; McKenzie, 1964.

OBEDIENCE "Obedience" is an important term in Romans. Its importance exceeds its numerical occurrence—the noun (*hypakoē*) is used seven times (out of 11 times in the letters of Paul and 15 times in the NT) while the verb (*hypakouō*) is used four times (out of 11 in the letters ascribed to Paul and 21 in the NT).

The word is a compound made up of the noun "hear" (*akoē*) and the preposition "under" (*hypo*). It literally means to "hear under," that is, to respond properly to hearing. Significantly, there is no word in Hebrew for "obey." The Septuagint translates the Hebrew Shema, *hear, O Israel, the Lord is our God, the Lord is one* (Dt. 6:4) as "obey," that is respond appropriately. To hear properly is intimately associated with the covenant—*love the Lord your God . . . keep the words I have commanded you . . . recite them to your children*.

Two things make obedience an important word in Romans. First, it defines the purpose of the letter in 1:5 and 16:26 as *the obedience of faith*. The letter is framed by this phrase. That framing is reinforced by another one—in 1:6 the faith of the Roman Christians *is proclaimed in all the world* while in 16:19 it is the obedience of the same people that *is known to all*. Faith and obedience are linked as equivalents in the frame of the letter.

This framing is significant also because Paul identifies the specific audience he has in mind when he speaks of *the obedience of faith—the obedience of faith among all the Gentiles in behalf of his [God's] name* (1:5) and *to the obedience of the Gentiles in word and work* (15:18). Paul is specifically concerned in Romans about the obedience of the Gentiles.

The second important thing about obedience in Romans is that it is a paradigmatic term, both in an eschatological and an ethical sense. The *obedience of the one*, that is Christ, reverses the *disobedience of one man*, that is Adam (5:12-21). The obedience of Christ makes many righteous just as Adam's disobedience made many sinners. Disobedience and obedience effect a cosmic and eschatological understanding of history. Disobedience introduces **Sin**, **Death**, and condemnation into the world. Obedience introduces life, grace, justice, and righteousness. Obedience is understood apocalyptically; it effects the change of the ages.

Precisely because obedience is eschatologically paradigmatic, it also is paradigmatic for the ethics of the Roman Christians. Paul defines life in Romans 6 as obedience to the slavery of **Sin** or to the slavery of righteousness. Everyone is conceived of as in slavery. Christians are people who were slaves of **Sin** and thus obeyed it. Now, however, they are people who have been set free from this slavery and become *obedient to righteousness* (6:16-18).

Obedience is also defined by its opposite in Romans. The problem of the Jews in 10:16 and 21 is that they have not *obeyed the gospel* which they heard. In 9:31-32 the problem was defined as *not out of faith*. Not trusting and not hearing properly are synonyms.

The answer to all humans being bound together in disobedience is the *obedience of faith*. The proper response to the end-time fulfillment of God's righteous salvation in Messiah Jesus is trusting and obeying. Faith expresses itself in obedience and obedience is evidence of faith. To speak of faith is to speak of obedience.

The linkage of faith and obedience in Romans underlines Paul's covenantal understanding of the Christian faith and church. Gentile Christians are becoming part of God's people and are expected to respond properly, that is, become *slaves of righteousness* and *obey the type of teaching* they have received (6:15-23).

See Miller, 2000; Nanos, 1996:218-37.

ORIGINAL SIN Romans 5:12 is the primary basis for the Christian doctrine of original sin. The words "original sin" are not found in this text, or in the Bible. They are a translation of the Latin *peccatum originale*, and stem from the fourth century Christian theologian Augustine.

Two things are important for understanding Augustine's interpretation. First, he was exegeting the Latin Vulgate, which translated the Greek *ep' hō pantes hēmarton, because* (literally, in which) *all sinned*, as in *quo omnes peccaverunt, in whom all have sinned*. The Vulgate translation does not identify the antecedent of "in whom," nor had anyone else before Augustine made this identification. Augustine identified the reference of "in whom" as Adam. So, for Augustine, "all sinned in Adam." Second, he formulated his theology of original sin in his conflict with Pelagius, who taught that Adam influenced humanity by being a bad example. Sin spread from Adam "by imitation," by people's voluntary imitation of Adam (the will is capable of choosing). Augustine responded that sin spread "by propagation, not imitation." He defined the link between Adam and subsequent human beings biologically; sin was transmitted from Adam through the male semen (the "seminal transmission of sin"). Therefore, human beings are totally corrupt and incapable of willing or doing good (the will is incapable of choosing).

It must be emphasized that the doctrine of original sin is an interpretation of the text, more accurately a misinterpretation of the text. Paul only asserts a causal connection between Adam and the spread of **Sin** as power in the world. He does not discuss or define the nature of the causality.

Despite the problematic of Augustine's interpretation, it became the dominant understanding of the text in western theology, and had enormous consequences in the development of Christian theology. For example, it served as the ground for infant baptism, the washing away of the inherited original sin with which every person was born. It is the basis for the interpretation of the virgin birth as necessary to break the seminal transmission from the male, Joseph, through the female carrier, Mary, to the child Jesus. No biblical text, of course, teaches either of these; they represent theological misinterpretations, built on a theological misinterpretation.

Scholars today generally reject Augustine's interpretation of Romans 5:12. The text simply asserts a causal connection that is best translated as *because all sinned*. The *because all sinned* does not point back directly to *the one person*, but explains the cause of the preceding statement, *and so death spread to all because all sinned*.

The sixteenth-century Anabaptists consistently rejected Augustine's notion of original sin, and thus also the crippling of the human will.

For a more detailed study of Augustine's interpretation, see De Brun, 1988; Burns, 1979; Greer, 1995:382-94; Reid, 1996; Rondet, 1972; Weaver, 1983 and 1985.

For the Anabaptist rejection of original sin, see Friedman, 1952; Weingart, 1994; van der Zijpp, 1959.

RIGHTEOUSNESS Righteousness language is used in the following ways in Romans: righteous (*dikaios*) seven out of 17 times in Paul; righteousness (*dikaiosunē*) 33/57; make righteous, the verb (*dikaiō*) 15/27; righteous requirement in 1:32; 2:26; 8:4 and rightwising act in 5:16, 18 (*dikaiōma*) 5/5; rightwiseness (*dikaiōsis*) 2/2; righteous judgment or Righteous Judge (*dikaiokrisia*) 1/1; righteousness of God (*dikaiosunē theou*) 8/10.

The Meaning of Righteousness
The Latin translated "righteousness" (*dikaiosunē*) with "justice" (*iustitia*). The sense of the Latin is impartiality, fairness, in judgment, especially in the giving of rewards and punishment. The standard for measuring fairness is deter-

mined by relation to an absolute norm, a legality. The norm in turn is derived from an absolute idea of justice. It is a legal term associated with the law courts. Righteousness is understood as distributive justice on the basis of this background. It is concerned with rendering to each what is fair.

The background to righteousness in Paul is Hebrew (*tsedeq/tsedaqah*) and the Greek (*dikaiosunē*), not Latin. In the ancient world righteousness language generally was relational, ethical language. The basic meaning was the right ordering of things. It was associated with the ancient Near Eastern concept of cosmic and/or social order. The essential idea was faithfulness within patterns of relationships that guarantee, preserve, and enhance the order of the world and society.

Righteousness in the *Old Testament* is faithfulness within the demands of a relationship, either with God or with fellow human beings. Action or behavior is righteous when it maintains and builds the relationship and supports the social order of which it is a part. Generally, the righteous person in Israel is the one who preserves the peace and wholeness of the community by fulfilling the demands of communal living. In fact, righteous (*tsedeq*) frequently stands parallel to peace (*shalom*, Isa. 48:18; 60:17; cf. Pss. 72:3, 7; 85:10). The unrighteous person is the "evildoer," because he/she destroys the community by failing to fulfill the demands of relationships.

Righteousness is often associated with "to judge" or "judgment" because determination of faithfulness in relationship occurs "at the gate," the legal context of ancient Israel. Thus, in one sense righteousness is a legal term. He/she who is righteous is judged to be in the right. That which is right is that which fulfills the demands of relationship in community. The function of the judge is to maintain the community, and to restore the right to those from whom it has been taken. Thus righteousness as legal language is not concerned with an impartial legal decision between two people but rather with protecting and restoring relationships in community.

The context for righteousness language in the Old Testament is the covenant. Righteousness is concerned with loyalty to the covenant in relationship to God and within the community. It speaks of faithfulness in covenant relationships, God as faithful in the covenant and Israel as faithful in relationship to God and to fellow Israelites. The concern is the right ordering of the world according to God's intention, with a special bias toward the poor and the outcast (a German writer H. H. Schmid, in *Righteousness as the Ordering of the World*, captures the meaning well). Righteousness is primarily social-ethical language, and only minimally a legal term. And when it is legal it is also ethical. The question answered by righteousness language is how to keep faith with God and the covenant.

The standard of righteousness in the OT is Yahweh. God's righteousness fulfills the demands of the covenant relationship and restores persons deprived of the covenant relationship, especially the needy, oppressed, and hungry. The righteousness of God is pictured as victory (Judg. 5:1; 1 Sam. 12:7; Mic. 6:5), as a king who regulates the life of his people (Pss. 50; 72), or as judge (Pss. 9:4, 8; 50:6; 96:13; Isa. 5:16; 58:2; Jer. 11:20). In some later writings (Isa. 40–66; Pss. 96; 98; 143) God's righteousness describes the redemptive acts by which God restores the covenant people. Righteousness becomes synonymous with salvation, and is universalized. These writings also increasingly picture God's righteousness as end-time (eschatological) action; God will save Israel in the future. And some associate the end-time manifestation of God's

402   **Essays**

righteousness with an expected messianic figure (Jer. 23:5-6; Pss. 72:1-4, 7; 96:13; Isa. 9:7; 11:1-2, 5; 53:10b-11; Mal. 4:2).

In the *Dead Sea Scrolls* the basic meaning of righteous is proper conduct according to the Torah as interpreted by the Teacher of Righteousness in the community. The concern is the right ordering of the community in light of the imminent end of history. The context is the covenant purity of the community in the desert. The means of righteousness is God's saving activity and obedience to the Teacher's interpretation of the Torah. The question answered by righteousness language is how to prepare a community for the end-time coming of the Kingdom of God.

The righteousness of God is pictured in contrast to the unrighteousness of the people (1QS 1:21-24; 1QH 1:26; 4:21), and in terms of divine mercy (1QH 1:31ff.; 5:6; 9:34; 11:14). But the righteousness of God is supremely God's eschatological saving power.

It is clear that righteousness in a Jewish context concerns social-ethical relations in the faith community. The same fundamental meaning is also apparent in *Aristotle*, the key definer of the term in Greek literature. Righteousness concerns behavior that is right and good for the city state (*polis*), the basic political association of Greek civilization. The concern is the right ordering and well-being of the community as a whole. The context of Aristotle's discussion of righteousness is the re-ordering of life in the city state in the midst of socio-political breakdown. The means of attaining righteousness is obedience to the law and the practice of virtue. The question answered by righteousness is how to live in community.

One other figure in the ancient world is critical to understanding what happens to the meaning of righteousness—Augustine. His discussion of righteousness is the first significant exposition in the early church, and it establishes the framework for future discussions. The language in Augustine shifts from Hebrew and Greek to Latin. That transference results in a fundamental alteration in the concept of righteousness, from a theologically centered understanding to a human centered one. A consequence of this shift is that righteousness in the western church becomes concerned with the meaning of the justification of humanity, i.e., with questions, such as: what was the nature of this righteousness within humanity, how did it get there, and where did it come from?

Augustine is preoccupied with how human beings become righteous. Because he is reacting against a Pelagian exaggeration of fallen humanity's abilities, the critical issues become a radical distinction between God's righteousness and human righteousness, and the nature of human free will. Augustine argues that while God is perfectly righteous, humanity can never be so. Second, Augustine teaches that human free will has been taken captive by sin and cannot function properly; it does not avail for righteousness unless it is set free by divine action. God initiates making humans righteous, and then cooperates with the renewed will to enable the human to perform righteous works. Making humans righteous, therefore, is an act of divine mercy, an entirely divine work, not a human one. At one level Augustine reads righteous language in light of a works/grace tension. Grace and righteousness become identical. Humans become righteous only by God's graceful action of "making them right," never by works. Righteousness language becomes individualistic and human centered. Central to this understanding is Augustine's view of the righteousness of God, which is not that righteousness by which God is righteous but that by which God makes righteous the sinner. In terms of the Reformation and post-Reformation debate, "the righteousness of God" is God's gift to humanity.

But at another level Augustine has an all-embracing understanding of righteousness. It includes both the event of making righteous (brought about by the operative grace of God) and the process of being made righteous (brought about by the cooperative grace of God). Augustine does not distinguish these two aspects of God's saving work, as the Reformation does. The renewal of the divine image in making righteous amounts to a new creation. Making humans righteous is inherent rather than imputed, again to use the language of the sixteenth century. The Christian does not merely receive the status of righteousness, but becomes a righteous person. Therefore, only the Christian can act righteously. Pagans can perform good deeds, but neither they are nor their actions are righteous. Thus Augustine's ethics is closely related to his doctrine of making righteous. And, similarly, his political theology is closely associated with his doctrine of righteousness. Only within the city of God can one find true justice, which is synonymous with the right ordering of human affairs according to the will of God. The context of the concern is the city of God in the midst of the collapsing Roman Empire. The question answered here is how to build a Christian social order in a collapsing world.

What is clear is that righteousness in the ancient world is fundamentally concerned with the proper ordering of life and community. It concerns proper relationships in community. Righteousness is consistently ethical-political-social language. Augustine, however, while sharing this larger ancient perspective also introduces a shift in his concern for the question of how human beings become righteous before God.

The shift introduced by Augustine becomes a landslide with Martin Luther. The basic meaning of righteousness becomes a legal (forensic) declaration that a person has right status with God, or is acceptable before God. "The righteousness of God" describes God's gift of right status to sinful human beings. In other words, righteousness involves a change of status, not of being or nature. To be made righteous is an act of God external to humanity. The alien righteousness of Christ is imputed to men and women. It is an act of God toward humanity, not an act of God within human beings. The wicked are not made righteous, as in Augustine, but only proclaimed righteous. Furthermore, righteousness is distinguished sharply from sanctification, the work of God within human beings. The concern is personal acceptance before God. The context is the Reformation preoccupation with God as the perfectly righteous judge and the scrupulous conscience of the medieval penance system. There is no salvation apart from the confession of and penance for *all* sins (conscious and unconscious). The means of making righteous is the divine declaration of right standing and the human act of faith. The question being answered is how sinful human beings can find acceptance in the sight of God.

Luther's interpretation is a completely new development. It takes the human centered half of Augustine, but not the ethical-political half. Luther transforms social-political-ethical language into psychological-salvation language. Righteousness has nothing to do with relationships in the believing community or with the ordering of the world. Being made righteous is something that happens to an individual believer when in faith he/she accepts Christ's atonement on the cross.

The Protestant Paradigm

A Protestant paradigm of the meaning of righteousness emerged out of Luther's understanding. That paradigm may be summarized as follows: 1) God is perfectly righteous; 2) righteousness is a requirement for personal salvation; 3) humanity is unable to be righteous; 4) humanity's only chance is God's merciful declaration of legal right standing; 5) God declares humans righteous by a legal declaration (a forensic act).

The ultimate concern of the Protestant paradigm is how people become righteous before God so that they can be saved. Righteousness concerns a quest for the gracious God. Acceptance before God is not by work, but by sheer grace. Being made righteous resolves the quest for a gracious God. It is an event between God and the individual that makes individual men and women acceptable before God.

This Protestant paradigm has dominated the understanding of righteousness and the interpretation of Romans since the Reformation. It takes on different forms in different eras, but the basic model remains the same. Righteousness gets translated in Rudolf Bultmann into an action by God in which the individual is removed from his/her inauthenticity, e.g., rebelliousness, hypocrisy. To be made righteous means to receive authentic self-understanding. It brings healing to the individual so that he/she can become a true self. In Robert Schuler, righteousness becomes self-acceptance; God accepts me so that I can accept myself. What we get in this Protestant model is a subjective, individualistic interpretation of righteousness. It concerns an event between God and "me." Righteousness does not address the questions of relationship in the believing community or in the world; it is not concerned with social and/or communal right ordering of relationships in the church or in the world.

The Challenge to the Protestant Paradigm

In 1900 H. Cremer launched a challenge to the Protestant way of reading Paul's righteousness language. Righteousness in Paul, he argued, is OT covenant language. Thus, it is a relational rather than a legal concept, and as such, is concerned with right relationships within the covenant community. Israelites entered the covenant relationship on the basis of God's election, an act of love and mercy, never by keeping the law. They maintained the covenant relationship by loyalty to the covenant, not by legal perfection. The righteousness of God describes God's covenant faithfulness. It is a statement about the nature of God as the covenant God. God is the One who keeps faith with the covenant by delivering Israel, by leading her to shalom, by keeping promises with Israel. God's righteousness pictures God's saving presence as warrior-king in Israel to order her life.

Cremer made little impact on the understanding of righteousness until E. Käsemann issued a new challenge in 1961. Käsemann argued that righteousness is OT relational and covenant language, and that the phrase "the righteousness of God" was a technical term in Jewish apocalyptic literature that focused on God's faithfulness to the covenant [*Essay: Righteousness of God*].

Käsemann's interpretation of righteousness (supported by a series of his students) shaped a new consensus among NT scholars by the mid-1970s that understands righteousness as being concerned with appropriate relationships within the covenant.

For further reading, see M. Barth, 1968; Beker, 1980; Dahl, 1977b:95-

120; Dunn and Suggate, 1993; Hays, 1992:1129-33; Hill, 1967; McGrath, 1986; J. Reumann, 1982; Scullion and Reumann, 1992:724-73; Stendahl, 1976; Stuhlmacher, 1986; Ziesler, 1972; Wright, 1980:13-37.

THE RIGHTEOUSNESS OF GOD Eighty percent of the *righteousness of God* phrases in Paul are found in Romans (1:17; 3:5, 21, 22, 25, 26; 10:3 [2x]). The other two occurrences are 2 Cor. 5:21; 9:9.

The critical issue is the meaning of the genitive, "of God," in the phrase. The genitive is the case of possession. There are three grammatical options to its interpretation. 1) It can be an objective genitive; the genitive is the object of the action implied by the noun. The righteousness of God means "the righteousness which is acceptable in God's sight." 2) It can be a genitive of author or origin; the genitive describes the source of the action implied in the noun. The righteousness of God is the righteousness which proceeds from God and is bestowed on the believer as an alien righteousness. 3) It can be a subjective genitive; the genitive describes the nature or character of the subject implied in the noun. The righteousness of God is the righteousness which belongs to God; it describes the character of God as the righteous God who is and acts righteously in all relationships.

The first two options are so similar that they can be treated as one (an increasingly common pattern in the literature dealing with this issue). The interpretive options then are: 1) genitive of authorship, God gives righteousness. The focus is on the gift of righteousness to humanity. The concern is the standing of the believer before God. The righteousness of God is the righteousness that comes from God to the believer. The believer receives "an alien righteousness" that gives him/her right standing with God. Righteousness is salvation seen in relation to human possibility. It answers the question, "how can I as an individual find a gracious God?" Righteousness is understood as a legal (forensic) term; it is not something a person has on his/her own, but something he/she receives in the verdict of the law court. Faith becomes the condition for the reception of righteousness. (So e.g., M. Luther, J. Calvin, R. Bultmann, A. Nygren, C. E. B. Cranfield). 2) Subjective genitive, God is righteous. The focus is God's nature and activity. The concern is the character of God. Righteousness speaks of a saving God and of God's saving activity. God's righteousness is the power which brings salvation to pass. The gift of righteousness which God gives partakes of the character of power. It is the means by which God subordinates creation to divine lordship. It answers the question, "is God faithful to the promises to Israel?" Righteousness is end-time language that depicts God faithfully keeping promises by the exercise of sovereign power in the world. Faith is the product of the righteousness of God (so Schlatter, Käsemann).

Luther interpreted the phrase as an objective genitive; it describes the gift of right status with God. Literally, Luther translated the righteousness of God as "the righteousness which is acceptable before God." Luther's interpretation dominated the understanding of the phrase and Romans until the early twentieth century. In 1900 Cremer challenged his interpretation and made the case that the righteousness of God refers to the covenant faithfulness of God (it is a subjective genitive). Cremer was followed in 1933 by A. Schlatter, who argued that the phrase describes the nature of God (a subjective genitive), not the legal gift of God (an objective genitive).

The critical turning point in interpretation came with Käsemann in 1961.

He argued not only that the phrase was a technical term in Jewish literature that focused on God's faithfulness to the covenant, but also that it pointed to the redemptive activity of God, not human oriented gift. Second, Käsemann made the case for the subjective genitive interpretation of the phrase (it describes the nature of God). Third, he argued that the gift character of God's righteousness in Jewish intertestamental literature is tied to the power character of God. The righteousness of God involves a change of lordship and a transformation of existence. It denotes God's extension of divine lordship over God's people and the entire creation to transform and make right.

Käsemann with the help of his students has again shaped a new consensus about the meaning of the righteousness of God. That consensus may be outlined as follows: 1) The OT concept of God's saving activity on behalf of Israel, seen in the context of God's faithfulness, is the theological backdrop of Paul's thinking on the righteousness of God. 2) The more immediate historical context of Paul's understanding is apocalyptic Judaism with its emphasis on God's righteousness as victory over all creation. 3) The genitive in the phrase is a subjective genitive that describes the nature and activity of God. 4) The meaning of "the righteousness of God" in the pre-Pauline tradition was determined by at least three different fields of meaning: a) the righteousness of God denotes the sovereignty of God as Lord over creation; b) the world (cosmos) is the forum for a judicial trial between God and Israel and/or the world; c) the end-time judgment in which God will manifest faithfulness once and for all is imminent. 5) Paul used the righteousness of God shaped by these connotations, and transformed it with his Christ centered gospel. 6) The righteousness of God for Paul is the end-time redemptive activity of God that renews and universalizes the covenant with Israel to include the entire creation. God acts redemptively in the Christ event on behalf of all humanity and creation. 7) The judicial-legal connotations of the righteousness of God are overshadowed by the lordship-eschatological meanings. The phrase asserts that God is establishing divine Lordship over the creation. God is putting humanity in the right, and thereby calling for life in obedience to divine lordship. In other words, the making righteous of human beings is more than simply a proclamation of right status; it is an "effective declaration" that places people under God's sovereign lordship and calls for their obedience to it.

This commentary understands the righteousness of God as a statement about God's nature and saving activity. That judgment is based on the following arguments. 1) The word cradle of the righteousness of God in vv. 16-18, the first and key use of the phrase in Romans, is gospel, the power of God, salvation, revelation, faithfulness, all words that describe God's nature and activity rather than gift. Furthermore, the two parallel phrases *power of God* and *wrath of God* are statements about the nature of God (subjective genitives). 2) Paul never associates the righteousness of God with giving (*didōnai*) or receiving (*lambanein*) language. The righteousness of God is not a gift that is received in Paul. This observation is especially clear when the righteousness of God and righteousness are compared. The righteousness of God is revealed, shown up, manifested, demonstrated, and can be known (1:17; 3:5, 21, 25; 10:3). What Paul says about the righteousness of God he does not say about righteousness (ch. 4; 5:17, 21; 8:10; 9:30; 10:4, 10; 14:17), and he does not say about righteousness what he says about the righteousness of God. Righteousness is a gift of God, the righteousness of God describes the activity of God. What is true of Paul is also true in prior Jewish literature. The righteousness of God refers to God's activity rather than gift (even Bultmann admits this). 3) Paul does not explain the meaning of the term. We, therefore, must assume that his readers were familiar with it from their scriptures, the Jewish Bible (our OT). As we have seen, the righteousness of God in the OT refers to God's covenant and saving faithfulness to Israel in history and in the eschatological future. 4) Whether the righteousness of God was a technical term in apocalyptic Judaism, as Käsemann and students argued, may be disputed because the precise phrase does not occur that often. But the meaning of God's sovereign and victorious extension of divine lordship over all creation is clear. Paul radicalized this understanding. The righteousness of God is God's sovereignty, God's power in v. 16, over the world revealing itself in Jesus Christ.

This understanding is confirmed by Paul's other uses of the phrase in Romans and 2 Corinthians.

The phrase occurs in 3:1-8 in the context of several contrasts:

human unfaithfulness	the faithfulness of God
human untruth	God is true
human unrighteousness	the righteousness of God
my untruthfulness	the truth of God

The righteousness of God is paralleled with *the faithfulness of God* and *the truth of God*. All three phrases describe the nature of God in contrast to human nature. The *righteousness of God* is the faithful and true saving power of God that overcomes human unfaithfulness, untruthfulness, and unrighteousness.

Romans 3:21-26 offers the clearest exposition of the righteousness of God in Paul. It is manifested *through the faithfulness of Jesus . . . to prove God's righteousness . . . that God may be righteous and the one making righteous* (see the explanatory notes on 3:21-26). It is the saving activity of God through Jesus Christ which demonstrates divine righteousness and the capacity to make righteous human beings.

In 10:1-4 the Jews do not know the righteousness of God, because they are seeking to establish their *own righteousness* rather than *submit* to the righteousness of God. The righteousness of God contrasts with Jewish national pride; their *own righteousness* refers to an exclusive ethnic definition that excludes other people. The righteousness of God has to describe the character of God; the issue is submitting to someone, not receiving or rejecting a gift. Christ is the one who makes righteousness available to everyone for salvation.

In 2 Corinthians 5:21 God made Christ sin so that believers could *become the righteousness of God in him*. God is the subject who makes believers like God. The righteousness of God describes God's saving and powerful activity.

His righteousness in 2 Corinthians 9:9 clearly describes the character of God. Psalm 111:9 is cited to assert that God's righteousness remains forever.

A similar, but slightly different, phrase in Philippians 3:2-11 confirms the preceding analysis. *The righteousness from God (ek theou)* is contrasted with confidence in the flesh and righteousness that comes from the law. The righteousness from God comes through the faith of Christ and is based on faith. The righteousness that comes from God is a saving power that profoundly changes Paul.

For further reading, see Dunn, 1992b; Dunn and Suggate, 1993; Hays, 1992:1129-33, and 1983; Käsemann, 1969b:168-82; Reumann, 1982; Soards, 1985 and 1991; Williams, 1980.

SALVATION-JUDGMENT BY WORKS Romans 2 contains a set of texts that have been very troubling in the interpretation of Paul. Does Paul teach salvation and judgment by works in vv. 6-7 (*he will render to everyone according to their works, to those who by patience in well-doing seek for glory and honor and immortality, he will give eternal life*), v. 10 (*. . . glory and honor and peace for everyone who does good*), v. 13 (*the ones doing the law will be made righteous*), v. 14 (*when Gentiles . . . do the things of the law . . .*), vv. 25-27 (*those who . . . keep the law will condemn those who do not*)?

Romans 2 seems to contradict what Paul says in 3:20, *no human being will be justified in his sight by works of law*, and the whole theology of justification by faith in the rest of the letter. The most common ways of interpreting these texts are: 1) they reflect a holdover from Paul's Jewish past which he has not yet overcome; 2) Paul is speaking hypothetically as if the law could be fulfilled (which we know is not possible); 3) Paul is speaking of Gentile Christians who fulfill the law through faith in Christ and life in the Spirit; 4) Paul contradicts himself. Each of these interpretations has serious problems.

The text should be read as is. The theme in 2:6-7 and 10 is impartial judgment according to works. The theme of judgment by works is an important teaching of Paul (see Rom. 14:10-12; 1 Cor. 3:13-15; 2 Cor. 5:10; 9:6; 11:15; Gal. 6:7; Eph. 6:8; Col. 3:25; 1 Tim. 5:24-25; 2 Tim. 4:14). It is a theme that is deeply rooted in the OT, Judaism, and early Christianity (see Pss. 9:8-21; 37:9, 37; 58:12; 62:10, 13; 96:10, 13; Job 34:11; Prov. 10:16; 24:12; Eccl. 12:14; Isa. 3:10-11; 59:18; Jer. 17:10; 25:14; 32:19; Lam. 3:64; Hos. 4:9; 1QS 5:6f.; 10:16-18; CD 7:9f.; 1QH 18:12f.; 1QpHab. 8:1f.; 10:3; 12:14–13:4; *Pss. Sol.* 2:17f., 38; 9:4; *2 Bar.* 13:8; 44:4; 54:21; 85:15; *4 Ezra* 6:19; *T. Gad* 7:5; *T. Ben.* 10:7f.; *1 En.* 1:7-9; 5:5-9; 16:2; 25:4f.; 41:2, 9; 50:1-4; 60:6; 62:2f.; 63:8; 100:7; *As. Moses* 12:10; *Sib. Or.* 4:183; Matt. 7:21; 12:36; 16:27; 25:35; John 3:20-21; 5:29; 1 Pet. 1:17; James 1:25; 2:24; Rev. 2:23; 14:13; 20:12-13; 22:12).

E. P. Sanders has shown decisively that Judaism was not a religion of works righteousness. Salvation in Judaism is always by grace, and judgment is according to works. God saves Israel by grace, by election, and within that framework of grace God rewards good deeds and punishes evil. Works are the condition of remaining within the covenant, within grace; they are never a condition for earning salvation (see Sanders, 1977:75, 94-101, 124, 137-47, 419-28, 543).

Romans 2 reflects an inner Jewish debate. Almost everything is standard Jewish teaching. That Jews are people who obey the law, that judgment is according to works, that circumcision is defined by doing the law are all taught in first century Judaism. The notion of righteous Gentiles—Gentiles who do the law—is not a common idea, but it is present in Jewish literature. Romans 2, therefore, essentially states a Jewish view of judgment.

But Romans 2 also radicalizes the judgment by universalizing it; it applies to both Jews and Gentiles equally. The general context in Romans is the just and inevitable retribution of God. The more immediate context is the reminder that God's judgment includes those who judge others, especially those who presume on God's mercy by refusing to repent. The principle of the judgment in 2:6 is corresponding retribution—each according to his/her works. Verses 7-10 show exactly how that works. Verse 12 states the principle of impartiality in a new way, within or without the law. Verses 14 and 27 illustrate the "without the law" principle.

What Romans 2 makes clear is that judgment is according to works without respect of persons. Salvation or eternal life is granted to those who live obediently in relation to the revelation they have received, whether within the law or without the law. Paul's real point is that judgment does not depend on whether one is within or without the people of the law. Both people will be judged by God because both sin.

The affirmation of judgment according to works in Romans 2 is part of a much larger biblical teaching that Protestants want to ignore. Judgment in the Bible is not according to grace, or faith, or mercy. It is according to works without respect of persons.

Does that mean Romans 2 teaches that people can be saved by works? It does not say that. As the larger message of Romans makes exceedingly clear, no human being can or will stand before God in his/her own righteousness—that is what Jesus is all about. The whole point of Romans 1:18–2:11 is that God is judging humanity because men/women did not center their lives in God—e.g., recognize, honor, glorify. Paul's concern here is not to offer a definition of the gospel, but to undercut exclusive understandings of righteousness and God's judgment.

Salvation in the Bible—both testaments—is always God's gracious gift; it can never be earned. God owes no one salvation. God judges all people by the evidence of their salvation—by their works.

Paul in Romans 2 is a Jew, just as Jesus and James were. Judgment by works does not contradict salvation by grace, but presupposes it. Salvation and ethics are flip sides of the same coin for Paul, as they were for the Jews and the other early Christians.

The teaching of Romans 2 regarding judgment by works is also consistent with another pattern that may be discerned in the Pauline "judgment" texts. As Nigel Watson has pointed out, they are consistently addressed to problems of presumption and arrogance, "puffed-upness," or to people living in a state of illusion. They are designed to evoke repentance and obedience.

See Donaldson, 1990; Donfried, 1976; Garlington, 1991b; Sanders, 1977, and 1983a:123-35; Snodgrass, 1986; Watson, 1983; Yinger, 1999.

SIN IN ROMANS Sin is a very important word in Romans, and Romans is very important for a Pauline understanding of sin. The key NT words for sin are found in Romans, and found more often than in any other writing. The major words for sin with their occurrence in Romans, Paul, and the NT are:

Term	Romans	Paul	NT
unrighteous (*adikia*)	7	12	25
sin (sing.) (*hamartia*)	48	64	173
lawless (*anomia*)	2	6	14
ungodly (*asebia*)	2	4	6
transgression (*parabasis*)	3	5	7
disobey (*parakoē*)	1	2	3
fall beside (*paraptōma*)	9	16	19

Sin in Romans is unrighteous or unjust behavior, lawlessness, ungodliness, breaking of a law, disobedience, falling beside or missing the mark. Sin concerns behavior, actions and attitudes by people. The description seems comprehensive. It also sounds very familiar; that is the way Christians have talked about sin for centuries. But that understanding by itself misunderstands Paul. His understanding of sin is much more profound. Paul talks about sin as **Sin** (singular, *hamartia*), as a personified power that rules. He defines sin as **Sin** primarily in Romans, 48 out of 64 occurrences. Furthermore, he concentrates this talk about **Sin** in chs. 5–8, 41 times (four times in chs. 1–4, one time each in chs. 9–11 and 12–16). Except for 7:5, all occurrences in chs. 5–8 are singular, **Sin** not sins.

Sin is a personal power. It has desires and passions (6:12; 7:5); it is opportunistic (7:8, 11); it revives from sleep (7:9); it deceives (7:11); it dwells in (7:17, 20, 23). As a personal power, it enters the world (5:12); it rules (5:21; 6:12, 13, 14); it enslaves (6:6, 16, 17, 20; 7:14; 8:2); it works (7:17, 20); it has its own law (7:23-8:2). Paul interprets **Sin** as a cosmic power. The categories of interpretation are apocalyptic theology.

Sin as cosmic, personal power is associated with the law (3:20; 5:13 [2x]; 6:14; 7:5, 7 [2x], 8, 9, 11, 23, 25; 8:2); with death, either as producing death (5:12 [2x], 21; 6:16, 23; 7:5, 8, 11, 13; 8:2, 10) or as something to die to (6:2, 6, 7, 10, 11); with slavery (6:6, 17, 18, 22; 7:14, 23; 8:2); with rulership (5:21; 6:12, 13, 14); with unrighteousness (6:13); with flesh (7:3).

Sin stands over against or is contrasted by grace (5:20, 21; 6:1, 14); life (5:21; 6:10, 11, 13, 22, 23); righteousness (6:13, 16, 18, 20; 8:3, 10); obedience (6:16, 17); freedom (6:7, 18, 20, 22; 8:2); law (7:14); God's son (8:7); faith (14:23).

Sin as inherited depravity or tendency (Augustine's misinterpretation of 5:12) or as sinful act/deed does not begin to tap the depth of Paul's interpretation of sin (see Original Sin essay). **Sin** is a cosmic power; it is a cosmic magnetic field that pulls all human beings, except Jesus, and all creation into its force field. Nothing is capable of bounding its power or freeing people or creation from its pull, not even the gift of God's revealed law. **Sin is Cosmic King** in Paul. **Sin's** kingship is total, with one exception (Jesus); no one and nothing can escape its tyrannical rule.

Sin was present in the cosmos before Adam. It is prior to acts of sin, either Adam's or his descendants. **Sin** exists and rules even when there is no system to define it; when it cannot be counted or tracked. Adam turned **Sin** loose in the world. His role is critical. He is the "trigger mechanism" or the enabler of **Sin**, but not its origin or cause. His fateful legacy is that he let **Sin** enter the world. Adam is thus the remote cause of death. But, he is not the immediate cause of all dying; all sin personally, all are pulled into the magnetic field of **Sin** by submitting to its rule as evidenced in sinful choices and actions.

Given this theology of **Sin**, Paul can say two things that seem contradictory but are not. First, all human beings are under the rule of **Sin** (Rom. 3:9). Second, not all sinful acts are transgressions; only those actions which violate a command or teaching of God constitute transgression or missing the mark. But people who are not guilty of transgressions, who have not violated the direct teaching of God because they do not have such a teaching, are still under the rule of **Sin** because they submit to **Sin**.

If Christians wish to use the traditional language of sin, "original sin," the theology must be redefined by Paul's explicit theology of **Sin**. Original sin refers to **Sin** as power that exists prior to and independent of any human sinful act, and that pulls all human beings, except one (Jesus), and all creation into its force field. Such a doctrine of original sin must be balanced by an emphasis on human responsibility—because all sinned. All humans, except one, choose to submit to **Sin's** rule by behaving sinfully. The exception of the one person's obedience is critical; it underlines free choice and human responsibility. Christ entered the world ruled by **Sin** but chose not to submit; instead his obedience both demonstrated and effected the saving power to overcome **Death** with **Life**.

Sin as cosmic ruler and magnetic field is the ultimate power that salvation must address. Forgiveness of sins does not triumph over **Sin** and **Death**. Salvation must achieve victory over **Sin** and **Death** for there to be forgiveness of sins. Romans 5:12-21 addresses the problem of **Sin** and **Death** by presenting Christ as the one who reverses Adam, who brings **Life** to replace **Death**.

The nature of **Sin** as cosmic ruler and magnetic field also explains Paul's repeated exhortations in chs. 6-8 that Christians continually resist **Sin**. Christ has triumphed over **Sin**, but because of its powerful force field that continues to pull people towards its center, Christians must intentionally resist **Sin** and depend on God's power via Christ and the Spirit to overcome its pull.

Paul's analysis of sin in Romans is profound. His interpretation of **Sin** in chs. 5–8 is among the most penetrating and insightful in the entire Bible. **Sin** here is not synonymous with "irreligious" or "impious." Earlier in Romans Paul argued that both Jews and Gentiles are very religious, in different and important ways to be sure, and yet "under **Sin**" (chs. 1:1–3:20, 23). **Sin** also is not synonymous with immorality. Paul says a great deal about immorality—immoral people will not participate in God's kingdom (1 Cor. 6:9-10). Immoral acts are sins, but these acts in themselves are not the real problem. Both religious and moral people, according to Paul, can be under **Sin**. The essence of **Sin** is wrong lordship, submission or enslavement to **Sin**. Sins are a function of **Sin**. Therefore, salvation must ultimately deal with **Sin** or it does not address the real and deeper human as well as cosmic dilemma and crisis. Salvation must involve the defeat of **Sin** and the establishment of a new lordship, a new power source that is stronger than **Sin**.

Beker, 1980:213-34; Dunn, 1998:102-27; Elliott, N., 1990:167-223; Guenther, 1978; Lyonnet, 1970:3-57; Staehlin and Grundmann, 1964; Wink, 1984, 1986, 1992.

UNIVERSALISM Romans 5:12-21 is one of the critical texts for people who argue that Paul taught universal or unlimited salvation (the others are: Rom. 11:26-36; 1 Cor. 15:22-28; 2 Cor. 5:19; Phil. 2:6-11; Col. 1:15-20). Universal salvation means that God will save all people. "All" in this argument is not limited to "Jews and Gentiles," the dominant meaning of "all" in Romans, but refers to all human beings in human history.

The argument from Romans 5 is particularly strong. The central image is of God as king. The action is carried by words for "reign" (*basileuō*); a form of it is used five times. The issue is, who rules the world and humanity? The passage begins with **Sin** and **Death** as the rulers of all humanity and all creation. Then, beginning with v. 15, Jesus establishes the powerful, gracious, and righteous rule of God over all people and creation. Adam is replaced by Jesus. The reign of **Sin** and **Death** is replaced by the reign of **Grace**, **Righteousness**, and **Life**. Both Adam and Christ are universal paradigms; whatever happened in Adam happens to all human beings, and whatever happened in Christ happens to all human beings. The picture is that one group composed of all human beings is first ruled by one king who is conquered by another king who becomes the ruler of all the people. A change of lordships takes place by a unilateral action of God. Human beings have no choice; they are transferred from Adam's people to Christ's people, from the lordship of **Sin** and **Death** to the lordship of **Grace** and **Life**. Verse 18 says it most clearly: "just as through one trespass there is condemnation for all human beings, so also through one righteous act there is righteousness of life for all human beings." Every statement between vv. 15 and 18 affirms that whatever humanity lost in Adam it "much more" regained in Christ.

Sin and **Death** are universal. Salvation—**Grace** and **Life**—is universal, determined by one person for all other human beings and for the entire cosmos. That is clearly the dominant message of Romans 5:12-21.

There is a minor theme in the text unit—human responsibility. The universality of sin is qualified in v. 12 by *because all sinned*. The universality of salvation is qualified in v. 17 by a participle, *the ones receiving* (*hoi lambanontes*). But the theme is a minor one, not major. That is why theologians have struggled so much about the relationship of Adam's sin and human responsibility in the interpretation of v. 12. The same issue applies to the relationship of Jesus' righteous act and human responsibility in vv. 15-19.

Romans 5:12-21, taken by itself, stresses universal salvation as the answer to universal **Sin**. That is the clear and plain meaning of the text.

The critical phrase is "taken by itself." Romans 5 presents one image of sin and one image of salvation. Sin is defined as **Sin**, as cosmic lord who pulls all people and all creation into its magnetic field. Salvation must always answer the problem of **Sin**. There are many different metaphors for salvation in the NT because sin is many different realities. Whatever the human predicament, whatever the nature of sin's expression, salvation must answer and correct it. Images of sin as broken relationships, or eneminess, or lost community are answered by righteousness, reconciliation, election, or adoption, not by the victory of Christ over **Sin**. But **Sin** as the powerful cosmic Lord requires an even more powerful cosmic lord to triumph over it and its child **Death**. Humans play no part in this drama because they are only slaves of a lord. Universal **Sin** requires universal salvation, an evil cosmic lord must be dethroned by an even more powerful cosmic lord, or talk about healing broken relationships, or reconciling enemies, or incorporating people into a family are only bandages on a totally dysfunctional world made up of totally dysfunctional communities filled with totally dysfunctional individuals. The government of the world has to be changed—**Sin** and **Death** have to be replaced by **Grace** and **Life**—so that sins can be corrected by appropriate salvific solutions.

Other texts make the minor theme here the major theme; they emphasize that humans are responsible to respond to the victory of Christ over **Sin**. One just has to think of the "trust" (faith) and obedience texts which assert that "trust in Christ" is a condition for salvation [*Essay: Faith*]. Paul also speaks often of "those who are perishing" or who face "the wrath of God" because of their rejection of God (Rom. 1:18-32; 2:7-8, 12-16; 6:23; 1 Cor. 1:18; 6:9; 8:11; 2 Cor. 2:15; 4:3; Phil. 1:28; 3:19; 2 Thess. 1:8-9). These texts make it clear that "trust in Christ" is essential for salvation, and that apart from Christ everyone will be condemned. Or, think of Romans 9–11; Paul genuinely worries that God's people Israel may be lost.

The difference between the two sets of text—universal or unlimited salvation and particular or limited salvation—is usually explained by subordinating one to the other (the majority subordinate the universal to the particular, a minority subordinate the particular to the universal), or by claiming that Paul is contradictory or at least incoherent, or by claiming that Paul says more than he intends in the universal texts.

But, Paul claims both the universal and particular. Why not let both stand as different answers to different questions? Each theme has its own inner logic and meaning, which should be accepted and respected in its respective answer to different issues. Both agree that there is salvation only through Christ. Both divide humanity into different groups, e.g., those subject to the rule of **Sin** or rule of Christ, those who reject Christ as God's way to salvation or those who "trust in Christ." There is universal salvation because Christ defeats the powers of **Sin** and **Death**, and there is particular salvation, because salvation is only through Christ. The universal does not deny the particular, but affirms it, and the particular needs the universal to be authentically and divinely transformative. God's grace is universal and humans are responsible to respond to that grace. It is "both/and" rather than "either/or."

For further study, see Boring, 1986; M. C. de Boer, 1988:173ff.; Marshall, 1989:313-28; Punt, 1980; Sanders, 1977:472-74 and 1983b:57; Theissen, 1992:159-86; Wright, 1979.

WORKS OF LAW The phrase "works of law" is a unique Pauline expression. It appears eight times in Galatians (2:16 [3x]; 3:2, 5, 10) and twice in Romans (3:20, 28). The question and answer in Romans 3:27, "through what kind of law? Of Works?" is probably a variant form of the same expression. The phrase does not occur elsewhere in the NT.

The phrase is used in contemporary Jewish literature only in two texts in the Dead Sea Scrolls (4QFlor., 4QMMT). In both texts the phrase, "deeds of law" (*ma'asey torah*), is used to distinguish the Qumran community, the "separated" brethren, from the Judaism represented by Jerusalem. In 4QFlor. "deeds of law" concern purity regulations that define the Qumran community as the Temple, that God has built to replace the Temple in Jerusalem. 4QMMT is a legal tractate (probably a letter from the leader of the community to leaders in Jerusalem) which outlines 24 rules of purity which contrast the community's (or the writer's) understanding with the practices of the Temple in Jerusalem. "Deeds of law" in the Qumran literature identify understandings and practices which define the identity of one sectarian group over against the establishment. They describe what one particular community understands the laws of purity require of the loyal members of that community. In short, works of law help define the group identity of one community in relationship to another community.

Several things are noteworthy about Paul's use of the phrase. First of all, it consists of a noun, works (*ergon*), with the genitive "of law" (*nomou*). The preposition, "out of" (*ek*), denoting source, is used seven times, "apart from" (*chōris*), indicating separation, is used once (Rom. 3:28). Second, the phrase occurs only in contexts concerned with the relation of Gentile Christians to Jewish Christians and to Judaism (Gal. 2:16-3:10, Rom. 3:20-28). Third, the phrase is polemical. It rejects one action in favor of another.

	Action	Not	But by
Gal. 2:16	one is justified	out of works of law	the faith of Christ
	we might be justified	out of works of law	the faith of Christ
Gal. 2:16	no flesh be justified	out of works of law	God's truth/righteousness
Rom. 3:20	no flesh be justified	out of works of law	God's truth/righteousness (based on Ps. 143:2)
Rom. 3:28	one is justified	apart from works of law	faithfulness
Gal. 3:2	you received the Spirit	out of works of law	hearing of faithfulness
Gal. 3:5	God supplies the Spirit	out of works of law	hearing of faithfulness
Gal. 3:10	under a curse	those out of works of law	

Five texts concern being made righteous (two with the use of Ps. 143:2), two the reception of the Spirit, one a curse. People are made righteous by divine action—the faithfulness of Christ, the truth, righteousness, and faithfulness of God (the "faithfulness" probably refers to God's or Christ's faithfulness given the prior and subsequent references)—not works of the law. People receive the Spirit through the hearing or obedience of faithfulness, not through works of the law. Those who rely on works of the law are under a curse that is so powerful it requires an act of God through Christ to liberate people.

There is no consensus about the meaning of this data. Four basic interpretive views have been proposed. The most popular interpretation in the history of the church is that works of law refer to the attempt of human beings to establish their own righteousness by meritorious deeds (so Luther, Calvin, Sanday and Headlam, Burton, Barrett, Bruce, Bultmann, Käsemann, Cranfield, Morris, Fung). Works of law are often equated with legalism in this interpretation. Second, works of law refers to actions performed in obedience to the law, to works which are commanded by the law (so Fuller, Cosgrove, Kaye). The third view argues that works of law refer to "nomistic service," service of the law (so especially Loymeyer, Tyson). Fourth, works of law signify distinctions between Jews and Gentiles, or the boundary markers which separate Jews from Gentiles (so Sanders, 1983a; Dunn, 1990a, 1990b, 1992c; Watson, 1983; Campbell, 1992a.).

E. P. Sanders has demonstrated that the first view is based on a faulty understanding of Judaism. Judaism and early Christianity were agreed that salvation comes from God's activity and is based on God's grace; it is not earned by any human effort or meritorious work.

The fact that the term appears exclusively in two letters of Paul suggests that its meaning can be determined only by the usage in these letters. Later theological interpretations of the phrase, e.g., works of law denote meritorious works designed to earn salvation, are not relevant and/or useful in understanding Paul's intention.

Pauline usage of the phrase favors the fourth interpretation—works of law refer to "covenantal nomism" (E. P. Sander's phrase for the basic theology of Judaism), to the Jewish conviction that status within the covenant is maintained by doing what the law requires. The specific laws of the covenant that became identity markers of Jewish identity during and following the Maccabean revolution (167 B.C.) were circumcision, food, and sabbath laws (cf. 1 Macc. 1:60-63). These specific laws became the test cases for Jews and non-Jews of faithfulness to the covenant. Both this theology and the specific identity markers served to separate Jews from Gentiles in Jewish and Gentile self-understanding in the first century.

Paul's first use of works of law occurs in Galatians 2:16. The context is an argument about the need for Gentile Christians to practice circumcision (the "false brothers") and to observe Jewish food laws "(the representatives of James and Jewish Christians in Antioch) in order to be members of the covenant people God was creating in the world through Messiah Jesus. Do Gentile converts have to become Jews—to adopt and practice the critical "identity markers" of Jewish identity—to be Christians? The issue in ch. 3 is identical. Did Gentile converts receive the Spirit by becoming Jews—by accepting circumcision and practicing Jewish dietary laws—or by the direct action of God? Paul's answer is that Gentile Christians are made righteous and receive the Spirit by the saving activity of God independent of Jewish ethnic identity.

The context for Paul's use of works of law in Romans is the universality of God's judgment and salvation over against a Jewish theology of superiority and exclusiveness. The first reference in Romans is in the closing argument that the Jews are equally under God's judgment as the Gentiles. The law itself is cited to demonstrate that the Jews are accountable to God, that no human being is made righteous by being Jewish. The second reference—the variant wording of 3:27—asserts that the revelation of the end-time righteousness of God in Jesus Christ excludes boasting that God is the God primarily, or even only, of the Jews—a reference back to Jewish boasting in God and the law in 2:17f. The third reference, immediately after in v. 28 and just before the affirmation that God is the God of all people, states that a human being is made righteous only by faithfulness, probably a reference to the faithfulness of Christ in vv. 22-26, not by works of the law, not by being a member of the Jewish covenant community.

Works of law in Galatians and Romans describe a theology and a self-understanding that differentiates the Jewish people from Gentiles. The critical symbols of the differentiation are circumcision and food laws, although the symbols point beyond themselves to the observance of the law as the means of covenant faithfulness. Circumcision—Romans 2—and dietary laws—Romans 14–15—are issues in the Roman churches that create tension between Jewish and Gentile Christians, because they differentiate the two peoples.

Such an understanding of works of law is consistent with the use of the parallel phrase in Qumran. They reflect the understanding of the covenant which distinguished the Qumran covenanters from fellow Jews.

Paul rejects works of law as defining marks of Christian identity. Gentiles do not have to become Jews to be Christian. Why? Because all people are made righteous by the saving righteousness of God in and through Messiah Jesus.

See Abegg, 1999 and 2001; Cranfield, 1991; Dunn, 1988, 1:153-160; 1990b; 1992c; 1997b; Gaston, 1987:100-6; Harrington, 1997:109-28; Kapera, 1991; H. B. P. Mijoga, 1999; Moo, 1983; Schreiner, 1991b; Wright, 1998.

WRATH Wrath, used 10 times in Romans (1:18; 2:5, 8; 3:5; 4:15; 5:9; 9:22; 12:19; 13:4, 5), comes from the OT and apocalyptic Jewish literature. The wrath of God describes God's action against those who offend in the covenant relationship (Deut. 28:15-68; 32:19-20). In other words, the wrath of God, like the righteousness of God, is a relational term. The wrathful action of God is personal, moral, and rational. It is God's reaction to sin, particularly idolatry. It is transitory in nature, operating in individual acts of punishment. God's love and righteousness are permanent; God's wrath represents a change in attitude caused by inappropriate behavior by the covenant partner (Isa. 54:7, 8).

This understanding of God's wrath is associated with end-times in the later OT writings (e.g., Zeph. 1:18; Dan. 8:19) and in the intertestamental literature. It is associated with the coming Day of the Lord, a day of judgment and vengeance (Isa. 2:10-22; Jer. 30; Joel 3:12), where the wrath of God becomes inescapable end-time doom. It is a permanent reality rather than a transitory one. "The wrath of God" became a technical term for the end-time power of God which operates as an aspect of divine justice to punish the wicked. It refers to corporate and cosmic judgment, not only to individual judgment. The wrath of God describes the end-time power of divine judgment on all forms of sin, especially sins in which human beings act as if they are Lord (see *Jub.* 5:6; 36:10; *1 En.* 5:6f.; 84:4; 92:9; 103:7f.). This wrath is poured out primarily on the Gentiles and apostate Jews in apocalyptic literature (*1 En.* 91:79; 2:9). God shows forbearance by holding back wrath in the present (*Jub.* 5:6). The wrath of God in Jewish literature is primarily a future reality.

Outline of Romans

3. The meaning of the revelation of the
righteousness of God through the
faithfulness of Jesus | 5:1–8:39
    A Peace with God | 5:1-11
       1) the basis | 5:1a
       2) the exhortations | 5:1b-8
       3) the basis | 5:9a
       4) the benefits | 5:9b-11

    B Victory of Christ over sin | 5:12-21
       1) the origin of death | 5:12-14
       2) the comparison of Adam and
Christ | 5:15-21

    C Death of the old humanity | 6:1-7:6
       1) first question | 6:1
       2) second question | 6:15
       3) third question | 7:1

    B Victory over the flesh/sin via
the Spirit | 7:7–8:11
       1) the weakness of the law due
to flesh/sin | 7:7-25
       2) the fulfillment of the law through
the victory of Christ and the Spirit | 8:1-11

    A Children of God | 8:12-39
       1) the Spirit and family relationships | 8:12-17
       2) the triumph of glory over suffering | 8:18-30
       3) the triumph of God in Christ | 8:31-39

4. The faithfulness of God to Jews and Gentiles | 9:1–11:36
    a. The lament of Paul for Israel | 9:1-5
       1) oath | 9:1-2
       2) wish | 9:3
       3) privileges | 9:4-5

    A God's word has not failed | 9:6-29
       1) thesis statement | 9:6a
       2) statement 1: God's call rather than
birth determines Jewish ancestry | 9:6-13
       3) statement 2: God's sovereignty is
just and serves God's purposes of
wrath and mercy | 9:14-21
       4) statement 3: God's election
purposes a new people | 9:22-29

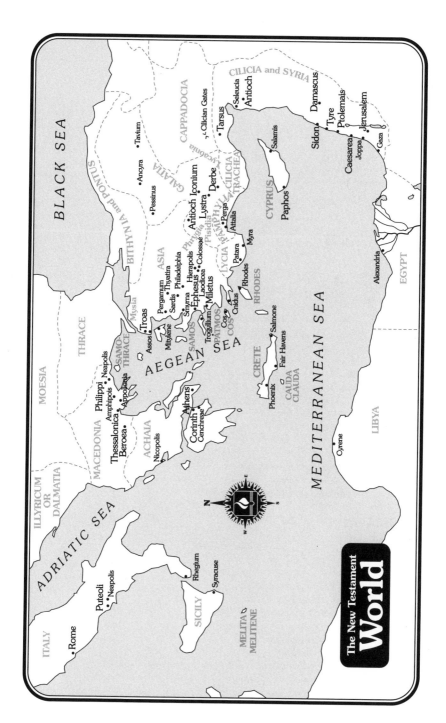

The New Testament World

BIBLIOGRAPHY

Abbreviations

ANRW	Aufstieg und Niedergang der römischen Welt
AsJT	Asian Journal of Theology
ATR	Anglican Theological Review
AusBR	Australian Biblical Review
BJRL	Bulletin of the John Rylands Library
BR	Biblical Research
BT	Bible Translator
BTB	Biblical Theology Bulletin
CBQ	Catholic Biblical Quarterly
ETL	Ephemerides theologicae lovanienses
EvQ	Evangelical Quarterly
ExpTim	Expository Times
HBT	Horizons in Biblical Theology
HTR	Harvard Theological Review
IBS	Irish Biblical Studies
Int	Interpretation
JBL	Journal of Biblical Literature
JES	Journal of Ecumenical Studies
JETS	Journal of the Evangelical Theological Society
JSNT	Journal for the Study of the New Testament
JTS	Journal of Theological Studies
LS	Louvain Studies
MQR	Mennonite Quarterly Review
NovT	Novum Testamentum
NTS	New Testament Studies
RefTR	Reformed Theological Review
SJT	Scottish Journal of Theology
ST	Studia theologica
TrinJ	Trinity Journal
TynBul	Tyndale Bulletin
TZ	Theologische Zeitschrift
WTJ	Westminster Theological Journal
ZNW	Zeitschrift für die neutestamentliche Wissenschaft

Bibliography

Only the primary works used in this commentary are included in the bibliography. More comprehensive bibliographies can be found in Brendan Byrne's commentary on *Romans* (Sacra Pagina, Liturgical Press, 1996), and in Joseph Fitzmyer's, *Romans* (Anchor Bible, Doubleday, 1993).

Aageson, J. W.
  1986 "Scripture and Structure in the Development of the Argument in Romans 9-11." *CBQ* 48:265-89.
Abegg, Martin G.
  1999 "4QMMT C 27, 31 and 'Works of Righteousness.'" *Dead Sea Discoveries* 6:139-47.
  2001 "4QMMT, Paul, and 'Works of the Law.'" In *The Bible at Qumran. Text, Shape and Interpretation*, ed. Peter W. Flint, 203-16. Grand Rapids: Eerdmans.
Achtemeier, P. J.
  1985 *Romans*. Atlanta: John Knox Press.
Applebaum, S.
  1974 "The Organization of the Jewish Communities in the Diaspora." In *The Jewish People in the First Century*, vol. 1, *Compendia Rerum Judaicarum ad Novum Testamentum*, ed. S. Safrai, M. Stern, and Van Gorcum. Philadelphia: Fortress Press, 464-503.
Aune, David E.
  1987 *The New Testament and Its Literary Environment*. Philadephia: Westminster.
Badenas, R.
  1985 *Christ the End of the Law*. Sheffield, UK: JOST Press.
Bailey, L. R.
  1979 *Biblical Perspectives on Death*. Philadelphia: Fortress Press.

Balch, David L., ed.
  2000 *Homosexuality, Science and the 'Plain Sense' of Scripture.*
        Grand Rapids: Eerdmans.
Barclay, William B.
  1999 "*Christ in You.*" Washington, D.C.: University Press of America.
Barrett, C. K.
  1957 *A Commentary on the Epistle to the Romans.* New York:
        Harper.
  1962 *From First Adam to Last.* New York: Scribners.
Barth, M.
  1968 "Jews and Gentiles: The Social Character of Justification in Paul."
        JES 5:241-67.
Bartsch, Hans-Werner
  1968 "The Concept of Faith in Paul's Letter to the Romans." *BR*
        13:41-53.
Bassler, J. M.
  1982 *Divine Impartiality.* Chico, CA: Scholars Press.
  1984 "Divine Impartiality in Paul's Letter to the Romans." *NovT* 26:43-
        58.
  2003 "Grace." *Int* 57:24-33.
Beasley-Murray, Paul
  1980 "Romans 1:3f.: An Early Confession of Faith in the Lordship of
        Jesus." *TynBul* 31:147-54.
Bechtler, Steven Richard
  1994 "Christ, the *Telos* of the Law: The Goal of Romans 10:4." *CBQ*
        56:288-308.
Beker, J. C.
  1980 *Paul the Apostle.* Philadelphia: Fortress Press.
  1985 "Paul's Letter to the Romans as Model for Biblical Theology:
        Some Preliminary Observations." In *Understanding the Word*,
        ed. J. T. Butler, et al., 359-67. Sheffield, UK: JSOT Press.
  1990 "The Relationship of Sin and Death in Romans." In *The
        Conversation Continues*, ed. R. T. Fortna and B. R. Gaventa,
        55-61. Nashville: Abingdon.
Benko, S.
  1969 "The Edict of Claudius of A.D. 49 and the Instigator Chrestus."
        TZ 25:407-18.
Best, Ernest
  1955 *One Body in Christ.* London: SPCK.
Betz, H. D.
  1995 "Transferring a Ritual: Paul's Interpretation of Baptism in Romans
        6." In *Paul in His Hellenistic Context*, ed. T. Engberg-Pedersen,
        84-118. Philadelphia: Fortress Press.
Black, David Alan
  1989 "The Pauline Love Command: Structure, Style, and Ethics in
        Romans 12:9-21." *Neotestamentica*, 2:3-22.
Black, C. Clifton
  1984 "Pauline Perspectives on Death in Romans 5-8." *JBL* 103:413-33.
Boers, Hendrikus
  1981 "The Problem of the Jews and Gentiles in the Macro-Structure of
        Romans." *Neotestamentica*, 15:1-11.

1992 "'We Who Are by Inheritance Jews; Not from the Gentiles, Sinners.'" *JBL* 111:273-81.
1994 *The Justification of the Gentiles*. Peabody, Mass.: Hendrickson.
Boomershine, Thomas E.
1989 "Epistemology at the Turn of the Ages in Paul, Jesus, and Mark: Rhetoric and Dialectic in Apocalyptic and the New Testament." In *Apocalyptic and the New Testament*, ed. Joel Marcus and Marion L. Soards, 147-67. Sheffield, UK: Sheffield Academic Press.
Borg, Marcus
1972 "A New Context for Romans XIII." *NTS* 19:205-18.
Boring, M. E.
1986 "The Language of Universal Salvation in Paul." *JBL* 105:269-92.
Bornkamm, Günther
1969 "The Revelation of God's Wrath." In *Early Christian Experience*, trans. Paul L. Hammer, New York: Harper & Row. Pp. 47-70.
Boswell, John
1980 *Christianity, Social Tolerance, and Homosexuality*. Chicago: University of Chicago Press.
Botha, J. E.
1987 "The Meanings of *Pisteu?* in the Greek New Testament: A Semantic-Lexicographical Study." *Neotestamentica* 21:225-40.
Boyarin, Daniel
1994 *A Radical Jew: Paul and the Politics of Identity*. Berkeley: University of California Press.
Branick, V. P.
1985 "The Sinful Flesh of the Son of God (Rom. 8.3): A Key Image of Pauline Theology." *CBQ* 47:246-62.
1989 *The House Church in the Writings of Paul*. Wilmington, Del.: Michael Glazier.
Breck, John
1982 "Biblical Chiasmus: Exploring Structure for Meaning." *BTB* 17:70-74.
Brooten, Bernadette J.
1996 *Love Between Women*. Chicago: University of Chicago Press.
Brown, R. E., and J. P. Meier
1983a "Not Jewish Christianity and Gentile Christianity, but Types of Jewish/Gentile Christianity." *CBQ* 45:74-79.
1983b *Antioch and Rome*. New York: Paulist Press.
1990 "Further Reflections on the Origins of the Church of Rome." In *The Conversation Continues*, ed. R. T. Fortna and B. R. Gaventa, 98-115. Nashville: Abingdon, .
Bultmann, Rudolf
Theology of the New Testament, 2 vols. New York: Scribners.
Burns, J. Patout
1979 "The Intepretation of Romans in the Pelagian Controversy," *Augustinian Studies* 10:43-74.
Byrne, Brendan
1979 "Sons of God"—"Seed of Abraham" Biblical Institute.
1981 "Living out the Righteousness of God: The Contribution of Rom. 6:1–8:13 to an Understanding of Paul's Ethical Presuppositions." *CBQ* 43:557-81.

1986   *Reckoning with Romans.* Wilmington, Del.: Michael Glazier.
1996   *Romans.* Sacra Pagina. Collegeville, Minn.: Liturgical Press.
2001   "Interpreting Romans Theologically in a Post-'New Perspective'
        Perspective." *HTR* 94:227-41.
Campbell, Douglas A.
1992   "The Meaning of *Pistis* and *Nomos* in Paul: A Linguistic and
        Structural Perspective." *JBL* 111:91-103.
1992   *The Rhetoric of Righteousness in Romans 3:21-26.* Sheffield,
        UK: JSOT Press.
1994   "Determining the Gospel through Rhetorical Analysis in Paul's
        Letter to the Roman Christians." In *Gospel in Paul*, ed. L. Ann
        Jervis and P. Richardson, 315-36. Sheffield, UK: Sheffield
        Academic Press.
1994   "Romans 1:17—A *Crux Interpretum* for the *Pistis Christou*
        Debate." *JBL* 113:265-85.
1997   "False Presuppositions in the *PISTIS CHRISTOU* Debate: A
        Response to Brian Dodd." *JBL* 116:713-19.
Campbell, William S.
1981   "The Freedom and Faithfulness of God in Relation to Israel."
        JSNT 13:27-45.
1981   "Romans III as a Key to the Structure and Thought of the Letter."
        NovT 23:22-40.
1981   "The Romans Debate." *JSNT* 10:19-28.
1982   "The Place of Romans ix-xi within the Structure and Thought of
        the Letter." In *Studia Evangelica VII*, ed. E. A. Livingstone, 121-
        31. Berlin: Akademie Verlag.
1984   "Christianity and Judaism: Continuity and Discontinuity."
        International Bulletin of Missionary Research, 8.54-58.
1991   *Paul's Gospel in an Intercultural Context.* Frankfurt am Main:
        Peter Lang.
1995   "The Rule of Faith in Romans 12:1–15:13: The Obligation of
        Humble Obedience to Christ as the only Adequate Response to
        the Mercies of God." In *Pauline Theology*, ed. D. M. Hay and
        E. E. Johnson, 3:259-86. Philadelphia: Fortress Press.
Calvin, John
1947   *Commentary on the Epistle of Paul the Apostle to the
        Romans.* Trans. John Owen. Grand Rapids: Eerdmans.
Carlson, R. P.
1993   "The Role of Baptism in Paul's Thought." *Int* 47:255-66.
Carras, G. P.
1992   "Romans 2:1-29: A Dialogue of Jewish Ideals." *Biblica* 73:183-207.
Carroll, John T. and Joel B. Green
1995   *The Death of Jesus in Early Christianity.* Peabody, Mass.:
        Hendrickson.
Cartwright, Michael C., and Peter Ochs. See Yoder, John H.
Chilton, Bruce
1988   "Romans 9-11 as Scriptural Interpretation and Dialogue with
        Judaism." *Ex Auditu* 4:27-37.
Colijin, B. D.
1991   "Paul's Use of the 'in Christ' Formula." *Ashland Theological
        Review*, 23:9-26.

1995   *Confession of Faith in Mennonite Perspective*. Scottdale, Pa.: Herald Press.

Corrigan, G. M.
1986   "Paul's Shame for the Gospel." *BTB* 16:23-27.

Corsani, B.
1984   "Ek Pisteōs in the Letters of Paul," *The New Testament Age*. W. C. Winrich, ed., Macon, Ga.: Mercer Press. Pp. 87-94.

Cosgrove, Charles H.
1987   "Justification in Paul: A Linguistic and Theological Reflection." *JBL* 106:653-70.
1987   "What If Some Have Not Believed? The Occasion and Thrust of Romans 3:1-8." *ZNW* 78:90-105.

Cranfield, C. E. B.
1975, 1979   *A Critical and Exegetical Commentary on the Epistle to the Romans*. 2 vols. Edinburgh, UK: T & T Clark.
1991   "The Works of the in the Law in the Epistle to the Romans." *JSNT* 43:89-101.

Cranford, Michael
1993   "Election and Ethnicity: Paul's View of Israel in Romans 9:1-13." *JSNT* 50:27-41.
1994   "Abraham in Romans 4: The Faith of All Who Believe." *NTS* 41:71-88.

Cremer, H.
1900   *Die paulinische Rechtferigunglehre im Zumsmmenhang ihrer geschichtlichen Voraussetzungen*. Berlin: Bertelsmann.

Dabourne, Wendy
1999   *Purpose and Cause in Pauline Exegesis*. Cambridge: Cambridge University Press.

Dahl, N. A.
1951   "Two Notes on Romans 5." *ST* 5:37-48.
1974   "Election and the People of God: Some Comments." In *Speaking of God Today*, ed. P. D. Opsahl and M. H. Tanenbaum, 31-38. Philadelphia: Fortress Press.
1977   *Studies in Paul*. Minneapolis: Augsburg.

Das, A. Andrew
2001   *Paul, the Law, and the Covenant*. Peabody, Mass.: Hendrickson.

Daube, David
1947   "Jewish Missionary Maxims in Paul." *ST* 1-2:158-69.
1981   "Conversion to Judaism and Early Christianity." In *Ancient Jewish Law*, 1-32. Leiden: Brill.

Davies, W. D.
1978   "Paul and the People of Israel." *NTS* 24:4-39.
1984a "Paul and the Gentiles: A Suggestion Concerning Romans 11:13-24." *Jewish and Pauline Studies*, 356-60. Philadelphia: Fortress Press.
1984b "Reflections on a Pauline Allegory in a French Context." In *The New Testament Age*, ed. W. C. Weinrich, 107-25. Macon, Ga.: Mercer University Press.

deBoer, Martinus C.
1988   *The Defeat of Death. Apocalyptic Eschatology in 1 Corinthians 15 and Romans 5*. Sheffield, UK: Sheffield Academic Press.
1989   "Paul and Jewish Apocalyptic Eschtology." In *Apocalyptic and*

the New Testament, ed. Joel Marcus and Marion L. Soards, 169-
90. Sheffield, UK: Sheffield Academic Press.
De Brun, T. S.
    1988   "Pelagius's Interpretation of Rom. 5:12-21," *Toronto Journal of
            Theology* 4:30-43.
Dillon, Richard J.
    1998   "The Spirit as Taskmaster and Troublemaker in Romans 8." *CBQ*
            60:682-702.
Dodd, Brian
    1995   "Romans 1:17—A *Crux Interpretum* for the *Pistis Christou*
            Debate." *JBL* 114:470-73.
    1999   *Paul's Paradigmatic 'I'.* Sheffield, UK: Sheffield Academic Press.
Dodd, C. H.
    1932   *The Epistle of Paul to the Romans.* London: Hodder and
            Stoughton.
Donaldson, T. L.
    1990   "Proselytes or 'Righteous Gentiles'? The Status of Gentiles in
            Eschatological Pilgrimage of Thought." *Journal for the Study of
            Pseudepigrapha*, 7:3-27.
    1993   "'Riches for the Gentiles' (Rom. 11:12): Israel's Rejection and
            Paul's Gentile Mission." *JBL* 112:81-98.
    1997   *Paul and the Gentiles.* Philadelphia: Fortress Press.
Donfried, Karl P., ed.
    1976   "Justification and Last Judgment in Paul." *ZNW* 67:90-110.
    1991   *The Romans Debate.* Peabody, Mass.: Hendrikson.
Donfried, Karl P., and Peter Richardson, eds.
    1998   *Judaism and Christianity in First-Century Rome.* Grand Rapids:
            Eerdmans.
Doughty, D. J.
    1973-74 "The Priority of XARIS." *NTS* 19:163-80.
Dunn, James D. G.
    1973   "Jesus—Flesh and Spirit: An Exposition of Romans 1:3-4." *JTS*
            24:40-68.
    1975   "Rom. 7:14-25 in the Theology of Paul." *TZ* 31:257-73.
    1982   "Salvation Proclaimed VI. Romans 6:1-11: Dead and Alive."
            ExpTim, 93:259-64.
    1983   "The New Perspective on Paul." *BJRL* 65:95-112.
    1985   "Works of the Law and the Curse of the Law (Galatians 3:10-
            14)." *NTS* 31:523-42. Reprinted in *Jesus, Paul and the Law*,
            215-41 (see 1990a below).
    1986   "Romans 13:1-7—A Charter for Political Quietism? *Ex Auditu*,
            2:55-68.
    1987   "'Righteousness from the Law' and 'Righteousness from Faith':
            Paul's Interpretation of Scripture in Romans 10:1-10." In
            Tradition and Interpretation in the New Testament, ed. G. F.
            Hawthrone and O. Betz, 216-28. Grand Rapids: Eerdmans.
    1988   *Romans.* 2 vols. Dallas: Word Books.
    1990a   *Jesus, Paul and the Law.* Louisville: Westminster/John Knox.
    1992a   "'The Body of Christ' in Paul." In *Worship, Theology and
            Ministry in the Early Church*, ed. M. J. Wilkins and T. Paige,
            146-62. Sheffield, UK: Sheffield Academic Press.

1992b "The Justice of God. A Renewed Perspective on Justification by Faith." *JTS* 43:1-22.

1992c "Yet Once More—The Works of the Law': A Response." *JSNT* 46:99-117.

1997a "Once More, PISTIS CHRISTOU." In *Pauline Theology*, ed. D. M. Hay and E. E. Johnson, 4:61-81. Atlanta: Scholars Press.

1997b "4QMMT and Galatians." *NTS* 43:147-53.

1998 *The Theology of Paul the Apostle*. Grand Rapids: Eerdmans.

1999 "Spirit Speech: Reflections on Romans 8:12-27." In *Romans and the People of God*, ed. Sven K. Soderlund and N. T. Wright, 82-91. Grand Rapids: Eerdmans.

2001a "In Search of Common Ground." In *Paul and the Mosaic Law*, ed. James D. G. Dunn, 309-34. Grand Rapids: Eerdmans.

Dunn, J. D. G., and A. M. Suggate

1994 *The Justice of God*. Grand Rapids: Eerdmans.

Du Toit, A. B.

1991 "Faith and Obedience in Paul." *Neotestamentica*, 25:65-74.

Earnshaw, J. D.

1994 "Reconsidering Paul's Marriage Analogy in Romans 7:1-4." *NTS* 40:68-88.

Eastman, Brad

1999 *The Significance of Grace in the Letters of Paul*. Berlin: Lang.

Edwards, J. R.

Romans. Peabody, Mass.: Hendrickson.

Elias, Jacob W.

1995 *1 and 2 Thessalonians*. Scottdale, Pa.: Herald Press.

Elliott, J. K.

1981 "The Language and Style of the Concluding Doxology to the Epistle to the Romans." *ZNW* 72:124-30.

Elliott, Neil

1990 *The Rhetoric of Romans*. Sheffield, UK: JSOT Press.

1994 *Liberating Paul*. Maryknoll, NY: Orbis.

1997a "Romans 13:1-7 in the Context of Imperial Propaganda." In *Paul and Empire*, ed. Richard A. Horsley, 184-204. Harrisburg, Pa.: Trinity Press International.

1997b "The Anti-Imperial Message of the Cross." In *Paul and Empire*, ed. Richard A. Horsley, 167-83. Harrisburg, Pa.: Trinity Press International.

1999 "Asceticism among the 'Weak' and 'Strong' in Romans 14-15." In *Asceticism and the New Testament*, ed. Leif E. Vaage and Vincent L. Wimbush, 231-51. New York: Routledge.

Ellis, Peter F.

1982 *Seven Pauline Letters*. Collegeville, Minn.: Liturgical Press.

Enz, Jacob J.

1990 "Judaism and Jews." In *Mennonite Encyclopedia*, 5:469-71. Scottdale, Pa.: Herald Press.

Espy, John M.

1985 "Paul's 'Robust Conscience' Re-Examined." *NTS* 31:161-88.

Evans, Craig A.

1984 "Paul and the Hermeneutics of 'True Prophecy': A Study of Romans 9-11." *Biblica*, 65:560-70.

1993 "Faith and Polemic: The New Testament and First Century Judaism." In *Anti-Semitism and Early Christianity*, ed. Craig A. Evans and Donald A. Hagner, 1-17. Philadelphia: Fortress Press.

1999 "Paul and the Prophets: Prophetic Criticism in the Epistle to the Romans." In *Romans and the People of God*, ed. Sven K. Soderlund and N. T. Wright, 115-38. Grand Rapids: Eerdmans.

Eskola, Timo
1998 *Theodicy and Predestination in Pauline Soteriology*. Tübingen: Mohr Siebeck.

Fee, Gordon
1994 "Christology and Pneumatology in Romans 8:9-11–and Elsewhere: Some Reflections on Paul as a Trinitarian." In *Jesus of Nazareth: Lord and Christ*, ed. J. B. Green and M. Turner, 312-31. Grand Rapids: Eerdmans.

1995 *God's Empowering Presence*. Peabody, Mass.: Hendrickson.

Finger, Reta Halteman
1993 *Paul and the Roman House Churches*. Scottdale, Pa.: Herald Press.

Fitzmyer, Joseph A.
1979 "The Gospel in the Theology of Paul." *Int* 33:339-50.

1981 *To Advance the Gospel*. Crossroad.

1993 *Romans*. Anchor Bible. New York: Doubleday.

1993 "The Consecutive Meaning of Ep' Ho in Romans 5:12." *NTS* 39:321-39.

Friedmann, Robert
1952 "Peter Riedemann on Original Sin and the Way of Redemption." *MQR* 26:210-15.

1959 "Original Sin." In *Mennonite Encyclopedia*, 4:79-82. Scottdale, Pa.: Herald Press.

1973 *The Theology of Anabaptism*. Scottdale, Pa.: Herald Press.

1994 "The Doctrine of Original Sin as Held by the Anabaptists of the Sixteenth Century." In *Essays in Anabaptist Theology*, ed. H. Wayne Pipkin, 147-56. Elkhart, Ind.: Institute of Mennonite Studies.

Friedrich, J., W. Poehlmann, and P. Stuhlmacher
1976 "Zur historischen Situation und Intention von Roem. 13:1-7." *Zeitschrift für Theologie und Kirche* 73:131-66.

Fiorenza, Elisabeth Schuessler
1986 "Missionaries, Apostles, Coworkers: Romans 16 and the Reconstruction of Women's Early Christian History." *Word and World* 6:420-33.

Fryer, N. S. L.
1981 "Reconciliation in Paul's Epistle to the Romans." *Neotestamentica* 15:34-68.

Fung, R. Y. K.
1988 *The Epistle to Galatians*. Grand Rapids, Eerdmans.

Funk, R. W.
1967 "The Apostolic Parousia: Form and Significance." In *Christian History and Interpretation*, ed. W. R. Farmer, C. F. D. Moule, R. R. Niebhur, 249-68. Cambridge: Cambridge University Press.

Gagnon, Robert A. J.
   1998   "The Meaning of HUPON TO AGATHON in Romans 14:16."
          JBL 117:675-89.
   2001   *The Bible and Homosexual Practice*. Nashville: Abingdon
Gamble, H.
   1977   *The Textual History of the Letter to the Romans*. Grand
          Rapids: Eerdmans.
Garlington, Don B.
   1990   "The Obedience of Faith in the Letter to the Romans." *WTJ*
          52:201-24.
   1991   *The Obedience of Faith*. Tübingen: Mohr Siebeck.
   1991   "The Obedience of Faith in the Letter to the Romans." *WTJ*
          53:47-72.
   1994   *Faith, Obedience and Perserverance*. Tübingen: Mohr Siebeck.
Gaston, Lloyd
   1980   "Abraham and the Righteousness of God." *HBT* 2:39-68.
   1982   "Israel's Enemies in Pauline Theology." *NTS* 28:400-23.
          Reprinted in *Paul and the Torah*, 80-99 (see 1987 below).
   1987   *Paul and the Torah*. Vancouver, BC: University of British
          Columbia Press.
   1998   "Faith in Romans 12 in the Light of the Common Life of the
          Roman Church." In *Common Life in the Early Church*, ed. Julian
          V. Hills, et al., 258-64. Harrisburg, Pa.: Trinity Press International.
Gathercole, Simon J.
   2002   *Where Is Boasting?* Grand Rapids: Eerdmans.
Geddert, Timothy J.
   2001   *Mark*. Scottdale: Herald Press.
Georgi, Dieter
   1991   *Theocracy*. Minneapolis: Fortress Press.
   1997   "God Turned Upside Down." In *Paul and Empire*, ed. Richard A.
          Horsley, 148-57. Harrisburg, Pa.: Trinity Press International.
Getty, M. A.
   1988   "Paul and the Salvation of Israel: A Perspective on Romans
          9–11." *CBQ* 50:456-69.
Gillman, F. A.
   1983   "Romans 6:5a: United to a Death Like Christ's." *ETL* 59:267-302.
   1987   "Another Look at Romans 8.3: 'In the Likeness of Sinful Flesh,'"
          CBQ 49:597-604.
Given, Mark D.
   1999   "Restoring the Inheritance in Romans 11:1." *JBL* 118:89-96.
Gorday, P.
   1983   *Principles of Patristic Exegesis*. Lewiston, NY: Edwin Mellen.
Gorman, Michael J.
   2001   *Cruciformity*. Grand Rapids: Eerdmans.
Green, Joel B. and Baker, Mark, D.
   2000   *Recovering the Scandal of the Cross*. Downers Grove, Ill.:
          InterVarsity.
Greer, Rowan
   1995   "Sinned We All in Adam's Fall." In *The Social World of the First
          Christians*, ed. L. Michael White and O. Larry Yarbrough, 382-
          94. Minneapolis: Fortress Press.

Grieb, A. Katherine
    2002   *The Story of Romans*. Louisville: Westminster John Knox Press.
Guenther, W.
    1978   "Sin." In *Dictionary of New Testament Theology*, 3:573-87.
            Grand Rapids: Zondervan.
Guerra, A. J.
    1988   "Romans 4 as Apologetic Theology." *HTR* 81:251-70.
    1990   "Romans: Paul's Purpose and Audience with Special Attention to
            Romans 9-11." *Revue Biblique* 97:219-37.
Hafemann, Scott
    1988   "The Salvation of Israel in Romans 11:25-32. A Response to
            Krister Stendahl." *Ex Auditu* 4:38-58.
Harder, Leland, trans. and ed.
    1985   *The Sources of Swiss Anabaptism*. Scottdale, Pa.: Herald Press.
Harrington, Hannah K.
    1997   "Holiness in the Laws of 4QMMT." In *Legal Texts and Legal
            Issues*, ed. Moshe Bernstein, Florentino G. Martinez, and John
            Kampen, 109-28. Leiden: Brill.
Harrison, J. R.
    1999   "Paul, Eschatology and the Augustan Age of Grace." *TynBul*
            50:79-91.
Harrisville, R. A.
    1994   "PISTIS CHRISTOU: Witness of the Fathers." *NovT* 36:233-41.
Hay, David M.
    1989   "Pistis as 'Ground for Faith' in Hellenized Judaism and Paul."*JBL*
            108:461-76.
    1995   *Pauline Theology*, vol. 3. Philadelphia: Fortress Press.
Hays, Richard B.
    1980   "Psalm 143 and the Logic of Romans 3." *JBL* 99:107-15.
    1983   *The Faith of Jesus Christ*. Chico, Calif.: Scholars Press.
    1985   "Have We Found Abraham to Be Our Forefather According to the
            Flesh? A Reconsideration of Romans 4:1." *NovT* 27:76-98.
    1986   "Relations Natural and Unnatural: A Response to John Boswell's
            Exegesis of Romans 1." *Journal of Religious Ethics*, 14:184-215.
    1989a   *Echoes of Scripture in the Letters of Paul*. New Haven, Conn.:
            Yale University Press.
    1989b   "'The Righteous One' as Eschatological Deliverer: A Case Study
            in Paul's Apocalyptic Hermeneutic." In *Apocalyptic and the New
            Testament*, ed. Joel Marcus and Marion L. Soards, 191-215.
            Sheffield, UK: Sheffield Academic Press.
    1991   "Awaiting the Redemption of Our Bodies." *Sojourners* 20:17-20.
    1992   "Justification." In *Anchor Bible Dictionary*, 3:1129-33. New
            York: Doubleday.
    1993   "Christ Prays the Psalms: Paul's Use of an Early Christian
            Exegetical Convention." In *The Future of Christology*, ed.
            Abraham J. Malherbe and Wayne A. Meeks, 122-36.
            Minneapolis: Fortress Press.
    1996   *The Moral Vision of the New Testament*. San Francisco: Harper.
    1997   "PISTIS and Pauline Christology: What Is at Stake?" In *Pauline
            Christology*, ed. D. M. Hay and E. E. Johnson, 4:35-60. Atlanta:
            Scholars Press.

2001   "Three Dramatic Roles: The Law in Romans 3-4." In *Paul and the Mosaic Law*, ed. James D. G. Dunn, 151-64. Grand Rapids: Eerdmans.

2002   *The Faith of Jesus Christ*. Revised ed. (with Hays's and Dunn's SBL Exchange on the "Faith of/in Jesus" issue). Grand Rapids: Eerdmans.

Heil, John Paul
2001   "Christ, the Termination of the Law (Romans 9:30-10:8)." *CBQ* 63:484-98.

Hill, David
1967   *Greek Words and Hebrew Meanings*. Cambridge: Cambridge University Press.

Hofius, Otfried
1990   "'All Israel will be Saved': Divine Salvation and Israel's Deliverance in Romans 9-11." *Princeton Seminary Bulletin* 11:19-39.

2001   "The Adam-Christ Antithesis and the Law." In *Paul and the Mosaic Law*, ed. James D. G. Dunn, 165-205. Grand Rapids: Eerdmans.

Hooker, M. D.
1959   "Adam in Romans 1." *NTS* 6:297-306.

1971   "Interchange in Christ." *JTS* 22:349-61.

1977   "Interchange and Atonement." *BJRL* 60:462-81.

1989   "Pistis Christou." *NTS* 35:321-42.

1990   *From Adam to Christ*. Cambridge: Cambridge University Press.

Hooker, M. D., and S. G. Wilson, eds.
1982   *Paul and Paulinism*. London: SPCK.

Horsley, Richard A.
1997   *Paul and Empire*. Harrisburg, Pa.: Trinity International Press.

2000   *Paul and Politics*. Harrisburg, Pa.: Trinity International Press.

Howard, George
1967   "On the 'Faith of Christ,'" *HTR* 60:459-65.

1969   "Christ the End of the Law: The Meaning of Romans 10:4f." *JBL* 88:331-37.

1970   "Romans 3:21-31 and the Inclusion of the Gentiles." *HTR* 63:223-33.

1973-74 "The 'Faith of Christ.'" *ExpTim* 85:212-15.

Hübner, Hans
1984   *Law in Paul's Thought*. Edinburgh: T &. T Clark.

2001   "Hermeneutics of Romans 7." In *Paul and the Mosaic Law*, ed. James D. G. Dunn, 207-14. Grand Rapids: Eerdmans.

Hultgren, Arland J.
1985   *Paul's Gospel and Mission*. Philadelphia: Fortress Press.

Humphrey, Edith M.
1999   "Why Bring the Word Down? The Rhetoric Demonstration and Disclosure in Romans 9:30–10:21." In *Romans and the People of God*, ed. Sven K. Soderlund and N. T. Wright, 129-48. Grand Rapids: Eerdmans.

Hurtado, Larry, W.
1981   "The Doxology at the End of Romans." In *New Testament Textual Criticism*, ed. Eldon Jay Epp and Gordon Fee, 185-200. New York: Clarendon Press.

1999   "Jesus' Divine Sonship in Paul's Epistle to the Romans." In
       Romans and the People of God, ed. Sven K. Soderlund and
       N. T. Wright, 217-33. Grand Rapids: Eerdmans.
Hvalvik, R.
1990   "A 'Sonderweg' for Israel. A Critical Examination of a Current
       Interpretation of Romans 11:25-27." *JSNT* 38:87-107.
Isaak, Jon
2003   "The Christian Community and Political Responsibility: Romans
       13:1-7." *Direction* 32,1 (Spring): 32-46.
Jervell, Jacob
1991   "The Letter to Jerusalem." In *The Romans Debate*, ed, K. P.
       Donfried, 53-64. Peabody, Mass.: Hendrickson.
Jervis, L. Ann
1991   *The Purpose of Romans*. Sheffield, UK: JSOT Press.
Jervis, L. Ann, and Peter Richardson, eds.
1994   *Gospel in Paul*. Sheffield, UK: Sheffield Academic Press.
Jewett, Robert
1969   "The Form and Function of the Homiletic Benediction." *ATR*
       51:18-34.
1971   *Paul's Anthropological Terms*. Leiden: Brill.
1982   *Christian Tolerance*. Philadelphia: Westminster.
1982   "Romans as an Ambassadorial Letter." *Int* 36:5-20.
1985   "The Redaction and Use of an Early Christian Confession in
       Romans 1:3-4." In *The Living Text*, ed. Dennis E. Groh and
       Robert Jewett, 99-122. Washington, D.C.: University Press of
       America.
1988   "Paul, Phoebe and the Spanish Mission." In *The Social World of
       Formative Judaism and Christianity*, ed. J. Neusner, et al., 142-
       61. Philadelphia: Fortress Press.
1991   "Following the Argument of Romans." In *The Romans Debate*,
       ed. K. P. Donfried, 265-77. Peabody, Mass.: Hendrickson.
1992   "Ecumenical Theology for the Sake of Mission: Romans 1:1-17 +
       15:14–16:24." In *SBL 1992 Seminar Papers*, 598-612.
       Atlanta: Scholars Press.
1998   "The God of Peace in Romans: Reflections on Crucial Lutheran
       Texts." *Currents in Theology and Mission* 25:186-94.
Johnson, E. Elizabeth
1989   *The Function of Apocalyptic and Wisdom Traditions in
       Romans 9-11*. Atlanta: Scholars Press.
Johnson, E. Elizabeth, and David M. Hay, eds.
1997   *Pauline Theology*. Vol. 4. Atlanta: Scholars Press.
Johnson, Luke T.
1997   *Reading Romans*. New York: Crossroad.
1982   "Rom. 3:21-26 and the Faith of Jesus." *CBQ* 44:77-90.
Johnston, George
1984   "'Kingdom of God' Sayings in Paul's Letters." In *From Jesus to
       Paul*, ed. P. Richardson and J. C. Hurd, 143-56. Waterloo, Ont.:
       Wilfrid Laurier Press.
Judge, E. A., and G. S. R. Thomas
1966   "The Origin of the Church at Rome: A New Solution." *RefTR*
       25:81-93.

Käsemann, Ernst
 1969 *New Testament Questions of Today.* London: SCM Press.
 1980 *Commentary on Romans.* Grand Rapids: Eerdmans.
Kapera, Zdzislaw J.
 1991 *Qumran Cave IV and MMT.* Krakow, Poland: Enigma Press.
Karlberg, Mark W.
 1986 "Israel's History Personified: Romans 7:7-13 in Relation to Paul's Teaching on the 'Old Man.'" *TrinJ* 7:65-74.
Karris, Robert J.
 1991 "Romans 14:1–15:13 and the Occasion of Romans." In *The Romans Debate*, ed. K. P. Donfried, 65-84. Peabody, Mass.: Hendrickson.
Kaylor, R. D.
 1988 *Paul's Covenant Community.* Atlanta: John Knox.
Keck, L. E.
 1969 "New Testament Views of Death." In *Perspectives on Death*, ed. L. O. Mills, 33-98. Abingdon.
 1977 "The Function of Rom. 3:10-18." In *God's Christ and His People*, ed. J. Jervell and W. A. Meeks, 141-57. Oslo, Norway: Universitets-forlaget.
 1980 "The Law and 'The Law of Sin and Death' (Rom. 8:1-4): Reflections on the Spirit and Ethics in Paul." In *The Divine Helmsman*, ed. J. L. Crenshaw and S. Sandmel, 41-57. New York: KTAV Publishing House.
 1986 "Romans 1:18-23." *Int.*" 40:402-6.
 1989 "Jesus in Romans." *JBL* 108:443-60.
 1990a "Christology, Soteriology, and the Praise of God (Romans 15:7-13)." In *The Conversation Continues*, ed. R. T. Fortna and B. R. Gaventa, 85-97. Nashville: Abingdon.
 1990b "Romans 15:4–An Interpolation?" In *Faith and History*, ed. J. T. Carroll, C. H. Cosgove, E. J. Johnson, 125-36. Atlanta: Scholars Press.
 1995 "What Makes Romans Tick?" In *Pauline Theology*, ed. D. M. Hay and E. E. Johnson, 3:3-29. Philadelphia: Fortress Press.
 1997 "Searchable Judgments and Scrutable Ways: A Response to Paul J. Achtemeier." In *Pauline Theology*, ed. E. E. Johnson and D. M. Hay, 4:22-32. Atlanta: Scholars Press.
Kennedy, George A.
 1984 *New Testament Interpretation Through Rhetorical Criticism.* Chapel Hill, N.C.: University of North Carolina Press.
Kertelge, K.
 1991 "The Sin of Adam in Light of Christ's Redemptive Act According to Romans 5:12-21." *Communio* 18:502-13.
Kinneavy, James L.
 1987 *Greek Rhetorical Origins of Christian Faith.* Oxford: Oxford University Press.
Kirby, J. T.
 1987 "The Syntax of Romans 5.12: A Rhetorical Approach." *NTS* 33:283-86.
Klaassen, Walter, Frank Friesen, and Werner Packull, trans. and eds.
 2001 *Sources of South German/Austrian Anabaptism.* Pandora, Ohio: Pandora Press.

Klassen, William
    1962   "Coals of Fire: Sign of Repentance or Revenge?" *NTS* 9:337-50.
    1998   "Pursue Peace: A Concrete Ethical Mandate (Romans 12:18-
            21)." In *Ja und Nein*, ed. Klaus Wengst and Gerhard Sass, 195-
            207. Neukirchen-Vluyn: Neukirchener Verlag.
Klassen, William, and Walter Klaassen, trans. and eds.
    1978   *The Writings of Pilgram Marpeck*. Scottdale, Pa.: Herald Press.
Klein, Guenther
    1991   "Paul's Purpose in Writing the Epistle to the Romans." In *The
            Romans Debate*, ed. K. P. Donfried, 29-43. Peabody, Mass.:
            Hendrickson.
Knox, John
    1964   "Romans 15:14-33 and Paul's Conception of His Apostolic
            Mission." *JBL* 83:1-11.
Koontz, Gale Gerber
    1989   "The Liberation of Atonement." *MQR* 64:171-92.
Kraftchick, Steve
    1987   "Paul's Use of Creation Themes: A Test of Romans 1–8." *Ex
            Auditu* 3:72-87.
Kraus, C. Norman
    1987   *Jesus Christ Our Lord*. Scottdale, Pa.: Herald Press.
Kreitzer, Larry
    1989   "Adam as Analogy: Help or Hindrance?" *New Blackfriars*
            70:278-84.
    1989   "Christ and Second Adam in Paul." *Communion Viatorum*
            32:55-101.
    1991   "The Sin of Adam in Light of Christ's Redemptive Act According
            to Romans 5:12-21." *Communio* 18:502-13.
Laato, T.
    1995   *Paul and Judaism*. Atlanta: Scholars Press.
Lambrecht, J.
    1974   "Man Before and Without Christ: Rom. 7 and Pauline
            Anthropology." *LS* 5:18-33.
    1984   "Why Is Boasting Excluded? A Note on Rom. 3:27 and 4:2." *ETL*
            61:364-69.
    1990   "The Groaning of Creation: A Study of Rom. 8:18-30." *LS* 15:3-
            18.
    1992   *The Wretched "I" and Its Liberation*. Grand Rapids: Eerdmans.
    2000   "Syntactical and Logical Remarks on Romans 15:8-9a." *NovT*
            42:257-61.
Lambrecht, J., and R. W. Thomson
    1989   *Justification by Faith*. Wilmington, Del.: Michael Glazier.
Lampe, Peter
    1991   "The Roman Christians of Romans 16." In *The Romans Debate*,
            ed. K. P. Donfried, 216-30. Peabody, Mass.: Hendrickson.
    1992   "Family in Church and Society in New Testament Times."
            Affirmation 5:1-20.
    2003   *From Paul to Valentinus*. Minneapolis: Fortress.
Lane, William
    1998   "Social Perspectives on Roman Christianity during the Formative
            Years from Nero to Nerva: Romans, Hebrews, 1 Clement." In

Judaism and Christianity in the First Century, ed. K. P. Donfried and P. Richardson, 196-244. Grand Rapids: Eerdmans.

LaPiana, G.
1925 "The Roman Church at the End of the Second Century." *HTR* 18:201-77.
1927 "Foreign Groups in Rome During the First Centuries of the Empire." *HTR* 20:183-403.

Lategan, B. C.
1991 "Reception: Theory and Practice in Reading Romans 13." In *Text and Interpretation*, ed. P. J. Hartin and J. H. Petzer, 145-69. Leiden: Brill.

Leenhardt, F.J.
1961 *The Epistle to the Romans*. London: Lutterworth.

Lehn, Cornelia
1980 *Peace Be With You*. Newton, Kan.: Faith & Life Press.

Leon, H. J.
1960 *The Jews of Ancient Rome*. Philadelphia: Jewish Publiciation Society of America.

Levison, J. R.
1988 *Portraits of Adam in Early Judaism*. Sheffield, UK: Sheffield Academic Press.

Lieu, Judith M.
1985 "'Grace to You and Peace': The Apostolic Greeting." *BJRL* 68:161-78.

Lincoln, Andrew T.
1992 "Abraham Goes to Rome: Paul's Treatment of Abraham in Romans 4." In *Worship, Theology and Ministry in the Early Church*, ed. Michael J. Wilkins and Terence Paige, 163-79. Sheffield, UK: Sheffield Academic Press.
1995 "From Wrath to Justification: Tradition, Gospel, and Audience in the Theology of Romans 1:18-4:25." In *Pauline Theology*, ed. D. M. Hay and E. E. Johnson, 3:130-59. Philadelphia: Fortress Press.

Lindsay, D. R.
1993a *Josephus and Faith*. Leiden: Brill.
1993b "The Root and Development of the *pis-* Word Group as Faith Terminology." *JSNT* 49:103-18.

Little, J. A.
1984 "Paul's Use of Analogy: A Structural Analysis of Romans 7:1-6." *CBQ* 46:82-90.

Lodge, John G.
1981 "James and Paul at Cross-Purposes? James 2:22." *Biblica* 62:195-213.

Lombard, H. A.
1981 "The Adam-Christ 'Typology' in Romans 5:12-21." *Neotestamentica* 15:69-100.

Longenecker, Bruce W.
1989 "Different Answers to Different Issues: Israel, the Gentiles and Salvation History in Romans 9-11." *JSNT* 36:95-123.
1991 *Eschatology and the Covenant in 4 Ezra and Romans 1-11*. Sheffield, UK: Sheffield Academic Press.

1993   "*Pistis* in Romans 3:25: Neglected Evidence for the 'Faithfulness of Christ.'" *NTS* 39:478-80.

Longenecker, Richard N.
1974   "The Obedience of Christ in the Theology of the Early Church." In *Reconciliation and Hope*, ed. R. Banks, 142-52. Grand Rapids: Eerdmans.
1999   "The Focus of Romans: The Central Role of 5:1-8:39 in the Argument of the Letter." In *Romans and the People of God*, ed. Sven K. Soderlund and N. T. Wright, 49-69. Grand Rapids: Eerdmans.

Lund, Nils W.
1942   *Chiasmus in the New Testament*. Chapel Hill, N.C.: University of North Carolina Press.

Luther, M.
1961   *Lectures on Romans*. Trans. W. Pauck. Philadelphia: Westminster.

Lyonnet, S.
1970   "The Notion of Sin." In *Sin, Redemption, and Sacrifice*, ed. S. Lyonnet and L. Sabourin, 3-57. Rome: Biblical Institute.

McGrath, A. E.
1986   *Iustitia Dei*. 2 vols. Cambridge: Cambridge University Press.

MacGregor, G. H. C.
1960   "The Concept of the Wrath of God in the New Testament." *NTS* 7:101-9.

McDonald, James I. H.
1987   "Romans 13:1-7 and Christian Social Ethics Today." *Modern Churchman* 29:19-25.
1989   "Romans 13:1-7: A Test Case for New Testament Interpretation." *NTS* 35:540-49.

McDonald, Patricia M.
1990   "Romans 5:1-11 as Rhetorical Bridge." *JSNT* 40:81-96.

McKenzie, John L.
1964   "Natural Law in the New Testament." *BR* 9:3-13.

McKnight, S.
1991   *A Light Among the Gentiles*. Minneapolis: Fortress Press.

Malan, F. S.
1981   "According to Romans 6:12-23 the New Life Must be Manifested by Doing What is Right." *Neotestamentica* 15:118-38.

Malina, Bruce J.
          "Some Observations on the Origin of Sin in Judaism and St. Paul." *CBQ* 31:18-34.
1981   *The New Testament World. Insights from Cultural Anthropology*. Atlanta: John Knox.
1993   *The New Testament World*. Louisville: Westminster John Knox Press.

Manson, T. W.
1991   "St. Paul's Letter to the Romans—and Others." In *The Romans Debate*, ed. K. P. Donfried, 3-16. Peabody, Mass.: Hendrickson.

Marcus, Joel
1986   "The Evil Inclination in the Letters of Paul." *IBS* 8:8-21.
1988   "'Let God Arise and End the Reign of Sin!' A Contribution to the Study of Pauline Parenesis." *Biblica* 69:386-95.

1989 "The Circumcision and the Uncircumcision in Rome." *NTS* 35:67-81.

2001 "'Under the Law': The Background of a Pauline Expression." *CBQ* 63:72-83.

Marshall, I. Howard

1989 "Does the New Testament Teach Universal Salvation?" In *Christ Is Our Place*, ed. T. Hart and D. Thimell, 313-28. Herfordshire, GB: Pickwick.

1999 "Romans 16:25-27–An Apt Conclusion." In *Romans and the People of God*, ed. Sven K. Soderlund and N. T. Wright, 170-84. Grand Rapids: Eerdmans.

Martin B. L.

1989 *Christ and the Law in Paul*. Leiden: Brill.

Martyn, J. Louis

1997 *Theological Issues in the Letters of Paul*, 37-46 Nashville: Abingdon.

Mason, Steve

1994 "'For I Am Not Ashamed of the Gospel' (Rom 1:16): The Gospel and the First Readers of Romans." In *Gospel in Paul*, ed. L. Ann Jervis and P. Richardson, 254-87. Sheffield, UK: Sheffield Academic Press.

Matlock, R. Barry

2000 "Detheologizing the *Pistis Christou* Debate: Cautionary Remarks from a Lexical Semantic Perspective." *NovT* 42:1-23.

2002 "Even the Demons Believe: Paul and pistis Christou," CBQ, 64:308-18.

Meeks, W. A.

1987 "Judgment and the Brother: Romans 14:1–15:13." In *Tradition and Interpretation in the New Testament*, ed. G. F. Hawthorne and O. Betz, 290-300. Grand Rapids: Eerdmans.

1990 "On Trusting an Unpredictable God: A Hermeneutical Meditation on Romans 9-11." In *Faith and History*, ed. J. T. Carroll, C. H. Cosgrove, and E. J. Johnson, 105-24. Atlanta: Scholars Press.

Melanchthon, Philip

1951 *Roemerbrief-Kommentar.* Guetersloh: Bertelsmann.

Meyer, Ben

1983 "The Pre-Pauline Formula in Rom. 3:25-26a." *NTS* 29:198-208.

1988 "Election—Historical Thinking in Romans 9–11, and Ourselves." *Ex Auditu* 4:1-7.

Meyer, P. W.

1980 "Romans 10.4 and the 'End' of the Law." In *The Divine Helmsman*, ed. J. L. Crenshaw and S. Sandmel, 59-78. New York: KTAV.

1990 "The Worm at the Core of the Apple: Exegetical Reflections on Romans 7." In *The Conversation Continues*, ed. R. T. Fortna and B. R. Gaventa, 62-84. Nashville: Abingdon.

Meyers, C. D.

1993 "Chiastic Inversion in the Argument of Romans 3–8." *NovT* 35:30-47.

Michaels, J. Ramsey

1999 The Redemption of Our Bodies: The Riddle of Romans 8:19-22."

In *Romans and the People of God*, ed. Sven K. Soderlund and N. T. Wright, 92-114. Grand Rapids: Eerdmans.

Mijoga, H. B. P.
1999 *The Pauline Notion of Deeds of the* Law. San Francisco: International Scholars Publications.

Miller, James C.
2000 *The Obedience of Faith, the Eschatological People of God, and the Purpose of Romans*. Atlanta: Society of Biblical Literature.

Minear, Paul S.
1971 *The Obedience of Faith*. Naperville, Ill.: Allenson.

Moiser, Jeremy
1990 "Rethinking Romans 12-15." *NTS* 36:571-82.

Moo, Douglas J.
1982 "Romans 6:1-14." *TrinJ* 3:215-20.
1983 "'Law,' 'Works of Law,' and Legalism in Paul." *WTJ* 45:73-100.
1986 "Israel and Paul in Romans 7:7-12." *NTS* 32:122-35.
1996 *The Epistle to the Romans*. Grand Rapids: Eerdmans.

Moody, R. M.
1981 "The Habakkuk Quotation in Romans 1:17." *ExpTim* 92:205-8.

Morgan, Florence A.
1983 "Romans 6:5a: United to a Death Like Christ's."*ETL* 59:267-302.

Morris, Leon
1970 "The Theme of Romans." In *Apostolic History and the Gospel*, ed. W. W. Gasque and R. P. Martin, 249-63. Grand Rapids: Eerdmans.
1988 *The Epistle to the Romans*. Grand Rapids: Eerdmans.

Moule, C. F. D.
1977 *The Origin of Christology*. Cambridge: Cambridge University Press.

Moxnes, Halvor
1980 *Theology in Conflict*. Leiden: Brill.
1988 "Honor and Righteousness in Romans." *JSNT* 32:61-77.
1988 "Honor, Shame, and the Outside World in Paul's Letter to the Romans." In *The Social World of Formative Christianity and Judaism*, ed. Jacob Neusner, et al., 207-18. Philadelphia: Fortress Press.
1995 "The Quest for Honor and the Unity of the Community in Romans 12 and in the Orations of Dio Chrysostom." In *Paul in His Hellenistic Context*, ed. Troels Engberg-Pedersen, 203-30. Minneapolis: Fortress Press..

Nanos, Mark D.
1996 *The Mystery of Romans*. Minneapolis: Fortress Press.

Nardoni, E.
1993 "The Concept of Charism in Paul." *CBQ* 55:68-80.

Neyrey, Jerome H.
1991 *The Social World of Luke-Acts*. Peabody, Mass.: Hendrickson.
1996a "Clean/Unclean, Pure/Polluted, and Holy/Profane: The Idea and the System of Purity." In *The Social Sciences and New Testament Interpretation*, ed. Richard Rohrbaugh, 80-104. Peabody, Mass.: Hendrickson.

1996b "Meals, Food, and Table Fellowship." In *The Social Sciences and New Testament Interpretation*, ed. Richard Rohrbaugh, 159-82. Peabody, Mass.: Hendrickson.

Nolland, John
1981 "Uncircumcised Proselytes." *Journal for the Study of Judaism* 12:173-94.

Nygren, A.
1949 *Commentary on Romans*. Philadelphia: Muhlenberg Press.

O'Brian, P.
1974 "Thanksgiving and the Gospel in Paul." *NTS* 21:144-55.

O'Rourke, John J.
1973 "Pistis in Romans," *CBQ*, 35:188-94.

Osiek, Carolyn
1987 "Women in House Churches." In *Common Life in the Early Church*, ed. Julian V. Hills, et al., 300-15. Harrisburg, Pa.: Trinity Press International.

Pedersen, Sigfred
2002 "Paul's Understanding of the Biblical Law." *NovT* 44:1-34.

Peristiany, J. D., ed.
1965 *Honor and Shame*. London: Weidenfeld & Nicholson.

Petersen, Norman R.
1990 "On the Ending(s) to Paul's Letter to Rome." In *The Future of Early Christianity*, ed. B. A. Pearson, 337-47. Minneapolis: Fortress Press.

Peterson, Anders Klostergaard
1998 "Shedding New Light on Paul's Understanding of Baptism: a Ritual Theoretical Approach to Romans 6." *ST* 52:3-28.

Pilgrim, Walter E.
1999 *Uneasy Neighbors: Church and State in the New Testament*. Minneapolis: Augsburg Fortress Press.

Piper, John
1980 "The Demonstration of the Righteousness of God in Romans 3:25,26." *JSNT* 7:2-32.
1980 "The Righteousness of God in Romans 3:1-8." *TZ* 36:3-16.
1983 *The Justification of God*. Grand Rapids: Baker.

Pipkin, Wayne, and John H. Yoder, trans. and eds.
1989 *Balthasar Hubmaier*. Scottdale, Pa.: Herald Press.

Pitt-Rivers, Julian
1968 "Honor." *International Encyclopedia of the Social Sciences*, ed. D. L. Sills, 6:503-11, New York: Macmillan.

Porter, Calvin L.
1994 "Romans 1:18-32: Its Role in the Developing Argument." *NTS* 40:210-28.

Porter, Stanley, E.
1991 "The Argument of Romans 5: Can a Rhetorical Question Make a Difference." *JBL* 110:655-77.

Pryor, John W.
1983 "Paul's Use of *Iesous*—A Clue for the Translation of Romans 3:26?" *Colloquium* 16:31-45.

Punt, N.
1980 *Unconditional Good News*. Grand Rapids: Eerdmans.

Quarles, Charles L.
  2003 "From Faith to Faith: A Fresh Examination of the Prepositional Series in Romans 1:17." *NovT* 45:1-21.
Räisänen, Heikki
  1983 *Paul and the Law.* Tübingen: Mohr Siebeck.
  1988 "Paul, God, and Israel: Romans 9–11 in Recent Recearch." In *The Social World of Formative Judaism and Christianity,* ed. J. Neusner, et al., 178-206. Philadelphia: Fortress Press.
  1992 *Jesus, Paul and the Torah.* Sheffield, UK: JSOT Press.
Reasoner, Mark
  1995 "The Theology of Romans 12:1–15:13." In *Pauline Theology,* ed. D. M. Hay and E. E. Johnson, 3:287-99. Fortress Press.
  1999 *The Strong and the Weak.* Cambridge: Cambridge University Press.
Reid, Marty L.
  1996 *Augustinian and Pauline Rhetoric in Romans Five.* Lewiston, NY: Mellen Biblical Press.
Reumann, John
  1982 *Righteousness in the New Testament.* Philadelphia: Fortress Press.
Rhyne, C. Thomas
  1985 "*Nomos Dikaiosynes* and the Meaning of Romans 10:4." *CBQ* 47:486-99.
Richardson, Peter
  1969 *Israel in the Apostolic Church.* Cambridge: Cambridge University Press.
  1986 "From Apostles to Virgins: Romans 16 and the Roles of Women in the Early Church." *Toronto Journal of Theology* 2:232-61.
  1998 "Augustus-Era Synagogues in Rome." In *Judaism and Christianity in First Century Rome,* ed. K. P. Donfried and Peter Richardson, 17-29. Grand Rapids: Eerdmans.
Richardson, Peter, and Stephen Westerholm
  1991 *Law in Religious Communities in the Roman World.* Wilfrid Laurier University Press.
Roberts, J. J. M.
  1987 "Yahweh's Foundation in Zion (Isa. 28:16)." *JBL* 106:27-45.
Roetzel, Calvin J.
  1997 "No 'Race of Israel' in Paul." *Putting Body and Soul Together,* ed. V. Wiles, A. Brown, and G. F. Snyder, 230-44. Valley Forge, Pa.: Trinity Press International.
Romaniuk, K.
  1991 "Was Phoebe in Romans 16:1 a Deaconess?" *ZNW* 81:132-34.
Rondet, Henri
  1972 *Original Sin: The Patristic and Theological Background.* New York: Alba House.
Rutgers, Leonard V.
  1998 "Romans Policy Toward the Jews: Expulsions from the City of Rome during the First Century C.E." In *Judaism and Christianity in First-Century Rome,* ed. K. P. Donfried and P. Richardson, 93-116. Grand Rapids: Eerdmans.

Sabourin, L.
    1981 "Original Sin Again." *Religious Study Bulletin* 4:88-101.
Sampley, J. Paul
    1995a "Different Light: A Response to Robert Jewett." In *Pauline Theology*, ed. D. M. Hay and E. E. Johnson, 3:109-29. Minneapolis: Fortress Press.
    1995b "The Weak and the Strong: Paul's Careful and Crafty Rhetorical Strategy in Romans 14:1–15:13." In *The Social World of the First Christians*, ed. L. Michael White and O. Larry Yarborough, 40-52. Minneapolis: Fortress Press.
Sanday, W., and A. C. Headlam
    1902 *A Critical and Exegetical Commentary on the Epistle to the Romans*. Edinburgh: T & T Clark.
Sanders, E. P.
    1977 *Paul and Palestinian Judaism*. Philadelphia: Fortress Press.
    1978 "Paul's Attitude Toward the Jewish People." *Union Seminary Quarterly Review* 33:175-91.
    1983a *Paul, the Law, and the Jewish People*. Philadelphia: Fortress Press.
    1983b "Romans 7 and the Purpose of the Law." *Proceedings of the Irish Biblical Association* 7:44-59.
    1985 *Jesus and Judaism*. Philadelphia: Fortress Press.
Schiffmann, L. H.
    1981 "At the Crossroads: Tannaitic Perspectives on the Jewish-Christian Schism." *Jewish and Christian Self-Definition*, ed. E. P. Sanders, 2:115-56. Philadelphia: Fortress Press.
Schlatter, A.
    1995 *Romans*. Trans. S. S. Schatzmann. Peabody, Mass.: Hendrickson.
Schmid, H. H.
    1968 *Gerechtigkeit as Weltordnung*. Tübingen: J. C. B. Mohr.
Schottroff, Luise
    1992 "'Give to Caesar What Belongs to Caesar and to God What Belongs to God': A Theological Response of the Early Christian Church to Its Social and Political Environment." In *The Love of Enemy and Nonretaliation in the New Testament*, ed. Willard Swartley, 223-57. Louisville: Westminster John Knox Press.
Schnabel, E. M.
    1985 *Law and Wisdom from Ben Sira to Paul*. Tübingen: Mohr Siebeck.
Schreiner, Thomas R.
    1983 "The Church as the New Israel and the Future of Ethnic Israel in Paul." *Studia Biblical et Theologica* 13-14:17-38.
    1991a "Israel's Failure to Attain Righteousness in Romans 9:30–10:3." *TrinJ* 12:209-20.
    1991b "'Works of Law' in Paul." *NovT* 33:215-44.
    1993a "Does Romans 9 Teach Individual Election unto Salvation? Some Exegetical and Theological Reflections." *JETS* 36:25-40.
    1993b *The Law and Its Fulfilment*. Grand Rapids: Baker.
    1998 *Romans*. Grand Rapids: Baker.
Schulz, Ray R.
    1990 "A Case for 'President' Phoebe in Romans 16:2." *Lutheran Theological Journal* 24:124-27.

Scott, J. M.
1992   *Adoptions as Sons of God*. Tübingen: Mohr Siebeck.
Scroggs, R.
1966   *The Last Adam*. Philadelphia: Fortress Press.
1983   *The New Testament and Homosexuality*. Minneapolis: Fortress Press.
Scullion J. J., and John Reumann
1992   "Righteousness." *Anchor Bible Dictionary*, 5:724-73. New York: Doubleday.
Segal, A. F.
1987   "The Sacrifice of Isaac in Early Judaism and Christianity." In *The Other Judaisms of Late Antiquity*, 107-30. Atlanta: Scholars Press.
1990a *Paul the Convert*. New Haven, Conn.: Yale.
1990b "Paul's Experience and Romans 9-11." *Princeton Seminary Bulletin* 11:56-70.
Seifrid, Mark A.
1985   "Paul's Approach to the Old Testament in Rom. 10:6-8." *TrinJ* 6:3-37.
1992a *Justification by Faith*. Leiden: Brill.
1992b "The Subject of Romans 7:14-25." *NovT* 34:313-33.
2000a *Christ Our Righteousness*. Downers Grove, Ill.: InterVarsity Press.
2000b "The 'New Perspective on Paul' and Its Problems." *Themelios* 25:5-18.
Seow, Choon-Leong, ed.
1996   *Homosexuality and Christian Community*. Louisville: Westminster John Knox Press.
Shillington, George
1998   *2 Corinthians*. Scottdale, Pa.: Herald Press.
Shogren, Gary S.
2000   "Is the Kingdom of God about Eating and Drinking or Isn't It? (Romans 14:17)." *NovT* 42:238-56.
2000   "The 'Wretched Man' of Romans 7:14-25 as Reductio ad absurdum." *EvQ* 72:119-34.
Siker, Jeffrey S.
1989   "From Gentile Inclusion to Jewish Exclusion: Abraham in Early Christian Controversy with Jews." *BTB* 19:30-36.
1991   *Disinheriting the Jews*. Louisville: Westminster.
Silberman, Lou H.
1990   "Paul's Midrash: Reflections on Romans 4." In *Faith and History*, ed. J. T. Carroll, C. H. Cosgrove, and E. J. Johnson, 99-104. Atlanta: Scholars Press.
Smallwood, E. M.
1976   *The Jews Under Roman Rule*. Leiden: Brill.
Smiga, George
1991   "Romans 12:1-2 and 15:30-32 and the Occasion of the Letter to the Romans." *CBQ* 53:257-73.
Smith, D. M.
1967   "O DE DIKAIOS EK PISTEOS ZĒSETAI." In *Studies in the History of the Text of the New Testament*, ed. B. L. Daniels and

M. J. Suggs, 13-25. Salt Lake City, Utah: University of Utah Press.

Snodgrass, K. R.
1986 "Justification by Grace—To the Doers: An Analysis of the Place of Romans 2 in the Theology of Paul." *NTS* 32:72-93.
1994 "The Gospel in Romans: A Theology of Revelation." In *Gospel in Paul*, ed. L. A. Jervis and P. Richardson, 288-314. Sheffield, UK: Sheffield Academic Press.

Snyman, A. H.
1984 "Style and Meaning in Romans 8:31-39." *Neotestamentica* 18:94-103.
1988 "Style and the Rhetorical Situation of Romans 8:31-39." *NTS* 34:218-31.

Soards, M. L.
1985 "The Righteousness of God in the Writings of the Apostle Paul." *BTB* 15:104-9.
1991 "One Again 'Righteousness of God' in the Writings of the Apostle Paul." *Biblebhashyam* 17:14-43.

Soderlund, Sven K., and N. T. Wright, eds.
1999 *Romans and the People of God*. Grand Rapids: Eerdmans.

Staehlin, W., and W. Grundmann
1964 "Hamarano." In *Theological Dictionary of the New Testament*, 1:293-316. Grand Rapids: Eerdmans.

Stanley, Christopher D.
1992 *Paul and the Language of Scripture*. Cambridge: Cambridge University Press.
1993 "'The Redeemer will come ek Zion': Romans 11:26-27 Revisited." In *Paul and the Scriptures of Israel*, ed. C. A. Evans and J. A. Sanders, 118-42. Sheffield, UK: Sheffield Academic Press.
1996 "'Neither Jew nor Greek': Ethnic Conflict in Graeco-Romans Society." *JSNT* 64:101-24.

Stegner, W. R.
1984 "Romans 9:6-29—A Midrash." *JSNT* 22:37-52.

Stein, Robert H.
1989 "The Argument of Romans 13:1-7." *NovT* 31:325-43.

Stendahl, K.
1976 *Paul Among Jews and Gentiles and Other Essays*. Philadelphia: Fortress Press.
1995 *Final Account*. Minneapolis: Fortress Press.

Stern, M.
1974 "The Jewish Diaspora." In *The Jewish People in the First Century*, vol. 1, *Compendia Rerum Judaicarum ad Novum Testamentum*, ed. S. Safrai and M. Stern, 117-83. Philadelphia: Van Gorcum.

Stirewalt, Martin Luther, Jr.
1991 "The Form and Function of the Greek Letter-Essay." In *The Romans Debate*, ed. K. P. Donfried, 147-71. Peabody, Mass.: Hendrickson.

Stowers, Stanley K.
1981 *The Diatribe and Paul's Letter to the Romans*. Chico, Calif.: Scholars Press.

1984   "Paul's Dialogue with a Fellow Jew in Romans 3:1-9." *CBQ* 46:707-22.

1986   *Letter Writing in Greco-Roman Antiquity.* Philadelphia: Westminister.

1988   "The Diatribe." *Greco-Roman Literature and the New Testament,* ed. D. E. Aune, 71-83. Atlanta: Scholars Press.

1989   "*Ek pisteōs* and *dia tēs pisteōs* in Romans 3:30." *JBL* 108:665-74.

1994   *A Rereading of Romans.* New Haven, Conn.: Yale University Press.

Stuhlmacher, Peter

1986   *Reconciliation, Law and Righteousness.* Philadelphia: Fortress Press.

1985   "Paul's Understanding of the Law." *Svensk exegetisk arsbok* 50:87-104.

1988   "The Theme of Romans." *AusBR* 36:31-44.

1991   "The Pauline Gospel." In *The Gospel and the Gospels,* ed. Peter Stuhlmacher, 149-72. Grand Rapids: Eerdmans.

1991   "The Purpose of Romans." In *The Romans Debate,* ed. K. P. Donfried, 231-42. Peabody, Mass.: Hendrickson.

1994   *Paul's Letter to the Romans.* Louisville: Westminster.

2001   *Revisiting Paul's Doctrine of Justification.* Downers Grove, Ill.: InterVarsity Press.

Suggs, Jack M.

1967   "'The Word Is Near You': Romans 10:6-10 Within the Purpose of the Letter." In *Christian History and Interpretation,* ed. W. R. Farmer, et al., 289-312. Cambridge: Cambridge University Press.

Swartley, Willard

2003   *Homosexuality: Biblical Interpretation and Moral Discernment.* Scottdale, Pa.: Herald Press.

Tannehill, R. G.

1967   *Dying and Rising with Christ.* Berlin: Toepelmann.

Thielman, Frank

1989   *From Plight to Solution.* Leiden: Brill.

1993   "The Story of Israel and the Theology of Romans 5-8." In *SBL 1993 Seminar Papers,* ed. E. H. Lovering, 227-49. Scholars Press. Reprinted in *Pauline Theology,* 3:169-295 ed. (see D. M. Hay 1995)

1994   *Paul and the Law.* Downers Grove, Ill.: InterVarsity Press.

Thiessen, Gerd

1987   *Psychological Aspects of Pauline Theology.* Philadelphia: Fortress Press.

1992   "Soteriological Symbolism in the Pauline Writings–A Structuralist Contribution." In *Social Reality and the Early Christians,* 159-86. Mineapolis: Fortress Press.

Thiselton, A. C.

1975   "Flesh in the New Testament." *Dictionary of New Testament Theology,* 1:674-82. Grand Rapids: Zondervan.

Thompson, Marianne Meye

2000a   "'Mercy Upon All': God as Father in the Epistle to the Romans." In *Romans and the People of God,* ed. Sven K. Soderlund and

N. T. Wright, 203-16. Grand Rapids: Eerdmans.

2000b *The Promise of the Father: Jesus and God in the New Testament.* Grand Rapids: Eerdmans.

Thompson, M.

1991 *Clothed with Christ.* Sheffield, UK: Sheffield Academic Press.

Thompson, R. W.

1986a "How Is the Law Fulfilled in Us? An Interpretation of Rom. 8:4." *LS* 11:31-40.

1986b "Paul's Double Critique of Jewish Boasting: A Study of Rom. 3:27 in Its Context." *Biblica* 67:520-31.

1988 "The Inclusion of the Gentiles in Rom. 3:27-30." *Biblica* 69:543-46.

Thorley, John

1996 "Junia, a Woman Apostle." *NovT* 38:18-29.

Tobin, T. H.

1993 "Controversy and Continuity in Romans 1:18–3:20." *CBQ* 55:198-218.

Tomson, P.

1990 *Paul and the Jewish Law.* Minneapolis: Fortress Press.

Towner, Philip H.

1999 "Romans 13:1-7 and Paul's Missiological Perspective: A Call to Political Quietism or Transformation?" *Romans and the People of God*, Sven K. Soderlund and N. T. Wright, eds. Grand Rapids: Eerdmans, 149-69.

van Daalen, D. H.

1982 "The emunah/pistis of Habakkuk 2:4 and Romans 1:17." In *Studia Evangelica*, ed. E. A. Livingston, 3:523-27. Academie Verlag.

van der Zijpp, N.

1959 "Original Sin." In *Mennonite Encyclopedia*, 4:79-83. Scottdale, Pa.: Herald Press.

Wagner, Ross J.

1997 "The Christ, Servant of Jew and Gentile: A Fresh Approach to Romans 15:8-9." *JBL* 116:473-85.

1998 "The Heralds of Isaiah and the Mission of Paul." In *Jesus and the Suffering Servant*, ed. William H. Bellinger Jr., and William R. Farmer, 193-222. Harrisburg, Pa.: Trinity Press International.

2002 *Heralds of the Good News.* Leiden: Brill.

Wallis, I. G.

1995 *The Faith of Jesus Christ in Early Christian Traditions.* Cambridge: Cambridge University Press.

Walters, James C.

1993 *Ethnic Issues in Paul's Letter to the Romans.* Harrisburg, Pa.: Trinity Press International.

1998 "Romans, Jews, and Christians: The Impact of the Romans on Jewish/Christian Relations in First-Century Rome." In *Judaism and Christianity in First-Century Rome*, ed. K. P. Donfried and P. Richardson, 175-95. Grand Rapids: Eerdmans.

Waltner, Erland

1999 *1 Peter.* Believers Church Bible Commentary. Scottdale, Pa.: Herald Press.

Watson, N. M.
  1983   "Justified by Faith; Judged by Works—An Antinomy?" *NTS* 29:209-21.
Watts, Rikki E.
  1999   "'For I Am Not Ashamed of the Gospel': Romans 1:16-17 and Habakkuk 2:4." In *Romans and the People of God*, ed. Sven K. Soderlund and N. T. Wright, 3-25. Grand Rapids: Eerdmans.
Weaver, D.
  1983   "From Paul to Augustine: Romans 5:12 in Early Christian Exegesis." *St. Vladimir's Theological Quarterly* 27:187-206.
  1985   "The Exegesis of Romans 5:12 among the Greek Fathers and Its Implications for the Doctrine of Original Sin: the 5th–12th Centuries." *St. Vladimir's Theological Quarterly* 29:113-59, 231-57.
Webster, Alexander F. C.
  1981   "St. Paul's Political Advice to the Haughty Gentile Christians in Rome: An Exegesis of Romans 13:1-7." *St. Vladimir Seminary Quarterly* 25:259-82.
Wedderburn, A. J. M.
  1971   "The Body of Christ and Related Concepts in 1 Corinthians." *SJT* 24:74-96.
  1973   "The Theological Structure of Romans V.12." *NTS* 19:332-54.
  1980   "Adam in Paul's Letter to the Romans." In *Studia Biblica 1978*, ed. E. A. Livingstone, 413-30. Sheffield, UK: JSOT Press.
  1983   "Hellenistic Christian Traditions in Romans 6." *NTS* 29:337-55.
  1985   "Some Observations on Paul's Use of the Phrases 'in Christ' and 'with Christ.'" *JSNT* 25:83-97.
  1987   *Baptism and Resurrection*. Tübingen: Mohr Siebeck.
  1987   "The Soteriology of the Mysteries and Pauline Baptismal Theology." *NovT* 29:53-72.
  1989   *The Reasons for Romans*. Minneapolis: T & T Clark.
  1991   "Purpose and Occasion of Romans Again." In *The Romans Debate*, ed. K. P. Donfried, 195-202. Peabody, Mass.: Hendrickson.
Weima, Jeffrey A. D.
  1994a   "Preaching the Gospel in Rome: A Study of the Epistolary Framework of Romans." In *Gospel in Paul*, ed. L. Ann Jervis and P. Richardson, 337-66. Sheffield, UK: Sheffield Academic Press.
  1994b   *Neglected Endings*. Sheffield, UK: Sheffield Academic Press.
Weingart, Richard
  1994   "The Meaning of Sin in the Theology of Menno Simons." In *Essays in Anabaptist Theology*, ed. H. Wayne Pipkin, 157-74. Elkhart, Ind.: Institute of Mennonite Studies.
Wenger, John C., trans. and ed.
  1955   *The Complete Writings of Menno Simons*. Scottdale, Pa.: Herald Press.
Westerholm, S.
  1988   *Israel's Law and the Church's Faith*. Grand Rapids: Eerdmans.
  2001   "Paul and the Law in Romans 9-11." In *Paul and the Mosaic Law*, ed. James D. G. Dunn, 215-37. Grand Rapids: Eerdmans.

White, J. L.
1971 "Introductory Formulae in the Body of the Pauline Letter." *JBL* 90:91-97.
1972 *The Body of the Greek Letter*. Missoula: Society of Biblical Literature.
1984 "New Testament Epistolary Literature in the Framework of Ancient Epistolography." *ANRW* II 25.2:1730-56.
Whitsett, Christopher G.
2000 "Son of God, Seed of David: Paul's Messianic Exegesis in Romans 2:3-4." *JBL* 119:661-81.
Wiefel, Wolfgang
1991 "The Jewish Community in Ancient Rome and the Origins of Roman Christianity." In *The Romans Debate*, ed. K. P. Donfried, 85-101. Peabody, Mass.: Hendrickson.
Wilckens, Ulrich
1974a "Roemer 13.1-7." In *Rechtfertigung als Freiheit*, 203-45. Neukirchen-Vluyn: Neukirchener.
1974b "Ueber Abfassunszweck und Aufbau des Roemerbriefes." In *Rechtfertigung als Freiheit*, 110-70. Neukirchen-Vluyn: Neukirchener.
Williams, S. K.
1975 *Jesus' Death as Saving Event*. Missoula: Scholars Press.
1980 "The 'Righteousness of God' in Romans." *JBL* 99:241-90.
1987 "Again Pistis Christou." *CBQ* 49:431-47.
Wilson, W. T.
1991 *Love Without Pretense*. Tübingen: Mohr Siebeck.
Winger, M.
1992 *By What Law?* Atlanta: Scholars Press.
Wink, Walter
1984 *Naming the Powers: The Language of Power in the New Testament*. Philadelphia: Fortress Press.
1986 *Unmasking the Powers: The Invisible Powers That Determine Human Existence*. Philadelphia: Fortress Press.
1992 *Engaging the Powers: Discernment and Resistance in a World of Domination*. Minneapolis: Fortress Press.
Wink, Walter, ed.
1999 *Homosexuality and Christian Faith*. Minneapolis: Fortress Press.
Witherington, Ben
1994 *Paul's Narrative Thought World*. Westminster John Knox Press.
Wright, N. Tom
1978 "The Paul of History and the Apostle of Faith." *TynBul* 29:61-88.
1979 "Towards a Biblical View of Universalism." *Themelios* 4:54-58.
1980 "Justification: The Biblical Basis and its Relevance for Contemporary Evangelicalism." In *The Great Acquital*, ed. G. Reid, 13-37, 109-19. London: Fount Paperbacks.
1983 "Adam in Pauline Christology." In *Society of Biblical Literature Seminar Papers, 1983*, ed. Kent H. Richard, 359-89. Chico, Calif.: Scholars Press.
1990 "The New Testament and the State." *Themelios* 16:11-17.
1991 *The Climax of the Covenant*. Minneapolis: Fortress Press.

1992a *Christian Origins and the Question of* God. Vol. 1. Minneapolis: Fortress Press.

1992b "Romans and the Theology of Paul." In *SBL Seminar Papers, 1992*, ed., E. H. Lovering, 184-213. Atlanta: Scholars Press. Reprinted in *Pauline Theology*, ed. D. M. Hay and E. E. Johnson, 3:30-67. Minneapolis: Fortress Press.

1996 "The Law in Romans 2." In *Paul and the Mosaic Law*, ed. James D. G. Dunn, 131-50. Grand Rapids: Eerdmans.

1997 *What Saint Paul Really Said?* Grand Rapids: Eerdmans.

1998 "Paul and Qumran." *Bible Review* 14:18, 54.

1999 "New Exodus, New Inheritance: The Narrative Structure of Romans 3-8." In *Romans and the People of God*, ed. Sven K. Soderlund and N. T. Wright, 26-35. Grand Rapids: Eerdmans.

2000 "Paul's Gospel and Caesar's Empire." In *Paul and Politics*, ed. Richard A. Horsley, 160-83. Harrisburg, Pa.: Trinity Press International.

2002 "The Letter to the Romans." In *The New Interpreters Bible*, 10:393-770. Nashville: Abingdon.

Wuellner, Wilhelm
1991 "Paul's Rhetoric of Argumentation in Romans: An Alternative to the Donfried-Karris Debate over Romans." In *The Romans Debate*, ed. K. P. Donfried, 128-46. Peabody, Mass.: Hendrickson.

Yeatts, John R.
2003 *Revelation*. Believers Church Bible Commentary. Scottdale, Pa.: Herald Press.

Yinger, Kent L.
1988 "Romans 12:14-21 and Nonretaliation in Second Temple Judaism: Addressing Persecution within the Community." *CBQ* 60:74-96.

1999 *Paul, Judaism, and Judgment According to Deeds*. Cambridge: Cambridge University Press.

Yoder, John H.
1994 *The Politics of Jesus*. Revised ed. Originally published 1972. Grand Rapids: Eerdmans.

2003 *The Jewish-Christian Schism Revisited*. Ed. Michael C. Cartwright and Peter Ochs. Grand Rapids: Eerdmans.

Yoder, John H., trans. and ed.
1973 *The Legacy of Michael Sattler*. Scottdale, Pa.: Herald Press.

Yoder Neufeld, Thomas R.
2002 *Ephesians*. Believers Church Bible Commentary. Scottdale, Pa.: Herald Press.

Zerbe, Gordon M.
1992 "Paul's Ethics of Nonretaliation and Peace." In *The Love of Enemy and Nonretaliation in the New Testament*, ed. Willard M. Swartley, 177-222. Louisville: Westminster John Knox Press.

1993 *Non-Retaliation in Early Christian and New Testament Texts*. Sheffield, UK: JSOT Press.

Ziesler, J. A.
1972 *The Meaning of Righteousness in Paul*. Cambridge: Cambridge University Press.

1987   "The Just Requirement of the Law (Romans 8.4)." *AusBR* 35:77-82.

1988   "The Role of the Tenth Commandment in Romans 7." *JSNT* 33:41-56.

1989   *Paul's Letter to the Romans.* Harrisburg, Pa.: Trinity Press International.

Zijpp, N. van der

1959   "Original Sin." In *Mennonite Encyclopedia*, 4:79-83. Scottdale, Pa.: Herald Press.

Zorn, W. D.

1998   "The Messianic Use of Habakkuk 2:4 in Romans." *Stone-Campbell Journal* 1:213-30.

Index of Ancient Sources

The Author

John E. Toews has a rich professional career in teaching biblical studies and serving as an academic dean and president at various Mennonite colleges and seminaries. He served at Fresno Pacific College (1961-68), Conrad Grebel University College (1970-73, 1996-2002), Tabor College (1973-77), Mennonite Brethren Biblical Seminary (1977-1995). At the end of December 2002, Toews retired as president of Conrad Grebel University College in Waterloo, Ontario.

Toews was born in Hepburn, Saskatchewan, and grew up in numerous communities in Canada and the U.S. He graduated with a B.A. in History (high honors) from Tabor College in 1958, and an M.A. in European Intellectual History from Wichita State University in 1960. Following studies in theology at Mennonite Brethren Bible College, Mennonite Brethren Biblical Seminary, University of Southern California, and Pacific School of Religion, he entered doctoral studies in New Testament at Garrett Theological Seminary/Northwestern University in 1968 and graduated with a Ph.D. in 1977.

Many of Toews' writings have been under assignment from church bodies such as the U.S. Conference and the General Conference of Mennonite Brethren Churches respectively. He edited the books, *The Power of the Lamb* and *Your Daughters Shall Prophesy*, in which he also contributed numerous chapters.

Toews and his wife Arlene are charter members of the College Community Church (Mennonite Brethren) in Clovis, California. They have three adult children–Delora Toews Schneider, Dawn Toews Hartman, and Mark Toews, and twin grandsons.